SAINS

THE STORY OF
THE CHURCH OF JESUS CHRIST
IN THE LATTER DAYS

SAINTS

THE STORY OF
THE CHURCH OF JESUS CHRIST
IN THE LATTER DAYS

Volume 1

THE STANDARD
OF TRUTH

1815–1846

Published by
The Church of Jesus Christ of Latter-day Saints
Salt Lake City, Utah

saints.lds.org

Cover art by Greg Newbold
Cover design and interior layout by Patric Gerber

Library of Congress Cataloging-in-Publication Data
Names: The Church of Jesus Christ of Latter-day Saints, issuing body.
Title: Saints : the story of the Church of Jesus Christ in the latter days.
    Volume 1, The standard of truth, 1815–1846.
Other titles: Story of the Church of Jesus Christ in the latter days | Standard of truth,
    1815–1846.
Description: Salt Lake City : The Church of Jesus Christ of Latter-day Saints, [2018] | Includes
    bibliographical references and index.
Identifiers: LCCN 2018010147 (print) | LCCN 2018014350 (ebook) | ISBN 9781629724928
    (paperbound) | ISBN 9781629737102 (ebook)
Subjects: LCSH: The Church of Jesus Christ of Latter-day Saints-History-19th century. |
    Mormon Church-History-19th century.
Classification: LCC BX8611 (ebook) | LCC BX8611 .S235 2018 (print) | DDC 289.309-dc23
LC record available at https://lccn.loc.gov/2018010147

10 9 8 7 6 5 4 3 2 1

The standard of truth has been erected.
No unhallowed hand can stop the work from
progressing; persecutions may rage,
mobs may combine, armies may assemble,
calumny may defame, but the truth of God will
go forth boldly, nobly, and independent till it
has penetrated every continent, visited every clime,
swept every country, and sounded in every ear,
till the purposes of God shall be accomplished and
the great Jehovah shall say the work is done.

—Joseph Smith, 1842

CONTRIBUTORS

SAINTS
THE STORY OF THE CHURCH OF JESUS CHRIST
IN THE LATTER DAYS

Church Historian and Recorder
Executive Director, Church History Department
Elder Steven E. Snow

Assistant Executive Director,
Church History Department
Elder J. Devn Cornish

Assistant Church Historian and Recorder
Managing Director, Church History Department
Reid L. Neilson

Director, Publications Division
Matthew J. Grow

Managing Historian
Steven C. Harper

Product Manager
Ben Ellis Godfrey

Digital Content Manager
Matthew S. McBride

Editorial Manager
Nathan N. Waite

VOLUME 1
THE STANDARD OF TRUTH
1815–1846

General Editors
Matthew J. Grow
Richard E. Turley Jr.
Steven C. Harper
Scott A. Hales

Writers
Scott A. Hales
James Goldberg
Melissa Leilani Larson
Elizabeth Palmer Maki
Steven C. Harper
Sherilyn Farnes

Historical Review Editors
Jed L. Woodworth
Lisa Olsen Tait

Editors
Leslie Sherman Edgington
Nathan N. Waite

Research Specialists
Kathryn Burnside
Chad O. Foulger
Brian D. Reeves

CONTENTS

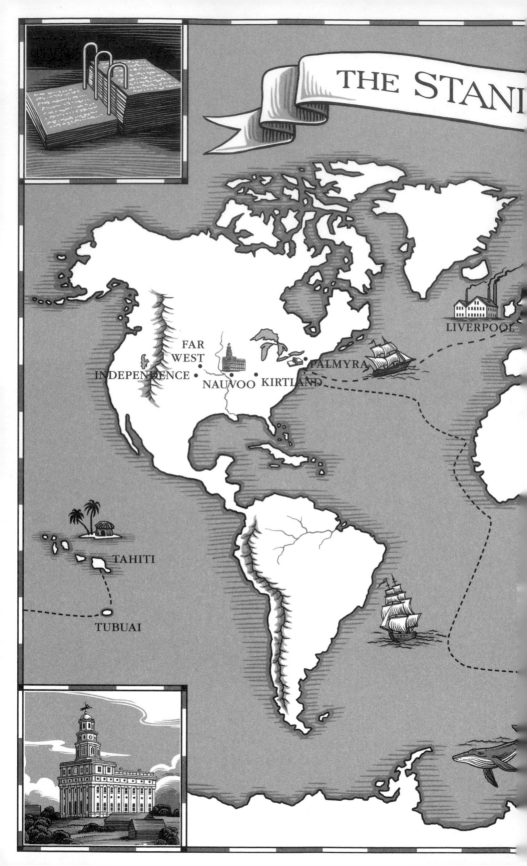

THE STAN[

LIVERPOOL

FAR
WEST
INDEPENDENCE · · PALMYRA
· KIRTLAND
NAUVOO

TAHITI

TUBUAI

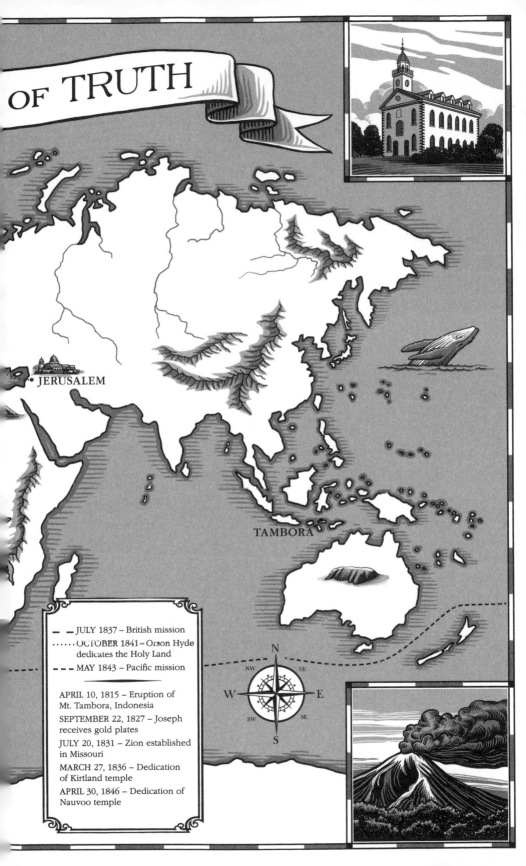

OF TRUTH

JERUSALEM

TAMBORA

— — JULY 1837 – British mission
······ OCTOBER 1841 – Orson Hyde
dedicates the Holy Land
— — MAY 1843 – Pacific mission

APRIL 10, 1815 – Eruption of
Mt. Tambora, Indonesia
SEPTEMBER 22, 1827 – Joseph
receives gold plates
JULY 20, 1831 – Zion established
in Missouri
MARCH 27, 1836 – Dedication
of Kirtland temple
APRIL 30, 1846 – Dedication of
Nauvoo temple

N
NW   NE
W   E
SW   SE
S

A MESSAGE FROM
THE FIRST PRESIDENCY

Throughout the scriptures the Lord asks us to *remember*. Remembering our shared legacy of faith, devotion, and perseverance gives us perspective and strength as we face the challenges of our day.

It is with this desire to remember "how merciful the Lord hath been unto the children of men" (Moroni 10:3) that we present *Saints: The Story of the Church of Jesus Christ in the Latter Days*. This is the first volume of a four-volume series. It is a narrative history that includes stories of faithful Latter-day Saints of the past. We encourage all to read the book and make use of the supplementary material available online.

You are an important part of the continuing history of this Church. We thank you for all you do to build on the foundation of faith laid by our forebears.

We testify that Jesus Christ is our Savior and that His gospel is the standard of truth today. The Lord called Joseph Smith to be His prophet, seer, and revelator in the latter days, and He continues to call living prophets and apostles to guide His Church.

We pray that this volume will enlarge your understanding of the past, strengthen your faith, and help you make and keep the covenants that lead to exaltation and eternal life.

Sincerely,
THE FIRST PRESIDENCY

PREFACE

True stories well told can inspire, caution, entertain, and instruct. Brigham Young understood the power of a good story when he counseled Church historians to do more than simply record the dry facts of the past. "Write in a narrative style," he advised them, and "write only about one tenth part as much."[1]

What follows is a narrative history designed to give readers a foundational understanding of Church history. Every scene, character, and line of dialogue is founded in historical sources, which are cited at the end of the book. Those who wish to read these sources, better understand related topics, and discover even more stories can find links to additional resources online at history.lds.org.

This book is the first of a four-volume history of The Church of Jesus Christ of Latter-day Saints. Together, the volumes tell the story of the Restoration of the gospel of Jesus Christ from the earliest days of the Church until now. They are written in an engaging style that is accessible to the Saints throughout the world.

The Church has published two multivolume histories in the past. The first was a documentary history begun by Joseph Smith in the 1830s and published beginning in 1842. The second was written by assistant Church historian B. H. Roberts and published in 1930.[2] The global reach of the restored gospel since then, and the Lord's command to keep the history continually for "the good of the church, and for the rising generations,"[3] signal that it is time to update and include more Saints in the story.

Even more than previous histories, *Saints* presents the lives and stories of ordinary men and women in the Church. It also provides new detail and insight into better-known people and events from Church history. Each chapter will help readers understand and appreciate the Saints who have made the Church what it is today. Woven together, their stories create the rich tapestry of the Restoration.

Saints is not scripture, but like the scriptures, each volume contains divine truth and stories of imperfect people trying to become Saints through the Atonement of Jesus Christ.[4] Their stories—like the stories of all Saints, past and present—remind readers how merciful the Lord has been to His people as they have joined together around the globe to further God's work.

PART 1

---◆---

My Servant Joseph

APRIL 1815–APRIL 1830

I the Lord, knowing the calamity
which should come upon the
inhabitants of the earth, called upon
my servant Joseph Smith, Jun., and
spake unto him from heaven . . . that mine
everlasting covenant might
be established.

Doctrine and Covenants 1:17, 22

1816–1830

CANADA

Lake Ontario

PALMYRA
Hill Cumorah
MANCHESTER
FAYETTE

NEW YORK

VERMONT

SHARON

N.H.

MASS.

Susquehanna River
COLESVILLE
HARMONY

CONN.

R.I.

PENNSYLVANIA

NEW YORK CITY

MARYLAND

N.J.

DEL.

CHAPTER 1

Ask in Faith

In 1815, the Indonesian island of Sumbawa was lush and green with recent rain. Families were preparing for the dry season ahead, as they had every year for generations, cultivating rice paddies in the shadow of a volcano called Tambora.

On April 5, after decades of slumber, the mountain roared awake, coughing up ash and fire. Hundreds of miles away, witnesses heard what sounded like cannon fire. Small eruptions continued for days. Then, on the evening of April 10, the whole mountain exploded. Three fiery plumes shot skyward, merging into one massive blast. Liquid fire flowed down the mountainside, enveloping the village at its base. Whirlwinds raged through the region, pulling up trees and sweeping away homes.[1]

The chaos continued all that night and into the next. Ash blanketed miles of land and sea, piling two feet high in places. Midday felt like midnight. Rough seas heaved over shorelines, spoiling crops and drowning villages. For weeks, Tambora rained cinders, stone, and fire.[2]

Over the next few months, the blast's effects rippled across the globe. Spectacular sunsets awed people around the world. But the vibrant colors masked the deadly effects of the volcano's ash as it circled the earth. In the coming year, the weather turned unpredictable and devastating.[3]

The eruption caused temperatures in India to drop, and cholera killed thousands, destroying families. In fertile Chinese valleys, summer snowstorms replaced a normally mild climate and flooding rains destroyed crops. In Europe, food supplies dwindled, leading to starvation and panic.[4]

Everywhere, people sought explanations for the suffering and death the strange weather caused. Prayers and chants from holy men echoed through Hindu temples in India. Chinese poets grappled with questions of pain and loss. In France and Britain, citizens fell to their knees, fearful the terrible calamities foretold in the Bible were upon them. In North America, ministers preached that God was punishing wayward Christians, and they sounded warnings to stoke religious feelings.

Across the land, people flocked to churches and revival meetings, anxious to know how they could be saved from the coming destruction.[5]

THE ERUPTION OF TAMBORA affected weather in North America through the following year. Spring gave way to snowfall and killing frosts, and 1816 passed into memory as the year without a summer.[6] In Vermont, in the northeast corner of the United States, rocky hills had frustrated a farmer named Joseph Smith Sr. for years. But that season, as he and his wife, Lucy Mack Smith, watched their crops shrivel under the relentless frosts, they knew they faced financial ruin and an uncertain future if they stayed where they were.

At forty-five, Joseph Sr. was no longer a young man, and the prospect of starting over on new land was daunting. He knew his oldest sons, eighteen-year-old Alvin and sixteen-year-old Hyrum, could help him clear the land, build a house, and plant and harvest crops. His thirteen-year-old daughter, Sophronia, was old enough to help Lucy with her work in the house and around the farm. His younger sons, eight-year-old Samuel and five-year-old William, were becoming more helpful, and three-year-old Katharine and newborn Don Carlos would one day be old enough to contribute.

But his middle son, ten-year-old Joseph Jr., was a different matter. Four years earlier, Joseph Jr. had undergone an operation to remove an infection in his leg. Since then he had walked with a crutch. Although his leg was starting to feel sturdy again, Joseph Jr. had a painful limp, and Joseph Sr. did not know if he would grow up to be as strong as Alvin and Hyrum.[7]

Certain they could rely on each other, the Smiths resolved to abandon their home in Vermont for better land.[8] Like others in the area, Joseph Sr. decided to travel to the state of New York, where he hoped to find a good farm they could buy on credit. He would then send for Lucy and the children, and the family could start over.

As Joseph Sr. set out for New York, Alvin and Hyrum walked him down the road before saying good-bye. Joseph Sr. loved his wife and children dearly, but he had not been able to provide them much stability in life. Bad luck and unsuccessful investments had kept the family poor and rootless. Maybe New York would be different.[9]

THE FOLLOWING WINTER, JOSEPH Jr. hobbled through the snow with his mother, brothers, and sisters. They were on their way west to a New York village named Palmyra, near where Joseph Sr. had found good land and was waiting for his family.

Since her husband could not help with the move, Lucy had hired a man named Mr. Howard to drive their wagon. On the road, Mr. Howard handled their belongings roughly and gambled and drank away the money they paid him. And after they joined up with another family traveling west, Mr. Howard kicked Joseph out of the wagon so the other family's daughters could sit with him as he drove the team.

Knowing how much it hurt Joseph to walk, Alvin and Hyrum tried to stand up to Mr. Howard a few times. But each time he knocked them down with the butt of his whip.[10]

If he had been bigger, Joseph probably would have tried to stand up to Mr. Howard himself. His hurt leg had kept him from work and play, but his strong will made up for his weak body. Before the doctors had cut into his leg and chipped away infected pieces of bone, they had wanted to tie him down or give him brandy to dull the pain. But Joseph had asked only that his father hold him.

He had stayed awake and alert the whole time, his face pale and dripping with sweat. His mother, who was usually so strong, had nearly fallen apart when she heard his screams. After that, she probably felt that she could bear anything.[11]

As Joseph limped along beside the wagon, he could see his mother was certainly bearing with Mr. Howard. They had already traveled two hundred miles, and so far she had been more than patient with the driver's bad behavior.

ABOUT A HUNDRED MILES from Palmyra, Lucy was preparing for another day on the road when she saw Alvin running toward her. Mr. Howard had thrown their goods and luggage onto the street and was about to leave with their horses and wagon.

Lucy found the man in a bar. "As there is a God in heaven," she declared, "that wagon and those horses as well as the goods accompanying them are mine."

She looked around the bar. It was filled with men and women, most of them travelers like her. "This man," she said, meeting their gaze, "is determined to take away from me every means of proceeding on my journey, leaving me with eight little children utterly destitute."

Mr. Howard said that he had already spent the money she paid him to drive the wagon, and he could go no farther.

"I have no use for you," Lucy said. "I shall take charge of the team myself."

She left Mr. Howard in the bar and vowed to reunite her children with their father, come what may.[12]

THE ROAD AHEAD WAS muddy and cold, but Lucy led her family safely to Palmyra. As she watched the children cling to their father and kiss his face, she felt rewarded for all they had suffered to get there.

The family soon rented a small house in town and discussed how to get their own farm.[13] The best plan, they decided, was to work until they had enough money for a down payment on land in the nearby woods. Joseph Sr. and the older sons dug wells, split fence rails, and harvested hay for cash, while Lucy and the daughters made and sold pies, root beer, and decorative cloths to provide food for the family.[14]

As Joseph Jr. got older, his leg grew stronger and he could easily walk through Palmyra. In town, he came in contact with people from all over the region, and many of them were turning to religion to satisfy spiritual yearnings and explain the hardships of life. Joseph and his family did not belong to a church, but many of their neighbors worshipped in one of the tall Presbyterian chapels, the Baptists' meetinghouse, the Quaker hall, or the campground where traveling Methodist preachers held revival meetings from time to time.[15]

When Joseph was twelve, religious debates swept Palmyra. Although he read little, he liked to think deeply about ideas. He listened to preachers, hoping to learn more about his immortal soul, but their sermons often left him unsettled. They told him he was a sinner in a sinful world, helpless without the saving grace of Jesus Christ. And while Joseph believed the message and felt bad about his sins, he was not sure how to find forgiveness.[16]

He thought going to church could help him, but he could not settle on a place to worship. The different churches argued endlessly about how people could be free of sin. After listening to these arguments for a while, Joseph was distressed to see people reading the same Bible but coming to different conclusions about its meaning. He believed God's truth was out there—somewhere—but he did not know how to find it.[17]

His parents were not sure either. Lucy and Joseph Sr. both came from Christian families and believed in the

Bible and Jesus Christ. Lucy attended church meetings and often brought her children with her. She had been seeking the true church of Jesus Christ since the death of her sister many years earlier.

Once, after falling gravely ill sometime before Joseph's birth, she had feared that she would die before finding the truth. She sensed a dark and lonely chasm between her and the Savior, and she knew she was unprepared for the next life.

Lying awake all night, she prayed to God, promising Him that if He let her live, she would find the church of Jesus Christ. As she prayed, the voice of the Lord spoke to her, assuring her that if she would seek, she would find. She had visited more churches since then, but she had still not found the right one. Yet even when it felt like the Savior's church was no longer on the earth, she kept searching, trusting that going to church was better than not.[18]

Like his wife, Joseph Sr. hungered for the truth. But he felt that attending no church at all was preferable to the wrong one. Following the counsel of his father, Joseph Sr. searched the scriptures, prayed earnestly, and believed that Jesus Christ had come to save the world.[19] Yet he could not reconcile what he felt to be true with the confusion and discord he saw in the churches around him. One night he had dreamed that contending preachers were like cattle, bellowing as they dug at the earth with their horns, which deepened his concern that they knew little about God's kingdom.[20]

Seeing his parents' dissatisfaction with local churches only confused Joseph Jr. more.[21] His soul was at stake, but no one could give him satisfying answers.

AFTER SAVING THEIR MONEY for more than a year, the Smiths had enough to make a payment on a hundred acres of forest in Manchester, just south of Palmyra. There, between jobs as hired hands, they tapped maple trees for their sugary sap, planted an orchard, and cleared fields to grow crops.[22]

As he worked the land, young Joseph continued to worry about his sins and the welfare of his soul. The religious revival in Palmyra had quieted down, but preachers continued to compete for converts there and throughout the region.[23] Day and night, Joseph watched the sun, moon, and stars roll through the heavens in order and majesty and admired the beauty of the earth teeming with life. He also looked at the people around him and marveled at their strength and intelligence. Everything seemed to testify that God existed and had created humankind in His own image. But how could Joseph reach Him?[24]

In the summer of 1819, when Joseph was thirteen, Methodist preachers gathered for a conference a few miles from the Smith farm and spread out across the countryside to spur families like Joseph's toward conversion. The success of these preachers worried other ministers in the area, and soon competition for converts was intense.

Joseph attended meetings, listened to soul-stirring preaching, and witnessed converts shout for joy. He wanted to shout with them, but he often felt like he was in the middle of a war of words and opinions. "Who of all these parties are right; or, are they all wrong together?" he asked himself. "If any one of them be right, which is it, and how shall I know it?" He knew he needed Christ's grace and mercy, but with so many people and churches clashing over religion, he did not know where to find it.[25]

Hope that he could find answers—and peace for his soul—seemed to slip away from him. He wondered how anyone could find truth amid so much noise.[26]

WHILE ATTENDING A SERMON, Joseph heard a minister quote from the first chapter of James in the New Testament. "If any of you lack wisdom," he said, "let him ask of God, that giveth to all men liberally, and upbraideth not."[27]

Joseph went home and read the verse in the Bible. "Never did any passage of scripture come with more power to the heart of man than this did at this time to mine," he later remembered. "It seemed to enter with great force into every feeling of my heart. I reflected on it again and again, knowing that if any person needed wisdom from God, I did." He had searched the Bible before as if it held all the answers. But now the Bible was telling him he could go directly to God for personal answers to his questions.

Joseph decided to pray. He had never prayed out loud before, but he trusted the Bible's promise. "Ask in faith, nothing wavering," it taught.[28] God would hear his questions—even if they came out awkwardly.

CHAPTER 2

Hear Him

Joseph rose early on a spring morning in 1820 and set out for the woods near his home. The day was clear and beautiful, and sunlight filtered through the branches overhead. He wanted to be alone when he prayed, and he knew a quiet spot in the woods where he had recently been clearing trees. He had left his ax there, wedged in a stump.[1]

Finding the place, Joseph looked around to make sure he was by himself. He was anxious about praying out loud and did not want to be interrupted.

Satisfied he was alone, Joseph knelt on the cool earth and began to share the desires of his heart with God. He asked for mercy and forgiveness and for wisdom to find answers to his questions. "O Lord," he prayed, "what church shall I join?"[2]

As he prayed, his tongue seemed to swell until he could not speak. He heard footsteps behind him but saw no one when he turned around. He tried to pray again, but the footsteps grew louder, as if someone was coming for him. He sprang to his feet and spun around, but still he saw no one.[3]

Suddenly, an unseen power seized him. He tried to speak again, but his tongue was still bound. A thick darkness closed in around him until he could no longer see the sunlight. Doubts and awful images flashed across his mind, confusing and distracting him. He felt as if some terrible being, real and immensely powerful, wanted to destroy him.[4]

Exerting all his strength, Joseph called once more to God. His tongue loosened, and he pleaded for deliverance. But he found himself sinking into despair, overwhelmed by the unbearable darkness and ready to abandon himself to destruction.[5]

At that moment, a pillar of light appeared over his head. It descended slowly and seemed to set the woods on fire. As the light rested on him, Joseph felt the unseen power release its hold. The Spirit of God took its place, filling him with peace and unspeakable joy.

Peering into the light, Joseph saw God the Father standing above him in the air. His face was brighter and more glorious than anything Joseph had ever seen. God called him by name and pointed to another being who appeared beside Him. "This is My Beloved Son," He said. "Hear Him!"[6]

Joseph looked into the face of Jesus Christ. It was as bright and glorious as the Father's.

"Joseph," the Savior said, "thy sins are forgiven."[7]

His burden lifted, Joseph repeated his question: "What church shall I join?"[8]

"Join none of them," the Savior told him. "They teach for doctrines the commandments of men, having a form of godliness, but they deny the power thereof."

The Lord told Joseph that the world was steeped in sin. "None doeth good," He explained. "They have turned aside from the gospel and keep not my commandments." Sacred truths had been lost or corrupted, but He promised to reveal the fullness of His gospel to Joseph in the future.[9]

As the Savior spoke, Joseph saw hosts of angels, and the light around them blazed brighter than the noonday sun. "Behold, and lo, I come quickly," the Lord said, "clothed in the glory of My Father."[10]

Joseph expected the woods to be devoured by the brilliance, but the trees burned like Moses's bush and were not consumed.[11]

WHEN THE LIGHT FADED, Joseph found himself lying on his back, looking up into heaven. The pillar of light had departed, and his guilt and confusion were gone. Feelings of divine love filled his heart.[12] God the Father and Jesus Christ had spoken to him, and he had learned for himself how to find truth and forgiveness.

Too weak from the vision to move, Joseph lay in the woods until some of his strength returned. He then struggled home and leaned against the fireplace for support. His mother saw him and asked what was wrong.

"All is well," he assured her. "I am well enough off."[13]

A few days later, while talking to a preacher, Joseph told him about what he had seen in the woods. The preacher had been active in the recent religious revivals, and Joseph expected him to take his vision seriously.

At first the preacher treated his words lightly. People claimed to have heavenly visions from time to time.[14] But then he became angry and defensive, and he told Joseph that his story was from the devil. The days of visions and revelations had ceased long ago, he said, and they would never return.[15]

Joseph was surprised, and he soon found that no one would believe his vision.[16] Why would they? He was only fourteen years old and had practically no education. He came from a poor family and expected to spend the rest of his life working the land and doing odd jobs to earn a meager living.

And yet his testimony bothered some people enough to ridicule him. How strange, he thought, that a simple boy of no consequence in the world could attract so much bitterness and scorn. "Why persecute me for telling the truth?" he wanted to ask. "Why does the world think to make me deny what I have actually seen?"

Joseph puzzled over these questions for the rest of his life. "I had actually seen a light, and in the midst of that light I saw two Personages, and they did in reality speak to me," he later recounted, "and though I was hated and persecuted for saying that I had seen a vision, yet it was true."

"I knew it, and I knew that God knew it," he testified, "and I could not deny it."[17]

ONCE JOSEPH DISCOVERED THAT sharing his vision only turned his neighbors against him, he kept it mostly to himself, content with the knowledge God had given him.[18] Later, after he moved away from New York, he tried to record his sacred experience in the woods. He described his yearning for forgiveness and the Savior's warning to a world in need of repentance. He wrote the words out himself, in halting language, trying earnestly to capture the majesty of the moment.

In the years that followed, he recounted the vision more publicly, drawing on scribes who could help him better express what defied all description. He told of his desire to find the true church and described God the Father appearing first to introduce the Son. He wrote less about his own search for forgiveness and more about the Savior's universal message of truth and the need for a restoration of the gospel.[19]

With each effort to record his experience, Joseph testified that the Lord had heard and answered his prayer. As a young man, he learned that the Savior's church was no longer on the earth. But the Lord had promised to reveal more about His gospel in due time. So Joseph resolved to trust in God, stay true to the commandment he had received in the woods, and wait patiently for further direction.[20]

CHAPTER 3

Plates of Gold

Three years passed, and three harvests. Joseph spent most days clearing land, turning soil, and working as a hired hand to raise money for the yearly cash payment on the family's property. The work made it impossible for him to attend school very often, and he spent most of his free time with family or other laborers.

Joseph and his friends were young and light-hearted. Sometimes they made foolish mistakes, and Joseph found that being forgiven once did not mean he would never need to repent again. Nor did his glorious vision answer every question or forever end his confusion.[1] So he tried to stay close to God. He read his Bible, trusted in Jesus Christ's power to save him, and obeyed the Lord's command not to join any church.

Like many people in the area, including his father, Joseph believed that God could reveal knowledge through objects like rods and stones, as He had done with Moses, Aaron, and others in the Bible.[2] One day, while Joseph was helping a neighbor dig a well, he came across a small stone buried deep in the earth. Aware that people sometimes used special stones to search for lost objects or hidden treasure, Joseph wondered if he had found such a stone. Looking into it, he saw things invisible to the natural eye.[3]

Joseph's gift for using the stone impressed family members, who saw it as a sign of divine favor.[4] But even though he had the gift of a seer, Joseph was still unsure if God was pleased with him. He could no longer feel the forgiveness and peace he had felt after his vision of the Father and Son. Instead, he often felt condemned for his weakness and imperfections.[5]

ON SEPTEMBER 21, 1823, SEVENTEEN-YEAR-OLD Joseph lay awake in the loft bedroom he shared with his brothers. He had stayed up late that evening, listening to his family talk about different churches and the doctrines they taught. Now everyone was asleep, and the house was quiet.[6]

In the darkness of his room, Joseph began to pray, pleading fervently that God would forgive his sins. He longed to commune with a heavenly messenger who could assure him of his standing before the Lord and give him the knowledge of the gospel he had been promised in the grove. Joseph knew God had answered his prayers before, and he had full confidence that He would answer again.

As Joseph prayed, a light appeared beside his bed and grew brighter until it filled the entire loft. Joseph looked up and saw an angel standing in the air. The angel wore a seamless white robe that came down to his wrists and ankles. Light radiated from him, and his face shone like lightning.

At first Joseph was afraid, but peace soon filled him. The angel called him by name and introduced himself as Moroni. He said God had forgiven Joseph of his sins and now had work for him to do. He declared that Joseph's name would be spoken of for good and evil among all people.[7]

Moroni spoke of gold plates buried in a nearby hill. On the plates was etched the record of an ancient people who once lived in the Americas. The record told of their origins and gave an account of Jesus Christ visiting them and teaching the fullness of His gospel.[8] Buried with the plates, Moroni said, were two seer stones, which Joseph later called the Urim and Thummim, or interpreters. The Lord had prepared these stones to help Joseph translate the record. The clear stones were fastened together and attached to a breastplate.[9]

For the rest of the visit, Moroni quoted prophecies from the biblical books of Isaiah, Joel, Malachi, and Acts.

The Lord was coming soon, he explained, and the human family would not fulfill the purpose of their creation unless God's ancient covenant was renewed first.[10] Moroni said that God had chosen Joseph to renew the covenant, and that if he chose to be faithful to God's commands, he would be the one to reveal the record on the plates.[11]

Before departing, the angel commanded Joseph to take care of the plates and show them to no one unless otherwise instructed, warning him that he would be destroyed if he disobeyed this counsel. Light then gathered around Moroni and he ascended to heaven.[12]

As Joseph lay thinking about the vision, light flooded the room again and Moroni reappeared, giving the same message as before. He then departed, only to appear once more and deliver his message a third time.

"Now, Joseph, beware," he said. "When you go to get the plates, your mind will be filled with darkness, and all manner of evil will rush into your mind to prevent you from keeping the commandments of God." Directing Joseph to someone who would support him, Moroni urged him to tell his father about his visions.

"He will believe every word you say," the angel promised.[13]

THE NEXT MORNING, JOSEPH said nothing about Moroni, even though he knew his father also believed in visions and angels. Instead, they spent the morning harvesting a nearby field with Alvin.

The work was difficult. Joseph tried to keep pace with his brother as they swung their scythes back and forth through the tall grain. But Moroni's visits had kept him awake all night, and his thoughts kept returning to the ancient record and the hill where it was buried.

Soon he stopped working, and Alvin noticed. "We must keep to work," he called out to Joseph, "or we shall not get our task done."[14]

Joseph tried to work harder and faster, but no matter what he did, he could not keep up with Alvin. After a while, Joseph Sr. noticed that Joseph looked pale and had stopped working again. "Go home," he said, believing his son was sick.

Joseph obeyed his father and stumbled back toward the house. But as he tried to cross a fence, he collapsed to the ground, exhausted.

While he lay there, gathering strength, he saw Moroni standing above him once more, surrounded by light. "Why did you not tell your father what I told you?" he asked.

Joseph said he was afraid his father would not believe him.

"He will," Moroni assured him, then repeated his message from the night before.[15]

JOSEPH SR. WEPT WHEN HIS son told him about the angel and his message. "It was a vision from God," he said. "Attend to it."[16]

Joseph set out immediately for the hill. During the night, Moroni had shown him a vision of where the plates were hidden, so he knew where to go. The hill, one of the biggest in the area, was about three miles from his house. The plates were buried beneath a large, round rock on the west side of the hill, not far from its summit.

Joseph thought about the plates as he walked. Even though he knew they were sacred, it was hard for him to resist wondering how much they were worth. He had heard tales of hidden treasures protected by guardian spirits, but Moroni and the plates he described were different from these stories. Moroni was a heavenly messenger appointed by God to deliver the record safely to His chosen seer. And the plates were valuable not because they were gold, but because they witnessed of Jesus Christ.

Still, Joseph could not help thinking that he now knew exactly where to find enough treasure to free his family from poverty.[17]

Arriving at the hill, Joseph located the place he had seen in the vision and began digging at the base of the rock until its edges were clear. He then found a large tree branch and used it as a lever to raise the stone and heave it aside.[18]

Beneath the boulder was a box, its walls and base made of stone. Looking inside, Joseph saw the gold plates, seer stones, and breastplate.[19] The plates were covered with ancient writing and bound together on one side by three rings. Each plate was about six inches wide, eight inches long, and thin. A portion of the plates also appeared to be sealed so no one could read it.[20]

Astonished, Joseph wondered again how much the plates were worth. He reached for them—and felt a shock pulse through him. He jerked his hand back but then reached for the plates twice more and was shocked each time.

"Why can I not obtain this book?" he cried out.

"Because you have not kept the commandments of the Lord," said a voice nearby.[21]

Joseph turned and saw Moroni. At once the message from the night before flooded his mind, and he understood that he had forgotten the record's true purpose. He started to pray, and his mind and soul awoke to the Holy Spirit.

"Look," Moroni commanded. Another vision unfolded before Joseph, and he saw Satan surrounded by his numberless host. "All this is shown, the good and the evil, the holy and impure, the glory of God and the power of darkness," the angel declared, "that you may know hereafter the two powers and never be influenced or overcome by that wicked one."

He instructed Joseph to purify his heart and strengthen his mind to receive the record. "If ever these sacred things are obtained they must be by prayer and faithfulness in obeying the Lord," Moroni explained. "They are not deposited here for the sake of accumulating gain and wealth for the glory of this world. They were sealed by the prayer of faith."[22]

Joseph asked when he could have the plates.

"The twenty-second day of September next," Moroni said, "if you bring the right person with you."

"Who is the right person?" Joseph asked.

"Your oldest brother."[23]

Ever since he was a child, Joseph knew he could rely on his oldest brother. Alvin was twenty-five years old now and could have acquired his own farm if he wanted. But he had chosen to stay on the family farm to help his parents get settled and secure on their land as they got older. He was serious and hardworking, and Joseph loved and admired him immensely.[24]

Maybe Moroni felt that Joseph needed his brother's wisdom and strength to become the kind of person the Lord could trust with the plates.

RETURNING HOME THAT EVENING, Joseph was tired. But his family crowded around him as soon as he came through the door, eager to know what he had found at the hill. Joseph started to tell them about the plates, but Alvin interrupted when he noticed how weary Joseph looked.

"Let us go to bed," he said, "and we will get up early in the morning and go to work." They would have plenty of time tomorrow to hear the rest of Joseph's story. "If Mother will get our suppers early," he said, "we will then have a fine long evening and all sit down and hear you talk."[25]

The next evening, Joseph shared what had happened at the hill, and Alvin believed him. As the oldest son in the family, Alvin had always felt responsible for his aging parents' physical welfare. He and his brothers had even started building a larger house for the family so they could be more comfortable.

Now it seemed Joseph was looking after their spiritual welfare. Night after night he captivated the family with talk of the gold plates and the people who wrote them. The family grew closer together, and their home was peaceful and happy. Everyone felt that something wonderful was about to happen.[26]

Then one autumn morning, less than two months after Moroni's visit, Alvin came home with an intense pain in his stomach. Bent over in agony, he begged his father to call for help. When a doctor finally arrived, he gave Alvin a large dose of a chalky medicine, but it only made things worse.

Alvin lay in bed for days, writhing in pain. Knowing he would probably die, he called for Joseph. "Do everything that lies in your power to obtain the records," Alvin said. "Be faithful in receiving instruction and keeping every commandment that is given you."[27]

He died a short time later, and sorrow settled over the house. At the funeral, a preacher all but said Alvin had gone to hell, using his death to warn others of what would happen unless God intervened to save them. Joseph Sr. was furious. His son had been a good young man, and he could not believe that God would damn him.[28]

With Alvin gone, talk of the plates ended. He had been such a staunch supporter of Joseph's divine call that any mention of them brought his death to mind. The family could not bear it.

Joseph missed Alvin terribly and took his death especially hard. He had hoped to rely on his oldest brother to help him get the record. Now he felt forsaken.[29]

WHEN THE DAY FINALLY came to return to the hill, Joseph went alone. Without Alvin, he was unsure if the Lord would trust him with the plates. But he thought he could keep every commandment the Lord had given him, as his brother had counseled. Moroni's instructions for retrieving the plates were clear. "You must take them into your hands and go straight to the house without delay," the angel had said, "and lock them up."[30]

At the hill, Joseph pried up the rock, reached into the stone box, and lifted out the plates. A thought then crossed his mind: the other items in the box were valuable and ought to be hidden before he went home. He set the plates down and turned to cover the box. But when he returned to the plates, they were gone. Alarmed, he fell to his knees and pleaded to know where they were.

Moroni appeared and told Joseph that he had failed to follow directions again. Not only had he set the plates down before safely securing them, he had also let them out of his sight. As willing as the young seer was to do the Lord's work, he was not yet able to protect the ancient record.

Joseph was disappointed in himself, but Moroni instructed him to return for the plates the following year. He also taught him more about the Lord's plan for the kingdom of God and the great work beginning to roll forth.

Still, after the angel left, Joseph slunk down the hill, worried what his family would think when he came home empty handed.[31] When he stepped inside the house, they were waiting for him. His father asked at once if he had the plates.

"No," he said. "I could not get them."

"Did you see them?"

"I saw them but could not take them."

"I would have taken them," Joseph Sr. said, "if I had been in your place."

"You do not know what you say," Joseph said. "I could not get them, for the angel of the Lord would not let me."[32]

CHAPTER 4

Be Watchful

Twenty-one-year-old Emma Hale first heard about
Joseph Smith when he came to work for Josiah Stowell
in the fall of 1825. Josiah had hired the young man and
his father to help him find buried treasure on his property.[1] Local legends claimed that a band of explorers
had mined a silver deposit and hidden the treasure in
the area hundreds of years earlier. Knowing Joseph had
a gift for using seer stones, Josiah offered him good
wages and a share of the findings if he would help in
the search.[2]

Emma's father, Isaac, supported the venture.
When Joseph and his father came to the Stowell farm
in Harmony, Pennsylvania—a village some 150 miles
south of Palmyra—Isaac served as a witness when they

signed their contracts. He also allowed the workers to live in his home.[3]

Emma met Joseph soon after. He was younger than she was, stood over six feet tall, and looked like someone who was used to hard work. He had blue eyes and a light complexion, and he walked with a faint limp. His grammar was uneven, and he sometimes used too many words to express himself, but he displayed a natural intelligence when he spoke. He and his father were good men who preferred to worship on their own rather than attend the church where Emma and her family worshipped.[4]

Both Joseph and Emma liked being outdoors. Since childhood, Emma had enjoyed riding horses and canoeing in the river near her home. Joseph was not a skilled horseman, but he excelled in wrestling and ball games. He was at ease around others and quick to smile, often telling jokes or humorous stories. Emma was more reserved, but she loved a good joke and could talk with anyone. She also liked to read and sing.[5]

As the weeks passed and Emma got to know Joseph better, her parents grew anxious about their relationship. Joseph was a poor laborer from another state, and they hoped their daughter would lose interest in him and marry into one of the prosperous families in their valley. Emma's father had also grown wary of the treasure hunt and was suspicious of Joseph's role in it. It did not seem to matter to Isaac Hale that Joseph had tried to convince Josiah Stowell to call the search off when it became clear nothing would come of it.[6]

Emma liked Joseph better than any other man she knew, and she did not stop spending time with him. After he succeeded in convincing Josiah to stop looking for silver, Joseph remained in Harmony to work on Josiah's farm. Sometimes he also worked for Joseph and Polly Knight, another farming family in the area. When he was not working, he visited Emma.[7]

JOSEPH AND HIS SEER stone soon became the subject of gossip in Harmony. Some of the older folks in town believed in seers, but many of their children and grandchildren did not. Josiah's nephew, claiming that Joseph had taken advantage of his uncle, brought the young man to court and charged him with being a fraud.

Standing before the local judge, Joseph explained how he had found the stone. Joseph Sr. testified that he had constantly asked God to show them His will for Joseph's marvelous gift as a seer. Finally, Josiah stood before the court and stated that Joseph had not swindled him.

"Do I understand," said the judge, "that you believe the prisoner can see by the aid of the stone?"

No, Josiah insisted. "I positively know it to be true."

Josiah was a well-respected man in the community, and people accepted his word. In the end, the hearing produced no evidence that Joseph had deceived him, so the judge dismissed the charge.[8]

In September 1826, Joseph returned to the hill for the plates, but Moroni said he was still not ready for them. "Quit the company of the money diggers," the angel told him. There were wicked men among them.[9] Moroni gave him one more year to align his will with God's. If he did not, the plates would never be entrusted to him.

The angel also told him to bring someone with him next time. It was the same request he had made at the end of Joseph's first visit to the hill. But since Alvin was dead, Joseph was confused.

"Who is the right person?" he asked.

"You will know," Moroni said.

Joseph sought the Lord's direction through his seer stone. The right person, he learned, was Emma.[10]

JOSEPH HAD BEEN DRAWN to Emma as soon as he met her. Like Alvin, she was someone who could help him become the man the Lord needed to carry out His work. But there was more to Emma than that. Joseph loved her and wanted to marry her.[11]

In December, Joseph turned twenty-one years old. In the past, he had let himself be pulled this way and that by the expectations of those who wanted to take advantage of his gift.[12] But after his last visit to the hill, he knew he had to do more to prepare himself to receive the plates.

Before returning to Harmony, Joseph spoke with his parents. "I have concluded to get married," he told them, "and, if you have no objections, Miss Emma Hale would be my choice." His parents were pleased with his decision, and Lucy urged him to come live with them after they married.[13]

Joseph spent as much time as he could with Emma that winter, sometimes borrowing the Knights' sleigh when snow made it hard to travel to the Hales' house. But her parents still did not like him, and his efforts to win over the family failed.[14]

In January 1827, Emma visited the Stowells' home, where she and Joseph could spend time together without her family's disapproving looks. Joseph proposed to Emma there, and at first, Emma seemed surprised. She knew her parents would oppose the marriage.[15] But Joseph urged her to think about it. They could elope right away.

Emma considered the proposal. Marrying Joseph would disappoint her parents, but it was her choice, and she loved him.[16]

A SHORT TIME LATER, on January 18, 1827, Joseph and Emma were married in the home of the local justice of the peace. They then went to Manchester and began life together in the new home of Joseph's parents. The house was comfortable, but Joseph Sr. and Lucy had overspent on it, fallen behind on their payments, and lost the property. They were now renting it from the new owners.[17]

The Smiths liked having Joseph and Emma with them. But their son's divine call made them anxious. People in the area had heard about the gold plates and sometimes went looking for them.[18]

One day, Joseph went to town on an errand. Expecting him back for dinner, his parents were alarmed when he did not return. They waited for hours, unable to sleep. At last Joseph opened the door and threw himself into a chair, exhausted.

"Why are you so late?" his father asked.

"I have had the severest chastisement that I ever had in my life," Joseph said.

"Who has been taking you to task?" demanded his father.

"It was the angel of the Lord," Joseph replied. "He says I have been negligent." The day of his next meeting with Moroni was coming soon. "I must be up and doing," he said. "I must set myself about the things which God has commanded me to do."[19]

AFTER THE FALL HARVEST, Josiah Stowell and Joseph Knight traveled to the Manchester area on business. Both men knew that the fourth anniversary of Joseph's visit to the hill was at hand, and they were eager to know whether Moroni would finally trust him with the plates.

Local treasure seekers also knew it was time for Joseph to get the record. Lately one of them, a man named Samuel Lawrence, had been roaming the hill, searching for the plates. Worried that Samuel would cause trouble, Joseph sent his father to Samuel's house on the evening of September 21 to keep an eye on him and confront him if it looked like he was going to the hill.[20]

Joseph then readied himself to retrieve the plates. His yearly visit to the hill was to take place the next day, but to keep ahead of the treasure seekers, he planned to arrive at the hill shortly after midnight—just as the morning of September 22 was beginning—when no one expected him to be out.

But he still needed to find a way to protect the plates once he got them. After most of the family had gone to bed, he quietly asked his mother if she had a lockbox. Lucy did not have one and got worried.

"Never mind," Joseph said. "I can do very well just now without it."[21]

Emma soon appeared, dressed for riding, and she and Joseph climbed into Joseph Knight's carriage and set out into the night.[22] When they arrived at the hill, Emma waited with the carriage while Joseph climbed the slope to the place where the plates were hidden.

Moroni appeared, and Joseph lifted the gold plates and seer stones from the stone box. Before Joseph set off down the hill, Moroni reminded him to show the plates to no one except those the Lord appointed, promising him that the plates would be protected if he did all within his power to preserve them.

"You will have to be watchful and faithful to your trust," Moroni told him, "or you will be overpowered by wicked men, for they will lay every plan and scheme that is possible to get them away from you. And if you do not take heed continually, they will succeed."[23]

Joseph carried the plates down the hill, but before he reached the carriage, he secured them in a hollow log where they would be safe until he obtained a lockbox. He then found Emma, and they returned home as the sun began to rise.[24]

AT THE SMITH HOME, Lucy waited anxiously for Joseph and Emma while she served breakfast to Joseph Sr., Joseph Knight, and Josiah Stowell. Her heart beat rapidly while she worked, fearful that her son would return without the plates.[25]

A short time later, Joseph and Emma came into the house. Lucy looked to see if Joseph had the plates but left the room trembling when she saw his empty hands.

Joseph followed her. "Mother," he said, "do not be uneasy." He handed her an object wrapped in a handkerchief. Through the fabric, Lucy felt what seemed to be a large pair of spectacles. They were the Urim and Thummim, the seer stones the Lord had prepared for translating the plates.[26]

Lucy was elated. Joseph looked as if a great weight had been lifted off his shoulders. But when he joined the others in the house, he made a sad face and ate his breakfast in silence. After he finished, he leaned his head forlornly on his hand. "I am disappointed," he said to Joseph Knight.

"Well," the older man said, "I am sorry."

"I am greatly disappointed," Joseph repeated, his expression changing to a smile. "It is ten times better than I expected!" He went on to describe the size and weight of the plates and talked excitedly about the Urim and Thummim.

"I can see anything," he said. "They are marvelous."[27]

THE DAY AFTER HE received the plates, Joseph went to work repairing a well in a nearby town to raise money for a lockbox. That same morning, while on an errand just over the hill from the Smith home, Joseph Sr. overheard a group of men plotting to steal the gold plates. "We will have the plates," one of them said, "in spite of Joe Smith or all the devils in hell."

Alarmed, Joseph Sr. returned home and told Emma. She said she did not know where the plates were, but she was sure Joseph had protected them.

"Yes," Joseph Sr. replied, "but remember that for a small thing Esau lost his blessing and birthright. It may be so with Joseph."[28]

To be sure the plates were secure, Emma mounted a horse and rode for more than an hour to the farm where Joseph was working. She found him by the well, caked in dirt and sweat from the day's work. Hearing of the danger, Joseph looked into the Urim and Thummim and saw that the plates were safe.

Back home, Joseph Sr. paced back and forth outside the house, glancing every minute down the road until he saw Joseph and Emma.

"Father," Joseph said as they rode up, "all is perfectly safe—there is no cause of alarm."[29]

But it was time to act.

HURRYING TO THE HILL, Joseph found the log where the plates were hidden and carefully wrapped them in a shirt.[30] He then ducked into the woods and headed for home, his eyes alert to danger. The forest concealed him from people on the main road, but it gave thieves plenty of places to hide.

Straining under the weight of the record, Joseph tramped through the woods as fast as he could. A fallen tree blocked the path ahead of him, and as he bounded over it, he felt something hard strike him from behind. Turning around, he saw a man coming at him, wielding a gun like a club.

Clutching the plates tightly with one arm, Joseph knocked the man to the ground and scrambled deeper into the thicket. He ran for about half a mile when another man sprang from behind a tree and struck him with the butt of his gun. Joseph fought the man off and darted away, desperate to be out of the woods. But before he could get very far a third man attacked, landing a heavy blow that sent him reeling. Gathering his strength, Joseph hit the man hard and ran for home.[31]

Back at the house, Joseph burst through the door with his heavy bundle tucked beneath one arm. "Father," he cried, "I have got the plates."

His fourteen-year-old sister, Katharine, helped him set the bundle on a table as the rest of the family gathered around him. Joseph could tell his father and younger brother William wanted to unwrap the plates, but he stopped them.

"Can we not see them?" Joseph Sr. asked.

"No," Joseph said. "I was disobedient the first time, but I intend to be faithful this time."

He told them they could feel the plates through the cloth, and his brother William picked up the bundle. It was heavier than stone, and William could tell that it had leaves that moved like the pages of a book.[32] Joseph also sent his youngest brother, Don Carlos, to get a lockbox from Hyrum, who lived down the road with his wife, Jerusha, and their newborn daughter.

Hyrum arrived soon after, and once the plates were securely in the box, Joseph collapsed onto a nearby bed and started telling his family about the men in the woods.

As he spoke, he realized his hand ached. Sometime during the attacks he had dislocated a thumb.

"I must stop talking, Father," he said suddenly, "and get you to put my thumb back in place."[33]

CHAPTER 5

All Is Lost

After Joseph brought the gold plates home, treasure seekers tried for weeks to steal them. To keep the record safe, he had to move it from place to place, hiding the plates under the hearth, beneath the floor of his father's shop, and in piles of grain. He could never let his guard down.

Curious neighbors stopped by the house and begged him to show them the record. Joseph always refused, even when someone offered to pay him. He was determined to care for the plates, trusting in the Lord's promise that if he did everything he could, they would be protected.[1]

These disruptions often kept him from examining the plates and learning more about the Urim and Thummim. He knew the interpreters were supposed to help him translate the plates, but he had never used seer stones to read an ancient language. He was anxious to begin the work, but it was not obvious to him how to do it.[2]

As Joseph studied the plates, a respected land-owner in Palmyra named Martin Harris had become interested in his work. Martin was old enough to be Joseph's father and had sometimes hired Joseph to help on his land. Martin had heard about the gold plates but had thought little about them until Joseph's mother invited him to visit with her son.[3]

Joseph was out working when Martin stopped by, so he questioned Emma and other family members about the plates. When Joseph arrived home, Martin caught him by the arm and asked for more details. Joseph told him about the gold plates and Moroni's instructions to translate and publish the writing on them.

"If it is the devil's work," Martin said, "I will have nothing to do with it." But if it was the Lord's work, he wanted to help Joseph proclaim it to the world.

Joseph let Martin heft the plates in the lockbox. Martin could tell something heavy was there, but he was not convinced it was a set of gold plates. "You must not blame me for not taking your word," he told Joseph.

When Martin got home after midnight, he crept into his bedroom and prayed, promising God to give all he had if he could know that Joseph was doing divine work.

As he prayed, Martin felt a still, small voice speak to his soul. He knew then that the plates were from

God—and he knew he had to help Joseph share their message.[4]

LATE IN 1827, EMMA learned she was pregnant and wrote to her parents. It had been almost a year since she and Joseph had married, and her father and mother were still unhappy. But the Hales agreed to let the young couple return to Harmony so Emma could give birth near her family.

Although it would take him away from his own parents and siblings, Joseph was eager to go. People in New York were still trying to steal the plates, and moving to a new place could provide the peace and privacy he needed to do the Lord's work. Unfortunately, he was in debt and had no money to make the move.[5]

Hoping to get his finances in order, Joseph went to town to settle some of his debts. While he was in a store making a payment, Martin Harris strode up to him. "Here, Mr. Smith, is fifty dollars," he said. "I give it to you to do the Lord's work."

Joseph was nervous about accepting the money and promised to repay it, but Martin said not to worry about it. The money was a gift, and he called on every-one in the room to witness that he had given it freely.[6]

Soon after, Joseph paid his debts and loaded his wagon. He and Emma then left for Harmony with the gold plates hidden in a barrel of beans.[7]

THE COUPLE ARRIVED AT the Hales' spacious home about a week later.[8] Before long, Emma's father demanded to see the gold plates, but Joseph said he could only show him the box where he kept them. Annoyed, Isaac picked up the lockbox and felt its weight, yet he remained skeptical. He said Joseph could not keep it in the house unless he showed him what was inside.[9]

With Emma's father around, translating would not be easy, but Joseph tried his best. Assisted by Emma, he copied many of the strange characters from the plates to paper.[10] Then, for several weeks, he tried to translate them with the Urim and Thummim. The process required him to do more than look into the interpreters. He had to be humble and exercise faith as he studied the characters.[11]

A few months later, Martin came to Harmony. He said he felt called by the Lord to travel as far as New York City to consult experts in ancient languages. He hoped they could translate the characters.[12]

Joseph copied several more characters from the plates, wrote down his translation, and handed the paper to Martin. He and Emma then watched as their friend headed east to consult with distinguished scholars.[13]

WHEN MARTIN ARRIVED IN New York City, he went to see Charles Anthon, a professor of Latin and Greek at Columbia College. Professor Anthon was a young man—about fifteen years younger than Martin—and was best known for publishing a popular encyclopedia on Greek and Roman culture. He had also begun collecting stories about American Indians.[14]

Anthon was a rigid scholar who resented interruptions, but he welcomed Martin and studied the characters and translation Joseph had provided.[15] Although the professor did not know Egyptian, he had read some studies on the language and knew what it looked like. Looking at the characters, he saw some similarities with Egyptian and told Martin the translation was correct.

Martin showed him more characters, and Anthon examined them. He said they contained characters from many ancient languages and gave Martin a certificate verifying their authenticity. He also recommended that he show the characters to another scholar named Samuel Mitchill, who used to teach at Columbia.[16]

"He is very learned in these ancient languages," Anthon said, "and I have no doubt he will be able to give you some satisfaction."[17]

Martin placed the certificate in his pocket, but just as he was leaving, Anthon called him back. He wanted to know how Joseph found the gold plates.

"An angel of God," Martin said, "revealed it unto him." He testified that the translation of the plates would change the world and save it from destruction. And now that he had proof of their authenticity, he intended to sell his farm and donate money to get the translation published.

"Let me see that certificate," Anthon said.

Martin reached into his pocket and gave it to him. Anthon tore it to pieces and said there was no such thing as ministering angels. If Joseph wanted the plates translated, he could bring them to Columbia and let a scholar translate them.

Martin explained that part of the plates were sealed and that Joseph was not allowed to show them to anyone.

"I cannot read a sealed book," said Anthon. He warned Martin that Joseph was probably cheating him. "Beware of rogues," he said.[18]

Martin left Professor Anthon and called on Samuel Mitchill. He received Martin politely, listened to his story, and looked at the characters and translation. He could not make sense of them, but he said they reminded him of Egyptian hieroglyphics and were the writings of an extinct nation.[19]

Martin left the city a short time later and returned to Harmony, more convinced than ever that Joseph had ancient gold plates and the power to translate them. He told Joseph about his interviews with the professors and reasoned that if some of the most educated men in America could not translate the book, Joseph had to do it.

"I cannot," Joseph said, overwhelmed by the task, "for I am not learned." But he knew the Lord had prepared the interpreters so he could translate the plates.[20]

Martin agreed. He planned to go back to Palmyra, set his business in order, and return as soon as possible to serve as Joseph's scribe.[21]

IN APRIL 1828, EMMA and Joseph were living in a home along the Susquehanna River, not far from her parents' house.[22] Now well along in her pregnancy, Emma often acted as Joseph's scribe after he began translating the record. One day, while he translated, Joseph suddenly grew pale. "Emma, did Jerusalem have a wall around it?" he asked.

"Yes," she said, recalling descriptions of it in the Bible.

"Oh," Joseph said with relief, "I was afraid I had been deceived."[23]

Emma marveled that her husband's lack of knowledge in history and scripture did not hinder the translation. Joseph could hardly write a coherent letter. Yet hour after hour she sat close beside him while he dictated the record without the aid of any book or manuscript. She knew only God could inspire him to translate as he did.[24]

In time, Martin returned from Palmyra and took over as scribe, giving Emma a chance to rest before the baby came.[25] But rest did not come easy. Martin's wife, Lucy, had insisted on coming with him to Harmony, and both Harrises had strong personalities.[26] Lucy was suspicious of Martin's desire to support Joseph financially and was angry that he had gone to New York City without her. When he told her he was going to Harmony to help with translation, she had invited herself along, determined to see the plates.

Lucy was losing her hearing, and when she could not understand what people were saying, she sometimes thought they were criticizing her. She also had little sense of privacy. After Joseph refused to show her the plates, she started searching the house, rifling through the family's chests, cupboards, and trunks. Joseph had little choice but to hide the plates in the woods.[27]

Lucy soon left the house and lodged with a neighbor. Emma had her chests and cupboards to herself again, but now Lucy was telling the neighbors that Joseph was out to get Martin's money. After weeks of causing trouble, Lucy went home to Palmyra.

With peace restored, Joseph and Martin translated quickly. Joseph was growing into his divine role as a seer and revelator. Looking into the interpreters or another seer stone, he was able to translate whether the plates were in front of him or wrapped in one of Emma's linen cloths on the table.[28]

Throughout April, May, and early June, Emma listened to the rhythm of Joseph dictating the record.[29] He spoke slowly but clearly, pausing occasionally to wait for Martin to say "written" after he had caught up to what Joseph had said.[30] Emma also took turns as scribe and was amazed how after interruptions and breaks, Joseph always picked up where he left off without any prompting.[31]

Soon it was time for Emma's baby to be born. The pile of manuscript pages had grown thick, and Martin had become convinced that if he could let his wife read the translation, she would see its value and stop interfering with their work.[32] He also hoped Lucy would be pleased with how he had spent his time and money to help bring forth God's word.

One day, Martin asked Joseph for permission to take the manuscript to Palmyra for a few weeks.[33] Remembering how Lucy Harris had acted when she visited the house, Joseph was wary of the idea. Yet he wanted to please Martin, who had believed him when so many others had doubted his word.[34]

Unsure what to do, Joseph prayed for guidance, and the Lord told him not to let Martin take the pages.[35] But Martin was sure showing them to his wife would change things, and he begged Joseph to ask again. Joseph did so, but the answer was the same. Martin pressed him to ask a third time, however, and this time God allowed them to do as they pleased.

Joseph told Martin he could take the pages for two weeks if he covenanted to keep them locked up and show them only to certain family members. Martin made the promise and returned to Palmyra, manuscript in hand.[36]

After Martin left, Moroni appeared to Joseph and took the interpreters from him.[37]

THE DAY AFTER MARTIN'S departure, Emma endured an agonizing labor and gave birth to a boy. The baby was frail and sickly and did not live long. The ordeal left Emma physically drained and emotionally devastated, and for a time it seemed she might die too. Joseph tended to her constantly, never leaving her side for long.[38]

After two weeks, Emma's health began to improve, and her thoughts turned to Martin and the manuscript. "I feel so uneasy," she told Joseph, "that I cannot rest and shall not be at ease until I know something about what Mr. Harris is doing with it."

She urged Joseph to find Martin, but Joseph did not want to leave her. "Send for my mother," she said, "and she shall stay with me while you are gone."[39]

Joseph took a stagecoach north. He ate and slept little during the journey, afraid that he had offended the Lord by not listening when He said not to let Martin take the manuscript.[40]

The sun was rising when he arrived at his parents' home in Manchester. The Smiths were preparing breakfast and sent Martin an invitation to join them. By eight o'clock, the meal was on the table but Martin had not come. Joseph and the family started to grow uneasy as they waited for him.

Finally, after more than four hours had passed, Martin appeared in the distance, walking slowly toward the house, his eyes fixed on the ground in front of him.[41] At the gate he paused, sat on the fence, and pulled his hat down over his eyes. He then came inside and sat down to eat in silence.

The family watched as Martin picked up his utensils, as if ready to eat, then dropped them. "I have lost my soul!" he cried, pressing his hands on his temples. "I have lost my soul."

Joseph jumped up. "Martin, have you lost that manuscript?"

"Yes," Martin said. "It is gone, and I know not where."

"Oh, my God, my God," Joseph groaned, clenching his fists. "All is lost!"

He started pacing the floor. He did not know what to do. "Go back," he ordered Martin. "Search again."

"It is all in vain," Martin cried. "I have looked every place in the house. I have even ripped open beds and pillows, and I know it is not there."

"Must I return to my wife with such a tale?" Joseph feared the news would kill her. "And how shall I appear before the Lord?"

His mother tried to comfort him. She said maybe the Lord would forgive him if he repented humbly. But Joseph was sobbing now, furious at himself for not obeying the Lord the first time. He could barely eat for the rest of the day. He stayed the night and left the next morning for Harmony.[42]

As Lucy watched him go, her heart was heavy. It seemed everything they had hoped for as a family—everything that had brought them joy over the last few years—had fled in a moment.[43]

CHAPTER 6

The Gift and Power of God

When Joseph returned to Harmony in the summer of 1828, Moroni appeared to him again and took the plates away. "If you are sufficiently humble and penitent," the angel said, "you will receive them again on the twenty-second of September."[1]

Darkness clouded Joseph's mind.[2] He knew he had been wrong to ignore God's will and trust Martin with the manuscript. Now God no longer trusted him with the plates or the interpreters. He felt like he deserved any punishment the heavens sent his way.[3]

Weighed down with guilt and regret, he went to his knees, confessed his sins, and pleaded for forgiveness. He reflected on where he had gone wrong and what he could do better if the Lord let him translate again.[4]

One day in July, as Joseph was walking a short distance from his house, Moroni appeared to him. The angel handed him the interpreters, and Joseph saw a divine message in them: "The works, and the designs, and the purposes of God cannot be frustrated, neither can they come to naught."[5]

The words were reassuring, but they soon gave way to reproof. "How strict were your commandments," the Lord said. "You should not have feared man more than God." He commanded Joseph to be more careful with sacred things. The record on the gold plates was more important than Martin's reputation or Joseph's desire to please people. God had prepared it to renew His ancient covenant and teach all people to rely on Jesus Christ for salvation.

The Lord urged Joseph to remember His mercy. "Repent of that which thou hast done," He commanded, "and thou art still chosen." Once again, He called Joseph to be His prophet and seer. Yet He warned him to heed His word.

"Except thou do this," He declared, "thou shalt be delivered up and become as other men, and have no more gift."[6]

THAT FALL, JOSEPH'S PARENTS traveled south to Harmony. Nearly two months had passed since Joseph left their home in Manchester, and they had heard nothing from him. They worried the summer's tragedies had devastated him. In a matter of weeks, he had lost his first child, nearly lost his wife, and lost the manuscript pages. They wanted to make sure he and Emma were well.

Less than a mile from their destination, Joseph Sr. and Lucy were overjoyed to see Joseph standing in the road ahead of them, looking calm and happy. He told them about losing the confidence of God, repenting of his sins, and receiving the revelation. The Lord's rebuke had stung him, but like prophets of old he wrote the revelation down for others to read. It was the first time he had ever recorded the Lord's word to him.

Joseph also told his parents that Moroni had since returned the plates and interpreters. The angel seemed pleased, Joseph recounted. "He told me that the Lord loved me for my faithfulness and humility."

The record was now safely stowed in the house, hidden in a trunk. "Emma writes for me now," Joseph told them, "but the angel said that the Lord would send someone to write for me, and I trust that it will be so."[7]

THE FOLLOWING SPRING, MARTIN Harris traveled to Harmony with some bad news. His wife had filed a complaint in court, claiming Joseph was a fraud who pretended to translate gold plates. Martin now expected a summons to testify in court. He would have to declare that Joseph had fooled him, or Lucy would charge him with deceit as well.[8]

Martin pushed Joseph to give him more evidence that the plates were real. He wanted to tell the court all about the translation, but he worried people would not believe him. Lucy, after all, had searched the Smiths' house and never found the record. And though he had served as Joseph's scribe for two months, Martin had never seen the plates either and could not testify that he had.[9]

Joseph took the question to the Lord and received an answer for his friend. The Lord would not tell Martin what to say in court, nor would He provide him any more evidence until Martin chose to be humble and exercise faith. "If they will not believe my words, they would not believe you, my servant Joseph," He said, "if it were possible that you should show them all these things which I have committed unto you."

The Lord promised to treat Martin mercifully, however, if he did as Joseph had done that summer and humbled himself, trusted in God, and learned from his mistakes. Three faithful witnesses would see the plates in due time, the Lord said, and Martin could be one of them if he stopped seeking the approval of others.[10]

Before closing His words, the Lord made a declaration. "If the people of this generation harden not their hearts," He said, "I will establish my church."[11]

Joseph reflected on these words as Martin copied the revelation. He and Emma then listened as Martin read it back to check its accuracy. As they read, Emma's father came into the room and listened. When they finished, he asked whose words they were.

"The words of Jesus Christ," Joseph and Emma explained.

"I consider the whole of it a delusion," Isaac said. "Abandon it."[12]

Ignoring Emma's father, Martin took his copy of the revelation and boarded the stagecoach for home. He had come to Harmony seeking evidence of the plates, and he left with a revelation testifying of their reality. He could not use it in court, but he returned to Palmyra knowing the Lord was aware of him.

Later, when Martin stood before the judge, he offered a simple, powerful testimony. With a hand raised to heaven, he witnessed of the truth of the gold plates and declared that he had freely given Joseph fifty dollars to do the Lord's work. With no evidence to prove Lucy's accusations, the court dismissed the case.[13]

Joseph, meanwhile, continued the translation, praying the Lord would soon send him another scribe.[14]

BACK IN MANCHESTER, A young man named Oliver Cowdery was staying with Joseph's parents. Oliver was a year younger than Joseph, and in the fall of 1828 he had begun teaching school about a mile south of the Smiths' farm.

Teachers often boarded with the families of their students, and when Oliver heard rumors about Joseph and the gold plates, he asked if he could stay with the Smiths. At first he gleaned few details from the family. The stolen manuscript and local gossip had made them wary to the point of silence.[15]

But during the winter of 1828–29, as Oliver taught the Smith children, he earned the trust of his hosts. Around this time, Joseph Sr. had come back from a trip to Harmony with a revelation declaring that the Lord was about to begin a marvelous work.[16] By then Oliver had proven to be a sincere seeker of truth, and Joseph's parents opened up to him about their son's divine calling.[17]

What they said captivated Oliver, and he longed to help with the translation. Like Joseph, Oliver was dissatisfied with modern churches and believed in a God of miracles who still revealed His will to people.[18] But Joseph and the gold plates were far away, and Oliver did not know how he could help the work if he stayed in Manchester.

Once spring day, as rain was falling hard against the Smiths' roof, Oliver told the family he wanted to go to Harmony to help Joseph when the school term was over. Lucy and Joseph Sr. urged him to ask the Lord if his desires were right.[19]

Retiring to his bed, Oliver prayed privately to know if what he had heard about the gold plates was true. The Lord showed him a vision of the gold plates and Joseph's efforts to translate them. A peaceful feeling rested over him, and he knew then that he should volunteer to be Joseph's scribe.[20]

Oliver told no one about his prayer. But as soon as the school term ended, he and Joseph's brother Samuel set out on foot for Harmony, more than a hundred miles away. The road was cold and muddy from spring rain, and Oliver had a frostbitten toe by the time he and Samuel arrived at Joseph and Emma's door. Yet he was eager to meet the couple and see for himself how the Lord worked through the young prophet.[21]

ONCE OLIVER ARRIVED IN Harmony, it was as if he had always been there. Joseph talked with him late into the night, listened to his story, and answered his questions. It was obvious Oliver had a good education, and Joseph readily accepted his offer to act as scribe.

After Oliver's arrival, Joseph's first task was to secure a place to work. He asked Oliver to draft a contract in which Joseph promised to pay his father-in-law for the small frame home where he and Emma lived, as well as the barn, farmland, and nearby spring.[22] Mindful of their daughter's well-being, Emma's parents agreed to the terms and promised to help calm neighbors' fears about Joseph.[23]

Meanwhile, Joseph and Oliver started translating. They worked well together, weeks on end, frequently with Emma in the same room going about her daily work.[24] Sometimes Joseph translated by looking through the interpreters and reading in English the characters on the plates.

Often he found a single seer stone to be more convenient. He would put the seer stone in his hat, place his face into the hat to block out the light, and peer at the stone. Light from the stone would shine in the darkness, revealing words that Joseph dictated as Oliver rapidly copied them down.[25]

Under the Lord's direction, Joseph did not try to retranslate what he had lost. Instead, he and Oliver continued forward in the record. The Lord revealed that Satan had enticed wicked men to take the pages, alter their words, and use them to cast doubt on the translation. But the Lord assured Joseph that He had inspired the ancient prophets who prepared the plates to include another, fuller account of the lost material.[26]

"I will confound those who have altered my words," the Lord told Joseph. "I will show unto them that my wisdom is greater than the cunning of the devil."[27]

Acting as Joseph's scribe thrilled Oliver. Day after day, he listened as his friend dictated the complex history of two large civilizations, the Nephites and the Lamanites. He learned of righteous and wicked kings, of people who fell into captivity and were delivered from it, of an ancient prophet who used seer stones to translate records recovered from fields filled with bones. Like Joseph, that prophet was a revelator and seer blessed with the gift and power of God.[28]

The record testified again and again of Jesus Christ, and Oliver saw how prophets led an ancient church and how ordinary men and women did the work of God.

Yet Oliver still had many questions about the Lord's work, and he hungered for answers. Joseph sought a revelation for him through the Urim and Thummim, and the Lord responded. "If you will ask of me you shall receive," He declared. "If thou wilt inquire, thou shalt know mysteries which are great and marvelous."

The Lord also urged Oliver to remember the witness he had received before coming to Harmony, which Oliver had kept to himself. "Did I not speak peace to your mind concerning the matter? What greater witness can you have than from God?" the Lord asked. "If I have told you things which no man knoweth have you not received a witness?"[29]

Oliver was astonished. He immediately told Joseph about his secret prayer and the divine witness he had received. No one could have known about it except God, he said, and he now knew the work was true.

They returned to work, and Oliver began to wonder if he could translate as well.[30] He believed that God could work through instruments like seer stones, and he had occasionally used a divining rod to find water and minerals. Yet he was unsure if his rod worked by the power of God. The process of revelation was still a mystery to him.[31]

Joseph again brought Oliver's questions to the Lord, and the Lord told Oliver that he had power to acquire knowledge if he asked in faith. The Lord confirmed that Oliver's rod worked by the power of God, like Aaron's rod in the Old Testament. He then taught Oliver more about revelation. "I will tell you in your mind and in your heart, by the Holy Ghost," He declared. "Behold, this is the spirit of revelation."

He also told Oliver that he could translate the record like Joseph did, as long as he relied on faith. "Remember," the Lord said, "without faith you can do nothing."[32]

After the revelation, Oliver was excited to translate. He followed Joseph's example, but when the words did not come easily, he grew frustrated and confused.

Joseph saw his friend's struggle and sympathized. It had taken him time to tune his heart and mind to the work of translation, but Oliver seemed to think he could master it quickly. It was not enough to have a spiritual gift. He had to cultivate and develop it over time for use in God's work.

Oliver soon gave up on translating and asked Joseph why he had not been successful.

Joseph asked the Lord. "You have supposed that I would give it unto you, when you took no thought save it was to ask me," the Lord replied. "You must study it out in your mind; then you must ask me if it be right."

The Lord instructed Oliver to be patient. "It is not expedient that you should translate now," He said. "The work which you are called to do is to write for my servant Joseph." He promised Oliver other opportunities to translate later, but for now he was the scribe and Joseph was the seer.[33]

CHAPTER 7

Fellow Servants

The spring of 1829 was cold and wet well into May. While farmers around Harmony stayed indoors, putting off their spring planting until the weather improved, Joseph and Oliver translated as much of the record as they could.[1]

They had come to an account of what happened among the Nephites and Lamanites when Jesus died in Jerusalem. It told of massive earthquakes and storms that devastated the people and altered the shape of the land. Some cities sank into the ground, while others caught fire and burned. Lightning split the sky for hours and the sun disappeared, shrouding the survivors in thick darkness. For three days people cried out, mourning for their dead.[2]

Finally, the voice of Jesus Christ pierced the gloom. "Will ye not now return unto me," He asked, "and repent of your sins, and be converted, that I may heal you?"[3] He lifted the darkness, and the people repented. Soon, many of them gathered to a temple in a place called Bountiful, where they spoke of the incredible changes to the land.[4]

While the people talked with one another, they saw the Son of God descend out of heaven. "I am Jesus Christ," He said, "whom the prophets testified shall come into the world."[5] He stayed among them for a time, taught His gospel, and commanded them to be baptized by immersion for the remission of sins.

"Whoso believeth in me, and is baptized, the same shall be saved," He declared. "They are they who shall inherit the kingdom of God."[6] Before ascending to heaven, He gave righteous men authority to baptize those who believed in Him.[7]

As they translated, Joseph and Oliver were struck by these teachings. Like his brother Alvin, Joseph had never been baptized, and he wanted to know more about the ordinance and the authority necessary to perform it.[8]

ON MAY 15, 1829, THE rains cleared and Joseph and Oliver walked into the woods near the Susquehanna River. Kneeling, they asked God about baptism and the remission of sins. As they prayed, the voice of the Redeemer spoke peace to them, and an angel appeared in a cloud of light. He introduced himself as John the

Baptist and placed his hands on their heads. Joy filled their hearts as God's love surrounded them.

"Upon you my fellow servants," John declared, "in the name of Messiah I confer the Priesthood of Aaron, which holds the keys of the ministering of angels, and of the gospel of repentance, and of baptism by immersion for the remission of sins."[9]

The angel's voice was mild, but it seemed to pierce Joseph and Oliver to the core.[10] He explained that the Aaronic Priesthood authorized them to perform baptisms, and he commanded them to baptize each other after he departed. He also said they would receive additional priesthood power later, which would give them authority to confer the gift of the Holy Ghost on each other and on those they baptized.

After John the Baptist left, Joseph and Oliver walked to the river and waded in. Joseph baptized Oliver first, and as soon as he came out of the water, Oliver began to prophesy about things that would soon happen. Oliver then baptized Joseph, who rose from the river prophesying about the rise of Christ's church, which the Lord had promised to establish among them.[11]

Following John the Baptist's instructions, they returned to the woods and ordained each other to the Aaronic Priesthood. In their study of the Bible, as well as their translation of the ancient record, Joseph and Oliver had often read about the authority to act in God's name. Now they carried that authority themselves.

After their baptism, Joseph and Oliver found that
scriptures that once seemed dense and mysterious suddenly became clearer. Truth and understanding flooded
their minds.[12]

BACK IN NEW YORK, Oliver's friend David Whitmer was
eager to learn more about Joseph's work. Though David
lived in Fayette, about thirty miles from Manchester, he
and Oliver had become friends while Oliver was teaching
school and living with the Smiths. They often talked about
the gold plates, and when Oliver moved to Harmony, he
promised to write to David about the translation.

Letters started arriving a short time later. Oliver
wrote that Joseph knew details about his life that no one
could have known except by revelation from God. He
described the Lord's words to Joseph and the translation
of the record. In one letter, Oliver shared a few lines of
the translation, testifying of its truthfulness.

Another letter informed David that it was God's will
for him to bring his team and wagon to Harmony to help
Joseph, Emma, and Oliver move to the Whitmer home
in Fayette, where they would finish the translation.[13]
People in Harmony had become less welcoming to the
Smiths. Some men had even threatened to attack them,
and had it not been for the influence of Emma's family,
they might have been seriously hurt.[14]

David shared Oliver's letters with his parents and
siblings, who agreed to welcome Joseph, Emma, and

Oliver into their home. The Whitmers were descendants of German-speaking settlers in the area and had a reputation for hard work and piety. Their farm was close enough to the Smith home for a visit but far enough away to keep thieves from disturbing them.[15]

David wanted to go to Harmony immediately, but his father reminded him that he had two days of heavy work to do before he could leave. It was planting season, and David needed to plow twenty acres and enrich the soil with plaster of paris to help their wheat grow. His father said he ought to pray first to learn if it was absolutely necessary to leave now.

David took his father's advice, and as he prayed, he felt the Spirit tell him to finish his work at home before going to Harmony.

The next morning, David walked out to the fields and saw rows of dark furrows in ground that had been unplowed the evening before. Exploring the fields further, he saw that about six acres had been plowed overnight, and the plow was waiting for him in the last furrow, ready for him to finish the job.

David's father was astonished when he learned what had happened. "There must be an overruling hand in this," he said, "and I think you had better go down to Pennsylvania as soon as your plaster of paris is sown."

David worked hard to plow the remaining fields and prepare the soil for a successful planting. When he finished, he hitched his wagon to a strong team of horses and set out for Harmony earlier than expected.[16]

ONCE JOSEPH, EMMA, AND Oliver moved to Fayette, David's mother had her hands full. Mary Whitmer and her husband, Peter, already had eight children between the ages of fifteen and thirty, and the few who did not still live at home resided nearby. Tending to their needs filled Mary's days with work, and the three houseguests added more labor. Mary had faith in Joseph's calling and did not complain, but she was getting tired.[17]

The heat in Fayette that summer was sweltering. As Mary washed clothes and prepared meals, Joseph dictated the translation in an upstairs room. Oliver usually wrote for him, but occasionally Emma or one of the Whitmers took a turn with the pen.[18] Sometimes, when Joseph and Oliver tired of the strain of translating, they would walk out to a nearby pond and skip stones across the surface of the water.

Mary had little time to relax herself, and the added work and the strain placed on her were hard to bear.

One day, while she was out by the barn where the cows were milked, she saw a gray-haired man with a knapsack slung across his shoulder. His sudden appearance frightened her, but as he approached, he spoke to her in a kind voice that set her at ease.

"My name is Moroni," he said. "You have become pretty tired with all the extra work you have to do." He swung the knapsack off his shoulder, and Mary watched as he started to untie it.[19]

"You have been very faithful and diligent in your labors," he continued. "It is proper, therefore, that you should receive a witness that your faith may be strengthened."[20]

Moroni opened his knapsack and removed the gold plates. He held them in front of her and turned their pages so she could see the writings on them. After he turned the last page, he urged her to be patient and faithful as she carried the extra burden a little longer. He promised she would be blessed for it.[21]

The old man vanished a moment later, leaving Mary alone. She still had work to do, but that no longer troubled her.[22]

AT THE WHITMER FARM, Joseph translated rapidly, but some days were challenging. His mind would wander to other matters, and he could not focus on spiritual things.[23] The Whitmers' small house was always busy and full of distractions. Moving there had meant giving up the relative privacy he and Emma had enjoyed in Harmony.

One morning, as he was getting ready to translate, Joseph became upset with Emma. Later, when he joined Oliver and David in the upstairs room where they worked, he could not translate a syllable.

He left the room and walked outside to the orchard. He stayed away for about an hour, praying. When he came back, he apologized to Emma and asked for forgiveness. He then went back to translating as usual.[24]

He was now translating the last part of the record, known as the small plates of Nephi, which would actually serve as the beginning of the book. Revealing a history similar to the one he and Martin had translated and lost, the small plates told of a young man named Nephi, whose family God had guided from Jerusalem to a new promised land. It explained the origins of the record and the early struggles between the Nephite and Lamanite peoples. More important, it bore a powerful testimony of Jesus Christ and His Atonement.

When Joseph translated the writing on the final plate, he found that it explained the record's purpose and gave it a title, The Book of Mormon, after the ancient prophet-historian who had compiled the book.[25]

Since he started translating the Book of Mormon, Joseph had learned much about his future role in God's work. In its pages, he recognized basic teachings he had learned from the Bible as well as new truths and insights about Jesus Christ and His gospel. He also uncovered passages about the latter days that prophesied of a chosen seer named Joseph, who would bring forth the Lord's word and restore lost knowledge and covenants.[26]

In the record, he learned that Nephi expanded on Isaiah's prophecy about a sealed book that learned men could not read. As Joseph read the prophecy, he thought of Martin Harris's interview with Professor Anthon. It affirmed that only God could bring forth the book out of the earth and establish the church of Christ in the last days.[27]

AS JOSEPH AND HIS friends finished the translation, their minds turned to a promise the Lord had given in the Book of Mormon and in His revelations—to show the plates to three witnesses. Joseph's parents and Martin Harris were visiting the Whitmer farm at the time, and one morning Martin, Oliver, and David pleaded with Joseph to let them be the witnesses. Joseph prayed and the Lord answered, saying that if they relied on Him wholeheartedly and committed to testify of the truth, they could see the plates.[28]

"You have got to humble yourself before your God this day," Joseph told Martin specifically, "and obtain if possible a forgiveness of your sins."[29]

Later that day, Joseph led the three men into the woods near the Whitmer home. They knelt, and each took a turn praying to be shown the plates, but nothing happened. They tried a second time, but still nothing happened. Finally, Martin rose and walked away, saying he was the reason the heavens remained closed.

Joseph, Oliver, and David returned to prayer, and soon an angel appeared in a brilliant light above them.[30] He had the plates in his hands and turned them over one by one, showing the men the symbols engraved on each page. A table appeared beside him, and on it were ancient artifacts described in the Book of Mormon: the interpreters, the breastplate, a sword, and the miraculous compass that guided Nephi's family from Jerusalem to the promised land.

The men heard the voice of God declare, "These plates have been revealed by the power of God, and they have been translated by the power of God. The translation of them, which you have seen, is correct, and I command you to bear record of what you now see and hear."[31]

When the angel departed, Joseph walked deeper into the woods and found Martin on his knees. Martin told him he had not yet received a witness from the Lord, but he still wanted to see the plates. He asked Joseph to pray with him. Joseph knelt beside him, and before their words were half-uttered, they saw the same angel displaying the plates and the other ancient objects.

"'Tis enough! 'Tis enough!" Martin cried. "Mine eyes have beheld! Mine eyes have beheld!"[32]

JOSEPH AND THE THREE Witnesses returned to the Whitmer house later that afternoon. Mary Whitmer was chatting with Joseph's parents when Joseph rushed into the room. "Father! Mother!" he said. "You do not know how happy I am!"

He flung himself down beside his mother. "The Lord has caused the plates to be shown to three more besides me," he said. "They know for themselves that I do not go about to deceive the people."

He felt as if a burden had been lifted off his shoulders. "They will now have to bear a part," he said. "I am not any longer to be entirely alone in the world."

Martin came into the room next, almost bursting with joy. "I have now seen an angel from heaven!" he cried. "I bless God in the sincerity of my soul that he has condescended to make me—even me—a witness of the greatness of His work!"[33]

A few days later, the Whitmers joined the Smith family at their farm in Manchester. Knowing the Lord had promised to establish His words "in the mouth of as many witnesses as seemeth him good," Joseph went into the woods with his father, Hyrum, and Samuel, as well as four of David Whitmer's brothers—Christian, Jacob, Peter Jr., and John—and their brother-in-law Hiram Page.[34]

The men gathered at a spot where the Smith family often went to pray privately. With the Lord's permission, Joseph uncovered the plates and showed them to the group. They did not see an angel as the Three Witnesses had, but Joseph let them hold the record in their hands, turn its pages, and inspect its ancient writing. Handling the plates affirmed their faith that Joseph's testimony about the angel and the ancient record was true.[35]

Now that the translation was over and he had witnesses to support his miraculous testimony, Joseph no longer needed the plates. After the men left the woods and went back to the house, the angel appeared and Joseph returned the sacred record to his care.[36]

CHAPTER 8

The Rise of the Church of Christ

In early July 1829, with manuscript in hand, Joseph knew the Lord wanted him to publish the Book of Mormon and spread its message far and wide. But the publishing business was unfamiliar to him and his family. He had to keep the manuscript safe, find a printer, and somehow get the book in the hands of people willing to consider the possibility of new scripture.

Publishing a book as long as the Book of Mormon would also not be cheap. Joseph's finances had not improved since he started the translation, and all the money he made went toward providing for his family. The same was true for his parents, who were still poor farmers working land they did not own. Joseph's only friend who could finance the project was Martin Harris.

Joseph set to work quickly. Before he completed the translation, he had filed for the book's copyright to protect the text from anyone who might steal or plagiarize it.[1] With Martin's assistance, Joseph also started looking for a printer who would agree to publish the book.

They went first to Egbert Grandin, a printer in Palmyra who was the same age as Joseph. Grandin declined the proposal at once, believing the book was a fraud. Undeterred, Joseph and Martin kept searching and found a willing printer in a nearby city. But before accepting his offer, they returned to Palmyra and asked Grandin once more if he wanted to publish the book.[2]

This time, Grandin seemed more willing to take the project, but he wanted to be paid $3,000 to print and bind five thousand copies before he even started work. Martin had already promised to help pay for the printing, but to come up with that kind of money, he realized he might need to mortgage his farm. It was an enormous burden for Martin, but he knew none of Joseph's other friends could help him with the money.

Troubled, Martin began to question the wisdom of financing the Book of Mormon. He had one of the best farms in the area. If he mortgaged his land, he risked losing it. Wealth he had spent a lifetime accruing could be gone in an instant if the Book of Mormon did not sell well.

Martin told Joseph his concerns and asked him to seek a revelation for him. In response, the Savior spoke of His sacrifice to do His Father's will, regardless of the cost. He described His ultimate suffering while paying the price for sin so that all might repent and be forgiven. He then commanded Martin to sacrifice his own interests to bring about God's plan.

"Thou shalt not covet thine own property," the Lord said, "but impart it freely to the printing of the Book of Mormon." The book contained the true word of God, the Lord assured Martin, and it would help others believe the gospel.[3]

Although his neighbors would not understand his decision, Martin obeyed the Lord and mortgaged his farm to guarantee payment.[4]

Grandin signed a contract and began to organize the massive project.[5] Joseph had translated the text of the Book of Mormon in three months, assisted by one scribe at a time. It would take Grandin and a dozen men seven months to print and bind the first copies of the 590-page work.[6]

WITH A PUBLISHER HIRED, Joseph returned to Harmony in October 1829 to work his farm and be with Emma. Oliver, Martin, and Hyrum, meanwhile, would oversee the printing and send Joseph regular updates on Grandin's progress.[7]

Remembering the despair he had felt after losing the first pages he translated, Joseph asked Oliver to copy the Book of Mormon manuscript page by page, making a duplicate to take to the printer so punctuation could be added and the type set.[8]

Oliver enjoyed copying the book, and letters he wrote at the time were saturated with its language. Echoing Nephi, Jacob, and Amulek from the Book of Mormon, Oliver wrote to Joseph about his gratitude for Christ's infinite Atonement.

"When I begin to write on the mercies of God," he told Joseph, "I know not when to stop, but time and paper fail."[9]

That same spirit drew others to the Book of Mormon as it was being printed. Thomas Marsh, a former printer's apprentice, had tried to find his place in other churches, but none of them seemed to preach the gospel he found in the Bible. He believed that a new church would soon arise that would teach restored truth.

That summer, Thomas felt led by the Spirit to travel hundreds of miles from his home in Boston to western New York. He stayed in the area three months before turning toward home, uncertain why he had traveled so far. At a stop along the way back, however, his host asked if he had heard about Joseph Smith's "golden book." Thomas told the woman he had not and felt compelled to learn more.

She told him he should talk to Martin Harris and directed him to Palmyra. Thomas went there immediately and found Martin at Grandin's printshop. The printer gave him sixteen pages of the Book of Mormon, and

Thomas took them back to Boston, eager to share the first taste of this new faith with his wife, Elizabeth.

Elizabeth read the pages, and she too believed they were the work of God.[10]

THAT FALL, WHILE THE printers made steady progress on the Book of Mormon, a former judge named Abner Cole began publishing a newspaper on Grandin's press. Working at night in the shop, after Grandin's staff went home, Abner had access to printed pages from the Book of Mormon, which was not yet bound or ready for sale.

Abner soon began poking fun at the "Gold Bible" in his newspaper, and during the winter he printed excerpts from the book alongside sarcastic commentary.[11]

When Hyrum and Oliver learned what Abner was doing, they confronted him. "What right have you to print the Book of Mormon in this way?" Hyrum demanded. "Do you not know that we have received a copyright?"

"It is none of your business," Abner said. "I have hired the press and I will print what I please."

"I forbid you to print any more of that book in your paper," Hyrum said.

"I don't care," Abner said.

Unsure what to do, Hyrum and Oliver sent word to Joseph in Harmony, who returned to Palmyra at once. He found Abner at the printing office, casually reading his own newspaper.

"You seem hard at work," Joseph said.

"How do you do, Mr. Smith," Abner replied dryly.

"Mr. Cole," Joseph said, "the Book of Mormon and the right of publishing it belong to me, and I forbid you meddling with it."

Abner threw off his coat and pushed up his sleeves. "Do you want to fight, sir?" he barked, pounding his fists together. "If you want to fight, just come on."

Joseph smiled. "You had better keep your coat on," he said. "It's cold, and I am not going to fight you." He calmly continued, "But you have got to stop printing my book."

"If you think you are the best man," Abner said, "just pull off your coat and try it."

"There is law," Joseph responded, "and you will find that out if you did not know it before. But I shall not fight you, for that will do no good."

Abner knew he was on the wrong side of the law. He calmed down and stopped printing excerpts from the Book of Mormon in his newspaper.[12]

SOLOMON CHAMBERLIN, A PREACHER on his way to Canada, first heard about the "Gold Bible" from a family he lodged with near Palmyra. Like Thomas Marsh, he had moved from church to church throughout his life but felt dissatisfied with what he saw. Some churches preached gospel principles and believed in spiritual gifts, but they did not have God's prophets or His priesthood.

Solomon felt the time was coming when the Lord would bring forth His church.

As Solomon listened to the family talk about Joseph Smith and the gold plates, he felt electrified from head to toe, and he determined to find the Smiths and learn more about the book.

He set out for the Smith house and met Hyrum at the door. "Peace be to this house," Solomon said.

"I hope it will be peace," Hyrum replied.

"Is there anyone here," asked Solomon, "that believes in visions or revelations?"

"Yes," Hyrum said, "we are a visionary house."

Solomon told Hyrum about a vision he had seen years before. In it, an angel had said that God had no church on the earth but would soon raise one up that had power like the apostles' church of old. Hyrum and the others in the house understood what Solomon said and told him they shared his belief.

"I wish you would make known some of your discoveries," Solomon said. "I think I can bear them."

Hyrum invited him to stay at the Smith farm as a guest and showed him the Book of Mormon manuscript. Solomon studied it for two days and went with Hyrum to Grandin's printing office, where a printer gave him sixty-four printed pages. With the unbound pages in hand, Solomon continued on to Canada, preaching everything he knew about the new faith along the way.[13]

BY MARCH 26, 1830, THE first copies of the Book of Mormon had been bound and were available for sale on the ground floor of Grandin's printing office. They were tightly bound in brown calfskin and smelled of leather and glue, paper and ink. The words *Book of Mormon* appeared on the spines in gold letters.[14]

Lucy Smith treasured the new scripture and saw it as a sign that God would soon gather His children and restore His ancient covenant. The title page declared that the book's purpose was to show the great things God had done for His people in the past, extend the same blessings to His people today, and convince all the world that Jesus Christ was the Savior of the world.[15]

In the back of the book were the testimonies of the Three Witnesses and the Eight Witnesses, telling the world that they had seen the plates and knew the translation was true.[16]

Despite these testimonies, Lucy knew some people thought the book was fiction. Many of her neighbors believed the Bible was enough scripture for them, not realizing that God had blessed more nations than one with His word. She also knew some people rejected its message because they believed God had spoken once to the world and would not speak again.

For these reasons and others, most people in Palmyra did not buy the book.[17] But some studied its pages, felt the power of its teachings, and went to their knees to ask the Lord if it was true. Lucy herself knew the Book of Mormon was the word of God and wanted to share it with others.[18]

ALMOST IMMEDIATELY AFTER THE Book of Mormon was published, Joseph and Oliver prepared to organize the church of Jesus Christ. Several months earlier, the Lord's ancient apostles Peter, James, and John had appeared to them and conferred on them the Melchizedek Priesthood, as John the Baptist had promised. This additional authority allowed Joseph and Oliver to confer the gift of the Holy Ghost on those they baptized. Peter, James, and John had also ordained them to be apostles of Jesus Christ.[19]

Around that time, while staying in the Whitmer home, Joseph and Oliver had prayed for more knowledge about this authority. In reply, the voice of the Lord commanded them to ordain each other elders of the church, but not until believers consented to follow them as leaders in the Savior's church. They were also told to ordain other church officers and confer the gift of the Holy Ghost on those who had been baptized.[20]

On April 6, 1830, Joseph and Oliver met in the Whitmer home to follow the Lord's commandment and organize His church. To fulfill the requirements of the law, they chose six people to become the first members of the new church. Around forty women and men also crowded into and around the small home to witness the occasion.[21]

In obedience to the Lord's earlier instructions, Joseph and Oliver asked the congregation to sustain them as leaders in the kingdom of God and indicate if they believed it was right for them to organize as a church. Every member of the congregation consented, and Joseph laid his hands on Oliver's head and ordained him an elder of the church. Then they traded places, and Oliver ordained Joseph.

Afterward, they administered the bread and wine of the sacrament in remembrance of Christ's Atonement. They then laid hands on those they had baptized, confirming them members of the church and giving them the gift of the Holy Ghost.[22] The Lord's Spirit was poured out on those in the meeting, and some in the congregation began to prophesy. Others praised the Lord, and all rejoiced together.

Joseph also received the first revelation addressed to the whole body of the new church. "Behold, there shall be a record kept among you," the Lord commanded, reminding His people that they were to write their sacred history, preserving an account of their actions and witnessing to Joseph's role as prophet, seer, and revelator.

"Him have I inspired to move the cause of Zion in mighty power for good," the Lord declared. "His word ye shall receive, as if from mine own mouth, in all patience in faith. For by doing these things the gates of hell shall not prevail against you."[23]

LATER, JOSEPH STOOD BESIDE a stream and witnessed the baptisms of his mother and father into the church. After years of taking different paths in their search for truth, they were finally united in faith. As his father came out of the water, Joseph took him by the hand, helped him onto the bank, and embraced him.

"My God," he cried, burying his face in his father's chest, "I have lived to see my father baptized into the true church of Jesus Christ!"[24]

That evening, Joseph slipped away into some nearby woods, his heart bursting with emotion. He wanted to be alone, out of sight of friends and family. In the ten years since his First Vision, he had seen the heavens open, felt the Spirit of God, and been tutored by angels. He had also sinned and lost his gift, only to repent, receive God's mercy, and translate the Book of Mormon by His power and grace.

Now Jesus Christ had restored His church and authorized Joseph with the same priesthood that apostles had held anciently when they carried the gospel to the world.[25] The happiness he felt was too much for him to hold in, and when Joseph Knight and Oliver found him later that night, he was weeping.

His joy was full. The work had begun.[26]

PART 2

---◆---

A House of Faith

APRIL 1830–APRIL 1836

Organize yourselves;
prepare every needful thing;
and establish a house,
even a house of prayer, a house of fasting,
a house of faith, a house of learning,
a house of glory,
a house of order, a house of God.

Doctrine and Covenants 88:119

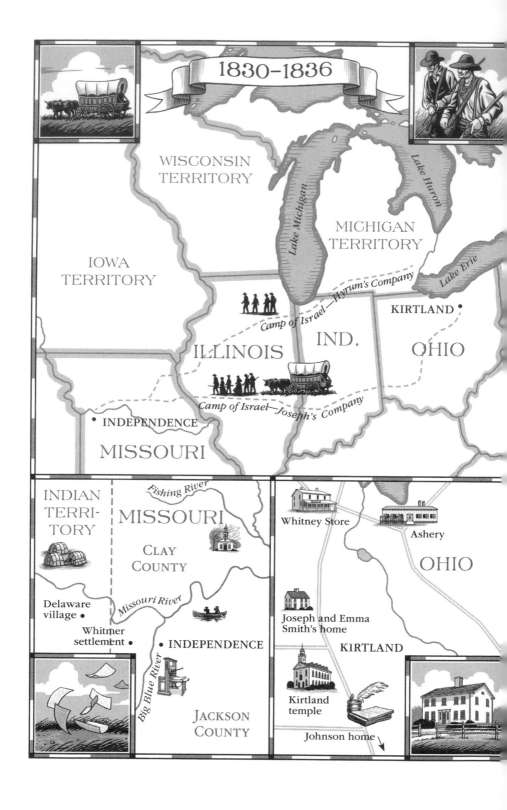

1830–1836

WISCONSIN TERRITORY

MICHIGAN TERRITORY

Lake Michigan

Lake Huron

Lake Erie

IOWA TERRITORY

Camp of Israel—Hyrum's Company

KIRTLAND

ILLINOIS

IND.

OHIO

Camp of Israel—Joseph's Company

INDEPENDENCE

MISSOURI

INDIAN TERRITORY

Fishing River

MISSOURI

CLAY COUNTY

Missouri River

Delaware village

Whitmer settlement

INDEPENDENCE

Big Blue River

JACKSON COUNTY

Whitney Store

Ashery

OHIO

Joseph and Emma Smith's home

KIRTLAND

Kirtland temple

Johnson home

CHAPTER 9

Come Life or Come Death

The Sunday after the church was organized, Oliver preached to the Whitmer family and their friends in Fayette. Many of them had supported the Book of Mormon translation but had not yet joined the church. After Oliver finished speaking, six people asked him to baptize them in a nearby lake.[1]

As more people joined the new church, the immensity of the Lord's commission to take the gospel to the world weighed on Joseph. He had published the Book of Mormon and organized the Lord's church, but the book was selling poorly and those who sought baptism were mostly his friends and relatives. And Joseph still had much to learn about heaven and earth.

People who joined the church often came seeking the gifts of the Spirit and other miracles they read about in the New Testament.[2] But the restored gospel promised believers something even greater than wonders and signs. Benjamin, a wise prophet and king in the Book of Mormon, had taught that if people yielded to the Holy Spirit, they could shed their sinful nature and become saints through the Atonement of Jesus Christ.[3]

For Joseph, the challenge now was how to move the Lord's work forward. He and Oliver knew they had to cry repentance to all people. The field was ready to harvest, and the worth of every soul was great in the eyes of God. But how could two young apostles—a farmer and a schoolteacher, both in their early twenties—move such a great work forward?

And how could a small church in rural New York rise above its humble beginnings and grow to fill the entire world?

AFTER THE BAPTISMS IN Fayette, Joseph began the hundred-mile trip back to his farm in Harmony. As busy as he was with the new church, he had to plant his fields soon if he wanted a successful fall harvest. His payments to Emma's father on the farm were already late, and if his crops failed, he would have to find another way to pay off his debt.

On his way home, Joseph stopped at Joseph and Polly Knight's farm in Colesville, New York. The Knights had long supported him, but they still had not joined the church. Joseph Knight in particular wanted to read the Book of Mormon before he embraced the new faith.[4]

Joseph stayed a few days in Colesville, preaching to the Knights and their friends. Newel Knight, one of Joseph and Polly's sons, often talked with the prophet about the gospel. One day, Joseph invited him to pray at a meeting, but Newel said he would rather pray alone in the woods.

The next morning, Newel went to the woods and tried to pray. An uneasy feeling came over him, and it grew worse as he started for home. By the time he reached his house, the feeling was so oppressive that he begged his wife, Sally, to get the prophet.

Joseph hurried to Newel's side and found family members and neighbors watching fearfully as the young man's face, arms, and legs contorted wildly. When Newel saw Joseph, he cried, "Cast the devil out!"

Joseph had never tried to rebuke the devil or heal someone before, but he knew Jesus had promised His disciples the power to do so. Acting quickly, he caught Newel by the hand. "In the name of Jesus Christ," he said, "depart from him."

As soon as Joseph spoke, the contortions stopped. Newel slumped to the floor, exhausted but unharmed, muttering that he had seen the devil leave his body.

The Knights and their neighbors were astonished by what Joseph had done. Helping them carry Newel to a bed, Joseph told them it was the first miracle performed in the church.

"It was done by God," he testified, "and by the power of godliness."[5]

HUNDREDS OF MILES TO the west, a farmer named Parley Pratt felt the Spirit urging him to leave his home and family to preach of the prophecies and spiritual gifts he found in the Bible. He sold his farm at a loss and trusted God would bless him for giving up everything for Christ.

With only a few items of clothing and just enough money to make the journey, he and his wife, Thankful, left their home and headed east to visit family before he set out to preach. As they traveled by canal, however, Parley turned to Thankful and asked her to go on without him. He felt the Spirit directing him to get off the boat.

"I will come soon," he promised. "I have a work to do in this region."[6]

Parley disembarked and walked ten miles into the countryside, where he came upon the home of a Baptist deacon who told him about a strange new book he had acquired. It claimed to be an ancient record, the man said, translated from gold plates with the help of angels and visions. The deacon did not have the book with him, but he promised to show it to Parley the following day.

The next morning, Parley returned to the deacon's house. He opened the book eagerly and read its title page. He then turned to the back of the book and read the testimonies of several witnesses. The words drew him in, and he started the book from the beginning. Hours passed, but he could not stop reading. Eating and sleeping were a burden. The Spirit of the Lord was upon him, and he knew the book was true.[7]

Parley soon made his way to the nearby village of Palmyra, determined to meet the translator of the book. People in town pointed him to a farm a few miles down the road. As Parley walked in that direction, he saw a man and asked him where he could find Joseph Smith. The man told him that Joseph lived in Harmony, a hundred miles south, but introduced himself as Hyrum Smith, the prophet's brother.

They talked most of the night, and Hyrum testified of the Book of Mormon, the restoration of the priesthood, and the Lord's work in the latter days. The next morning, Parley had preaching appointments to fulfill, so Hyrum gave him a copy of the book and sent him on his way.

Parley opened the book at his next opportunity and discovered, to his joy, that the resurrected Lord had visited the people of ancient America and taught them His gospel. The message of the book, Parley realized, was worth more than all the riches of the world.

When his preaching appointments were over, Parley returned to the Smith house. Hyrum welcomed him back and invited him to visit the Whitmer farm, where he could meet a growing congregation of church members.

Eager to learn more, Parley accepted the invitation. A few days later, he was baptized.[8]

IN LATE JUNE 1830, Emma traveled with Joseph and Oliver to Colesville. Word of Joseph's miracle that spring had spread throughout the area, and now the Knights and several other families wanted to join the church.

Emma was also ready to be baptized. Like the Knights, she believed in the restored gospel and in her husband's prophetic call, but she had not yet joined the church.[9]

After arriving in Colesville, Joseph worked with others to dam a nearby stream so they could hold a baptismal meeting the following day. When morning came, however, they discovered that someone had wrecked the dam overnight to prevent the baptisms from taking place.

Disappointed, they held a Sabbath-day meeting instead, and Oliver preached on baptism and the Holy Ghost. After the sermon, a local minister and some members of his congregation broke up the meeting and tried to drag one of the believers away.

Emma was all too familiar with opposition to Joseph and his message. Some people called him a fraud and accused him of trying to profit off his followers. Others mocked believers, calling them "Mormonites."[10] Wary of trouble, Emma and the others returned to the stream early the next day and repaired the dam. Once the water was deep enough, Oliver waded into the middle of the pool and baptized Emma, Joseph and Polly Knight, and ten others.

During the baptisms, some men stood along the bank, a short distance back, and heckled the believers. Emma and the others tried to ignore them, but when the group headed back to the Knight farm, the men followed, shouting threats at the prophet along the way. At the Knights' house, Joseph and Oliver wanted to confirm the newly baptized women and men, but the group of hecklers outside swelled to a noisy mob of fifty.

Worried they might be attacked, the believers fled to a neighboring house, hoping to finish the confirmations in peace. But before they could perform the ordinances, a constable arrested Joseph and carried him off to jail for causing an uproar in the community by preaching the Book of Mormon.

Joseph spent the night in custody, unsure if the mob would capture him and carry out their threats. Emma, meanwhile, waited anxiously at her sister's house while she and their Colesville friends prayed for Joseph's safe release.[11]

OVER THE NEXT TWO days, Joseph was tried in court and acquitted, only to be arrested and tried again on similar charges. After his second hearing he was set free, and he and Emma returned to their farm in Harmony before she and the Colesville Saints could be confirmed as members of the church.¹²

Back home, Joseph tried again to work on his farm, but the Lord gave him a new revelation on how he should spend his time. "Thou shalt devote all thy service in Zion," the Lord declared. "In temporal labors thou shalt not have strength, for this is not thy calling." Joseph was told to plant his fields and then set off to confirm the new members in New York.¹³

The revelation left much uncertainty in Emma's life. How would they earn a living if Joseph devoted all his time to the Saints? And what would she do while he was away serving the church? Was she supposed to stay at home, or did the Lord want her to go with him? And if He did, what would be her role in the church?

Knowing Emma's desire for guidance, the Lord spoke to her in a revelation given through Joseph. He forgave her sins and called her an "elect lady." He directed her to go with Joseph in his travels and promised, "Thou shalt be ordained under his hand to expound scriptures, and to exhort the church."

He also calmed her fears about their finances. "Thou needest not fear," He assured her, "for thy husband shall support thee."

The Lord then instructed her to make a selection of sacred hymns for the church. "For my soul delighteth in the song of the heart," He said.¹⁴

Soon after the revelation, Joseph and Emma traveled to Colesville, where Emma and the Saints there were finally confirmed. As the new members received the gift of the Holy Ghost, the Spirit of the Lord filled the room. Everyone rejoiced and praised God.[15]

LATER THAT SUMMER, JOSEPH and Emma paid off their farm with the help of friends and moved to Fayette so Joseph could devote more time to the church.[16] After they arrived, however, they learned that Hiram Page, one of the Eight Witnesses and a teacher in the Aaronic Priesthood, had started to seek revelations for the church through what he thought was a seer stone.[17] Many Saints, including Oliver and some members of the Whitmer family, believed these revelations were from God.[18]

Joseph knew he was facing a crisis. Hiram's revelations mimicked the language of scripture. They spoke of the establishment of Zion and the organization of the church, but at times they contradicted the New Testament and truths the Lord had revealed through Joseph.

Unsure of what to do, Joseph stayed up praying one night, pleading for guidance. He had experienced opposition before, but not from his friends. If he acted too forcefully against Hiram's revelations, he could offend those who believed in them or discourage faithful Saints from seeking revelation on their own.[19] But if he did not condemn the false revelations, they could undermine the authority of the Lord's word and divide the Saints.

After many sleepless hours, Joseph received a revelation directed to Oliver. "No one shall be appointed to receive commandments and revelations in this church excepting my servant Joseph Smith," the Lord declared, "for all things must be done in order, and by common consent in the church." The Lord directed Oliver to teach this principle to Hiram.

The revelation then called Oliver to go nearly a thousand miles to the western edge of the United States to preach the restored gospel to American Indians, who were remnants of the house of Israel. The Lord said that the city of Zion would be built near these people, echoing the Book of Mormon's promise that God would establish the New Jerusalem on the American continent prior to the Second Coming of Christ. He did not identify the city's exact location, but He promised to reveal that information at a later time.[20]

A few days later, at a conference of the church, the Saints renounced Hiram's revelations and unanimously sustained Joseph as the only one who could receive revelation for the church.[21]

The Lord called Peter Whitmer Jr., Ziba Peterson, and Parley Pratt to join Oliver on the mission to the West.[22] Emma and other women, meanwhile, began making clothes for the missionaries. Working long hours, they spun wool into yarn, wove or knitted the yarn into cloth, and stitched the cloth together piece by piece.[23]

Parley had recently returned to Fayette with Thankful after sharing the gospel with her and other members of his family. When he left for the West, she moved in with Mary Whitmer, who gladly welcomed her into her home.

On the way to Missouri, Parley planned to take the other missionaries to the state of Ohio, where his former pastor, Sidney Rigdon, lived. Parley hoped he would be interested in their message.[24]

THAT SAME SUMMER, IN a town two days' journey from Fayette, Rhoda Greene found Samuel Smith, the prophet's brother, on her doorstep. Rhoda had met Samuel earlier that year when he left a copy of the Book of Mormon at her house. Her husband, John, was a traveling preacher for another faith, and he thought the book was nonsense, but he had promised to take it with him on his circuit and collect the names of anyone interested in its message.

Rhoda invited Samuel inside and told him no one had shown any interest in the Book of Mormon so far. "You will have to take the book," she said. "Mr. Greene does not seem to feel like buying it."

Samuel took the Book of Mormon and was turning to leave when Rhoda mentioned that she had read it and liked it. Samuel paused. "I will give you this book," he said, returning the copy. "The Spirit of God forbids my taking it away."

Rhoda felt overcome with emotion as she took the book back. "Ask God to give you a testimony of the truth of the work," Samuel said, "and you will feel a burning sensation in your breast, which is the Spirit of God."

Later, after her husband came home, Rhoda told him about Samuel's visit. At first John was reluctant to pray about the book, but Rhoda convinced him to trust Samuel's promise.

"I do know that he would not tell an untruth," she said. "I know he must be a good man if there ever was one."

Rhoda and John prayed about the book and received a testimony of its truth. They then shared it with their family and neighbors, including Rhoda's younger brother Brigham Young and his friend Heber Kimball.[25]

IN THE FALL, THIRTY-EIGHT-YEAR-OLD Sidney Rigdon listened politely as Parley Pratt and his three companions testified of a new work of scripture, the Book of Mormon. But Sidney was not interested. For years, he had exhorted people in and around the village of Kirtland, Ohio, to read the Bible and return to the principles of the New Testament church. The Bible had always guided his life, he told the missionaries, and it was enough.[26]

"You brought the truth to me," Parley reminded Sidney. "I now ask you as a friend to read this for my sake."[27]

"You must not argue with me on the subject," Sidney insisted. "But I will read your book and see what claim it has upon my faith."[28]

Parley asked Sidney if they could preach to his congregation. Although he was skeptical of their message, Sidney gave them permission.

After the missionaries left, Sidney read parts of the book and found he could not dismiss it.[29] By the time Parley and Oliver preached to his congregation, he had no desire to warn anyone against the book. When he rose to speak at the end of the meeting, he quoted the Bible.

"Prove all things," he said, "and hold fast that which is good."[30]

But Sidney remained uncertain about what to do. Accepting the Book of Mormon would mean losing his employment as a pastor. He had a good congregation, and they provided him, his wife, Phebe, and their six children with a comfortable life. Some people in the congregation were even building a home for them.[31] Could he really ask his family to walk away from the comfort they enjoyed?

Sidney prayed until a sense of peace rested over him. He knew the Book of Mormon was true. "Flesh and blood hath not revealed it unto me," he exclaimed, "but my Father which is in heaven."[32]

Sidney shared his feelings with Phebe. "My dear," he said, "you have once followed me into poverty. Are you again willing to do the same?"

"I have counted the cost," she replied. "It is my desire to do the will of God, come life or come death."[33]

CHAPTER 10

Gathered In

In the fall of 1830, not far from Kirtland, fifteen-year-old Lucy Morley finished her usual housework and took a seat beside her employer, Abigail Daniels. As Abigail worked her loom, moving a weaving shuttle back and forth through crisscrossing threads, Lucy wound yarn onto thin spools. The cloth they wove would go to Lucy's mother in exchange for Lucy's services around the Daniels house. With many children under her roof, and no teenage daughters, Abigail relied on Lucy to help keep her family clean and fed.

While the two worked side by side, they heard a knock at the door. "Come in," Abigail called out.

Glancing up from her spool, Lucy saw three men enter the room. They were strangers, but they were well dressed and looked friendly. All three of them appeared to be a few years younger than Abigail, who was in her early thirties.

Lucy stood up and brought more chairs into the room. As the men sat down, she took their hats and returned to her seat. The men introduced themselves as Oliver Cowdery, Parley Pratt, and Ziba Peterson, preachers from New York who were passing through town on their way to the West. They said the Lord had restored His true gospel to their friend, a prophet named Joseph Smith.

As they spoke, Lucy quietly attended to her work. The men talked about angels and a set of gold plates the prophet had translated by revelation. They testified that God had sent them on their mission to preach the gospel one last time before the Second Coming of Jesus Christ.

When they finished their message, the rhythmic clatter of Abigail's loom stopped, and the woman turned around on her bench. "I do not want any of your damnable doctrine taught in my house," she said, angrily waving the shuttle in their faces.

The men tried to persuade her, testifying that their message was true. But Abigail ordered them to leave, saying she did not want them polluting her children with false doctrine. The men asked if she would at least feed them. They were hungry and had not eaten all day.

"You cannot have anything to eat in my house," Abigail snapped. "I do not feed impostors."

Suddenly, Lucy spoke up, horrified that Abigail would speak to servants of God so rudely. "My father lives one mile from here," she said. "He never turns anyone hungry from his door. Go there and you will be fed and cared for."

Fetching their hats, Lucy followed the missionaries outside and showed them how to get to her parents' house. The men thanked her and started down the road.

"God bless you," they said.

After the men were out of sight, Lucy went back into the house. Abigail was at her loom again, running the shuttle back and forth. "I hope you feel better now," she said to Lucy, clearly irritated.

"Yes, I do," replied Lucy.[1]

As Lucy promised, the three missionaries found a hearty meal at the Morley home. Her parents, Isaac and Lucy, were members of Sidney Rigdon's congregation, and they believed that followers of Christ should share their goods and property with each other as one large family. Following the example of saints in the New Testament who tried to have "all things common," they had opened their large farm to other families who wanted to live together and practice their beliefs separate from the competitive, often selfish world around them.[2]

That evening, the missionaries taught the Morleys and their friends. The families responded to the missionaries' message of preparing for the Savior's return and millennial reign, and around midnight, seventeen people were baptized.

In the days that followed, more than fifty people around Kirtland flocked to the missionaries' meetings and asked to join the church.[3] Many of them were living on the Morleys' farm, including Pete, a freed slave whose mother had come from West Africa.[4] Even Abigail Daniels, who had rejected the missionaries so quickly, embraced their message after she and her husband listened to them preach.[5]

As the church grew in Ohio, particularly among Sidney's followers, Oliver reported the good news to Joseph. Every day more people were asking to hear their message. "There is considerable call here for books," he wrote, "and I wish you would send five hundred."[6]

As pleased as he was with their success in Ohio, though, Oliver knew the Lord had called them to preach to the American Indians who lived beyond the western border of the United States. He and the other missionaries soon left Kirtland, taking with them a new convert named Frederick Williams. Frederick was a doctor, and at forty-three, he was the oldest man in the company.[7]

Heading west in late fall 1830, they trudged across snowy flatlands and gently rising hills. They stopped briefly to preach to Wyandot Indians in central Ohio before booking passage on a steamboat bound for Missouri, the westernmost state in the nation.

The missionaries made steady progress on the river until ice blocked their way. Undeterred, they disembarked and walked hundreds of miles along the frozen riverbank. By then, snow had fallen thick and deep, making it more difficult to travel over the wide prairies. Sometimes the winds that cut across the landscape seemed sharp enough to take the skin off their faces.[8]

AS THE MISSIONARIES TRAVELED west, Sidney traveled east with his friend Edward Partridge, a thirty-seven-year-old hatmaker from his congregation. The two men were headed to Manchester, nearly three hundred miles from Kirtland, to meet Joseph. Sidney had already joined the church, but Edward wanted to get to know the prophet before deciding whether he should do the same.[9]

When they arrived, the friends went first to the farm of Joseph's parents, only to learn that the Smiths had moved closer to Fayette. But before trekking another twenty-six miles to the Smiths' home, Edward wanted to look over the property, thinking the Smiths' handiwork might reveal something about their character. He and Sidney saw their well-kept orchards, their homes and outbuildings, and the low stone walls they had constructed. Each testified of the family's order and industry.[10]

Edward and Sidney returned to the road and walked all day, reaching the Smiths' home by evening. When they got there, a church meeting was in progress. They slipped into the house and joined a small congregation listening to Joseph preach. When the prophet finished, he said anyone in the room could stand and speak as he or she felt inspired.

Edward stood and told the Saints what he had seen and felt on his trip. Then he said, "I am ready to be baptized, Brother Joseph. Will you baptize me?"

"You have traveled a long way," Joseph said. "I think you had better take some rest and refreshment and tomorrow morning be baptized."

"Just as you think proper," Edward replied. "I am ready at any time."[11]

BEFORE THE BAPTISM TOOK place, Joseph received a revelation calling Edward to preach and prepare for the day when Christ would come to His temple.[12] Edward was baptized and quickly left to share the gospel with his parents and relatives.[13] Sidney, meanwhile, stayed in Fayette to act as Joseph's scribe and was soon assisting him in a new project.[14]

Months earlier, Joseph and Oliver had begun an inspired translation of the Bible. From the Book of Mormon, they knew that precious truths had been corrupted through the ages and taken away from the Old and New Testaments. Using a Bible that Oliver purchased from Grandin's bookstore, they had begun to study the book of Genesis, seeking inspiration about passages that seemed incomplete or unclear.[15]

Before long, the Lord had revealed to Joseph a vision first received by Moses, which was missing from the Old Testament. In the newly restored scripture, God showed Moses "worlds without number," told him that God created everything spiritually before He created it physically, and taught that the purpose of this glorious creation was to help men and women receive eternal life.[16]

After Oliver left on his mission to the West, Joseph had continued to translate with John Whitmer and Emma as scribes until Sidney arrived. Most recently, the Lord had begun to reveal more of the history of the prophet Enoch, whose life and ministry received only a brief mention in Genesis.[17]

As Sidney recorded Joseph's dictation, they learned that Enoch had been a prophet who gathered together an obedient and blessed people. Like the Nephites and Lamanites who created a righteous society after the Savior's visit to the Americas, Enoch's people learned to live peacefully with each other. "They were of one heart and one mind, and dwelt in righteousness," the scripture recorded, "and there was no poor among them."[18]

Under Enoch's leadership, the people built a holy city called Zion, which God eventually received into His presence. There Enoch spoke with God as they looked down on the earth, and God wept over the wickedness and suffering of His children. The day would come, He told Enoch, when truth would be brought forth from the earth and His people would build another city of Zion for the righteous.[19]

As Sidney and Joseph reflected on the revelation, they knew the day had come when the Lord would again establish Zion on the earth. Like Enoch's people, the Saints needed to prepare themselves, uniting in heart and mind, so they would be ready to build the holy city and its temple as soon as the Lord revealed its location.

AT THE END OF December, the Lord instructed Joseph and Sidney to pause their work on the translation. "A commandment I give unto the church," He declared, "that they should assemble together at the Ohio." They were to gather with the new converts in the Kirtland area and wait for the missionaries to return from the West.

"Here is wisdom," the Lord stated, "and let every man choose for himself until I come."[20]

The call to move to Ohio seemed to bring the Saints closer to fulfilling ancient prophecies about the gathering of God's people. The Bible and Book of Mormon both promised that the Lord would gather together His covenant people to safeguard them against the perils of the last days. In a recent revelation, the Lord had told Joseph that this gathering would soon begin.[21]

But the call still came as a shock. At the church's third conference, held at the Whitmers' home soon after the new year, many of the Saints were troubled, their minds full of questions about the commandment.[22] Ohio was sparsely settled and hundreds of miles away. Most church members knew little about it.

Many of them had also worked hard to improve their property and cultivate prosperous farms in New

York. If they moved as a group to Ohio, they would have to sell their property quickly and would probably lose money. Some might even be ruined financially, especially if the land in Ohio proved less rich and fertile than their land in New York.

Hoping to ease concerns about the gathering, Joseph met with the Saints and received a revelation.[23] "I hold forth and deign to give unto you greater riches, even a land of promise," the Lord declared, "and I will give it unto you for the land of your inheritance, if you seek it with all your hearts." By gathering together, the Saints could flourish as a righteous people and be protected from the wicked.

The Lord also promised two additional blessings to those who gathered to Ohio. "There I will give unto you my law," He said, "and there you shall be endowed with power from on high."[24]

The revelation calmed the minds of most of the Saints in the room, although a few people refused to believe it came from God. Joseph's family, the Whitmers, and the Knights were among those who believed and chose to follow it.[25]

As the leader of the Colesville branch of the church, Newel Knight returned home and began to sell what he could. He also spent much of his time visiting church members. Following the example of Enoch's people, he and other Saints in Colesville worked together and sacrificed to ensure the poor could make the journey before spring.[26]

Joseph, meanwhile, felt an urgent need to get to Kirtland and meet the new converts. Although Emma was pregnant with twins and was recovering from a long bout of sickness, she climbed aboard the sleigh, determined to go with him.[27]

BACK IN OHIO, THE church was struggling. After the missionaries left for the West, the number of converts in Kirtland continued to grow, but many of the Saints were unsure how to practice their new faith. Most looked to the New Testament for guidance as they had before they joined the church, but without prophetic direction there seemed to be as many ways to interpret the New Testament as there were Saints in Kirtland.[28]

Elizabeth Ann Whitney was among those who longed to experience the spiritual gifts of the early Christian church. Before the missionaries came to Kirtland, Ann and her husband, Newel, had prayed many times to know how they could receive the gift of the Holy Ghost.

One night, while praying for divine direction, they had seen a vision of a cloud resting over their home. The Spirit filled them, and their house faded away as the cloud enveloped them. They heard a voice from heaven: "Prepare to receive the word of the Lord, for it is coming."[29]

Ann had not grown up in a religious home, and neither of her parents had attended church. Her father did not like clergymen, and her mother was always busy with household duties or tending to Ann's younger siblings. Both of them had encouraged Ann to enjoy life rather than seek God.[30]

But Ann had always been drawn to spiritual things, and when she married Newel, she expressed a desire to find a church. At her insistence, they joined Sidney Rigdon's congregation because she believed its principles were nearest to those she found in scripture. Later, when she first heard Parley Pratt and his companions preach the restored gospel, she knew what they taught was true.[31]

Ann joined the church and rejoiced in her new faith, but the different ways people practiced it confused her. Her friends Isaac and Lucy Morley continued to invite people to live on their farm and share their resources.[32] Leman Copley, who owned a large farm east of Kirtland, continued to hold on to some teachings from his time among the Shakers, a religious community that had a settlement nearby.[33]

Some of the Saints in Kirtland took their beliefs to wild extremes, reveling in what they took to be gifts of the Spirit. Several people claimed to have visions they could not explain. Others believed the Holy Ghost made them slide or scoot across the ground.[34] One man bounced around rooms or swung from ceiling joists whenever he thought he felt the Spirit. Another acted like a baboon.[35]

Seeing this behavior, some converts grew discouraged and gave up on the new church. Ann and Newel continued to pray, confident the Lord would show them the way forward.[36]

On February 4, 1831, a sleigh arrived at the store Newel owned and operated in Kirtland. A twenty-five-year-old man stepped out, bounded inside, and reached his hand across the counter. "Newel K. Whitney!" he cried. "Thou art the man!"

Newel shook his hand. "You have the advantage of me," he said. "I could not call you by name, as you have me."

"I am Joseph the prophet," the man exclaimed. "You have prayed me here, now what do you want of me?"[37]

CHAPTER 11

Ye Shall Receive My Law

Ann and Newel Whitney were grateful to have Joseph and Emma in Kirtland. Although the Whitneys had three small children and an aunt living with them, they invited the Smiths to stay in their house until they found a place of their own. Since Emma was far along in her pregnancy, Ann and Newel moved into an upstairs room so she and Joseph could have the bedroom on the ground floor.[1]

After settling into the Whitney home, Joseph began to visit new converts. Kirtland was a small cluster of houses and shops on a hill south of the Whitneys' store. A small creek ran alongside the town, powering mills and feeding a larger river to the north. About a thousand people lived there.[2]

As Joseph visited church members, he saw their enthusiasm for spiritual gifts and their sincere desire to pattern their lives after the saints in the New Testament.[3] Joseph loved the gifts of the Spirit himself and knew they had a role in the restored church, but he worried that some Saints in Kirtland were getting carried away in their pursuit of them.

He could see that he had serious work to do. The Kirtland Saints had more than doubled the size of the church, but it was clear they needed additional direction from the Lord.

EIGHT HUNDRED MILES TO the west, Oliver and the other missionaries arrived in the small town of Independence in Jackson County, Missouri, on the western border of the United States. They found lodging and work to support themselves and then made plans to visit the Delaware Indians who lived on territory a few miles west of town.[4]

The Delaware had recently moved to the territory after they were forced off their land by Indian removal policies of the United States government. Their leader, Kikthawenund, was an old man who had struggled for more than twenty-five years to hold his people together while settlers and the U.S. Army pushed them west.[5]

On a cold day in January 1831, Oliver and Parley set out to meet Kikthawenund. They found him sitting beside a fire in the center of a large cabin in the Delaware settlement. The chief shook their hands warmly and motioned for them to sit on some blankets.

His wives then placed a tin pan full of steaming beans and corn in front of the missionaries, and they ate with a wooden spoon.

Aided by a translator, Oliver and Parley spoke to Kikthawenund about the Book of Mormon and asked for a chance to share its message with his governing council. Kikthawenund was normally opposed to letting missionaries speak to his people, but he told them he would think about it and give them his decision soon.

The missionaries returned to the cabin the next morning, and after some discussion, the chief called a council together and invited the missionaries to speak.

Thanking them, Oliver looked into the faces of his audience. "We have traveled the wilderness, crossed the deep and wide rivers, and waded in the deep snows," he said, "to communicate to you great knowledge which has lately come to our ears and hearts."

He introduced the Book of Mormon as a history of the ancestors of the American Indians. "The book was written on plates of gold," he explained, "and handed down from father to son for many ages and generations." He told how God had helped Joseph find and translate the plates so their writings could be published and shared with all people, including the Indians.

After he finished speaking, Oliver handed Kikthawenund a Book of Mormon and waited as he and the council examined it. "We feel truly thankful to our white friends who have come so far, and been at such pains to tell us good news," the old man said, "and especially this new news concerning the book of our forefathers."

But the severe winter weather had been hard on his people, he explained. Their shelters were poor, and their animals were dying. They had to build homes and fences and prepare farms for the spring. For now, they were not ready to host missionaries.

"We will build a council house and meet together," Kikthawenund promised, "and you shall read to us and teach us more concerning the book of our fathers and the will of the Great Spirit."[6]

A FEW WEEKS LATER, Joseph received a report from Oliver. After describing the missionaries' visit with Kikthawenund, Oliver admitted he was still unsure if the Delaware would accept the Book of Mormon. "How the matter will go with this tribe to me is uncertain," he wrote.[7]

Joseph remained optimistic about the Indian mission, even as he turned his attention to strengthening the church in Kirtland. Shortly after meeting the Saints there, he received a revelation for them. "By the prayer of your faith ye shall receive my law," the Lord again promised, "that ye may know how to govern my church and have all things right before me."[8]

From his study of the Bible, Joseph knew that God had given Moses a law as he led his people to the promised land. He also knew that Jesus Christ had come to earth and clarified the meaning of His law throughout

His ministry. Now He would once more reveal the law to His covenant people.

In the new revelation, the Lord praised Edward Partridge for his pure heart and called him to be the first bishop of the church. The Lord did not describe a bishop's duties in detail, but He said Edward was to devote his time completely to the church and help the Saints obey the law the Lord would give them.[9]

A week later, on February 9, Edward met with Joseph and other elders of the church to pray to receive the law. The elders asked Joseph a series of questions about the law, and the Lord revealed answers through him.[10] Some of these answers repeated familiar truths, affirming the principles of the Ten Commandments and the teachings of Jesus. Others gave the Saints new insights into how to keep the commandments and help those who transgressed them.[11]

The Lord also gave commandments to help the Saints become like Enoch's people. Rather than share common property, as the people on the Morleys' farm did, they were to think of all their land and wealth as a sacred stewardship from God, given to them so they could care for their families, relieve the poor, and build Zion.

Saints who chose to obey the law were to consecrate their property to the church by deeding it to the bishop. He would then return land and goods to them as an inheritance in Zion, according to the needs of their families. Saints who obtained inheritances were to act as God's stewards, using the land and tools they had received and returning whatever was unused to help the needy and build Zion and the temple.[12]

The Lord urged the Saints to obey this law and continue seeking truth. "If thou shalt ask, thou shalt receive revelation upon revelation, knowledge upon knowledge," He promised, "that thou mayest know the mysteries and peaceable things—that which bringeth joy, that which bringeth life eternal."[13]

Joseph received other revelations that brought order to the church. Responding to the extreme behaviors of some Saints, the Lord warned that false spirits were abroad on the earth, deceiving people into thinking that the Holy Ghost caused them to act wildly. The Lord said that the Spirit did not alarm and confuse people, but rather uplifted and instructed them.

"That which doth not edify is not of God," He declared.[14]

SOON AFTER THE LORD revealed His law in Kirtland, the Saints in New York made final preparations to gather to Ohio. They sold their land and property at great loss, packed their belongings in wagons, and said goodbye to family and friends.

Elizabeth and Thomas Marsh were among the Saints preparing to move. After Thomas received the pages from the Book of Mormon and returned home to Boston, they had moved to New York to be closer to Joseph and the church. The call to gather to Ohio came just a few months later, so Elizabeth and Thomas packed up once more, resolved to gather with the Saints and build Zion wherever the Lord directed.

Elizabeth's determination grew out of her conversion. Although she believed the Book of Mormon was the word of God, she had not been baptized right away. After giving birth to a son in Palmyra, however, she asked the Lord for a witness that the gospel was true. A short time later, she received the testimony she sought and joined the church, unwilling to deny what she knew and ready to lend a hand to the work.

"There has a great change taken place with me, both in body and mind," Elizabeth wrote Thomas's sister shortly before they left for Ohio. "I feel a desire to be thankful for what I have received and still look for more."

In the same letter, Thomas shared the news of the gathering. "The Lord calleth for all to repent," he declared, "and assemble at Ohio speedily." He did not know if the Saints were going to Ohio to build Zion or if they were preparing for a more ambitious move in the future. But it did not matter. If the Lord commanded them to gather to Missouri, or even to the Rocky Mountains a thousand miles beyond the nation's western border, he was ready to go.

"We know nothing of what we are to do, save it be revealed to us," he explained to his sister. "But this we know: a city will be built in the promised land."[15]

WITH THE LORD'S LAW revealed and Saints from New York gathering to Ohio, Joseph and Sidney resumed the inspired translation of the Bible.[16] They moved on from the account of Enoch to the story of the patriarch Abraham, whom the Lord promised to make a father of many nations.[17]

The Lord did not reveal extensive changes to the text, but as Joseph read Abraham's story, he pondered much about the patriarch's life.[18] Why had the Lord not condemned Abraham and other Old Testament patriarchs for marrying multiple wives, a practice Bible-reading Americans abhorred?

The Book of Mormon provided one answer. In the days of Jacob, Nephi's younger brother, the Lord commanded Nephite men to have only one wife. But He also declared that He could direct them otherwise, if circumstances required it, to raise up righteous children.[19]

Joseph prayed about the matter, and the Lord revealed that He sometimes commanded His people to practice plural marriage. The time to restore the practice was not yet, but a day would come when He would ask some of the Saints to do so.[20]

THE GROUND WAS STILL cold when the first group of Saints left New York. The second group, including Lucy Smith and about eighty others, left a little later. They booked passage on a canal boat that would bring them to a large lake to the west. At the lake, they would then board a steamboat that would carry them to a harbor near Kirtland. From there, they would travel overland for the final leg of their three-hundred-mile journey.[21]

At first the journey proceeded smoothly, but halfway to the lake, a broken lock on the canal stranded Lucy's group on shore. Since they had not planned on the delay, many people had not brought enough food. Hunger and anxiety about the gathering caused some of them to complain.

"Be patient, and stop your murmuring," Lucy told them. "I have no doubt that the hand of the Lord is over us."

The next morning, workmen repaired the canal, and the Saints started moving again. They arrived at the lake a few days later, but to their disappointment, thick ice blocked the harbor, preventing them from going any farther.[22]

The company hoped to rent a house in town while they waited, but they found only one large room to share. Fortunately, Lucy met a steamship captain who knew her brother, and she arranged for her group to move onto his boat while they waited for the ice to break.[23]

On the boat, the Saints seemed discouraged. Many were hungry, and everyone was wet and cold. They saw no way forward and started to argue with each other.[24] The arguments grew heated and attracted the attention of onlookers. Worried the Saints were making a spectacle of themselves, Lucy confronted them.

"Where is your faith? Where is your confidence in God?" she demanded. "If you will all of you raise your desires to heaven, that the ice may be broken up and we be set at liberty, as sure as the Lord lives, it will be done."

At that moment Lucy heard a noise like bursting thunder as the ice in the harbor split wide enough for the boat to steam through. The captain ordered his men to their posts, and they steered the craft through the narrow opening, passing dangerously close to the ice on both sides of them.[25]

Stunned and grateful, the Saints joined together in prayer on the deck.[26]

WHILE HIS MOTHER AND the New York Saints traveled west, Joseph moved with Emma to a small cabin on the Morley farm. His leadership and the newly revealed law had brought more order, understanding, and harmony to the Saints in Ohio. Now many elders and their families were making great sacrifices to spread the gospel to neighboring towns and villages.

In Missouri, missionary efforts were less encouraging. For a time, Oliver had believed they were making progress with Kikthawenund and his people. "The principal chief says he believes every word of the book," he had reported to Joseph, "and there are many more in the nation who believe."[27] But after a government agent threatened to arrest the missionaries for preaching to

Indians without permission, Oliver and the missionaries had to stop their efforts.[28]

Oliver considered taking the message to another Indian nation, the Navajo, who lived a thousand miles to the west, but he did not feel authorized to travel that far. Instead, he sent Parley back east to get a preaching license from the government while he and the other missionaries tried to convert settlers in Independence.[29]

Joseph and Emma, meanwhile, faced another tragedy. On the last day of April, Emma delivered twins—a girl and a boy—with the help of women from the Morley family. But like their brother before them, the twins were frail and died within a few hours of birth.[30]

On the same day, a recent convert named Julia Murdock passed away after giving birth to twins. When Joseph heard about her death, he sent a message to her husband, John, letting him know that he and Emma were willing to raise them. Heartbroken at his loss and unable to care for the newborns on his own, John accepted the offer.[31]

Joseph and Emma were overjoyed to welcome the babies into their home. And when Joseph's mother arrived safely from New York, she was able to cradle her new grandchildren in her arms.[32]

CHAPTER 12

After Much Tribulation

In the spring of 1831, seven-year-old Emily Partridge lived in a town northeast of Kirtland with her parents, Edward and Lydia, and four sisters. They had a fine frame house with a large room and two bedrooms on the ground floor. Upstairs was a bedroom, another large room, and a closet where they stored clothes. In the basement there was a kitchen and a vegetable cellar so dark it frightened Emily.

Outside, the Partridges' large yard provided Emily a place to play and explore. They had a flower garden and fruit trees, a barn, and a vacant lot where her father planned to build an even nicer home someday. Her father's hat shop was also nearby. Beneath the counter in the shop, she could always find bright ribbons and other treasures. The whole building was full of tools and machines her father used to dye fabrics and furs and shape them into hats for his customers.[1]

Her father did not spend much time making hats now that he was the bishop of the church. With Saints gathering to Ohio from New York, he had to help them settle into homes and find work. Among the new arrivals were the Knight family and their church branch from Colesville. Knowing Leman Copley had a large farm twenty miles northeast of Kirtland, which he had agreed to consecrate to the Lord, Emily's father sent the Colesville Saints there to settle.[2]

Some of the New York Saints came to Ohio with measles, and since they often stayed at the Partridge house, it was not long before Emily and her sisters developed high fevers and rashes. Emily recovered after a while, but her eleven-year-old sister, Eliza, came down with pneumonia. Her parents soon watched helplessly as her breathing grew labored and her fever soared.[3]

As the family cared for Eliza, her father attended an important church conference at a schoolhouse near the Morley farm. He was gone several days, and when he returned, he told the family he had to leave again.[4] Joseph had received a revelation that said the next conference would be held in Missouri. Several church leaders, including her father, were called to go there as soon as possible.[5]

Many people started making plans for the journey. In the revelation, the Lord called Missouri the land of the Saints' inheritance, echoing biblical descriptions of a promised land "flowing with milk and honey." There the Saints were to build the city of Zion.[6]

Emily's father was not eager to leave his family. Eliza was still sick and might die while he was away.[7] Emily could see that her mother was worried as well. As committed as Lydia Partridge was to the cause of Zion, she was not used to being left to care for the children and home by herself. She seemed to know that her trials were only beginning.[8]

POLLY KNIGHT WAS SICK when she and the Colesville Saints settled on Leman Copley's land. The farm had more than seven hundred acres of choice ground, offering enough space for many families to build homes, barns, and shops.[9] Here the Knights could start over and practice their new faith in peace, although many worried that Polly would not be long with them.

Polly's husband and sons worked quickly, making fences and planting fields to improve the land. Joseph and Bishop Partridge also encouraged the Colesville Saints to consecrate their property according to the law of the Lord.[10]

After the settlement started taking shape, however, Leman withdrew from the church and told the Colesville Saints to get off his property.[11] With nowhere else to go, the evicted Saints asked Joseph to seek the Lord's direction for them.

"You shall take your journey into the regions westward," the Lord told them, "unto the land of Missouri."[12]

Now that they knew Zion would be in Missouri, not Ohio, the Colesville Saints realized they would be among the first church members to settle there. They began to prepare for the journey, and about two weeks after the revelation, Polly and the rest of the branch left the Kirtland area and boarded riverboats that would take them west.[13]

As Polly and her family floated down the river, her greatest desire was to set foot in Zion before she died. She was fifty-five years old, and her health was failing. Her son Newel had already gone ashore to buy lumber for a coffin in case she died before getting to Missouri.

But Polly was determined to be buried nowhere else but in Zion.[14]

SHORTLY AFTER THE COLESVILLE Saints left, the prophet, Sidney, and Edward Partridge set out for Missouri with several elders of the church. They traveled mostly on land, preaching the gospel along the way and talking about their hopes for Zion.[15]

Joseph spoke optimistically about the church in Independence. He told some of the elders that Oliver and the other missionaries were sure to have built up a strong branch of the church there, as they had in Kirtland. Some of the elders took it as a prophecy.

As they neared Jackson County, the men admired the gently rolling prairie around them. With plenty of land for the Saints to spread out, Missouri seemed like the ideal location for Zion. And Independence, with its proximity to a large river and Indian lands, could be the perfect place to gather God's covenant people.[16]

But when they reached the town, the elders were unimpressed by what they saw. Ezra Booth, a former minister who had joined the church after seeing Joseph heal a woman's paralyzed arm, thought the area looked dreary and undeveloped. It had a courthouse, a few stores, several log houses—and little else. The missionaries had baptized only a handful of people in the area, so the branch was not as strong as Joseph had expected. Feeling misled, Ezra and others began to question Joseph's prophetic gifts.[17]

Joseph was disappointed too. Fayette and Kirtland were small villages, but Independence was little more than a backwater trading post. The town was a point of departure for trails going west, so it drew fur trappers and teamsters along with farmers and small businessmen. Joseph had known people in most of these trades all his life, but he found the men in Independence especially godless and rough. What's more, government agents in the town were suspicious of the missionaries and would likely make preaching to Indians difficult, if not impossible.[18]

Discouraged, he took his concerns to the Lord. "When will the wilderness blossom as the rose?" he asked. "When will Zion be built up in her glory, and where will Thy temple stand?"[19]

On July 20, six days after his arrival, Joseph's prayers were answered. "This land," the Lord told him, "is the land which I have appointed and consecrated for the gathering of the saints."

They had no reason to look elsewhere. "This is the land of promise," He declared, "and the place for the city of Zion." The Saints were to purchase as much of the available land as possible, build homes, and plant fields. And on a bluff west of the courthouse, they were to build a temple.[20]

EVEN AFTER THE LORD revealed His will for Zion, some Saints remained skeptical about Independence. Like Ezra Booth, Edward had expected to find a large branch of the church in the area. Instead, he and the Saints were to build Zion in a town where people were wary of them and not at all interested in the restored gospel.

As bishop of the church, he also understood that much of the responsibility for laying the foundation of Zion fell on his shoulders. To prepare the promised land for the Saints, he would have to buy as much of it as possible to distribute as inheritances to those who came to Zion and kept the law of consecration.[21] This meant that he would have to stay in Missouri and move his family permanently to Zion.

Edward wanted to help establish Zion, but so much about the revelation, his new responsibilities, and the area troubled him. One day, as he inspected the land in and around Independence, he pointed out to Joseph that it was not as good as other land nearby. He was frustrated with the prophet and did not see how the Saints could establish Zion there.

"I see it," Joseph testified, "and it will be so."[22]

A few days later, the Lord again revealed his word to Joseph, Edward, and the other elders of the church. "Ye cannot behold with your natural eyes, for the present time, the design of your God concerning those things which shall come hereafter, and the glory which shall follow after much tribulation," He declared. "For after much tribulation come the blessings."

In the revelation, the Lord also chastened Edward's unbelief. "If he repent not of his sins," He said of the bishop, "let him take heed lest he fall. Behold his mission is given unto him, and it shall not be given again."[23]

The warning humbled Edward. He asked the Lord to forgive his blindness of heart and told Joseph that he would stay in Independence and prepare the land of Zion for the Saints. Yet he still worried he was not up to the enormous task that lay ahead.

"I fear my station is above what I can perform to the acceptance of my Heavenly Father," he confessed in a letter to Lydia. "Pray for me that I may not fall."[24]

AFTER THREE WEEKS OF travel, Polly Knight arrived in Independence with the Colesville Saints. She stood feebly on the ground, grateful she had reached the land of Zion. Her body was rapidly failing, though, and two recent converts from the area brought her into their home so she could rest in relative comfort.

As the Knights searched the area for a place to settle, they found the countryside beautiful and pleasant, with rich land they could develop and farm. The people also seemed friendly, even though they were strangers. Unlike some of the elders from Kirtland, the Colesville members believed the Saints could build Zion there.

On August 2, the Saints in Missouri assembled several miles west of Independence to begin work on the first house in Zion. Joseph and twelve men from the Colesville Branch, who symbolically represented the tribes of Israel, laid the first log for the building. Sidney then dedicated the land of Zion for the gathering of the Saints.

The next day, on a plot west of the courthouse in Independence, Joseph carefully laid a single stone to mark the corner of the future temple.[25] Someone then opened a Bible and read from the eighty-seventh psalm: "The Lord loveth the gates of Zion more than all the dwellings of Jacob. Glorious things are spoken of thee, O city of God."[26]

A few days later, Polly died, praising the Lord for supporting her in her suffering.[27] The prophet preached the funeral sermon, and her husband buried her body in a patch of woods not far from the temple site. She was the first Saint laid to rest in Zion.[28]

The same day, Joseph received another revelation: "Blessed, saith the Lord, are they who have come up unto this land with an eye single to my glory, according to my commandments. For those that live shall inherit the earth, and those that die shall rest from all their labors."[29]

Soon after the funeral, Ezra and other church elders started their journey back to Kirtland with Joseph, Oliver, and Sidney. Ezra was relieved to be returning home to Ohio. Unlike Edward, he had not had a change of heart about Joseph or the location of Zion.

The men launched canoes onto the wide Missouri River, just north of Independence, and paddled downstream. At the end of the first day of travel, they were in good spirits and enjoyed a dinner of wild turkey along the riverbank. On the following day, however, the August weather was hot and the river was wild and difficult to navigate. The men quickly grew tired and soon began criticizing each other.[30]

"As the Lord God liveth," Oliver finally shouted at the men, "if you do not behave better, some accident will befall you."

Joseph took the lead in his canoe the next afternoon, but some of the elders were upset with him and Oliver and refused to paddle. At a dangerous bend in the river, they hit a submerged tree and nearly capsized. Fearing for the lives of everyone in the company, Joseph and Sidney ordered the elders off the river.[31]

After they set up camp, Joseph, Oliver, and Sidney tried to talk to the group and ease tensions. Irritated, the men called Joseph and Sidney cowards for getting off the river, mocked the way Oliver paddled his canoe, and accused Joseph of acting like a dictator. The quarrel lasted long into the night.

Rather than stay up with the company, Ezra went to bed early, deeply critical of Joseph and the elders. Why, he wondered, would the Lord trust the keys of His kingdom to men like these?[32]

LATER THAT SUMMER, LYDIA Partridge received Edward's letter from Missouri. Along with sharing his anxieties about his calling, he explained that he was not coming home as planned but instead staying in Jackson County to purchase land for the Saints. Attached to the letter was a copy of the revelation to Edward, which directed their family to settle in Zion.

Lydia was surprised. When Edward left, he had told their friends that he would return to Ohio as soon as his work in Missouri was finished. Now, with so many responsibilities in Zion, he was unsure if he could return to help Lydia and the children make the journey. Yet he knew other families in Ohio were moving to Missouri that fall, including his counselors in the bishopric. So too were Sidney Gilbert, a Kirtland storekeeper, and William Phelps, a printer, both of whom would be establishing businesses for the church in Zion.[33]

"It will probably be for the best if you should come with them," he wrote.[34]

Knowing Independence offered few luxuries, Edward also gave Lydia a long list of things to pack and things to leave behind. "We have to suffer," he warned her, "and shall for some time have many privations here, which you and I have not been much used to."[35]

Lydia began preparing for the move. The children were now healthy enough to travel, and she arranged to journey with the Gilbert and Phelps families. As she sold her family's property, her neighbors expressed disbelief that she and Edward would give up their beautiful home and prosperous business to follow a young prophet into the wilderness.[36]

Lydia had no desire to turn her back on the Lord's command to build Zion. She knew abandoning her fine home would be a trial, but she believed it would be an honor to help lay the foundation of the city of God.[37]

CHAPTER 13

The Gift Has Returned

When Joseph returned to Kirtland in late August 1831, tension still lingered between him and a few of the elders who had gone with him to Independence. After their quarrel on the banks of the Missouri River, Joseph and most of the elders traveling with him had humbled themselves, confessed their sins, and sought forgiveness. The next morning, the Lord had forgiven them and offered reassurance and encouragement.[1]

"Inasmuch as you have humbled yourselves before me," He had said, "the blessings of the kingdom are yours."[2]

Other elders, Ezra Booth among them, did not heed the revelation or resolve their differences with Joseph. When Ezra returned to Kirtland, he continued to criticize Joseph and complain about his actions on the mission.[3]

A conference of Saints soon revoked Ezra's preaching license, and he began writing his friends scathing letters attacking Joseph's character.[4]

The Lord rebuked these attacks in early September and called on the elders to stop condemning Joseph's errors and criticizing him without cause. "He has sinned," the Lord acknowledged, "but verily I say unto you, I, the Lord, forgive sins unto those who confess their sins before me and ask forgiveness."

He admonished the Saints to be forgiving as well. "I, the Lord, will forgive whom I will forgive," He declared, "but of you it is required to forgive all men."

He also urged the Saints to do good and build up Zion, rather than let their disagreements divide them. "Be not weary in well-doing, for ye are laying the foundation of a great work," He reminded them. "The Lord requireth the heart and a willing mind; and the willing and obedient shall eat the good of the land of Zion in these last days."

Before concluding His words, the Lord called a few church members to sell their property and go to Missouri. Most of the Saints were to stay in Ohio, however, and continue sharing the gospel there. "For I, the Lord, will," He told Joseph, "to retain a strong hold in the land of Kirtland, for the space of five years."[5]

ELIZABETH MARSH LISTENED EAGERLY as the elders returning to Ohio described the land of Zion. They spoke of deep, black soil, tumbling prairies as vast as the ocean, and a roiling river that seemed to have a life of its own. Although they had little good to say about the Missourians, many of the returning elders were optimistic about Zion's future.

Writing to her sister-in-law in Boston, Elizabeth recounted everything she knew about the promised land. "They have erected a stone for both the temple and city," she reported, "and purchased land as far as circumstances would admit for the inheritance of the faithful." The temple site itself was in a forest west of the courthouse, she noted, fulfilling biblical prophecies that the forest would be "esteemed a fruitful field" and that "solitary places shall be made glad."[6]

Elizabeth's husband, Thomas, was still in Missouri preaching the gospel, and she expected him to come home in a month or so. According to the elders, most people in Missouri were not interested in the message he was sharing, but missionaries were baptizing people elsewhere and sending them on to Zion.[7]

Before long, hundreds of Saints would be gathering to Independence.

HUNDREDS OF MILES SOUTHWEST of Kirtland, twenty-five-year-old William McLellin visited the graves of his wife, Cinthia Ann, and their baby. William and Cinthia Ann had been married for less than two years when she and the baby died. As a schoolteacher, William had a quick mind and a gift for writing. But he found nothing to comfort him in the lonely hours since he lost his family.[8]

One day, after teaching his class, William heard two men preach about the Book of Mormon. One of them, David Whitmer, declared that he had seen an angel who testified that the Book of Mormon was true. The other, Harvey Whitlock, astonished William with the power and clarity of his preaching.

William invited the men to teach him more, and he was again struck by Harvey's words. "I never heard such preaching in all my life," William wrote in his journal. "The glory of God seemed to encircle the man."[9]

Eager to meet Joseph Smith and investigate his claims, William followed David and Harvey to Independence. Joseph had already returned to Kirtland by the time they arrived, but William met Edward Partridge, Martin Harris, and Hyrum Smith and heard their testimonies. He also spoke with other men and women in Zion and marveled at the love and peace he saw among them.[10]

While taking a long walk through the woods one day, he talked with Hyrum about the Book of Mormon and the beginning of the church. William wanted to believe, but in spite of everything he had heard so far, he still was not convinced to join the church. He wanted a witness from God that he had found the truth.

Early the next morning, he prayed for direction. Reflecting on his study of the Book of Mormon, William realized it had opened his mind to new light. He knew then that it was true and felt honor bound to testify of it. He was certain he had found the living church of Jesus Christ.[11]

Hyrum baptized and confirmed William later that day, and the two men soon set out for Kirtland.[12] As they preached along the way, William discovered he had a talent for captivating audiences and debating ministers. He sometimes acted arrogantly when he preached, however, and he felt bad when his boasting drove the Spirit away.[13]

Once they arrived in Kirtland, William was anxious to speak with Joseph. He had several specific questions he wanted answered, but he kept them to himself, praying that Joseph would discern them on his own and reveal their answers. William was now unsure where to go and what to do with his life. Without a family, he could devote himself fully to the Lord's work. But part of him wanted to look out for his own welfare first.

That night, William went home with Joseph and asked him for a revelation from the Lord, as he knew many others had done. Joseph agreed, and as the prophet received the revelation, William heard the Lord answer each of his questions. His anxiety gave way to joy. He knew he had found a prophet of God.[14]

A FEW DAYS LATER, on November 1, 1831, Joseph called a council of church leaders together. Ezra Booth had recently published a letter in a local newspaper accusing

Joseph of making false prophecies and hiding his revelations from the public. The letter was widely read, and
many people had begun to grow wary of the Saints and
their message.[15]

Many Saints also wanted to read the Lord's word
themselves. Since there were only handwritten copies
of the revelations Joseph had received, they were not
well known among most church members. Elders who
wanted to use them in missionary work had to copy
them by hand.

Knowing this, Joseph proposed publishing the revelations in a book. He was confident that such a book
would help missionaries share the Lord's word more
easily and provide correct information about the church
to curious neighbors.

The council talked the matter over for hours. David
Whitmer and a few others opposed publishing the revelations, worried that making the Lord's plans for Zion
more public might cause problems for the Saints in
Jackson County. Joseph and Sidney disagreed, insisting
that the Lord wanted the church to publish His words.[16]

After more debate, the council agreed to publish
ten thousand copies of the revelations as the Book of
Commandments. They assigned Sidney, Oliver, and
William McLellin to write a preface to the book of revelations and present it to them later that day.[17]

The three men began writing immediately, but
when they returned with a preface, the council was
unhappy with it. They read it over, picking it apart line

by line, and asked Joseph to seek the Lord's will on it. Joseph prayed, and the Lord revealed a new preface for the book. Sidney recorded His words as Joseph spoke them.[18]

In the new preface, the Lord commanded all people to hearken to His voice. He declared that He had given Joseph these commandments to help His children increase their faith, trust in Him, and receive and proclaim the fullness of His gospel and everlasting covenant. He also addressed the fears of those like David who worried about the content of the revelations.

"What I the Lord have spoken, I have spoken, and I excuse not myself," He declared, "and though the heavens and the earth pass away, my word shall not pass away, but shall all be fulfilled, whether by mine own voice or by the voice of my servants, it is the same."[19]

After Joseph spoke the words of the preface, several members of the council said they were willing to testify of the truth of the revelations. Others in the room were still reluctant to publish the revelations in their current form. They knew Joseph was a prophet, and they knew the revelations were true, but they were embarrassed that the word of the Lord had come to them filtered through Joseph's limited vocabulary and weak grammar.[20]

The Lord did not share their concern. In His preface, He had testified that the revelations came from Him, given to His servants "in their weakness, after the manner of their language."[21] To help the men know the revelations came from Him, He issued a new revelation, challenging the council to select the wisest man in the room to write a revelation like the ones Joseph had received.

If the man selected for the task was unable to do it, everyone in the room would know and be responsible to testify that the Lord's revelations to Joseph were true, despite their imperfections.[22]

Taking up a pen, William tried to write a revelation, confident in his mastery of language. When he finished, though, he and the other men in the room knew what he had written had not come from the Lord.[23] They admitted their error and signed a statement testifying that the revelations had been given to the prophet by the inspiration of God.[24]

In council, they resolved that Joseph should review the revelations and "correct those errors or mistakes which he may discover by the Holy Spirit."[25]

AROUND THIS TIME, ELIZABETH Marsh welcomed a traveling preacher named Nancy Towle into her home in Kirtland. Nancy was a small, wiry woman with large eyes that burned with the intensity of her convictions. At thirty-five, Nancy had already made a name for herself preaching to large congregations of women and men in schools, churches, and camp meetings across the United States. After talking with her, Elizabeth could tell that she was well educated and firm in her beliefs.[26]

Nancy had come to Kirtland with a purpose. Although she usually kept an open mind about other Christian churches, even when she disagreed with them, Nancy was sure the Saints were deluded. She wanted to learn more about them so she could help others resist their teachings.[27]

Elizabeth did not support such a mission, but she could understand that Nancy was defending what she thought was the truth. She listened to them preach and saw some baptisms in a nearby river. Later in the day, she and Elizabeth attended a confirmation meeting with Joseph, Sidney, and other church leaders.[28]

At the meeting, William Phelps confronted Nancy about doubting the truth of the Book of Mormon. "You shall not be saved unless you believe that book," he told her.

Nancy glared at William. "If I had that book, sir, I would burn it," she said. Nancy was shocked that so many talented and intelligent people could follow Joseph Smith and believe in the Book of Mormon.

"Mr. Smith," she said, addressing the prophet, "can you, in the presence of Almighty God, give your word by oath that an angel from heaven showed you the place of those plates?"

"I will not swear at all," said Joseph wryly. Instead, he approached those who had just been baptized, placed his hands on their heads, and confirmed them.

Turning to Nancy, Elizabeth testified of her own confirmation. "No sooner his hands fell upon my head," she said, "than I felt the Holy Ghost as warm water go over me."

Nancy was offended, as if Elizabeth had accused her of not knowing what the Spirit of the Lord felt like. She looked at Joseph again. "Are you not ashamed of such pretentions?" she said. "You who are no more than any ignorant plowboy of our land!"

Joseph testified simply: "The gift has returned back again, as in former times, to illiterate fishermen."[29]

CHAPTER 14

Visions and Nightmares

In January 1832, Joseph, Emma, and the twins were living in the home of Elsa and John Johnson in Hiram, Ohio, about thirty miles south of Kirtland.[1] The Johnsons were around the same age as Joseph's parents, so most of their children had married and moved out of their spacious farmhouse, leaving plenty of room for Joseph to meet with church leaders and work on his translation of the Bible.

Before their baptisms, Elsa and John had been members of Ezra Booth's congregation. In fact, it had been Elsa who was miraculously healed by Joseph, leading Ezra to join the church.[2] But while Ezra had lost his faith, the Johnsons continued to support the prophet, just as the Whitmers and Knights had done in New York.

That winter, Joseph and Sidney spent much of their time translating in an upstairs room at the Johnson home. In mid-February, as they read in the Gospel of John about the resurrection of just and unjust souls, Joseph wondered if there was not more to know about heaven or the salvation of humankind. If God rewarded His children according to their deeds on earth, were traditional notions of heaven and hell too simple?[3]

On February 16, Joseph, Sidney, and about twelve other men sat in an upstairs room in the Johnson home.[4] The Spirit rested on Joseph and Sidney, and they grew still as a vision opened before their eyes. The glory of the Lord surrounded them, and they saw Jesus Christ at the right hand of God. Angels worshipped at His throne, and a voice testified that Jesus was the Only Begotten of the Father.[5]

"What do I see?" Joseph asked as he and Sidney marveled at the wonders they saw. He then described what he beheld in the vision, and Sidney said, "I see the same." Sidney then asked the same question and described the scene before him. Once he finished, Joseph said, "I see the same."

They spoke like this for an hour, and their vision revealed that God's plan of salvation started before life on earth and that His children would be resurrected after death through the power of Jesus Christ. They also described heaven in a way no one in the room had ever imagined. Rather than being a single kingdom, it was organized into various kingdoms of glory.

Expanding on the apostle Paul's description of the Resurrection in 1 Corinthians 15, Joseph and Sidney saw and described specific details about each kingdom. The Lord prepared telestial glory for those who had been wicked and unrepentant on earth. Terrestrial glory was for those who had lived honorably in life but had not fully obeyed the gospel of Jesus Christ. Celestial glory was for those who accepted Christ, made and kept gospel covenants, and inherited the fullness of God's glory.[6]

The Lord revealed more about heaven and the Resurrection to Joseph and Sidney but told them not to record it. "They are only to be seen and understood by the power of the Holy Spirit," He explained, "which God bestows on those who love him, and purify themselves before him."[7]

When the vision closed, Sidney looked limp and pale, overcome by what he had seen. Joseph smiled and said, "Sidney is not used to it as I am."[8]

AS THE SAINTS IN Kirtland learned of Joseph's grand vision of heaven, William Phelps was setting up the church's printing office in Independence. He had been a newspaper editor much of his adult life, and along with working on the Book of Commandments, he hoped to publish a monthly newspaper for the Saints and their neighbors in Missouri.

Writing in a strong, confident voice, William penned a public announcement for the paper, which he planned to call *The Evening and the Morning Star.* "The *Star* will borrow its light from sacred sources," he declared, "and be devoted to the revelations of God." He believed the last days had arrived, and he wanted his newspaper to warn the righteous and wicked alike that the gospel was restored and that the Savior would soon return to the earth.

He wanted to print other items of interest as well, including news reports and poetry. But even though he was a man of strong opinions who rarely passed up the chance to speak his mind, William insisted that the newspaper would not meddle in politics or local disputes.

He had been a politically active editor for other newspapers and had sometimes peppered his articles and editorials with opinions that irritated his opponents.[9] Staying above the fray in Missouri would be challenging. Still, the prospect of writing news articles and editorials thrilled him.

William was sincere in his plan to focus the paper on the gospel, and he understood that his first priority as church printer was publishing the revelations. "From this press may be expected, as soon as wisdom directs, many sacred records," he promised his readers.[10]

BACK IN OHIO, JOSEPH and Sidney's vision was causing a stir. Many Saints quickly embraced the newly revealed truths about heaven, but others had a hard time squaring the vision with their traditional Christian beliefs.[11] Did this new view of heaven save too many souls? A few Saints rejected the revelation and left the church.

The vision further troubled some of their neighbors, who were already bothered by the letters Ezra Booth had published in a local newspaper. As the letters spread Ezra's criticisms against Joseph, other former members of the church joined in, raising questions in the minds of people whose family and friends worshipped with the Saints.[12]

As the sun set one evening in late March 1832, a group of men met in a brickyard half a mile from the Johnsons' home. In the kiln, the men built a fire to heat pine tar. As the sky grew darker, they covered their faces in soot and slipped away into the night.[13]

EMMA WAS LYING AWAKE in bed when she heard faint tapping on the window. The noise was loud enough to catch her attention, but not unusual. She thought nothing of it.

Nearby, Joseph lay on a trundle bed, his steady breathing a sign that he was asleep. The twins had measles, and earlier that night Joseph had stayed up with the sicker of the two so Emma could sleep. After a while, she awoke, took the baby from him, and told him to rest. He had to preach in the morning.

Emma was drifting off to sleep when the bedroom door swung open and a dozen men burst into the room.

They seized Joseph by the arms and legs and started to drag him from the house. Emma screamed.

Joseph thrashed wildly as the men tightened their grip. Someone grabbed him by the hair and yanked him toward the door. Wrenching one of his legs free, Joseph kicked a man in the face. The man stumbled backward and toppled down the doorstep, clutching his bleeding nose. Laughing hoarsely, he scrambled back to his feet and shoved a bloody hand into Joseph's face.

"I'll fix you," he snarled.

The men wrestled Joseph out of the house and into the yard. He fought against their grip, trying to free his powerful limbs, but someone seized him by the throat and squeezed until his body went limp.[14]

JOSEPH AWOKE IN A meadow some distance from the Johnson house. The men were still holding him tightly, a little off the ground, so he could not break free. A few feet away, he saw the half-naked figure of Sidney Rigdon stretched out in the grass. He looked dead.

"Have mercy," Joseph begged the men. "Spare my life."

"Call on your God for help," someone shouted. Joseph looked around and saw more men joining the mob. One man stepped out of a nearby orchard with a wooden plank, and the men stretched Joseph across it and carried him deeper into the meadow.

151

After they had gone some distance from the house, they tore away his clothes and held him down while a man approached with a sharp knife, ready to mutilate him. But the man took a look at Joseph and refused to cut him.

"Damn you," another man howled. He leapt on Joseph and raked his sharp fingernails across the prophet's skin, leaving it raw and lacerated. "That's the way the Holy Ghost falls on folks," he said.

Joseph could hear other men a short distance off, arguing over what to do with him and Sidney. He could not hear every word they said, but he thought he heard a familiar name or two.

Once the arguing stopped, someone said, "Let's tar up his mouth." Filthy hands forced his jaw open while a man tried to pour a bottle of acid down his throat. The bottle broke on Joseph's teeth, chipping one of them.

Another man tried to cram a paddle of sticky tar into his mouth, but Joseph shook his head back and forth. "Damn you!" the man cried. "Hold up your head." He jammed the paddle into Joseph's mouth until the tar oozed over his lips.

More men came with a vat of tar and poured it over him. The tar ran down his lacerated skin and through his hair. They covered him with feathers, dumped him on the cold ground, and fled the scene.

After they left, Joseph tore the tar from his lips and gasped for air. He struggled to his feet, but his strength failed him. He tried again and this time managed to stay upright. Stray feathers flitted in the air around him.[15]

WHEN SHE SAW JOSEPH stumbling to the Johnsons' door, Emma fainted, sure the mob had mangled him beyond recognition. Hearing the commotion, several women in the neighborhood had rushed to the house. Joseph asked for a blanket to cover his battered body.

For the rest of the night, people tended to Joseph and to Sidney, who had lain in the meadow a long time, barely breathing. Emma scraped the tar from Joseph's limbs, chest, and back. Elsa Johnson, meanwhile, used lard from her pantry to ease the hardened tar from his skin and hair.[16]

The next day, Joseph got dressed and preached a sermon from the Johnsons' doorstep. He recognized some of the men from the mob in the congregation, but he said nothing to them. In the afternoon, he baptized three people.[17]

Still, the attack had caused plenty of damage. His body was bruised and aching from the beating. Sidney lay in bed, delirious, teetering between life and death. The mob had dragged him out of his house by his heels, leaving his head unprotected as it bounced down the steps and across the cold March ground.

Joseph and Emma's babies also suffered. While his twin sister Julia's health improved steadily, little Joseph grew worse, and he died later that week. The prophet blamed his son's death on the cold air that poured into the house when the mob dragged him away.[18]

A FEW DAYS AFTER the baby's burial, Joseph returned to the work despite his grief. Following the Lord's commandment, he set out for Missouri on April 1 with Newel Whitney and Sidney, who was still weak from the attack but had recovered enough to travel.[19] The Lord had recently called Newel to serve as a bishop of the Saints in Ohio and directed him to consecrate surplus money from his profitable businesses to help support the store, printing office, and land purchases in Independence.[20]

The Lord wanted the three men to go to Missouri and covenant to cooperate economically with leaders in Zion to benefit the church and better care for the poor. He also wanted them to strengthen the Saints so they would not lose sight of their sacred responsibility to build the city of Zion.[21]

When they arrived in Independence, Joseph convened a council of church leaders and read a revelation that called on him, Edward Partridge, Newel Whitney, and other church leaders to covenant with each other to manage the church's business concerns.[22]

"I give unto you this commandment, that ye bind yourselves by this covenant," the Lord declared, "every man seeking the interest of his neighbor, and doing all things with an eye single to the glory of God." Bound thus together, they called themselves the United Firm.[23]

While he was in Missouri, Joseph also visited members of the old Colesville Branch and others who had settled in the area. Church leaders seemed to be working well together, the new printing office was preparing to publish the first issue of *The Evening and the Morning Star,* and many church members were eager to build up the city.[24]

But Joseph sensed hard feelings toward him from some of the Saints, including a few of their leaders. They seemed to resent his choice to stay in Kirtland rather than move permanently to Missouri. And some still seemed upset about what had happened on his last visit to the area, when he and some of the elders had disagreed about where to establish Zion in Missouri.

Their resentment surprised him. Did they not realize he had left his grieving family and traveled eight hundred miles just to help them?[25]

WHILE JOSEPH WAS VISITING the Saints in Independence, William McLellin was struggling spiritually in Ohio. After being called as a missionary, he had spent the winter preaching the gospel, first in towns and villages east of Kirtland and later to the south. Although he had enjoyed some success early on, poor health, bad weather, and uninterested people now left him discouraged.[26]

As a teacher, he was used to obedient students who listened to his lessons and did not talk back. As a missionary, however, he was often at odds with people who did not respect his authority. Once, while delivering a long sermon, he was interrupted several times and called a liar.[27]

After months of setbacks, he started to question whether it was the Lord or Joseph Smith who had called him on a mission.[28] Unable to settle the matter in his mind, he left the mission field and found a job clerking at a store.[29] In his free time, he scoured the Bible for evidence of the restored gospel and argued with skeptics about religion.

In time, he chose not to return to his mission. Instead, he married a church member named Emeline Miller and decided to accompany a group of about a hundred Saints to Jackson County, where land was readily available. In a revelation to Joseph, God had rebuked William for abandoning his mission, but William believed he could start over in Zion.

He wanted to do it on his own terms, however. In the summer of 1832, he and his company moved to Missouri without a recommendation from church leaders, which the Lord required migrating Saints to obtain so that Zion would not grow too quickly and strain resources. When he arrived, he also did not go to Bishop Partridge to consecrate his property or receive an inheritance. Instead he bought two lots in Independence from the government.[30]

The arrival of William and the others overwhelmed Bishop Partridge and his counselors. Many of the newcomers were poor and had little to consecrate. The bishop did his best to get them settled, but it was a challenge to arrange homes, farms, and employment for them while Zion's economy was still fragile.[31]

William, however, believed his large company fulfilled Isaiah's prophecy that many people would come to Zion. He found work as a schoolteacher and wrote his relatives about his faith.

"We believe that Joseph Smith is a true prophet or seer of the Lord," he testified, "and that he has power and does receive revelations from God, and that these revelations when received are of divine authority in the Church of Christ."[32]

Such notions were beginning to unnerve his neighbors in Missouri, though, especially when they heard some church members say that God had appointed Independence to be the center place of their promised land.[33] With the arrival of William's company, the Saints in Zion numbered around five hundred. Already resources were getting scarce, driving up prices on local goods.[34]

"They are crowding in," one woman observed as more Saints settled around her. "I do think they ought to be punished."[35]

CHAPTER 15

Holy Places

In August 1832, Phebe Peck watched proudly as three of her children were baptized near their home in Missouri. They were among eleven children baptized in Zion that day. Along with the children of Lydia and Edward Partridge and Sally and William Phelps, they belonged to the first generation of young Saints growing up in a land the Lord had set apart as holy.

Phebe and her children had moved to Zion with the Colesville Saints a year earlier. Phebe's late husband, Benjamin, was Polly Knight's brother, so Phebe had a place in the extended Knight family. But she still missed her own family and friends in New York who had not joined the church.

Shortly after her children's baptisms, she wrote to two of her old friends about Zion. "You would not think it a hardship to come here," she told her friend Anna, "for the Lord is revealing the mysteries of the heavenly kingdom unto His children."[1]

Recently, William Phelps had published Joseph and Sidney's vision of heaven in *The Evening and the Morning Star,* and Phebe shared with Anna its promise that those who were baptized and remained valiant in the testimony of Christ would enjoy the highest degree of glory and the fullness of God's blessings.

With such a promise in mind, Phebe urged another friend, Patty, to listen to the gospel message. "Could you but see and believe as I do," she wrote, "the way would be opened and you would come to this land, and we should behold each other and rejoice in the things of God."

Phebe testified of the prophet's recently revealed vision and the peace it brought her, encouraging Patty to read its words if she ever got the chance.

"I hope you will read with a careful and a prayerful heart," she told her friend, "for these things are worthy of notice, and I desire that you may search into them."[2]

THAT FALL, JOSEPH TRAVELED with Newel Whitney to New York City to preach the gospel and make purchases for the United Firm. The Lord had called Newel to warn people in large cities of the calamities that were coming in the last days. Joseph accompanied him to help fulfill the Lord's commandment.[3]

Lately, the prophet had felt an increasing urgency to preach the gospel and build up the gathering place of the Saints. Shortly before he left Kirtland, he received a revelation that priesthood holders had a responsibility to preach the gospel and lead the faithful to the safety of Zion and the temple, where the Lord promised to visit them with His glory.

The priesthood, therefore, brought with it a duty to administer ordinances to those who accepted Christ and His gospel. Only through these ordinances, the Lord taught, could His children be ready to receive His power and return to His presence.[4]

As he left on his journey, though, Joseph had reason to worry about the effort to build Zion in Missouri. The church in Ohio was thriving, despite opposition from former church members, but the church in Missouri struggled to maintain order as more people moved to the area without permission. With tensions between him and some of Zion's leaders still unresolved, something had to be done to unify the church.

Arriving in New York City, Joseph was astonished by its size. Tall buildings towered over narrow streets that stretched for miles. Everywhere he looked were shops with expensive goods, large houses and office buildings, and banks where wealthy men transacted business. People of many ethnicities, occupations, and classes hurried by him, seemingly indifferent to others around them.[5]

He and Newel lodged at a four-story hotel near the warehouses where Newel hoped to make his purchases for the United Firm. Joseph found the work of selecting goods tedious and was discouraged by the pride and wickedness he saw in the city, so he often returned to the hotel to read, meditate, and pray. He soon became homesick. Emma was nearing the end of another difficult pregnancy, and he longed to be with her and their daughter.

"Thoughts of home, of Emma and Julia, rush upon my mind like a flood," he wrote, "and I could wish for a moment to be with them."

Sometimes Joseph would leave the hotel to explore and preach. New York City had a population of more than two hundred thousand, and Joseph sensed that the Lord was pleased with the wonderful architecture and extraordinary inventions of its people. Yet no one seemed to glorify God for the marvelous things around them or take interest in the restored gospel of Jesus Christ.

Undeterred, Joseph continued to share his message. "I am determined to lift up my voice," he wrote Emma, "and leave the event with God, who holdeth all things in His hands."[6]

ONE MONTH LATER, AFTER Joseph and Newel had returned to Ohio, thirty-one-year-old Brigham Young arrived in Kirtland with his older brother Joseph and his best friend, Heber Kimball. They were recent converts from central New York, not far from where Joseph Smith had grown up. Brigham had wanted to meet the prophet since he first learned about the Book of Mormon. Now that he was in Kirtland, he planned to shake Joseph's hand, look into his eyes, and know his heart. Brigham had been preaching from the Book of Mormon since his baptism, but he knew little about the man who translated it.

Joseph and Emma now lived in the apartment above the Whitneys' store in Kirtland, but when the three men stopped there, the prophet was out chopping firewood in a forest about a mile away. They set out for the place immediately, unsure what they would find when they got there.

Walking into the woods, Brigham and the others came to a clearing where Joseph was splitting logs. He was taller than Brigham and dressed in simple work clothes. From the skillful way Joseph swung his ax, Brigham could see he was no stranger to manual labor.

Brigham approached him and introduced himself. Setting down his ax, Joseph shook Brigham's hand. "I am glad to see you," he said.

As they talked, Brigham offered to chop wood while his brother and Heber helped load it into a wagon. The prophet seemed cheerful, hardworking, and friendly. Like Brigham, he had come from a humble background, but he was not crude the way some laborers were. Brigham knew at once he was a prophet of God.[7]

After a while, Joseph invited the men back to his house for a meal. When they arrived, he introduced them to Emma, who lay in bed, cradling a healthy baby boy.

The baby had been born a few days earlier, only hours before Joseph and Newel returned from New York. Emma and Joseph had named him Joseph Smith III.[8]

Following the meal, Joseph held a small meeting and invited Brigham to pray. As he bowed his head, Brigham felt the Spirit move him to speak in an unknown language. The people in the room were startled. Over the last year, they had seen many people mimic the gifts of the Spirit with wild behavior. What Brigham did was different.

"Brethren, I shall never oppose anything that comes from the Lord," Joseph said, sensing their discomfort. "That tongue is from God."

Joseph then spoke in the same language, declaring that it was the language Adam had spoken in the Garden of Eden and encouraging the Saints to seek the gift of tongues, as Paul had done in the New Testament, for the benefit of the children of God.[9]

BRIGHAM LEFT KIRTLAND a week later as a peaceful winter settled over the small village. A few days before Christmas, however, a local newspaper published reports that government leaders in the state of South Carolina were fighting taxes on imported goods and threatening to declare independence from the United States. Some people were calling for war.[10]

As Joseph read reports of the crisis, he reflected on the wickedness and destruction that the Bible said would precede the Savior's Second Coming.[11] The whole world groaned under the bondage of sin, the Lord had told him recently, and God would soon visit the wicked with His wrath, rending the kingdoms of the earth and causing the heavens to tremble.[12]

After praying to know more about these calamities, Joseph received a revelation on Christmas Day. The Lord told him that the time would come when South Carolina and other southern states would rebel against the rest of the nation. The rebellious states would call on other countries for help, and enslaved peoples would rise up against their masters. War and natural disaster would then pour out upon all nations, spreading misery and death across the earth.

The revelation was a bleak reminder that the Saints could no longer delay the building of Zion and the temple. They had to prepare now if they hoped to avoid the coming devastation.

"Stand ye in holy places," the Lord urged them, "and be not moved, until the day of the Lord come."[13]

TWO DAYS AFTER RECEIVING the revelation on war, Joseph met with church leaders in Newel Whitney's store. He believed that the Saints in Missouri were growing more critical of his leadership. If they did not repent and restore harmony in the church, he feared, they could lose their inheritances in Zion and forfeit their chance to build the temple.[14]

After opening the meeting, Joseph asked the church leaders to pray to know God's will for building Zion. The men bowed their heads and prayed, each expressing his willingness to keep God's commandments. Joseph then received a revelation while Frederick Williams, his new scribe, wrote it down.[15]

It was a message of peace for the Saints, urging them to be holy. "Sanctify yourselves," the Lord commanded, "that your minds become single to God." To their surprise, He directed them to build a temple in Kirtland and prepare to receive His glory.

"Organize yourselves," the Lord said. "Prepare every needful thing; and establish a house, even a house of prayer, a house of fasting, a house of faith, a house of learning, a house of glory, a house of order, a house of God."

The Lord also counseled them to start a school. "As all have not faith," He declared, "seek ye diligently and teach one another words of wisdom; yea, seek ye out of the best books words of wisdom; seek learning, even by study and also by faith."[16]

Joseph sent a copy of the revelation to William Phelps in Missouri, calling it an "olive leaf" and "the Lord's message of peace" to the Saints in Kirtland. He warned the Saints in Zion that if they did not sanctify themselves as the Lord instructed, He would choose others to build His temple.

"Hear the warning voice of God, lest Zion fall," Joseph pleaded. "The brethren in Kirtland pray for you unceasingly, for knowing the terrors of the Lord, they greatly fear for you."[17]

ON JANUARY 22, 1833, JOSEPH and the Saints in Kirtland opened the School of the Prophets in the Whitneys' store. One of Joseph's clerks, Orson Hyde, was appointed to teach the class. Like Joseph and many of the other students, Orson had spent most of his childhood working rather than attending school. He was an orphan, and his guardian had allowed him to attend school only in the winter, after the harvest and before the next planting. Orson had a good memory and learned quickly, however, and he had attended a nearby academy as an adult.[18]

In the School of the Prophets, Orson taught the men spiritual lessons in addition to history, grammar, and arithmetic, as the Lord had commanded.[19] Those who attended his classes were not just pupils. They addressed each other as brothers and bound themselves with a covenant of fellowship.[20] They studied together, had discussions, and prayed as a group.[21]

One day, Joseph invited Orson and others in the class to take off their shoes. Following Christ's example, Joseph knelt before them one by one and washed their feet.

When he finished, he said, "As I have done, so do ye." He asked them to serve one another and to keep themselves clean from the sins of the world.[22]

WHILE THE SCHOOL OF the Prophets was in session, Emma watched the students arrive and make their way up the stairs to the small, tightly packed room where they met. Some men came to the school freshly washed and neatly dressed out of respect for the sacred nature of the school. Some also skipped breakfast so they could come to the meeting fasting.[23]

After class got out and the men left for the day, Emma and some young women hired to help would clean the schoolroom. Since the men smoked pipes and chewed tobacco during the lessons, the room was hazy and the floorboards were covered in tobacco spit when they left. Emma would scrub with all her might, but tobacco stains remained on the floor.[24]

She complained to Joseph about the mess. Joseph did not normally use tobacco, but he did not mind if the other men did. Emma's complaints, however, caused him to question if tobacco use was right in God's eyes.

Emma was not alone in her concerns. Reformers in the United States and other countries throughout the world thought smoking and chewing tobacco, as well as drinking alcohol, were filthy habits. But some doctors believed tobacco could cure a host of ailments. Similar claims were made about drinking alcohol and hot drinks like coffee and tea, which people drank liberally.[25]

When Joseph took the matter to the Lord, he received a revelation—a "word of wisdom for the benefit of the Saints in these last days."[26] In it, the Lord cautioned His people against consuming alcohol, declaring that distilled liquor was for washing their bodies while wine was for occasions like the sacrament. He also warned them against tobacco and hot drinks.

The Lord emphasized a healthy diet, encouraging the Saints to eat grains, herbs, and fruits and to consume meat sparingly. He promised blessings of health, knowledge, and strength to those who chose to obey.[27]

The revelation had been declared not as a commandment but as a caution. Many people would find it hard to give up using these powerful substances, and Joseph did not insist on strict conformity. He continued to drink alcohol occasionally, and he and Emma sometimes drank coffee and tea.[28]

Still, after Joseph read the words to the School of the Prophets, the men in the room tossed their pipes and plugs of chewing tobacco into the fire to show their willingness to obey the Lord's counsel.[29]

THE FIRST SESSION OF the School of the Prophets closed in March, and its members dispersed to serve missions or fill other assignments.[30] Church leaders in Kirtland, meanwhile, worked to buy a brickyard and raise funds to build the temple.[31]

Around this time, Joseph received a letter from Missouri. After reading the "olive leaf" revelation, Edward and others had urged the Saints to repent and reconcile with the church in Kirtland. Their efforts worked, and they now asked Joseph to forgive them.[32]

Ready to put the conflict behind him, Joseph sought ways to fulfill the Lord's commandments for Zion. In June, he prayed with Sidney Rigdon and Frederick Williams to learn how to build a temple. As they prayed, they saw a vision of the temple and examined its exterior, observing the structure of its windows, roof, and steeple. The temple then seemed to move over the top of them, and they found themselves inside it, inspecting its interior halls.[33]

After their vision, the men drew up plans for temples in Kirtland and Independence. Outside, the buildings would look like large churches, but inside they would have two spacious assembly rooms, one on the upper floor and one on the lower, where the Saints could meet and learn.[34]

Joseph next focused on helping the Saints in Zion make a city of their settlement, which had more than doubled in size since his last visit.[35] With the help of Frederick and Sidney, he drew up plans for a one-square-mile city. Long, straight streets in a grid pattern crisscrossed the map, with brick and stone houses set on deep lots with groves of trees in the front and garden space in back.

Land was to be divided into lots of a half acre each, for rich and poor alike. Farmers would live in the city and work in fields on the outskirts of town. At the center of the city were the temple and other sacred buildings intended for worship, education, administration, and caring for the poor. Each public building was to be inscribed with the words "Holiness to the Lord."[36]

The city could accommodate fifteen thousand people, which would make it far smaller than New York City, but still one of the largest cities in the country. Once the city was full, the plan could be replicated over and over, until all the Saints had an inheritance in Zion. "Lay off another in the same way," Joseph directed, "and so fill up the world in these last days."[37]

In June 1833, Joseph, Sidney, and Frederick sent the plan for the city from Kirtland to Independence, along with detailed instructions for how to build the temple.

"We have commenced building the House of the Lord in this place, and it goes on rapidly," they reported in a letter that accompanied the plans. "Day and night, we pray for the salvation of Zion."[38]

CHAPTER 16

Only a Prelude

While the plans for Zion and the temple traveled by mail to Missouri, nine-year-old Emily Partridge leapt from her bed and rushed outside in her nightclothes. In the yard behind her house, not far from the temple site in Independence, she saw one of her family's large haystacks engulfed in flames. The fire reached high into the night sky, its bright yellow light casting long shadows behind those who stood by, helplessly watching the blaze.

Accidental fires were common on the frontier, but this one was no accident. Small mobs had been vandalizing the Saints' property all through the summer of 1833, hoping to scare the newcomers away from Jackson County. No one had been hurt so far, but the mobs seemed to grow more aggressive with every attack.

Emily did not understand all the reasons why people in Jackson County wanted the Saints to leave. She knew her family and friends were unlike their neighbors in many ways. The Missourians she overheard in the streets had a different way of speaking, and the women wore a different style of dress. Some of them walked around barefoot in the summer and washed their clothes with large paddles instead of the washboards Emily was used to in Ohio.

These were trivial differences, but there were also major disagreements Emily knew little about. People in Independence did not like that the Saints preached to Indians and disapproved of slavery. In the northern states, where most church members had lived, owning slaves was against the law. But in Missouri, enslaving black people was legal, and the longtime settlers staunchly defended it.

The fact that the Saints usually kept to themselves did not help ease suspicions. As more of them arrived in Zion, they worked together to build and furnish homes, cultivate farms, and raise children. They were eager to lay the foundation of a holy city that would endure through the Millennium.

The Partridges' own house, situated in the middle of Independence, was a step toward making the town into Zion. It was a simple two-story house lacking the refinement of Emily's old home in Ohio, but it signaled that the Saints were in Independence to stay.

As the blazing haystack showed, it also made them a target.[1]

WITH TENSIONS RISING BETWEEN the Saints and their
neighbors in Jackson County, William Phelps decided to
use the pages of the local church newspaper to calm fears.
In the July 1833 issue of *The Evening and the Morning
Star,* he published a letter to immigrating church members, counseling them to pay their debts before coming
to Zion to avoid being a burden on the community.

In writing this and other words of advice, he hoped
that Jackson County residents would read the paper too
and see that the Saints were law-abiding citizens whose
beliefs posed no threat to them or the local economy.[2]

William also addressed church members' attitudes
toward black people. Although he sympathized with
those who wished to free enslaved people, William
wanted his readers to know that the Saints would obey
Missouri's laws restricting the rights of free blacks. There
were only a few black Saints in the church, and he recommended that if they chose to move to Zion, they act
carefully and trust in God.

"So long as we have no special rule in the church
as to people of color," he wrote vaguely, "let prudence
guide."[3]

SAMUEL LUCAS, A COUNTY judge and colonel in the
Jackson County militia, was livid when he read the letter in *The Evening and the Morning Star.* In Samuel's
mind, William was inviting free black people to become
Mormons and move to Missouri. William's statements

discouraging black Saints from settling in Missouri did nothing to calm his fears.[4]

With mobs already harassing the Saints in Independence and nearby settlements, it was not hard for Samuel to find others who agreed with him. For more than a year, town leaders had been rallying their neighbors against the Saints. Some had distributed handbills and called town meetings, urging people to drive the newcomers out of the area.[5]

Initially, most of the locals thought the Saints were harmless fanatics who pretended to receive revelations, heal by the laying on of hands, and perform other miracles. But as more and more church members settled in the county, claiming that God had given them Independence as a promised land, Samuel and other town leaders saw them and their revelations as threats to their property and their political power.

And now William's letter stoked one of their greatest fears. Just two years before, dozens of enslaved people in another state had rebelled and killed more than fifty white men and women in less than two days. Slave owners in Missouri and across the southern states dreaded something similar happening in their communities. Some people feared that if the Saints invited free blacks to Jackson County, their presence could cause slaves to yearn for freedom and rebel.[6]

Since there were laws protecting the Saints' freedom of religion and speech, Samuel and the others understood they could not put down this threat through legal means. But they would not be the first town to use violence to drive unwanted people from their midst. Acting together, they could expel the Saints from the county and get away with it.

Town leaders soon met to take action against the newcomers. Samuel and others listed their complaints against the Saints and presented the statement to the people of Independence.

The document declared the town leaders' intention to drive the Saints from Jackson County by any means necessary. They appointed July 20 for a meeting at the courthouse to decide what to do with the Saints. Hundreds of Jackson County residents signed their names to the statement.[7]

WHEN HE LEARNED OF the uproar, William Phelps tried desperately to undo any offense his newspaper article had caused. The Book of Mormon declared that Christ invited all to come unto Him, "black and white, bond and free," but William was more concerned about the entire county turning against the Saints.[8]

Acting quickly, he printed a single-page leaflet recanting what he had written about slavery. "We are opposed to having free people of color admitted into the state," he insisted, "and we say that none will be admitted into the church."[9] The leaflet misrepresented the church's stance on baptizing black members, but he hoped it would prevent future violence.[10]

On July 20, William, Edward, and other church leaders went to the Jackson County courthouse to meet with county leaders. The weather was unusually mild for July, and hundreds of people left their homes, farms, and businesses to attend the meeting and prepare to take action against the Saints.

Deciding to give church leaders a last-minute warning before resorting to violence, Samuel Lucas and twelve other men representing the community demanded that William stop printing *The Evening and the Morning Star* and that the Saints leave the county immediately.[11]

As the bishop in Zion, Edward knew how much the Saints would lose if they gave in to the demands. Shutting down the printing press would delay the publication of the Book of Commandments, which was almost finished. And leaving the county would mean not only losing valuable property but also giving up their inheritances in the promised land.[12]

Edward asked for three months to consider the proposal and seek Joseph's counsel in Kirtland. But the Jackson County leaders refused to grant his request. Edward asked for ten days to consult the other Saints in Missouri. Community leaders gave him fifteen minutes.[13]

Unwilling to be pressured into a decision, the Saints ended the negotiations. As the Jackson County delegation left, one man turned to Edward and told him the work of destruction would begin immediately.[14]

DOWN THE STREET FROM the courthouse, Sally Phelps was at home on the ground floor of the church's printing office, tending to her sick newborn. Her four other children were nearby. William had left hours earlier to attend the meeting at the courthouse. He had still not returned, and Sally anxiously waited for news of the meeting.

A heavy thump rattled the front door, startling her and the children. Outside, men pounded a large log against the door, trying to break it down. A crowd of men, women, and children formed around the printing office, some cheering the men on and others watching in silence.[15]

Once the door broke open, armed men rushed into the house and dragged Sally and the children into the street.[16] They threw the family's furniture and belongings out the front door and smashed windows. Some of the attackers climbed up to the second floor of the printing office and dumped type and ink onto the floor as other men began to tear the building down.[17]

Standing with her children huddled around her, Sally watched as men broke the second-floor window of the printing office and tossed out paper and type. They then heaved the printing press out the window and sent it crashing to the ground.[18]

In the chaos, a few of the men emerged from the printing office with their arms full of unbound pages from the Book of Commandments. "Here is the book of revelations of the damned Mormons," one of them shouted to the crowd as he threw the pages into the street.[19]

CROUCHED TOGETHER BESIDE A nearby fence, fifteen-year-old Mary Elizabeth Rollins and her thirteen-year-old sister, Caroline, watched as the men scattered the pages of the Book of Commandments.

Mary had seen some of the pages before. She and Caroline were nieces of Sidney Gilbert, who operated the Saints' store in Independence. One evening, at their uncle's house, Mary had listened as church leaders read and discussed the revelations on the newly printed pages. While the men talked, the Spirit came upon the meeting, and some spoke in tongues while Mary interpreted their words. She now felt a deep reverence for the revelations, and seeing them lying in the street upset her.

Turning to Caroline, Mary said she wanted to get the pages before they were ruined. The men had started to pry the roof off the printing office. Soon they would pull down its walls, leaving nothing but rubble.

Caroline wanted to save the pages, but she was frightened of the mob. "They will kill us," she said.

Mary understood the danger, but she told Caroline that she was determined to get the pages. Unwilling to leave her sister's side, Caroline agreed to help.

The sisters waited until the men turned their backs, then sprang from their hiding place and grabbed as many pages as their arms could hold. As they turned to retreat to the fence, some men caught sight of them and ordered them to stop. The sisters gripped the pages tighter and ran as fast as they could into a nearby cornfield as two men followed after them.

The corn was six feet high, and Mary and Caroline could not see where they were going. Throwing themselves to the ground, they hid the pages beneath their bodies and listened breathlessly as the two men tramped back and forth through the corn. The sisters could hear them getting closer and closer, but after a while, the men gave up the search and left the cornfield.[20]

EMILY PARTRIDGE AND HER older sister Harriet were fetching water from a spring when they saw a mob of about fifty armed men approaching their house. Taking cover beside the spring, the girls watched in terror as the men surrounded the house, drove their father outside, and marched him away.[21]

The mob led Edward to the public square, where a crowd of more than two hundred people surrounded Charles Allen, another Saint who had been captured. Russell Hicks, who had led the town meeting earlier that day, approached Edward and told him to leave the county or face the consequences.

"If I must suffer for my religion," Edward said, "it is no more than others have done before me."[22] He told Hicks that he had done nothing wrong and refused to leave town.[23]

"Call upon your Jesus!" a voice cried out.[24] The mob shoved Edward and Charles to the ground, and Hicks began stripping off the bishop's clothes. Edward resisted, and someone in the crowd demanded that Hicks let the bishop keep his shirt and trousers on.

Relenting, Hicks tore away Edward's hat, coat, and vest and turned him over to the mob. Two men stepped forward and covered the prisoners head to foot in tar and feathers. The tar burned, eating away at their skin like acid.[25]

Nearby, a convert named Vienna Jaques was collecting scattered pages from the Book of Commandments off the street. Vienna had consecrated her considerable savings to help build up Zion, and now everything was falling apart.

As she clutched the loose pages, a man from the mob came up to her and said, "This is only a prelude to what you have to suffer." He pointed to Edward's haggard figure. "There goes your bishop, tarred and feathered."[26]

Vienna looked up and saw Edward limping away. Only his face and the palms of his hands were not covered in tar. "Glory to God!" she exclaimed. "He will receive a crown of glory for tar and feathers."[27]

SALLY PHELPS HAD NO home to go back to that evening. She found shelter in an abandoned log stable next to a cornfield. With help from her children, she gathered brush to make beds.

As she and the children worked, two figures appeared from the cornfield. In the waning light, Sally saw it was Caroline and Mary Rollins. In their arms, the sisters cradled stacks of paper. Sally asked what they had, and they showed her the pages they had collected from the Book of Commandments.

Sally took the pages from the sisters and hid them safely beneath her brush-pile bed.[28] Night was fast approaching, and she did not know what tomorrow held for Zion.

CHAPTER 17

Though the Mob Kill Us

W hen violence erupted in the streets of Independence, William McLellin fled his home and hid in the woods, terrified of the mobs. After destroying the church's printing office, the people of Jackson County had ransacked Sidney Gilbert's store and driven many Saints from their homes. Some men had been captured and whipped until they bled.[1]

Hoping to avoid their fate, William stayed in the woods for days. When he learned that a mob was offering a cash reward to anyone who captured him or other prominent church members, he slipped away to the Whitmer family's settlement along the Big Blue River, several miles to the west, and kept out of sight.

Alone and afraid, William was racked with doubts. He had come to Independence believing the Book of Mormon was the word of God. But now he had a price on his head. What would happen if a mob found him? Could he stand by his testimony of the Book of Mormon then? Could he declare his faith in the restored gospel? Was he willing to suffer and die for it?

As William agonized over these questions, he met David Whitmer and Oliver Cowdery in the woods. Even though there was a reward out for Oliver too, the men had reason to believe the worst had passed. The people of Independence were still determined to drive the Saints out of the county, but the attacks had stopped and some church members were returning to their homes.

Looking for reassurance, William turned to his friends. "I have never seen an open vision in my life," he told them, "but you men say you have." He had to know the truth. "Tell me, in the fear of God," he demanded, "is that Book of Mormon true?"

Oliver looked at William. "God sent His holy angel to declare the truth of the translation of it to us, and therefore we know," he said. "And though the mob kill us, yet we must die declaring its truth."

"Oliver has told you the solemn truth," David said. "I most truly declare to you its truth."

"I believe you," William said.[2]

ON AUGUST 6, 1833, BEFORE Joseph learned the extent of the violence in Missouri, he received a revelation about the persecution in Zion. The Lord told the Saints not to fear. He had heard and recorded their prayers, and He promised with a covenant to answer them. "All things wherewith you have been afflicted," the Lord assured the Saints, "shall work together for your good."[3]

Three days later, Oliver arrived in Kirtland with a full report of the attacks in Missouri.[4] To quiet the mobs, Edward Partridge and other church leaders had signed a pledge, promising the people of Independence that the Saints would leave Jackson County by the spring. None of them wanted to abandon Zion, but refusing to sign the pledge would have only put the Saints in more peril.[5]

Horrified by the violence, Joseph approved of the decision to evacuate. The next day, Oliver wrote church leaders in Missouri, instructing them to look for another place to settle. "Be wise in your selection," he advised. "Another place of beginning will be no injury to Zion in the end."

"If I were with you, I should take an active part in your sufferings," Joseph added at the end of the letter. "My spirit would not let me forsake you."[6]

Afterward, Joseph remained shaken for days. The terrible news had come while he was facing intense criticism in Kirtland. That summer, a church member named Doctor Philastus Hurlbut had been excommunicated for immoral behavior while on a mission. Soon Hurlbut had started speaking out against Joseph at well-attended meetings and collecting money from critics of the church. With this money, Hurlbut planned to travel to New York to look for stories he could use to embarrass the church.[7]

As pressing as the problems in Ohio were, however, Joseph knew the situation in Missouri needed his full attention. Reflecting on the violence, Joseph realized that the Lord had neither revoked His command to build Zion in Independence nor authorized the Saints to give up their land in Jackson County. If they abandoned their property now, or sold it to their enemies, getting it back would be nearly impossible.

Desperate to receive specific directions for the Missouri Saints, Joseph prayed to the Lord. "What more dost Thou require at their hands," he asked, "before Thou wilt come and save them?" He waited for an answer, but the Lord gave him no new instructions for Zion.

On August 18, Joseph wrote personally to Edward and other leaders in Zion. "I know not what to say to you," he admitted. He had sent them a copy of the August 6 revelation, and he assured them that God would deliver them from danger. "I have His immutable covenant that this shall be the case," Joseph testified, "but God is pleased to keep it from mine eyes the means how exactly the thing will be done."

In the meantime, Joseph urged, the Saints should trust in the promises the Lord had already given them. He counseled the Saints to be patient, rebuild the printing office and store, and seek legal ways to recover their losses. He also implored them not to abandon the promised land, and he sent them a more detailed plan for the city.

"It is the will of the Lord," he wrote, "that not one foot of land purchased should be given to the enemies of God or sold to them."[8]

JOSEPH'S LETTER REACHED EDWARD in early September, and the bishop agreed that the Saints should not sell their property in Jackson County.[9] Although mob leaders had threatened to harm the Saints if they tried to seek compensation for their losses, he collected accounts of the abuses the Saints had endured that summer and sent them to Missouri's governor, Daniel Dunklin.[10]

Privately, Governor Dunklin had contempt for the Saints, but he encouraged them to take their grievances to the courts. "Ours is a government of laws," he told them. If the court system in Jackson County failed to execute the law peacefully, the Saints could notify him and he would step in to help. Until then, however, he recommended they trust in the laws of the land.[11]

The governor's letter gave Edward and the Saints hope. They began to rebuild their community, and Edward and other church leaders in Zion hired lawyers from a neighboring county to take their case.[12] They resolved that they would defend themselves and their property if they were attacked.[13]

Town leaders in Independence were furious. On October 26, a group of more than fifty residents voted to force the Saints from Jackson County as soon as they could.[14]

FIVE DAYS LATER, AT sunset, Saints in the Whitmer settlement learned that armed men from Independence were headed in their direction. Lydia Whiting and her husband, William, fled their home and took their two-year-old son and newborn twins to a house where other church members were gathering to defend themselves.

At ten o'clock that night, Lydia heard a commotion outside. The men from Independence had arrived and were tearing down cabins. They spread out through the settlement, throwing stones through windows and breaking down doors. Men climbed on top of houses and tore away the roofs. Others drove families from their homes with clubs.

Lydia heard the mob coming closer. A short distance away, they broke open the door of Peter and Mary Whitmer's house, where many church members had taken cover. Screams broke out as men with clubs forced their way into the house. The women scrambled to reach their children and begged their attackers for mercy. The mob drove the men outside and beat them with clubs and whips.

In the house where Lydia was hiding, fear and confusion gripped the Saints. With few firearms and no plan to defend themselves, some people panicked and fled, racing for cover in the nearby woods. Afraid for her family, Lydia handed her twins to two girls huddled beside her and sent them running for safety. She then scooped up her son and followed after them.

Outside was chaos. Women and children darted past her as the mob pulled down more houses and toppled chimneys. Men lay slumped on the ground, badly beaten and bleeding. Lydia clutched her son to her chest and ran for the woods, losing sight of her husband and the girls who carried her babies.

When she reached the cover of the trees, Lydia could find only one of her twins. She took the baby and sat down with her toddler, shivering in the autumn cold. From their hiding place, they could hear the mob tearing down their house. As a long night passed, she had no idea if her husband had made it out of the settlement.

In the morning, Lydia stepped cautiously out of the woods and looked for her husband and missing baby among the bleary-eyed Saints in the settlement. To her relief, the baby was unharmed and William had not been caught by the mob.

Elsewhere in the settlement, other families were reunited. No one had been killed in the attack, but nearly a dozen homes had been leveled. For the rest of the day, the Saints picked through the rubble, trying to salvage what remained of their property, and cared for the wounded.[15]

OVER THE NEXT FOUR days, Zion's leaders told the Saints to gather in large groups to defend themselves against attacks. Mobs from Independence rode throughout the countryside, terrorizing outlying settlements. Church leaders begged a local judge to stop the mobs, but he ignored them. The people of Jackson County were determined to drive every last Saint from their midst.[16]

Soon the mob struck the Whitmer settlement again, this time with more intensity. When twenty-seven-year-old Philo Dibble heard gunfire in the direction of the settlement, he and other Saints nearby rushed to its defense. They found fifty armed men on horseback, trampling through cornfields and scattering the frightened Saints into the woods.

Catching sight of Philo and his company, the mob fired their guns, mortally wounding one man. The Saints fired back in force, killing two of their attackers and dispersing the rest.[17] Smoke from their black powder guns filled the air.

As the mob scattered, Philo felt a pain in his abdomen. Looking down, he saw that his clothes were torn and bloody. He had been hit by a lead ball and buckshot.[18]

Still clutching his gun and powder, he staggered back toward home. Along the way he saw women and children huddled in wrecked houses, hiding from mobs that threatened to kill anyone who helped the wounded. Faint and thirsty, Philo stumbled on until he came to the house where his family was hiding.

Cecelia, his wife, saw his wound and took off into the woods, frantic to find help. She lost her way and found no one. When she returned to the house, she said that most of the Saints had fled three miles away to the settlement where the Colesville Saints lived.[19]

Other Saints were scattered across the countryside, hiding in cornfields or wandering the endless prairie.[20]

AS THE SAINTS BATTLED mobs along the Big Blue River, Sidney Gilbert stood before a judge in the Independence courthouse along with Isaac Morley, John Corrill, William McLellin, and a few other Saints. The men had been arrested after a man they had caught looting Sidney's store had charged them with assault and false imprisonment when they tried to have him arrested.

The courtroom was full as the judge heard their case. With the whole town in an uproar over the Saints' decision to defend their rights and property, Sidney and his friends had little reason to hope they would get a fair hearing. The trial felt like a sham.

While the judge listened to testimonies, false rumors reached Independence that the Saints had slaughtered twenty Missourians at the Big Blue River. Anger and confusion filled the courtroom as the spectators cried out to lynch the prisoners. Unwilling to turn them over to a mob, one of the court clerks ordered the men back to the jail for protection before the crowd could murder them.[21]

That night, after the outrage had cooled, William stayed behind in the jail while the sheriff and two deputies escorted Sidney, Isaac, and John to a meeting with Edward Partridge. The church leaders discussed their options. They knew they had to get out of Jackson County quickly, but they hated to leave their land and homes in the hands of their enemies. In the end, they decided it was better to lose their property than their lives. They had to abandon Zion.[22]

Their discussion finished at two o'clock in the morning, and the sheriff led the prisoners back to jail. When they arrived, a half dozen armed men were waiting for them.

"Don't fire! Don't fire!" the sheriff called out when he saw the mob.

The men leveled their guns at the prisoners, and John and Isaac bolted. Some of the mob fired after them and missed. Sidney stood his ground as two other men came up to him and aimed their guns at his chest. Bracing himself, Sidney heard the hammers snap and saw a flash of gunpowder.

Stunned, he searched his body for wounds but found that he was uninjured. One of the guns had broken, and the other had misfired. The sheriff and his deputies hurried him off to the safety of the jail cell.[23]

Much of Jackson County was now mobilizing for battle. Messengers canvased the countryside, enlisting armed men to help drive the Saints from the area. A church member named Lyman Wight, meanwhile, led a company of one hundred Saints, some armed with guns and others with clubs, toward Independence to rescue the prisoners.

To prevent more bloodshed, Edward began to prepare the Saints to leave the county. The sheriff set the prisoners free, and Lyman disbanded his company. The county militia was called out to keep order as the Saints left their homes, but since most of the men in the militia had been part of the attacks on the settlements, they did little to prevent more violence.[24]

There was nothing the Saints could do now but run.

ON NOVEMBER 6, WILLIAM PHELPS wrote to church leaders in Kirtland. "It is a horrid time," he told them. "Men, women, and children are fleeing, or preparing to, in all directions."[25]

Most of the Saints trudged north, ferrying across the frigid Missouri River into neighboring Clay County, where scattered family members found each other. Wind and rain beat against them, and soon snow began to fall. Once the Saints crossed the river, Edward and other leaders set up tents and built rough log shelters to shield them from the elements.[26]

Too injured to flee, Philo Dibble languished in his house near the Whitmer settlement. A doctor told him he would die, but he clung to life. Before David Whitmer headed north, he sent word to Philo promising him he would live. Newel Knight then came, sat beside his bed, and silently placed his hand on Philo's head.

Philo felt the Spirit of the Lord rest over him. As the feeling spread through his body, he knew that he would be healed. He stood up, and his wounds discharged blood and ragged bits of cloth. He then got dressed and went outside for the first time since the battle. Overhead, he saw countless shooting stars streak across the night sky.[27]

At the camp along the Missouri River, Saints emerged from their tents and hovels to see the meteor shower. Edward and his daughter Emily watched with delight as stars seemed to cascade around them like a heavy summer rain. To Emily, it was as if God had sent the lights to cheer the Saints in their afflictions.

Her father believed they were tokens of God's presence, a reason to rejoice amid so much tribulation.[28]

IN KIRTLAND, A KNOCK at the door woke the prophet. "Brother Joseph," he heard a voice say, "come get up and see the signs in the heaven."

Joseph got up and looked outside, and he saw the meteors falling from the sky like hailstones. "How marvelous are Thy works, O Lord!" he exclaimed, remembering New Testament prophecies about stars falling from the heavens before the Second Coming, when the Savior would return and reign a thousand years in peace.

"I thank Thee for Thy mercy unto me, Thy servant," he prayed. "O Lord, save me in Thy kingdom."[29]

CHAPTER 18

The Camp of Israel

For days following the meteor shower, Joseph expected something miraculous to happen. But life continued as normal, and no other signs appeared in the heavens. "My heart is somewhat sorrowful," he confided in his journal. More than three months had passed since the Lord had revealed anything for the Saints in Zion, and Joseph still did not know how to help them. The heavens seemed closed.[1]

Adding to Joseph's anxiety, Doctor Philastus Hurlbut had recently returned from Palmyra and Manchester with stories—some false, others exaggerated—about Joseph's early life. As the stories spread around Kirtland, Hurlbut also swore he would wash his hands in Joseph's blood. The prophet soon began using bodyguards.[2]

On November 25, 1833, a little more than a week after the meteor shower, Orson Hyde arrived in Kirtland and reported on the Saints' expulsion from Jackson County.[3] The news was harrowing. Joseph did not understand why God had let the Saints suffer and lose the promised land. Nor could he foresee Zion's future. He prayed for guidance, but the Lord simply said to be still and trust in Him.

Joseph wrote Edward Partridge immediately. "I know that Zion, in the own due time of the Lord, will be redeemed," he testified, "but how many will be the days of her purification, tribulation, and affliction, the Lord has kept hid from my eyes."

With little else to offer, Joseph tried to comfort his friends in Missouri, despite the eight hundred miles between them. "When we learn of your sufferings, it awakens every sympathy of our hearts," he wrote. "May God grant that notwithstanding your great afflictions and sufferings, there may not anything separate us from the love of Christ."[4]

JOSEPH CONTINUED TO PRAY, and in December he finally received a revelation for the Saints in Zion. The Lord declared that they had been afflicted for their sins, but He had compassion on them and promised they would not be forsaken. "They must needs be chastened and tried, even as Abraham," He explained to Joseph, "for all those who will not endure chastening, but deny me, cannot be sanctified."

As He had before, the Lord instructed the Saints to purchase land in Zion and seek legal, peaceful means to get back what they had lost. "Zion shall not be moved out of her place," He declared. "They that remain, and are pure in heart, shall return, and come to their inheritances."[5]

While the revelation urged peaceful negotiations with the people of Independence, the Lord also indicated that Zion could be reclaimed by power. He told a parable about a vineyard that had been taken from slothful servants and destroyed by an enemy. When the lord of the vineyard saw the destruction, he chastised the servants for their negligence and called them to action.

"Go and gather together the residue of my servants, and take all the strength of mine house," he commanded, "and go ye straightway unto the land of my vineyard, and redeem my vineyard." The Lord did not interpret the parable, but He told the Saints that it reflected His will for the redemption of Zion.[6]

Two months later, Parley Pratt and Lyman Wight came to Kirtland with more news from Missouri. Friendly people across the river from Jackson County had given the Saints food and clothes in exchange for labor, but they were still scattered and discouraged. They wanted to know when and how Zion would be rescued from its enemies.[7]

After hearing the report, Joseph rose from his chair and announced that he was going to Zion. For six months, he had offered encouraging words and hope to the Saints there as he dealt with other challenges in Kirtland.

Now he wanted to do something for them—and he wanted to know who would join him.[8]

IN APRIL 1834, AT a meeting of a small branch of the church in New York, twenty-seven-year-old Wilford Woodruff listened to Parley Pratt recount the Lord's latest revelation to Joseph Smith. It called on the Saints to raise five hundred men to march with the prophet to Missouri. "The redemption of Zion must needs come by power," the Lord declared. "Let no man be afraid to lay down his life for my sake."[9]

Parley invited the young and middle-aged men in the branch to go to Zion. Every man who could be spared was expected to go.

At the end of the meeting, Wilford introduced himself to Parley. He and his older brother Azmon had joined the church three months earlier, and both were teachers in the Aaronic Priesthood. Wilford said he was willing to go to Zion, but he had bills to pay and accounts to collect before he could leave. Parley told him it was his duty to get his finances in order and join the march.[10]

Later, Wilford spoke to Azmon about going to Zion. Although the Lord had called on every able-bodied man in the church to join the march, Azmon decided to stay, reluctant to leave his home, family, and farm. But Wilford was unmarried, and he was eager to go to Zion with the prophet.[11]

Wilford arrived in Kirtland a few weeks later and met Brigham Young and Heber Kimball, who had recently moved to Ohio with their families. Heber worked as a potter, and he and his wife, Vilate, had two children. Brigham was a carpenter with two small daughters. Recently, he had married a convert named Mary Ann Angell after his first wife, Miriam, had passed away.[12] Both men were willing to join the march, despite the sacrifices their families would have to make.

Mary Ann's cousins, Joseph and Chandler Holbrook, were also joining the march, along with their wives, Nancy and Eunice, and their young children. Nancy and Eunice planned to help the few other women in camp, who would cook, wash clothes, and nurse the sick and wounded along the way to Missouri.[13]

Women who stayed home found other ways to support the march. Shortly before leaving for Zion, Joseph said, "I want some money to help fit out Zion, and I know that I shall have it." The next day, he received $150 from a Sister Vose in Boston.[14]

Wilford and a handful of Saints left for Zion on May 1. Joseph, Brigham, Heber, and the Holbrooks—along with about a hundred other volunteers—left

Kirtland several days later and joined up with Wilford along the road.

Once assembled, the force was only a small fraction of the five hundred the Lord had called for.[15] But they headed west in good spirits, determined to fulfill the Lord's word.

JOSEPH HAD HIGH HOPES for his small band, which he called the Camp of Israel. Although they were armed and willing to fight, as the ancient Israelites had been when they battled for the land of Canaan, Joseph wanted to resolve the conflict peacefully. Government officials in Missouri had told church leaders there that Governor Dunklin was willing to send the state militia to accompany the Saints back to their lost lands. He could not, however, promise to keep mobs from driving them out again.[16]

Joseph planned to request the governor's aid once the Camp of Israel arrived in Missouri, then work with the militia to return the Saints to Jackson County. The camp would remain in Zion for a year to keep the Saints safe from their enemies.[17]

To ensure that everyone in camp was provided for, camp members put their money in a general fund. Following Old Testament patterns, Joseph divided the men into companies, with each group electing a captain.[18]

As the Camp of Israel moved farther west, Joseph worried about entering enemy territory with his small force. His brother Hyrum and Lyman Wight had recruited additional men among the branches of the church north-west of Kirtland, but they had not yet joined up with the Camp of Israel and Joseph did not know where they were. He also worried that spies were watching the camp's movements and counting their numbers.[19]

On June 4, after a month of marching, the camp reached the Mississippi River. Joseph was tired and sore from the journey, but he felt ready to confront the challenges that lay ahead.[20] He learned that reports and rumors of the camp's movements had already reached Missouri, and hundreds of settlers were preparing for a fight. He wondered whether the Saints were strong enough to face them.

"Camp is in as good a situation as could be expected," he wrote Emma while sitting on the riverbank, "but our numbers and means are altogether too small."[21]

THE NEXT DAY WAS hot and muggy as the Camp of Israel waited to cross the river into Missouri. The Mississippi was more than a mile wide, and the camp had only one boat to ferry them across. As they waited, some camp members hunted and fished while others fought off boredom and looked for shade to escape the summer sun.

The camp spent two tedious days crossing the river. By the end of the second day, they were tired and on edge. Now that they were in Missouri, many of them feared surprise attacks. That evening, Joseph's watchdog startled everyone when it began barking at the last company to arrive in camp.

Sylvester Smith, the captain of the arriving company, threatened to kill the dog if it did not stop barking. Joseph calmed the animal, but Sylvester and his company were still complaining about it the next morning.[22]

Hearing their complaints, Joseph called camp members together. "I will descend to the spirit that is in the camp," he announced, "for I want to drive it from the camp." He started to mimic Sylvester's behavior from the night before, repeating the captain's threats against the dog. "This spirit keeps up division and bloodshed throughout the world," he said.

Sylvester, who was no relation to Joseph, was unamused. "If that dog bites me," he said, "I *will* kill him."

"If you kill that dog," Joseph said, "I will whip you."

"If you do," said Sylvester, "I shall defend myself!"[23]

The camp watched the two men stare each other down. So far, no fights had broken out among them, but weeks of marching had frayed everyone's nerves.

At last, Joseph turned away from Sylvester and asked the Saints if they were as ashamed as he was of the feeling in the camp. He said they were acting like dogs rather than men. "Men ought never to place themselves on a level with beasts," he said. "They ought to be above it."[24]

THE MOOD IN CAMP settled down after that, and the small band trekked deeper into Missouri. Nancy and Eunice Holbrook stayed busy attending to their daily tasks, yet they understood that every step they took toward Jackson County placed them in more and more danger.[25]

Not long after the main body of the camp crossed the Mississippi, Hyrum Smith and Lyman Wight arrived with their recruits, increasing the camp's numbers to more than two hundred volunteers.[26] Camp leaders were still worried about an attack, however, and Joseph told the men who had families with them to seek shelter for their wives and children.

Several women in camp objected to being left behind. But just as the men were about to leave, Joseph called everyone together. "If the sisters are willing to undergo a siege with the camp," he said, "they can all go along with it."[27]

Nancy, Eunice, and the other women in camp said they were willing to go, happy that Joseph let them choose to continue on the march.[28]

SEVERAL DAYS LATER, PARLEY Pratt and Orson Hyde came to camp with unwelcome news: Governor Dunklin had refused to provide militia support for the Saints.[29] Without the governor's aid, the camp knew, they would not be able to help the Missouri Saints return to their land in Zion peacefully. Joseph and his captains decided to press on. They hoped to reach the exiled Saints in Clay County, north of the Missouri River, and help them negotiate a compromise with the people of Jackson County.[30]

The Camp of Israel cut across the central Missouri prairie. About a day's journey from their destination, a black woman—possibly a slave—called out to them nervously. "There is a company of men here who are calculating to kill you this morning as you pass through," she said.[31]

The camp marched cautiously on. Plagued by wagon problems, they were forced to stop for the night on a hill overlooking a fork in the Fishing River, still ten miles from the exiled Saints. As they pitched their tents, they heard the rumbling of horse hooves as five men rode into camp. The strangers brandished weapons and boasted that more than three hundred men were on their way to wipe the Saints out.[32]

Alarm rippled through the Camp of Israel. Knowing they were outnumbered, Joseph posted guards around the area, certain an attack was imminent. One man begged him to strike the mob first.

"No," Joseph said. "Stand still and see the salvation of God."[33]

Overhead the clouds looked heavy and gray. Twenty minutes later, hard rains tore through camp, driving the men from their tents as they scrambled to find better shelter. The banks of the Fishing River disappeared as the water rose and surged downstream.[34] Wind whipped through the camp, blowing down trees and upending tents. Bright lightning streaked the sky.

Wilford Woodruff and others in the camp found a small church nearby and huddled inside while hail pelted the roof.[35] After a moment, Joseph burst into the church, shaking the water from his hat and clothes. "Boys, there is some meaning to this," he exclaimed. "God is in this storm!"

Unable to sleep, the Saints stretched out on the benches and sang hymns through the night.[36] In the morning, they found their tents and gear soaked and scattered throughout camp, but nothing was damaged beyond repair and no attack had come.

The rivers remained swollen, cutting the camp off from their enemies on the opposite bank.[37]

OVER THE NEXT FEW days, the Camp of Israel made contact with the Saints in Clay County while Joseph met with officials from surrounding counties to explain the purpose of the march and plead for the Saints in Zion. "We are anxious for a settlement of the difficulties existing between us," Joseph told them. "We want to live in peace with all men, and equal rights is all we require."[38]

The officials agreed to help calm the anger of their fellow citizens, but they warned the camp not to go into Jackson County. If the Saints tried to march into Independence, a bloody battle could break out.[39]

The next day, June 22, in a council with church leaders, Joseph received a revelation for the Camp of Israel. The Lord accepted the sacrifices of its members but redirected their efforts to obtaining divine power. "Zion cannot be built up," He declared, "unless it is by the principles of the law of the celestial kingdom."

The Lord told the Saints that they should wait to redeem Zion until they had prepared themselves through learning and experience to do the will of God. "And this cannot be brought to pass," He explained, "until mine elders are endowed with power from on high." This endowment was to come in the Lord's house, the temple in Kirtland.

The Lord was pleased, however, with those who had marched in the Camp of Israel. "I have heard their prayers, and will accept their offering," He said, "and it is expedient in me that they should be brought thus far for a trial of their faith."[40]

AFTER THEY HEARD THE revelation, some members of the camp accepted it as the word of the Lord. Others protested, feeling that it denied them a chance to do more for the Missouri Saints. A few people were angry and ashamed that they had to return home without a fight.[41]

The camp disbanded soon after, and what little was left of its common fund was divided out to its members. Some people in camp planned to stay in Missouri to work and help the Saints start over, while Brigham, Heber, and others readied themselves to return to their families, finish the temple, and prepare to receive the endowment of power.[42]

Although the camp had not redeemed Zion, Wilford Woodruff was grateful for the knowledge he had gained on the march. He had traveled close to a thousand miles with the prophet and had seen him reveal the word of God.[43] The experience left him wanting to preach the gospel.

Wilford did not yet know if preaching was in his future, but he decided to stay in Missouri and do whatever the Lord required of him.[44]

CHAPTER 19

Stewards over This Ministry

As the Camp of Israel disbanded, a devastating outbreak of cholera attacked its ranks. Saints who had been healthy only hours before collapsed, unable to move. They vomited again and again and suffered intense stomach pains. The cries of the sick filled the camp, and many men were too weak for guard duty.

Nancy Holbrook was one of the first to get sick. Her sister-in-law Eunice soon joined her, overcome with excruciating muscle cramps.[1] Wilford Woodruff spent much of the night and the next day tending to a sick man in his company.[2] Joseph and the elders in camp gave blessings to the sick, but the disease soon struck many of them as well. Joseph fell ill after a few days and languished in his tent, unsure if he would survive.[3]

When people began to die, Heber Kimball, Brigham Young, and others wrapped the bodies in blankets and buried them along a nearby stream.[4]

THE CHOLERA RAN ITS course after several days, clearing up in early July. By that time, more than sixty Saints had fallen sick. Joseph recovered, as did Nancy, Eunice, and most people in the camp. But more than a dozen Saints died during the outbreak, including Sidney Gilbert and Betsy Parrish, one of the few women in the camp. Joseph mourned for the victims and their families. The last person to die was Jesse Smith, his cousin.[5]

Joseph's own brush with death was a reminder of how easily his life could be taken from him. At twenty-eight years old, he was becoming more worried about completing his divine mission.[6] If he died now, what would happen to the church? Was it strong enough to outlast him?

Following the Lord's direction, Joseph had already made changes in church leadership to share the burdens of administration. By this time, Sidney Rigdon and Frederick Williams were serving with him in the presidency of the church. He had also designated Kirtland to be a stake of Zion, or an official gathering place for the Saints.[7]

More recently, after receiving a vision of how Peter organized the Lord's church anciently, Joseph had organized a high council of twelve high priests in Kirtland to help him govern the stake and lead it in his absence.[8]

Soon after the cholera subsided, Joseph organized the church further. Meeting with church leaders in Clay County in July 1834, he formed a high council in Missouri and appointed David Whitmer to preside over the church there with the help of two counselors, William Phelps and John Whitmer.[9] He then set out for Kirtland, eager to finish the temple and obtain the endowment of power that would help the Saints redeem Zion.

Joseph knew major problems lay ahead. When he left Kirtland that spring, the temple's sandstone walls were four feet high, and the arrival of several skilled workers in town had given him hope that the Saints would realize the Lord's plan for His house. But the losses in and around Independence—the printing office, the store, and many acres of land—had hurt the Saints financially. Joseph, Sidney, and other church leaders had also gone deeply into debt, taking out heavy loans to purchase land for the Kirtland temple and finance the Camp of Israel.

With church businesses stalled or struggling, and no reliable system for collecting donations from the Saints, the church could not pay for the temple. If Joseph and the other leaders fell behind on their payments, they could lose the sacred building to creditors. And if they lost the temple, how could they receive the endowment of power and redeem Zion?[10]

BACK IN KIRTLAND, SIDNEY Rigdon shared Joseph's anxiety about finishing the temple. "We should use every effort to accomplish this building by the time appointed," he told the Saints. "On it depends the salvation of the church and also of the world."[11]

Sidney had monitored the progress on the temple while Joseph was in Missouri. Lacking younger men to do the work, Artemus Millet, the superintendent of construction, had enlisted older men as well as women and children to work on the building. Many of the women took on jobs men usually filled, assisting the masons and driving wagons to and from the quarry site to haul stone for the temple. By the time Joseph and the Camp of Israel returned to Kirtland, the walls had risen several more feet above the foundation.

The return of the camp spurred construction in the summer and fall of 1834.[12] The Saints quarried stone, hauled it to the temple lot, and built up the temple walls day by day. Joseph labored alongside workers as they cut stone blocks from a nearby creek. Some worked in the church's sawmill preparing lumber for beams, ceilings, and floors. Others helped lift wood and rock up the scaffolding to where it was needed.[13]

Emma and other women, meanwhile, made clothes for the workers and kept them fed. Vilate Kimball, Heber's wife, spun one hundred pounds of wool into thread, wove it into cloth, and sewed clothes for the workers, not keeping so much as an extra pair of stockings for herself.

The Saints' enthusiasm for completing the temple encouraged Sidney, but the church's debts were increasing by the day, and having signed his name to many of the heaviest loans, he knew he would be financially ruined if the church failed to repay them. When he saw the poverty of the Saints and the sacrifices they were making to finish the temple, Sidney also feared that they would never have the resources or resolve to complete it.

Overcome with worry, he would sometimes climb on top of the temple walls and plead with God to send the Saints the funds they needed to finish the temple. As he prayed, tears fell from his eyes to the stones beneath his feet.[14]

FIVE HUNDRED MILES NORTHEAST of Kirtland, twenty-one-year-old Caroline Tippets carefully stowed a large sum of money among the clothes and other items she was taking from New York to Missouri. She and her younger brother Harrison were moving west, hoping to settle somewhere near Jackson County. They had heard about the persecution of the Saints there, but they wanted to obey the Lord's command to gather to Missouri and purchase land in Zion before enemies of the church snatched it up.[15]

The commandment had been part of the revelation Joseph received after he learned about the Saints' expulsion from Zion. "Purchase all the lands," it read, "which can be purchased in Jackson County, and the counties round about." The funds were to come by donation. "Let all the churches gather together all their moneys," the Lord directed, "and let honorable men be appointed, even wise men, and send them to purchase these lands."[16]

When Caroline's branch leaders learned about the revelation, they called on the small group of Saints to fast and pray for the Lord's help in collecting money to purchase land in Missouri. Some members of the branch gave large donations of cash and property to the fund. Others gave a few dollars.

Caroline had about $250 she could place in the fund. It was more money than anyone else in the branch had donated and probably more than anyone expected her to give, but she knew it would help the Saints redeem the promised land. When she added her donation to the fund, the total came to about $850, a substantial amount of money.

Following the meeting, Harrison and his cousin John were selected to travel to Missouri to purchase the land. Caroline decided to go with them and safeguard her share of the donation. After John settled some business and family members prepared a team and wagon for them, the three were ready to set out for Missouri.

Climbing into the wagon, Caroline looked forward to starting a new life in the West. Since the Tippetses planned to stop at Kirtland along the way, their branch leaders gave them a letter of introduction to the prophet, explaining where their money came from and what they intended to do with it.[17]

ALL THROUGH THE FALL of 1834, Joseph and other church leaders slipped further and further behind in their payments on the temple land, and interest on the loans continued to accumulate. Some workers volunteered their time to labor on the temple, easing the church's financial burden somewhat. When families had extra cash or goods, they sometimes offered it to the church for the temple project.[18]

Other people, both inside and outside the church, extended credit, loaning money to keep construction moving forward. The donations and loans, in turn, paid for materials and allowed people who might have otherwise been unemployed to work.[19]

These efforts kept the temple walls rising higher, and in the final months of the year, they were high enough for woodworkers to begin laying the beams for the upper floor. But money was always tight, and church leaders prayed constantly for more funds.[20]

In early December, the Tippets family arrived in Kirtland, and Harrison and John delivered their branch's letter to the high council. With winter almost upon them, they asked the council if they should continue on to Missouri or spend the season in Kirtland. After some discussion, the high council recommended that the family stay in Ohio until the spring.

Desperate for funds, the council also asked the young men to loan the church some money, promising to repay it before their spring departure. Harrison and John agreed to loan the church part of the $850 from their branch.

Since a large portion of that money was Caroline's, the council called her into the meeting and explained the terms of the loan, which she willingly accepted.

The next day, Joseph and Oliver rejoiced as they thanked the Lord for the financial relief the Tippets family had brought.[21]

MORE LOANS AND DONATIONS came to the church that winter, but Joseph knew they would still not be enough to cover the growing cost of the temple. Caroline Tippets and her family had shown, however, that many Saints in the far-flung branches of the church wanted to do their part in the work of the Lord. As a new year dawned, Joseph realized that he needed to find a way to strengthen these branches and seek their help in finishing the temple so the Saints could be endowed with power.

The solution came from a revelation Joseph had received several years earlier that commanded Oliver Cowdery and David Whitmer to search out twelve apostles to preach the gospel to the world. Like the apostles in the New Testament, these men were to act as special witnesses of Christ, baptizing in His name and gathering converts to Zion and its branches.[22]

As a quorum, the twelve apostles were also to function as a traveling high council and minister to areas that fell outside the jurisdiction of the high councils in Ohio and Missouri.[23] In this capacity, they could direct missionary work, oversee branches, and raise funds for Zion and the temple.

One Sunday in early February, Joseph invited Brigham and Joseph Young to his home. "I wish you to notify all the brethren living in the branches, within a reasonable distance from this place, to meet at a general conference on Saturday next," he told the brothers. At that conference, he explained, twelve men would be appointed to the new quorum.

"And you," Joseph said to Brigham, "will be one of them."[24]

THE NEXT WEEK, ON February 14, 1835, the Saints in Kirtland assembled for the conference. Under Joseph's direction, Oliver, David, and their fellow Book of Mormon witness, Martin Harris, announced the members of the Quorum of the Twelve Apostles. Each of the men called had served preaching missions, and eight of them had marched in the Camp of Israel.[25]

Thomas Marsh and David Patten, both in their mid-thirties, were the oldest of the Twelve. Thomas was one of the earliest converts, having gained a testimony of the Book of Mormon while the first copies were still being printed. David had served mission after mission in the three years since his conversion.[26]

As Joseph had stated a week earlier, Brigham was also called to the quorum. So too was his best friend, Heber Kimball. Both men had served faithfully as captains in the Camp of Israel. Now Brigham would again leave his carpenter's bench and Heber his potter's wheel to go on the Lord's errand.

Like the New Testament apostles Peter and Andrew and James and John, two pairs of brothers were called to the Twelve. Parley and Orson Pratt had spread the gospel to the east and the west and were now to dedicate themselves to serving the church branches everywhere. Luke and Lyman Johnson had preached to the south and the north and would go out again, now with apostolic authority.[27]

The Lord selected both the educated and the unschooled. Orson Hyde and William McLellin had taught in the School of the Prophets and brought their keen intellects to the quorum. Though only twenty-three years old, John Boynton had seen great success as a missionary and was the only one of the apostles who had attended a university. The prophet's younger brother William did not have the same benefit of formal education, but he was a passionate speaker, fearless in the face of opposition, and quick to defend the needy.[28]

After calling the apostles, Oliver gave them a special charge. "Never cease striving until you have seen God, face to face," he told them. "Strengthen your faith, cast off your doubts, your sins, and all your unbelief, and nothing can prevent you from coming to God."

He promised them that they would preach the gospel in faraway nations and gather many of God's children to the safety of Zion.

"You will be stewards over this ministry," he testified. "We have a work to do that no other men can do. You must proclaim the gospel in its simplicity and purity, and we commend you to God and the word of His grace."[29]

TWO WEEKS AFTER ORGANIZING the Twelve, Joseph formed another priesthood quorum to join the apostles in spreading the gospel, strengthening the branches, and collecting donations for the church. The members of this new quorum, called the Quorum of the Seventy, were all veterans of the Camp of Israel. They were to travel far and wide, following the New Testament example of seventy disciples journeying two by two into every city to preach Jesus's word.[30]

The Lord selected seven men to preside over the quorum, including Joseph Young and Sylvester Smith, the company captain who had quarreled with the prophet during the march of the Camp of Israel. With the help of the Kirtland high council, the two men had resolved their differences that summer and made amends.[31]

Shortly after their call, the prophet spoke to the new quorums. "Some of you are angry with me because you did not fight in Missouri," he said. "But let me tell you, God did not want you to fight." Instead, Joseph explained, God had called them to Missouri to test their willingness to sacrifice and consecrate their lives to Zion, and to increase the power of their faith.

"He could not organize His kingdom with twelve men to open the gospel door to the nations of the earth, and with seventy men under their direction to follow in their tracks," he taught, "unless He took them from a body of men who had offered their lives and who had made as great a sacrifice as did Abraham."[32]

CHAPTER 20

Do Not Cast
Me Off

During the summer of 1835, while the apostles left on missions to the eastern states and Canada, the Saints worked together to finish the temple and prepare for the endowment of power. Spared the violence and loss the Saints in Missouri had suffered, Kirtland grew and prospered spiritually as converts gathered to the town and lent their hands to the Lord's work.[1]

In July, a poster advertising "Egyptian Antiquities" appeared in town. It told of the discovery of hundreds of mummies in an Egyptian tomb. Some of the mummies, as well as several ancient papyrus scrolls, had been exhibited throughout the United States, attracting large crowds of spectators.[2]

Michael Chandler, the man showcasing the artifacts, had heard of Joseph and come to Kirtland to see if he wanted to purchase them.[3] Joseph examined the mummies, but he was more interested in the scrolls. They were covered with strange writing and curious images of people, boats, birds, and snakes.[4]

Chandler permitted the prophet to take the scrolls home and study them overnight. Joseph knew Egypt played an important role in the lives of several prophets in the Bible. He also knew Nephi, Mormon, and other writers of the Book of Mormon had recorded their words in what Moroni called "reformed Egyptian."[5]

As he examined the writings on the scrolls, he discerned that they contained vital teachings from the Old Testament patriarch Abraham. Meeting with Chandler the next day, Joseph asked how much he wanted for the scrolls.[6] Chandler said he would only sell the scrolls and mummies together, for $2,400.[7]

The price was far more than Joseph could afford. The Saints were still struggling to finish the temple with limited funds, and few people in Kirtland had money to loan him. Yet Joseph believed the scrolls were worth the price, and he and others quickly raised enough money to buy the artifacts.[8]

Excitement rippled through the church as Joseph and his scribes began trying to make sense of the ancient symbols, confident the Lord would soon reveal more of their message to the Saints.[9]

WHEN JOSEPH WAS NOT poring over the scrolls, he put them and the mummies on display for visitors. Emma took a keen interest in the artifacts and listened carefully as Joseph explained his understanding of the writings of Abraham. When curious people asked to see the mummies, she often exhibited them herself, sharing what Joseph had taught her.[10]

It was a thrilling time to live in Kirtland. While critics of the church still hounded the Saints, and debts continued to worry Joseph and Sidney, Emma could see the Lord's blessings all around her. Workers on the temple completed the roof in July and immediately began constructing a tall steeple.[11] Joseph and Sidney began holding Sabbath meetings in the unfinished structure, sometimes drawing a crowd as large as one thousand people inside to hear them preach.[12]

Emma and Joseph now lived in a house near the temple, and from her yard, Emma could see Artemus Millet and Joseph Young covering the temple's outer walls with a blue-gray stucco, which they scored to look like cut stone blocks.[13] Under Artemus's direction, children helped collect pieces of broken glass and crockery to crush into tiny shards and mix into the stucco. In the sunlight, the shards made the temple walls sparkle as light reflected off them like the facets of a gem.[14]

Emma's house was always busy. Many people boarded with the Smiths, including some of the men who ran the church's new printing office. Aside from printing a new church newspaper, the *Latter Day Saints' Messenger and Advocate,* these men worked on several other projects, including the hymnal Emma had compiled with the help of William Phelps.[15]

Emma's book included new hymns by Saints and older works from other Christian churches. William wrote some of the new pieces, as did Parley Pratt and a recent convert named Eliza Snow. The final hymn was William's "The Spirit of God like a Fire Is Burning," an anthem praising God for restoring the gospel.

Emma knew the printers were also publishing a new collection of revelations called the Doctrine and Covenants. Compiled under Joseph and Oliver's supervision, the Doctrine and Covenants was a combination of revelations from the unpublished Book of Commandments and more recent revelations, together with a series of lectures on faith that church leaders had given to the elders.[16] The Saints accepted the Doctrine and Covenants as a work of scripture, as important as the Bible and Book of Mormon.[17]

That fall, as these projects neared completion, church leaders from Missouri came to Kirtland to prepare for the temple dedication and the endowment of power. On October 29, Emma and Joseph held a dinner in honor of Edward Partridge and others who had arrived. As they all rejoiced in the unity they felt with each other, Newel Whitney told Edward that he hoped to dine with him the next year in Zion.

Looking at her friends, Emma said she hoped everyone at the table might be able to join them in the promised land as well.

"Amen," Joseph said. "God grant it."[18]

AFTER THE DINNER, JOSEPH and Emma attended a meeting of the Kirtland high council. Joseph's younger brother William had charged a woman in the church with physically abusing her stepdaughter. Among the witnesses who spoke in the case was Lucy Smith, Joseph and William's mother. During her testimony, Joseph interrupted when she started speaking about something the council had already heard and resolved.[19]

Leaping to his feet, William accused Joseph of doubting their mother's words. Joseph turned to his brother and told him to sit down. William ignored him and remained standing.

"Sit down," Joseph repeated, trying to stay calm.

William said he would not sit unless Joseph knocked him down.

Agitated, Joseph turned to leave the room, but his father stopped him and asked him to stay. Joseph called the council to order and finished the hearing. By the end of the meeting, he had relaxed enough to say a cordial goodbye to William.

But William was seething, still convinced that Joseph was wrong.[20]

AROUND THIS TIME, HYRUM Smith and his wife, Jerusha, hired Lydia Bailey, a twenty-two-year-old convert, to help out in their boardinghouse. Joseph had baptized Lydia a couple years earlier when he and Sidney were on a short mission to Canada.[21] Lydia had moved to Kirtland not long after, and Hyrum and Jerusha promised to care for her like family.

The work kept Lydia busy. With church leaders from Missouri in town to prepare for the temple dedication, she and Jerusha cooked meals, made beds, and cleaned the house constantly. She rarely had time to talk with the boarders, although Newel Knight, a longtime friend of the Smiths, had caught her eye.[22]

"Brother Knight is a widower," Jerusha told her one day as they worked.

"Oh," said Lydia, pretending not to be interested.

"He lost his wife last fall," Jerusha said. "His heart was almost broken."

Hearing about Newel's loss caused Lydia to remember her own.[23] When she was sixteen, she had married a young man named Calvin Bailey. After their marriage, Calvin drank heavily and sometimes hit her and their daughter.

In time, they lost their farm because of Calvin's drinking, forcing them to rent a smaller home. Lydia gave birth to a son there, but the baby lived only a day. Calvin abandoned Lydia soon after, and she and her daughter moved back in with her parents.

Life seemed to be getting better, but then her daughter got sick. When she died, it was as though the last of Lydia's happiness died too. To help her cope with the loss, her parents sent her to friends in Canada. There she heard the gospel and was baptized, and since then, her life had been happier and more hopeful. But she was lonely and longed for companionship.[24]

One day, Newel approached her in an upper room of the Smith home. "I think your situation, as well as mine, is rather lonely," he said, taking her hand. "Perhaps we might be some company for each other."[25]

Lydia sat in silence. "I suppose you are aware of my situation," she said sadly. "I have not the slightest knowledge where my husband is, or whether he is alive or dead." Without a divorce from Calvin, she did not feel she could marry Newel.

"I would rather sacrifice every feeling of my own, and even life," she told him before leaving the room, "than step aside from virtue or offend my Heavenly Father."[26]

THE DAY AFTER ARGUING with his brother, Joseph received a letter from him. William was upset because the high council had blamed him, and not Joseph, for the dispute. Believing he had been right to reprimand Joseph in front of the high council, he insisted on meeting privately with Joseph to defend his actions.[27]

Joseph agreed to meet with William, suggesting that they each share their version of what had happened, acknowledge their errors, and apologize for any wrongdoing. Since Hyrum had a calming influence in the family, Joseph invited him to join them and make a fair judgment on who was at fault.[28]

William came to Joseph's house the next day, and the brothers took turns explaining the dispute. Joseph said he was upset that William had spoken out of turn in front of the council and failed to respect his position as president of the church. William denied that he had been disrespectful and insisted that Joseph was in the wrong.

Hyrum listened carefully to his brothers. When they finished, he started to give his opinion, but William interrupted, accusing him and Joseph of heaping all the blame on him. Joseph and Hyrum tried to calm him down, but he stormed out of the house. Later that day, he sent Joseph his preaching license.

Soon all of Kirtland knew about the dispute. It divided the normally tight-knit Smith family, setting Joseph's brothers and sisters against each other. Worried that his critics would use the feud against him and the church, Joseph kept his distance from William, hoping his brother's anger would cool.[29]

But William continued to rail against Joseph in the early weeks of November, and soon some of the Saints took sides as well. The apostles condemned William's behavior and threatened to eject him from the Quorum of the Twelve. Joseph, however, received a revelation urging them to be patient with William.[30]

Watching divisions unfold around him, Joseph grew sad. That summer, the Saints had worked together with purpose and goodwill, and the Lord had blessed them with the Egyptian records and great progress on the temple.

But now, with the endowment of power almost within their reach, they could not come together in heart and mind.[31]

THROUGHOUT THE FALL OF 1835, Newel Knight remained determined to marry Lydia Bailey. Believing Ohio law allowed women who had been abandoned by their husbands to remarry, he urged Lydia to leave her past behind. But as much as Lydia wanted to marry Newel, she needed to know that it was right in the eyes of God.

Newel fasted and prayed for three days. On the third day, he asked Hyrum to find out from Joseph if it was right to marry Lydia. Hyrum agreed to talk to his brother, and Newel left to work on the temple on an empty stomach.

Newel was still working when Hyrum approached him later that day. Hyrum told him that Joseph had asked the Lord and received an answer that Lydia and Newel should marry. "The sooner they are married, the better," Joseph had said. "Tell them no law shall hurt them. They need not fear either the law of God or man."

Newel was ecstatic. Dropping his tools, he ran to the boardinghouse and told Lydia what Joseph had said. Lydia was overjoyed, and she and Newel thanked God for His goodness. Newel asked her to marry him, and she accepted. He then rushed to the dining room to break his fast.

Hyrum and Jerusha agreed to host the wedding the following day. Lydia and Newel wanted Joseph to perform the ceremony, but they knew he had never performed a marriage before and did not know if he had legal authority to do it.

The next day, however, while Hyrum was inviting guests to the ceremony, he told Joseph he was still looking for someone to marry the couple. "Stop!" Joseph exclaimed. "I will marry them myself!"

Ohio law allowed ministers of formally organized churches to marry couples.[32] More importantly, Joseph believed his office in the Melchizedek Priesthood divinely authorized him to perform marriages. "The Lord God of Israel has given me authority to unite the people in the holy bonds of matrimony," he declared, "and from this time forth I shall use that privilege."

Hyrum and Jerusha welcomed wedding guests into their home on an icy evening in November. The aroma of the wedding feast filled the room as the Saints prayed and sang to celebrate the occasion. Joseph stood and asked Lydia and Newel to join him at the front of the room and take each other's hands. He explained that marriage was instituted by God in the Garden of

Eden and should be solemnized by the everlasting priesthood.

Turning to Lydia and Newel, he had them covenant that they would accompany each other through life as husband and wife. He pronounced them married and encouraged them to start a family, blessing them with long life and prosperity.[33]

LYDIA AND NEWEL'S WEDDING was a bright spot in an otherwise difficult winter for Joseph. Since his falling out with William, he had not been able to focus on the Egyptian scrolls or on preparing the Saints for the endowment of power. He tried to lead cheerfully, following the Spirit of the Lord. But the turmoil within his family and the burdens of leading the church could be taxing, and sometimes he spoke harshly to people when they made mistakes.[34]

In December, William began holding an informal debating society at his home. Hoping the debates would provide opportunities for learning and teaching by the Spirit, Joseph decided to participate. The society's first two meetings went smoothly, but during the third gathering, the mood grew tense when William interrupted another apostle during a debate.

William's interruption led some people to question if the society should continue. William grew angry and an argument broke out. Joseph intervened, and soon he and William were exchanging insults.[35] Joseph Sr. tried to calm his sons down, but neither man relented, and William lunged at his brother.

Scrambling to defend himself, Joseph tried to remove his coat, but his arms got tangled in the sleeves. William struck hard, again and again, aggravating an injury Joseph had received when he was tarred and feathered. By the time some of the men wrestled William away, Joseph lay on the floor, barely able to move.[36]

A few days later, as he recovered from the fight, Joseph received a message from his brother. "I feel as though it was a duty to make a humble confession," William stated. Afraid that he was unworthy of his calling, he asked Joseph to remove him from the Quorum of the Twelve.[37]

"Do not cast me off for what I have done, but strive to save me," he begged. "I do repent of what I have done to you."[38]

Joseph responded to the letter, expressing hope that they could reconcile. "May God take away enmity from between me and thee," he declared, "and may all blessings be restored, and the past be forgotten forever."[39]

On the first day of the new year, the brothers met with their father and Hyrum. Joseph Sr. prayed for his sons and pleaded for them to forgive each other. As he spoke, Joseph could see how much his feud with William had pained their father. The Spirit of God filled the room, and Joseph's heart melted. William too looked contrite. He confessed his fault and asked again for Joseph's forgiveness.

Knowing he had been at fault as well, Joseph apologized to his brother. They then covenanted to try harder to build each other up and resolve their differences in meekness.

Joseph invited Emma and his mother into the room, and he and William repeated their covenant. Joyful tears ran down their faces. They bowed their heads, and Joseph prayed, grateful that his family was once more united.[40]

CHAPTER 21

The Spirit of God

After reconciling with his brother, Joseph focused again on finishing the temple. While modest compared to the soaring cathedrals of Europe, the temple was taller and grander than most buildings in Ohio. Travelers on the road to Kirtland could easily spot its colorful bell tower and gleaming red roof peeking above the treetops. The sparkling stucco walls, vibrant green doors, and peaked Gothic windows made it a stunning sight.[1]

By the end of January 1836, the inside of the temple was nearly completed, and Joseph was preparing church leaders for the endowment of divine power the Lord had promised to give them. No one knew for sure what the endowment would be like, but Joseph had explained that it would come after he had administered symbolic washing and anointing ordinances to men ordained to the priesthood, as Moses had washed and anointed the priests of Aaron in the Old Testament.[2]

The Saints had also read New Testament passages that offered insight into the endowment. After His Resurrection, Jesus had counseled His apostles not to leave Jerusalem to preach the gospel until they were "endowed with power from on high." Later, on the day of Pentecost, Jesus's apostles received this power when the Spirit descended upon them like a rushing wind, and they spoke in tongues.[3]

As the Saints prepared for their endowment, they anticipated a similar spiritual outpouring.

On the afternoon of January 21, Joseph, his counselors, and his father climbed the stairs to a loft in the printing office behind the temple. There the men symbolically washed themselves with clean water and blessed each other in the name of the Lord. Once they were cleansed, they went next door to the temple, where they joined with the bishoprics of Kirtland and Zion, anointed each other's heads with consecrated oil, and blessed one another.

When it was Joseph's turn, his father anointed his head and blessed him to lead the church as a latter-day Moses, pronouncing on him the blessings of Abraham, Isaac, and Jacob. Joseph's counselors then laid their hands on his head and blessed him.[4]

When the men completed the ordinance, the heavens opened and Joseph saw a vision of the future. He beheld the celestial kingdom, its beautiful gate blazing before him like a circle of fire. He saw God the Father and Jesus Christ seated on glorious thrones. The Old Testament prophets Adam and Abraham were there as well, along with Joseph's mother and father and his older brother Alvin.

Seeing his brother made Joseph wonder. Alvin had died soon after Moroni's first visit, and he had never had a chance to be baptized by proper authority. How could he inherit celestial glory? Joseph's family had refused to believe that Alvin was in hell, as a preacher once suggested, but his eternal fate remained a mystery to them.

While Joseph marveled at the sight of his brother, he heard the voice of the Lord say, "All who have died without a knowledge of this gospel, who would have received it if they had been permitted to tarry, shall be heirs of the celestial kingdom of God."

The Lord explained that He would judge all people by their works and the desires of their hearts. People in Alvin's situation would not be damned for lacking opportunities on earth. The Lord also taught that small children who died before reaching the age of accountability, like the four infants Joseph and Emma had buried, would be saved in the celestial kingdom.[5]

After the vision closed, Joseph and his counselors anointed the members of the high councils of Kirtland and Zion, who had been waiting prayerfully in another room. As the men received the ordinance, more visions of heaven unfolded before them. Some saw angels, and others beheld the face of Christ.

Filled with the Spirit, the men prophesied of things to come and glorified God long into the night.[6]

TWO MONTHS LATER, ON the morning of March 27, 1836, Lydia Knight sat shoulder to shoulder with other Saints in the temple's lower court. All around her, people squeezed together as ushers packed more people into the pews. About a thousand Saints were already in the room, and many more were crowding the front entrances, hopeful the doormen would let them in.[7]

Lydia had visited the temple a few times since her marriage to Newel four months earlier. She and Newel had occasionally gone there to hear a sermon or lecture.[8] But this visit was different. Today the Saints had assembled to dedicate the temple to the Lord.

From her seat, Lydia could watch church leaders take their places behind the three rows of ornately carved pulpits at both ends of the room. In front of her, on the west end of the building, were pulpits for the First Presidency and other leaders in the Melchizedek Priesthood. Behind her, along the east wall, were pulpits for the bishoprics and Aaronic Priesthood leaders. As a member of the Missouri high council, Newel sat in a row of box seats beside these pulpits.

As she waited for the dedication to begin, Lydia could also admire the beautiful woodwork along the pulpits and the row of tall columns that ran the length of the room. It was still early in the morning, and sunlight poured into the court through the tall windows along the side walls. Overhead hung large canvas curtains, which could be rolled down between the pews to divide the space into temporary rooms.[9]

When the ushers could squeeze no one else into the room, Joseph stood and apologized to those who were unable to find a place to sit. He suggested holding an overflow meeting in the nearby schoolroom on the first floor of the printshop.[10]

A few minutes later, after the congregation settled into their seats, Sidney opened the service and spoke with great force for more than two hours. After a brief intermission, during which almost everyone in the congregation stayed seated, Joseph stood and offered the dedicatory prayer, which he had prepared with the help of Oliver and Sidney the day before.[11]

"We ask thee, O Lord, to accept of this house," Joseph said, "the workmanship of the hands of us, thy servants, which thou didst command us to build." He asked that the missionaries might go out, armed with power, to spread the gospel to the ends of the earth. He prayed for a blessing on the Saints in Missouri, for the leaders of the nations of the world, and for scattered Israel.[12]

He also petitioned the Lord to endow the Saints with power. "Let the anointing of thy ministers be sealed upon them with power from on high," he said. "Put upon thy servants the testimony of the covenant, that when they go out and proclaim thy word they may seal up the law, and prepare the hearts of thy saints." He asked that the Lord might fill the temple with His glory, like the rushing of wind the ancient apostles had experienced.[13]

"O hear, O hear, O hear us, O Lord," he pleaded, "and answer these petitions, and accept the dedication of this house unto thee."[14]

As soon as Joseph pronounced his final "amen," the choir sang William Phelps's new hymn:

> *The Spirit of God like a fire is burning;*
> *The latter-day glory begins to come forth.*
> *The visions and blessings of old are returning;*
> *The angels are coming to visit the earth.*[15]

Lydia felt the glory of God fill the temple. Rising to her feet with the other Saints in the room, she joined her voice with theirs as they shouted, "Hosanna! Hosanna! Hosanna to God and the Lamb!"[16]

AFTER THE TEMPLE DEDICATION, manifestations of the Lord's Spirit and power enveloped Kirtland. On the evening of the dedication, Joseph met with church leaders in the temple, and the men began to speak in tongues, as the Savior's apostles had done at Pentecost. Some at the meeting saw heavenly fire resting on those who spoke. Others saw angels. Outside, Saints saw a bright cloud and a pillar of fire rest over the temple.[17]

On March 30, Joseph and his counselors met in the temple to wash the feet of about three hundred church leaders, including the Twelve, the Seventy, and other men called to missionary labor, much like the Savior had done with His disciples before His Crucifixion. "This is a year of Jubilee to us and a time of rejoicing," Joseph declared. The men had come to the temple fasting, and he asked a few of them to purchase bread and wine for later. He had others bring in tubs of water.

Joseph and his counselors first washed the feet of the Quorum of the Twelve, then proceeded to wash the feet of the members of other quorums, blessing them in the name of the Lord.[18] As the hours passed, the men blessed each other, prophesied, and shouted hosannas until the bread and wine arrived in the early evening.

Joseph spoke as the Twelve broke the bread and poured the wine. He told them their short stay in Kirtland would soon be over. The Lord was endowing them with power and would then send them on missions. "Go in all meekness, in sobriety, and preach Jesus Christ," he said. He instructed them to avoid arguments over religious beliefs, urging them to stay true to their own.

"Bear the keys of the kingdom to all nations," he told the apostles, "and unlock them, and call upon the seventies to follow." He said the organization of the church was now complete and the men in the room had received all of the ordinances the Lord had prepared for them at that time.

"Go forth and build up the kingdom of God," he said.

Joseph and his counselors went home, leaving the Twelve to take charge of the meeting. The Spirit again descended on the men in the temple, and they began to prophesy, speak in tongues, and exhort one another in the gospel. Ministering angels appeared to some men, and a few others had visions of the Savior.

Outpourings of the Spirit continued until the early morning hours. When the men left the temple, their souls were soaring from the wonders and glories they had just experienced. They felt endowed with power and ready to take the gospel to the world.[19]

ONE WEEK AFTER THE dedication, on the afternoon of Easter Sunday, a thousand Saints again came to the temple to worship. After the Twelve administered the Lord's Supper to the congregation, Joseph and Oliver lowered the canvas curtains around the uppermost pulpit on the west side of the lower court and knelt behind them to pray silently, out of sight from the Saints.[20]

After their prayers, the Savior appeared in front of them, His face beaming brighter than the sun. His eyes were like fire and His hair was like snow. Beneath His feet, the breastwork of the pulpit looked like it was pure gold.[21]

"Let the hearts of all my people rejoice, who have, with their might, built this house to my name," the Savior declared, His voice like rushing water. "Behold, I have accepted this house, and my name shall be here; and I will manifest myself to my people in mercy."[22] He urged the Saints to keep it sacred and confirmed that they had received the endowment of power.

"The hearts of thousands and tens of thousands shall greatly rejoice," He declared, "in consequence of the blessings which shall be poured out, and the endowment with which my servants have been endowed in this house."

Finally the Lord promised, "The fame of this house shall spread to foreign lands; and this is the beginning of the blessing which shall be poured out upon the heads of my people."[23]

The vision closed around Joseph and Oliver, but instantly the heavens opened again. They saw Moses standing in front of them, and he committed the keys of the gathering of Israel to them so the Saints could take the gospel to the world and bring the righteous to Zion.

Elias then appeared and committed the dispensation of the gospel of Abraham to them, saying all generations would be blessed through them and those who came after them.

After Elias departed, Joseph and Oliver had another glorious vision. They saw Elijah, the Old Testament prophet who ascended to heaven in a chariot of fire.

"The time has fully come, which was spoken of by the mouth of Malachi," Elijah declared, referring to the Old Testament prophecy that he would turn the hearts of the fathers to the children and the children to the fathers.

"The keys of this dispensation are committed into your hands," Elijah continued, "and by this ye may know that the great and dreadful day of the Lord is near, even at the doors."[24]

The vision closed, leaving Joseph and Oliver to themselves.[25] Sunlight filtered through the arched window behind the pulpit, but the breastwork in front of them no longer shone like gold. The heavenly voices that had shaken them like thunder gave way to the muted stirrings of the Saints on the other side of the curtain.

Joseph knew the messengers had conveyed important priesthood keys on him. Later, he taught the Saints that the priesthood keys restored by Elijah would seal families together eternally, binding in heaven what was bound on earth, linking parents to their children and children to their parents.[26]

IN THE DAYS THAT followed the dedication of the temple, missionaries left in every direction to preach the gospel, strengthened by the endowment of power. Bishop Partridge and the other Saints who came from Missouri headed west again with new resolve to build Zion.[27]

Lydia and Newel Knight also wanted to go west, but they needed money. Newel had spent most of his time in Kirtland working without pay on the temple, and Lydia had loaned almost all of her money to Joseph and the church when she first arrived in town. Neither regretted their sacrifice, but Lydia could not help thinking that the money she had loaned the church would have more than covered the cost of travel.

As they puzzled over how to pay for their journey, Joseph stopped by to see them. "So, Newel, you are about to depart for your western home," he said. "Are you amply provided for?"

"We are rather cramped just now for means," Newel said.

"I have not forgotten how generously you helped me when I was in trouble," Joseph said to Lydia. He stepped out of the house and returned a short time later with more than the sum she had loaned him.

He told them to purchase what they needed to be comfortable on the journey to their new home. Hyrum also provided a team of horses to take them to the Ohio River, where they could catch a steamer all the way to Missouri.

Before the Knights left, they visited Joseph Smith Sr. so Lydia could receive a blessing from him. More than a year earlier, the Lord had called Joseph Sr. to be the patriarch of the church, granting him authority to give the Saints special patriarchal blessings, as Abraham and Jacob had done for their children in the Bible.

Placing his hands on Lydia's head, Joseph Sr. spoke the words of the blessing. "Thou hast been afflicted much in thy past days, and thy heart has been pained," he said to Lydia. "But thou shalt be comforted."

He told her the Lord loved her and had given her Newel to comfort her. "Your souls shall be knit together, and nothing shall be able to dissolve them. Neither distress nor death shall separate you," he promised. "You shall be preserved in life and go safely and speedily to the land of Zion."[28]

Soon after the blessing, Lydia and Newel set out for Missouri, optimistic about the future of the church and Zion. The Lord had endowed the Saints with power, and Kirtland was flourishing beneath the towering steeple of the temple. The visions and blessings that season had given them a foretaste of heaven. The veil between earth and heaven seemed ready to burst.[29]

PART 3

---⊸✦⊷---

Cast into the Deep

APRIL 1836–APRIL 1839

If thou be cast into the deep; if the
billowing surge conspire against thee;
if fierce winds become thine enemy; if the heavens
gather blackness, and all the elements
combine to hedge up the way; and above all,
if the very jaws of hell shall gape open
the mouth wide after thee, know thou, my son,
that all these things shall give thee experience,
and shall be for thy good.

Doctrine and Covenants 122:7

1836–1839

MISSOURI

• ADAM-ONDI-AHMAN

GALLATIN •

Grand River

DAVIESS
COUNTY

FAR WEST •

Shoal Creek

• HAWN'S MILL

CALDWELL
COUNTY

CARROLL
COUNTY

CLAY
COUNTY

Crooked River

DE WITT •

• LIBERTY

RAY
COUNTY

Missouri River

THE BRITISH MISSION 1837

PRESTON •

• WALKER FOLD

LIVERPOOL •

• MANCHESTER

• INDEPENDENCE

JACKSON
COUNTY

GREAT
BRITAIN

HEREFORDSHIRE

CHAPTER 22

Try the Lord

After the temple dedication, Joseph basked in the hope and goodwill that rested over Kirtland.[1] Saints witnessed an outpouring of spiritual gifts throughout the spring of 1836. Many saw hosts of angels, clothed in brilliant white, standing on the roof of the temple, and some people wondered if the Millennium had begun.[2]

Joseph could see evidence of the Lord's blessings everywhere. When he had moved to Kirtland five years earlier, the church had been disorganized and unruly. Since then, the Saints had embraced the word of the Lord more fully and transformed a simple village into a strong stake of Zion. The temple stood as a testament to what they could accomplish when they followed God and worked together.

But even as he rejoiced in Kirtland's success, Joseph could not forget the Saints in Missouri, who were still huddled in small communities just outside of Jackson County, along the Missouri River. He and his counselors trusted in the Lord's promise to redeem Zion after the elders received the endowment of power. Yet no one knew how and when He would carry the promise out.

Turning their attention to Zion, the church leaders fasted and prayed to know the Lord's will.[3] Joseph then recalled the revelation in which the Lord had asked the Saints to purchase all the lands in and around Jackson County.[4] The Saints had already started purchasing some land in Clay County, but as always, the problem was finding the money to make more purchases.

In early April, Joseph met with members of the church's printing firm to discuss church finances. The men believed they needed to contribute all their resources to the redemption of Zion, and they recommended that Joseph and Oliver lead fund-raising efforts to purchase more land in Missouri.[5]

Unfortunately, the church was already tens of thousands of dollars in debt from building the temple and from earlier land purchases, and money was still scarce in Kirtland, even with missionaries collecting donations. Much of the Saints' wealth was in land, which meant few people could make cash donations. And without cash, the church could do little to pull itself out of debt or buy more land in Zion.[6]

Once again, Joseph had to find a way to finance the Lord's work.

TWO HUNDRED MILES NORTH, Parley Pratt stood on the outskirts of a town called Hamilton, in southern Canada. He was headed to Toronto, one of the largest cities in the province, to serve his first mission since receiving the endowment of power. He had no money, no friends in the area, and no idea how to accomplish what the Lord had sent him to do.

A few weeks earlier, as the Twelve and Seventy were leaving Kirtland to preach the gospel, Parley had planned to stay home with his family. Like many Saints in Kirtland, he was steeped in debt, having purchased land in the area and built a house on credit. Parley was also concerned about his wife, Thankful, who was sick and needed his care. As eager as he was to preach, a mission seemed out of the question.[7]

But then Heber Kimball had come to his house and given him a blessing as his friend and fellow apostle. "Go forth in the ministry, nothing doubting," Heber had said. "Take no thoughts for your debts, nor the necessaries of life, for the Lord will supply you with abundant means for all things."

Speaking by inspiration, Heber told Parley to go to Toronto, promising that he would find people who were ready for the fullness of the gospel. He said Parley would lay the foundation for a mission to England and find relief from his debts. "You shall yet have riches, silver and gold," Heber prophesied, "till you will loathe the counting thereof."

He also spoke of Thankful. "Thy wife shall be healed from this hour," he promised, "and shall bear thee a son."[8]

The blessing had been marvelous, but its promises seemed impossible. Parley had experienced plenty of success in the mission field, but Toronto was new and unfamiliar to him. He had never made much money in his life, and it was unlikely that he would receive enough money on the mission to pay off his debts.

The promises about Thankful were the most unlikely of all. She was almost forty years old and had often been sickly and frail. After ten years of marriage, she and Parley had no children.[9]

But with faith in the Lord's promises, Parley had headed northeast, traveling by stagecoach over muddy roads. When he reached Niagara Falls and crossed into Canada, he had set off on foot until he reached Hamilton. Thoughts of home and the immensity of his mission soon overwhelmed him, and he yearned to know how he was supposed to exercise faith in a blessing when its promises seemed so far out of reach.

"Try the Lord," the Spirit suddenly whispered to him, "and see if anything is too hard for Him."[10]

MEANWHILE, IN MISSOURI, TWELVE-YEAR-OLD Emily Partridge was relieved to see spring return to Clay

County. With her father in Kirtland for the temple dedication, she and the rest of her family shared a one-room log cabin with the family of Margaret and John Corrill, her father's counselor in the bishopric. The cabin had been used as a stable before the two families moved in, but her father and Brother Corrill had cleaned out the muck that caked the floor and had made the place livable. There was a large fireplace, and the families had spent the frigid winter huddled around its warmth.[11]

That spring, Emily's father returned to Missouri to resume his duties as bishop. He and other church leaders had received the endowment of power in Kirtland, and they seemed hopeful about the future of Zion.[12]

As the weather grew warmer, Emily prepared to return to school. Soon after the Saints arrived in Clay County, they had set up a school in a cabin near a grove of fruit trees. Emily loved to play with her friends in the grove and eat the fruit that fell from the branches overhead. When Emily and her friends were not studying, they made houses out of sticks and used vines as jump ropes.[13]

Most of Emily's classmates belonged to the church, but some were the children of longtime settlers in the area. They were often better dressed than Emily and the other poor children, and some made fun of the young Saints' tattered clothes. But for the most part, everyone got along well enough, despite their differences.

The same was not true of their parents. As more Saints moved to Clay County and purchased large tracts of land, the longtime settlers grew uneasy and impatient. They had initially welcomed the Saints into their county, offering refuge until they could return to their homes across the river. No one had expected church members to make a permanent home in Clay County.[14]

At first, the strain between the Saints and their neighbors had little effect on the routine of Emily's school days.[15] But as the spring wore on and their neighbors grew more hostile, Emily and her family had reason to fear that the nightmare of Jackson County would be repeated, and they would again be without a home.

As Parley continued his journey north, he asked the Lord to help him reach his destination. A short time later, he met a man who gave him ten dollars and a letter of introduction to someone in Toronto named John Taylor. Parley used the money to book passage on a steamship to the city and arrived at the Taylor home soon after.

John and Leonora Taylor were a young couple from England. As Parley chatted with them, he learned that they belonged to a group of Christians in the area who rejected any doctrine that could not be supported by the Bible. Lately, they had been praying and fasting that God would send them a messenger from His true church.

Parley talked to them about the restored gospel, but they showed only a mild interest. The next morning, he left his bag with the Taylors and introduced himself to the city's clergymen, hoping they would let him preach to their congregations. Parley then met with city officials to see if they would let him hold a meeting in the courthouse or some other public space. They all denied his request.

Discouraged, Parley went into the woods nearby and said a prayer. Then he returned to the Taylors' home to retrieve his bag. As he was leaving, John stopped him and spoke of his love for the Bible.[16] "Mr. Pratt," he said, "if you have any principles to advance of any kind, I should wish you, if you can, to sustain them by that record."

"That is a thing that I think I shall be able to do," Parley said. He asked John if he believed in apostles and prophets.

"Yes," John replied, "because the Bible teaches me all these things."

"We teach baptism in the name of Jesus Christ for the remission of sins," Parley said, "and the laying on of hands for the gift of the Holy Ghost."

"What about Joseph Smith and the Book of Mormon and some of your new revelations?" John asked.

Parley testified that Joseph Smith was an honest man and a prophet of God. "As to the Book of Mormon," he said, "I am as able to bring as strong testimony in favor of that book as you can of the authenticity of the Bible."[17]

As they spoke, Parley and John overheard Leonora talking with a neighbor, Isabella Walton, in another room. "There is a gentleman here from the United States who says the Lord sent him to the city to preach the gospel," Leonora told Isabella. "I am sorry to have him depart."

"Tell the stranger he is welcome to my house," Isabella said. "I have a spare room and bed, and food in plenty." She also had space where he could preach to her friends and relatives that night. "I feel by the Spirit that he is a man sent by the Lord with a message which will do us good," she said.[18]

AFTER HIS CONVERSATION WITH Parley, John Taylor began reading the Book of Mormon and comparing its teachings to the Bible. He had studied the doctrines of other churches before, but he found something compelling in the Book of Mormon and the principles Parley taught him. Everything was clear and consistent with the word of God.

John soon introduced Parley to his friends. "Here is a man come in answer to our prayers," he announced, "and he says the Lord has established the true church."

"Are you going to be a Mormon?" someone asked him.

"I don't know," John said. "I am going to investigate and pray for the Lord to help me. If there is truth in this thing, I will embrace it—and if error, I want nothing to do with it."[19]

A short time later, he and Parley traveled to a nearby farming village where Isabella Walton's relatives lived. John's friend Joseph Fielding also lived there with his sisters, Mercy and Mary. They too were from England and held religious views similar to the Taylors'.

As John and Parley rode up to the Fieldings' home, they saw Mercy and Mary run to a neighbor's house. Their brother stepped outside and greeted the men coolly. He said he wished they had not come. His sisters, and many other people in town, did not want to hear them preach.

"Why do they oppose Mormonism?" Parley asked.

"I don't know," Joseph said. "The name has such a contemptible sound." He said they were not looking for new revelation or any doctrine that contradicted the teachings of the Bible.

"Oh," said Parley, "if that is all, we shall soon remove your prejudices." He told Joseph to call his sisters back to the house. He knew there was a religious meeting in the village that evening, and he wanted to preach at it.

"We will take supper with you and all go over to the meeting together," Parley said. "If you and your sisters will agree to this, I will agree to preach the old Bible gospel and leave out all new revelations which are opposed to it."[20]

That evening, Joseph, Mercy, and Mary Fielding sat in a crowded room and were captivated by Parley's sermon. Nothing he said about the restored gospel or the Book of Mormon contradicted the teachings of the Bible.

Soon after, Parley baptized the Taylors, Fieldings, and enough people in the area to organize a branch. The Lord's promises in Heber's blessing had begun to be fulfilled, and Parley was eager to return home to Thankful. Some of his debts were due, and he still needed to earn the money to pay them.

As Parley set off for Kirtland, he shook hands with his new friends. One by one, they pressed money into his palms, amounting to several hundred dollars. It was enough to pay off his most urgent debts.[21]

WHEN PARLEY ARRIVED IN Kirtland, he saw that Thankful was healthy, a fulfillment of another of the Lord's promises. After Parley paid off some debts, he collected pamphlets and copies of the Book of Mormon and returned to Canada to continue his mission, this time bringing his wife with him.[22] The journey wearied Thankful, and when the Saints in Canada saw her frailty, they doubted she was strong enough to bear the son promised in Parley's blessing. Soon after, however, Parley and Thankful were expecting their first child.[23]

While the Pratts were away, their friends Caroline and Jonathan Crosby rented their house in Kirtland. The Crosbys were a young couple who had moved to Kirtland a few months before the temple dedication. They met often with friends to worship, sing hymns, or share a meal.[24]

With the temple completed, more Saints were moving to Kirtland. There was plenty of land in the area, but much of it was undeveloped. The Saints hurried to construct more houses, often on credit because there was not much cash in the community. But they could not build fast enough to accommodate the new arrivals, so established families often opened their homes to these people or rented out spare rooms.

As housing in town grew scarcer, John Boynton, one of the apostles, approached the Crosbys about renting the Pratts' house to his family. He offered them more than what they paid the Pratts.[25]

The offer was generous, and Caroline knew she and Jonathan could use the money to help pay for the house they were building. But they enjoyed living by themselves, and Caroline was now pregnant with their first child. If they moved out of the Pratts' home, they would have to move in with an elderly neighbor, Sabre Granger, whose cramped cottage had only one bedroom.

Jonathan asked Caroline to make the decision about moving. Caroline did not want to leave the comfort and space of the Pratts' home, and she was reluctant to move in with Sister Granger. The money did not concern her much, no matter how much she and Jonathan could use it.

But knowing they would be helping the large Boynton family gather to Kirtland was worth the small sacrifice Caroline had to make. After a few days, she told Jonathan she was willing to move.[26]

IN LATE JUNE, WILLIAM Phelps and other church leaders in Clay County wrote the prophet to tell him that local officials had summoned church leaders to the court-house, where they discussed the Saints' future in their county. The officials had spoken calmly and politely, but their words left no room for compromise.

Since the Saints could not return to Jackson County, the officials recommended that they look for a new place to live—somewhere they could be by themselves. The church leaders in Clay County agreed to leave rather than risk another violent expulsion.[27]

The news shattered Joseph's hopes of returning to Jackson County that year, but he could not blame the Saints in Missouri for what happened. "You are better acquainted with circumstances than we are," he wrote back, "and of course have been directed in wisdom in your moves, relative to leaving the county."[28]

With the Saints in Missouri needing a new place to settle, Joseph felt even more pressure to raise money to buy lands. He decided to open a church store near Kirtland and borrowed more money to purchase goods to sell there.[29] The store had some success, but many Saints took advantage of Joseph's kindness and trust, knowing he would not refuse them credit at the store. Several of them also insisted on trading for what they needed, making it difficult to turn a cash profit on the goods.[30]

By the end of July, neither the store nor anything else church leaders tried had eased the church's debt. Desperate, Joseph left Kirtland with Sidney, Hyrum, and Oliver for Salem, a city on the East Coast, after hearing from a church member who thought he knew where to find a cache of hidden money. No money came of the lead when they arrived in the city, and Joseph turned to the Lord for guidance.[31]

"I, the Lord your God, am not displeased with your coming on this journey, notwithstanding your follies," came the response. "Concern not yourselves about your debts, for I will give you power to pay them. Concern not yourselves about Zion, for I will deal mercifully with her."[32]

The men all returned to Kirtland about a month later with church finances still weighing on their minds. But that fall Joseph and his counselors proposed a new project that just might raise the money they needed for Zion.

CHAPTER 23

Every Snare

Jonathan Crosby worked on his new home in Kirtland throughout the fall of 1836. By November he had put up the walls and the roof, but the house still had an unfinished floor and no windows or doors. With the baby coming soon, Caroline had been urging him to finish the house as quickly as possible. Things were working out fine with their landlady, Sister Granger, but Caroline was anxious to move out of the tight quarters and into her own house.[1]

While Jonathan labored feverishly to make the house livable before the baby came, church leaders announced their plans to start the Kirtland Safety Society, a village bank designed to boost Kirtland's struggling economy and raise money for the church. Like other small banks in the United States, it would provide loans to borrowers so they could purchase property and goods, helping the local economy grow. As borrowers paid these loans back with interest, the bank would turn a profit.[2]

Loans would be issued in the form of banknotes backed by the Safety Society's limited reserve of silver and gold coins. To build up this reserve of hard money, the bank would sell shares of stock to investors, who committed to make payments on their shares over time.[3]

By early November, the Kirtland Safety Society had more than thirty stockholders, including Joseph and Sidney, who invested much of their own money in the bank.[4] The stockholders elected Sidney as president of the institution and Joseph as cashier, making him responsible for the bank's accounts.[5]

With plans for the bank in place, Oliver went east to purchase materials for printing banknotes, and Orson Hyde went to apply for a charter from the state legislature so they could operate the bank legally. Joseph, meanwhile, urged all the Saints to invest in the Safety Society, quoting Old Testament scriptures that called on the ancient Israelites to bring their gold and silver to the Lord.[6]

Joseph felt that God approved of their efforts, and he promised that all would be well if the Saints heeded the Lord's commandments.[7] Trusting the prophet's word, additional Saints invested in the Safety Society, although others were more cautious about purchasing stock in an untried institution. The Crosbys thought about purchasing shares, but the high cost of building their home had left them no money to spare.[8]

Around the start of December, Jonathan had finally installed windows and doors for the house, and he and Caroline moved in. The interior was still unfinished, but they had a good cooking stove to keep them warm and fed. Jonathan had also dug a well nearby where they could fetch water easily.

Caroline was happy to have a home of her own, and on December 19, she gave birth to a healthy baby boy as a blinding snowstorm swirled outside.[9]

WINTER ENVELOPED KIRTLAND, AND in January 1837, the Kirtland Safety Society opened for business.[10] On its first day, Joseph issued crisp banknotes, fresh from the printing press, with the institution's name and his signature on the front.[11] As more Saints took out loans, often using their land as collateral, the notes began circulating around Kirtland and elsewhere.[12]

Phebe Carter, who had recently moved to Kirtland from the northeastern United States, did not invest in the Safety Society or take out a loan. But she stood to benefit from the prosperity it promised. She was nearly thirty years old and unmarried, and she had no family in Kirtland to rely on for support. Like other women in her situation, she had few options for employment, but she could earn a modest income sewing and teaching school, as she had done before moving to Ohio.[13] If

Kirtland's economy improved, more people would have money to spend on new clothes and education.

For Phebe, though, the decision to come to Kirtland had been spiritual, not economic. Her parents had opposed her baptism, and after she announced her plans to gather with the Saints, her mother protested. "Phebe," she had said, "will you come back to me if you find Mormonism false?"

"Yes, Mother, I will," Phebe promised.[14]

But she knew she had found the restored gospel of Jesus Christ. Some months after arriving in Kirtland, she had received a patriarchal blessing from Joseph Smith Sr. that assured her great rewards on earth and in heaven. "Be comforted, for thy troubles are over," the Lord told her. "Thou shalt have long life and see good days."[15]

The blessing confirmed the feelings Phebe had when she left home. Too sad to say goodbye in person, she had written a letter and left it on the family table. "Be not anxious for your child," it read. "I believe that the Lord will take care of me and give me that which is for the best."[16]

Phebe had faith in the promises of her patriarchal blessing. It said she would be the mother of many children and marry a man with wisdom, knowledge, and understanding.[17] But so far Phebe had no prospects of marriage, and she knew she was older than most women who married and started having children.

One evening in January 1837, Phebe was visiting friends when she met a dark-haired man with pale blue eyes. He was a few days older than she was and had recently returned to Kirtland after marching with the Camp of Israel and then serving a mission in the southern United States.

His name, she learned, was Wilford Woodruff.[18]

THROUGHOUT THE WINTER, THE Saints in Kirtland continued to borrow large sums of money to purchase property and goods. Employers sometimes paid workers in banknotes, which could be used as currency or redeemed for hard money at the Kirtland Safety Society office.[19]

Soon after the Safety Society opened for business, a man named Grandison Newell began hoarding banknotes. A longtime resident of a nearby town, Grandison hated Joseph and the Saints. He had enjoyed some prominence in the county until the Saints arrived, and now he often looked for ways, legal or otherwise, to harass them.[20]

If church members came to him for work, he would refuse to hire them. If missionaries preached near his home, he would organize a group of men to pelt them with eggs. When Doctor Philastus Hurlbut began collecting slanderous statements against Joseph, Grandison helped finance his work.[21]

Yet despite his efforts, the Saints kept gathering to the area.[22]

The opening of the Kirtland Safety Society gave Grandison a new point of attack. Concerned about the rising number of banks in Ohio, the state legislature had refused to grant Orson Hyde a charter. Without this approval, the Safety Society could not call itself a bank, but it could still take deposits and issue loans. Its success relied on stockholders making payments on their shares so the institution could maintain its reserves. Few stockholders had enough hard money to do that, however, and Grandison suspected the Safety Society's reserves were too small to sustain it for long.[23]

Hoping the business would collapse if enough people redeemed notes for gold or silver coins, Grandison traveled around the countryside purchasing Safety Society notes.[24] He then brought his stack of notes to the Safety Society office and demanded cash in return. If the officers did not redeem them, he threatened, he would press charges.[25]

Cornered, Joseph and the Safety Society officers had no choice but to redeem the notes and pray for more investors.

ALTHOUGH HE HAD LITTLE money, Wilford Woodruff purchased twenty shares in Kirtland Safety Society stock.[26] His good friend Warren Parrish was the Safety Society's secretary. Wilford had traveled west with Warren and his wife, Betsy, as part of the Camp of Israel. After Betsy died in the cholera outbreak, Warren and Wilford served a mission together before Warren returned to Kirtland and became Joseph's scribe and trusted friend.[27]

Since his mission, Wilford had moved from place to place, often living off the kindness of friends like Warren. But after meeting Phebe Carter, he began thinking about marriage, and investing in the Safety Society was one way he could establish himself financially before starting a family.

By the end of January, however, the Safety Society was facing a crisis. While Grandison Newell was trying to wipe out its reserves, newspapers in the area were publishing articles that cast doubt on its legitimacy. Like others around the country, some Saints had also speculated in land and goods, hoping to get rich with little effort. Others neglected to make the required payments on their stock. Before long, many workers and businesses in and around Kirtland refused to accept Safety Society notes.[28]

Fearing failure, Joseph and Sidney temporarily shut down the Safety Society and traveled to another city to try to partner with an established bank there.[29] But the Safety Society's poor start had shaken the faith of many Saints, leading them to question the prophet's spiritual leadership that had spurred their investment.[30]

In the past, the Lord had revealed scripture through Joseph, making it easy for them to exercise faith that he was a prophet of God. But when Joseph's statements about the Safety Society appeared to go unfulfilled, and their investments began to slip away, many Saints became uneasy and critical of Joseph.

Wilford continued to trust that the Safety Society would succeed. After the prophet partnered with the other bank, he returned to Kirtland and responded to the complaints of his critics.[31] Later, at the church's general conference, Joseph spoke to the Saints about why the church borrowed money and established institutions like the Safety Society.

The Saints had begun the latter-day work poor and destitute, he reminded them, yet the Lord had commanded them to sacrifice their time and talents to gather to Zion and build a temple. These efforts, though costly, were vital to the salvation of God's children.[32] To move the Lord's work forward, church leaders had to find a way to finance it.

Still, Joseph regretted how much they owed creditors. "We are indebted to them, to be sure," he admitted, "but our brethren abroad have only to come with their money." He believed that if Saints gathered to Kirtland and consecrated their property to the Lord, it would do much to relieve the church of its burden of debt.[33]

As Joseph spoke, Wilford felt the power of his words. "Oh, that they might be written upon our hearts as with an iron pen," he thought, "to remain forever that we might practice them in our lives." He wondered how anyone could hear the prophet speak and still doubt that he had been called of God.[34]

Yet doubts persisted. By mid-April, Kirtland's economy worsened as a financial crisis overwhelmed the nation. Years of excessive lending had weakened banks in England and the United States, causing widespread fear of economic collapse. Banks called in debts, and some stopped issuing loans altogether. Panic soon spread from town to town as banks closed, businesses failed, and unemployment soared.[35]

In this climate, a struggling institution like the Kirtland Safety Society stood little chance. Joseph could not do much to fix the dilemma, yet some found it easier to blame him than the national economic panic.

Soon creditors were hounding Joseph and Sidney constantly. One man filed a lawsuit against them over an unpaid debt, and Grandison Newell brought false criminal charges against Joseph, claiming the prophet was conspiring against him. With each passing day, the prophet grew more concerned that he would be arrested or killed.[36]

Wilford and Phebe were now engaged, and they had asked Joseph to marry them. But on the day of their wedding, he was nowhere to be found, leaving Frederick Williams to perform the ceremony.[37]

SHORTLY AFTER JOSEPH'S SUDDEN disappearance, Emma received a letter from him, assuring her he was safe.[38] He and Sidney had fled Kirtland, putting distance between themselves and those who wished to harm them. Their location was secret, but Newel Whitney and Hyrum knew how to contact them and were advising them from afar.[39]

Emma understood the dangers Joseph faced. When his letter arrived, some men—probably friends of

Grandison Newell—examined its postmark, trying to learn where he was. Others were spying on his struggling store.

Although she remained optimistic, Emma worried about the children. Their one-year-old son, Frederick, was too young to understand what was happening, but six-year-old Julia and four-year-old Joseph became anxious when they learned their father would not be coming home soon.[40]

Emma knew she had to trust in the Lord, especially now that so many people in Kirtland were turning to doubt and disbelief. "If I had no more confidence in God than some I could name, I should be a sad case indeed," Emma wrote Joseph at the end of April. "But I still believe that if we humble ourselves and are as faithful as we can be, we shall be delivered from every snare that may be laid at our feet."[41]

Even so, she worried that Joseph's creditors would take advantage of his absence and seize whatever property or money they could. "It is impossible for me to do anything," she lamented, "as long as everybody has so much better right to all that is called yours than I have."

Emma was ready for him to come home. There were few people she trusted now, and she was reluctant to give anyone anything that did not help to pay off Joseph's debts. And to make matters worse, she feared their children had been exposed to measles.

"I wish it could be possible for you to be at home when they are sick," she wrote. "You must remember them, for they all remember you."[42]

AMID THIS TURMOIL, PARLEY and Thankful returned to Kirtland for the birth of their baby. As Heber had prophesied, Thankful delivered a baby boy, whom they named after Parley. But she suffered severely during the labor, and she died a few hours later. Unable to care for his newborn son alone, Parley placed him in the arms of a woman who could nurse the infant and returned to Canada. There he began planning a mission to England with the help of Saints like Joseph Fielding, who had been writing about the restored gospel to friends and relatives across the ocean.[43]

After he finished his mission to Canada, Parley returned to Ohio and married a young widow in Kirtland named Mary Ann Frost. He also received a letter from Thomas Marsh, the president of the Quorum of the Twelve, urging him to postpone the mission to England until the apostles could meet as a quorum that summer in Kirtland.[44]

While Parley waited for the other apostles to assemble, Joseph and Sidney returned to Kirtland and tried to resolve their debts and ease tensions among the Saints.[45]

A few days later, Sidney visited Parley and told him he had come to collect an overdue debt. Sometime earlier, Joseph had loaned Parley $2,000 to purchase some land in Kirtland. To relieve his own debts, Joseph had since sold Parley's debt to the Safety Society, and Sidney was now collecting the money.

Parley told Sidney he did not have the $2,000 but offered to return the land as payment. Sidney told him he would have to give up his house as well as the land to satisfy the debt.[46]

Parley was outraged. When Joseph first sold him the land, he had told Parley that he would not be hurt in the deal. And what of Heber Kimball's blessing promising him countless riches and freedom from debt? Now Parley felt like Joseph and Sidney were taking away everything he had. If he lost his land and home, what would he and his family do?[47]

The next day, Parley sent an angry letter to Joseph. "I have at length become fully convinced that the whole scene of speculation in which we have been engaged is of the devil," he wrote, "which has given rise to lying, deceiving, and taking advantage of one's neighbor." Parley told Joseph he still believed in the Book of Mormon and the Doctrine and Covenants, but he was disturbed by the prophet's actions.

He demanded that Joseph repent and accept the land as payment for the debt. Otherwise, he would have to take legal action.

"I shall be under the painful necessity of preferring charges against you," he warned, "for extortion, covetousness, and taking advantage of your brother."[48]

ON MAY 28, A FEW days after Parley sent his letter to Joseph, Wilford Woodruff went to the temple for a Sunday meeting. As dissent mounted in Kirtland, Wilford remained one of Joseph's staunchest allies. But Warren

Parrish, who had worked side by side with Joseph for years, had begun criticizing the prophet for his role in the financial crisis and was quickly becoming a leader of the dissenters.

Wilford prayed that the contentious spirit in the church would dissipate.[49] But he would not be in Kirtland much longer to help. Lately, he had felt impressed to take the gospel to the Fox Islands, off the coast of the northeastern state of Maine, near the home of Phebe's parents. He hoped that on the way there, he would have the chance to teach his own parents and younger sister the gospel. Phebe would join him to meet his family and take him farther north to meet hers.[50]

As eager as he was to be with family, Wilford could not help worrying about Joseph and the state of the church in Kirtland. Taking a seat in the temple, he saw Joseph at the pulpit. In the face of so much opposition, the prophet appeared cast down. He had lost thousands of dollars in the collapse of the Safety Society, far more than anyone else.[51] And, unlike many others, he had not abandoned the institution when it began to fail.

Gazing out across the congregation, Joseph defended himself against his critics, speaking in the name of the Lord.

As Wilford listened, he could see that the power and Spirit of God rested over Joseph. He also felt it descend on Sidney and others as they took the stand and testified of Joseph's integrity.[52] But before the meeting closed, Warren stood up and denounced Joseph in front of the congregation.

Wilford's heart sank as he listened to the tirade. "Oh, Warren, Warren," he grieved.[53]

CHAPTER 24

Truth Shall Prevail

Late in the spring of 1837, apostles Thomas Marsh, David Patten, and William Smith left their homes in Missouri and set out for Kirtland. Many of the Saints in Zion were now settled along a stream called Shoal Creek, about fifty miles northeast of Independence. There they had founded a town called Far West, using Joseph's plan for the city of Zion as their guide to lay out the settlement. Hoping to find a peaceful solution to the Saints' ongoing problems with their neighbors, the Missouri legislature had organized Caldwell County, which encompassed the land around Far West and Shoal Creek, for the settlement of the Saints.[1]

Thomas was anxious to reunite with the rest of the Twelve, especially when he learned of Parley's desire to take the gospel to England. Preaching the gospel overseas was an important step in the Lord's work, and as president of the quorum, Thomas wanted to assemble the apostles and plan the mission together.

He also worried about reports he had received of the dissent in Kirtland. Three of the dissenters—Luke and Lyman Johnson and John Boynton—were members of his quorum. Unless the Twelve could become more united, Thomas feared that the mission to England would not prosper.[2]

BACK IN OHIO, HEBER Kimball could see just how divided the Quorum of the Twelve had become since the Kirtland Safety Society had opened six months earlier. As Joseph's efforts to pull the church out of debt failed, Orson Hyde, William McLellin, and Orson Pratt also began to grow angry with him. With Parley Pratt now speaking out against Joseph, Brigham Young and Heber were the only loyal apostles left in Kirtland.[3]

One day, as Heber sat with the prophet in the pulpits of the temple, Joseph leaned over to him and said, "Brother Heber, the Spirit of the Lord has whispered to me, 'Let my servant Heber go to England and proclaim my gospel, and open the door of salvation to that nation.'"

Heber was stunned. He was a simple potter with little education. England was the most powerful nation in the world, and its people were famous for their learning and religious devotion. "O Lord," he prayed, "I am a man of stammering tongue and altogether unfit for such a work. How can I go to preach in that land?"[4]

And what about his family? Heber could hardly bear the thought of leaving Vilate and their children to preach overseas. He was sure other apostles were more qualified to lead the mission. Thomas Marsh was the senior apostle and had been among the first to read the Book of Mormon and join the church. Why would the Lord not send him?

Or what about Brigham? Heber asked Joseph if Brigham could at least go with him to England. Brigham had more seniority in the quorum because he was older than Heber.

No, Joseph said. He wanted Brigham to stay in Kirtland.[5]

Reluctantly, Heber accepted the call and prepared to leave. He prayed at the temple daily, asking for the Lord's protection and power. Soon word of his call spread through Kirtland, and Brigham and others eagerly supported his decision to go. "Do as the prophet has told you," they told Heber, "and be blessed with power to do a glorious work."

John Boynton was less encouraging. "If you are such a damned fool as to go at the call of the fallen prophet," he scoffed, "I will not make an effort to help you." Lyman Johnson was also opposed, but after seeing Heber's determination to go, he removed his cloak and placed it on Heber's shoulders.[6]

Soon Joseph Fielding came to Kirtland with a group of Canadian Saints, and he and several others were assigned to the mission, fulfilling Heber's prophecy that Parley's mission to Canada would lay a foundation for a mission to England. Orson Hyde repented of his disaffection and also joined the mission. Finally, Heber invited Brigham's cousin Willard Richards to go with them.[7]

On the day of his departure, Heber knelt with Vilate and their children. He prayed that God would grant him a safe voyage across the ocean, make him useful in the mission field, and provide for his family while he was away. Then, with tears rolling down his cheeks, he blessed each of his children and left for the British Isles.[8]

THE NATIONAL ECONOMIC CRISIS continued into the summer of 1837. With no money and little food, Jonathan Crosby quit work on his house to join a crew building a house for Joseph and Emma. But Joseph could only pay the workmen with Safety Society banknotes, which fewer and fewer businesses in Kirtland were accepting as payment. Soon the notes would be almost worthless.

Little by little, men on the crew left to seek better-paying work. But the financial panic had left few jobs in and around Kirtland—or anywhere else in the nation. As a result, the cost of goods rose and land values fell sharply. Few people in Kirtland had means to support themselves or workers. To pay church debts, Joseph had to mortgage the temple, putting it at risk of foreclosure.[9]

While Jonathan worked on the prophet's house, his wife, Caroline, often lay in bed, recovering from a severe cold. An infection in her breast kept her from nursing her son, and as their food supply dwindled, she worried about where the family would get their next meal. They had a small vegetable garden that provided some food, but no cow, forcing them to buy milk from neighbors to feed their son.

Caroline knew many of their friends were in the same situation. Occasionally, someone would share food with them, but with so many Saints struggling to make ends meet, it seemed no one had enough to share.

As time passed, Caroline watched Parley Pratt, the Boyntons, and other close friends blame the church for their hardships. She and Jonathan had not lost money to the Safety Society, but they had not been immune to the crisis either. Like many others, they were barely getting by, yet neither she nor Jonathan felt like leaving the church or forsaking the prophet.

Jonathan, in fact, worked on the Smiths' house until he was the only one left on the crew. When he and Caroline ran out of food, he took a day off work to find provisions for his family, but he came home empty-handed.[10]

"Now what shall we do?" Caroline asked.

Jonathan knew that despite Joseph and Emma's own financial struggles, they sometimes had food to give to those who had less than they did. "In the morning," he said, "I will go and tell Sister Emma how it is with us."

The next day, Jonathan returned to work on the Smith house, but before he had a chance to speak with Emma, she came to him. "I don't know how you are off for provisions," she said, "but you have stopped and worked while the others are all gone." In her hands she held a large ham. "I thought I would make you a present."[11]

Surprised, Jonathan thanked her and mentioned his empty pantry and Caroline's illness. When Emma heard this, she told Jonathan to get a sack and take away as much flour as he could carry.

Jonathan brought the food home later that day, and as Caroline ate her first real meal in days, she thought that nothing had ever tasted so good.[12]

BY THE END OF June, dissenters in Kirtland had become more aggressive. Led by Warren Parrish, they disrupted Sunday meetings in the temple and accused Joseph of all manner of sins. If any of the Saints tried to defend the prophet, the dissenters shouted them down and threatened their lives.[13]

Mary Fielding, who had moved to Kirtland with her brother before he left for England, was dismayed by the turmoil in Ohio. At a meeting in the temple one morning, Parley Pratt called Joseph to repentance and declared that nearly all the church had departed from God.

Parley's words pained Mary.[14] The same voice that had taught her the gospel was now denouncing the prophet of God and condemning the church. Parley's angry letter to Joseph had circulated all over Kirtland, and Parley himself made no secret of his grievances. When John Taylor was in town, Parley had taken him aside and warned him not to follow Joseph.

"Before you left Canada, you bore a strong testimony to Joseph Smith being a prophet of God," John had reminded him, "and you said you knew these things by revelation and the gift of the Holy Ghost."

John had then testified, "I now have the same testimony that you then rejoiced in. If the work was true six months ago, it is true today. If Joseph Smith was then a prophet, he is now a prophet."[15]

Joseph, meanwhile, became sick and could not leave his bed. Intense pain racked his body, and he grew too weak to lift his head. Emma and his doctor remained at his side as he slipped in and out of consciousness. Sidney said he did not believe Joseph would live much longer.[16]

Joseph's critics reveled in his suffering, saying God was punishing him for his sins. Many of the prophet's friends, however, went to the temple and prayed all night that he would be healed.[17]

In time, Joseph began to recover, and Mary visited him with Vilate Kimball. He said the Lord had comforted him during his sickness. Mary was glad to see he was doing better and invited him to visit the Saints living in Canada when he was well again.

The following Sunday, Mary attended another meeting in the temple. Joseph was still too weak to attend, so Warren Parrish strode up to the pulpits and sat down in the prophet's seat. Hyrum, who led the meeting, did not respond to the provocation, but he preached a long sermon about the state of the church. Mary admired Hyrum's humility as he reminded the Saints of their covenants.

"My heart is soft," Hyrum told the congregation, "and I now feel as a little child." His voice full of emotion, he promised the Saints that the church would begin to rise from that very hour.

Mary wrote her sister Mercy a few days later. "I truly feel encouraged to hope that we shall ere long have order and peace restored to the church," she said. "Let us all unite to pray for this with all our hearts."[18]

A MONTH LATER, MARY'S brother Joseph Fielding stepped off a stagecoach onto the streets of Preston. The town was an industrial center of western England, nestled in the heart of green pastureland. Tall chimneys from the town's many factories and mills belched clouds of gray smoke into the air, obscuring its many church steeples behind a sooty haze. The River Ribble cut through the center of town, winding its way to the sea.[19]

The missionaries to England had landed at the port of Liverpool just two days earlier. Following a prompting from the Spirit, Heber had directed the men to go to

Preston, where Joseph Fielding's brother James was a preacher.[20] Joseph and his sisters had been corresponding with James, telling him about their conversion and testifying of the restored gospel of Jesus Christ. James had seemed interested in what they wrote and told his congregation about Joseph Smith and the Latter-day Saints.

The missionaries arrived in Preston on the day of an election, and as they walked along the streets, workers unfurled a campaign banner outside a window just over their heads. Its message, written in gold letters, was not meant for the missionaries, but it encouraged them all the same: TRUTH SHALL PREVAIL.

"Amen!" they cheered. "Thanks be to God, truth will prevail!"[21]

Joseph Fielding set out immediately to find his brother. Since leaving Kirtland, he had been praying that the Lord would prepare James to receive the gospel. Like Joseph, James cherished the New Testament and sought to live by its precepts. If he accepted the restored gospel, he could be a great help to the missionaries and the work of the Lord.

When Joseph and the missionaries found James at his home, he invited them to preach from his pulpit at Vauxhall Chapel the next morning. Joseph believed his brother's interest in their message was the Lord's doing, but he also understood all his brother could lose by opening his doors to them.

Preaching was James's livelihood. If he accepted the restored gospel, he would find himself without a job.[22]

ON THE ROAD FROM Far West to Kirtland, Thomas Marsh, David Patten, and William Smith were surprised to meet Parley Pratt headed the other direction. Trying to recover his losses, Parley had sold some land, cashed out his shares in the Safety Society, and struck out for Missouri alone.[23]

Still determined to reunite the Quorum of the Twelve, Thomas urged Parley to come back to Kirtland with them. Parley was not eager to go back to a place where he had suffered so much heartache and disappointment.[24] Yet Thomas pressed him to reconsider, confident he could be reconciled with the prophet.

Parley thought it over. When he had written his letter to Joseph, he had told himself that the letter was for the prophet's own good. But Parley knew he was fooling himself. He had not called Joseph to repentance in a spirit of meekness. Rather, he had lashed out at him, seeking retribution.

Parley also realized that his feeling of betrayal had blinded him to Joseph's own hardships. Speaking out against the prophet and accusing him of selfishness and greed had been wrong.[25]

Ashamed, Parley decided to return to Kirtland with Thomas and the other apostles. Once they arrived, he went to the prophet's house. Joseph was still recovering from his illness, but he was getting stronger. Parley wept when he saw him and apologized for everything he had said and done to hurt him. Joseph forgave him, prayed for him, and blessed him.[26]

Thomas, meanwhile, tried to reunify the other members of the Twelve. He succeeded in reconciling Orson Pratt and Joseph, but William McLellin had moved away and the Johnson brothers and John Boynton could not be placated.[27]

Thomas himself began to grumble when he learned that Joseph had sent Heber Kimball and Orson Hyde to England without consulting him. As president of the Twelve, was it not his responsibility to direct missionary work and lead the mission to England? Had he not come to Kirtland to rally the Twelve and send them overseas?[28]

He prayed for Heber and Orson and the work they were doing abroad, but his resentment and damaged pride were hard to stifle.[29]

On July 23, Thomas discussed the matter with Joseph. As they met, they resolved their differences and Joseph received a revelation addressed to Thomas.[30] "Thou art the man whom I have chosen to hold the keys of my kingdom, as pertaining to the Twelve, abroad among all nations," the Lord assured him. He forgave his sins and urged him to be of good cheer.

But the Lord affirmed that the Twelve acted under the authority of Joseph and his counselors in the First Presidency, even in matters related to missionary work. "Whithersoever they shall send you, go ye," the Lord said, "and I will be with you." He told Thomas that following the First Presidency's direction would lead to greater success in the mission field.[31]

"In whatsoever place ye shall proclaim my name," He promised, "an effectual door shall be opened unto you."

The Lord also helped Thomas know how to repair his fractured quorum. "Be thou humble," He said, "and the Lord thy God shall lead thee by the hand, and give thee answer to thy prayers."

He urged Thomas and the Twelve to lay aside their differences with Joseph and focus on their mission. "See to it that ye trouble not yourselves concerning the affairs of my church in this place," He continued, "but purify your hearts before me; and then go ye into the world, and preach my gospel unto every creature."

"Behold," the Lord said, "how great is your calling."[32]

CHAPTER 25

Move On to
the West

When Jennetta Richards made a short trip to Preston, England, in August 1837, her friends Ann and Thomas Walmesley had much to say about a group of missionaries from America.

Ann had been sick for years, slowly wasting away until she was little more than skin and bones. When Heber Kimball preached to her, he promised that she would be healed if she had faith, repented, and entered the waters of baptism. Ann was baptized into the new church soon after, along with eight others, and her health began to improve steadily.

Many of the people who were baptized had belonged to the congregation of James Fielding. Although Reverend Fielding had allowed the missionaries to preach in his church, he refused baptism himself and had come to resent the loss of his parishioners.[1]

Jennetta was intrigued by the message of the American missionaries. She lived in a small rural village called Walkerfold, fifteen miles from Preston's smokestacks and crowded streets. Her own father was a Christian minister in the village, so she had grown up with the word of God in her home.

Now, only weeks away from her twentieth birthday, she was curious to learn more of God's truth. When she visited the Walmesleys, she met Heber and was struck by what he said about angels, an ancient record written on gold plates, and a living prophet who received revelations from God, like prophets of old.

Heber invited Jennetta to hear him preach that evening. She went and listened and wanted to hear more. The following day, she heard him preach again and knew his words were true.

The next morning, Jennetta asked Heber to baptize her. He and Orson Hyde followed her to the banks of the River Ribble, and Heber immersed her in the water. They then confirmed her at the river's edge.

Jennetta wanted to stay in Preston with the other Saints after her baptism, but she needed to return to her parents in Walkerfold. She was eager to share her new faith with them, yet she was unsure how her father would respond to her decision to join with the Saints.

"The Lord will soften the heart of thy father," Heber told her. "I will yet have the privilege of preaching in his chapel."

Hoping he was right, Jennetta asked Heber to pray for her.[2]

JOSEPH TRAVELED THAT SAME summer to Canada to visit the Saints in Toronto. In his absence, Joseph Sr. spoke at a Sunday meeting in the Kirtland temple about the floundering Safety Society. He defended his son's character and condemned the actions of the dissenters, who were sitting at the other end of the room.

As the patriarch addressed the Saints, Warren Parrish stood and demanded to speak. Joseph Sr. told him not to interrupt, but Warren bounded across the room and forced his way onto the stand. He seized Joseph Sr. and tried to pull him away from the pulpit. The patriarch cried out for Oliver Cowdery, who served as the local justice of the peace, but Oliver did nothing to help his old friend.

Seeing his father in danger, William Smith sprang to his feet, threw his arms around Warren, and dragged him off the stand. John Boynton lunged forward, unsheathing a sword. He pointed the blade at William's chest and threatened to run his fellow apostle through if he took another step. Other dissenters drew knives and pistols from their pockets and surrounded William.

The temple erupted in chaos. People scrambled for doorways or escaped out nearby windows. Constables burst into the room, pushed through the fleeing crowd, and grappled with the armed men.[3]

When Joseph returned to Kirtland a few weeks later and learned what had happened, he convened an emergency conference of the Saints and called for a sustaining vote of each leader in the church.[4] The Saints sustained him and the First Presidency but rejected John Boynton, Luke Johnson, and Lyman Johnson as members of the Quorum of the Twelve.[5]

The vote of confidence was assuring, though Joseph knew Kirtland's problems were far from over. As the only stake in the church, Kirtland was supposed to provide a gathering place for the Saints. But the town was struggling economically and spiritually—and the dissenters were turning vulnerable church members against him. For many people, Kirtland had ceased to be a place of peace and spiritual strength.

Recently, through a vision, the Lord had urged Joseph to create new stakes of Zion and enlarge the borders of the church. Joseph and Sidney now believed it was time to go to Missouri, inspect the new settlement at Far West, and establish other stakes as gathering places for the Saints.[6]

Joseph needed to visit Missouri for other reasons as well. He worried that the apostasy in Kirtland had carried over to church leaders in Zion. When they founded Far West, John Whitmer and William Phelps had not counseled with the bishopric or high council, as directed by revelation. They had also bought land with donated money in their own names and sold it for personal profit.

Although both men had admitted their error, Joseph and other church leaders suspected that they were still being dishonest in their management of land in Missouri.[7]

Joseph also worried about the influence of members of his own First Presidency who were preparing to move to Far West. Frederick Williams had clashed with him over the management of the Kirtland Safety Society, and it had hurt their friendship.[8] Oliver, meanwhile, had become uncomfortable with Joseph taking a more active role in local economics and politics. Both he and David Whitmer, the president of the church in Missouri, felt that Joseph was exerting too much influence over temporal matters in his role as prophet.[9]

While these men were not in league with Warren Parrish or the other dissenters, their loyalty to Joseph had waned over the last eight months, and he worried about them causing problems in Zion.

Before leaving Kirtland, Joseph asked his brother Hyrum and Thomas Marsh to go to Far West ahead of him to warn the faithful Saints about the growing rift between him and these men.[10] Hyrum accepted the mission, though it meant leaving his wife, Jerusha, when she was just weeks away from delivering their sixth child.[11]

OLIVER'S FALLING OUT WITH the prophet went beyond disagreements over how to lead the church. Since

learning about plural marriage during his inspired translation of the Bible, Joseph had known that God sometimes commanded His people to practice the principle.
Joseph had not acted on this knowledge immediately,
but a few years later an angel of the Lord had commanded him to marry an additional wife.[12]

After receiving the commandment, Joseph struggled to overcome his natural aversion to the idea. He
could foresee trials coming from plural marriage, and
he wanted to turn from it. But the angel urged him to
proceed, instructing him to share the revelation only with
people whose integrity was unwavering. The angel also
charged Joseph to keep it private until the Lord saw fit to
make the practice public through His chosen servants.[13]

During the years Joseph lived in Kirtland, a young
woman named Fanny Alger worked in the Smith home.
Joseph knew her family well and trusted them. Her
parents were faithful Saints who had joined the church
in its first year. Her uncle, Levi Hancock, had marched
in the Camp of Israel.[14]

Following the Lord's command, Joseph proposed
marriage to Fanny with the help of Levi and the approval
of her parents.[15] Fanny accepted Joseph's teachings and
his proposal, and her uncle performed the ceremony.[16]

Since the time had not come to teach plural marriage in the church, Joseph and Fanny kept their marriage
private, as the angel had instructed.[17] But rumors spread
among some people in Kirtland.[18] By the fall of 1836,
Fanny had moved away.[19]

Oliver was deeply critical of Joseph's relationship with Fanny, although how much he knew about it is unclear.[20] What Emma knew about the marriage is also uncertain. In time, Fanny married another man and lived apart from the main body of the Saints. Later in life, she received a letter from her brother asking about her plural marriage to Joseph.

"That is all a matter of our own," Fanny wrote back, "and I have nothing to communicate."[21]

IN THE FALL OF 1837, as Joseph and Sidney left for Far West, Wilford Woodruff was living as a missionary among fishermen and whalers on the Fox Islands in the northern Atlantic Ocean.[22] He and his companion, Jonathan Hale, had arrived on one of the weather-beaten islands in the final weeks of August. Neither of them knew much about the place, which was covered in shaggy evergreen trees, but they wanted to help fulfill Isaiah's prophecy that the Lord's people would gather from the islands of the sea.[23]

Before the two men left Kirtland, some of the dissenters had tried to discourage Jonathan from going to the Fox Islands, predicting that he would not baptize anyone there. He did not want to prove them right.[24]

Wilford and Jonathan had already been working together for several months. After leaving Kirtland, they had tried to share the gospel with Wilford's family in the state of Connecticut, but only his uncle, aunt, and cousin were baptized.[25] Phebe Woodruff had joined them soon after, and they had journeyed up the coast to her parents' home in Maine, where she was now staying while they continued their mission.[26]

One of Wilford and Jonathan's first contacts on the islands was a minister named Gideon Newton. Wilford and Jonathan shared a meal with his family and gave him a Book of Mormon. Afterward, the missionaries went to his church and Wilford preached from the New Testament.[27]

Over the next few days, Wilford and Jonathan preached daily, often in schoolhouses. They found the people on the islands to be intelligent, hardworking, and kind. Gideon and his family attended most of their meetings. The minister studied the Book of Mormon and felt the Spirit testify of its truth. But he did not know if he could accept it—especially if it meant giving up his congregation.[28]

One morning, after more than a week on the islands, Wilford preached a sermon to a large congregation at Gideon's church. The sermon's warm reception worried the minister, who confronted the missionaries later that day. He told them that he had read quite enough of the Book of Mormon and could not accept it. He planned to use what influence he had on the islands to put a stop to their preaching.

Gideon went to the church to preach his own sermon, leaving Wilford and Jonathan in doubt about their future success on the island. But when Gideon arrived at his church, he found it empty. No one had come to hear him preach.[29]

That night, Wilford and Jonathan stayed in the home of a sea captain named Justus Eames and his wife, Betsy. The Eameses took interest in the missionaries' message, and after one Sunday meeting, Wilford invited them to be baptized. To his joy, they accepted.[30]

Turning to Jonathan, Wilford recalled how the Kirtland dissenters had predicted their failure on the islands. "Go and baptize him," Wilford said, pointing to Justus, "and prove those men false prophets."[31]

GOING ABOUT HIS WORK in Far West, Hyrum waited for his brother's arrival, hoping every day that Joseph would bring word from Jerusha. Hyrum and Thomas had found Far West thriving. The Saints had surveyed wide streets and spacious city blocks for houses and gardens. Children laughed and played in the streets, dodging the horses, wagons, and carts that rumbled past them. The town had houses and cabins, a hotel, and several shops and stores, including a bishop's storehouse. At the center of town was a site for a temple.[32]

Joseph and Sidney rode into Far West in early November, but they had no news for Hyrum. When they left Kirtland a few weeks earlier, Jerusha had not yet given birth.[33]

Joseph quickly convened a conference in Far West to discuss ways to expand the settlement for future growth. He and Sidney could see that the area had room for the Saints to gather and grow without crowding neighbors and risking more violence. At the conference, Joseph announced their plans for expansion and postponed further work on the new temple until the Lord revealed His will concerning the building.

The prophet also called for a vote of the Saints in Far West to sustain church leaders. This time, Frederick Williams was removed from his office in the First Presidency, and Sidney Rigdon nominated Hyrum to fill the vacancy. The Saints approved the nomination.[34]

A few days later, Hyrum received the long-awaited news in a letter from Kirtland. But it was written by his brother Samuel, not Jerusha. "Dear Brother Hyrum," it began, "this evening I sit down to write to you to perform a duty, knowing that every reasonable man wants to know exactly the state of his family."

Hyrum's eyes moved back and forth across the page. Jerusha had delivered a healthy baby girl, but the labor had left her weak. The Smith family tried to nurse her back to health, but she had passed away after a few days.[35]

HYRUM AND JOSEPH IMMEDIATELY began preparing to return to Kirtland. Before departing, Joseph met privately with Thomas and Oliver.[36] They talked about Oliver's objections to Joseph's marriage to Fanny Alger, but their differences remained unresolved.[37] Finally, Joseph extended his hand to Oliver and said he wanted to drop any disagreement that had come between them. Oliver shook his hand, and they parted ways.[38]

Joseph, Sidney, and Hyrum arrived back in Kirtland a few weeks later. In the homes of relatives, Hyrum found his five children still mourning the sudden loss of their mother, who lay buried in a cemetery beside the temple. With his new responsibilities in the First Presidency, Hyrum had no idea how he would care for them on his own.[39]

Joseph encouraged his brother to marry again and recommended Mary Fielding.[40] She was kind, well educated, and committed to the church. She would be an excellent companion for Hyrum and a caring mother for his children.

Hyrum proposed to Mary a short time later. At thirty-six, she had received more than one marriage proposal in her life, but she had always declined them. Once, her mother had warned her never to marry a widower with children. If she agreed to marry Hyrum, she would instantly become a mother of six.

Mary considered the proposal and accepted. She already admired the Smith family, thought of Joseph as a brother, and respected Hyrum for his humility.[41] They were married the day before Christmas.[42]

MANY SAINTS WERE RELIEVED to have Joseph back in Kirtland, but any hope that he could restore harmony to the church soon evaporated. Warren Parrish, Luke Johnson, and John Boynton were meeting weekly with Grandison Newell and other enemies of the church to denounce the First Presidency. Former stalwarts like Martin Harris soon joined them, and by the end of the year, the leading dissenters had organized a church of their own.[43]

A short time later, Vilate Kimball wrote her husband in England about the state of the church in Ohio. Knowing Heber's love for Luke Johnson and John Boynton, who had been his fellow quorum members, Vilate hesitated to tell him the terrible news.[44]

"I have no doubt but it will pain your heart," she wrote Heber. "They profess to believe the Book of Mormon and Doctrine and Covenants but in works deny them."[45]

At the end of the letter, Marinda Hyde added a note to her husband, Orson. Marinda's older brother was Luke Johnson, and the apostasy was just as heartbreaking for her. "Such times in Kirtland you never witnessed as we now have," she wrote, "for it seems that all confidence in each other is gone." She had to watch and pray to know for herself the right course to take through the perilous times.

"If ever I wanted to see you in my life," she told Orson, "it is now."[46]

Nothing seemed to temper the dissenters' feelings. They claimed that Joseph and Sidney had mismanaged the Kirtland Safety Society and cheated the Saints.

Warren believed that a prophet should be more godly than other people, and he used the Safety Society's demise to show how Joseph fell short of this standard.[47]

After months of trying to reconcile with the leading dissenters, the Kirtland high council excommunicated them. The dissenters then seized the temple for their own church meetings and threatened to drive anyone who was still loyal to Joseph out of Kirtland.

Vilate believed the dissenters were wrong to turn away from the Saints, yet she felt sorrow for them rather than anger. "After all that I have said about this dissenting party," she wrote Heber, "there are some of them that I love, and I have great feeling and pity for them."[48] She knew the collapse of the Safety Society had tried them spiritually and temporally. She too thought that Joseph had made mistakes while managing the institution, but she had not lost faith in the prophet.

"I have every reason to believe that Joseph has humbled himself before the Lord and repented," she told Heber. And she trusted that the church would weather the storm.

"The Lord says, he that cannot endure chastisement but denies me cannot be sanctified," she wrote. That might mean facing hostility in Kirtland alone while she and the children waited for Heber to return from his mission. Or if things got worse, it could mean abandoning their home and moving to Missouri.

"If we shall have to flee," she told Heber, "I shall."[49]

THE KIRTLAND DISSENTERS GREW more bitter and aggressive as the new year dawned. Threats of mob violence hung over the church, and debt and false legal charges hounded the prophet. Soon a local sheriff, armed with an arrest warrant, began searching for him. If caught, Joseph could face a costly trial and possibly imprisonment.[50]

On January 12, 1838, the prophet sought the Lord's help and received a revelation. "Let the presidency of my church take their families," the Lord instructed, "and move on to the west as fast as the way is made plain."

The Lord urged Joseph's friends and their families to gather to Missouri as well. "Be at peace among yourselves, O ye inhabitants of Zion," He declared, "or there shall be no safety for you."[51]

The Smiths and Rigdons planned their escape immediately. The two men would slip out of Kirtland that night, and their families would follow a short time later in wagons.

That night, well after darkness had fallen over Kirtland, Joseph and Sidney climbed onto their horses and rode out of town.[52] They traveled south until morning, covering nearly sixty miles. When their horses were spent, the men stopped to wait for their wives and children.

Neither Joseph nor Sidney expected to see Kirtland again. When their families arrived, the men joined them in their wagons and set out for Far West.[53]

CHAPTER 26

A Holy and Consecrated Land

The winter of 1838 was long and cold. As the families of Joseph and Sidney pushed west, Oliver Cowdery trudged through northern Missouri, battling rain and snow to scout locations for new stakes of Zion. The land was some of the choicest he had ever seen, and he surveyed dozens of spots where the Saints could go to establish towns and mills. Yet he had little to eat in the sparsely settled wilderness, and nothing but the damp earth to sleep on at night.

When he returned to Far West three weeks later, he was physically exhausted.[1] As his health recovered, he learned that Thomas Marsh, David Patten, and the high council were investigating him and the presidency of the Missouri church—David Whitmer, John Whitmer, and William Phelps—for wrongdoing.[2]

The charges centered on their handling of land in the area. Some time ago, John and William had sold church property in Far West and kept the profits for themselves, and the matter had never been resolved. Oliver, John, and William, moreover, had recently sold some of their land in Jackson County. Although they had a legal right to sell the Jackson County land, which was their personal property, it had been consecrated to the Lord, and a revelation had forbidden them to sell it. Not only had the three men broken a sacred covenant, they had showed a lack of faith in Zion.

Oliver appeared before the Missouri high council and insisted that since he and the others had paid for the Jackson County land with their own money, they could sell it as they pleased. Privately, he also questioned the motives of some on the council. He mistrusted men like Thomas Marsh and others who seemed to covet position and authority. Oliver suspected that they had somehow turned Joseph against him, further straining his already troubled friendship with the prophet.[3]

"My soul is sick of such scrambling for power," he confided to his brother. "I came to this country to enjoy peace. If I cannot, I shall go where I can."

Because Oliver was in the First Presidency, he was outside the jurisdiction of the high council and retained his calling. David, John, and William, however, were removed from their positions.[4]

Four days later, Oliver met with the three men and several others who were eager to break away from the church. Many of them sympathized with Warren Parrish and his new church in Kirtland. Like Warren, they were determined to oppose the prophet.[5]

Day by day, as the Saints awaited Joseph's return to Far West, Oliver's disdain for church leaders grew. He doubted they would understand why he acted as he did. "With the unreasonable and ignorant," he scoffed, "we do not expect to be applauded or approved."[6]

He still had faith in the Book of Mormon and the restoration of the gospel, and he could not forget or deny the sacred experiences he had shared with the prophet. They had been brothers and the best of friends, fellow servants of Jesus Christ.

But now those days were a distant memory.[7]

AFTER JENNETTA RICHARDS RETURNED to her home in Walkerfold, England, her parents, John and Ellin Richards, learned with interest about Heber Kimball and her baptism. Taking out a pen and paper, her father composed a short letter to the missionary, inviting him to preach at his chapel.

"You are expected to be here next Sunday," he wrote. "Although we be strangers to one another, yet I hope we are not strangers to our blessed Redeemer."

Heber arrived the following Saturday, and the reverend greeted him warmly. "I understand you are the minister lately from America," he said. "God bless you." He ushered Heber into his home and offered him something to eat.

The family visited with Heber late into the night.[8] As Jennetta watched the men get acquainted, their differences were apparent. Her father was seventy-two years old and had preached from the pulpit in Walkerfold for more than forty years. He was a small man who wore a brown wig and read Greek and Latin.[9] Heber, on the other hand, was tall and broad and had a bald head. He was not yet forty and had little education or social polish.

And yet they became fast friends. The next morning, the two men walked to the Walkerfold chapel together. Knowing an American missionary would be preaching, more people than usual had come to the meeting, and the tiny chapel was filled to overflowing. After the reverend opened the meeting with singing and prayer, he invited Heber to preach.

Heber took the stand and spoke to the congregation in the language of a common man. He talked about the importance of faith in Jesus Christ and sincere repentance. He said a person needed to be baptized by immersion and receive the gift of the Holy Ghost by someone who had proper authority from God.

Like the converts in Canada a year earlier, the people in Walkerfold responded readily to the message, which fit with their understanding of the Bible. That afternoon, more people came to the chapel to hear Heber preach again. When he finished, the congregation was in tears and Jennetta's father invited him to preach the next day.

Soon Jennetta was not the only believer in Walkerfold. After Heber's Monday sermon, the people in the congregation begged him to preach again on Wednesday. By the end of the week, he had baptized six members of the congregation—and the people of Walkerfold were pleading to hear more.[10]

ON MARCH 14, 1838, JOSEPH, Emma, and their three children arrived in Far West after nearly two months on the road. Eager to welcome the prophet to Zion, the Saints greeted the family with a joyful reception. Their friendly words and kind embraces were a happy change from the dissent and hostility Joseph had left in Kirtland. The Saints that crowded around him had a spirit of unity, and love abounded among them.[11]

Joseph wanted to make a fresh start in Missouri. Saints from Kirtland and from branches of the church in the eastern United States and Canada would soon arrive. To accommodate them, the church needed to establish stakes of Zion where they could gather in peace and have the chance to prosper.

Oliver had already scouted the area for new gathering places, and his report was promising. But Joseph knew he had to address the growing dissent in Far West before the Saints could begin any new settlements. It grieved him to see friends like Oliver falling away from the church, but he could not allow discord to flourish in Missouri as it had in Kirtland.

Joseph credited the leadership of Thomas Marsh and the high council for the relative peace in Far West.

Since removing William Phelps and John Whitmer from office, the high council had excommunicated both men, and Joseph approved their decision. Now he believed it was time to address Oliver's apostasy.[12]

On April 12, Edward Partridge convened a bishop's council to review Oliver's standing in the church. His defiance was well known. He had stopped attending his church meetings, ignored the counsel of other church leaders, and written insulting letters to Thomas and the high council. He was also charged with selling his lands in Jackson County contrary to revelation, falsely accusing Joseph of adultery, and forsaking the cause of God.[13]

Oliver chose not to attend the hearing, but he sent a letter for Bishop Partridge to read in his defense. In the letter, Oliver did not deny selling his Jackson County land or opposing church leaders. Rather, he once more insisted that he had a legal right to sell the lands, regardless of any revelation, covenant, or commandment. He also resigned his membership in the church.[14]

For the rest of the day, the council reviewed evidence and heard several Saints testify of Oliver's actions. Joseph stood, spoke of his former trust in Oliver, and explained his relationship with Fanny Alger in response to Oliver's accusations.[15]

After hearing more testimonies, the council discussed Oliver's case. Like him, they cherished the principles of individual agency and liberty. Yet for nearly a decade, the Lord had also urged the Saints to be united, setting aside individual desires to consecrate what they had to building the kingdom of God.

Oliver had turned away from these principles and relied instead on his own judgment, treating the church, its leaders, and the commandments of the Lord with contempt. After reviewing the charges one more time, Bishop Partridge and his council made the painful decision to remove Oliver from the church.[16]

IN ENGLAND'S RIVER RIBBLE Valley, spring weather brought an end to winter's bitter cold.[17] Traveling through green pastureland near a town close to Walkerfold, Willard Richards plucked a tiny white flower from the hedges that lined the road.[18] He was on a tour of branches of the church in the area and planned to listen to Heber Kimball and Orson Hyde preach that afternoon at a meeting five miles away.

Since arriving in England eight months earlier, Willard and his companions had baptized more than a thousand people in towns and villages throughout the valley. Many of the new Saints were young, working-class laborers who were drawn to the message of hope and peace found in the gospel of Jesus Christ. Heber's plain manners put them at ease and quickly won their trust.[19]

Better educated than Heber and trained in herbal medicine, Willard lacked the plainspoken appeal of his fellow missionary, who sometimes had to remind Willard to keep his message simple and focus on the first principles of the gospel. But Willard had established a strong branch of the church south of Preston, near the city of Manchester, despite opposition. Many people he baptized worked long hours in factories where the air was bad and they were paid a pittance. When they heard the restored gospel, they felt the Spirit and found joy in its promise that the day of the Lord's coming was near.[20]

Arriving at the home of a church member, Willard entered the kitchen and hung up the white flower just before two young women entered the room. One of them, he discovered, was Jennetta Richards.

He had heard about Jennetta. Although they shared the same last name, they were not related. After she had joined the church, Heber had written Willard about her. "I baptized your wife today," he noted.

Willard was thirty three years old, far older than most unmarried men in the church. He did not know what—if anything—Heber had told Jennetta about him.

Since the young women were headed to the same meeting he was, Willard walked with them, giving them plenty of time to talk.

"Richards is a good name," Willard said as they walked. "I never want to change it." Then he added boldly, "Do you, Jennetta?"

"No, I do not," she replied. "And I think I never will."[21]

Willard saw more of Jennetta after that. Both were in Preston a few weeks later when Heber and Orson announced that they were returning to the United States.

As they prepared to depart, the apostles held an all-day conference in a large building where the Preston Saints often met.[22] In between preaching and singing hymns, the missionaries confirmed forty people, blessed more than a hundred children, and ordained several men to the priesthood.

Before saying goodbye to the Saints, Heber and Orson set Joseph Fielding apart as the new president of the mission and called Willard and a young factory clerk named William Clayton to be his counselors. They then shook hands with the new presidency as a token of oneness between the Saints in England and America.[23]

THAT SPRING, A REVELATION came to the prophet in Far West. "Arise and shine forth," the Lord told the Saints, "that thy light may be a standard for the nations." He proclaimed the name of the church to be The Church of Jesus Christ of Latter-day Saints and affirmed that Far West was a holy and consecrated land.

"It is my will that the city of Far West should be built up speedily by the gathering of my saints," He declared, "and also that other places should be appointed for stakes in the regions round about." He commanded the Saints to build a temple in Far West, appointing July 4, 1838, as the day to lay its foundation.[24]

Not long after, Joseph and several men traveled to Daviess County, just north of Caldwell County, to visit a settlement of church members at a place called Spring

Hill. Joseph hoped the area would be a suitable gathering place for Saints coming to Missouri.[25]

Although Caldwell County had been created specifically for the Latter-day Saints, the government had already surveyed most of its land, making it too expensive for poorer Saints to purchase. In Daviess County, however, vast tracts of unsettled land had not yet been surveyed. Church members could settle there for free, and by the time the government surveyed the area, they would have already worked the land and acquired enough money to buy it.[26]

There was some risk in moving Saints to the neighboring county, however. Believing the Saints had promised to settle only in Caldwell County, some Daviess County men had warned the Saints in the area to stay away, but since no laws restricted the Saints from settling there, the protests soon ended.[27]

As he traveled north, Joseph marveled at the beauty of the country around him. From what he could see, Daviess County offered unbounded freedom and provided everything the Saints needed to establish new settlements.

Although the prairie had few trees, it seemed to have plenty of wild game. Joseph saw wild turkeys, hens, deer, and elk. Creeks and rivers kept the land lush and fertile. The Grand River, the largest in the county, was wide and deep enough to allow a steamboat to pass through, which could make travel and commerce easier for gathering Saints.

Pushing on, Joseph and his companions rode their horses along the banks of the river for ten miles until they arrived at Spring Hill. The small settlement was situated at the base of a bluff overlooking a spacious green valley. Lyman Wight, the leader of the outpost, earned a small living operating a ferry across the Grand River.[28]

The men climbed the bluff and set up camp, then rode back down to the ferry. Joseph said he wanted to claim the area for the Saints and build a city near the river. The Lord revealed to him that this was the valley of Adam-ondi-Ahman, where Adam, the first man, had blessed his children before he died.[29] In this valley, Joseph explained, Adam would come to visit his people when the Savior returned to earth, as foretold by the prophet Daniel.[30]

The settlement was everything Joseph had hoped it would be. On June 28, 1838, in a grove near Lyman's home, he organized a new stake of Zion on the sacred ground—and bid the Saints to gather.[31]

CHAPTER 27

We Proclaim
Ourselves Free

In the middle of June 1838, Wilford Woodruff stood on his parents' doorstep, once more determined to share the restored gospel of Jesus Christ with them. After starting a branch in the Fox Islands, he had returned to the mainland to visit Phebe, who would soon give birth to their first child. He then spent time preaching in Boston, New York, and other cities along the coast. His parents' house was his last stop before returning north.[1]

Wilford wanted nothing more than to see his family embrace the truth. His father, Aphek, had spent a lifetime seeking truth to no avail. His sister Eunice also longed for more light in her life.[2] But as Wilford talked with them about the church over several days, he sensed that something was keeping them from accepting its teachings.

"These are days of great suspense," Wilford noted.[3] His time at home was running out. If he stayed with his parents much longer, he would miss the baby being born.

Wilford prayed harder for his family, but they became even less eager to accept baptism. "The devil fell upon the whole household with great wrath and temptations," he confided in his journal.[4]

On July 1, he preached one more time to his family, declaring the words of Christ as fervently as he could. At last his words reached their hearts, and their concerns faded away. They felt the Spirit of God and knew that Wilford had spoken the truth. They were ready to act.

Wilford led his family immediately to a canal near their house. At the water's edge, they sang a hymn and Wilford said a prayer. He then waded into the water and baptized his father, his stepmother, and his sister, along with an aunt, a cousin, and a family friend.

When he raised the last person from the water, Wilford climbed out of the canal, rejoicing. "Forget this not," he told himself. "Regard it as the mercy of thy God."

With their hair and clothes dripping, the family returned to the house. Wilford placed his hands on their heads, one by one, and confirmed them members of the church.[5]

Two days later, he said goodbye to his parents and hurried back to Maine, hoping he would arrive in time to welcome his first child into the world.[6]

THAT SPRING AND SUMMER, Saints gathered to Missouri in droves. John Page, a missionary who had experienced enormous success in Canada, set out for Zion at the head of a large company of converts from the Toronto area.[7] In Kirtland, the Quorum of the Seventy labored to prepare poor families to travel to Missouri together. By sharing resources and assisting each other along the way, they hoped to arrive safely in the promised land.[8]

The Saints in Far West held a parade on July 4 to celebrate the nation's independence day and to lay the cornerstones of the new temple. Leading the parade were Joseph Smith Sr. and a small military unit. Behind them came the First Presidency and other church leaders, including the temple architect. A unit of cavalry proudly brought up the rear.[9]

As he marched with the Saints, Sidney Rigdon could see their unity. Over the last few weeks, though, the church had disciplined more dissenters. Shortly after Oliver Cowdery's hearing, the high council had excommunicated David Whitmer and Lyman Johnson.[10] Not long after that, the bishop's council had rebuked William McLellin for losing confidence in the First Presidency and indulging in lustful desires.[11]

William had since left the church and moved away from Far West, but Oliver, David, and other dissenters had remained in the area. In June, Sidney had condemned these men publicly. Echoing language from the Sermon on the Mount, he compared them to salt that had lost its savor, good for nothing but to be cast out and trodden underfoot. Afterward, Joseph expressed his support for the rebuke, although he urged the Saints to obey the law as they dealt with dissent.[12]

Sidney's sermon had emboldened some Saints who had banded together a week earlier to defend the church against dissenters.[13] These men went by several names, but they were best known as the Danites, after the tribe of Dan in the Old Testament. Joseph did not organize the group, yet he likely sanctioned some of their actions.[14]

In their eagerness to defend the church, the Danites vowed to protect the Saints' rights against what they saw as threats from inside and outside the church. Many of them had seen how dissent had unraveled the community in Kirtland, placed Joseph and others at risk of mob attacks, and endangered the ideals of Zion. Together they pledged to protect the community at Far West against any similar threat.

Around the time of Sidney's public condemnation of the dissenters, the Danites had warned Oliver, David, and others to leave Caldwell County or face dire consequences. Within days, the men fled the area for good.[15]

As the Fourth of July parade arrived at the town square, the Saints raised the American flag to the top of a tall pole and circled around the excavated temple site. From the edges of the groundwork, they watched the workers carefully set the cornerstones in place. Sidney then climbed a nearby stand to address the congregation.[16]

Following the American tradition of giving fiery, emotional speeches on Independence Day, Sidney spoke forcefully to the Saints about freedom, the persecution they had endured, and the important role of temples in their spiritual education. At the end of the speech, he warned the enemies of the church to leave the Saints alone.

"Our rights shall no more be trampled on with impunity," he asserted. "The man or the set of men who attempts it does it at the expense of their lives."

The Saints would not be the aggressors, he assured his audience, but they would defend their rights. "That mob that comes on us to disturb us," he cried out, "it shall be between us and them a war of extermination, for we will follow them till the last drop of their blood is spilled, or else they will have to exterminate us."

No more would the Saints abandon their homes or crops. No more would they bear their persecution meekly. "We this day then proclaim ourselves free," Sidney declared, "with a purpose and a determination that never can be broken! *No, never!!*"[17]

"Hosanna!" the Saints cheered. "Hosanna!"[18]

AS THE SAINTS RALLIED in Far West, a missionary named Elijah Able was preaching in eastern Canada, hundreds of miles away. One night he had a troubling dream. He saw Eunice Franklin, a woman he had baptized in New York, racked with doubts about the Book of Mormon and Joseph Smith. Her uncertainty robbed her of sleep. She could not eat. She felt deceived.[19]

Elijah set out for New York immediately. He had met Eunice and her husband, Charles, that spring while preaching in their town.[20] The sermon Elijah had preached to them was rough and uneven. As a black man born in poverty, he had found few opportunities for schooling.

But like other missionaries, he had been ordained to the Melchizedek Priesthood, participated in ordinances in the Kirtland temple, and received the endowment of power.[21] What he lacked in education he made up for in faith and in the power of the Spirit.

His sermon had thrilled Eunice, but Charles stood up afterward and tried to argue with him. Elijah approached Charles, placed his hand on his shoulder, and said, "Tomorrow I will come and see you and have a little chat."

The next day Elijah had visited the Franklin house and taught them about Joseph Smith, but Charles remained unconvinced.

"Is it a sign that you require for to make you believe?" Elijah had asked.

"Yes," said Charles.

"You shall have what you asked," Elijah told him, "but it will make your heart ache."

When Elijah had returned a short time later, he learned that Charles had suffered many sorrows before he finally prayed for forgiveness. By then, both he and Eunice were ready to join the church, and Elijah baptized them.[22]

Eunice had been certain of her faith at the time. What had happened to her since?

ONE SUNDAY MORNING A short time later, Eunice was surprised to find Elijah standing at her doorstep. She had been storing up things to say when she saw him again. She wanted to tell him that the Book of Mormon was a work of fiction and Joseph Smith was a false prophet. But when she saw Elijah at her door, she instead invited him inside.

"Sister," Elijah said after some conversation, "you have not been tempted as long as the Savior was after He was baptized. He was tempted one way and you in another." He told Eunice and Charles that he was preaching that afternoon at a nearby schoolhouse. He asked them to tell their neighbors, then said goodbye.

Eunice did not want to go to the meeting, but that afternoon she turned to her husband and said, "I will go and see the coming out of it."

When she sat down in the schoolhouse, Eunice was once again moved by Elijah's words. He preached on a verse from the New Testament. "Beloved," it read, "think it not strange concerning the fiery trial which is to try you."[23] Elijah's voice and the message of the restored gospel opened Eunice's heart to the Spirit. The certainty she had once felt flooded back. She knew Joseph Smith was a prophet of God and the Book of Mormon was true.

Elijah promised Eunice he would return in two weeks. But after he left, Eunice saw handbills in town falsely claiming that Elijah had murdered a woman and five children. The notices offered a reward for his capture.

"Now what do you think of your Mormon elder?" some of her neighbors asked. They swore Elijah would be arrested before he had another chance to preach in their town.

Eunice did not believe Elijah had murdered anyone. "He will come and fill his appointment," she said, "and God will protect him."[24]

She suspected opponents of the church had fabricated the story. It was not uncommon for white people to spread lies about black people, even in places where slavery was illegal. Strict laws and customs restricted interactions between blacks and whites, and sometimes people found cruel ways to enforce them.[25]

As promised, Elijah returned after two weeks to preach another sermon. The schoolhouse was crowded. Everyone, it seemed, wanted to see him be arrested—or worse.

Elijah took a seat. After a few moments, he stood and said, "My friends, I am advertised for murdering a woman and five children, and a great reward is offered for my person. Now here I am."

Eunice looked around the room. No one stirred.

"If anyone has anything to do with me, now is your time," Elijah continued. "But after I commence my services, don't you dare to lay your hands on me."

Elijah paused, waiting for a response. The congregation watched him in startled silence. Another moment passed, then he sang a hymn, said a prayer, and delivered a powerful sermon.

Before he left town, Elijah spoke with Eunice and Charles. "Sell out and go further west," he advised them. Prejudice against the Saints was increasing in the area, and there was a branch of the church forty miles away. The Lord did not want His people to live their religion alone.

Eunice and Charles took his advice and soon gathered to the branch.[26]

BACK IN MISSOURI, JOSEPH was optimistic about the future of the church. He had Sidney's Fourth of July speech published as a pamphlet. He wanted everyone in Missouri to know that the Saints would no longer be intimidated by mobs and dissenters.[27]

Yet old problems nagged at him. Much of the church's debt was still unpaid, and many Saints had been left destitute by ongoing persecution, the national economic problems, the financial collapse in Kirtland, and the costly move to Missouri. Furthermore, the Lord had forbidden the First Presidency to borrow more money.[28] The church needed funds but still had no reliable system for collecting them.[29]

Recently, the bishops of the church, Edward Partridge and Newel Whitney, had proposed tithing as a way to obey the law of consecration. Joseph knew the Saints should consecrate their property, but he was unsure how much of it the Lord required as a tithe.[30]

Joseph also worried about the Quorum of the Twelve. Two days earlier, a letter from Heber Kimball and Orson Hyde reached Far West, reporting that both apostles had arrived safely in Kirtland after their mission to England. Heber had been reunited with Vilate and their children, and they were now preparing to move to Missouri.[31] Six other apostles—Thomas Marsh, David Patten, Brigham Young, Parley and Orson Pratt, and William Smith—were in Missouri or on missions, still firm in their faith. But the remaining four apostles had left the church, leaving vacancies in the quorum.[32]

On July 8, Joseph and other church leaders prayed about these problems and received a flood of revelation. The Lord appointed a Saint named Oliver Granger to represent the First Presidency in paying off the church's debts. The properties the Saints had given up in Kirtland were to be sold and applied toward the debt.[33]

The Lord then answered Joseph's questions about tithing. "I require all their surplus property to be put into the hands of the bishop of my church in Zion," He declared, "for the building of mine house, and for the laying of the foundation of Zion." After offering what they could spare, the Lord continued, the Saints were to pay a tenth of their increase from year to year.

"If my people observe not this law, to keep it holy," the Lord declared, "it shall not be a land of Zion unto you."[34]

Concerning the Twelve, the Lord commanded Thomas Marsh to remain in Far West to help with church publishing and called the other apostles to preach. "If they will do this in all lowliness of heart, in meekness and humility, and long-suffering," the Lord promised, "I will provide for their families; and an effectual door shall be opened for them, from henceforth."

The Lord wanted the Twelve to go abroad in the coming year. He directed the quorum to assemble at the temple site in Far West on April 26, 1839, a little less than a year away, and embark from there on another mission to England.[35]

Finally, the Lord named four men to fill the vacancies in the quorum. Two of the new apostles, John Taylor and John Page, were in Canada. One of the others, Willard Richards, was serving in the mission presidency in England. The fourth, Wilford Woodruff, was in Maine, only days away from becoming a father.[36]

PHEBE WOODRUFF GAVE BIRTH to a daughter, Sarah Emma, on July 14. Wilford was overjoyed that the baby was healthy and that his wife had made it through the delivery.[37] As she recovered, Wilford passed the time doing work for Sarah, Phebe's widowed sister. "I spent the day mowing grass," he reported in his journal. "It being rather new business, I felt weary at night."[38]

Several days later, a message from Joseph Ball, a missionary laboring in the Fox Islands, reported that dissenters in Kirtland had sent letters to Wilford's converts there, trying to sway their faith. Most of the Saints in the Fox Islands had ignored the letters, but a few had left the church—including some Wilford wanted to bring to Missouri later that year.[39]

Two weeks after the birth of Sarah Emma, Wilford hurried to the Fox Islands to strengthen the Saints and help them prepare for the journey to Zion. "O my God, prosper my way," Wilford prayed as he left Phebe's side. "Bless my wife and the babe which Thou has given us while I am absent."[40]

When he arrived on the islands a little more than a week later, a letter was waiting for him from Thomas Marsh in Missouri. "The Lord has commanded that the Twelve assemble in this place as soon as possible," it read. "Know then, Brother Woodruff, by this that you are appointed to fill the place of one of the Twelve Apostles." The Lord expected Wilford to come to Far West as soon as possible to prepare for a mission to England.

Wilford was not entirely surprised by the news. A few weeks before, he had received an impression that he would be called as an apostle, but he had told no one. Still, that night he lay awake, a thousand thoughts tumbling through his mind.[41]

CHAPTER 28

Tried Long Enough

August 6, 1838, was Election Day in Missouri. That morning, John Butler rode to the town of Gallatin, the seat of Daviess County government, to vote.[1]

John had been a Latter-day Saint for a few years. He and his wife, Caroline, had moved to a small settlement near Adam-ondi-Ahman that summer. He was a captain in the local militia and a Danite.[2]

Founded just a year earlier, Gallatin was little more than a cluster of houses and saloons. When John arrived at the town square, he found it teeming with men from around the county. A polling place had been set up in a small house on the edge of the square.[3] As men filed in to cast their votes, campaigners mingled with the crowd outside.[4]

John joined a small group of Saints standing apart from the main group. Attitudes in Daviess County had never favored the Saints. After Joseph had established a stake in Adam-ondi-Ahman, the settlement blossomed and more than two hundred houses had been built. The Saints could now influence the county vote, and that angered many other settlers. To avoid problems, John and his friends planned to vote together and return home quickly.[5]

As John approached the polling place, William Peniston, a candidate for state representative, climbed on top of a whiskey barrel to make a speech. William had tried to court the Saints' vote earlier that year, but when he learned that most of them favored the other candidate, he lashed out against them.

"The Mormon leaders are a set of horse thieves, liars, and counterfeiters," William bellowed to the men gathered nearby. John grew uneasy. It would not take much for William to turn the crowd against him and his friends. Most of the men were already angry with them, and many had been drinking whiskey since the polls opened.

William warned the voters that the Saints would steal their property and overwhelm their vote.[6] They did not belong in the county, he said, and had no right to take part in the election. "I headed a mob to drive you out of Clay County," he boasted, turning to John and the other Saints, "and would not prevent you from being mobbed now."[7]

More whiskey passed through the crowd. John heard some men curse the Saints. He started to back away. He was over six feet tall and powerfully built, but he had come to Gallatin to vote, not fight.[8]

Suddenly, a man in the crowd tried to punch one of the Latter-day Saints. Another Saint leapt to his defense, but the crowd knocked him back. A third Saint grabbed a piece of lumber from a nearby woodpile and clubbed the attacker across the head. The man fell close to John's feet. Men on both sides grabbed clubs and pulled out knives and whips.[9]

The Saints were outnumbered four to one, but John was determined to protect his fellow Saints and their leaders. Spotting a pile of fence rails, he grabbed a thick piece of oak and rushed to the fight. "Oh yes, you Danites," he cried out, "here is a job for us!"

He clubbed the men attacking the Saints, measuring each swing to knock his opponents down, not kill them. His friends fought back as well, improvising weapons from sticks and rocks. They knocked down anyone who rushed at them, ending the fight after two minutes.[10]

Catching his breath, John looked out across the town square. Wounded men lay motionless on the ground. Others were slinking away. William Peniston had jumped off his whiskey barrel and fled up a nearby hill.

A man from the crowd approached John and said the Saints could vote now. "Put down your stick," he said. "There's no use for it."[11]

John gripped the fence rail tighter. He wanted to cast his vote, but he knew he would be trapped if he went into the small house and tried to vote unarmed. Instead, he turned around and started to walk away.

"We must take you prisoner," another man called out. He said some of the men John had struck would probably die.

"I am a law-abiding man," John said, "but I do not intend to be tried by a mob." He mounted his horse and left town.[12]

THE NEXT DAY, JOHN rode to Far West and told Joseph about the fight. Reports of deaths at Gallatin were spreading rapidly through northern Missouri, and mobs were preparing to attack the Saints. Fearing John would be a target for retaliation, Joseph asked him if he had moved his family out of Daviess County yet.

"No," said John.

"Then go and move them directly," Joseph told him, "and do not sleep another night there."

"But I don't like to be a coward," John replied.

"Go and do as I tell you," Joseph said.[13]

John left immediately for home, and Joseph soon rode out with a group of armed volunteers to defend the Saints in Daviess County. When they arrived in Adam-ondi-Ahman, they learned that no one on either side of the fight at Gallatin had died. Relieved, Joseph and his company stayed the night with Lyman Wight.

The next morning, Lyman and an armed band of
Saints rode out to the home of Adam Black, the local justice of the peace. Rumors claimed that Adam was rallying
a mob to come after the Saints. Lyman wanted him to sign
a statement saying that he would guarantee fair treatment
of the Saints in Daviess County, but Adam refused.

Later that day, Joseph and more than a hundred
Saints returned to Adam's cabin. Sampson Avard, a
leader of the Danites in Far West, took three of his men
into the house and tried to force the justice of the peace
to sign the statement. Adam again refused, demanding
to see Joseph. At that point the prophet joined the negotiations and settled the matter peacefully, agreeing
to let the justice write up and sign his own statement.[14]

But the peace did not last long. Soon after the
meeting, Adam demanded that Joseph and Lyman be
arrested for surrounding his cabin with an armed force
and intimidating him. Joseph avoided arrest by asking
to be tried in his home county of Caldwell rather than
Daviess, where so many of the citizens were outraged
at the Saints.[15]

People throughout northern Missouri, meanwhile,
called meetings to discuss the reports from Gallatin
and the rising numbers of Saints settling among them.
Small mobs vandalized church members' homes and
barns in Daviess County and targeted Latter-day Saint
settlements nearby.[16]

To calm tensions, Joseph returned to Daviess
County in early September to answer the charges against

him. During the hearing, Adam admitted that Joseph had not forced him to sign the statement. Even so, the judge ordered the prophet to return in two months for a trial.[17]

The Saints had some allies in the Missouri government, and soon the state militia was mustered to disperse vigilante groups. But people in and around Daviess County were still set on driving the Saints from their borders.

"The persecutors of the Saints," Joseph wrote to a friend, "are not asleep in Missouri."[18]

ON THE LAST DAY of August, Phebe and Wilford Woodruff rode along a white sandy beach not far from her parents' house in Maine. It was low tide. Waves rolled in from the Atlantic Ocean and crashed on the shoreline. In the distance, not far from the horizon, ships passed silently by, their heavy canvas sails billowing in the breeze. A flock of birds circled overhead and alighted on the water.

Halting her horse, Phebe dismounted and collected seashells that lay scattered in the sand. She wanted to take them with her as a keepsake when she and Wilford moved west to Zion. Phebe had lived near the ocean for most of her life, and shells were part of the landscape of home.[19]

Since his call to the Quorum of the Twelve, Wilford had been anxious to get to Missouri. His recent visit to the Fox Islands had lasted only long enough to urge the small group of Saints to go with him and Phebe to

Zion. He returned to the mainland disappointed. Some members of the branch had agreed to go with them. Others—including Justus and Betsy Eames, the first people baptized on the islands—were staying behind.

"They will all see their folly when it is too late," Wilford said.[20]

But Phebe was not especially eager to go, either. She had loved living with her parents again. Their home was comfortable, warm, and familiar. If she stayed in Maine, she would never be far from family and friends.[21] Missouri, on the other hand, was fifteen hundred miles away. If she left, she might not see her family again. Was she ready to make that sacrifice?

Phebe confided her feelings to Wilford. He was sympathetic to her anxiety about leaving family, but he did not share her attachment to home. He knew, as she did, that Zion was a place of safety and protection.

"I would go to the land of Zion or wherever God sent me," he noted in his journal, "if I had to forsake as many fathers, mothers, brothers, and sisters as could stand between Maine and Missouri—and subsist upon boiled herbs on the way."[22]

Through September, Phebe and Wilford waited for the Fox Islands branch to come to the mainland and start their journey west. But as each day passed and the branch members did not appear, Wilford became impatient. It was getting late in the year. The longer they delayed their journey, the more likely they were to encounter bad weather on the road.

Other circumstances were making Phebe more hesitant to leave. Their daughter, Sarah Emma, had come down with a severe cough, and Phebe wondered if it was wise to take her on such a long journey in cold weather.[23] Then an exaggerated report of the election-day brawl in faraway Daviess County appeared in the local newspaper. The news startled everyone.

"It will not do to go," neighbors told Phebe and Wilford. "You will be killed."[24]

A few days later, about fifty Fox Islands Saints arrived, ready to journey to Zion. Phebe knew it was time to leave, that Wilford had to join the Twelve in Missouri. But she felt the strong pull of home and family. The road to Missouri would be hard, and Sarah Emma's health was still frail. And there was no guarantee that they would be safe from mobs once they arrived in their new home.

Still, Phebe believed in the gathering. She had left home to follow the Lord before, and she was willing to do it again. When she said goodbye to her parents, she felt like Ruth in the Old Testament, forsaking home and family for her faith.

As hard as it was to leave, she placed her trust in God and climbed into the wagon.[25]

IN LATE SEPTEMBER, TWENTY-ONE-YEAR-OLD Charles Hales arrived with a company of Canadian Saints in De Witt, Missouri. One of thousands answering the call to gather to Zion, he had left Toronto with his parents and siblings earlier that year. De Witt was seventy miles south-east of Far West and provided wagon trains a place to rest and resupply before pushing on to Caldwell County.[26]

But when Charles arrived, the town was under siege. About four hundred Saints lived in De Witt, and neighbors in and around the settlement were pressuring them to move out of the area, insisting they go by October 1 or face expulsion. George Hinkle, the leader of the Saints in De Witt, refused to leave. He said the Saints would stay and fight for their right to live there.[27]

Feeding tensions in De Witt were rumors that Danites were preparing to wage war against the Missourians. Many citizens had begun to mobilize against the Saints and were now camped on the outskirts of De Witt, ready to attack the town at any moment. The Saints had sent an appeal to Missouri governor Lilburn Boggs for protection.[28]

Most of the Canadian Saints pushed on to Far West, anxious to avoid conflict, but George asked Charles to stay and defend De Witt against mobs. As a farmer and musician, Charles was more accustomed to a plow or trombone than a gun. But George needed men to build up fortifications around De Witt and prepare for battle.[29]

On October 2, the day after the Saints' deadline to abandon the settlement, the mob started shooting at them. At first, the Saints did not return fire. But after two days, Charles and some two dozen Saints took positions along their fortifications and fired back, wounding one man.

The mob charged the fortifications, sending Charles and the others scrambling for cover in some log homes nearby.[30] The mob blocked roads going into De Witt, cutting the Saints off from food and other supplies.

Two nights later, on October 6, Joseph and Hyrum Smith slipped into town with Lyman Wight and a small band of armed men. They found the Saints nearly out of food and other provisions. Unless the siege ended soon, hunger and sickness would weaken the Saints before the mob had to fire another shot.[31]

Lyman was ready to defend De Witt to the end, but after Joseph saw how desperate the situation was, he wanted to broker a peaceful solution.[32] He was sure that if any Missourians were killed in the siege, mobs would descend on the town and wipe the Saints out.

Joseph sent a plea for Governor Boggs's help, enlisting a friendly Missourian to carry the appeal. The messenger returned four days later with news that the governor would not defend the Saints against attacks. Boggs insisted the conflict was between them and the mob.

"They must fight it out," he said.[33]

With enemies assembling in nearly every nearby county, and the Saints receiving no reliable support from the state militia, Joseph knew he had to end the siege. He hated to give in to the mob, but the Saints in De Witt were exhausted and desperately outnumbered. Defending the settlement further could be a fatal mistake. Reluctantly, he decided it was time to abandon De Witt and retreat to Far West.

On the morning of October 11, the Saints loaded up what little property they could carry in wagons and set out across the prairie.[34] Charles wanted to go with them, but another Canadian Saint, who was not yet ready to leave, asked him to stay behind and help him. Charles agreed, expecting that he and his friend would quickly be able to catch up with the rest of the Saints.

But after they finally slipped out of town, his friend turned back when his horse gave out. Unwilling to stay any longer in hostile territory, Charles set off alone and on foot over the unfamiliar prairie. He headed northwest, in the direction of Caldwell County, with only a vague idea of where he was going.[35]

ON OCTOBER 15, A FEW days after the De Witt Saints arrived in Far West, Joseph called together every man in town. Hundreds of Saints had retreated to Far West, fleeing mob activities across northern Missouri. Many of them now lived in wagons or tents scattered throughout the town. The weather had turned cold, and the Saints were cramped and miserable.[36]

Joseph could see the situation was spiraling out of control. He was getting reports that their enemies were gathering from all directions. When mobs had attacked them in Jackson and Clay counties, the Saints had tried to bear it meekly, retreating from conflicts and relying on lawyers and judges to restore their rights. But where had it gotten them? He was tired of the abuse, and he wanted to take a bolder stand against their enemies. The Saints were out of options.

"We have tried long enough," Joseph cried out to the men around him. "Who is so big a fool as to cry, 'The law! The law!' when it is always administered against us and never in our favor?"

Years of stolen land and unpunished crimes against the Saints had left him with little trust in politicians and lawyers, and the governor's unwillingness to help the Saints only reinforced that view. "We will take our affairs into our own hands and manage for ourselves," Joseph said. "We have applied to the governor, and he will do nothing for us. The militia of the county we have tried, and they will do nothing."

He believed the state itself was no better than a mob. "We have yielded to the mob in De Witt," he said, "and now they are preparing to strike a blow in Daviess." He refused to let anything else be taken from the Saints.[37]

They would defend themselves, the prophet declared, or die in the attempt.[38]

CHAPTER 29

God and Liberty

After the fall of De Witt, the men who laid siege to the town headed north to Adam-ondi-Ahman. In neighboring counties, other mobs began forming to attack Far West and the settlements along Shoal Creek, vowing to drive the Saints from Daviess to Caldwell County, and from Caldwell to hell.[1] General Alexander Doniphan, an officer in the state militia who had provided legal help to the church in the past, strongly encouraged the Caldwell County militia, an official unit of the state militia composed mainly of Latter-day Saints, to defend their communities against enemy forces.

Knowing the Saints in Daviess County were in grave danger, Joseph and Sidney ordered the Caldwell County militia and other armed men to Adam-ondi-Ahman.

Mounting horses, Joseph and Hyrum rode north with the group.[2]

On October 16, 1838, as the troops set up camp outside Adam-ondi-Ahman, a heavy snowfall blanketed the county. Downriver, Agnes Smith was settling in for the night. Agnes was married to Joseph's youngest brother, Don Carlos, who was away. Aside from her two small daughters, she was alone in the house.

Sometime before midnight, a group of men broke into her house and surrounded her. Terrified, Agnes gathered up her daughters as the mob drove them out into the snow at gunpoint.

Without coats or blankets to keep them warm, Agnes and the girls huddled together as the men set fire to the house. The blaze spread quickly, throwing heavy black smoke into the night sky. Everything Agnes owned was soon engulfed in flames.

Agnes knew she had to flee. The safest place to go was Adam-ondi-Ahman, only three miles away, but it was dark, the snow was ankle-deep, and her girls were not old enough to walk far on their own. The journey would take hours, but what choice did she have? She could not stay at home.

Holding a daughter on each hip, Agnes trudged west as the mob drove more Saints into the snow and set fire to their houses. Her feet became wet and numb with cold, and her arms and back ached from carrying her children.

Soon she came to an icy stream stretching for miles in both directions. The water was deep, but not too deep to wade across. Getting wet was dangerous in weather this cold, but help was only a few miles away. Fording it was her only option if she wanted to get her daughters to safety.

Lifting the girls higher, Agnes waded into the creek until the current closed in around her and she was waist-deep in the water.[3]

SOMETIME IN THE EARLY morning of October 17, Agnes and her daughters staggered into Adam-ondi-Ahman, desperately cold and weary. Other victims of the attack arrived in similar distress. Many of them were women and children wearing little more than their nightclothes. They said the mob had chased them off their land, torched their homes, and scattered their cattle, horses, and sheep.[4]

The sight of the refugees horrified Joseph. In his Fourth of July speech, Sidney had said the Saints would not go on the offensive. But if their enemies went unchecked, what had happened to the Saints in De Witt could happen in Adam-ondi-Ahman.

Hoping to weaken the mobs and bring a rapid end to the conflict, the Saints decided to march on nearby settlements that supported and equipped their enemies. Dividing their men into four units, church and militia leaders ordered raids on Gallatin and two other settlements. The fourth unit would patrol the surrounding area on foot.[5]

The next morning, October 18, was shrouded in fog. David Patten rode out of Adam-ondi-Ahman with a hundred armed men, bound for Gallatin.[6] When they arrived in town, the men found it empty except for some stragglers who fled as the men approached.

Once the streets were clear, the men broke into the general store and filled their arms with goods and supplies the refugee Saints needed in Adam-ondi-Ahman. Several men emerged from the store with heavy crates and barrels, which they hefted onto wagons they had brought with them. When the shelves were empty, the men went into other shops and dwellings, taking quilts, bedding, coats, and clothing.

The raid lasted several hours. Once they packed away all they could carry, the men torched the store and other buildings and rode out of town.[7]

FROM THE TOP OF the hill overlooking Adam-ondi-Ahman, Saints could see a distant ribbon of smoke curling into the sky over Gallatin.[8] Thomas Marsh, who had come to the settlement with the militia, dreaded such signs of conflict, certain the raids would turn the state government against the church and cause innocent people to suffer. Thomas believed Joseph and Sidney had exaggerated the threat of mob attacks in their fiery speeches and sermons. Even when the battered refugees had poured into the settlement, he had refused to believe that the attacks on their homes were anything but isolated incidents.

Thomas rarely agreed with Joseph anymore. The previous year, when he had gone to Kirtland to prepare the apostles for the mission to England, Thomas had been disappointed to learn that the mission had started without him. The Lord counseled him to be humble and not rebel against the prophet. Yet he had continued to question the success of the British mission, and he doubted it would thrive without his leadership.

Later, after moving to Missouri, his wife, Elizabeth, had argued with another woman over an agreement they had made to exchange milk for cheese-making. After the bishop and high council heard the case and ruled against Elizabeth, Thomas had appealed the case to Joseph and the First Presidency. They too had decided against her.[9]

The incident had bruised Thomas's pride, and he struggled to hide his resentment. He grew angry, and he wanted everyone else to be angry. Twice already Joseph had asked him if he was going to fall away. "When you see me leave the church," Thomas had replied, "you will see a good fellow leave."[10]

It was not long before he saw only the worst in the prophet. He blamed Joseph for the crisis in Missouri and found fault with his response to the violence. He also knew others who felt the same way, including fellow apostle Orson Hyde, whose faith had faltered again after returning from England.[11]

Shortly after the raiding parties returned to Adam-ondi-Ahman, reports arrived that mobs were closing in on Far West. Alarmed, the Saints' forces hurried back to Caldwell County to protect the town and their families.[12]

Thomas returned with them, but not to defend the town. Instead, he packed his belongings and left Far West under the cover of night. He believed divine punishment was about to rain down on Joseph and the Saints who followed him. If the mob or the government leveled Far West, he thought, it was because God willed it to happen.[13]

Traveling south, Thomas wanted to get far away from Missouri. But before he left the state, he had a document to write.[14]

As raiding and fighting raged across northern Missouri, Charles Hales was lost. After leaving De Witt, he had roamed the prairie, unsure if the road he was on led to Far West. Weeks had passed since he had last seen his family. He had no way of knowing if they had made it to Far West, nor if they were safe from mobs.

The best he could do was keep moving, avoid any direct confrontations, and hope he found someone who could point him in the right direction.

One evening he saw a man harvesting corn in a cultivated field. It looked like the man was alone and unarmed. If he was unsympathetic or hostile to the Saints, the worst he could do was chase Charles off his property. But if he turned out to be friendly, he might offer a place to sleep and something to eat.

Approaching the farmer, Charles asked if he could shelter him for the night. The farmer did not answer the question but instead asked if Charles was a Mormon.

Knowing it could cost him a meal and a warm place to sleep, Charles said he was. The farmer then said he had nothing to offer him and told him he was a long way from Far West.

"I am a perfect stranger in the county," Charles told the farmer. He said he had lost his way and could not walk any farther. His feet were blistered and sore. It was sunset, and he had another cold night on the prairie ahead of him.

The farmer appeared to take pity on him. He told Charles that some men had stayed at his house during the siege of De Witt. They belonged to the mob and had made him swear never to let a Mormon stay with him.

But he then told Charles where he could find shelter nearby and gave him directions to Far West. It was not much, but it was all he could offer.

Charles thanked the man and set off again in the fading light.[15]

ON THE NIGHT OF October 24, Drusilla Hendricks peered fearfully out the window of her home in Caldwell County. In nearby Far West, the Saints were on the alert. Their raids in Daviess County had caused many of their allies in the Missouri militia to turn against them and blame them for the whole conflict.[16] Now, a few miles to the south of Drusilla's house, a mob had starting setting wildfires, turning the prairie black with smoke.[17]

With uncertainty in the air, Drusilla and her husband, James, prepared to abandon their house and flee to Far West. Knowing food might be scarce in the coming weeks, they picked and shredded cabbage from their garden and layered it with salt to make sauerkraut.

They worked well into the night. Around ten o'clock, Drusilla and James went into the yard to find a stone to weigh down the cabbages and keep them submerged in the brine. Walking behind James, Drusilla could see his tall form clearly in the dim moonlight. She was struck by how tall he was—and startled when the thought came to her that she might never see him stand so tall again.

Later, after the work was finished and Drusilla and James had gone to bed, their neighbor, Charles Rich, knocked at the door. The mob had attacked settlements to the south, he reported. Families of Saints had been driven from their homes, and two or three men had been beaten and taken prisoner. He and David Patten were now organizing a rescue party to take them back.

Drusilla arose and lit a fire while James fetched his horse. She then grabbed James's pistols and placed them in the pockets of his coat. When he returned, she picked up his sword and carefully fastened it to his waist. Donning his overcoat, James said goodbye and climbed on his horse. Drusilla then handed another gun up to him.

"Don't get shot in the back," she said.[18]

ALMOST AS SOON AS Charles Hales stumbled into Far
West, he was asked to join the rescue party. Although he
was exhausted and footsore, Charles borrowed a horse
and gun and set off with forty other men.[19]

They rode south, gathering men from outlying settlements until their force numbered around seventy-five.
The prisoners were being held in a camp along the
Crooked River, twelve miles from Far West. Among the
men riding with Charles was Parley Pratt, the apostle
who had baptized him in Canada.

The night was dark and solemn. The only noises
they heard were the rumble of hooves and the clank-
ing of weapons in their scabbards and holsters. In the
distance, they could see the glow of prairie fires. Now
and then a meteor flashed overhead.[20]

The men arrived at the Crooked River before dawn.
As they neared the enemy camp, they dismounted and
formed into companies. "Trust in the Lord for victory,"
David Patten said once they assembled. He ordered
them to follow him to the ford on the river.[21]

Charles and the other men marched silently up a
low hill until they could see campfires along the river.
Cresting the hill, they heard the sharp voice of a sentry:
"Who comes there?"

"Friends," said David.

"Are you armed?" asked the sentry.

"We are."

"Then lay down your arms."

"Come and get them."[22]

"Lay them down!"

In the confusion that followed, the sentry fired at the Saints, and a young man standing near Charles doubled over as the bullet struck his torso. The sentry retreated instantly, scrambling down the hill.[23]

"Fight for liberty," David shouted. "Charge, boys!"

Charles and the men raced down the hill and formed lines along a road and behind a row of trees and hazel brush. Below them, men in the camp were rushing from their tents and taking cover along the riverbank. Before the rescue party could fire a volley at the camp, they heard the enemy captain cry out, "Boys, let them have it!"[24]

Enemy fire whistled harmlessly over Charles's head, but James Hendricks, who had taken a position along the road, took a bullet to the neck and slumped to the ground.[25]

"Fire!" David Patten cried, and the morning erupted with gunshots.

As men from both sides reloaded their weapons, an eerie quiet rested on the battlefield. Charles Rich cried out, "God and liberty!" and the Saints echoed him again and again until David Patten ordered another charge.

The Saints stormed down the hill as the Missourians fired another round before retreating across the river. As he charged, David caught sight of a stray man and chased after him. The man spun around and, glimpsing David's white coat, fired point-blank at the apostle. The ball tore through his abdomen and he fell.[26]

With the Missourians scattered, the skirmish was over. A member of the camp and one of the Saints lay dead on the field. David Patten and one other Saint were dying.[27] James Hendricks was still conscious, but he could not feel anything below his neck.[28]

Charles Hales and most of the men in the party were unhurt or had only minor injuries. They searched the enemy camp and found the captured Saints. They then carried James and David up the hill to a wagon with the rest of the wounded.

By sunrise, the Saints were back on their horses, riding north to Far West.[29]

EXAGGERATED REPORTS OF THE skirmish at the Crooked River arrived at the desk of Missouri governor Lilburn Boggs soon after the fighting ended. Some reports claimed the Saints had massacred fifty Missourians in the fight. Others said the death toll was closer to sixty. With so many rumors spreading about the battle, Boggs had no way of knowing what had actually happened.

In times of frontier conflict, hastily organized militias often looked and acted like lawless vigilantes. That morning, the Saints had attacked not a mob, as they had supposed, but a company of Missouri state militia. And that was considered insurrection against the state.[30]

A longtime resident of Independence, Boggs had supported the Saints' expulsion from Jackson County and had no desire to protect their rights. Yet he had stayed neutral in the fight so far, even when both sides begged for his help.[31] As reports of Mormon aggression spread, citizens across the state wrote him, urging action against the Saints.

Among the letters and statements that crossed the governor's desk was an affidavit from a church apostle, Thomas Marsh, claiming that Joseph intended to overrun the state, the nation, and ultimately the world.

"It is believed by every true Mormon that Smith's prophecies are superior to the law of the land," Thomas warned.[32] Attached to the affidavit was a statement from Orson Hyde attesting to its truth.[33]

The documents gave Boggs everything he needed to make a case against the Saints. Soon after the confrontation at the Crooked River, he ordered several divisions of Missouri militiamen to quell the Mormon forces and bring the Saints into submission. He also issued an executive order to the general in charge of the First Division of Missouri troops.

"Information of the most appalling character," the governor wrote on October 27, 1838, "places the Mormons in the attitude of an open and armed defiance of the laws and of having made war upon the people of this state. Your orders are therefore to hasten your operations with all possible speed. The Mormons must be treated as enemies and must be exterminated or driven from the state."[34]

CHAPTER 30

Fight like Angels

The afternoon of October 30, 1838, was crisp and pleasant at Hawn's Mill, a small settlement in Caldwell County. Children played beneath a blue sky on the banks of Shoal Creek. Women washed clothes at the river and prepared meals. Some men were in the fields, gathering crops for the winter, while others worked in the mills along the river.[1]

Amanda Smith sat in a tent while her daughters, Alvira and Ortencia, played nearby. Her husband, Warren, was at the blacksmith shop with their three young sons, Willard, Sardius, and Alma.[2]

The Smiths were only passing through Hawn's Mill. They belonged to the company of poor Saints who had left Kirtland earlier that summer. One problem after another had delayed the family's journey, forcing them to separate from the others. Most of the company had already arrived in Far West, and Amanda and Warren were anxious to move on.[3]

As Amanda rested in the tent, she saw a flicker of movement outside and froze. A group of armed men, their faces blackened, were descending on the settlement.[4]

Like other Saints in the area, Amanda had worried about mob attacks. Before stopping at Hawn's Mill, her small company had been accosted by men who raided their wagons, confiscated their weapons, and placed them under guard for three days before releasing them.[5]

When her company arrived at Hawn's Mill, local leaders had assured them that the settlement was safe. David Evans, the leader of the Saints there, had made a truce with their neighbors, who said they wanted to live peacefully with the Saints. But as a precaution, he had posted guards around the settlement.

Now danger was upon the Saints at Hawn's Mill. Snatching up her little girls, Amanda ran to the woods by the millpond. She heard the crack of gunfire behind her, and a volley of bullets whistled past her and the others scrambling for the trees.[6]

Near the blacksmith shop, David waved his hat and shouted for a cease-fire. The mob ignored him and continued to advance, firing again at the fleeing Saints.[7]

Clinging to her daughters, Amanda ran down into a ravine as more bullets flew past her. When she reached the bottom, she and the girls hurried across a plank bridging the pond and started up a hill on the other side.

Mary Stedwell, a woman running next to her, raised her hands to the mob and begged for peace. The mob fired again, and a bullet ripped through her hand.

Amanda shouted for Mary to take cover behind a fallen tree. She and her daughters ran deeper into the woods and ducked behind some bushes on the other side of the hill.

Out of sight from the mob, Amanda pulled her girls close and listened as shots echoed throughout the settlement.[8]

WHEN THE SHOOTING BEGAN, Amanda's six-year-old son, Alma, and his older brother Sardius followed their father into the blacksmith shop, where the Saints had stored what few guns they owned. Inside, dozens of men were trying desperately to fend off the attackers, using the shop as a fort. Those who had guns fired at the mob through gaps in the log walls.

Terrified, Alma and Sardius crawled under the blacksmith bellows with another young boy. The mob outside surrounded the shop and closed in on the Saints. Some men rushed out the door, shouting for peace, but withering fire from the mob cut them down.[9]

Alma stayed hidden beneath the bellows as the gunfire grew louder and more intense. The mob pressed in around the shop, thrust their guns through the gaps in the walls, and fired into the men at close range. One after another, the Saints fell to the ground with bullet holes in their chests, arms, and thighs.[10] From under the bellows, Alma could hear men groaning in pain.

The mob soon stormed the entrance, firing at more men as they tried to escape. Three bullets struck the boy hiding beside Alma, and his body went limp. One man caught sight of Alma and fired at him, blasting a gaping wound in his hip.[11] Another man spotted Sardius and dragged him outside. He shoved the muzzle of his gun roughly against the ten-year-old's head and pulled the trigger, killing him instantly.[12]

One of the mob turned his head away. "It was a damned shame to kill those little boys," he said.

"Nits make lice," replied another.[13]

UNAWARE OF THE GOVERNOR'S extermination order, the Saints in Far West held out hope that Boggs would send help before mobs laid siege to their town. When they saw an approaching army of about two hundred and fifty troops in the distance on October 30, joy swept over them. Finally, they thought, the governor had sent the state militia to protect them.[14]

Commanding the force was General Alexander Doniphan, who had helped the Saints in the past. General Doniphan formed his troops into a line opposite the Saints' forces positioned just outside Far West, and the Saints hoisted a white flag of truce. The general was still waiting for written orders from the governor, but he and his troops had not come to protect Far West. They were there to subdue the Saints.[15]

Although he knew the Saints' forces outnumbered the Missouri troops, George Hinkle, the Latter-day Saint in charge of the Caldwell County regiment, grew uneasy and commanded his troops to retreat. As the men fell back, Joseph rode up through their ranks, confused by George's order.

"Retreat?" he exclaimed. "Where in the name of God shall we retreat to?" He told the men to return to the field and re-form their lines.[16]

Messengers from the Missouri militia then approached the Saints with orders to ensure the safe removal of Adam Lightner and his family from the town. Adam was not a member of the church, but he was married to twenty-year-old Mary Rollins, the young woman who had rescued pages of the Book of Commandments from a mob years before in Independence.

Adam and Mary were summoned from Far West along with Adam's sister Lydia and her husband, John Cleminson. When they learned what the soldiers wanted, Mary turned to Lydia and asked her what she thought they should do.

"We will do as you say," Lydia said.

Mary asked the messengers if the women and children in Far West could leave before the attack.

"No," they responded.

"Will you let my mother's family go out?" Mary asked.

"The governor's orders were that no one but your two families should go," she was told.[17]

"If that is the case, I refuse to go," said Mary. "Where they die, I will die, for I am a full-blooded Mormon, and I am not ashamed to own it."

"Think of your husband and child," the messengers said.

"He can go and take the child with him, if he wants to," Mary said, "but I will suffer with the rest."[18]

As the messengers were leaving, Joseph rode up to them and said, "Go tell that army to retreat in five minutes or we'll give them hell!"[19]

The militiamen rode back to their line, and soon the Missouri troops retreated to their main camp.[20] Later that day, eighteen hundred more troops arrived under the command of General Samuel Lucas, who had been a leader in driving the Saints from Jackson County five years earlier.[21]

There were no more than three hundred armed Saints in Far West, but they were determined to defend their families and homes. The prophet gathered the Saints' forces to the town square and told them to prepare for battle.[22]

"Fight like angels," Joseph said. He believed that if the Missouri militia attacked, the Lord would send the Saints two angels for every man they lacked.[23]

But the prophet did not want to go on the offensive. That night, the Saints piled up anything they could, making a barricade that stretched a mile and a half along the city's eastern, southern, and western borders. While men wedged fence rails between house logs and wagons, women gathered supplies in anticipation of an attack. Guards stood watch all night.[24]

AT HAWN'S MILL, ELEVEN-YEAR-OLD Willard Smith— Amanda Smith's oldest son—emerged from behind a large tree near the millpond and crept to the blacksmith shop. When the attack began, he had tried to stay with his father and brothers, but he had been unable to push his way into the shop and instead took cover behind a woodpile. As the mob spread out and discovered his location, he had moved from house to house, dodging bullets as he ran, until the mob left the settlement.

At the blacksmith shop, Willard found his father's lifeless body slumped over in the doorway. He saw the body of his brother Sardius, whose head had been horribly mutilated from the gunshot. Other bodies—more than a dozen—lay heaped on the floor inside the shop. Willard searched among them and found his brother Alma. The boy lay limp and motionless in the dirt, but he was still breathing. His trousers were covered in blood where he had been shot.[25]

Willard gathered Alma in his arms and carried him outside. He saw their mother coming toward them from the woods. "They have killed my little Alma!" Amanda cried when she saw them.

"No, Mother," Willard said, "but Father and Sardius are dead."

He carried his brother to their camp and carefully laid him down. The mob had ransacked the tent, sliced open the mattresses, and scattered the straw. Amanda smoothed out the straw as best she could and covered it with clothing to make a bed for Alma. She then cut off his trousers to see the damage.[26]

The wound was raw and ghastly. The hip joint was entirely gone. Amanda had no idea how to help him.

Perhaps she could send Willard for help, but where would he go? Through the thin fabric of her tent, Amanda could hear the groans of the wounded and the weeping of Saints who had lost husbands and fathers, sons and brothers. Anyone who might be able to help her was already tending to someone else or grieving. She knew she would have to rely on God.[27]

When Alma regained consciousness, Amanda asked him if he thought the Lord could make him a new hip. Alma said he did if she thought so.

Amanda gathered her three other children around Alma. "Oh, my Heavenly Father," she prayed, "Thou seest my poor wounded boy and knowest my inexperience. Oh, Heavenly Father, direct me what to do."[28]

She finished her prayer and heard a voice direct her actions. The family's fire still smoldered outside, and she quickly mixed its ashes with water to make lye. She soaked a clean cloth in the solution and gently washed Alma's wound, repeating the procedure over and over until the wound was clean.

She then sent Willard to gather roots from an elm tree. When he returned, Amanda ground the roots to a pulp and folded them into a poultice. She placed the poultice on Alma's wound and wrapped it with linen.

"Now you lie like that, and don't move," she told her son, "and the Lord will make you another hip."[29]

Once she knew he was asleep and the other children were safe in the tent, Amanda stepped outside and wept.[30]

THE NEXT MORNING, OCTOBER 31, George Hinkle and other leaders of the Saints' militia met with General Doniphan under a white flag of truce. Doniphan had still not received the governor's orders, but he knew they authorized the extermination of the Saints. Any talk of peace, he explained, would have to wait until he saw the orders. He also told George that General Lucas, the Saints' old enemy, was now in command of the militia forces.[31]

Returning to Far West, George reported what he had learned to Joseph. Around this time, messengers from Hawn's Mill arrived with news of the massacre. Seventeen people had been killed and more than a dozen wounded.[32]

Both reports sickened Joseph. The conflict with the Missourians had escalated beyond raids and minor skirmishes. If mobs and militias breached the Saints' barricade, the people in Far West could suffer the same fate as those at Hawn's Mill.[33]

"Beg like a dog for peace," Joseph urged George. The prophet said he would rather die or go to prison for twenty years than have the Saints massacred.[34]

Later that day, the governor's orders came, and George and other militia leaders arranged to meet with General Lucas on a hill near Far West. The general arrived in the afternoon and read the extermination order aloud. The Saints were shocked. Far West, they knew, was surrounded by almost three thousand Missouri militiamen, most of them hungry for a fight. All Lucas had to do was sound the order and his troops would overrun the city.

Yet the general said that he and his troops were willing to show some mercy if the Saints turned over their leaders, surrendered their arms, and agreed to sell their land and leave the state for good. He gave George one hour to agree to the terms. Otherwise, nothing would stop his troops from annihilating the Saints.[35]

George returned to Far West that evening, unsure if Joseph would commit to the terms. As commander of the Caldwell County militia, George had the authority to negotiate with the enemy. Yet Joseph wanted him to consult with the First Presidency before agreeing to any proposals from the state troops.

With time running out and the Missouri militia poised to strike the town, George told Joseph that

General Lucas wanted to speak with him and other church leaders about ending the conflict. Eager to place the Saints out of danger, Joseph agreed to talk under a flag of truce. Although he was not a member of the militia, Joseph wanted to do whatever he could to resolve the conflict.[36]

He and George left Far West shortly before sundown with Sidney Rigdon, Parley Pratt, Lyman Wight, and George Robinson. Halfway to the Missouri camp, they saw General Lucas riding out to meet them with several soldiers and a cannon. Joseph assumed they were coming to escort them safely to the Missouri camp.

The general halted his horse in front of the men and ordered his troops to surround them. George Hinkle stepped up to the general and said, "These are the prisoners I agreed to deliver up."

General Lucas drew his sword. "Gentlemen," he said, "you are my prisoners." The Missouri troops erupted into shrill war whoops and closed in on the captives.[37]

Joseph was stunned. What had George done? The prophet's confusion turned to anger, and he demanded to speak to Lucas, but the general ignored him and rode away.

The troops marched Joseph and the other men to the Missouri camp. A crowd of soldiers greeted them with vicious threats and insults. As Joseph and his friends passed through their lines, the men howled triumphantly and spat in their faces and on their clothes.

General Lucas placed Joseph and his friends under heavy guard and forced them to sleep on the cold ground. Their days as free men were over. They were now prisoners of war.[38]

CHAPTER 31

How Will This End?

Lydia Knight feared something was wrong when she heard wild whooping and yelling coming from the Missouri camp. She knew the prophet had gone there to negotiate peace. But the noise she heard sounded like a pack of wolves, hungry for prey.

Gazing anxiously out the window, Lydia saw her husband running toward the house. "Pray as you never prayed before," Newel told her. The militia had captured the prophet.

Lydia felt weak. The night before, two veterans of the skirmish at the Crooked River had knocked at her door, looking for a place to hide. The Missouri militia had sworn to punish the Saints who had taken part in the fight, so harboring the men would put her family at risk. But she could not turn them away and had hidden them in her home.

Now she had to wonder if the men were safe enough. Newel would be gone again that night on guard duty. If the militia entered the city while he was away and found the men hiding in her home, they might kill them. And what would they do to her and the children?

As he left for the night, Newel warned her to be cautious. "Do not go outside," he said. "Prowlers are around."

Once Newel was gone, Lydia began to pray. When she and Newel had come west after the temple dedication, they had made a home and now had two children. It had been a good life before the mob attacks started. She did not want everything to fall apart.

She could still hear the distant shrieks of the Missourians. The noise made her flesh crawl, but praying calmed her. She knew that God ruled the heavens. Whatever happened would not change that.[1]

THE NEXT MORNING, NOVEMBER 1, 1838, Newel returned briefly to the house. George Hinkle had ordered the Saints' forces to assemble at the town square. The Missouri militia was lined up outside their camp and in position to march on Far West.

"How will this end?" Lydia asked. "My heart is torn with anxious fears, and yet the Spirit tells me all will yet be well."

"God grant it," Newel said, picking up his rifle. "Goodbye, and God protect you."[2]

While the Saints' forces gathered in the square, General Lucas marched his troops to the prairie southeast of Far West and ordered them to stand ready to put down any resistance from the Saints. At ten o'clock that morning, George led his troops from the square and positioned them near the Missouri line. He then rode up to General Lucas, removed the sword and pistols from his belt, and handed them to the general.[3]

The Missourians brought out a writing desk and placed it in front of their line. George rode back to his men and ordered the Saints to approach the desk, one by one, and surrender their weapons to a pair of Missouri militia clerks.[4]

Surrounded and vastly outnumbered, Newel and the Saints had little choice but to comply. When his turn came to surrender his gun, Newel strode up to the desk and glared at General Lucas. "Sir, my rifle is my own private property," he said. "No one has a right to demand it from me."

"Lay down your arms," said the general, "or I will have you shot."

Furious, Newel gave up his rifle and returned to the ranks.[5]

After every Saint had been disarmed, the city stood defenseless. General Lucas marched the Saints' forces back into Far West and held them as prisoners on the town square.

He then ordered his troops to seize the city.[6]

THE MISSOURI MILITIA WASTED little time breaking into houses and tents, rummaging through chests and barrels, and searching for weapons and valuables. They carried off bedding, clothes, food, and money. Some built bonfires from house logs, fence rails, and barns. Others shot cattle, sheep, and hogs and left them to die in the streets.[7]

At the Knight house, Lydia braced herself as three militiamen approached the door. "Have you any men in the house?" one of them demanded.

"You have our men under guard," Lydia said, blocking the way to her home. If she let him inside, he would find the men she was hiding.

"Have you any arms in the house?" he asked.

"My husband took his rifle with him," Lydia said. Behind her, the children started to cry, frightened at the sight of the stranger. Drawing up her courage, Lydia turned back to the man. "Go away!" she shouted. "Do you not see how frightened my little ones are?"

"Well," the man said, "have you no men or arms in the house?"

"I tell you again," Lydia said, "my husband is a prisoner on the square, and he took his rifle with him."

The man grumbled and stormed off with the others.

Lydia went back into her house. She was trembling, but the militiamen were gone and everyone in her house was safe.[8]

AT THE TOWN SQUARE, under heavy guard with the rest of the Saints' troops, Heber Kimball heard a familiar voice call his name. Looking up, he saw William McLellin, the former apostle, coming toward him. William was dressed in a hat and shirt decorated with garish red patches.[9]

"Brother Heber," William said, "what do you think of Joseph Smith the fallen prophet now?" William had a group of soldiers with him. They had been moving from house to house, plundering the town at will.

"Look and see yourself," William went on. "Poor, your family stripped and robbed, and your brethren in the same fix. Are you satisfied with Joseph?"[10]

Heber could not deny that things looked bleak for the Saints. Joseph was a captive, and the Saints were disarmed and under assault.

But Heber knew he could not forsake Joseph and the Saints, as William, Thomas Marsh, and Orson Hyde had done. Heber had stayed loyal to Joseph through every trial they had faced together, and he was determined to remain loyal even if that meant losing everything he owned.[11]

"Where are you?" Heber asked, turning the question back on William. "What are you about?" Heber's testimony of the restored gospel of Jesus Christ and his refusal to abandon the Saints answered William's question well enough.

"I'm more satisfied with him a hundredfold than ever I was before," Heber continued. "I tell you Mormonism is true, and Joseph is a true prophet of the living God."[12]

AS THE MILITIA PILLAGED the town, General Lucas did nothing to stop his troops from terrorizing the Saints and taking their property. Across the settlement, Missouri militiamen were chasing Saints from their homes, cursing them as they fled into the streets. The troops whipped and beat those who resisted them.[13] Some soldiers assaulted and raped women they found hiding in the houses.[14] General Lucas believed the Saints were guilty of insurrection, and he wanted them to pay for their actions and feel the power of his army.[15]

Throughout the day, Lucas's officers rounded up more church leaders. With the help of George Hinkle, troops forced their way into the home of Mary and Hyrum Smith. Hyrum was sick, but the troops drove him outside at the point of a bayonet and placed him with Joseph and the other prisoners.[16]

That evening, as General Lucas prepared to try the prisoners in a military court, a militia officer named Moses Wilson took Lyman Wight aside, hoping to convince him to testify against Joseph at the trial.

"We do not wish to hurt you nor kill you," Moses told Lyman. "If you will come out and swear against him, we will spare your life and give you any office you want."

"Joseph Smith is not an enemy to mankind," Lyman said hotly. "Had it not been that I had given heed to his counsel, I would have given you hell before this time."

"You are a strange man," said Moses. "There is to be a court-martial held this night, and will you attend?"

"I will not, unless compelled by force."[17]

Moses threw Lyman back in with the other prisoners, and General Lucas soon convened the court. Several militia officers participated, including George Hinkle. General Doniphan, the only lawyer present, opposed the trial, arguing that the militia had no authority to try civilians like Joseph.

Paying no attention to him, General Lucas proceeded with the trial and rushed through the hearing without any of the prisoners present. George wanted Lucas to show mercy to the prisoners, but the general instead sentenced them to be shot for treason. A majority of the officers present sustained the ruling.[18]

After the trial, Moses told Lyman the verdict. "Your doom is fixed," he said.

Lyman looked at him contemptuously. "Shoot and be damned," he said.[19]

Later that evening, General Lucas ordered General Doniphan to march Joseph and the other prisoners into the town square at nine o'clock the following morning and execute them in front of the Saints. Doniphan was outraged.[20]

"I will be damned if I will have any of the honor of it, or the disgrace of it," he told the prisoners in private. He said he planned to withdraw with his troops before sunrise.[21]

He then sent a message to General Lucas. "It is cold-blooded murder. I will not obey your order," he stated. "If you execute those men, I will hold you responsible before an earthly tribunal, so help me God!"[22]

AS PROMISED, GENERAL DONIPHAN'S forces were gone the next morning. Rather than execute Joseph and the other prisoners, General Lucas ordered his men to escort them to his headquarters in Jackson County.[23]

Flanked by armed guards, Joseph was led through the ravaged streets of Far West to gather some belongings from his home. Emma and the children were in tears when he arrived, but they were relieved that he was still alive. Joseph begged his guards to let him visit with his family privately, but they refused.

Emma and the children clung to him, unwilling to part. The guards drew their swords and pried them away. Five-year-old Joseph held his father tightly. "Why can't you stay with us?" he sobbed.[24]

A guard thrust his sword at the boy. "Get away, you rascal, or I will run you through!"[25]

Back outside, troops marched the prisoners through a crowd of Saints and ordered them to climb inside a covered wagon. The militia then surrounded the wagon, creating a wall of armed men between the Saints and their leaders.[26]

As Joseph waited for the wagon to roll away, he heard a familiar voice above the noise of the crowd. "I am the mother of the prophet," Lucy Smith called out. "Is there not a gentleman here who will assist me through this crowd!"

The wagon's heavy canvas cover prevented the prisoners from seeing outside, but at the front of the wagon, Hyrum pushed his hand under the cover and took his mother's hand. The guards immediately ordered her back, threatening to shoot her. Hyrum felt his mother's hand slip away, and it seemed that the wagon would roll out at any moment.

Just then, Joseph, who was at the back of the wagon, heard a voice on the other side of the canvas. "Mister Smith, your mother and sister are here."

Joseph pushed his hand beneath the cover and felt his mother's hand. "Joseph," he heard her say, "I cannot bear to go till I hear your voice."

"God bless you, Mother," Joseph said, just before the cart lurched and drove away.[27]

SEVERAL NIGHTS LATER, THE prisoners lay on the floor of a log house in Richmond, Missouri. After taking them to Jackson County, General Lucas had put them on display like animals before he was ordered to send them to Richmond for a legal hearing.

Now each man tried to sleep with a shackle around his ankle and a heavy chain binding him to the other prisoners. The floor was hard and cold, and the men had no fire to keep them warm.[28]

Lying awake, Parley Pratt felt sick as their guards told obscene stories about raping and killing Saints. He wanted to stand up and rebuke the men—to say something that would make them stop talking—but he kept silent.

Suddenly, he heard chains clank beside him as Joseph rose to his feet. "Silence, ye fiends of the infernal pit!" the prophet thundered. "In the name of Jesus Christ, I rebuke you and command you to be still! I will not live another minute and hear such language!"

The startled guards gripped their weapons and looked up. Joseph stared back at them, radiating majesty. "Cease such talk," he commanded, "or you or I die *this instant!*"

The room went quiet, and the guards lowered their guns. Some of them retreated to the corners. Others crouched in fear at Joseph's feet. The prophet stood still, looking calm and dignified. The guards begged his pardon and fell silent until their replacements came.[29]

ON NOVEMBER 12, 1838, JOSEPH and more than sixty other Saints were taken to the Richmond courthouse to determine if there was enough evidence to try them on charges of treason, murder, arson, robbery, burglary, and larceny. The judge, Austin King, would decide if the prisoners would go to trial.[30]

The hearing lasted for more than two weeks. The star witness against Joseph was Sampson Avard, who had been a Danite leader.[31] During the siege of Far West, Sampson had tried to flee Missouri, but the militia had captured him and threatened to prosecute him if he refused to testify against the prisoners.[32]

Eager to save himself, Sampson claimed that everything he had done as a Danite had been done under orders from Joseph. He testified that Joseph believed it was the will of God for the Saints to fight for their rights against the governments of Missouri and the nation.

Sampson also said that Joseph believed the church was like the stone spoken of by Daniel in the Old Testament, which would fill the earth and consume its kingdoms.[33]

Alarmed, Judge King questioned Joseph about Daniel's prophecy, and Joseph testified that he believed it.

"Write that down," the judge told his clerk. "It is a strong point for treason."

Joseph's attorney objected. "Judge," he said, "you had better make the Bible treason."[34]

The prosecution called more than forty witnesses to testify against the prisoners, including several former church leaders. Afraid of being prosecuted themselves, John Corrill, William Phelps, John Whitmer, and others had struck a deal with the state of Missouri to testify against Joseph in exchange for their own freedom. Under oath, they described outrages they had witnessed during the conflict, and all of them blamed Joseph.

The Saints' defense, meanwhile, consisted of a few witnesses who did little to sway the judge's opinion. Other witnesses could have testified in Joseph's behalf, but they were harassed or scared away from the courtroom.[35]

By the time the hearing was over, five Saints, including Parley Pratt, were jailed in Richmond to await trial on murder charges related to the fight at Crooked River.

Those who remained—Joseph and Hyrum Smith, Sidney Rigdon, Lyman Wight, Caleb Baldwin, and

Alexander McRae—were transferred to a jail in a town called Liberty to await trial on charges of treason. If convicted, they could be executed.[36]

A blacksmith shackled the six men together and led them to a large wagon. The prisoners climbed in and sat on the rough wood, their heads barely above the high sides of the wagon box.

The journey took all day. When they arrived in Liberty, the wagon rolled through the center of town, past the courthouse, then north to a small, stone jail. The door stood open, waiting for the men in the cold of the December day.

One by one, the prisoners climbed down from the wagon and made their way up the steps to the entryway of the jail. A crowd of curious people pressed in around them, hoping to catch sight of the prisoners.[37]

Joseph was the last man off the wagon. As he reached the door, he looked at the crowd and raised his hat in polite greeting. He then turned and descended into the dark prison.[38]

CHAPTER 32

Though All
Hell Should Endeavor

By mid-November 1838, the Saints in Far West were suffering from hunger and exposure. The Missouri militia had destroyed homes and depleted most of the food supplies in the city. What crops remained in the fields were frozen.[1]

General John Clark, who replaced General Lucas as the head of the Missouri forces at Far West, had no more sympathy for the Saints than his predecessor did.[2] He accused them of being the aggressors and disobeying the law. "You have brought upon yourselves these difficulties," he told them, "by being disaffected and not being subject to rule."

Since winter was almost upon them, General Clark agreed to let the Saints stay in Far West until the spring. But he advised them to scatter after that. "Never again organize yourselves with bishops and presidents," he warned, "lest you excite the jealousies of the people and subject yourselves to the same calamities that have now come upon you."[3]

Conditions at Hawn's Mill were even worse. The day after the massacre, the mob ordered the Saints to leave the state or be killed. Amanda Smith and other survivors wanted to leave, but the mob had stolen horses, clothing, food, and other supplies they needed to make the long journey. Many of the wounded, like Amanda's son Alma, were in no condition to move so far.[4]

The women in the settlement held prayer meetings, asking the Lord to heal their wounded. When mob members learned about these meetings, they threatened to wipe out the settlement if the women continued. After that, the women prayed quietly, trying desperately not to draw attention to themselves as they prepared to leave.

After a while, Amanda moved her family from their tent to a cabin.[5] As she continued to grieve for her murdered husband and son, she had four small children to care for on her own. She worried about staying too long in Hawn's Mill while her son mended. But even if she and her children could leave, where would they go?

It was a question Saints were asking all over northern Missouri. They feared the militia would carry out the governor's extermination order if they did not leave by the spring. But without leaders to guide them, they had no idea how to make the journey out of Missouri—or where to gather once they did.[6]

AS THE SAINTS PREPARED to abandon Far West, Phebe Woodruff lay in a roadside inn in western Ohio, suffering from severe headaches and a fever. She and Wilford had been traveling west for two months with the Fox Islands Saints, plodding through snow and rain to reach Zion. Illness had attacked many of the children, including her daughter, Sarah Emma.[7] Two families had already dropped out of the company, convinced they could not make it to Zion that winter.[8]

Before stopping at the inn, Phebe had been in agony every time the wagon jostled over the rough road.[9] After she almost stopped breathing one day, Wilford had halted the company so she could recover.

Phebe was certain she was dying. Wilford blessed her and tried everything to relieve her suffering, but the fever grew worse. Finally she called Wilford to her side, testified of the gospel of Jesus Christ, and urged him to have faith amid his trials. The next day, her breathing stopped altogether, and she felt her spirit leave her.[10]

She watched as Wilford gazed down at her lifeless body. She saw two angels enter the room. One of them told her she had a choice to make. She could go with them to rest in the spirit world or return to life and endure the trials that lay ahead.

Phebe knew that if she stayed, the road would not be easy. Did she want to return to her careworn life and uncertain future? She saw the faces of Wilford and Sarah Emma, and her answer came swiftly.

"Yes," she said, "I will do it!"

As Phebe made her decision, Wilford's faith was renewed. He anointed her with consecrated oil, placed his hands on her head, and rebuked the power of death. When he finished, Phebe's breathing returned. She opened her eyes and watched the two angels leave the room.[11]

BACK IN MISSOURI, JOSEPH, Hyrum, and the other prisoners in the Liberty jail huddled together, trying to stay warm. The small, dank dungeon was mostly below ground, enclosed in walls of stone and timber four feet thick. Two tiny windows near the ceiling let in some light but did little to eliminate the dungeon's rancid stench. Piles of dirty straw on the stone floor served as the prisoners' beds, and when the men were desperate enough to eat the revolting meals they were given, the food sometimes made them vomit.[12]

Emma visited Joseph in early December, relaying news about the Saints in Far West.[13] As Joseph listened to stories of their suffering, his indignation toward those who had betrayed him grew. He dictated a letter to the Saints, condemning the treachery of these men and encouraging the Saints to persevere.

"Zion shall yet live, though she seemeth to be dead," he assured them. "The very God of peace shall be with you and make a way for your escape from the adversary of your souls."[14]

In February 1839, Hyrum's wife, Mary, and her sister Mercy visited the prisoners with Hyrum's newborn son, Joseph F. Smith. Mary had not seen Hyrum since before she gave birth in November. The delivery and a severe cold had left her almost too weak to travel to Liberty. But Hyrum had asked her to come, and she did not know if she would have another chance to see him.[15]

Inside the prison, the jailer opened the trapdoor and the women descended into the dungeon to stay the night with the prisoners. He then shut the door over them and secured it with a heavy lock.[16]

No one slept much that night. The sight of Joseph, Hyrum, and the other prisoners—gaunt and filthy in their cramped quarters—shocked the women.[17] Hyrum held his infant son and talked quietly with Mary. He and the other prisoners were anxious. The jailer and guards were always on alert, certain Joseph and Hyrum were plotting an escape.

The next morning, Mary and Mercy said goodbye to the prisoners and climbed out of the dungeon. As the guards showed them out, the hinges of the trapdoor squealed as it slammed shut.[18]

THAT WINTER IN FAR West, Brigham Young and Heber Kimball received a letter from Joseph. "The management of the affairs of the church devolves on you, that is, the Twelve," he stated. He instructed them to appoint the oldest of the original apostles to replace Thomas Marsh as president of the quorum.[19] David Patten had been oldest, but he had died after being shot at the Crooked River, meaning that Brigham, now thirty-seven years old, was to lead the Saints out of Missouri.

Already Brigham had enlisted the help of the Missouri high council to keep order in the church and make decisions in Joseph's absence.[20] But more needed to be done.

General Clark had given the Saints until spring to leave the state, but armed mobs were now riding through the city, promising to kill anyone who was still there by the end of February. Frightened, many Saints who had the means got away as soon as possible, leaving the poor to fend for themselves.[21]

On January 29, Brigham urged the Saints in Far West to covenant to help each other evacuate the state. "We will never desert the poor," he told them, "till they shall be out of the reach of the exterminating order."

To ensure that every Saint was taken care of, he and the other leaders in Far West appointed a committee of seven men to direct the evacuation.[22] The committee collected donations and supplies for the poor and made a careful assessment of the Saints' needs. Several men scouted trails across the state, keeping mostly to established roads and avoiding areas hostile to the Saints. The chosen routes all converged at the Mississippi River, the eastern border of the state, 160 miles away.

The exodus out of Missouri, they determined, would begin at once.[23]

IN EARLY FEBRUARY, EMMA left Far West with her four children—eight-year-old Julia, six-year-old Joseph III, two-year-old Frederick, and seven-month-old Alexander.[24] Almost everything she and Joseph owned had been stolen or left behind in Far West, so she traveled with friends who supplied a wagon and horses for the journey. She also carried with her Joseph's important papers.[25]

The family traveled across Missouri's frozen ground for more than a week. Along the way, one of their horses died. When they reached the Mississippi, they found that the bitterly cold winter had created a sheet of ice across the wide river. No ferries could operate, but the ice was just thick enough for the group to cross on foot.

With Frederick and Alexander in her arms, Emma stepped out onto the ice. Little Joseph clutched one side of her skirt while Julia clung tightly to the other. All three walked carefully across the slippery path until their feet at last found the far riverbank.[26]

Safely out of Missouri, Emma found the people in the nearby town of Quincy, Illinois, kinder than she had expected. They assisted the Saints across the icy river, donated food and clothing, and supplied shelter and employment for those in greatest need.[27]

"I still live and am yet willing to suffer more, if it is the will of kind heaven that I should, for your sake," she wrote her husband soon after her arrival. The children were also doing well, except that Frederick was ill.

"No one but God knows the reflections of my mind and the feelings of my heart," she expressed, "when I left our house and home and almost all of everything that we possessed, excepting our little children, and took my journey out of the state of Missouri, leaving you shut up in that lonesome prison."

Still, she trusted in divine justice and hoped for better days. "If God does not record our sufferings and avenge our wrongs on them that are guilty," she wrote, "I shall be sadly mistaken."[28]

As Saints fled Missouri, Alma Smith's wound still prevented his family from leaving Hawn's Mill. Amanda cared for her son, continuing to trust that the Lord would mend his hip.

"Do you think that the Lord can, Mother?" Alma asked her one day.

"Yes, my son," she said. "He has showed it all to me in a vision."[29]

In time, the mob near the settlement grew more hostile and set a deadline for the Saints to leave. When that day came, Alma's hip was still raw, and Amanda refused to go. Afraid, and longing to pray out loud, she hid in a bundle of cornstalks and asked the Lord for strength and assistance. When she finished her prayer, a voice spoke to her, repeating a familiar line from a hymn:

The soul that on Jesus hath leaned for repose,
I will not, I cannot desert to his foes;
That soul, though all hell should endeavor to shake,
I'll never, no never, no never forsake![30]

The words strengthened Amanda, and she felt as if nothing could hurt her.[31] Not long after, as she was fetching water from a stream, she heard her children screaming in the house. Terrified, she rushed to the door—and saw Alma running around the room.

"I'm well, Ma, I'm well!" he cried. Flexible cartilage had formed in place of his hip, allowing him to walk.

With Alma able to travel, Amanda packed up her family, headed to the home of the Missourian who had stolen her horse, and demanded the animal. He told her she could have it back if she paid five dollars to compensate him for feeding it.

Ignoring him, Amanda went into the yard, took her horse, and set out for Illinois with her children.[32]

WITH MORE SAINTS LEAVING Far West every day, Drusilla Hendricks worried that she and her family would be left behind. Isaac Leany, a fellow Saint who had taken four bullets at Hawn's Mill, assured her that they would not be abandoned. But Drusilla did not know how her husband could make the journey.

James was still paralyzed from his neck wound at Crooked River. When the fight was over, Drusilla had found him lying among the other wounded men at the home of a neighbor. Though overcome with grief, she had composed herself, brought James home, and tried several remedies to restore feeling to his limbs. Nothing seemed to help.

In the weeks after the surrender of Far West, she sold their land and worked to make money for the move east, earning enough to purchase some supplies and a small wagon, but not a team of animals to haul it.

Without a way to pull her wagon, Drusilla knew they would be stuck in Missouri. James had regained some movement in his shoulders and legs after receiving a priesthood blessing, but he could not walk very far. To get him safely out of the state, they needed a team.

With the deadline for evacuation approaching, Drusilla grew more anxious. She began receiving threats from the mob, warning her that they were coming to kill her husband.

One night, as Drusilla nursed her baby on the bed beside James, she heard a dog barking outside. "Mother!" cried William, her oldest son. "The mob is coming!" Moments later they heard pounding on the door.

Drusilla asked who was there. A voice from outside said it was none of her business and threatened to break down the door if she did not open it. Drusilla told one of her children to open the door, and soon the room was filled with armed men wearing false whiskers to disguise their faces.

"Get up," they ordered Drusilla.

Fearing the men would kill James if she left his side, Drusilla did not move. One man grabbed a candle from a nearby table and began searching the house. The mob said they were looking for a Danite in the area.

They rummaged under the bed and in the back of the house. Then they pulled the covers off James and tried to interrogate him, but he was too weak to say much. In the dim light, he looked fragile and pale.

The mob asked for water, and Drusilla told them where to find some. As the men drank, they loaded their pistols. "All is ready," one of them said.

Drusilla watched the men place their fingers on the triggers of their guns. They stood up, and Drusilla braced herself for gunfire. The men lingered in the room for a minute, then they stepped outside and rode away.

A short time later, a doctor took pity on James and gave Drusilla advice on how to help him. Slowly James gained strength. Their friend Isaac also found a yoke of cattle for the family.

It was all they needed to leave Missouri for good.[33]

WHEN WILFORD AND PHEBE Woodruff arrived in Illinois with the Fox Islands branch, they learned of the Saints' expulsion from Missouri. In mid-March, as more church members settled in Quincy, the Woodruffs set out for the bustling river town to reunite with the Saints and meet with church leaders.[34]

Edward Partridge, who had suffered for weeks in a Missouri jail before being released, was helping lead the church in Quincy despite his poor health. Heber and other senior leaders, meanwhile, were still directing the evacuation from Missouri.[35]

Wilford and Phebe found Emma and her children living in the home of Sarah and John Cleveland, a local judge. They also saw that the prophet's parents and siblings were now living in and around Quincy, as were Brigham and Mary Ann Young and John and Leonora Taylor.[36]

The next day, Brigham announced that the evacuation committee in Far West needed money and teams of animals to help fifty poor families leave Missouri. Although the Saints in Quincy were poor themselves, he asked them to extend the hand of charity to those who were even worse off. In response, the Saints donated fifty dollars and several teams.[37]

Wilford went to the banks of the Mississippi River the following day to visit a camp of newly arrived church members. The day was cold and rainy, and the refugees were huddled in the mud, tired and hungry.[38] As kind as the people of Quincy had been, Wilford knew the Saints would soon need a place of their own.

Fortunately, Bishop Partridge and others had been talking with a man named Isaac Galland, who wanted to sell them some swampy land along a bend in the river north of Quincy. It was hardly the land of milk and honey they envisioned for Zion, but it was readily available and could provide a new gathering place for the Saints.[39]

CHAPTER 33

O God, Where Art Thou?

The days dragged on for the prisoners in the Liberty jail. During their first months in prison, they often received visits from family and friends who brought kind words, clothing, and food. But by the end of winter, the number of letters and friendly visitors to the prison had dropped sharply as the Saints fled to Illinois, leaving the prisoners feeling even more isolated.[1]

In January 1839 they had tried to appeal their case before a county judge, but only Sidney Rigdon, who was gravely ill, was released on bail. The rest—Joseph, Hyrum, Lyman Wight, Alexander McRae, and Caleb Baldwin—returned to their dungeon to await trial in the spring.[2]

Life in prison wore Joseph down. Hecklers would peek through the barred windows to gawk or shout obscenities at him. He and the other prisoners often had nothing but a little cornbread to eat. The straw they had used for bedding since December was now matted and provided no comfort. When they lit a fire to try to warm themselves, the dungeon filled with smoke and choked them.[3]

With their day in court rapidly approaching, each man knew he stood a good chance of being convicted by a biased jury and executed. More than once they tried to break out, but their guards caught them every time.[4]

Since receiving his divine call, Joseph had pressed forward in the face of opposition, striving to obey the Lord and gather the Saints. And yet, as much as the church had flourished over the years, it seemed to now be on the verge of collapse.

Mobs had driven the Saints out of Zion in Jackson County. Internal dissent had divided the church in Kirtland and left the temple in the hands of creditors. And now, after a terrible war with their neighbors, the Saints were scattered along the eastern bank of the Mississippi River, disheartened and homeless.

If only the people of Missouri had left them alone, Joseph thought, there would have been nothing but peace and quiet in the state. The Saints were good people who loved God. They did not deserve to be dragged from their homes, beaten, and left to die.[5]

The injustice angered Joseph. In the Old Testament, the Lord often rescued His people from danger, vanquishing their enemies with the strength of His arm.

But now, when the Saints had been threatened with extermination, He had not intervened.

Why?

Why did a loving Heavenly Father allow so many innocent men, women, and children to suffer while those who drove them from their homes, stole their lands, and committed unspeakable violence against them went free and unpunished? How could He let His faithful servants wallow in a hellish prison, far from their loved ones? What purpose did it serve to abandon the Saints at the very time they needed Him the most?

"O God, where art thou?" Joseph cried out. "How long shall thy hand be stayed?"[6]

WHILE JOSEPH WRESTLED WITH the Lord, the apostles in Quincy had an important—and potentially life-threatening—decision to make. The previous year, the Lord had commanded them to meet at the Far West temple site on April 26, 1839, where they were to continue laying the foundation of the temple and then leave for another mission to England. With the appointed date a little over a month away, Brigham Young insisted that the apostles return to Far West and fulfill the Lord's commandment to the letter.

Several church leaders in Quincy believed it was no longer necessary for the apostles to obey the revelation and thought it was foolish to return to a place where mobs had sworn to kill the Saints. Surely, they reasoned, the Lord would not expect them to risk their lives traveling hundreds of miles into enemy territory and back when they were needed so badly in Illinois.[7]

Besides, their quorum was in disarray. Thomas Marsh and Orson Hyde were in apostasy, Parley Pratt was in prison, and Heber Kimball and John Page were still in Missouri. The most recently called apostles, Wilford Woodruff, Willard Richards, and Joseph's cousin George A. Smith, had not even been ordained yet, and Willard was preaching the gospel in England.[8]

But Brigham felt that it was within their power to meet in Far West as the Lord commanded, and that they should try to carry it out.

He wanted the apostles in Quincy to be united in their decision. To make the journey, they would have to leave their families at a time when the future of the church was uncertain. If the apostles were captured or killed, their wives and children would have to face the coming trials alone.

Knowing what was at stake, Orson Pratt, John Taylor, Wilford Woodruff, and George A. Smith agreed to do whatever was required to follow the Lord's command.

"The Lord God has spoken," Brigham said after they made their decision. "It is our duty to obey and leave the event in His hands."[9]

BACK IN THE LIBERTY jail, concern for the Saints and the wrongs committed against them consumed Joseph's mind. On the evening of March 19, he received letters from Emma, his brother Don Carlos, and Bishop Partridge.[10] The letters cheered him and the other prisoners a little, but he could not forget that he was trapped in a filthy dungeon while the Saints were scattered and needed help.

The day after the letters arrived, Joseph began writing a pair of epistles to the Saints, unburdening his soul as he never had in writing. Dictating to a fellow prisoner, who acted as scribe, the prophet tried to shore up the Saints in their despair.

"Every species of wickedness and cruelty practiced upon us," he assured them, "will only tend to bind our hearts together and seal them together in love."[11]

Yet he could not ignore the months of persecution that had driven them to their desperate state. He railed against Governor Boggs, the militia, and those who had harmed the Saints. "Let thine anger be kindled against our enemies," he cried out to the Lord in prayer, "and, in the fury of thine heart, with thy sword avenge us of our wrongs!"[12]

Joseph knew, however, that their enemies were not the only ones at fault. Some Saints, including church leaders, had tried to cover their sins, gratify their pride and ambition, and use force to compel others to obey them. They had abused their power and position among the Saints.

"We have learned by sad experience," Joseph said under inspiration, "that it is the nature and disposition of almost all men, as soon as they get a little authority, as they suppose, they will immediately begin to exercise unrighteous dominion."[13]

Righteous Saints were to act on higher principles. "No power or influence can or ought to be maintained by virtue of the priesthood," the Lord declared, "only by persuasion, by long suffering, by gentleness and meekness, and by love unfeigned." Those who tried to do otherwise lost the Spirit and the authority to bless the lives of others with the priesthood.[14]

Still, Joseph cried out in behalf of the innocent Saints. "O Lord," he pleaded, "how long shall they suffer these wrongs and unlawful oppressions, before thine heart shall be softened toward them?"[15]

"My son, peace be unto thy soul," the Lord responded. "Thine adversity and thine afflictions shall be but a small moment; and then, if thou endure it well, God shall exalt thee on high; thou shalt triumph over all thy foes."[16]

The Lord assured Joseph that he was not forgotten. "If the very jaws of hell shall gape open the mouth wide after thee," the Lord told Joseph, "know thou, my son, that all these things shall give thee experience, and shall be for thy good."

The Savior reminded Joseph that the Saints could not suffer more than He had. He loved them and could end their pain, but He chose instead to suffer affliction with them, carrying their grief and sorrow as part of His atoning sacrifice. Such suffering filled Him with mercy, giving Him power to succor and refine all who turned to him in their trials. He urged Joseph to hold on and promised never to forsake him.

"Thy days are known and thy years shall not be numbered less," the Lord assured him. "Therefore, fear not what man can do, for God shall be with you for ever and ever."[17]

AS THE LORD SPOKE peace to Joseph in prison, Heber Kimball and other Saints in Missouri lobbied the state supreme court tirelessly to get the prophet released. The judges seemed sympathetic to Heber's pleas, and some even questioned the legality of Joseph's imprisonment, but they ultimately refused to take action on the case.[18]

Discouraged, Heber returned to Liberty to report to Joseph. The guards would not let him into the dungeon, so he stood outside the prison window and called down to his friends. He had tried his best, he said, but it had made no difference.

"Be of good cheer," Joseph called back, "and get all the Saints away as fast as possible."[19]

Heber slipped into Far West a few days later, wary of the dangers that still lurked in the area. Aside from a handful of leaders and a few families, the city was empty. Heber's own family had left two months earlier, and he had heard nothing from them since. As he thought about them and the prisoners and those who had suffered and died at the hands of mobs, he felt downcast and lonely. Like Joseph, he longed for the suffering to end.

As Heber thought about their miserable situation, and his failure to gain Joseph's freedom, the Lord's love and gratitude filled him. Steadying a piece of paper on his knee, he recorded the impressions that came to him.

"Remember that I am always with you, even to the end," he heard the Lord say. "My Spirit shall be in your heart to teach you the peaceable things of the kingdom."

The Lord told him not to worry about his family. "I will feed them and clothe them and make unto them friends," He promised. "Peace shall rest upon them forever, if thou wilt be faithful and go forth and preach my gospel to the nations of the earth."[20]

When Heber finished writing, his heart and mind were calm.

AFTER THE LORD SPOKE to him in the dark, miserable dungeon, Joseph no longer feared that God had forsaken him and the church. In letters to Edward Partridge and the Saints, he testified boldly of the latter-day work. "Hell may pour forth its rage like the burning lava of Mount Vesuvius," he declared, "yet shall Mormonism stand." He was sure of this.

"Truth is Mormonism," he exclaimed. "God is the author of it. He is our shield. It is by Him we received our birth. It was by His voice that we were called to a dispensation of His gospel in the beginning of the fullness of times."[21]

He urged the Saints to compile an official record of the wrongs they had suffered in Missouri so they could deliver it to the president of the United States and other government officials for review. He believed it was the Saints' duty to seek legal reparations for their losses.

"Let us cheerfully do all things that lie in our power," he counseled, "and then may we stand still, with the utmost assurance, to see the salvation of God, and for his arm to be revealed."[22]

A few days after Joseph sent his letters, he and his fellow prisoners left the jail to appear before a grand jury in Gallatin. Before they left, Joseph penned a letter to Emma. "I want to see little Frederick, Joseph, Julia, and Alexander," he wrote. "Tell them Father loves them with a perfect love, and he is doing all he can to get away from the mob to come to them."[23]

When the prisoners arrived in Gallatin, some of the lawyers in the room were drinking, while a crowd of men loitered outside, idly peeking through the windows. The judge on the bench had served as the attorney prosecuting the Saints in their November hearing.[24]

Convinced they could not get a fair hearing in Daviess County, Joseph and the other prisoners asked for a change of venue. Their request was granted, and the prisoners set out for a courthouse in another county with a sheriff and four new guards.[25]

The guards were lenient with the prisoners and treated them humanely as they traveled to the new venue.[26] In Gallatin, Joseph had won their respect by beating the strongest of them in a good-natured wrestling match.[27] Public opinion about the Saints was also shifting. Some Missourians were growing uncomfortable with the governor's extermination order and simply wished to drop the whole matter and be rid of the prisoners.[28]

The day after they left Daviess County, the men stopped at a way station, and the prisoners bought whiskey for their guards. Later that night, the sheriff approached the prisoners. "I shall take a good drink of grog and go to bed," he told them, "and you may do as you have a mind to."

As the sheriff and three of the guards got drunk, Joseph and his friends saddled two horses with the help of the remaining guard and headed east into the night.[29]

TWO DAYS LATER, AS Joseph and the other prisoners were fleeing to safety, five of the apostles started in the opposite direction, crossing the Mississippi toward Far West. Brigham Young, Wilford Woodruff, and Orson Pratt rode in one carriage, while John Taylor and George A. Smith rode with Alpheus Cutler, who had been the temple's master workman, in another.

They traveled quickly across the prairie, anxious to arrive in Far West on the appointed day. Along the way, they came upon apostle John Page, who was moving east with his family out of Missouri, and persuaded him to join them.[30]

After seven days on the road, the apostles entered Far West on the moonlit night of April 25. Grass had already grown over its deserted streets, and all was quiet. Heber Kimball, who had returned to Far West after learning of Joseph's escape, emerged from his hiding place and welcomed them to the town.

The men passed a few hours together. Then, as sunlight stretched across the eastern horizon, they rode quietly into the town square and walked with the few Saints who remained in the city to the temple site. There they sang a hymn and Alpheus rolled a large stone to the southeast corner of the temple site, fulfilling the Lord's commandment to recommence laying the foundation of the temple.[31]

Wilford took a seat on the stone as the apostles formed a circle around him. They placed their hands on his head, and Brigham ordained him to the apostleship. When he finished, George took Wilford's place on the stone and was ordained as well.

Recognizing they had done all they could, the apostles bowed their heads and took turns praying in the morning light. When they finished, they sang "Adam-ondi-Ahman," a hymn that looked forward to the Second Coming of Jesus Christ and the day when the peace of Zion would spread across Missouri's war-torn prairie and fill the world.

Alpheus then rolled the stone back to where he found it, leaving the foundation in the Lord's hands until the day when He would prepare a way for the Saints to return to Zion.[32]

The next day, the apostles rode thirty-two miles to catch up with the last families struggling to leave Missouri. They expected to depart for Great Britain soon. But first they wanted to reunite with their loved ones in Illinois and settle them in the new gathering place, wherever it might be.[33]

AROUND THIS TIME, A ferry landed at Quincy and several rough-looking passengers came ashore. One of them—a pale, thin man—wore a wide-brimmed hat and a blue jacket with an upturned collar that concealed his unshaven face. His ragged trousers were tucked into worn-out boots.[34]

Dimick Huntington, a former sheriff among the Saints in Far West, watched the unkempt stranger climb up the bank. Something familiar about the man's face and the way he carried himself caught Dimick's attention. But he could not say why until he got a better look.

"Is it you, Brother Joseph?" he exclaimed.

Joseph raised his hands to quiet his friend. "Hush!" he said cautiously. "Where is my family?"[35]

Since their escape, Joseph and the other prisoners had been on guard and on the run, following Missouri's back roads to the Mississippi River and the freedom that awaited them on the other side, beyond the reach of Missouri authorities.[36]

Still shocked to see the prophet, Dimick explained that Emma and the children lived four miles out of town.

"Take me to my family as quick as you can," Joseph said.

Dimick and Joseph rode to the Cleveland home, following back streets through the town to avoid being seen. When they arrived, Joseph dismounted and started for the house.

Emma appeared at the door and recognized him immediately. She broke into a run and embraced him halfway to the gate.[37]

PART 4

---◆---

Fullness of Times

APRIL 1839–FEBRUARY 1846

Let this house be built unto my name,
that I may reveal mine ordinances
therein unto my people; for I deign to reveal
unto my church things which have been kept hid
from before the foundation of the world,
things that pertain to the dispensation
of the fulness of times.

Doctrine and Covenants 124:40–41

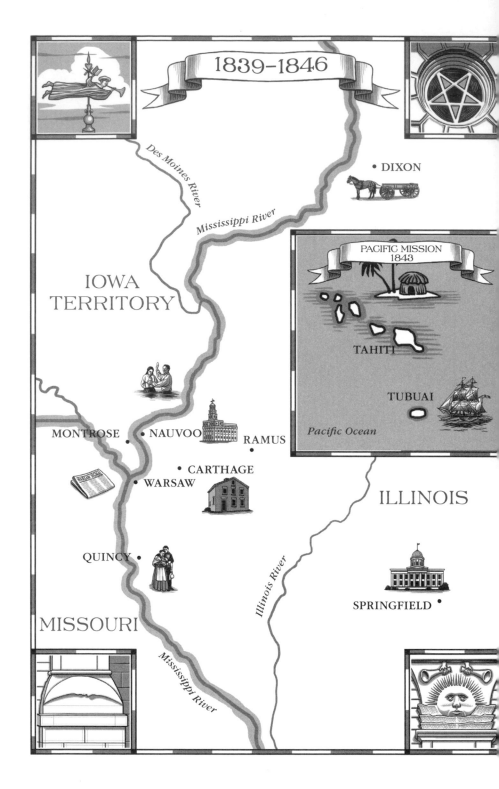

1839–1846

DIXON

IOWA
TERRITORY

PACIFIC MISSION
1843

TAHITI

TUBUAI

Pacific Ocean

MONTROSE • NAUVOO RAMUS

CARTHAGE

WARSAW

ILLINOIS

QUINCY

Mississippi River

Des Moines River

Illinois River

SPRINGFIELD

MISSOURI

Mississippi River

CHAPTER 34

Build Up a City

In late April 1839, days after reuniting with the Saints, Joseph rode north to inspect land that church leaders wanted to buy in and around Commerce, a town fifty miles from Quincy. For the first time in more than six months, the prophet was traveling without armed guards or the threat of violence looming over him. He was finally among friends, in a state where people welcomed the Saints and seemed to respect their beliefs.

While in jail, Joseph had written to a man who was selling land around Commerce, expressing interest in settling the church there. "If there is not anyone who feels particular interest in making the purchase," Joseph had told him, "we will purchase it of you."[1]

After the fall of Far West, however, many Saints questioned the wisdom of gathering to a single area.

Edward Partridge wondered if the best way to avoid conflict and provide for the poor was to gather in small communities scattered throughout the country.[2] But Joseph knew the Lord had not revoked His commandment for the Saints to gather.

Arriving in Commerce, he saw a marshy floodplain that rose gently to a wooded bluff overlooking a wide bend in the Mississippi River. A few homes dotted the area. Across the river in Iowa Territory, near a town called Montrose, stood some abandoned army barracks on more land available for purchase.

Joseph believed the Saints could build thriving stakes of Zion in this area. The land was not the choicest he had ever seen, but the Mississippi River was navigable all the way to the ocean, making Commerce a good place for gathering the Saints from abroad and establishing commercial enterprises. The area was also sparsely settled.

Still, gathering the Saints there would be risky. If the church grew, as Joseph hoped it would, their neighbors might become alarmed and turn against them, as people had in Missouri.

Joseph prayed. "Lord, what wilt Thou have me to do?"

"Build up a city," the Lord replied, "and call my Saints to this place."[3]

THAT SPRING, WILFORD AND Phebe Woodruff moved into the barracks in Montrose. Among their new neighbors were Brigham and Mary Ann Young and Orson and Sarah Pratt. After they settled their families, the three apostles planned to leave on their mission for Britain with the rest of the quorum.[4]

Thousands of Saints soon moved to the new gathering place, pitching tents or living in wagons as they went to work building homes, acquiring food and clothes, and clearing farmland on both sides of the river.[5]

As the new settlement grew, the Twelve met often with Joseph, who preached with new vigor as he prepared them for their mission.[6] The prophet taught that God did not reveal anything to him that He would not also make known to the Twelve. "Even the least Saint may know all things as fast as he is able to," Joseph declared.[7]

He instructed them in the first principles of the gospel, the Resurrection and the Judgment, and the building of Zion. Remembering the betrayal of former apostles, he also urged them to be faithful. "See to it that you do not betray heaven," he said, "that you do not betray Jesus Christ, that you do not betray your brethren, and that you do not betray the revelations of God."[8]

Around this time, Orson Hyde expressed a desire to return to the Quorum of the Twelve, ashamed that he had denounced Joseph in Missouri and abandoned the Saints. Fearing Orson would betray them again when the next difficulty came along, Sidney Rigdon was reluctant to restore his apostleship. Joseph, however, welcomed him back and restored his place among the Twelve.[9] In

July, Parley Pratt escaped from prison in Missouri and was also reunited with the apostles.[10]

By then swarms of mosquitos had risen from the marshlands to feast on the new settlers, and many Saints came down with deadly malarial fevers and bone-rattling chills. Most of the Twelve were soon too sick to leave for Britain.[11]

On the morning of Monday, July 22, Wilford heard Joseph's voice outside his home: "Brother Woodruff, follow me."

Wilford stepped outside and saw Joseph standing with a group of men. All morning they had been moving from house to house, tent to tent, taking the sick by the hand and healing them. After blessing the Saints in Commerce, they had taken a ferry across the river to heal the Saints in Montrose.[12]

Wilford walked with them across the village square to the home of his friend Elijah Fordham. Elijah's eyes were sunken and his skin ashen. His wife, Anna, was weeping as she prepared his burial clothes.[13]

Joseph approached Elijah and took his hand. "Brother Fordham," he asked, "have you not faith to be healed?"

"I am afraid it is too late," he said.

"Do you not believe that Jesus is the Christ?"

"I do, Brother Joseph."

"Elijah," the prophet declared, "I command you, in the name of Jesus of Nazareth, to arise and be made whole."

The words seemed to shake the house. Elijah rose from his bed, his face flush with color. He dressed, asked for something to eat, and followed Joseph outside to help minister to many others.[14]

Later that evening, Phebe Woodruff was astonished when she visited Elijah and Anna. Only a few hours earlier, Anna had all but given up on her husband. Now Elijah said he felt strong enough to work in his garden. Phebe had no doubt his recovery was the work of God.[15]

JOSEPH'S EFFORTS TO BLESS and heal the sick did not end the spread of disease in Commerce and Montrose, and some Saints perished. As more people died, eighteen-year-old Zina Huntington worried that her mother would succumb to the illness as well.

Zina cared for her mother daily, leaning on her father and brothers for support, but soon the entire family was sick. Joseph checked on them from time to time, seeing what he could do to help the family or make Zina's mother more comfortable.

One day, Zina's mother called for her. "My time has come to die," she said weakly. "I am not afraid." She testified to Zina of the Resurrection. "I shall come forth triumphant when the Savior comes with the just to meet the Saints on the earth."

When her mother died, Zina was overcome with grief. Knowing the family's suffering, Joseph continued to attend to them.[16]

During one of Joseph's visits, Zina asked him, "Will I know my mother as my mother when I get over on the other side?"

"More than that," he said, "you will meet and become acquainted with your eternal Mother, the wife of your Father in Heaven."

"Have I then a Mother in Heaven?" Zina asked.

"You assuredly have," said Joseph. "How could a Father claim His title unless there were also a Mother to share that parenthood?"[17]

IN EARLY AUGUST, WILFORD departed for England with John Taylor, the first of the apostles to leave on the new mission. At the time, Phebe was expecting another baby, and John's wife, Leonora, and their three children were sick with fevers.[18]

Parley and Orson Pratt were the next apostles to depart, even though Orson and Sarah were still mourning for their daughter, Lydia, who had died just eleven days before. Mary Ann Pratt, Parley's wife, was joining the apostles on the mission, and she set out with them. George A. Smith, the youngest apostle, was still sick when he began his mission, postponing marriage to his fiancée, Bathsheba Bigler.[19]

Mary Ann Young said goodbye to Brigham in the middle of September. He was sick again, but he was determined to do what was required of him. Mary Ann was ill herself and had little money to support their five children while Brigham was away, but she wanted him to do his duty.

"Go and fill your mission, and the Lord will bless you," she said. "I will do the best I can for myself and the children."[20]

A few days after Brigham left, Mary Ann learned that he had made it only as far as the Kimball house, on the other side of the Mississippi, before collapsing from exhaustion. She immediately crossed the river to care for him until he was strong enough to leave.[21]

At the Kimballs', Mary Ann found Vilate sick in bed with two of her boys, leaving no one but their four-year-old son to carry heavy water jugs from the well. Heber was too sick to stand up, but he was committed to leaving with Brigham the following day.

Mary Ann tended to Brigham until a wagon arrived in the morning. As Heber stood to go, he looked distraught. He embraced Vilate, who lay in bed shaking with fever, then said goodbye to his children and climbed unsteadily into the wagon.

Brigham tried in vain to look healthy when he said goodbye to Mary Ann and his sister Fanny, who urged him to stay until he was well again.

"I never felt better in my life," he said.

"You lie," said Fanny.

Brigham climbed with effort into the wagon and took a seat beside Heber. As the wagon rolled down the hill, Heber felt terrible about leaving his family when they were so sick. He turned to the wagon driver and told him to stop. "This is pretty tough," he said to Brigham. "Let's rise up and give them a cheer."

Back at the house, a noise from outside startled Vilate out of bed. Staggering to the door, she joined Mary Ann and Fanny, who were looking at something a short distance away. Vilate looked too, and a smile spread across her face.

It was Brigham and Heber, standing in the back of the wagon and leaning on each other for support. "Hurrah! Hurrah!" the men cried, waving their hats in the air. "Hurrah for Israel!"

"Goodbye!" the women called out. "God bless you!"[22]

WHILE THE APOSTLES WERE leaving for Britain, Saints in Illinois and Iowa composed statements detailing their harsh treatment in Missouri, as Joseph had instructed them to do when he was in jail. By the fall, church leaders had collected hundreds of these accounts and prepared a formal petition. In total, the Saints asked for more than two million dollars to compensate for lost homes, land, livestock, and other property. Joseph planned to deliver these claims personally to the president of the United States and to Congress.

Joseph considered President Martin Van Buren to be a high-minded statesman—someone who would champion the rights of citizens. Joseph hoped that the president and other lawmakers in Washington, DC, would read about the Saints' suffering and agree to recompense them for the land and property they had lost in Missouri.[23]

On November 29, 1839, after traveling nearly a thousand miles from his home in Illinois, Joseph arrived at the front door of the presidential mansion in Washington. Beside him were his friend and legal adviser, Elias Higbee, and John Reynolds, a congressman from Illinois.[24]

A porter greeted them at the door and motioned them inside. The mansion had recently been redecorated, and Joseph and Elias were awed by the elegance of its rooms, which contrasted sharply with the Saints' ramshackle dwellings in the West.

Their guide led them upstairs to a room where President Van Buren was speaking with visitors. As they waited outside the door, with the petition and several letters of introduction in hand, Joseph asked Congressman Reynolds to introduce him simply as a "Latter-day Saint." The congressman seemed surprised and amused by the request, but he agreed to do as Joseph wished. Though not eager to assist the Saints, Congressman Reynolds knew their large numbers could influence politics in Illinois.[25]

Joseph had not expected to meet the president with such a small delegation. When he left Illinois in October, his plan had been to let Sidney Rigdon take the lead in these meetings. But Sidney was too sick to travel and had stopped along the way.[26]

At last the president's parlor doors opened, and the three men entered the room. Like Joseph, Martin Van

Buren was the son of a New York farmer, but he was a much older man, short and squat, with a light complexion and a shock of white hair framing most of his face.

As promised, Congressman Reynolds introduced Joseph as a Latter-day Saint. The president smiled at the unusual title and shook the prophet's hand.[27]

After greeting the president, Joseph handed him the letters of introduction and waited. Van Buren read them and frowned. "Help you?" he said dismissively. "How can I help you?"[28]

Joseph did not know what to say.[29] He had not expected the president to dismiss them so quickly. He and Elias urged the president to at least read about the Saints' suffering before deciding to reject their pleas.

"I can do nothing for you, gentlemen," the president insisted. "If I were for you, I should go against the whole state of Missouri, and that state would go against me in the next election."[30]

Disappointed, Joseph and Elias left the mansion and delivered their petition to Congress, knowing it would be weeks before legislators could review and discuss it.[31]

While they waited, Joseph decided to visit the eastern branches of the church. He would also preach in Washington and in the surrounding towns and cities.[32]

WILFORD WOODRUFF AND JOHN Taylor arrived in Liverpool, England, on January 11, 1840. It was Wilford's first trip to England, but John was back among family and friends. After retrieving their luggage, they went to the home of John's brother-in-law George Cannon. George and his wife, Ann, were surprised to see them and invited them to dinner.

The Cannons had five children. Their oldest, George, was a bright thirteen-year-old who enjoyed reading. After dinner, Wilford and John gave the family a Book of Mormon and *A Voice of Warning,* a book-length missionary tract Parley Pratt had published in New York City a few years earlier. John taught the family the first principles of the gospel and invited them to read the books.[33]

The Cannons agreed to store the missionaries' luggage while Wilford and John caught a train to Preston to meet with Joseph Fielding and Willard Richards.[34] Both Joseph and Willard had married British Saints since Heber Kimball and Orson Hyde left the mission a year earlier. As Heber had predicted, Willard had married Jennetta Richards.

Following the meeting in Preston, John returned to Liverpool while Wilford made his way southeast to the industrial Staffordshire region, where he quickly established a branch. One evening, while meeting with the Saints there, Wilford felt the Spirit rest upon him. "This is the last meeting that you will hold with this people for many days," the Lord told him.

The message astonished Wilford. The work in Staffordshire had only just begun, and he had many preaching appointments in the area. But the next morning he prayed for more guidance, and the Spirit inspired him to go farther south, where many souls were waiting for God's word.

He left the next day with William Benbow, one of the Staffordshire Saints, and traveled south to the farm of John and Jane Benbow, William's brother and sister-in-law.[35] John and Jane owned a spacious white brick home on a prospering three-hundred-acre farm. When Wilford and William arrived, they stayed up with the Benbows until two o'clock in the morning talking about the Restoration.

The couple had made a good life for themselves, but they were spiritually unfulfilled. Recently, they had joined others in breaking away from their church to look for the true gospel of Jesus Christ. Calling themselves the United Brethren, the group had built chapels at Gadfield Elm, several miles south of the Benbow farm, and at other sites. They chose preachers from among their own number and asked God for further light.[36]

As John and Jane listened to Wilford that evening, they believed they had finally found the fullness of the gospel. The next day, Wilford preached a sermon in the Benbows' home to a large group of neighbors, and he soon baptized John and Jane in a nearby pond.

In the coming weeks, Wilford baptized more than one hundred and fifty members of the United Brethren, including forty-six lay ministers. With more people asking to be baptized, he wrote Willard Richards for help.[37]

"I am called to baptize four or five times a day!" he exclaimed. "I cannot do the work alone!"[38]

On February 5, sixty-seven-year-old Matthew Davis heard that Joseph Smith, the Mormon prophet, was preaching that evening in Washington. Matthew was a correspondent for a popular newspaper in New York City. Knowing his wife, Mary, was curious about the Latter-day Saints, he was eager to hear the prophet speak and to report his teachings back to her.

At the sermon, Matthew discovered that Joseph was a plainly dressed farmer with a strong build, handsome face, and dignified bearing. His preaching revealed that he was not formally educated, but Matthew could tell he was strong-minded and knowledgeable. The prophet seemed sincere, with no trace of levity or fanaticism in his voice.

"I will state to you our beliefs, so far as time will permit," Joseph began his sermon. He testified of God and His attributes. "He reigns over all things in heaven and on earth," he declared. "He foreordained the fall of man, but all-merciful as He is, He foreordained at the same time a plan of redemption for all mankind."

"I believe in the divinity of Jesus Christ," he continued, "and that He died for the sins of all men, who in Adam had fallen." He stated that all people were born pure and undefiled and that all children who died at an early age would go to heaven, because they did not know good from evil and were incapable of sinning.

Matthew listened, impressed by what he heard. Joseph taught that God was eternal, without beginning or end, as was the soul of every man and woman. Matthew noted that the prophet said very little about rewards or punishments in the next life except that he believed that God's punishment would have a beginning and an end.

After two hours, the prophet closed his sermon with his testimony of the Book of Mormon. He declared that he was not the author of the book but that he had received it from God, direct from heaven.

Reflecting on the sermon, Matthew realized that he had heard nothing that evening that would harm society. "There was much in his precepts, if they were followed," Matthew told his wife the next day in a letter, "that would soften the asperities of man towards man, and that would tend to make him a more rational being."

Matthew had no intention of accepting the prophet's teachings, but he appreciated his message of peace. "There was no violence, no fury, no denunciation," he wrote. "His religion appears to be the religion of meekness, lowliness, and mild persuasion."

"I have changed my opinion of the Mormons," he concluded.[39]

AS JOSEPH WAITED FOR Congress to review the Saints' petition, he grew weary of being away from his family. "My dear Emma, my heart is entwined around you and those little ones," he wrote that winter. "Tell all the children that I love them and will come home as soon as I can."[40]

When Joseph married Emma, he had believed that their union would end at death.[41] But the Lord had since revealed to him that marriages and families could endure beyond the grave through the power of the priesthood.[42] Recently, while visiting church branches in the eastern states with Parley Pratt, Joseph had told him that righteous Saints could cultivate family relationships forever, allowing them to grow and increase in affection. No matter how much distance separated faithful families on earth, they could trust in the promise that one day they would be united in the world to come.[43]

While waiting in Washington, Joseph also grew tired of hearing politicians make grand speeches full of lofty language and empty promises. "There is such an itching disposition to display their oratory on the most trivial occasions and so much etiquette, bowing and scraping, twisting and turning to make a display of their witticism," he told his brother Hyrum in a letter. "It seems to us rather a display of folly and show more than substance and gravity."[44]

After an unsuccessful meeting with John C. Calhoun, one of the most influential senators in the nation, Joseph realized that he was wasting his time in Washington and decided to go home. Everyone spoke of liberty and justice, but no one seemed willing to hold the people of Missouri accountable for their treatment of the Saints.[45]

After the prophet returned to Illinois, Elias Higbee continued to seek compensation for the Saints' losses. In March, the Senate reviewed the Saints' petition and allowed delegates from Missouri to defend the actions of their state. After considering the case, the legislators decided to do nothing. They acknowledged the Saints' distress but believed Congress had no power to interfere with the actions of a state government. Only Missouri could compensate the Saints for their losses.[46]

"Our business is at last ended here," Elias wrote Joseph in disappointment. "I have done all I could in this matter."[47]

CHAPTER 35

A Beautiful Place

As the malaria epidemic in Commerce continued into 1840, Emily Partridge and her sister Harriet visited the tents, wagons, and unfinished homes of the sick. Now sixteen years old, Emily was used to stark living conditions. For almost a decade, her family had been driven out of one humble dwelling after another, never enjoying the stable home life they had known in Ohio.

The sisters attended the sick until they too came down with fevers and shakes. Realizing their daughters' lives were in peril, Edward and Lydia Partridge moved them from a tent to a small rented room in an abandoned storehouse beside the river. Edward then went to work building a house for his family on a lot a mile away.

But the trials of Missouri had broken the bishop's health, and he was in no condition to work. He soon had a fever as well, which he treated with medicine until he was strong enough to do a week or two of work on the house. When the sickness returned, he took more medicine and went back to work.

Meanwhile, the cramped, stifling room in the storehouse did little to help Emily, Harriet, or their siblings, who also took sick. Emily's fever remained steady through the spring of 1840, but Harriet's grew worse and worse. She died in the middle of May at the age of eighteen.[1]

Harriet's death crushed the Partridges. After the funeral, Edward tried to move the family to an unfinished cow stable on their property, hoping it would provide better shelter. But the exertion wore him out and he collapsed. To help the family, fellow Saints William and Jane Law took Emily and her siblings into their home and nursed them back to health.

Edward languished in bed several days before passing away, just a week and a half after Harriet's death. The losses left Emily grief-stricken. She had been close to Harriet, and she knew her father had sacrificed everything to provide for his family and the church—even when grumbling Saints, faithless dissenters, and hostile neighbors wore his soul weary.[2]

In time, Emily emerged from the fog of sickness and grief, but her life was different now. To help provide for their destitute family, she and her nineteen-year-old sister, Eliza, had to find work. Eliza had the skills to hire out as a seamstress, but Emily had no trade. She could wash dishes, sweep and scrub floors, and do other household chores, of course, but so could most everyone else in the community.[3]

Fortunately, the Saints did not forget how much her father had sacrificed for the church. "No man had the confidence of the church more than he," read the obituary for Bishop Partridge in the *Times and Seasons,* the Saints' new newspaper. "His religion was his all; for this he spent his life, and for this he laid it down."[4]

To honor his memory and care for his family, the Saints finished the house the bishop had begun, giving his family a place they could call their own.[5]

BY THE SPRING OF 1840, the new city on the Mississippi was off to a promising start. The Saints dug ditches and canals to drain the swamps along the river and make the land more livable. They plotted streets, laid foundations, framed houses, planted gardens, and cultivated fields. By June, around two hundred and fifty new homes stood as a testament to their hard work.[6]

Unsatisfied with the name Commerce, Joseph had rechristened the place Nauvoo almost as soon as he arrived. "The name of our city," he explained in a First Presidency proclamation, "is of Hebrew origin and signifies a beautiful situation or place, carrying with it also the idea of *rest*."[7] Joseph hoped Nauvoo would live up to its name and give the Saints a reprieve from the conflicts of recent years.

Yet he knew peace and rest would not come easily. To avoid the dissent and persecution they had experienced in Ohio and Missouri, the Saints needed to forge stronger bonds with each other and create lasting friendships with their neighbors.[8]

Around this time, Joseph received a letter from William Phelps, who had moved to Ohio after forsaking the church and testifying against Joseph in a Missouri court. "I know my situation, you know it, and God knows it," William wrote, "and I want to be saved if my friends will help me."[9]

Knowing William to be a sincere man despite his faults, Joseph wrote back a short time later. "It is true that we have suffered much in consequence of your behavior," he stated. "However, the cup has been drunk, the will of our Heavenly Father has been done, and we are yet alive." Happy to put the dark days of Missouri behind them, Joseph forgave William and put him back to work in the church.

"Come on, dear brother, since the war is past," Joseph wrote, "for friends at first are friends again at last."[10]

Joseph also felt an urgency to give the Saints more spiritual direction. In the Liberty jail, the Lord had told him that his days were known, and Joseph confided to friends that he did not think he would live to be forty. He needed to teach the Saints more of what God had revealed to him before it was too late.[11]

Building a city and managing the church's temporal concerns, however, consumed most of Joseph's time.

He had always taken an active part in church business, and he had long relied on men like Bishop Partridge to help shoulder the burden. Now that Edward was gone, Joseph began leaning more on Bishop Newel Whitney and the additional bishops that were called in Nauvoo. Yet he knew he needed still more help directing the temporal side of church administration so he could focus on his spiritual ministry.[12]

Soon after, Joseph received another letter, this time from a stranger named John Cook Bennett. John said he intended to move to Nauvoo, join the church, and offer his services to the Saints. He was a physician and a high-ranking officer in the Illinois state militia who had also been a minister and a professor. "I believe I should be much happier with you," he said. "Write me immediately."[13]

In the days that followed, Joseph received two more letters from John. "You can rely upon me," John promised. "I hope that time will soon come when your people will become my people and your God my God." He told Joseph that his public-speaking skills and untiring energy would be invaluable to the Saints.[14]

"My anxiety to be with you is daily increasing," he insisted, "and I shall wind up my professional business immediately and proceed to your blissful abode, if you think it best!"[15]

Joseph reviewed the letters, encouraged that someone with John's credentials wanted to unite with the Saints. A man with his abilities could certainly help the church establish itself in Illinois.

"Were it possible for you to come here this season to suffer affliction with the people of God," Joseph wrote John, "no one will be more pleased or give you a more cordial welcome than myself."[16]

AS NAUVOO TOOK FORM, Joseph's mind turned to the gathering. In England, the apostles had recently sent a company of forty-one Saints across the ocean, headed to Nauvoo. Joseph expected to welcome even more companies in the coming months and years.

"This is the principal place of gathering," he announced in a sermon that July. "Whosoever will, let him come and partake of the poverty of Nauvoo freely!"

He knew the expulsion from Missouri and the failed petition to the government had left many people uncertain about the future of Zion and the gathering. Joseph wanted them to understand that Zion was more than a parcel of land in Jackson County. "Where the Saints gather is Zion," he declared.

The Lord now commanded them to establish stakes in Nauvoo and the surrounding area. In time, as more Saints gathered to Zion, the church would organize additional stakes and the Lord would bless the land.

Before closing his sermon, Joseph announced, "I obligate myself to build as great a temple as ever Solomon did, if the church will back me up." He stretched out his hand and pointed to a spot high on the bluff where the Saints would build the sacred structure. "If it should be the will of God that I might live to behold that temple complete," he said longingly, "I will say, 'Oh, Lord, it is enough. Lord, let thy servant depart in peace.' "[17]

A few weeks later, as high temperatures continued in Nauvoo and sickness claimed still more lives, Joseph's friend Seymour Brunson passed away.[18] At the funeral, Joseph offered words of comfort to Seymour's widow, Harriet, and the thousands of Saints in the congregation. As he spoke, he looked at Jane Neyman, whose teenage son Cyrus had died before being baptized.

Knowing that Jane was worried about the welfare of her son's soul, Joseph decided to share what the Lord had taught him about the salvation of those, like his own brother Alvin, who had died without baptism.[19]

Opening the Bible, Joseph read the words of the apostle Paul to the Corinthians: "Else what shall they do which are baptized for the dead, if the dead rise not at all? Why are they then baptized for the dead?"[20] He noted that Paul's words were evidence that a living person could be baptized vicariously for a deceased person, extending the benefits of baptism to those who were dead in body but whose spirits lived on.

Joseph said God's plan of salvation was designed to save all those who were willing to obey the law of God, including the countless people who had died never knowing about Jesus Christ or His teachings.[21]

Shortly after the sermon, Jane went to the river with an elder of the church and was baptized for Cyrus. When Joseph heard about the baptism later that evening, he asked what words the elder had used in the ordinance. When they were repeated back to him, Joseph confirmed that the elder had performed the baptism correctly.[22]

JOHN BENNETT ARRIVED IN Nauvoo in September 1840, and Joseph eagerly sought his advice on managing the legal and political concerns of Nauvoo and the church. John was about the prophet's age but more educated. He was a short man with graying black hair, dark eyes, and a thin, handsome face. He readily accepted baptism.[23]

Lucy Smith was too worried about her ailing husband to take much notice of the popular newcomer. Like Bishop Partridge, Joseph Sr. had left Missouri in poor health, and Nauvoo's sickly summer climate only weakened him more. Lucy hoped he would eventually recover, but after he vomited blood one day, she feared his death was near.

When Joseph and Hyrum learned about their father's worsening condition, they rushed to his bedside.[24]

Lucy sent word to the rest of the family while Joseph kept his father company. He told his father about baptism for the dead and the blessings it afforded all of God's children. Overjoyed, Joseph Sr. begged him to perform the ordinance for Alvin.

Soon Lucy sat with most of her children around the bed of their father. Joseph Sr. wanted to give each of them a parting blessing while he still had strength to speak. When it was Joseph's turn, Joseph Sr. placed his hands on his son's head.

"Hold out faithful and you shall be blessed, and your family shall be blessed and your children after you," he said. "You shall live to finish your work."

"Oh, Father," Joseph cried, "shall I?"

"Yes, you shall," said the patriarch, "and you shall lay out the plan of all the work that God requires at your hand."

When Joseph Sr. finished blessing his children, he turned to Lucy. "Mother," he said, "you are one of the most singular women in the world."

Lucy protested, but her husband continued. "We have often wished that we might both die at the same time," he said, "but you must not desire to die when I do, for you must stay to comfort the children when I am gone."

After a pause, Joseph Sr. exclaimed, "I see Alvin." He then folded his hands together and began to breathe slowly, until his breaths grew shorter and shorter, and he passed quietly away.[25]

A FEW WEEKS AFTER Joseph Sr.'s death, the Saints gathered in Nauvoo for the October 1840 general conference. Joseph taught them more about baptism for the dead, explaining that the spirits of the dead were waiting for their living kindred to receive the saving ordinance in their behalf.[26]

Between sessions of the conference, the Saints rushed to the Mississippi River, where several elders stood waist-deep in the water, beckoning them to be baptized for their deceased grandparents, fathers, mothers, siblings, and children. Soon after, Hyrum was baptized for his brother Alvin.[27]

As Vilate Kimball watched the elders in the river, she longed to be baptized for her mother, who had died more than a decade earlier. She wished Heber was back from England to perform the ordinance, but since Joseph had urged the Saints to redeem the dead as soon as possible, she decided to be baptized for her mother right away.[28]

Emma Smith's thoughts were also on family. Her father, Isaac Hale, had passed away in January 1839. He had never reconciled with her and Joseph. Some years before his death, he had even allowed critics of the church to publish a letter he had written condemning Joseph and calling the Book of Mormon "a silly fabrication of falsehood and wickedness."[29]

Still, Emma loved her father and was baptized for him in the river.[30] He had not accepted the restored gospel in this life, but she hoped it would not be that way forever.

THAT FALL, JOSEPH AND John Bennett drafted a charter of laws for Nauvoo. The document was designed to give the Saints as much freedom as possible to govern themselves and protect against the kinds of injustices that had afflicted them in Missouri. If the state legislature approved the charter, the citizens of Nauvoo could pass their own laws for the city, operate local courts, found a university, and organize a militia.[31]

Joseph's plans for the church continued to grow as well. Anticipating more and more Saints gathering, the prophet founded several stakes in new settlements near Nauvoo. He also called Orson Hyde and John Page to embark on a mission to Palestine, where they would dedicate Jerusalem for the gathering of the children of Abraham. To get there, the apostles would have to cross Europe, giving them opportunities to preach the gospel in many of its cities.[32]

"We may soon expect to see flocking to this place, people from every land and from every nation," Joseph and the First Presidency proclaimed, "persons of all languages and of every tongue and of every color, who shall with us worship the Lord of Hosts in His holy temple."[33]

In early December, John Bennett successfully lobbied the Illinois state legislature to approve the Nauvoo charter, granting the Saints power to carry out their plans for the city. When John returned to Nauvoo in triumph, Joseph praised him at every opportunity.[34]

A little over a month later, on January 19, 1841, the Lord blessed the Saints with a new revelation. He assured them that He had welcomed Edward Partridge and Joseph Smith Sr. into His care, alongside David Patten, who had been killed at the Crooked River skirmish.

Hyrum Smith was called to take his father's place as patriarch of the church and was also appointed to serve as a prophet, seer, and revelator alongside Joseph, filling the role Oliver Cowdery once held in the church.[35]

Additionally, the Lord instructed John Bennett to stand by Joseph and continue speaking to those outside the church in the Saints' behalf, promising him blessings on the condition of righteous works. "His reward shall not fail if he receive counsel," the Lord declared. "I have seen the work which he hath done, which I accept if he continue."[36]

The Lord also accepted the Saints' past efforts to build Zion in Jackson County, but He commanded them now to build up Nauvoo, establish more stakes, and build a hotel called the Nauvoo House, which would provide visitors a place to rest and contemplate the word of God and the glory of Zion.[37]

Most important, the Lord commanded the Saints to construct the new temple. "Let this house be built unto my name," He declared, "that I may reveal mine ordinances therein unto my people."[38]

Baptism for the dead was one of these ordinances. So far the Lord had allowed the Saints to perform the baptisms in the Mississippi River, but now He commanded them to stop the ordinance until they had dedicated a special baptismal font in the temple. "This ordinance," He declared, "belongeth to my house."[39]

Other temple ordinances and inspiring new truths would come later. "I deign to reveal unto my church things which have been kept hid from before the foundation of the world, things that pertain to the dispensation of the fulness of times," the Lord promised. "And I will show unto my servant Joseph all things pertaining to this house, and the priesthood thereof."[40]

Promising to reward their diligence and obedience, the Lord urged the Saints to labor with all their might on the temple. "Build a house to my name, even in this place, that you may prove yourselves unto me that ye are faithful in all things," He commanded, "that I may bless you, and crown you with honor, immortality, and eternal life."[41]

As the new year dawned, the future looked bright for the Saints. On February 1, 1841, they elected John Bennett mayor of Nauvoo, which also made him the chief justice of the city court. He also became chancellor of the new university, major general of the militia, and an assistant president in the First Presidency.[42] Joseph and other church leaders had confidence in his ability to lead the city and make it great.

As John's authority and responsibilities expanded, Emma could not deny that he had helped the Saints immensely. But she did not share the Saints' affection for him. She thought John paraded himself through town like a pompous general, and when he was not trying to impress Joseph, he seemed self-absorbed and inconsiderate.

For all his talents and usefulness, something about John Bennett worried her.[43]

CHAPTER 36

Incline Them to Gather

In the spring of 1841, Mary Ann Davis took a final look at her husband's face before the lid closed on his coffin and his friends carried his remains to a quiet corner of a churchyard cemetery in Tirley, England. John Davis had been in his prime, only twenty-five years old, when he died. As Mary watched the men bear his coffin away, she felt suddenly alone, standing in her black mourning dress in a village where she was now the only Latter-day Saint.

John had died because of his beliefs. He and Mary had met at a meeting of Saints a year earlier, not long after Wilford Woodruff had baptized hundreds of the United Brethren in nearby Herefordshire. Neither she nor John had worshipped with the United Brethren, but the restored gospel had spread quickly through the area, attracting the notice of many people.[1]

Mary and John had opened their home to missionaries hoping to establish a congregation in the area. The British mission had grown larger and larger, and after just four years, there were more than six thousand Saints in England and Scotland.[2] Even in London, where street preachers from many churches competed fiercely for souls, the missionaries had established a branch of around forty Saints, led by a young American elder named Lorenzo Snow.[3]

Opposition remained strong throughout the country, though. Cheap pamphlets littered the streets in most cities, proclaiming every kind of religious idea.[4] Some were reprints of anti-Mormon tracts from the United States and warned readers against the Latter-day Saints.[5]

Hoping to correct false reports, Parley Pratt had begun writing his own pamphlets and editing a monthly newspaper, the *Latter-day Saints' Millennial Star,* which printed news from the Saints in Nauvoo and throughout Britain. Brigham Young also arranged to have a hymnal and the Book of Mormon printed for the British Saints.[6]

In Tirley, Mary and John had faced hostility as soon as missionaries began preaching in their home. Rough men often broke up meetings and ran the missionaries off. Things only grew worse until one day, the men had knocked John to the floor and kicked him mercilessly. He had never recovered. A short time later, he took a bad fall and began coughing up blood. The missionaries tried to visit the couple, but hostile neighbors kept them away. Confined to bed, John grew weaker until he died.

After the funeral, Mary decided to join the gathering to Nauvoo. Several apostles, including Brigham Young and Heber Kimball, had recently announced that they were returning home that spring, taking with them a large company of British Saints. Mary planned to leave for North America soon after with a smaller company of Saints.

Since she was the only member of her family in the church, Mary visited her parents and siblings to say goodbye. She expected her father to protest, but he simply asked her when she would be leaving and on what ship.

On the day Mary set out for the port town of Bristol, she was sick with grief. Passing the church where she and John had been married a few months earlier, she thought about everything that had happened to her since.

Now a twenty-four-year-old widow, she was going alone to a new land, casting her lot with the people of God.[7]

BACK IN NAUVOO, NEWSPAPER editor Thomas Sharp took a seat beside Joseph Smith on a raised platform and looked out over a crowd of several thousand Saints. It was April 6, 1841, the eleventh anniversary of the church and the first day of a general conference. A brass band played over the chatter of the congregation. In a few moments, the Saints would commemorate the important day by laying the cornerstones of a new temple.

Thomas did not belong to their church, but Nauvoo's mayor, John Bennett, had invited him to spend the day with the Saints.[8] It was not hard to guess why. As a newspaper editor, Thomas could make or break a reputation with a handful of words, and he had been brought to Nauvoo as a potential ally.

Like the Saints, Thomas was new to the region. Not yet twenty-three years old, he had come west the previous year to practice law and had settled in the city of Warsaw, about a day's journey south of Nauvoo. Within months of his arrival, he had become the editor of the only non-Mormon newspaper in the county and gained a reputation for his forceful writing.[9]

He was indifferent to the Saints' teachings and only mildly impressed by their devotion to their faith.[10] But he had to admit that today's events were striking.

The day had begun with deafening volleys of cannon fire followed by a parade of the city militia, called the Nauvoo Legion, which was made up of 650 men. Joseph Smith and John Bennett, dressed in the crisp blue coats and golden epaulets of military officers, had marched the Legion through town and up the bluff to the freshly dug foundation of the temple. Out of respect, the Saints had placed Thomas near the head of the procession, not far from Joseph and his militia aides.[11]

Sidney Rigdon began the cornerstone ceremony with a stirring hour-long speech about the Saints' recent tribulations and their efforts to build temples. Following the speech, Joseph stood and directed workers to lower the massive stone at the southeast corner of the foundation.

"This principal cornerstone, in representation of the First Presidency, is now duly laid in honor of the great God," he announced, "that the Saints may have a place to worship God, and the Son of Man have where to lay His head."[12]

After the sacred celebration, Joseph invited Thomas and other honored guests to his home for a turkey dinner. He wanted them to know they were welcome in Nauvoo. If they did not share his faith, he hoped they would at least accept his hospitality.[13]

JOSEPH WAS PLEASED TO learn that Thomas printed a favorable account of the cornerstone ceremony in his newspaper the next day. For the first time since the organization of the church, it seemed the Saints had the sympathies of their neighbors, government support, and friends in important places.[14]

As much as Joseph welcomed a time of goodwill and peace in Nauvoo, however, he knew the Lord expected him to obey all His commandments, even if doing so tried the faith of the Saints. And no commandment would be a greater trial than plural marriage.[15]

Joseph understood through revelation that marriage and family were central to God's plan. The Lord had sent Elijah the prophet to the Kirtland temple to restore priesthood keys that sealed generations together like links in a chain. Under the Lord's direction, Joseph had begun to teach more Saints that husbands and wives could be sealed together for time and eternity, becoming heirs to the blessings of Abraham and fulfilling God's eternal plan for His children.[16]

The prophet Jacob in the Book of Mormon taught that no man should have "save it be one wife," unless God commanded otherwise.[17] As the story of Abraham and Sarah showed, God sometimes commanded faithful followers to participate in plural marriage as a way to extend these blessings to more individuals and raise a covenant people to the Lord. Despite the trials it brought, Abraham's marriage to his plural wife Hagar had brought forth a great nation. Plural marriage would likewise try the Saints who practiced it, yet the Lord promised to exalt them for their obedience and sacrifice.[18]

The years following Joseph's departure from Kirtland had been turbulent, and he had not introduced the Saints to plural marriage then. But the situation was different in Nauvoo, where the Saints had finally found a measure of safety and stability.

Joseph also had confidence in the United States Constitution, which protected the free exercise of religion. Earlier that year, the Nauvoo City Council had affirmed this right when it passed an ordinance declaring that all religious groups were permitted to worship freely in Nauvoo. The law extended to Christians and non-Christians alike. Even though no one in Nauvoo followed Islam, the ordinance even specifically protected Muslims, who sometimes practiced polygamy.[19] Although politicians had disappointed him in the nation's capital, Joseph believed in and trusted the founding principles of the American republic to protect his right to live according to God's will.[20]

Still, he knew the practice of plural marriage would shock people, and he remained reluctant to teach it openly. While other religious and utopian communities often embraced different forms of marriage, the Saints had always preached monogamy. Most Saints—like most Americans—associated polygamy with societies they considered less civilized than their own.

Joseph himself left no record of his own views on plural marriage or his struggle to obey the commandment. Emma too disclosed nothing about how early she learned of the practice or what impact it had on her marriage. The writings of others close to them, however, make clear that it was a source of anguish for both of them.

Yet Joseph felt an urgency to teach it to the Saints, despite the risks and his own reservations. If he introduced the principle privately to faithful men and women, he could build strong support for it, preparing for the time when it could be taught openly. To accept plural marriage, people would have to overcome their prejudices, reconsider social customs, and exercise great faith to obey God when He commanded something so foreign to their traditions.[21]

Around the fall of 1840, Joseph had begun speaking with twenty-five-year-old Louisa Beaman about the practice. Louisa's family had been among the first to believe in the Book of Mormon and embrace the restored gospel. After her parents died, she had moved in with her older sister Mary and her sister's husband, Bates Noble, a veteran of the Camp of Israel.[22]

Bates was present during Joseph's discussions with Louisa about plural marriage.[23] "In revealing this to you, I have placed my life in your hands," Joseph told him. "Do not in an evil hour betray me to my enemies."[24]

Sometime later, Joseph proposed marriage to Louisa. She left no record of how she reacted to the offer, or when or why she accepted it. But on the evening of April 5, 1841, the day before general conference, Joseph met Louisa and Bates for the ceremony. Authorized by Joseph, Bates sealed the two together, repeating back the words of the ordinance as Joseph spoke them to him.[25]

THAT SUMMER, THE SAINTS rejoiced when John Bennett was appointed to an important position in the county court system. But others in the county were outraged, fearful of the Saints' growing political power. They saw John's appointment as an attempt by rival politicians to win the Saints' votes.[26]

Thomas Sharp, who was a member of the rival party, openly questioned John's qualifications for the position, his reputation, and the sincerity of his recent baptism. In a newspaper editorial, he urged citizens to oppose the appointment.[27]

Thomas also exaggerated reports of dissatisfaction among the hundreds of British Saints gathering to the area. "It is said that many have determined to leave," he reported, "and that letters have been sent to England, warning their friends, who had designed to emigrate, of the sad state of things in the City of the Church." At the heart of their discontent, he claimed, was a lack of faith in the prophet's mission.[28]

Livid after reading the editorial, Joseph dictated a letter and sent it to Thomas, canceling his subscription:

> *Sir—You will discontinue my paper—its contents are calculated to pollute me, and to patronize the filthy sheet—that tissue of lies—that sink of iniquity—is disgraceful to any moral man.*
>
> *Yours, with utter contempt,*
> *Joseph Smith*
>
> *P.S. Please publish the above in your contemptible paper.*[29]

Irritated by the letter, Thomas printed it in the next issue alongside sarcastic commentary about Joseph's prophetic call. Some people had accused Thomas of using his newspaper to flatter the Saints.[30] He now wanted his readers to know that he saw the Saints as a growing political threat to the rights of other citizens in the county.

As proof, Thomas reprinted a proclamation Joseph had recently published that called on Saints everywhere to gather and build up Nauvoo. "If his will is to be their law," Thomas warned his readers, "what may—nay, what *will*—become of your dearest rights and most valued privileges?"[31]

As Thomas grew more critical, Joseph worried that he would turn others in the county against the Saints.[32] With the temple's cornerstones in place and British immigrants coming by the shipload, so much was at stake. The Saints could not lose Nauvoo as they had lost Independence and Far West.

SAILING VESSELS LARGE AND small crowded the busy docks of Bristol Harbor in southwest England.[33] Stepping aboard the ship that would take her to North America, Mary Ann Davis found her bed clean and saw no signs of fleas. She and the other passengers were allowed to keep only one trunk beside their beds while the rest of their belongings were stowed in the ship's hold.

Mary remained in Bristol a week as the ship was being outfitted. For privacy, she and the other passengers hung curtains between their beds, partitioning the large room into tiny compartments. They also explored Bristol's narrow streets, taking in the sights and smells of the city.

Mary expected her parents to arrive any day to see her off. Why else would her father want to know the name of her ship and point of departure?

But her parents never came. Instead, lawyers—hired by her father to compel her not to leave—began visiting the ship daily, asking about a young widow with dark eyes and a black dress. Disappointed, but determined to gather to Zion, Mary packed away her mourning clothes and started dressing like the other young women on board.

The ship soon set sail for Canada. When it landed two months later, Mary and her company traveled south by steamship, train, and canal boat until they arrived at a harbor near Kirtland. Eager to be among the Saints, Mary and her friends made their way to the town, where they found William Phelps leading a small branch of the church.[34]

Kirtland was a shadow of what it had once been. On Sundays, William held meetings in the temple, often sitting alone in the pulpits. From her place in the congregation, Mary thought the temple looked forsaken.

Some weeks later, another company of British Saints arrived in Kirtland. One member of the company, Peter Maughan, planned to push on, taking a steamship across the Great Lakes to Chicago and then traveling overland to Nauvoo. Eager to finish their journey, Mary and several other Saints joined him and his six young children.[35]

On the way to Nauvoo, Mary and Peter became better acquainted. He was a widower who had worked in the lead mines of northwest England. His wife, Ruth, had died in childbirth shortly before the family planned to emigrate. Peter had considered staying in England, but Brigham Young had convinced him to come to Nauvoo.[36]

When Mary arrived in Nauvoo, she searched the city for friends from England. Making her way through the streets, she saw a man preaching atop a barrel and stopped to listen. The preacher was a cheerful man, and his plainspoken sermon captivated the small crowd. Now and then, he would lean forward and place his hands on the shoulders of a tall man in front of him, as if he were leaning on a desk.

Mary knew at once that he was Joseph Smith. After five months of traveling, she was finally standing among the Saints in the presence of the prophet of God.[37]

MEANWHILE, ON THE OTHER side of the world, Orson Hyde was overcome with emotion as he gazed for the first time on Jerusalem. The ancient city sat atop a hill bordered by valleys and surrounded by thick walls. As he approached the western gate of the city, weary from his travels, Orson caught glimpses of its walls and the towers looming behind them.[38]

Orson had hoped to enter Jerusalem with John Page, but John had gone home before leaving the United States. Setting off alone, Orson had traveled through England and across Europe, passing through some of the continent's great cities. He then headed southeast to Constantinople and caught a steamship to the coastal city of Jaffa, where he arranged to travel to Jerusalem with a company of English gentlemen and their heavily armed servants.

Over the next few days, Orson navigated Jerusalem's dusty, uneven streets and met with the city's religious and civic leaders. About ten thousand people, mostly Arabic speakers, lived in Jerusalem. The city was in a dilapidated state, with parts of it reduced to rubble after centuries of conflict and neglect.

Even so, as Orson visited places he had read about in the Bible, he was in awe of the city and its sacred history. When he saw people doing the everyday tasks described in the Savior's parables, he imagined himself transported back to the time of Jesus. In Gethsemane, he plucked a twig from an olive tree and contemplated the Atonement.[39]

On October 24, 1841, Orson rose before dawn and hiked down a slope near where Jesus had walked the night before His Crucifixion. Climbing the Mount of Olives, Orson looked back across the valley at Jerusalem and saw the spectacular Dome of the Rock, rising near the site where the temple had stood in the Savior's time.[40]

Knowing the Lord had promised that some of Abraham's posterity would be gathered to Jerusalem before the Second Coming, the apostle sat down and wrote out a prayer, asking God to lead the scattered remnants to their promised land.[41]

"Incline them to gather in upon this land according to thy word," Orson prayed. "Let them come like clouds and like doves to their windows."

When he finished his prayer, Orson made a pile of stones at the site and walked back across the valley to pile more stones on Mount Zion as a simple monument to the completion of his mission. He then began the long journey home.[42]

CHAPTER 37

We Will Prove Them

On January 5, 1842, Joseph opened a store in Nauvoo and cheerfully greeted his many customers. "I love to wait upon the Saints and be a servant to all," he told a friend in a letter, "hoping that I may be exalted in the due time of the Lord."[1]

The doctrine of exaltation weighed heavily on Joseph's mind.[2] In February, he turned his attention back to the Egyptian scrolls he had purchased in Kirtland and the unfinished translation of Abraham's writings.[3] The new scripture taught that God had sent His children to earth to test their faithfulness and willingness to obey His commandments.

"We will prove them herewith," the Savior had declared before the creation of the earth, "to see if they will do all things whatsoever the Lord their God shall command them." Those who were obedient to His commandments would be exalted to greater glory. Those who chose not to obey God lost these eternal blessings.[4]

Joseph wanted to help the Saints learn these truths so they could progress toward exaltation and enter into God's presence. In Kirtland, the endowment of power had fortified many men for the rigors of the mission field. But God had promised to bestow a greater spiritual endowment in the Nauvoo temple. By revealing additional ordinances and knowledge to faithful men and women of the church, the Lord would make them kings and queens, priests and priestesses, as John the Revelator had prophesied in the New Testament.[5]

Joseph urged the Twelve and other trusted friends to be obedient to the Lord as he prepared them to receive this endowment of divine power. He also taught the principle of plural marriage to a few more Saints and testified of its divine origin. The previous summer, less than a week after the apostles returning from England arrived in Nauvoo, he had taught the principle to a few of them and instructed them to obey it as a commandment of the Lord.[6] While plural marriage was not necessary for exaltation or the greater endowment of power, obedience to the Lord and a willingness to dedicate one's life to Him were.

Like Joseph, the apostles at first resisted the new principle. Brigham felt such agony over the decision to marry another wife that he longed for an early grave. Heber Kimball, John Taylor, and Wilford Woodruff wanted to delay obedience as long as possible.[7]

Following the Lord's command, Joseph had also been sealed to other women since his marriage to Louisa Beaman. When teaching a woman about plural marriage, he would instruct her to seek her own spiritual confirmation that being sealed to him was right. Not every woman accepted his invitation, but several did.[8]

In Nauvoo, some Saints entered plural marriages for time and eternity, which meant their sealing would last through this life and the next. Like monogamous marriages, these marriages could involve sexual relations and having children. Other plural marriages were for eternity only, and the participants understood that their sealing would take effect in the next life.[9]

In some cases, a woman who was married for time to a disaffected Saint, or to a man who was not a member of the church, or even to a church member in good standing, could be sealed for eternity to another man. After the sealing ceremony, the woman continued to live with her current husband while anticipating the blessings of an eternal marriage and exaltation in the life to come.[10]

Early in 1842, Joseph proposed such a sealing to Mary Lightner, whose husband, Adam, was not a member of the church. During their discussion, Joseph told Mary that the Lord had commanded them to be sealed together for the next life.[11]

"If God told you that," Mary asked, "why does He not tell me?"

"Pray earnestly," Joseph replied, "for the angel said to me you should have a witness."[12]

JOSEPH'S INVITATION UNSETTLED MARY. In teaching her about plural marriage, Joseph had described the everlasting blessings of the eternal marriage covenant.[13] When Mary had married Adam, they had made promises to each other for this life only. Now she understood that she could not make eternal covenants with him unless he first agreed to be baptized by proper authority.[14]

Mary spoke to Adam about baptism, pleading with him to join the church. Adam told her that he respected Joseph but he did not believe in the restored gospel and would not be baptized.[15]

Longing for the blessings of eternal marriage, yet knowing she could not receive them with Adam, Mary wondered what to do. Doubts flooded her mind. Finally, she prayed that the Lord would send an angel to confirm to her that Joseph's invitation was right.[16]

One night, while she was staying with her aunt, Mary saw a light appear in her room. Sitting up in bed, she was startled to see an angel, dressed in white, standing beside her. The angel's face was bright and beautiful, with eyes that pierced her like lightning.

Frightened, Mary threw the covers over her head, and the angel departed.

The following Sunday, Joseph asked Mary if she had received an answer.

"I have not had a witness, but I have seen something I have never seen before," Mary admitted. "I saw an angel and I was almost frightened to death. I did not speak."

"That was an angel of the living God," Joseph said. "If you are faithful you shall see greater things than that."[17]

Mary continued to pray. She had seen an angel, which strengthened her faith in Joseph's words. And she received other spiritual witnesses over the coming days that she could not deny or ignore. Adam would still be her husband in this life, but she wanted to ensure that she received all the blessings available to her in the life to come.[18]

She soon accepted Joseph's invitation, and Brigham Young sealed them together for the next life.[19]

UNDER JOSEPH'S DIRECTION, JOHN Taylor and Wilford Woodruff began publishing the prophet's translation of the book of Abraham in the March 1842 issues of the *Times and Seasons*. As the Saints read the record, they were thrilled to discover new truths about the creation of the world, the purpose of life, and the eternal destiny of God's children. They learned that Abraham had possessed a Urim and Thummim and had spoken with the Lord face-to-face. They read that the earth and everything in it had been organized from existing materials to bring about the exaltation of the Father's spirit children.[20]

Amid the excitement over the publication of the book of Abraham and the soul-expanding doctrine it taught, the Saints continued making sacrifices to build up their new city and construct the temple.

By this time, Nauvoo had more than a thousand log cabins, with many frame houses and solid brick homes completed or in the works.[21] To better organize the city, Joseph had divided it into four units called wards and appointed bishops to preside over them. Each ward was expected to assist with temple building by sending laborers to work on the Lord's house every tenth day.[22]

Margaret Cook, an unmarried woman who supported herself as a seamstress in Nauvoo, watched as work on the temple progressed. She had been working for Sarah Kimball, one of the earliest converts to the church, who had married a successful merchant who was not a Latter-day Saint.

As Margaret worked, she and Sarah sometimes talked about efforts to build the temple. The walls were still only a few feet high, but already craftsmen had built a temporary space in the temple's basement and installed a large font for baptisms for the dead. The font was an oval pool of expertly shaped pine boards sitting on the backs of twelve hand-carved oxen and finished with fine moldings. Once the font was dedicated, the Saints had begun performing baptisms for the dead again.[23]

Eager to contribute to the temple herself, Margaret noticed that many workers lacked adequate shoes, trousers, and shirts. She suggested to Sarah that they work together to provide new shirts for the workers. Sarah said she could supply the materials for the shirts if Margaret did the sewing. They could also enlist the help of other women in Nauvoo and organize a society to direct the work.[24]

A short time later, Sarah invited about a dozen women to her home to discuss the new society. They asked Eliza Snow, who was known for her writing talents, to draft a constitution. Eliza went to work immediately on the document and showed it to the prophet when she finished.

Joseph said it was the best constitution of its kind. "But this is not what you want," he said. "Tell the sisters their offering is accepted of the Lord and He has something better for them." He asked the society to meet with him in a few days at his store.

"I will organize the women under the priesthood, after the pattern of the priesthood," Joseph said.[25] "I now have the key by which I can do it."[26]

THE FOLLOWING THURSDAY, MARCH 17, 1842, Emma Smith climbed the steps to the large room above Joseph's store. Nineteen other women, including Margaret Cook, Sarah Kimball, and Eliza Snow, had come to organize the new society. Joseph was also there with Willard Richards, who had begun working as Joseph's scribe after returning from England, and John Taylor.[27]

The youngest woman in attendance was fifteen-year-old Sophia Marks. The oldest, Sarah Cleveland, was fifty-four. Most of the women were about Emma's age. Aside from Leonora Taylor, who was born in England, the women were all from the eastern United States and had come west with the Saints. A few of them, like Sarah Kimball and Sarah Cleveland, were well-off, while others owned little more than the dresses they wore.

The women knew each other well. Philinda Merrick and Desdemona Fullmer had survived the massacre at Hawn's Mill. Athalia Robinson and Nancy Rigdon were sisters. Emma Smith and Bathsheba Smith were cousins by marriage, as were Eliza Snow and Sophia Packard. Both Sarah Cleveland and Ann Whitney had helped Emma at difficult times in her life, taking her and her family into their homes when they had nowhere else to go. Elvira Cowles boarded in Emma's home and helped care for her children.[28]

Emma liked the idea of starting a society for women in Nauvoo. Lately, Joseph and other men in town had entered into a centuries-old fraternal society called Freemasonry, after longtime Masons like Hyrum Smith and John Bennett had helped to organize a Masonic lodge in the city. But the women in Nauvoo would have a different kind of society.[29]

After everyone sang "The Spirit of God" and John Taylor offered a prayer, Joseph stood and explained that the new society was to encourage women to seek out and care for the needy, offer righteous correction to those in error, and strengthen the community. He then invited the women to choose a president, who would select two counselors, just as in priesthood quorums. For the first time, women would have official authority and responsibilities in the church.[30]

Emma's friend Ann Whitney nominated her to be president, and the women in the room unanimously agreed. Emma then appointed Sarah Cleveland and Ann to be her counselors.

Joseph read the revelation he had received for Emma in 1830 and noted that she had been ordained or set apart at that time to expound scriptures and teach the women of the church. The Lord had called her an "elect lady," Joseph explained, because she was chosen to preside.

John Taylor then ordained Sarah and Ann as counselors to Emma and confirmed Emma in her new calling, blessing her with the strength she needed. After offering additional instructions, Joseph turned the meeting over to her, and John proposed that they decide on a name for the society.

Emma's counselors recommended that they call it the Nauvoo Female Relief Society, but John suggested the Nauvoo Female Benevolent Society instead, echoing the names of other women's societies across the country.[31]

Emma said she preferred "relief" over "benevolent," but Eliza Snow suggested that "relief" implied an extraordinary response to a great calamity. Wasn't their society going to focus more on the problems of everyday life?

"We are going to do something extraordinary," Emma insisted. "When a boat is stuck on the rapids with a multitude of Mormons on board, we shall consider that a loud call for relief. We expect extraordinary occasions and pressing calls."

Her words settled over the room. "I shall have to concede the point," John said. "Your arguments are so potent I cannot stand before them."

Ever attentive to the poetry of words, Eliza recommended a slight change in the name. Instead of the Nauvoo Female Relief Society, she proposed "the Female Relief Society of Nauvoo." The women all agreed.

"Each member should be ambitious to do good," Emma told them. Above all else, charity should motivate their society. As Paul taught in the New Testament, good works profited them nothing if charity did not abound in their hearts.[32]

JOSEPH MET FREQUENTLY WITH the Relief Society that spring. The organization grew rapidly, adding long-time Saints and newly baptized immigrants to its numbers. By its third meeting, the women hardly had space in Joseph's store for everyone who wished to attend. Joseph wanted the Relief Society to prepare its members for the endowment of power they would receive in the temple. He taught the women that they must be a select society, standing apart from evil and operating according to the pattern of the ancient priesthood.[33]

Meanwhile, Joseph was concerned by reports that a few men in Nauvoo were having sexual relations outside of marriage and claiming such behavior was permissible as long as they were kept secret. The seductions, which corrupted the Lord's teachings on chastity, were spread by men who cared nothing for the commandments. If these men continued unchecked, they could become a serious stumbling block for the Saints.

On March 31, Joseph asked Emma to read a letter to the Relief Society, advising them that church authorities never sanctioned such actions. "We want to put a stop to them," the letter declared, "for we wish to keep the commandments of God in all things."[34]

More than anything, Joseph wanted the Saints to be worthy of the blessings of exaltation. "If you wish to go where God is, you must be like God or possess the principles which God possesses," he told the Saints that spring. "As far as we degenerate from God, we descend to the devil and lose knowledge, and without knowledge we cannot be saved."[35]

He trusted the presidency of the Relief Society to lead the women of the church and to help them nurture such knowledge and righteousness in themselves.

"This society is to get instruction through the order which God has established—through the medium of those appointed to lead," he declared. "I now turn the key to you in the name of God, and this society shall rejoice, and knowledge and intelligence shall flow down from this time."[36]

ON MAY 4, 1842, BRIGHAM Young, Heber Kimball, and Willard Richards found the upper room of Joseph's store transformed. On the wall was a newly painted mural. Small trees and plants stood nearby, suggesting a garden setting. Another part of the room was sectioned off with a rug hung up like a curtain.[37]

Joseph had invited the three apostles to come to the store that morning for a special meeting. He had invited his brother Hyrum and William Law as well, both members of the First Presidency and two of his closest advisers. Also in attendance were bishops Newel Whitney and George Miller, Nauvoo's stake president, William Marks, and church leader James Adams.[38]

For the rest of the afternoon, the prophet introduced an ordinance to the men. Part of it involved washings and anointings, similar to the ordinances given in the Kirtland temple and the ancient Hebrew tabernacle. The men were given a sacred undergarment that covered their bodies and reminded them of their covenants.[39]

The new ordinance God revealed to Joseph taught exalting truths. It drew upon scriptural accounts of the Creation and the Garden of Eden, including the new account found in the Abraham translation, to guide the men step-by-step through the plan of salvation. Like Abraham and other ancient prophets, they received knowledge that would enable them to return to the presence of God.[40] Along the way, the men made covenants to live righteous, chaste lives and dedicate themselves to serving the Lord.[41]

Joseph called the ordinance the endowment and trusted the men not to reveal the special knowledge they learned that day. Like the endowment of power in Kirtland, the ordinance was sacred and meant for the spiritually minded. Yet it was more than an outpouring of spiritual gifts and divine power on the elders of the church. As soon as the temple was finished, both men and women would be able to receive the ordinance, strengthen their covenant relationship to God, and find greater power and protection in consecrating their lives to the kingdom of God.[42]

When the ceremony was finished, Joseph gave some instructions to Brigham. "This is not arranged right," he told the apostle, "but we have done the best we could under the circumstances in which we are placed, and I wish you to take this matter in hand and organize and systematize all these ceremonies."[43]

As they left the store that day, the men were in awe of the truths they had learned from the endowment. Some aspects of the ordinance reminded Heber Kimball of Masonic ceremonies. In Freemasonry meetings, men acted out an allegorical story about the architect of Solomon's temple. Masons learned gestures and words they pledged to keep secret, all of which symbolized that they were building a solid foundation and adding light and knowledge to it by degrees.[44]

Yet the endowment was a priesthood ordinance meant for men and women, and it taught sacred truths not contained in Masonry, which Heber was eager for others to learn.

"We have received some precious things through the prophet on the priesthood that would cause your soul to rejoice," Heber wrote Parley and Mary Ann Pratt in England. "I cannot give them to you on paper, for they are not to be written, so you must come and get them for yourself."[45]

CHAPTER 38

A Traitor or a True Man

Steady rain pelted the streets of Independence, Missouri, on the evening of May 6, 1842. At home, Lilburn Boggs finished his dinner and settled into a chair to read the newspaper.[1]

Although his term as the governor of Missouri had ended more than a year earlier, Boggs was still active in politics and was now running for an open seat in the state senate. He had made enemies over the years, and his election was hardly certain. Besides criticizing him for issuing the extermination order that drove thousands of Saints from the state, some Missourians were displeased with the governor's aggressive handling of a border dispute with Iowa Territory. Others raised questions about the way he had raised funds for a new state capitol building.[2]

As Boggs glanced at the headlines, he sat with his back to a window. The evening was cool and dark, and he could hear the faint patter of the rain outside.

At that moment, unbeknownst to Boggs, someone stole silently across his muddy yard and aimed a heavy pistol through the window. A flash of light erupted from the barrel, and Boggs slumped over his newspaper. Blood flowed from his head and neck.

Hearing the gunshot, Boggs's son rushed into the room and called for help. By then the shooter had tossed the weapon to the ground and fled unseen, leaving only footprints in the mud.[3]

WHILE INVESTIGATORS TRIED TO track down Boggs's shooter, Hyrum Smith was in Nauvoo investigating crimes of a different nature. In the early weeks of May, several women had accused Mayor John Bennett of appalling acts. In the presence of a city alderman, they told Hyrum that John had come to them in secret insisting that it was not sinful to have a sexual relationship with him as long as they told no one. Calling his practice "spiritual wifery," John had lied to them, assuring them that Joseph approved of such behavior.[4]

At first, the women had refused to believe John. But he insisted and had his friends swear to the women that he was telling the truth. If he was lying, he said, the sin would fall squarely on him. And if they became pregnant, he promised that as a physician, he would perform an abortion. The women eventually gave in to John—and to a few of his friends when they came making similar requests.

Hyrum was horrified. He had known for a while that John was not the man of character he had first claimed to be. Rumors about John's past had surfaced shortly after he moved to Nauvoo and became mayor. Bishop George Miller had been sent by Joseph to investigate the rumors and soon learned that John had a history of moving from place to place, using his many talents to take advantage of people.

George also discovered that John had children and was still married to a woman he had abused and cheated on for many years.[5]

After William Law and Hyrum had verified these findings, Joseph confronted John and rebuked him for his past wickedness. John had promised to reform, but Joseph had lost confidence in him and no longer trusted him as before.[6]

Now, as Hyrum listened to the women's testimony, he knew something more had to be done. Together Hyrum, Joseph, and William drew up a document excommunicating John from the church, which other church leaders signed. Because they were still investigating the extent of John's sins and hoped to settle the matter without creating a public scandal, they decided to withhold the excommunication notice.[7]

But one thing was certain: the mayor had become a danger to the city and the Saints, and Hyrum felt compelled to stop him.

JOHN PANICKED WHEN HE learned about Hyrum's investigation. With tears streaming down his cheeks, he went to Hyrum's office and begged for mercy. He said he would be ruined forever if others learned he had deceived so many women. He wanted to talk to Joseph and make things right.

The two men stepped outside, and John saw the prophet crossing the yard to his store. Reaching for him, John cried out, "Brother Joseph, I am guilty." His eyes were red with tears. "I acknowledge it, and I beg of you not to expose me."

"Why are you using my name to carry on your hellish wickedness?" Joseph demanded. "Did I ever teach you anything that was not virtuous?"

"Never!"

"Did you ever know anything unvirtuous or unrighteous in my conduct or actions at any time, either in public or in private?"

"I did not."

"Are you willing to make oath to this before an alderman of the city?"

"I am."

John followed Joseph to his office, and a clerk handed him a pen and paper. When the alderman arrived, Joseph stepped out of the room while John hunched over a desk and wrote out a confession stating that the prophet had not taught him anything contrary to the laws of God.[8] He then resigned his position as mayor of Nauvoo.[9]

Two days later, on May 19, the city council accepted John's resignation as mayor and appointed Joseph to the office. Before he closed the meeting, Joseph asked John if he had anything to say.

"I have no difficulty with the heads of the church, and I intend to continue with you, and hope the time may come when I may be restored to full confidence and fellowship," John said. "Should the time ever come that I may have the opportunity to test my faith, it will then be known whether I am a traitor or a true man."[10]

THE FOLLOWING SATURDAY, AN Illinois newspaper gave an update on the Lilburn Boggs shooting. The former governor was still clinging to life, it was reported, despite the serious wounds to his head. Police investigations into the identity of the shooter had proved fruitless. Some people accused Boggs's political rivals of pulling the trigger, but the newspaper argued that the Saints were behind it, claiming that Joseph had once prophesied a violent end for Boggs.

"Hence," it declared, "there is plenty of foundation for rumor."[11]

The report offended Joseph, who was tired of being accused of crimes he did not commit. "You have done me manifest injustice in ascribing to me a prediction of the demise of Lilburn W. Boggs," he wrote the editor of the newspaper. "My hands are clean, and my heart pure, from the blood of all men."[12]

The accusation came when he had little time to defend himself publicly. He was in the middle of a weeklong investigation into John Bennett's actions.[13] Day after day, the First Presidency, Quorum of the Twelve, and Nauvoo high council listened to the testimonies of John's victims. As they told their stories, Joseph discovered how much John had distorted the laws of God, making a mockery of the eternal covenant relationships Joseph had been trying to forge among the Saints.

During the hearings, he heard the testimony of Catherine Warren, the widow of a victim of the Hawn's Mill massacre. As a mother of five children, she was desperately poor and struggling to provide for her family.

Catherine said John Bennett was the first man to take advantage of her in Nauvoo. "He said he wished his desires granted," she told the high council. "I told him I was not guilty of such conduct and thought it would bring a disgrace on the church if I should become pregnant." She gave in to him after he had lied to her, telling her that church leaders approved of it.

Soon some of John's friends had also used the same lies to take advantage of her.

"Last winter I became alarmed at my conduct," Catherine told the high council. When she learned that Joseph and other church leaders did not sanction what John was doing, she decided to speak out against him. Joseph and the high council listened to Catherine, continued to fellowship her, and excommunicated the men who had deceived her.[14]

When the investigation concluded, John received his official excommunication notice as well. Once more, he begged for mercy and urged the council to handle his punishment quietly. He said the news would break his aging mother's heart and surely kill her with grief.[15]

Like Hyrum, Joseph was repulsed by John's sins, but with accusations about the Boggs shooting hanging over the Saints, and newspaper editors eager to find scandal in Nauvoo, he and other church leaders acted cautiously to avoid drawing attention to the matter. They decided not to publicize John's excommunication and waited to see if he would reform.[16]

Still, Joseph worried about the women John had deceived. It was not uncommon for communities to cruelly ostracize women they perceived to be guilty of sexual misconduct, even when the women were innocent of wrongdoing. Joseph urged the women of the Relief Society to be charitable and slow to condemn others.

"Repent, reform, but do it in a way to not destroy all around you," he counseled. He did not want the Saints to tolerate wickedness, but he did not want them to shun people either. "Be pure in heart. Jesus designs to save the people out of their sins," he reminded them. "Said Jesus, 'Ye shall do the work which ye see me do.' These are the grand key words for the society to act upon."

"All idle rumor and idle talk must be laid aside," Emma agreed. Yet she mistrusted quiet discipline. "Sin must not be covered," she told the women, "especially those sins which are against the law of God and the laws of the country." She believed in bringing sinners to light to prevent others from making the same errors.[17]

Joseph, however, continued to handle the matter privately. John's past behavior showed he tended to withdraw from a community after he was exposed and stripped of authority. Perhaps, if they waited patiently, John would simply leave town on his own.[18]

THE RELIEF SOCIETY MET for its tenth meeting on May 27, 1842, near a grove of trees where the Saints often went for worship services. Hundreds now belonged to the organization, including Phebe Woodruff, who had joined a month earlier with Amanda Smith, Lydia Knight, Emily Partridge, and dozens of other women.[19]

The weekly meetings were a time for Phebe to set aside the concerns of her busy life, learn about the needs of the people around her, and listen to sermons prepared specifically for the women of the church.

Often Joseph and Emma spoke at the meetings, but on this day Bishop Newel Whitney spoke to the women about the blessings the Lord would soon give them. Having just received the endowment, Bishop Whitney urged the women to stay focused on the work of the Lord and prepare to receive His power. "Without the female, all things cannot be restored to the earth," he declared.

He promised them that God had many precious things to bestow on the faithful Saints. "We must lose sight of vain things and remember that the eye of God is upon us. If we are striving to do right, although we may err in judgment many times, yet we are justified in the sight of God if we do the best we can."[20]

Two days after Newel's sermon, Phebe and Wilford climbed the bluff to the unfinished temple. As a family, they had endured hardships, including the death of their daughter Sarah Emma while Wilford was in England. Now they were more settled than they had ever been since their marriage, and they had welcomed two more children into their family.

Wilford managed the *Times and Seasons* office, which provided steady work so he could support their family. The Woodruffs lived in a modest home in the city while building a new brick home on land south of the temple. They had plenty of friends to visit in the area, including John and Jane Benbow, who had sold their large farm in England to gather with the Saints.[21]

Still, as Bishop Whitney had taught, the Saints had to keep striving to do right, engaging in the work of the Lord and avoiding distractions that would lead them astray.

More and more the temple was becoming crucial to keeping that focus. Descending to its basement, Phebe entered the baptismal font on May 29 and was baptized for her grandfather, grandmother, and great-uncle.[22] As

Wilford immersed her in the water, she had faith that her kindred dead would accept the restored gospel and make covenants to follow Jesus Christ and remember His sacrifice.

JOHN BENNETT WAS STILL in Nauvoo two weeks after he learned of his excommunication. By then the Relief Society had warned the women in the city about his crimes and fervently condemned the kind of lies he had spread about church leaders.[23] More unsavory information about John's past had also surfaced, and Joseph realized it was time to announce the former mayor's excommunication and publicly expose his grave sins.

On June 15, Joseph published a short notice of John's excommunication in the *Times and Seasons*.[24] A few days later, in a sermon at the temple site, he spoke plainly to more than a thousand Saints about John's lies and exploitation of women.[25]

John stormed out of Nauvoo three days later, saying the Saints were unworthy of his presence and threatening to send a mob after the Relief Society. Unfazed, Emma proposed that the Relief Society put together a pamphlet that denounced John's character. "We have nothing to do but fear God and keep the commandments," she told the women, "and in so doing we shall prosper."[26]

Joseph published an additional indictment against John, detailing the ex-mayor's long history of deviance. "Instead of manifesting a spirit of repentance," Joseph declared, "he has to the last proved himself to be unworthy of the confidence or regard of any upright person by lying to deceive the innocent and committing adultery in the most abominable and degraded manner."[27]

John, meanwhile, rented a room in a nearby town and sent bitter letters about Joseph and the Saints to a popular newspaper in Illinois. He accused Joseph of a host of crimes, including many that he himself had committed, and wove wildly false and exaggerated stories to support his claims and cover his sins.

In one letter, John accused Joseph of ordering the May shooting of Lilburn Boggs, repeating the story from the newspaper that the prophet had foretold Boggs's violent death and adding that Joseph had sent his friend and bodyguard Porter Rockwell to Missouri "to fulfill prophecy."[28]

The Saints could see lie after lie in John's writing, but the letters fed a fire that was already burning among their critics in Missouri. After recovering from the attack, Boggs had demanded that his would-be assassin be brought to justice. When he learned that Porter Rockwell had been visiting family in Independence at the time, Boggs accused Joseph of being an accomplice to his attempted murder. He then urged Thomas Reynolds, the new governor of Missouri, to request that Illinois officials arrest Joseph and send him back to Missouri for trial.[29]

Governor Reynolds agreed, and he in turn demanded that Thomas Carlin, the governor of Illinois, treat Joseph like a fugitive from justice who had fled Missouri after the crime.[30]

Knowing that Joseph had not been to Missouri since escaping the state three years earlier, and that there was no evidence of his involvement in the shooting, the Saints were outraged. The Nauvoo City Council and a group of Illinois citizens who were friendly to the Saints immediately petitioned the governor not to arrest Joseph.[31] Emma, Eliza Snow, and Amanda Smith traveled to Quincy to meet with the governor and personally deliver a Relief Society petition in support of Joseph. Governor Carlin listened to their entreaties, but he ultimately issued warrants for Joseph and Porter anyway.[32]

A deputy sheriff and two officers arrived in Nauvoo on August 8 and arrested the two men, charging Porter with shooting Boggs and Joseph with being an accessory. Before the sheriff could take them away, however, the Nauvoo City Council demanded the right to investigate the warrant. Joseph had been charged falsely before, and the Nauvoo charter granted the Saints power to protect themselves against abuses of the legal system.

Unsure if the council had the right to question the warrant, the sheriff delivered Joseph and Porter over to the city marshal and left town to ask the governor what he should do. When he returned two days later, the sheriff searched for his prisoners, but they were nowhere to be found.[33]

CHAPTER 39

The Seventh Trouble

On August 11, 1842, a sliver of moon reflected in the dark current as Joseph and his friend Erastus Derby silently paddled a skiff down the Mississippi. Ahead, they could see the outline of two wooded islands in the stretch of river between Nauvoo and Montrose. Steering between the islands, the men caught sight of another boat beached along a bank and paddled toward it.[1]

The day before, Joseph and Porter had slipped out of Nauvoo to avoid arrest, worried they would not get a fair trial. Porter had gone east to leave the state while Joseph had gone west, crossing the river to his uncle John's house in Iowa Territory, beyond the jurisdiction of the Illinois sheriff and his men. He had been hiding there all day, but he had grown anxious to see family and friends.

When Joseph and Erastus landed their skiff on the island, Emma, Hyrum, and some of Joseph's close friends greeted them. Taking Emma's hand, Joseph listened as the group sat in the boat and spoke quietly about the situation in Nauvoo.[2]

The danger was greater than Joseph had expected. His friends had heard that the governor of Iowa had issued an arrest warrant for him and Porter as well, meaning it was no longer safe for Joseph to hide at his uncle's house. They now expected sheriffs on both sides of the river to be searching for him.

Still, Joseph's friends believed the arrest attempts were illegal, a shameless scheme by his enemies in Missouri to capture the prophet. For now, the best thing for Joseph to do was to hide out at a friend's farm back on the Illinois side of the river and wait until things calmed down.[3]

As Joseph left the island, his heart overflowed with gratitude. Others had abandoned and betrayed him time and time again in the face of adversity. But these friends had come to help him in the dark of night, choosing to stand beside him and the truths he cherished.

"They are my brethren," he thought, "and I shall live."

Yet he felt the most gratitude for Emma. "Again she is here," he thought, "even in the seventh trouble, undaunted, firm and unwavering, unchangeable, affectionate Emma!"[4]

EMMA COMMUNICATED REGULARLY WITH Joseph over
the following days and weeks. When they could not
meet in person, they exchanged letters. When she
could evade the lawmen who watched her every action, she joined him at a safe house and strategized
about their next move. Often she relayed Joseph's
messages to and from the Saints, choosing which people he should trust and dodging those who meant
him harm.[5]

With sheriffs threatening to search every house in
Illinois if necessary, Joseph knew the Saints worried that
he would soon be captured and taken back to Missouri.
Some of his friends urged him to escape to the pine
forests north of Illinois, where Saints were harvesting
timber for the temple.[6]

Joseph hated the idea of running away, preferring
to stay in Illinois and see the crisis to the end. But he was
willing to go if that was what Emma wanted to do. "My
safety is with you," he wrote. "If you and the children
go not with me, I don't go."

Part of him yearned to take his family somewhere
else, if only for a short time. "I am tired of the mean,
low, and unhallowed vulgarity of some portions of the
society in which we live," he told Emma, "and I think
if I could have a respite of about six months with my
family, it would be a savor of life unto life."[7]

Emma responded to his letter later that day. "I am
ready to go with you if you are obliged to leave," she
wrote, "but still I feel good confidence that you can be

protected without leaving this country. There are more ways than one to take care of you."[8]

The next evening, she wrote a letter to Illinois governor Thomas Carlin assuring him of Joseph's innocence. Joseph was not in Missouri when the assassination attempt took place, she reasoned, and he was innocent of the charges against him. She believed that Joseph would never get a fair trial in Missouri and would likely be murdered instead.

"I beg you to spare my innocent children the heart-rending sorrow of again seeing their father unjustly dragged to prison, or to death," she pleaded.[9]

The governor responded to Emma a short time later. His letter was polite and carefully worded, insisting that his actions against Joseph were motivated strictly by a sense of duty. He expressed hope that Joseph would submit to the law, and he gave no indication that he was willing to change his mind on the matter.[10]

Undeterred, Emma wrote a second letter, this time explaining why arresting her husband was illegal.

"What good can accrue to this state or the United States, or any part of this state or the United States, or to yourself, or any other individual," she asked the governor, "to continue this persecution upon this people, or upon Mr. Smith?"

She sent the letter and waited for a reply.[11]

MEANWHILE, MOST SAINTS IN Nauvoo were unaware that Joseph was hiding only a few miles away. Some of them believed he had returned to Washington, DC. Others thought he had gone to Europe. As they watched the sheriff and his officers prowl the streets of Nauvoo, searching for clues to Joseph's whereabouts, the Saints grew anxious about his safety.[12] Yet they trusted that the Lord would protect His prophet, and they went on with day-to-day life.

Like other British immigrants, Mary Davis was still adjusting to her new home in Nauvoo. Since arriving in the city, she had married Peter Maughan, the young widower she had met in Kirtland, becoming stepmother to his children. Together they rented the home of Orson Hyde, who was still on his mission to Jerusalem, and struggled to find suitable work to support their family.[13]

Nauvoo provided plenty of jobs for farm laborers and builders but fewer opportunities for skilled laborers like Peter, who had lived and worked in the busy mining and manufacturing centers of England. Local entrepreneurs were trying to establish mills, factories, and foundries in Nauvoo, but these businesses were only getting started and could not employ all the skilled laborers pouring in from England.[14]

Lacking steady work, Mary and Peter had survived their first winter by selling some of their possessions to buy food and firewood. When Joseph learned about Peter's work as a miner in England, he had hired him to extract a vein of coal discovered on land he owned south of Nauvoo. The coal proved to be of superior quality, and Peter retrieved three wagonloads for Joseph before exhausting the vein.[15]

Some poor immigrant families left Nauvoo to find better-paying work in neighboring towns and cities, but Mary and Peter chose to stay in the city and make do with what they had. They laid out wooden planks on the unfinished floor of the Hyde house and put down feather mattresses for beds. They used a chest for a table and stored their dishes out in the open because they had no cupboards.[16]

Summertime heat in Nauvoo could be stifling, but when temperatures cooled in the afternoons and evenings, families like the Maughans set their chores aside and strolled together through the city. The streets were often full of people chatting about politics, local news, and the gospel. Sometimes the Saints held lectures, attended plays, or listened to the newly formed Nauvoo Brass Band fill the air with the popular music of the day. Groups of children were never far away, shooting marbles, jumping rope, and playing other outdoor games until the sun dipped behind the Mississippi and stars flickered in the darkening sky.[17]

BY THE END OF August, the letters John Bennett had published earlier that summer were being reprinted in newspapers across the country, damaging the church's reputation and making it harder for missionaries to share the message of the restored gospel. In response, church leaders called hundreds of elders on missions to combat the negative press.

On August 29, the elders met in the grove near the temple site to receive instruction. During Hyrum's address, a stir passed through the congregation when Joseph climbed onto the stand and took a seat. Many of the elders had not seen him since he went into hiding earlier that month.

Illinois authorities were still hunting Joseph, but they had recently left the area, allowing Joseph to relax his guard somewhat. For a little more than a week, he had been living quietly at home with his family and meeting privately with the Twelve and other church leaders.[18]

Two days after the conference with the elders, Joseph felt safe enough to attend a Relief Society meeting. He spoke to the women about his recent trials and the accusations made against him. "Although I do wrong, I do not the wrongs that I am charged with doing," he said. "The wrong that I do is through the frailty of human nature, like other men. No man lives without fault."

He thanked Emma and the other women for defending him and petitioning the governor in his behalf. "The Female Relief Society has taken the most active part in my welfare against my enemies," he said. "If these measures had not been taken, more serious consequences would have resulted."[19]

That weekend, he and Emma hosted former apostle John Boynton. Although John had been a dissenter— and had even threatened Joseph's brother with a sword in the Kirtland temple—he had put his differences with Joseph behind him. As the family ate their noonday meal, an Illinois sheriff and two armed officers barged into the house with new orders to arrest the prophet. John distracted the men, giving Joseph time to duck out the back door, cut through the cornstalks in his garden, and take cover in his store.

At the house, Emma demanded to see the sheriff's search warrant. He told her he did not have one and pushed past her with his men. They rummaged from room to room, searching behind every door and curtain, but found nothing.

That night, after the lawmen had left town, Joseph moved into the home of his friends Edward and Ann Hunter.[20] "I have thought it expedient and wisdom in me to leave the place for a short season, for my own safety and the safety of this people," Joseph wrote the Saints a few days later. He did not wish to dwell on his trials, though, and he shared a new revelation with them about baptism for the dead.

"Verily thus saith the Lord," read the revelation, "let the work of my temple, and all the works which I have appointed unto you, be continued on and not cease." The Lord instructed the Saints to keep a record of the proxy baptisms they performed and to provide witnesses for them, so that the redemption of the dead might be recorded on earth and in heaven.[21]

A few days later, Joseph sent the Saints additional instructions about the ordinance. "The earth will be smitten with a curse, unless there is a welding link of some kind or other between the fathers and the children," he wrote, paraphrasing Malachi. He explained that generations past and present were to work together to redeem the dead and bring about the fullness of times, when the Lord would reveal all the keys, powers, and glories He held in reserve for the Saints, including things He had never revealed before.

Joseph's joy in God's mercy toward the living and dead could not be contained. Even in hiding, unjustly hunted by his enemies, he exulted in the restored gospel of Jesus Christ.

"What do we hear in the gospel?" he asked the Saints. "A voice of gladness! A voice of mercy from heaven; and a voice of truth out of the earth!" He wrote jubilantly of the Book of Mormon, of angels restoring the priesthood and its keys, and of God revealing His plan line upon line and precept upon precept.

"Shall we not go on in so great a cause?" he asked. "Let your hearts rejoice, and be exceedingly glad. Let the earth break forth into singing. Let the dead speak forth anthems of eternal praise to the King Immanuel." All creation testified of Jesus Christ, and His victory over sin and death was certain.

"How glorious is the voice we hear from heaven!" Joseph rejoiced.[22]

IN THE FALL OF 1842, Governor Carlin responded to Emma's second letter, expressing admiration for her devotion to her husband but ultimately refusing to help her.[23] Around the same time, John Bennett published a book-length exposé of Joseph and the Saints. He also started giving lectures on what he called "The Secret Wife System at Nauvoo," tantalizing audiences with wild rumors he had heard—and plenty he had made up himself—about Joseph's plural marriages.[24]

With John's aggressive campaign in full swing, and Governor Carlin refusing to intervene, Joseph felt more and more cornered. He knew he could not give himself up and stand trial as long as his enemies in Missouri wanted him dead. But neither could he stay in hiding for the rest of his life. How long could he evade arrest before the state turned on his family and the Saints for protecting him?[25]

In December, after Joseph had been in hiding for three months, Governor Carlin's term ended. Although the new governor, Thomas Ford, refused to interfere directly in Joseph's case, he expressed sympathy for the prophet's plight and confidence that the courts would rule in his favor.[26]

Joseph did not know if he could trust the new governor, but he had no better option. The day after Christmas 1842, he surrendered himself to Wilson Law, a general in the Nauvoo Legion and William Law's brother. They then made their way to Springfield, the state capital, for a hearing to determine whether the Missouri governor's demand for Joseph's arrest was legal and whether he would be sent back to Missouri to stand trial.[27]

Joseph's arrival in Springfield caused an uproar. Curious spectators crowded the courtroom across the street from the new capitol building, pressing together and craning their necks to catch a glimpse of the man who called himself a prophet of God.

"Which is Joe Smith?" someone asked. "Is it that big man?"

"What a sharp nose!" said someone else. "He is too smiling for a prophet!"[28]

Judge Nathaniel Pope, one of the most respected men in Illinois, presided over the courtroom. Joseph sat with his lawyer, Justin Butterfield, at the front of the courtroom. Nearby, Willard Richards, acting as Joseph's secretary, hunched over an open notebook, taking down a record of the proceedings. Several other Saints crowded into the room.[29]

In Judge Pope's mind, Joseph's case was not about whether the prophet was an accomplice in the Boggs shooting, but whether he had been in Missouri when the crime occurred and then fled the state. Josiah Lamborn, Illinois's young district attorney, focused his opening statements on Joseph's alleged prophecy about Boggs's demise. He reasoned that if Joseph had prophesied Boggs's shooting, then he ought to be held accountable and tried in Missouri.[30]

When Mr. Lamborn finished his statement, Joseph's lawyer argued that Governor Boggs's accusations and the charges against Joseph were faulty, since Joseph had not been in Missouri when the shooting took place. "There is not a particle of testimony that Joseph has fled from Missouri," Mr. Butterfield reasoned. "He is not subject to be transported till it is proven that he is a fugitive. They must prove he had fled!"

He then presented the court with witness testimonies confirming Joseph's innocence. "I do not think the defendant ought under any circumstances to be delivered up to Missouri," he concluded.[31]

The next morning, January 5, 1843, the courtroom buzzed with anticipation as Joseph and his lawyers returned to hear the judge's ruling. The Saints waited anxiously, knowing that if Judge Pope decided against Joseph, the prophet could easily be in the hands of his enemies by nightfall.

Judge Pope arrived shortly after nine o'clock. Taking his seat, he thanked the attorneys and began to voice his decision. He had much to say on the case, and as he spoke, Willard Richards hurried to write down every word.

As the defense attorney had argued the day before, the judge concluded that Joseph had been summoned to stand trial in Missouri illegally. "Smith must be discharged," he declared, seeing no reason to detain Joseph any longer.

Joseph rose from his chair and bowed to the court. After five months of hiding, he was finally free.[32]

CHAPTER 40

United in an Everlasting Covenant

When Joseph returned to Nauvoo on January 10, 1843, friends and relatives flocked to his house to congratulate him. Soon after, he and Emma held a dinner party to celebrate his victory and their sixteenth wedding anniversary. Wilson Law and Eliza Snow composed songs for the occasion, and Joseph and Emma served the meal while their guests laughed and shared stories.[1]

Joseph enjoyed being among loved ones. "If I had no expectation of seeing my mother, brothers, and sisters and friends again," he soon mused, "my heart would burst in a moment."[2] He took comfort knowing that baptisms for the living and dead, the endowment, and eternal marriage provided ways for the Saints to make sacred covenants that sealed them together and ensured that their relationships continued beyond the grave.

Yet up to now no women and only a handful of men had received the endowment, and many Saints were still unaware of the eternal marriage covenant. Joseph clung to the promise that he would live to finish his mission, and he yearned for the temple to be completed so he could introduce the Saints to these ordinances. He continued to feel like time was running out.

Still he sprinted forward, urging the Saints to keep pace. He believed extraordinary blessings were available to those who received sacred ordinances and obeyed God's laws. Now, more than ever, his goal was to extend the divine knowledge he had received to a greater number of Saints, to help them make and keep covenants that would uplift and exalt them.[3]

THE MISSISSIPPI RIVER FROZE solid that winter, blocking the usual traffic of rafts and riverboats up and down the water. Snow fell often, and icy winds cut across the flatlands and over the bluff. Few Saints stayed outside long since many of them had only low shoes, thin jackets, and threadbare shawls to protect them from the cold and slush.[4]

As the end of winter approached, a bitter chill still hung in the air while Emily Partridge washed clothes and tended children at the Smith home. For more than two years, she and her older sister Eliza had been living and working with the Smiths, not far from where their mother lived with her new husband.[5]

Emily belonged to the Relief Society and talked often with the women around her. Occasionally she would hear whispers about plural marriage. More than thirty Saints had quietly embraced the practice, including two of her stepsisters and one of her stepbrothers. Emily herself knew nothing about it firsthand.[6]

A year earlier, however, Joseph had mentioned that he had something to tell her. He had offered to write it in a letter, but she asked him not to do so, worried that it might say something about plural marriage. Afterward, she had regretted her decision and told her sister about the conversation, sharing what little she knew about the practice. Eliza appeared upset, so Emily said nothing more.[7]

With no one to confide in, Emily felt like she was struggling alone in deep water. She turned to the Lord and prayed to know what to do, and after some months, she received divine confirmation that she should listen to what Joseph had to say to her—even if it had to do with plural marriage.[8]

On March 4, a few days after her nineteenth birthday, Joseph asked to speak with Emily at the home of Heber Kimball. She set out as soon as she finished work, her mind ready to receive the principle of plural marriage. As expected, Joseph taught it to her and asked if she would be sealed to him. She agreed, and Heber performed the ordinance.[9]

Four days later, her sister Eliza was sealed to Joseph too. The sisters could now talk to each other and share what they understood and felt about the covenants they made.[10]

THE SAINTS CONTINUED TO defend Joseph against the accusations in John Bennett's exposé. Much of what John had written was embellished or flatly untrue, but his claim that Joseph had married multiple women was correct. Unaware of this fact, Hyrum Smith and William Law fiercely denied all of John's statements and unwittingly condemned the actions of Saints who obediently practiced plural marriage.[11]

This made Brigham Young uneasy. As long as members of the First Presidency remained unaware of the practice, he believed, their condemnation of polygamy could prevent Joseph and others from fulfilling the commandment of the Lord.

Joseph had already tried without success to teach his brother and William about plural marriage. Once, during a council meeting, he had barely broached the issue when William interrupted. "If an angel from heaven was to reveal to me that a man should have more than one wife," he said, "I would kill him!"

Brigham could see that Hyrum's and William's actions exhausted Joseph. One Sunday, as Brigham finished his evening chores, Joseph arrived unexpectedly at his door. "I want you to go to my house and preach," Joseph said.

Normally Brigham enjoyed meeting with the Saints, but he knew Hyrum would be preaching that evening as well. "I would rather not go," he said.[12]

Both Brigham and his wife Mary Ann had come to know through prayer and inspiration that they should practice plural marriage. With Mary Ann's consent, Brigham had been sealed to a woman named Lucy Ann Decker in June 1842, a year after Joseph had first taught him the principle. Lucy had separated from her first husband and had young children to care for.[13]

"Brother Brigham," Joseph insisted, "if you do not go with me, I will not go home to my house tonight."

Reluctantly, Brigham agreed to preach, and he walked home with the prophet. They found Hyrum standing beside the fireplace, speaking to a full house. He held the Bible, Book of Mormon, and Doctrine and Covenants in his hand and declared that they were the law God had given them to build up His kingdom.

"Everything more than these," Hyrum said, "is of man and is not of God."

Brigham listened to Hyrum's sermon, his emotions rising. Beside him, Joseph sat with his face buried in his hands. When Hyrum finished, Joseph nudged Brigham and said, "Get up."

Brigham stood and picked up the scriptures Hyrum had set down. He laid the books in front of him, one by one, so everyone in the room could see. "I would not give the ashes of a rye straw for these three books," he declared, "without the living oracles of God."[14] Lacking a latter-day prophet, he said, the Saints were no better off than they were before God revealed the gospel through Joseph Smith.

When he finished, Brigham could tell his sermon had moved Hyrum. Rising to his feet, Hyrum humbly asked the Saints to forgive him. Brigham was right, he said. As valuable as the scriptures were, they were no substitute for a living prophet.[15]

THAT SPRING, JOSEPH OFTEN left Nauvoo to visit the smaller stakes of the church nearby. Everywhere he went, he was accompanied by his new clerk William Clayton, a bright young man from England. William had gathered to Nauvoo with his wife, Ruth, in 1840 and had been hired by the prophet soon after.[16]

On April 1, William traveled a half a day with Joseph and Orson Hyde, who had recently returned from Jerusalem, to a meeting in a town called Ramus.[17] The next morning, William listened as Orson preached that it was the Saints' privilege to have the Father and Son dwell in their hearts until the Second Coming.[18]

Later, while they enjoyed a meal at the home of Joseph's sister Sophronia, Joseph said, "Elder Hyde, I am going to offer some corrections to you."

"They shall be thankfully received," Orson replied.

"To say that the Father and the Son dwell in a man's heart is an old sectarian notion and is not correct,"

Joseph said. "We shall see Him as He is. We shall see that He is a man like ourselves."[19]

Joseph had more to say on the matter when the conference continued later that evening. "The Father has a body of flesh and bones as tangible as man's, and the Son also," he taught, "but the Holy Ghost is a personage of spirit."[20]

As Joseph spoke, William wrote down as much of the sermon as he could in his diary. He was drawn to the profound truths Joseph shared and hungered to know more.

William recorded Joseph's teaching that the knowledge and intelligence people acquired in life rose with them in the Resurrection. "If a person gains more knowledge in this life, through his diligence and obedience, than another," Joseph explained, "he will have so much the advantage in the world to come."[21]

A month later, Joseph and William returned to Ramus and stayed in the home of Benjamin and Melissa Johnson. Joseph taught the Johnsons that a woman and man could be sealed together for eternity in the new and everlasting covenant of marriage. Only by entering into this covenant, which was an order of the priesthood, he taught, could they obtain exaltation. Otherwise, their relationship would cease beyond the grave, putting an end to their eternal progress and increase.

Joseph's description of eternal marriage awed William. "I feel desirous to be united in an everlasting covenant to my wife," he wrote in his diary, "and pray that it may soon be."[22]

ORSON HYDE'S RETURN FROM Jerusalem meant that Peter and Mary Maughan had to move their family out of the Hyde home in Nauvoo. Having nowhere else to stay, they camped on a city lot they acquired from the temple committee, with the understanding that Peter would work on the temple to pay for the land. Mary, meanwhile, bartered spools of cotton she had brought from England for food.

Peter soon started work as a stonemason, cutting and shaping limestone blocks for the temple.[23] By now, the walls were twelve feet high in some places, and a temporary floor had been installed to allow the Saints to hold meetings in the temple.[24]

The building was going to be bigger and grander than the temple Peter and Mary had visited in Kirtland. It would still have assembly rooms on its first and second floors. But the exterior of the temple in Nauvoo would be adorned with ornate stone carvings of stars, moons, and suns, evoking the kingdoms of glory described in Joseph's vision of the Resurrection as well as John the Revelator's description of the church as "a woman clothed with the sun, and the moon under her feet, and upon her head a crown of twelve stars."[25]

Week after week, workers used gunpowder to extract stone from quarries north of town. They then chiseled the rock into rough blocks and used ox-drawn carts to haul them to a workshop near the temple. There, men like Peter cut and polished the blocks to the right fit while skilled artisans carved and sculpted the more decorative stones. When a stone was ready, workers attached it to a tall crane and hoisted it into place.[26]

With steady work and land of their own, Peter and Mary planted a vegetable garden, worked on building their house, and looked forward to comfortable days ahead.[27]

TWO MONTHS AFTER HER sealing to Joseph, Emily Partridge still worked every day in the Smith home, washing and mending clothes and tending the children. Julia Smith turned twelve that spring and took painting lessons.[28] The boys too were getting older. Young Joseph was ten, Frederick was six, and Alexander was nearly five. The older children attended school with Emily's younger sister Lydia. Young Joseph also played with her nine-year-old brother, Edward Jr.[29]

In choosing to be sealed to Joseph, Emily trusted in her witness that she was acting in obedience to the Lord's commandment. She and her sister Eliza continued to keep their marriages private. They and the others who practiced plural marriage never referred to it as polygamy, which they considered a worldly term, not a priesthood ordinance.[30] When Joseph or someone else condemned "polygamy" or "spiritual wifery" in public, those who practiced plural marriage understood that they were not referring to their covenant relationships.[31]

Aside from the Bible, Joseph had no models or precedents to follow, and the Lord did not always give him exact instructions on how to obey His word. As with other commandments and revelations, Joseph had to move forward according to his best judgment. Only many years later did Emily and others write recollections of Joseph's obedience to the principle and their own experiences with plural marriage in Nauvoo. Their accounts were often brief and fragmented.[32]

Because neither Joseph nor Emma wrote down how they felt about plural marriage, many questions are left unanswered. In her writings, Emily recorded some of their struggles with the practice. At times Emma rejected it completely while at other times reluctantly accepting it as a commandment. Torn between the Lord's mandate to practice plural marriage and Emma's opposition, Joseph sometimes chose to marry women without Emma's knowledge, creating distressing situations for everyone involved.[33]

In early May, Emma took Emily and Eliza aside and explained the principle of plural marriage to them.[34] She had told Joseph that she would consent to him being sealed to two additional wives as long as she could choose them, and she had chosen Emily and Eliza, apparently unaware that Joseph had already been sealed to them.[35]

Rather than mention her former sealing, Emily believed that keeping silent on the matter was the best thing for her to do.[36] A few days later, she and Eliza were again sealed to Joseph, this time with Emma as a witness.[37]

On May 14, while Joseph was away at another conference, Hyrum preached in the temple against men having more than one wife. Referring to Jacob's condemnation of unauthorized plural marriages in the Book of Mormon, Hyrum called the practice an abomination before God.[38]

After the sermon, Hyrum began to question his own certainty about what he taught. Discussions about plural marriage swirled around Nauvoo, and rumors that Joseph had several wives were also common.[39]

Hyrum wanted to believe this was not the case, but he wondered if Joseph was not telling him something. There had been times, after all, when Joseph had alluded to the practice, perhaps testing Hyrum to see how he would react. And Hyrum sensed there were some things that Joseph told the Twelve that he had not taught him.

One day soon after the sermon, Hyrum saw Brigham near his home and asked if they could talk. "I know there is something or other which I do not understand that is revealed to the Twelve," he said. "Is this so?"

The men sat down on a pile of fence rails. "I do not know anything about what you know," Brigham answered cautiously, "but I know what I know."

"I have mistrusted for a long time that Joseph had received a revelation that a man should have more than one wife," Hyrum said.

"I will tell you about this," Brigham said, "if you will swear with an uplifted hand before God that you will never say another word against Joseph and his doings and the doctrines he is preaching."

Hyrum stood up. "I will do it with all my heart," he said. "I want to know the truth."

As Brigham taught him about the Lord's revelation to Joseph on plural marriage, Hyrum wept, convinced that Joseph acted under commandment.[40]

IN LATE MAY 1843, Emma and Joseph were sealed together for eternity in a room above Joseph's store, solemnizing at last what they had long desired.[41] Joseph then invited Brigham and Mary Ann Young, Willard and Jennetta Richards, Hyrum and Mary Fielding Smith, and Mary's widowed sister, Mercy Thompson, to meet with him the following morning to receive the same ordinance.[42]

Before the meeting, Hyrum worried about his complicated family situation. If the blessings of eternal marriage belonged only to those who had been sealed together by the priesthood, what would happen to his first wife, Jerusha, who had died six years earlier?

"You can have her sealed to you upon the same principle as you can be baptized for the dead," Joseph said.

"What can I do for my second wife?" Hyrum asked.

"You can also make a covenant with her for eternity," Joseph said.

Mary agreed to serve as Jerusha's proxy in the special sealing. "And I will be sealed to you for eternity myself," she told Hyrum. "I love you and I do not want to be separated from you."[43]

On the morning of May 29, Joseph and the others met above his store, and each couple was sealed together, uniting them for eternity. As the only widow in the room, Mercy Thompson could not help feeling different from the others. But learning that she could still be sealed to her late husband, Robert, who had died of a malarial fever a few years earlier, made her feel like God was mindful of her and her situation.[44]

When Mercy's turn came to receive the ordinance, Joseph said he could think of no one better than her brother-in-law Hyrum to stand in for Robert. He sealed her to Robert, then sealed Hyrum to Jerusha with Mary serving as proxy.[45]

Brigham closed their meeting with a hymn and a prayer, and the friends spent the rest of the morning talking about the things of God. A pleasant harmony seemed to quiet everything that had troubled the Saints for the last few years.[46]

CHAPTER 41

God Must Be the Judge

On June 1, 1843, Addison and Louisa Pratt walked with their daughters to one of Nauvoo's steamboat landings. Addison was leaving that day for a three-year mission to the Hawaiian Islands. In his arms he carried Anne, their youngest daughter, while her older sisters, Ellen, Frances, and Lois, followed gloomily behind, dreading their father's departure.[1]

Recently, while talking with Brigham Young, Addison had spoken fondly about Hawaii and his years as a young whaler in the Pacific Ocean. Since the church had no presence on the islands, Brigham asked if Addison would be willing to open a mission there. Addison said he was willing if others would go with him. Soon after, Joseph and the Twelve called him to lead a group of elders to the islands.[2]

Louisa had cried for three days when she learned of Addison's assignment. Hawaii was thousands of miles away, in a part of the world that sounded strange and dangerous. She had no home of her own in Nauvoo, no money, and few goods to barter. Her daughters would need clothes and schooling, and without Addison, she would have to provide every-thing for them.

As Louisa walked to the steamboat with her family, her heart still felt weak, but she had come to rejoice that Addison was worthy of his call. She was not the only woman in the city who would be alone while her husband left to preach the gospel. Missionaries were leaving in all directions that summer, and Louisa had resolved to face her trials and trust the Lord.

Addison struggled to restrain his emotions. Stepping onto the deck of the steamboat that would carry him far from his family, he raised a handkerchief to his eyes and wiped away tears. On shore, his daughters started crying as well. Frances said she did not think she would ever see him again.[3]

Knowing the sea as he did, Addison understood the dangers ahead of him. But when the Twelve had set him apart for his mission, they had blessed him to have power over the elements and courage in the face of tempests. If he proved faithful, they promised by the Spirit, he would return home safely to his family.[4]

SEVERAL DAYS LATER, EMMA, Joseph, and their children left Nauvoo to visit Emma's sister in Dixon, Illinois, several days' journey to the north. Before departing, she instructed Ann Whitney to encourage the women of the Relief Society to continue helping the poor and to assist the men in building the temple.[5]

Recently, Joseph had spoken to the Saints about the ordinances of the temple, teaching them that they were building it so the Lord could give them the endowment. Emma had told Ann that she had felt a deep interest in the temple since then and wanted the Relief Society to discuss what they could do to hurry the work along.

"We might speak to the temple committee," Emma suggested, "and whatever they wished and we could, we might do."[6]

With this charge, Ann called to order the first Relief Society meeting of the year and asked the women to suggest ways to help the temple effort. Some said they were willing to ask for donations and collect wool and other materials to make new clothes. Others said they were willing to knit, sew, or repair old clothes as needed. One woman suggested furnishing older women with yarn to knit socks for the temple workmen in the winter.

Polly Stringham and Louisa Beaman said they would make clothing for the workers. Mary Felshaw said she could donate soap. Philinda Stanley proposed donating flax to make linen and giving a quart of milk every day to the effort. Esther Gheen offered to donate thread of her own spinning.

"Angels are rejoicing over you!" Sister Chase testified, praising the women's willingness to help build the house of the Lord.

Before closing the meeting, Ann urged the mothers in the room to prepare their daughters to enter the temple. Instruct them in love, she counseled, and teach them to act with sobriety and propriety within its sacred walls.[7]

TWO HUNDRED MILES AWAY, the Smiths' visit with Emma's sister was interrupted on June 21 when William Clayton and Stephen Markham arrived with alarming news. The governor of Missouri was again demanding that Joseph stand trial in Missouri, this time on the old charge of treason, and Governor Ford of Illinois had just issued another warrant for the prophet's arrest.

"I have no fear," Joseph said. "Missourians cannot hurt me."[8]

A few days later, two men claiming to be Latter-day Saint elders knocked at the door while the family was eating dinner. Emma's brother-in-law told them that Joseph was out in the yard, near the barn.

Moments later Emma and the family heard a commotion outside. Rushing to the door, they saw the men pointing cocked pistols at Joseph's chest. One man held Joseph by the collar. "If you stir one inch," he snarled, "I'll shoot you!"

"Shoot away!" Joseph said, baring his chest. "I am not afraid of your pistols."

Stephen Markham ran outside and charged toward the men. Startled, they turned their guns on him but quickly turned them back to Joseph, jabbing the barrels into his ribs. "Stand still!" they shouted at Stephen.

They wrestled Joseph into the back of their wagon and held him there. "Gentlemen," Joseph said, "I wish to obtain a writ of habeas corpus." The writ would allow a local judge to rule on whether Joseph's arrest was legal.

"Damn you!" they said, once again striking him in the ribs with their pistols. "You shan't have one!"

Stephen sprang at the wagon and seized the horses by their bits as Emma rushed into the house and grabbed Joseph's coat and hat. At that instant, Joseph saw a man passing by the house. "These men are kidnapping me!" he cried out. When the man kept walking, Joseph turned to Stephen and told him to get help.

"Go!" he shouted.[9]

JOSEPH'S CAPTORS WERE LAW enforcement officers from Illinois and Missouri. That afternoon they locked him in a nearby tavern and refused to let him see a lawyer. Acting quickly, Stephen reported Joseph's mistreatment to local authorities, who soon had the officers arrested for kidnapping and abuse. Stephen then helped to secure a writ of habeas corpus from a nearby court official. The writ required Joseph to attend a hearing sixty miles away.

When they found out the judge was not in town, Joseph, his captors, and his captors' captors set out to find another court that could sort out the legal mess.[10]

In Nauvoo, Wilson Law and Hyrum learned of Joseph's capture and enlisted more than a hundred men to rescue him. They sent some men up the river on a steamer while they ordered others to ride on horseback in every direction and search for the prophet.

When his first two rescuers came into sight, Joseph was relieved. "I am not going to Missouri this time," he told his captors. "These are my boys." Soon the two rescuers became twenty—and then more. They turned the party toward Nauvoo, where they believed the municipal court could rule on the legality of the warrant.[11]

By midday the prophet approached the city, flanked by a few lawmen and his rescuers on horseback. Emma, who had already returned to Nauvoo with the children, rode out with Hyrum to meet Joseph as the Nauvoo Brass Band played patriotic songs and people fired guns and cannons in celebration. A parade of carriages soon joined them, drawn by horses decorated with prairie flowers.

Crowds lined both sides of the street to cheer the prophet's safe return as the procession passed in front of them, winding its way slowly to Joseph's home. When it arrived, Lucy Smith embraced her son, and his children rushed out of the house to see him.

"Pa," said seven-year-old Frederick, "the Missourians won't take you again, will they?"

"I am out of the hands of the Missourians again, thank God," Joseph said, climbing atop a fence to address the hundreds of Saints who had gathered around him. "I thank you all for your kindness and love to me," he cried. "I bless you all in the name of Jesus Christ."[12]

As expected, the Nauvoo court declared Joseph's arrest illegal. Outraged, the two arresting officers demanded that the governor challenge the ruling. But Governor Ford refused to interfere with the court's decision, angering the Saints' critics across the state. They began to fear that Joseph would once again escape prosecution.[13]

Meanwhile, hundreds of Saints continued to gather to Nauvoo and its neighboring stakes. In the eastern state of Connecticut, a young woman named Jane Manning boarded a canal boat with her mother, several siblings, and other members of her branch to begin their journey to Nauvoo. Leading them was Charles Wandell, a missionary who served as their branch president.

Unlike the other members of their branch, all of whom were white, Jane and her family were free black Saints. Jane had been born and raised in Connecticut and had worked most of her life for a wealthy white couple. She had joined a Christian church, but she quickly grew dissatisfied with it.

When she learned that a Latter-day Saint elder was preaching in the area, she decided she wanted to hear him. Her pastor told her not to attend the sermon, but Jane went anyway and was convinced that she had found the true gospel. The largest branch in the area was only a few miles away, and she was baptized and confirmed the following Sunday.[14]

Jane had been an eager new convert. Three weeks after her baptism, the gift of tongues had come upon her while she prayed. Now, a year later, she and her family were gathering to Zion.[15]

On the canal, Jane and her family traveled without incident across New York. From there they expected to travel with their branch south through Ohio and on to Illinois, but canal officials refused to let the Mannings continue on their journey until they paid their travel fare.

Jane was confused. She thought her family would not have to pay until they reached Ohio. Why did they have to pay now? None of the white members of her branch were required to pay their fares in advance.

The Mannings counted their money, but they did not yet have enough to pay for the journey. They turned to Elder Wandell for assistance, but he refused to help them.

As the boat pulled away and disappeared from sight, Jane and her family had almost no money and more than eight hundred miles between them and Nauvoo. With nothing but her feet to carry her west, Jane resolved to lead the small company to Zion.[16]

ON THE MORNING OF July 12, William Clayton was in Joseph's office when the prophet and Hyrum entered. "If you will write the revelation," Hyrum told Joseph, "I will take and read it to Emma, and I believe I can convince her of its truth, and you will hereafter have peace."

"You do not know Emma as well as I do," Joseph said. That spring and summer, he had been sealed to additional women, including a few whom Emma had personally selected.[17] Yet helping Joseph choose wives had not made obeying the principle easy for Emma.

"The doctrine is so plain," Hyrum said. "I can convince any reasonable man or woman of its truth, purity, and heavenly origin."

"We will see," Joseph said. He asked William to take out paper and write as he spoke the word of the Lord.[18]

Much of the revelation was already known to Joseph. It described the new and everlasting covenant of eternal marriage, along with associated blessings and promises. It also revealed the terms governing plural marriage, which Joseph had learned while translating the Bible in 1831. The remainder of the revelation was new counsel for him and Emma, addressing their questions and current struggles with plural marriage.

The Lord revealed that for a marriage to continue beyond the grave, the man and woman must marry by priesthood authority, have their covenant sealed by the Holy Spirit of Promise, and remain faithful to their covenant. Those who met these conditions would inherit glorious blessings of exaltation.[19]

"Then shall they be gods, because they have no end," the Lord declared. "Then shall they be above all, because all things are subject unto them."[20]

The Lord went on to speak about plural marriage and His covenant to bless Abraham with an innumerable posterity for his faithfulness.[21] From the beginning, the Lord had ordained marriage between one man and one woman to fulfill His plan. Sometimes, however, the Lord authorized plural marriage as a way to raise up children in righteous families and bring about their exaltation.[22]

Although the revelation was directed to the Saints, it ended with counsel for Emma about Joseph's plural wives. "Let mine handmaid, Emma Smith, receive all those that have been given unto my servant Joseph," the Lord instructed. He commanded her to forgive Joseph, stay with him, and keep her covenants, promising to bless and multiply her and give her reason to rejoice if she did. He also warned her of the dire consequences that befell those who broke their covenants and disobeyed the law of the Lord.[23]

When Joseph finished dictating the revelation, William had filled ten pages. He put down the pen and read the revelation back to Joseph. The prophet said it was correct, and Hyrum took it to Emma.[24]

HYRUM RETURNED TO JOSEPH'S office later that day and told his brother that he had never been talked to more severely in his life. When he read the revelation to Emma, she had become angry and rejected it.

"I told you you did not know Emma as well as I did," Joseph said quietly. He folded the revelation and put it in his pocket.[25]

The next day, Joseph and Emma spent hours in heart-wrenching discussion. Sometime before noon, Joseph called William Clayton into the room to help mediate between them. Both Joseph and Emma seemed caught in an impossible dilemma. Each loved and cared deeply for the other and wanted to honor the eternal covenant they had made. But their struggle to keep the Lord's commandment was splitting them apart.[26]

Emma seemed especially worried about the future. What if Joseph's enemies found out about plural marriage? Would he go to prison again? Would he be killed? She and the children depended on Joseph for support, but the family's finances were entwined with the church's. How would they get by if something happened to him?

Joseph and Emma wept as they spoke, but by the end of the day they had worked through their problems. To provide Emma additional financial security, Joseph deeded some property to her and their children.[27] And after that fall, he entered into no more plural marriages.[28]

AT THE END OF August 1843, the Smiths moved into a two-story home near the river. Called the Nauvoo Mansion, the new home was large enough to accommodate their four children, Joseph's aging mother, and the people who worked for and boarded with them. Joseph planned to use much of the house as a hotel.[29]

Several weeks later, as summer turned to autumn in Nauvoo, Jane Manning and her family arrived at Joseph and Emma's door looking for the prophet and a place to stay. "Come in!" Emma told the weary group. Joseph showed them where they could sleep that night and found chairs for everyone.

"You have been the head of this little band, haven't you?" Joseph said to Jane. "I would like you to relate your experience in your travels."

Jane told Joseph and Emma about their long journey from New York. "We walked until our shoes were worn out and our feet became sore and cracked open and bled," she said. "We asked God the Eternal Father to heal our feet, and our prayers were answered and our feet were healed."

They had slept beneath the stars or in barns near the road. Along the way, some men had threatened to throw them in jail because they did not have "free papers," or documents proving that they were not runaway slaves.[30] At another time, they had to cross a deep stream without a bridge. They endured dark nights and frosty mornings and helped others when they could. Not far from Nauvoo, they had blessed a sick child, and the child was healed by their faith.

"We went on our way," Jane said of their journey, "rejoicing, singing hymns, and thanking God for His infinite goodness and mercy to us."

"God bless you," Joseph said. "You are among friends now."

The Mannings stayed in the Smith home for a week. During that time, Jane searched for a trunk she had shipped to Nauvoo, but as far as she could tell it had been lost or stolen along the way. Her family members, meanwhile, found places to work and live and soon moved out.

One morning, Joseph noticed that Jane was crying and asked her why. "The folks have all gone and got themselves homes," she said, "and I have got none."

"You have a home right here if you want it," Joseph assured her. He took Jane to see Emma and explained the situation. "She has no home," he said. "Haven't you a home for her?"

"Yes, if she wants one," Emma said.

Jane quickly became a part of the busy household, and the other family members and boarders welcomed her. Her trunk never turned up, but Joseph and Emma soon provided her with new clothes from the store.[31]

THAT FALL, AS HER family settled into their new house, Emma became increasingly troubled over plural marriage.[32] In His revelation to her thirteen years earlier, the Lord had promised to crown her with righteousness if she honored her covenants and kept the commandments continually. "Except thou do this," He had said, "where I am you cannot come."[33]

Emma wanted to keep the covenants she had made with Joseph and the Lord. But plural marriage often seemed too much to bear. Although she had allowed some of Joseph's plural wives into her household, she resented their presence and sometimes made life unpleasant for them.[34]

Eventually, Emma demanded that Emily and Eliza Partridge leave the house for good. With Joseph at her side, Emma called the sisters into her room and told them that they had to end their relationships with him at once.[35]

Feeling cast off, Emily left the room, angry at Emma and Joseph. "When the Lord commands," she told herself, "His word is not to be trifled with." She intended to do as Emma wished, but she refused to break her marriage covenant.

Joseph followed the sisters out of the room and found Emily downstairs. "How do you feel, Emily?" he asked.

"I expect I feel as anybody would under the circumstances," she said, glancing at Joseph. He looked like he was ready to sink into the earth, and Emily felt sorry for him. She wanted to say something more, but he left the room before she could speak.[36]

Decades later, when Emily was an old woman, she reflected on these painful days. By then, she better understood Emma's complicated feelings about plural marriage and the pain it caused her.[37]

"I know it was hard for Emma, and any woman, to enter plural marriage in those days," she wrote, "and I do not know as anybody would have done any better than Emma did under the circumstances."[38]

"God must be the judge," she concluded, "not I."[39]

CHAPTER 42

Round Up Your
Shoulders

In early November 1843, Phebe Woodruff welcomed Wilford home from a four-month mission to the eastern states. He arrived with gifts for his family and a wagon laden with printing supplies for the *Times and Seasons* office, where Phebe and the children had been living.[1]

Phebe had given birth to another daughter in July, and she had been anticipating Wilford's arrival for about a month. The Woodruffs were very close and hated being apart when Wilford was on missions. Unlike other apostles and their wives, though, they had not yet been sealed together for time and eternity, and they were anxious to receive the ordinance.

While Wilford was away, Phebe had written to him, asking if he thought their love would ever be divided in eternity. He responded with a poem expressing his hope that their love would thrive beyond the tomb.[2]

On November 11, a week after Wilford's return, the Woodruffs visited the home of John and Leonora Taylor. There Hyrum Smith taught about resurrection, redemption, and exaltation through the new and everlasting covenant. He then sealed Phebe and Wilford together for time and eternity, and they all enjoyed a pleasant evening together.[3] The Woodruffs soon began preparing to receive the endowment.

Earlier that fall, for the first time in more than a year, Joseph had started to endow more Saints. As promised, he had extended the endowment to women, and on September 28 he administered the ordinance to Emma in the Nauvoo Mansion.[4] Soon after, Emma had washed and anointed Jane Law, Rosannah Marks, Elizabeth Durfee, and Mary Fielding Smith. It was the first time a woman had officiated in a temple ordinance in the latter days.[5]

In the weeks that followed, Emma performed the ordinance for Lucy Smith, Ann Whitney, Mercy Thompson, Jennetta Richards, Leonora Taylor, Mary Ann Young, and others. Soon other women performed the ordinance under Emma's supervision.[6]

In December, Phebe and Wilford were washed, anointed, and endowed.[7] By the end of the year, forty-two women and men had received the endowment. They met together often in the room above Joseph's store to pray and learn about the things of eternity.[8]

THAT FALL, WHILE MEETING regularly with the endowed Saints, William Law hid from Joseph and Hyrum the fact that he was guilty of adultery. In committing the sin, William felt like he had transgressed against his own soul.[9]

Around this time, Hyrum gave him a copy of the revelation on marriage. "Take it home and read it," Hyrum instructed, "then be careful with it and bring it back again." William studied the revelation and showed it to his wife, Jane. He doubted its authenticity, but she was sure it was real.

William took the revelation to Joseph, who confirmed that it was genuine.[10] William begged him to renounce its teachings, but Joseph testified that the Lord had commanded him to teach plural marriage to the Saints and that he would stand condemned if he disobeyed.[11]

At some point, William became sick and finally confessed his adultery to Hyrum, admitting to his friend that he did not feel worthy to live or die. Yet he wanted to be sealed for eternity to Jane, and he asked Joseph if that were possible. Joseph took the question to the Lord, and the Lord revealed that William could not receive the ordinance because he was adulterous.[12]

Now William's heart began to burn with anger against Joseph.[13] In late December, he and Jane stopped meeting with the endowed Saints.[14] Jane advised that they sell their property quietly and simply leave Nauvoo. But William wanted to crush Joseph.[15] He began plotting secretly with others who opposed the prophet, and not long after, he lost his place in the First Presidency.

William declared that he was glad to be free of his association with Joseph. But instead of leaving Nauvoo and moving on, as Jane had recommended, he became more determined than ever to work against the prophet and bring about his demise.[16]

WILLIAM LAW'S APOSTASY WAS upsetting but not unprecedented. "I have tried for a number of years to get the minds of the Saints prepared to receive the things of God," Joseph told a congregation on a chilly Sunday early in 1844, "but we frequently see some of them, after suffering all they have for the work of God, will fly to pieces like glass as soon as anything comes that is contrary to their traditions."

Since the organization of the church, Joseph had seen men and women leave the faith when they disagreed with the principles he taught or when he fell short of their notions of what a prophet should be. Those who broke with the church often left peacefully. But as men like Ezra Booth, Warren Parrish, and John Bennett had shown, sometimes those who fell away fought against the prophet, the church, and its teachings, often leading to violence against the Saints. The course William would take was yet to be seen.

In the meantime, Joseph continued to prepare the Saints to receive the saving ordinances found in the temple. "I would to God that this temple was now done that we might go into it," he told the large congregation of men and women. "I would advise all the Saints to go to with their might and gather together all their living relatives to this place that they may be sealed and saved."[17]

He knew, however, that the Saints could do so only if they were able to finish the temple. Already Joseph was worried about growing unrest in the communities around Nauvoo. After a statewide election the previous summer, his critics had met in protest, accusing him of swaying the Saints' votes. "Such an individual," they declared, "cannot fail to become a most dangerous character, especially when he shall have been able to place himself at the head of a numerous horde."[18]

Knowing how quickly tensions could escalate, Joseph hoped to find allies in the national government who could defend the Saints in the public sphere. A few months earlier, he had written five candidates for president in the upcoming national election, hoping to learn if they would support the Saints' efforts to recoup their losses in Missouri. Three of the candidates wrote back. Two of them argued that considering redress was a matter for the state, not the president. The third was sympathetic but ultimately noncommittal.[19]

Frustrated by the candidates' unwillingness to help, Joseph decided to run for president of the United States himself. Winning the election was unlikely, but he wanted to use his candidacy to publicize the grievances of the Saints and champion the rights of others who had been treated unjustly. He anticipated that hundreds of Saints would campaign throughout the nation on his behalf.

On January 29, 1844, the Quorum of the Twelve formally nominated Joseph as a candidate for the presidency, and he accepted their nomination. "If I ever get in the presidential chair," he promised, "I will protect the people in their rights and liberties."[20]

MEANWHILE, ON A WHALING ship off the coast of South Africa, Addison Pratt watched his shipmates lower four small boats into the ocean and row with all their might after a large whale. Drawing their boats alongside the beast, the men cast harpoons into its back, causing it to dive deep beneath the water and pull the boats over the mountainous crest of a wave.

The swift motion snapped the tow line, and the whale surfaced again, this time near the ship. Climbing atop the mast to get a better view, Addison saw the massive creature lash back and forth, bellowing and spouting water as it tried to free itself of the two harpoons snagged in its powerful flesh. When the boats got nearer, it dove again to dodge another assault, resurfacing farther out to sea. The men tried to pursue it once more, but the whale got away.

Watching the chase reminded Addison of the patriarchal blessing he had received shortly after moving to Nauvoo. In it, Hyrum Smith had promised him that he would "go out and come in and go forth upon the face of the earth." After the blessing, Hyrum had said, "I guess you have got to go a-whaling."[21]

Addison and his fellow missionaries had been at sea now for several months, sailing south across the Atlantic Ocean and around the Cape of Good Hope, toward the islands beyond Australia. Unable to find a ship bound for Hawaii, they had booked passage on a whaling vessel headed farther south to Tahiti. The voyage would last the better part of a year, and already Addison and the missionaries had tried discussing the restored gospel with shipmates.

Most days aboard the whaler were pleasant, but Addison's nights were sometimes troubled with ominous dreams. One night, he dreamed that Joseph and the Saints were aboard a ship sailing directly into a storm. The ship ran across a shoal and struck the ocean floor, shredding the hull. As water poured into the ship, its prow began to sink beneath the water. Some of the Saints drowned while others managed to flee the sinking vessel, only to be devoured by ravenous sharks.[22]

In another dream, a few nights later, he saw his family and the church leaving Nauvoo. He searched a long time before he found them settled in a fertile valley. In the dream, Louisa and the children lived on a hillside in a small cabin surrounded by plowed fields. She greeted Addison and invited him to walk with her to see the stable and cow pasture on the upper end of the field. The yard was not fenced and the hogs were giving her trouble, but Louisa had a good dog to watch over the property.[23]

Addison awoke from these dreams anxious for his family and afraid that enemies were once again afflicting the Saints.[24]

THAT WINTER, MERCY FIELDING Thompson and Mary Fielding Smith collected pennies from the women in Nauvoo as part of a fund-raising effort for the temple. Late the previous year, while praying to know what she could do to help build up Zion, Mercy had been inspired to start the penny drive. "Try to get the sisters to subscribe one cent per week," the Spirit had whispered to her, "for the purpose of buying glass and nails for the temple."

Mercy proposed the idea to Joseph, and he told her to go ahead with it and the Lord would bless her. The women responded enthusiastically to Mercy's plan. Every week, she and Mary collected pennies and carefully recorded the names of the women who had pledged their support.

Hyrum also assisted the women in the drive and gave it the First Presidency's full endorsement. He declared that every woman who contributed her pennies should have her name written in the Book of the Law of the Lord, where Joseph and his scribes recorded tithing, revelations, and other sacred writings.[25]

Once the penny drive was under way in Nauvoo, the sisters sent a letter to the office of the *Millennial Star* in England to solicit pennies from the women of the church there. "This is to inform you that we have here entered into a small weekly subscription for the benefit of the temple funds," they wrote. "One thousand have already joined it, while many more are expected, by which we trust to help forward the great work very much."[26]

Soon women in the British mission were sending their pennies across the ocean to Nauvoo.

WITH THE HELP OF William Phelps, Joseph developed an independent presidential platform and drafted a pamphlet to publicize it across the nation.[27] He proposed granting the president more power to put down mobs, liberating slaves by compensating their owners, turning prisons into places of learning and reform, and expanding the nation westward, but only with the full consent of the American Indians. He wanted voters to know that he was the champion of all people, not just the Latter-day Saints.[28]

He believed that a theocratic democracy, where the people chose to live in harmony with God's laws, could establish a just and peaceful society to prepare the world for the Second Coming. But if his campaign were to fail and the oppressed and downtrodden were left unprotected, he wanted to establish a place to protect them in the last days, somewhere outside the United States.

Constant threats in Missouri and Illinois, along with the ever-increasing number of Saints, had lately prompted Joseph to look westward for such a place. He did not intend to abandon Nauvoo, but he expected the church to grow beyond what the city could accommodate. Joseph wanted to find a place where the Saints could establish the kingdom of God on earth and institute just laws that would govern the Lord's people into the Millennium.

With this in mind, Joseph thought of places like California, Oregon, and Texas, all of which were then outside the borders of the United States. "Send out a delegation and investigate the locations," he directed the Twelve. "Find a good location where we can remove after the temple is completed and build a city in a day and have a government of our own in a healthy climate."[29]

On March 10 and 11, the prophet formed a new council of men that would oversee the establishment of the Lord's kingdom on earth.[30] The council came to be known as the Council of the Kingdom of God, or the Council of Fifty. Joseph wanted vigorous debate in the council and encouraged its members to speak their minds and say what was in their hearts.

Before adjourning their first meeting, council members spoke enthusiastically about creating a government of their own under a new constitution that reflected the mind of God. They believed it would serve as a standard to the people and fulfill Isaiah's prophecy that the Lord would establish an ensign to the nations to gather His children together in the last days.[31]

During this time, Joseph appeared weighed down in meetings with church leaders. He believed something important was about to happen. "It may be that my enemies will kill me," he said, "and in case they should, and the keys and power which rest on me not be imparted to you, they will be lost from the earth." He said he felt compelled to confer upon the Twelve Apostles all priesthood keys so he could rest assured that the work of the Lord would continue.[32]

"Upon the shoulders of the Twelve must the responsibility of leading this church henceforth rest until you shall appoint others to succeed you," he said to the apostles. "Thus can this power and these keys be perpetuated in the earth."

The way ahead would not be easy, Joseph warned them. "If you are called to lay down your lives, die like men," he said. "After they have killed you, they can harm you no more. Should you have to walk right into danger and the jaws of death, fear no evil. Jesus Christ has died for you."[33]

Joseph sealed on the heads of the apostles all the priesthood keys they needed to carry on the Lord's work without him, including the sacred keys of the sealing power.[34] "I roll the burden and responsibility of leading this church off from my shoulders and onto yours," he said. "Now round up your shoulders and stand under it like men, for the Lord is going to let me rest a while."

Joseph no longer appeared weighed down. His face was clear and full of power. "I feel as light as a cork—I feel that I am free," he told the men. "I thank my God for this deliverance."[35]

CHAPTER 43

A Public Nuisance

After his dismissal from the First Presidency, William Law avoided Joseph. In late March 1844, Hyrum tried to reconcile the two men, but William refused to make amends as long as the prophet upheld plural marriage.[1] Around the same time, Joseph heard that William and several others in town were conspiring to kill him and his family.[2]

Joseph spoke out confidently against the conspirators. "I won't swear out a warrant against them, for I don't fear any of them," he told the Saints. "They would not scare off an old setting hen."[3] Yet he was concerned about the growing dissent in Nauvoo, and the death threats only added to the feeling that his time to teach the Saints was nearing an end.[4]

That spring, a church member named Emer Harris informed Joseph that the conspirators had invited him and his nineteen-year-old son, Denison, to attend their meetings. "Brother Harris," Joseph said, "I would advise you not to attend those meetings, nor pay any attention to them." But he told Emer that he wanted Denison to attend the meetings and learn what he could about the conspirators.

Later, Joseph met with Denison and his friend Robert Scott to prepare them for their assignment. Knowing the conspirators were dangerous, he cautioned the young men to say as little as possible while they were there and to offend no one.[5]

ON APRIL 7, 1844, THE second day of the church's general conference, Joseph set aside his concerns about conspiracy to address the Saints. A strong wind blew through the congregation as he took the stand. "It will be hardly possible for me to make you all hear unless there is profound attention," the prophet called out above the weather. He announced that he was going to speak about his friend King Follett, who had died recently, and offer comfort to everyone who had lost loved ones.[6]

He also desired to give every Saint a glimpse of what awaited them in the world to come. He wanted to pull back the spiritual veil, if only for a moment, and teach them about the nature of God and their divine potential.

"What kind of a being is God?" he asked the Saints. "Does any man or woman know? Have any of you seen Him, heard Him, communed with Him?" Joseph let his questions linger over the congregation. "If the veil was rent today," he said, "and the great God, who holds this world in its orbit, and upholds all things by His power—if you were to see Him today, you would see Him in all the person, image, and very form as a man."

Joseph explained that seeking knowledge and keeping covenants would help the Saints fulfill the Father's ultimate plan for them. "You have got to learn how to be gods yourselves," Joseph said, "by going from a small degree to another, from grace to grace, from exaltation to exaltation, until you are able to sit in glory as do those who sit enthroned in everlasting power."

This plan, he reminded them, conquered death. "How consoling to the mourner," he said, "to know that although the earthly tabernacle shall be dissolved, they shall rise in immortal glory, not to sorrow, suffer, or die anymore, but they shall be heirs of God and joint-heirs with Jesus Christ."[7]

The process would take time, requiring much patience, faith, and learning. "It is not all to be comprehended in this world," the prophet assured the Saints. "It will take a long time after the grave to understand the whole."

As his sermon drew to a close, Joseph became reflective. He spoke about his family members and friends who had died. "They are only absent for a moment," he said. "They are in the spirit, and when we depart we shall hail our mothers, fathers, friends, and all whom we love." He assured mothers who had lost infants that they would be reunited with their children. In the eternities, he said, the Saints would no longer live in fear of mobs, but instead dwell in joy and happiness.[8]

Standing before the Saints, Joseph was no longer the rough, unschooled farm boy who had sought wisdom in a grove of trees. Day by day, year by year, the Lord had polished him like a stone, slowly shaping him into a better instrument for His hands.[9] Yet the Saints understood so little of his life and mission.

"You never knew my heart," he said. "I don't blame you for not believing my history. Had I not experienced it, I could not believe it myself." He hoped that one day, after his life had been weighed in the balance, the Saints would know him better.

When Joseph finished, he took a seat and the choir sang a hymn. He had spoken for almost two and a half hours.[10]

JOSEPH'S SERMON INSPIRED THE Saints and filled them with the Spirit. "The teachings which we heard made our hearts rejoice," wrote Ellen Douglas to her parents in England a week after the conference. Ellen and her husband and children had been among the first British converts to sail for Nauvoo in 1842, and the truths Joseph taught in his sermon were a reminder of why they had sacrificed so much to gather with the Saints.

Like many British converts, the Douglases had spent most of their savings immigrating to Nauvoo, leaving them in poverty. Ellen's husband, George, had died shortly after their arrival, and she had come down with a terrible fever, leaving her unable to support her eight children. A friend soon recommended that she get help from the Relief Society, which Ellen had joined after arriving in the city.

"I refused to do so," Ellen told her parents in the letter she wrote after the conference, "but she said I needed something and that I had been so long sick, and if I would not do it myself, she would do it for me." Ellen knew her children needed many things, especially clothes, so she finally agreed to ask a member of the Relief Society for help.

"She asked me what I needed most," Ellen explained, "and they brought the wagon and fetched me such a present as I never received before from any place in the world."

She and her children now had a cow and raised dozens of chickens on the lot they rented while they saved money to purchase land of their own. "I never in my life enjoyed myself better than I do now," she told her parents. "I for one feel to rejoice and to praise my God that He ever sent the elders of Israel to England, and that He ever gave me a heart to believe them."

She closed her letter by bearing testimony of the prophet Joseph Smith. "The day will come," she told her parents, "when you will know that I have told you the truth."[11]

THAT SPRING, DENISON HARRIS and Robert Scott attended William Law's secret meetings and reported what they learned to Joseph.[12] By now, William saw himself as a church reformer. He still professed to believe in the Book of Mormon and Doctrine and Covenants, but he was furious about plural marriage and Joseph's recent teachings about the nature of God.[13]

Among the conspirators, Denison and Robert recognized William's wife, Jane, and his older brother Wilson. They also saw Robert and Charles Foster, who had been Joseph's friends until they had clashed with him over land development around the temple.[14] John Bennett's old allies Chauncey and Francis Higbee attended as well, along with a local roughneck named Joseph Jackson.[15]

The prophet was touched that Denison and Robert were willing to risk their lives for him. Following their second meeting with the conspirators, he instructed the young men to attend once more. "Be strictly reserved," he advised, "and make no promises to conspire against me or any portion of the community." He warned them that the conspirators might try to kill them.

The following Sunday, Denison and Robert found men guarding the usual meeting place with muskets and bayonets. The two entered the house and quietly listened as the conspirators debated. Everyone agreed that Joseph had to die, but no one could settle on a plan.

Before the meeting closed, Francis Higbee administered an oath of solidarity to each conspirator. One by one, the men and women in the room raised a Bible in their right hand and took the oath. When Denison and Robert's turn came, they refused to step forward.

"Have you not heard the strong testimony of all present against Joseph Smith?" the conspirators reasoned. "We deem it our solemn duty to accomplish his destruction and rescue the people from this peril."

"We came to your meetings because we thought you were our friends," the young men said. "We did not think there was any harm in it."

The leaders ordered guards to seize Denison and Robert and march them down into the cellar. Once there, the young men were given one more chance to take the oath. "If you are still determined to refuse," they were told, "we will have to shed your blood."

The young men again said no and braced themselves for death.

"Hold on there!" someone in the cellar cried. "Let's talk this matter over!"

In an instant the conspirators were arguing again, and the young men heard one man say that it was too dangerous to kill them. "The boys' parents," he reasoned, "may institute a search that would be very dangerous to us."

Denison and Robert were taken down to the river by armed guards and released. "If you ever open your mouths," the guards warned, "we will kill you by night or by day, wherever we find you."[16]

The young men left—and immediately reported back to Joseph and a bodyguard who was with him. As the prophet listened to their story, grateful they were unharmed, a grave expression crossed his face. "Brethren," he said, "you do not know what this will terminate in."

"Do you think they are going to kill you?" asked the bodyguard. "Are you going to be slain?"

Joseph did not answer the question directly, but he assured the young men that William Law and the other conspirators were wrong about him. "I am no false prophet," he testified. "I have had no dark revelations. I have had no revelations from the devil."[17]

AMID THE TURMOIL OF the spring, Joseph met regularly with the Council of Fifty to discuss the ideal attributes of a theocratic democracy and the laws and practices that governed it. At one meeting, shortly after the April conference, the council voted to receive Joseph as prophet, priest, and king.

The men had no political authority, so the motion had no temporal consequences. But it affirmed Joseph's priesthood offices and responsibilities as head of the Lord's earthly kingdom prior to the Second Coming.

It also alluded to John the Revelator's testimony that Christ had made righteous Saints kings and priests unto God, giving added meaning to the Savior's title King of Kings.[18]

Later that afternoon, Joseph noted that a few members of the council were not members of the church. He proclaimed that in the Council of Fifty, men were not consulted about their religious opinions, no matter what they were. "We act upon the broad and liberal principle that all men have equal rights and ought to be respected," he said. "Every man has a privilege in this organization of choosing for himself voluntarily his God and what he pleases for religion."

As he spoke, Joseph picked up a long ruler and gestured broadly with it, as a schoolmaster might do. "When a man feels the least temptation to such intolerance, he ought to spurn it," he told the council. He said the spirit of religious intolerance had drenched the earth in blood. "In all governments or political transactions," he declared, "a man's religious opinions should never be called in question. A man should be judged by the law, independent of religious prejudice."

When Joseph finished speaking, he accidentally snapped the ruler in half, to the surprise of everyone in the room.

"As the rule was broken in the hands of our chairman," Brigham Young quipped, "so might every tyrannical government be broken before us."[19]

BY THE END OF April, William and Jane Law's increasingly public dissent led a council of thirty-two church leaders to excommunicate them and Robert Foster for unchristian conduct. Since no one had summoned them to defend themselves at the hearing, William was outraged, and he rejected the council's decision.[20]

Afterward, the church's critics became more vocal as several apostles and scores of elders left Nauvoo to serve missions and campaign for Joseph's presidency. Robert Foster and Chauncey Higbee rummaged for evidence that could be used in lawsuits against the prophet.[21] William Law held a public meeting on April 21 at which he denounced Joseph as a fallen prophet and organized a new church.

At the meeting, William's followers installed him as president of the new church. After that, they met every Sunday and planned ways to attract other disaffected Saints to their cause.[22]

Meanwhile, Thomas Sharp, the young newspaper editor who had turned against the Saints shortly after they arrived in Illinois, filled his paper with criticisms of Joseph and the church.

"You know nothing of the repeated insults and injuries received by our citizens from the heads of the Mormon church," he declared, defending his attacks on the Saints. "You can know nothing of these things, or you could not undertake to lecture us for endeavoring to expose such a gang of outlaws, blacklegs, and bloodsuckers."[23]

Then, on May 10, William and his followers announced their plans to publish the *Nauvoo Expositor,* a newspaper that would give, as they put it, "a full, candid, and succinct statement of facts, as they really exist in the city of Nauvoo."[24] Francis Higbee also brought charges against Joseph, accusing him of defaming his character in public, while William and his brother Wilson used Joseph's plural marriages as grounds for charging him with adultery.[25]

"The devil always sets up his kingdom at the very same time in opposition to God," Joseph told the Saints in a sermon as false charges mounted against him. Afterward, he and the other endowed Saints met above his store and prayed to be delivered from their enemies.[26] Joseph wanted to avoid arrest, but he did not want to go into hiding again. Emma was pregnant and very ill, and he was reluctant to leave her side.[27]

Finally, at the end of May, he decided that it was best to go to Carthage, the county seat, and face a legal investigation into the accusations against him.[28] Around two dozen of Joseph's friends accompanied him to the town. When the case came before a judge, the prosecutors were missing a witness and were not able to proceed with the investigation. The hearings were put off for a few months, and the sheriff permitted Joseph to return home.[29]

Joseph's release enraged Thomas Sharp. "We have seen and heard enough to convince us that Joe Smith is not safe out of Nauvoo, and we would not be surprised to hear of his death by violent means in a short time," he declared in an editorial. "The feeling of this country is now lashed to its utmost pitch, and it will break forth in fury upon the slightest provocation."[30]

WHILE OPPOSITION TO JOSEPH intensified, the Saints continued to build up their city. Louisa Pratt struggled to shelter and feed her four daughters while her husband was away on his mission in the South Pacific. Before leaving, Addison had purchased some lumber, but not enough for Louisa to build a house on their city lot. Since she owned some land in a neighboring state, she went to a nearby lumber mill and asked to purchase lumber on credit, with her land as collateral.

"You need not doubt a woman," she told the miller, worried he would deny her credit because of her gender. "As a general thing, they are more punctual than men."

The miller had no qualms about selling to her on credit, and Louisa soon had the wood she needed to build a small frame house. Unfortunately, the men she hired to do the work were a continual disappointment, forcing her to hire others until she found reliable workers.

While the house was under construction, Louisa worked as a seamstress. When her daughters came down with measles, she watched over them night and day, praying for their recovery until they got well. From all appearances, she seemed to be managing well under the circumstances. But she often felt lonely, inadequate, and helpless to bear the burden on her shoulders.

Once the house was finished, Louisa moved her family in. She installed a rug she had made herself and furnished the home with items she purchased from her earnings.

As the months passed, Louisa and the girls survived on her small income, bartering and purchasing on credit while she paid off her debt to the miller. When their food ran out and Louisa had new debts to pay, the children asked, "What shall we do, Mother?"

"Complain to the Lord," Louisa said dryly. She wondered what her prayer would sound like. Would she complain about the people who owed her money? Would she rail against those who had not paid her for the work they hired her to do?

Just then a man arrived with a heavy load of wood for her, which she could sell. Then another man arrived with a hundred pounds of flour and twenty-five pounds of pork.

"Why, Mother," her daughter Frances said, "what a lucky woman you are!"

Overwhelmed with gratitude, Louisa decided to withhold her complaint.[31]

AS WILLIAM LAW PROMISED, the *Nauvoo Expositor* appeared on Nauvoo's streets in early June. "We are earnestly seeking to explode the vicious principles of

Joseph Smith," it declared in its preamble, "which we verily know are not accordant and consonant with the principles of Jesus Christ and the apostles."

In the newspaper, William and his followers insisted that Joseph had strayed from the restored gospel by introducing the endowment, practicing plural marriage, and teaching new doctrine about exaltation and the nature of God.[32]

They also warned the county's citizens that the Saints' political power was rising. They condemned Joseph's blurring of the roles of church and state and denounced his candidacy for the presidency.

"Let us arise in the majesty of our strength," they declared ominously, "and sweep the influence of tyrants and miscreants from the face of the land."[33]

The day after the paper appeared, Joseph convened the Nauvoo City Council to discuss what to do about the *Expositor*. Many of the Saints' neighbors were already hostile to the church, and he worried that the *Expositor* would provoke them to violence. "It is not safe that such things should exist," he said, "on account of the mob spirit which they tend to produce."[34]

Hyrum reminded the city council of the mobs that had driven them out of Missouri. Like Joseph, he worried that the newspaper would stir people up against the Saints unless they passed a law to stop it.

It was getting late on a Saturday night, and the men adjourned the meeting until Monday.[35] On that day, the city council met from morning until evening, again discussing what they could do. Joseph proposed declaring the newspaper a public nuisance and destroying the press that printed it.[36]

John Taylor agreed. As the editor of the *Times and Seasons,* John valued a free press and free speech, but both he and Joseph believed they had a constitutional right to protect themselves against libel. Destroying the *Expositor* and its press would be controversial, but they believed the laws permitted them to do it legally.

Joseph read aloud from the Illinois state constitution about freedom of the press so that all in the room understood the law. Retrieving a respected law book, another councilor read a legal justification for destroying a nuisance disturbing the peace of a community. With the legal reasoning set forth, Hyrum repeated Joseph's proposal that they destroy the press and scatter the type.[37]

William Phelps told the council that he had reviewed the United States Constitution, the Nauvoo city charter, and the laws of the land. In his mind, the city was fully and legally justified to declare the press a nuisance and destroy it immediately.

The council voted to destroy the press, and Joseph sent orders to the city marshal to carry out the measure.[38]

THAT EVENING, THE NAUVOO marshal arrived at the *Expositor* office with about a hundred men. They broke into the shop with a sledgehammer, dragged the printing press into the street, and smashed it into pieces. They then dumped out drawers of type and set fire to the rubble. Any copies of the newspaper they could find were added to the blaze.[39]

The next day, Thomas Sharp reported the destruction of the press in an extra edition of his newspaper. "War and extermination is inevitable! Citizens *arise, one and all!!!*" he wrote. "We have no time for comment, every man will make his own. *Let it be made with powder and ball!!!*"[40]

CHAPTER 44

A Lamb to the Slaughter

After Thomas Sharp sounded his call to arms, anger against the Saints in Nauvoo spread through the area like wildfire. Citizens rallied in nearby Warsaw and Carthage to protest the destruction of the *Expositor.* Town leaders called on men in the region to join them in rising up against the Saints.[1] Within two days an armed mob of three hundred men had formed in Carthage, ready to march on Nauvoo and annihilate the Saints.[2]

One hundred miles northeast of Nauvoo, Peter Maughan and Jacob Peart sat down for a meal at a hotel. Under Joseph's direction, they had come to the area to find a coal bed for the church to purchase. Joseph believed it would be profitable to mine the coal and ship it down the Mississippi on the *Maid of Iowa,* the church's steamboat.[3]

While they waited for their food, Peter opened the newspaper and read a report claiming that a massive battle had taken place in Nauvoo, killing thousands. Shocked, and afraid for Mary and his children, Peter showed the report to Jacob.

The two men took the next riverboat home. When they were about thirty miles from Nauvoo, they learned to their relief that no battle had taken place. But it seemed to be only a matter of time before violence erupted.[4]

DESPITE THE CITY COUNCIL'S studied decision to destroy the printing press, they had underestimated the outcry that followed. William Law had fled the city, but some of his followers were now threatening to destroy the temple, set fire to Joseph's house, and tear down the church's printing office.[5] Francis Higbee charged Joseph and other members of the city council with inciting a riot when the press was destroyed. He swore that in ten days' time there would not be a single Mormon left in Nauvoo.[6]

On June 12, an officer from Carthage arrested Joseph and other members of the city council. Nauvoo's municipal court found the charges baseless and released the men, angering Joseph's critics even more. The following day, Joseph learned that three hundred men had assembled in Carthage, ready to march on Nauvoo.[7]

Hoping to prevent another all-out war with their neighbors, as they had seen in Missouri, Joseph and others wrote urgent letters to Governor Ford, explaining the city council's actions and pleading for help against mob attacks.[8] Joseph spoke to the Saints, admonishing them to stay calm, prepare for the defense of the city, and make no disturbances. Then he mustered the Nauvoo Legion and put the city under martial law, suspending the usual rule of law and putting the military in charge.[9]

On the afternoon of June 18, the Legion assembled in front of the Nauvoo Mansion. As the militia commander, Joseph dressed in full military uniform and climbed atop a nearby platform, where he spoke to the men. "It is thought by some that our enemies would be satisfied with my destruction," he said, "but I tell you that as soon as they have shed my blood, they will thirst for the blood of every man in whose heart dwells a single spark of the spirit of the fullness of the gospel."

Drawing his sword and raising it to the sky, Joseph urged the men to defend the liberties that had been denied them in the past. "Will you all stand by me to the death," Joseph asked, "and sustain, at the peril of your lives, the laws of our country?"

"Aye!" roared the crowd.

"I love you with all my heart," he said. "You have stood by me in the hour of trouble, and I am willing to sacrifice my life for your preservation."[10]

AFTER HEARING FROM JOSEPH about the city council's reasons for destroying the press, Governor Thomas Ford understood that the Saints had acted in good faith. There were legal grounds and precedents for declaring and destroying nuisances in a community. But he disagreed with the council's decision and did not believe their actions could be justified. The legal destruction of a newspaper, after all, was uncommon in an age when communities usually left such work to illegal mobs, as when vigilantes destroyed the Saints' newspaper in Jackson County more than a decade earlier.[11]

The governor also placed high value on the free speech protections in the Illinois state constitution, regardless of what the law may have allowed. "Your conduct in the destruction of the press was a very gross outrage upon the laws and the liberties of the people," he wrote the prophet. "It may have been full of libels, but this did not authorize you to destroy it."

The governor further argued that the Nauvoo city charter did not grant the local courts as much power as the prophet seemed to think. He advised him and the other city council members who had been charged with riot to turn themselves in and submit to the courts outside of Nauvoo. "I am anxious to preserve the peace," he told them. "A small indiscretion may bring on war." If the city leaders gave themselves up and stood trial, he promised to protect them.[12]

Knowing that Carthage was swarming with men who hated the Saints, Joseph doubted the governor could keep his promise. Yet staying in Nauvoo would only anger his critics more and draw mobs to the city, putting the Saints in danger. More and more, it seemed the best way to protect the Saints was to leave Nauvoo for the West or seek help in Washington, DC.

Writing the governor, Joseph told him of his plans to leave the city. "By everything that is sacred," he wrote, "we implore Your Excellency to cause our helpless women and children to be protected from mob violence." He insisted that if the Saints had done anything wrong, they would do everything in their power to make it right.[13]

That night, after saying goodbye to his family, Joseph climbed into a skiff with Hyrum, Willard Richards, and Porter Rockwell and set out across the Mississippi. The boat was leaky, so the brothers and Willard bailed water with their boots while Porter rowed. Hours later, on the morning of June 23, they arrived in Iowa Territory, and Joseph instructed Porter to return to Nauvoo and bring back horses for them.[14]

Before Porter left, Joseph gave him a letter for Emma, instructing her to sell their property if necessary to support herself, the children, and his mother. "Do not despair," he told her. "If God opens a door that is possible for me, I will see you again."[15]

Later that morning, Emma sent Hiram Kimball and her nephew Lorenzo Wasson to Iowa to convince Joseph to come home and turn himself in. They told Joseph that the governor intended to occupy Nauvoo with troops until he and his brother Hyrum gave themselves up. Porter returned soon after with Reynolds Cahoon and a letter from Emma, again begging him to return to the city. Hiram Kimball, Lorenzo, and Reynolds all called Joseph a coward for leaving Nauvoo and exposing the Saints to danger.[16]

"I will die before I will be called a coward," Joseph said. "If my life is of no value to my friends, it is of none to myself." He knew now that leaving Nauvoo would not protect the Saints. But he did not know if he would survive going to Carthage. "What shall I do?" he asked Porter.

"You are the oldest and ought to know best," Porter said.

"You are the oldest," Joseph said, turning to his brother. "What shall we do?"

"Let us go back and give ourselves up, and see the thing out," said Hyrum.

"If you go back, I shall go with you," Joseph said, "but we shall be butchered."

"If we live or have to die," Hyrum said, "we will be reconciled to our fate."

Joseph considered that for a moment, then asked Reynolds to get a boat. They would turn themselves in.[17]

EMMA'S HEART SANK WHEN Joseph arrived home late that afternoon. Now that she saw him again, she feared she had called him back to his death.[18] Joseph longed to preach once more to the Saints, but he stayed home with his family instead. He and Emma gathered their children together, and he blessed them.

Early the next morning Joseph, Emma, and their children stepped out of the house. He kissed each of them.[19]

"You are coming back," Emma said through tears.

Joseph mounted his horse and set off with Hyrum and the other men for Carthage. "I am going like a lamb to the slaughter," he told them, "but I am calm as a summer's morning. I have a conscience void of offense towards God and towards all men."[20]

The riders climbed the hill to the temple as the sun rose, casting golden light over the building's unfinished walls. Joseph stopped his horse and looked out over the city. "This is the loveliest place and the best people under the heavens," he said. "Little do they know the trials that await them."[21]

JOSEPH DID NOT STAY away long. Three hours after leaving Nauvoo, he and his friends encountered troops who had orders from the governor to confiscate the state-issued arms of the Nauvoo Legion. Joseph decided to return and see the order carried out. If the Saints resisted, he knew, it might give the mobs reason to attack them.[22]

Back in Nauvoo, Joseph rode home to see Emma and their children again. He said another goodbye and asked Emma if she would come with him, but she knew she had to stay with the children. Joseph appeared solemn and thoughtful, grimly certain of his fate.[23] Before he left, Emma asked him for a blessing. With no time to spare, Joseph asked her to write the blessing she desired and promised he would sign it when he returned.

In the blessing she penned, Emma asked for wisdom from Heavenly Father and the gift of discernment. "I desire the Spirit of God to know and understand myself," she wrote. "I desire a fruitful, active mind, that I may be able to comprehend the designs of God."

She asked for wisdom to raise her children, including the baby she expected in November, and expressed hope in her eternal marriage covenant. "I desire with all my heart to honor and respect my husband," she wrote, "ever to live in his confidence and by acting in unison with him retain the place which God has given me by his side."

Finally, Emma prayed for humility and hoped to rejoice in the blessings God prepared for the obedient. "I desire that whatever may be my lot through life," she wrote, "I may be enabled to acknowledge the hand of God in all things."[24]

HOWLING AND SWEARING GREETED the Smith brothers when they arrived at Carthage a little before midnight on Monday, June 24. The militia unit that had collected the Saints' arms in Nauvoo now escorted Joseph and Hyrum through the commotion of Carthage's streets. Another unit, known as the Carthage Greys, was camped on the public square near the hotel where the brothers planned to stay the night.

As Joseph passed the Carthage Greys, the troops pushed and shoved to get a look. "Where is the damned prophet?" one man yelled. "Clear the way and let us have a view of Joe Smith!" The troops whooped and yelled and threw their guns into the air.[25]

The next morning, Joseph and his friends turned themselves over to a constable. A little after nine o'clock, Governor Ford invited Joseph and Hyrum to walk with him through the assembled troops. The militia and the mob that pressed in around them were quiet until a company of the Greys began to jeer again, tossing their hats into the air and drawing their swords. As they had done the night before, they howled and sneered at the brothers.[26]

That day in court, Joseph and Hyrum were released to await trial on the riot charges. But before the brothers could leave town, two of William Law's associates brought complaints against them for declaring martial law in Nauvoo. They were charged with treason against the government and people of Illinois, a capital offense that prevented the men from being released on bail.

Joseph and Hyrum were confined in the county jail, locked together in a cell for the night. Several of their friends chose to stay with them, to protect them and keep them company. That night Joseph wrote a letter to Emma with encouraging news. "The governor has just agreed to march his army to Nauvoo," he reported, "and I shall come along with him."[27]

THE NEXT DAY, THE prisoners were moved to a more comfortable room on the second floor of the Carthage jail. The room had three large windows, a bed, and a wooden door with a broken latch. That evening, Hyrum read aloud from the Book of Mormon and Joseph bore powerful witness of its divine authenticity to the guards on duty. He testified that the gospel of Jesus Christ had been restored, that angels still ministered to humanity, and that the kingdom of God was once more on the earth.

After the sun set, Willard Richards sat up late writing until his candle burned out. Joseph and Hyrum lay on the bed, while two visitors, Stephen Markham and John Fullmer, lay on a mattress on the floor. Near them, on the hard floor, lay John Taylor and Dan Jones, a Welsh riverboat captain who had joined the church a little more than a year earlier.[28]

Sometime before midnight, the men heard a gunshot outside the window nearest Joseph's head. The prophet rose and moved to the floor beside Dan. Joseph quietly asked him if he was afraid to die.[29]

"Has that time come?" Dan asked in his thick Welsh accent. "Engaged in such a cause I do not think that death would have many terrors."

"You will see Wales," Joseph whispered, "and fulfill the mission appointed you ere you die."

Around midnight, Dan awoke to the sound of troops marching past the jail. He got up and looked out the window. Below, he saw a crowd of men outside. "How many shall go in?" he heard someone ask.

Startled, Dan quickly woke up the other prisoners. They heard footsteps coming up the stairs and threw themselves against the door. Someone picked up a chair to use as a weapon in case the men outside stormed the room. A tomb-like silence surrounded them as they waited for an attack.

"Come on!" Joseph finally shouted. "We are ready for you!"

Through the door, Dan and the other prisoners could hear shuffling back and forth, as if the men outside could not decide whether to attack or leave. The commotion continued until dawn, when the prisoners at last heard the men retreat down the stairs.[30]

THE FOLLOWING DAY, JUNE 27, 1844, Emma received a letter from Joseph, in the handwriting of Willard Richards. Governor Ford and a band of militia were on their way to Nauvoo. But despite his promise, the governor had not taken Joseph with him. Instead, he had disbanded one militia unit at Carthage and retained only a small group of Carthage Greys to guard the jail, leaving the prisoners more vulnerable to an attack.[31]

Still, Joseph wanted the Saints to treat the governor cordially and not raise any alarms. "There is no danger of any exterminating order," he told her, "but caution is the parent of safety."[32]

After the letter, Joseph wrote out a postscript in his own hand. "I am very much resigned to my lot, knowing

547

I am justified and have done the best that could be done," he declared. He asked her to give his love to the children and his friends. "As for treason," he added, "I have not committed any, and they cannot prove an appearance of anything of the kind." He told her not to worry about harm falling on him and Hyrum. "God bless you all," he wrote in closing.[33]

Governor Ford arrived in Nauvoo later that day and addressed the Saints. He blamed them for the crisis and threatened to hold them responsible for its aftermath. "A great crime has been done by destroying the *Expositor* press and placing the city under martial law," he stated. "A severe atonement must be made, so prepare your minds for the emergency."[34]

He warned the Saints that Nauvoo could be reduced to ashes and its people exterminated if they rebelled. "Depend upon it," he said. "A little more misbehavior from the citizens, and the torch which is now already lighted will be applied."[35]

The speech offended the Saints, but since Joseph had asked them to preserve the peace, they pledged to heed the governor's warning and sustain the laws of the state. Satisfied, the governor finished his speech and paraded his troops down Main Street. As the soldiers marched, they drew their swords and swung them menacingly.[36]

TIME PASSED SLOWLY IN the Carthage jail that afternoon. In the summer heat, the men left their coats off and opened the windows to let in a breeze. Outside, eight men from the Carthage Greys guarded the jail while the rest of the militia camped nearby. Another guard sat just on the other side of the door.[37]

Stephen Markham, Dan Jones, and others were running errands for Joseph. Of the men who had stayed there the night before, only Willard Richards and John Taylor were still with Joseph and Hyrum. Earlier in the day, visitors had smuggled two guns to the prisoners—a six-shooter revolver and a single-shot pistol—in case of an attack. Stephen had also left behind a sturdy walking stick he called the "rascal beater."[38]

To ease the mood and pass the time, John sang a British hymn that had lately become popular with the Saints. Its lyrics spoke of a humble stranger in need who ultimately revealed himself as the Savior:

> *Then in a moment to my view,*
> *The stranger darted from disguise;*
> *The tokens in his hands I knew,*
> *My Savior stood before mine eyes;*
> *He spake—and my poor name He named,—*
> *"Of me thou hast not been ashamed,*
> *These deeds shall thy memorial be;*
> *Fear not, thou didst them unto me."*

When John finished the song, Hyrum asked him to sing it again.[39]

At four o'clock in the afternoon, new guards relieved the old ones. Joseph struck up a conversation with a guard at the door while Hyrum and Willard talked quietly together. After an hour, their jailer entered the room and asked the prisoners if they wanted to be moved to the more secure jail cell in case of an attack.

"After supper we will go in," said Joseph. The jailer left and Joseph turned to Willard. "If we go in the jail," Joseph asked, "will you go with us?"

"Do you think I would forsake you now?" Willard answered. "If you are condemned to be hung for treason, I will be hung in your stead and you shall go free."

"You cannot," said Joseph.

"I will," said Willard.[40]

A FEW MINUTES LATER, the prisoners heard a rustling at the door and the crack of three or four gunshots. Willard glanced out the open window and saw a hundred men below, their faces blackened with mud and gunpowder, storming the entry to the jail. Joseph grabbed one of the pistols while Hyrum seized the other. John and Willard picked up canes and gripped them like clubs. All four men pressed themselves against the door as the mob rushed up the stairs and tried to force their way inside.[41]

Gunfire sounded in the stairwell as the mob shot at the door. Joseph, John, and Willard sprang to the side of the doorway as a ball splintered through the wood. It struck Hyrum in the face and he turned, stumbling away from the door. Another ball struck him in the lower back. His pistol fired and he fell to the floor.[42]

"Brother Hyrum!" Joseph cried. Gripping his six-shooter, he opened the door a few inches and fired once. More musket balls flew into the room, and Joseph fired haphazardly at the mob while John used a cane to beat down the gun barrels and bayonets thrust through the doorway.[43]

After Joseph's revolver misfired two or three times, John ran to the window and tried to climb the deep windowsill. A musket ball flew across the room and struck him in the leg, tipping him off balance. His body went numb and he crashed against the windowsill, smashing his pocket watch at sixteen minutes past five o'clock.

"I am shot!" he cried.

John dragged himself across the floor and rolled under the bed as the mob fired again and again. A ball ripped into his hip, tearing away a chunk of flesh. Two more balls struck his wrist and the bone just above his knee.[44]

Across the room, Joseph and Willard strained to put all their weight against the door as Willard knocked away the musket barrels and bayonets in front of him. Suddenly, Joseph dropped his revolver to the floor and darted for the window. As he straddled the windowsill, two balls struck his back. Another ball hurtled through the window and pierced him below the heart.

"O Lord, my God," he cried. His body lurched forward and he pitched headfirst out the window.

Willard rushed across the room and stuck his head outside as lead balls whistled past him. Below, he saw the mob swarming around Joseph's bleeding body. The prophet lay on his left side next to a stone well. Willard watched, hoping to see some sign that his friend was still alive. Seconds passed, and he saw no movement.

Joseph Smith, the prophet and seer of the Lord, was dead.[45]

CHAPTER 45

An Almighty Foundation

Before sunrise on June 28, Emma answered an urgent knock at her door. She found her nephew Lorenzo Wasson standing on the doorstep, covered in dust. His words confirmed her greatest fear.[1]

Soon the whole city awoke as Porter Rockwell rode through the streets shouting the news of Joseph's death.[2] A crowd gathered outside the Smiths' home almost instantly, but Emma kept herself and her children inside with only a handful of friends and boarders. Her mother-in-law, Lucy Smith, paced the floor of her bedroom, looking absently out the windows. The children huddled together in another room.[3]

Emma sat alone, grieving silently. After a while, she buried her face in her hands and cried, "Why am I a widow and my children orphans?"

Hearing her sobs, John Greene, the Nauvoo city marshal, entered the room. Trying to comfort her, he said her affliction would be a crown of life to her.

"My husband was my crown," she said sharply. "Why, O God, am I thus deserted?"[4]

LATER THAT DAY, WILLARD Richards and Samuel Smith rode into Nauvoo with wagons carrying the bodies of Joseph and Hyrum. To shield them from the hot summer sun, the bodies had been placed in wooden boxes and covered with brush.[5]

Both Willard and Samuel were deeply shaken from the previous day's attack. Samuel had tried to visit his brothers in jail, but before he could reach Carthage, a mob had fired on him and chased him for more than two hours on horseback.[6] Willard, meanwhile, had survived the assault with only a small wound on his earlobe, fulfilling a prophecy Joseph had made a year earlier that balls would fly around Willard, strike his friends on the right and left, but leave not a hole in his clothing.[7]

John Taylor, on the other hand, hovered between life and death in a hotel in Carthage, too injured to leave town.[8] The night before, Willard and John had written a short letter to the Saints, pleading with them not to retaliate for Joseph and Hyrum's murder. When Willard finished the letter, John had been so weak from blood loss that he could scarcely sign his name to it.[9]

As Willard and Samuel neared the temple, a group of Saints met the wagons and followed them into town. Nearly everyone in Nauvoo joined the procession as the wagons moved slowly past the temple site and down the hill to the Nauvoo Mansion. Saints wept openly as they walked through the city.[10]

When the procession arrived at the Smiths' home, Willard climbed the platform where Joseph had last addressed the Nauvoo Legion. Looking over a crowd of ten thousand people, Willard could see that many were angry with the governor and the mob.[11]

"Trust in the law for redress," he pleaded. "Leave vengeance to the Lord."[12]

THAT EVENING, LUCY SMITH braced herself as she waited with Emma, Mary, and her grandchildren outside the dining room of the Nauvoo Mansion. Earlier, several men had carried the bodies of Joseph and Hyrum into the house to wash and dress them. Since then Lucy and her family had been waiting to view the bodies. Lucy could barely hold herself together, and she prayed that she would have the strength to see her murdered sons.

When the bodies were ready, Emma went in first but quickly sank to the floor and had to be carried from the room. Mary followed her, trembling as she walked. With her two youngest children clinging to her, she knelt beside Hyrum, gathered his head in her arms, and sobbed. "Have they shot you, my dear

Hyrum?" she said, smoothing his hair with her hand. Grief overtook her.

With the help of friends, Emma soon returned to the room and joined Mary at Hyrum's side. She placed her hand on her brother-in-law's cold forehead and spoke softly to him. She then turned to her friends and said, "Now I can see him. I am strong now."

Emma stood and walked unassisted to Joseph's body. She knelt beside him and placed her hand on his cheek. "Oh, Joseph, Joseph!" she said. "Have they taken you from me at last!"[13] Young Joseph knelt and kissed his father.

Lucy was so overwhelmed by the sadness around her that she could not speak. "My God," she prayed silently. "Why hast thou forsaken this family?" Memories of her family's trials flooded her mind, but as she looked on her sons' lifeless faces, they appeared peaceful. She knew Joseph and Hyrum were now beyond the reach of their enemies.

"I have taken them to myself," she heard a voice say, "that they might have rest."[14]

The next day, thousands of people lined up outside the Nauvoo Mansion to honor the brothers. The summer day was hot and cloudless. Hour after hour, Saints entered one door, passed by the coffins, and exited another door. The brothers had been enclosed in fine coffins lined with white linen and soft black velvet. A plate of glass over their faces allowed mourners to see them one last time.[15]

After the viewing, William Phelps preached the prophet's funeral sermon to a crowd of thousands of Saints. "What shall I say of Joseph the seer?" he asked. "He came not in the whirlwind of public opinion, but in the simple name of Jesus Christ."

"He came to give the commandments and law of the Lord, to build temples, and teach men to improve in love and grace," William testified. "He came to establish our church upon earth, upon the pure and eternal principles of revelation, prophets, and apostles."[16]

FOLLOWING THE FUNERAL, MARY Ann Young wrote about the tragedy to Brigham, who was hundreds of miles to the east campaigning for Joseph with several members of the Twelve. "We have had great afflictions in this place since you left home," she related. "Our dear brother Joseph Smith and Hyrum have fallen victims to a ferocious mob." Mary Ann assured Brigham that their family was in good health, but she did not know how safe they were. For the last three weeks, incoming mail to Nauvoo had all but stopped, and the threat of mob attacks was constant.

"I have been blessed to keep my feelings calm during the storm," Mary Ann wrote. "I hope you will be careful on your way home and not expose yourself to those that will endanger your life."[17]

On the same day, Vilate Kimball wrote Heber. "Never before did I take up my pen to address you under so trying circumstances as we are now placed," she told him. "God forbid that I should ever witness another like unto it."

Vilate had heard that William Law and his followers were still seeking revenge against church leaders. Fearing for Heber's safety, she was reluctant for her husband to come home. "My constant prayer now is for the Lord to preserve us all to meet again," she wrote. "I have no doubt but your life will be sought, but may the Lord give you wisdom to escape their hands."[18]

A short time later, Phebe Woodruff wrote her parents and described the attack at Carthage. "These things will not stop the work any more than Christ's death did, but will roll it on with a greater rapidity," Phebe testified. "I believe Joseph and Hyrum are where they can do the church much more good now than when with us."

"I am stronger in the faith than ever," she affirmed. "I would not give up the faith of true Mormonism if it cost me my life within one hour from the time I am writing this, for I know of a surety that it is the work of God."[19]

AS THE LETTERS OF Mary Ann, Vilate, and Phebe traveled east, Brigham Young and Orson Pratt heard rumors that Joseph and Hyrum had been killed, but no one could confirm the story. Then, on July 16, a member of the church in the New England branch they were visiting received a letter from Nauvoo detailing the tragic news.

When he read the letter, Brigham felt like his head was going to crack. He had never felt such despair.

His thoughts turned instantly to the priesthood. Joseph had held all the keys necessary to endow the Saints and seal them together for eternity. Without those keys, the work of the Lord could not move forward. For a moment, Brigham feared that Joseph had taken them to the grave.

Then, in a burst of revelation, Brigham remembered how Joseph had bestowed the keys on the Twelve Apostles. Bringing his hand down hard on his knee, he said, "The keys of the kingdom are right here with the church."[20]

Brigham and Orson traveled to Boston to meet with the other apostles in the eastern states. They decided to return home immediately and advised all missionaries who had families in Nauvoo to return as well.[21]

"Be of good cheer," Brigham told the Saints in the area. "When God sends a man to do a work, all the devils in hell cannot kill him until he gets through." He testified that Joseph had given the Twelve all the keys of the priesthood before his death, leaving the Saints everything they needed to carry on.[22]

BACK IN NAUVOO, AS Emma mourned her husband, she began to worry about supporting her children and mother-in-law alone. Joseph had made extensive legal efforts to separate his family's property from what belonged to the church, but he had still left behind considerable debts and no will. Unless the church quickly appointed a trustee-in-trust to replace Joseph as manager of the church's property, Emma feared, her family would be left destitute.[23]

Church leaders in Nauvoo were divided over who had the authority to make the appointment. Some people believed the responsibility should fall on Samuel Smith, the prophet's oldest living brother, but he had taken sick after the mob chased him away from Carthage, and he died suddenly at the end of July.[24] Others believed that local stake leaders should select the new trustee. Willard Richards and William Phelps wanted to postpone the decision until the Twelve had returned from their mission to the eastern states so they could participate in the selection.

But Emma was anxious for a decision and wanted church leaders to appoint a trustee-in-trust right away. Her choice for the position was William Marks, the Nauvoo stake president.[25] Bishop Newel Whitney strongly opposed the choice, however, because William had rejected plural marriage and cared little for the ordinances of the temple.

"If Marks is appointed," the bishop declared privately, "our spiritual blessings will be destroyed, inasmuch as he is not favorable to the most important matters." Knowing the church was much more than a corporation with financial holdings and legal obligations, Newel believed the new trustee-in-trust ought to be someone who fully supported what the Lord had revealed to Joseph.[26]

Around this time, John Taylor recovered enough from his wounds to return to Nauvoo. Parley Pratt also returned from his mission and joined John, Willard Richards, and William Phelps in urging Emma and William Marks to wait for the return of the other apostles. They believed it was far more important to select the new trustee through the proper authority than to reach a quick decision.[27]

Then, on August 3, Sidney Rigdon returned to Nauvoo. As Joseph's running mate in the presidential campaign, Sidney had moved to another state to meet legal requirements for the position. But when he learned of the prophet's death, Sidney rushed back to Illinois, certain his position in the First Presidency entitled him to lead the church.

To strengthen his claim, Sidney also announced that he had received a vision from God showing him that the church needed a guardian—someone who would care for the church in Joseph's absence and continue to speak for him.[28]

Sidney's arrival concerned Parley and the other apostles in Nauvoo. The conflict over the trustee-in-trust made it clear the church needed a presiding authority to make important decisions. But they knew that Sidney, like William Marks, had rejected many of the teachings and practices the Lord had revealed to Joseph. More important, they knew that Joseph had depended less on Sidney in recent years and had not bestowed all the keys of the priesthood on him.[29]

The day after his arrival, Sidney publicly offered to lead the church. He said nothing about finishing the temple or endowing the Saints with spiritual power. Rather, he warned them that perilous times were ahead and promised to guide them boldly through the last days.[30]

Later, at a meeting of church leaders, Sidney insisted on assembling the Saints in two days to select a new leader and appoint a trustee-in-trust. Alarmed, Willard and the other apostles called for more time to review Sidney's claims and await the return of the rest of their quorum.

William Marks compromised and scheduled the meeting for August 8, four days away.[31]

ON THE EVENING OF August 6, word spread rapidly that Brigham Young, Heber Kimball, Orson Pratt, Wilford Woodruff, and Lyman Wight had arrived in Nauvoo by steamboat. Soon the Saints were greeting the apostles in the streets as they made their way home.[32]

The next afternoon, the newly arrived apostles joined Willard Richards, John Taylor, Parley Pratt, and George A. Smith at a meeting with Sidney and the other councils of the church.[33] By this time, Sidney had changed his mind about selecting a new leader on August 8. Instead, he said he wanted to hold a prayer meeting with the Saints on that day, postponing the decision until church leaders could come together and "warm up each other's hearts."[34]

Still, Sidney insisted on his right to direct the church. "It was shown to me that this church must be built up to Joseph," he told the councils, "and that all the blessings we receive must come through him." He said that his recent vision had simply been a continuation of the grand vision of heaven he had seen with Joseph more than a decade earlier.

"I have been ordained a spokesman to Joseph," he continued, referring to a revelation Joseph had received in 1833, "and I must come to Nauvoo and see that the church is governed in a proper manner."[35]

Sidney's words did not impress Wilford. "It was a kind of second-class vision," he noted in his journal.[36]

After Sidney finished speaking, Brigham arose and testified that Joseph had conferred all the keys and powers of the apostleship on the Twelve. "I do not care who leads the church," he said, "but one thing I must know, and that is what God says about it."[37]

On August 8, the day of Sidney's prayer meeting, Brigham missed an early-morning meeting with his quorum, something he had never done before.[38] Stepping outside, he saw that thousands of Saints had gathered in the grove near the temple. The morning was blustery, and Sidney stood in a wagon with his back to a strong, steady wind. Rather than holding a prayer meeting, Sidney was again offering himself as guardian of the church.

Sidney spoke for more than an hour, bearing witness that Joseph and Hyrum would hold their priesthood authority through eternity and had organized the church councils sufficiently to lead the church after their deaths. "Every man will stand in his own place and stand in his own calling before Jehovah," Sidney declared. He again proposed that his own place and calling was as Joseph's spokesman. He did not wish the congregation to vote on the matter, but he wanted the Saints to know his views.[39]

When Sidney finished speaking, Brigham called out to the crowd to stay a few moments longer. He said that he had wanted time to mourn Joseph's death before settling any church business, but he sensed an urgency among the Saints to choose a new leader. He worried that some among them were grasping for power against the will of God.

To resolve the matter, Brigham asked the Saints to return later that afternoon to sustain a new leader of the church. They would vote by quorum and as a church body. "We can do the business in five minutes," he said. "We are not going to act against each other, and every man and woman will say amen."[40]

THAT AFTERNOON, EMILY HOYT returned to the grove for the meeting. A cousin of the prophet, Emily was in her late thirties and a graduate of a teacher's academy. Over the last few years, she and her husband, Samuel, had grown close to Joseph and Hyrum, and the sudden deaths of the brothers had saddened them. Although they lived across the river in Iowa Territory, Emily and Samuel had come to Nauvoo that day to attend Sidney's prayer meeting.[41]

Around two o'clock, the priesthood quorums and councils took their seats together on and around the stand. Brigham Young then stood to address the Saints.[42] "There has been much said about President Rigdon being president of the church," he said, "but I say unto you that the Quorum of the Twelve have the keys of the kingdom of God in all the world."[43]

As Emily listened to Brigham speak, she caught herself glancing up at him to make sure it was not Joseph speaking. He had Joseph's expressions, his method of reasoning, and even the sound of his voice.[44]

"Brother Joseph, the prophet, has laid the foundation for a great work, and we will build upon it," Brigham continued. "There is an almighty foundation laid, and we can build a kingdom such as there never was in the world. We can build a kingdom faster than Satan can kill the Saints off."

But the Saints needed to work together, Brigham declared, following the will of the Lord and living by faith. "If you want Sidney Rigdon or William Law to lead you, or anybody else, you are welcome to them," he said, "but I tell you in the name of the Lord that no man can put another between the Twelve and the prophet Joseph. Why? He has committed into their hands the keys of the kingdom in this last dispensation, for all the world."[45]

Feeling that the Spirit and the power that had rested on Joseph now rested on Brigham, Emily watched the apostle call on the Saints to sustain the Twelve as the leaders of the church. "Every man, every woman, every quorum is now put in order," he said. "All that are in favor of this in all the congregation of the Saints, manifest it by holding up the right hand."

Emily and the whole congregation raised their hands.[46]

"There is much to be done," Brigham said. "The foundation is laid by our prophet, and we will build thereon. No other foundation can be laid but that which is laid, and we will have our endowment if the Lord will."[47]

Seven years later, Emily recorded her experience of watching Brigham speak to the Saints, testifying how much he looked and sounded like Joseph on the stand. In the years to come, dozens of Saints would add their witness to hers, describing how they saw Joseph's prophetic mantle fall on Brigham that day.[48]

"If anyone doubts the right of Brigham to manage the affairs for the Saints," Emily wrote, "all I have to say to them is this: Get the Spirit of God and know for yourselves. The Lord will provide for His own."[49]

THE DAY AFTER THE conference, Wilford sensed a gloominess still hanging over the city. "The prophet and patriarch are gone," he wrote in his journal, "and there appears to be but little ambition to do anything." Even so, Wilford and the Twelve went to work immediately. They met that afternoon and appointed bishops Newel Whitney and George Miller to serve as trustees-in-trust for the church and resolve the issues related to Joseph's finances.[50]

Three days later, they called Amasa Lyman to the Quorum of the Twelve and divided the eastern United States and Canada into districts to be presided over by high priests. Brigham, Heber, and Willard would call men to these positions and oversee the church in America while Wilford would travel with Phebe to England to preside over the British mission and manage its printing establishment.[51]

While Wilford prepared for his mission, the other apostles strove to strengthen the church in Nauvoo. The Saints at the August 8 meeting had sustained the Twelve, but some men were already trying to divide the church and draw people away. One of them, James Strang, was a new member of the church who claimed to have a letter from Joseph appointing him to be his true successor. James had a home in Wisconsin Territory and wanted the Saints to gather there.[52]

Brigham cautioned the Saints not to follow dissenters. "Don't scatter," he urged them. "Stay here in Nauvoo, and build up the temple and get your endowment."[53]

Completing the temple remained the focus of the church. On August 27, the night before they left for England, Wilford and Phebe visited the temple with friends. Standing at the base of its walls, which reached almost to the top of the second story, Wilford and Phebe admired the way the moonlight brought out the structure's grandeur and sublimity.

They climbed a ladder to the top of the walls and knelt down to pray. Wilford expressed his gratitude to the Lord for giving the Saints power to build the temple and pleaded that they might be able to finish it, receive the endowment, and plant the work of God throughout the world. He also asked the Lord to preserve him and Phebe in the mission field.

"Enable us to fill our mission in righteousness," he prayed, "and be enabled to again return to this land and tread the courts of the Lord's house in peace."[54]

The next day, just before the Woodruffs left, Brigham gave Phebe a blessing for the work ahead of her. "You shall be blessed on your mission in common with your husband, and thou shalt be the means of doing much good," he promised. "If thou wilt go in all humility, thou shalt be preserved to return and meet with the Saints in the temple of the Lord and shall rejoice therein."

Later that afternoon, Wilford and Phebe set out for England. Among the missionaries traveling with them were Dan Jones and his wife, Jane, who were headed to Wales to fulfill Joseph's prophecy.[55]

CHAPTER 46

Endowed with Power

In the fall of 1844, the Quorum of the Twelve sent an epistle to all Saints everywhere. "The temple," they announced, "necessarily claims our first and most strict attention." They encouraged the Saints to send money, supplies, and laborers to speed the work along. An endowment of power awaited them. All they needed was a place to receive it.[1]

The Saints shared the apostles' urgency. In late September, Peter Maughan wrote Willard Richards about the Saints' new coal mine a hundred miles up the Mississippi River. Peter and Mary had recently sold their home in Nauvoo, used the money to purchase the mine for the church, and moved their family to a rough cabin near the work site. But already Peter longed to be back in Nauvoo cutting stone for the house of the Lord.

"The only thing that rests on my mind," he told Willard, "is that the temple is being built right up and I am cut off from the privilege of helping."[2]

With the temple walls climbing higher, Brigham was determined to continue the work Joseph had begun. Following the prophet's example, he prayed often with the endowed Saints and asked the Lord to preserve and unify the church. Baptisms for the dead, which had stopped after Joseph's death, began again in the basement of the temple. Elders and seventies returned to the mission field in greater numbers.[3]

But challenges were never far away. In September, Brigham and the Twelve learned that Sidney Rigdon was conspiring against them and denouncing Joseph as a fallen prophet. They charged him with apostasy, and Bishop Whitney and the high council excommunicated him. Sidney left Nauvoo soon after, predicting that the Saints would never complete the temple.[4]

Still concerned about her family's well-being, Emma Smith also refused to give her full support to the apostles. She cooperated with the trustees-in-trust they had appointed to sort out Joseph's estate, but disputes over Joseph's papers and other property rankled her. It also troubled her that the apostles continued to teach and practice plural marriage privately.[5]

The women who had been sealed to Joseph as plural wives made no claim to his estate. After his death, some of them returned to their families. Others married members of the Twelve, who covenanted to care and provide for them in Joseph's absence. Quietly, the apostles continued to introduce plural marriage to more Saints, married new plural wives, and started families with them.[6]

At the start of 1845, the Saints' greatest challenges came from outside the church. Thomas Sharp and eight other men had been charged with murdering Joseph and Hyrum, but none of the Saints expected them to be convicted. State legislators, meanwhile, sought to weaken church members' political power by repealing the Nauvoo city charter. Governor Ford supported their efforts, and by the end of January 1845, the legislature stripped the Saints living in Nauvoo of their right to make and enforce laws and disbanded the Nauvoo Legion as well as the local police force.[7]

Without these protections, Brigham feared, the Saints would be vulnerable to attacks from their enemies. Yet the temple was far from finished, and if the Saints fled the city, they could hardly expect to receive their endowment. They needed time to complete the work the Lord had given them. But staying in Nauvoo, if only for another year, could put everyone's lives at risk.

Brigham went to his knees and prayed to know what the Saints should do. The Lord responded with a simple answer: stay and finish the temple.[8]

ON THE MORNING OF March 1, thirty-eight-year-old Lewis Dana became the first American Indian to join the

Council of Fifty. After Joseph's death, council meetings had stopped, but once the Nauvoo charter was repealed and the Saints realized their days in Nauvoo were numbered, the Twelve had called the council together to help govern the city and plan its evacuation.

A member of the Oneida nation, Lewis had been baptized with his family in 1840. He had served several missions, including one to the Indian territory west of the United States, and had ventured as far away as the Rocky Mountains. Knowing Lewis had friends and relatives among Indian nations to the west, Brigham invited him to join the council and share what he knew about the people and lands there.

"In the name of the Lord," Lewis told the council, "I am willing to do all I can."[9]

Over the years, the Saints had grown deeply resentful of their nation's leaders for refusing to help them. Church leaders were now resolved to leave the country and carry out Joseph's plan to establish a new gathering place where they could raise an ensign to the nations, as the prophet Isaiah foretold, and live the laws of God in peace. Like Joseph, Brigham wanted the new gathering place to be in the West, among the Indians, whom he hoped to gather together as a branch of scattered Israel.

Addressing the council, Brigham proposed sending Lewis and several other members of the council west on an expedition to meet with Indians from several nations and explain the Saints' purpose for moving west. They would also identify possible sites for gathering.[10]

Heber Kimball agreed with the plan. "While these men are finding this location," he said, "the temple will be finished and the Saints get their endowment."[11]

The council approved the expedition, and Lewis agreed to lead it. For the rest of March and April, he attended council meetings and advised fellow councilmen on how best to outfit the expedition and achieve its goals.[12] By the end of April, the council had appointed four men to join Lewis on the journey, including Brigham's brother Phineas and a recent convert named Solomon Tindall, a Mohegan Indian who had been adopted by the Delaware.[13]

The expedition left Nauvoo soon after, traveling southwest through Missouri to the territory beyond.[14]

ON THE ISLAND OF Tubuai in the South Pacific, Addison Pratt calculated that it had been almost two years since he left his wife and children in Nauvoo. Although Louisa had doubtlessly written him, just as he had written home at every opportunity, he had received no mail from his family.

Still, he was grateful to the people of Tubuai, who had made him feel at home. The small island had about two hundred inhabitants, and Addison had worked hard, learned their language, and made many friends. After a year on the island, he had baptized sixty people, including Repa, the oldest daughter of the local king. He also baptized a couple named Nabota and Telii, who had shared all they had with him and treated him like family. For Addison, it was a spiritual feast to hear Nabota and Telii pray for the Saints in Nauvoo and thank the Lord for sending Addison on a mission.[15]

Although thinking about Louisa and his daughters made Addison long for home, it also gave him a chance to reflect on the reason for their sacrifice. He was on Tubuai because of his love for Jesus Christ and his desire for the salvation of God's children. As he crisscrossed the island to visit the Tubuaian Saints, Addison often felt a warmth and love that brought him and those around him to tears.

"I have friends here that nothing but the bonds of the everlasting gospel could have created," he noted in his journal.[16]

Three months later, in July 1845, Addison learned of Joseph's and Hyrum's deaths in a letter from Noah Rogers, his fellow missionary, who was then serving farther away in Tahiti. As Addison read about the murders, the blood in his veins seemed to chill.[17]

About a week later Noah wrote Addison again. Missionary labors in Tahiti and the surrounding islands had been less successful than Addison's on Tubuai, and the news from Nauvoo unsettled Noah. He had a wife and nine children back home and was concerned for their safety. They had suffered much during the conflict in Missouri, and he did not want them to endure more trials without him. He planned to take the next ship home.[18]

Addison had every reason to follow Noah. With Joseph gone, he too feared for his family and the church. "What the results will be," he wrote in his journal, "the Lord only knows."[19]

Noah sailed away a few days later, but Addison chose to stay with the Tubuaian Saints. The following Sunday, he preached three sermons in the local dialect and one in English.[20]

IN ILLINOIS, LOUISA PRATT visited her friends Erastus and Ruhamah Derby in Bear Creek, a small settlement south of Nauvoo.[21] While she was there, mobs set fire to a neighboring settlement of Saints. Erastus left immediately to defend the settlement, leaving the two women to guard the house should mobs attack Bear Creek as well.

That night, Ruhamah was too scared to sleep and insisted on standing guard while Louisa slept. When she awoke in the morning, Louisa found her friend exhausted but still on the alert. A tense day passed without incident, and when night came again, Louisa tried to convince Ruhamah to let her stand watch that night. At first, Ruhamah seemed too afraid to trust her, but Louisa finally coaxed her to sleep.

By the time Erastus returned a few days later, the two women were worn out but unharmed. Erastus told them that Saints at the neighboring settlement were living in tents and wagons, exposed to the rain and the night air.[22] When the news reached Brigham, he called the Saints living outside Nauvoo to gather to the safety of the city. Hoping to curb mob aggression and gain more time to fulfill the Lord's commandment to finish the temple, he promised Governor Ford that the Saints would leave the area by spring.[23]

When Louisa learned this, she did not know what to do. With Addison on the other side of the globe, she did not feel she had the ability or resources to move her family on her own. The more she thought about abandoning Nauvoo, the more anxious she grew.[24]

AFTER A WEEK OF rain, the skies above Nauvoo cleared in time for the church's October 1845 conference. The day was unusually warm as Saints from every part of the city climbed the hill to the temple and found a seat in its newly built first-floor assembly hall. While the rest of its interior was still largely unfinished, the building's outer walls and roof were completed and the domed bell tower stood gleaming in the sunlight.[25]

As Brigham watched the Saints file into the assembly hall, he felt torn. He did not want to abandon the temple or Nauvoo, but the recent mob attacks were only a taste of what would happen if the Saints stayed in the city much longer.[26] That spring, the men accused of murdering Joseph and Hyrum had also been acquitted, giving the Saints further proof that their rights and liberties would not be honored in Illinois.[27]

Reports from Lewis Dana on the expedition to the Indians were good, and over the past few weeks, the apostles and the Council of Fifty had been debating possible sites for the new gathering place. Church leaders had taken interest in the valley of the Great Salt Lake, on the far side of the Rocky Mountains. Descriptions of the Salt Lake Valley were promising, and Brigham believed the Saints could settle near there, eventually spreading out and settling along the Pacific Coast.[28]

But the valley lay fourteen hundred miles away across a vast, unfamiliar wilderness with few roads and almost no stores where they could purchase food and supplies. The Saints already knew they had to leave Nauvoo, but could they undertake such a long and potentially dangerous journey?

With the Lord's help, Brigham was confident they could, and he planned to use the conference to bolster and reassure church members. Parley Pratt spoke first in the afternoon session, alluding to the church's plans to move west. "The Lord designs to lead us to a wider field of action, where there will be more room for the Saints to grow and increase," he declared, "and where we can enjoy the pure principles of liberty and equal rights."

George A. Smith stood at the pulpit next and spoke of the persecution the Saints had faced in Missouri. Threatened by an extermination order, they had evacuated the state together, covenanting to leave no one behind. George wanted the Saints to do the same now, to give their all to help those who could not make the journey on their own.

When George finished, Brigham proposed that they covenant with each other and with the Lord to leave no one behind who wished to go west. Heber Kimball called for a sustaining vote, and the Saints raised their hands as a sign of their willingness to carry out their pledge.

"If you will be faithful to your covenant," Brigham promised, "I will now prophesy that the great God will shower down means upon this people to accomplish it to the very letter."[29]

IN THE MONTHS FOLLOWING the conference, the Saints made use of every saw, hammer, anvil, and sewing needle to build and outfit wagons for the westward trek. Workers also redoubled their efforts on the temple so they could complete enough of it to allow the Saints to receive the ordinances there before they left the city.[30]

As the workers prepared the attic of the temple for the endowment and sealings, baptisms for the dead continued in the basement. Under the Lord's direction, Brigham instructed that men should no longer be baptized for women nor women for men.[31]

"Joseph in his lifetime did not receive everything connected with the doctrine of redemption," Brigham had taught the Saints earlier that year, "but he has left the key with those who understand how to obtain and teach to this great people all that is necessary for their salvation and exaltation in the celestial kingdom of our God."

The change to the ordinance showed how the Lord continued to reveal His will to His people. "The Lord has led this people all the while in this way," Brigham declared, "by giving them here a little and there a little. Thus He increases their wisdom, and he that receives a little and is thankful for that shall receive more and more and more."[32]

By December the temple's attic was finished, and the apostles prepared it for the endowment. With the help of other Saints, they hung heavy curtains to divide the large hall into several rooms decorated with plants and murals. At the east end of the attic, they partitioned off a large space for the celestial room, the most sacred place in the temple, and adorned it with mirrors, paintings, maps, and a magnificent marble clock.[33]

The apostles then invited the Saints to enter the temple to receive their blessings. Men and women who had previously been endowed now took turns performing the various roles in the ceremony. Guiding the Saints through the rooms of the temple, they taught them more about God's plan for His children and placed them under additional covenants to live the gospel and consecrate themselves to building His kingdom.[34]

Vilate Kimball and Ann Whitney administered the washing and anointing ordinances to the women. Eliza Snow then ushered the women through the rest of the ordinances, aided by other previously endowed women. Brigham called Mercy Thompson to move into the temple full-time to assist in the work there.[35]

After the start of the new year, the apostles began sealing couples together for time and eternity. Soon, more than a thousand couples received the new and everlasting covenant of marriage. Among them were Sally and William Phelps, Lucy and Isaac Morley, Ann and Philo Dibble, Caroline and Jonathan Crosby, Lydia and Newel Knight, Drusilla and James Hendricks, and other women and men who had followed the church from place to place, consecrating their lives to Zion.

The apostles also sealed children to parents and men and women to spouses who had passed away. Joseph Knight Sr., who had rejoiced with Joseph on the morning he brought the gold plates home, was sealed vicariously to his wife, Polly, the first Saint buried in Jackson County, Missouri. Some Saints also participated in special adoption sealings that joined them to the eternal families of close friends.[36]

With each ordinance, the Lord's plan of a welded chain of Saints and their families, bound to Him and to each other by the priesthood, became a reality.[37]

THAT WINTER, ENEMIES OF the church were restless, doubtful the Saints would keep their promise to leave in the spring. Brigham and other apostles were falsely charged with crimes, which forced them to keep out of sight and sometimes even hide in the temple.[38] Rumors circulated that the U.S. government questioned the Saints' loyalty and wanted to send troops to keep them from leaving the country and aligning with the foreign powers that controlled the western lands.[39]

Feeling intense pressure to leave, the apostles decided that church leaders, their families, and others who were targets of persecution should go as soon as possible. They believed crossing the Mississippi River into Iowa might hold off their enemies a while longer and prevent further violence.

In early January 1846, the apostles finalized their plans for the exodus with the Council of Fifty. Before leaving, they appointed agents to manage the property they were leaving and sell what they could to help the poor make the journey. They also wanted some men to stay behind to finish and dedicate the temple.

Brigham and the Twelve were now determined to gather the Saints to the valleys beyond the Rocky Mountains. After fasting and praying daily in the temple, Brigham had seen a vision of Joseph pointing to a mountaintop with a flag flying atop it as an ensign. Joseph had told him to build a city under the shadow of that mountain.

Brigham believed few people would covet the region, which was less fertile than the plains east of the mountains. He hoped the mountains would also protect them against enemies and provide a moderate climate. Once they settled themselves in the valleys, he hoped, they could establish ports on the Pacific Coast to receive emigrants from England and the eastern United States.[40]

The council reconvened two days later, and Brigham again reflected on Joseph's desire to fulfill Isaiah's prophecy and raise an ensign to the nations. "The saying of the prophets would never be verified," Brigham told the council, "unless the house of the Lord should be reared in the tops of the mountains and the proud banner of liberty wave over the valleys that are within the mountains."

"I know where the spot is," he declared, "and I know how to make the flag."[41]

ON FEBRUARY 2, AFTER THOUSANDS of Saints had received temple ordinances, the apostles announced that they would halt the work in the temple and instead prepare boats to ferry wagons across the icy Mississippi River. Brigham sent messengers to the captains of wagon companies, instructing them to be ready to leave within four hours. He then continued to administer the endowment to the Saints until late in the evening, keeping the temple recorders there until every ordinance had been properly recorded.[42]

When Brigham arose the next day, a crowd of Saints met him outside the temple, eager for their endowment. Brigham told them it was unwise to delay their departure. If they stayed to do more endowments, their way out of the city could be impeded or cut off. He promised they would build more temples and have more opportunities to receive their blessings out west.

Then Brigham walked away, expecting the Saints to disperse, but instead they climbed the steps to the temple and filled its halls. Turning around, Brigham followed them inside. He saw their anxious faces, and he changed his mind. They knew they needed the endowment of power to endure the hardships ahead, overcome the sting of death, and return to the presence of God.

For the rest of that day, temple workers administered the ordinances to hundreds of Saints.[43] The next day, February 4, 1846, an additional five hundred Saints received their endowment as the first wagons rolled out of Nauvoo.

Finally, on February 8, Brigham and the apostles met on the temple's upper floor. They knelt around the altar and prayed, asking God's blessing upon the people heading west and upon those staying in Nauvoo to finish the temple and dedicate it to Him.[44]

OVER THE COMING DAYS and weeks, companies of Saints loaded their wagons and oxen onto flatboats and ferried them across the river, joining others who had already made the crossing. As they climbed a high bluff a few miles west of the river, many Saints looked back on Nauvoo to bid an emotional farewell to the temple.[45]

Day by day, Louisa Pratt watched her friends and neighbors leave the city. She still dreaded the thought of going west without Addison's help and companionship. Everyone expected the journey to be full of unforeseen dangers, yet so far no one had asked her if she was prepared to make it. And none of the men who had called Addison on a mission had offered to help her move.

"Sister Pratt," a friend said one day after she voiced her feelings, "they expect you to be smart enough to go yourself without help, and even to assist others."

Louisa thought about that for a moment. "Well," she said, "I will show them what I can do."[46]

WITH SNOW SWIRLING AROUND her, Emily Partridge shivered as she sat on a fallen tree along the western bank of the Mississippi. Her mother and sisters had crossed the river six days earlier and had camped nearby, but Emily did not know where. Like many Saints who had left Nauvoo, she was tired, hungry, and anxious about the journey ahead. This was the fourth time she had been driven from her home because of her faith.[47]

For almost as long as she could remember, she had been a Latter-day Saint. As a young girl, she had watched her father and mother suffer persecution and poverty to serve Jesus Christ and establish Zion. By sixteen, when mobs forced her family out of Missouri, Emily had already spent much of her life searching for a place of refuge and peace.

Almost twenty-two now, she was starting another journey. After Joseph's death, she had married Brigham

Young as a plural wife. The previous October, they had a son, Edward Partridge Young, named for her father. Two months later, Emily entered the temple and received her endowment.

If her baby survived the journey, he would grow up in the mountains, safe from the mobs of his mother's youth. Yet he would never know, as Emily had, what it was like to live in Jackson County or Nauvoo. He would never meet Joseph Smith or hear him preach to the Saints on a Sunday afternoon.

Before crossing the river, Emily had called at the Nauvoo Mansion to see Joseph and Emma's infant son, David Hyrum, born five months after the prophet's death. The hard feelings that had once existed between Emma and Emily were gone, and Emma invited her into her home and treated her kindly.

Emma and the children were not going west. Her struggle to accept plural marriage, as well as ongoing disputes over property, continued to complicate her relationship with the church and the Twelve. She still believed in the Book of Mormon and had a powerful testimony of her husband's prophetic call. But rather than follow the apostles, she had chosen to stay in Nauvoo with other members of the Smith family.[48]

Sitting along the Mississippi, Emily grew colder as large snowflakes collected on her clothes. Brigham was still in Nauvoo, overseeing the exodus, so she rose and carried her baby from one campfire to another, searching for warmth and a familiar face. Before long, she reunited with her sister Eliza and joined her in an encampment of Saints at a place called Sugar Creek. There she saw families huddled in tents and wagons, clinging together for warmth and comfort against the cold and an unknown future.[49]

No one in the camp knew what the morning would bring. Yet they were not leaping blindly into the dark. They had made covenants with God in the temple, strengthening their faith in His power to guide and sustain them on their journey. Each trusted that somewhere to the west, across the summits of the Rocky Mountains, they would find a place to gather together, build another temple, and establish the kingdom of God on earth.[50]

NOTES

Some sources are referred to with a shortened citation. The "Sources Cited" section provides full citation information for all sources. Many sources are available digitally and are linked from the electronic version of the book, available at saints.lds.org and in Gospel Library.

The word Topic *in the notes indicates additional information online at saints.lds.org.*

PREFACE

1. Woodruff, Journal, Oct. 20, 1861.
2. Joseph Smith and others, *History of the Church of Jesus Christ of Latter-day Saints,* edited by B. H. Roberts (Salt Lake City: Deseret News, 1902–1912 [vols. 1–6], 1932 [vol. 7]); B. H. Roberts, *A Comprehensive History of the Church of Jesus Christ of Latter-day Saints: Century I.* 6 vols. (Salt Lake City: Deseret News, 1930).
3. Doctrine and Covenants 69:8 (Revelation, Nov. 11, 1831–A, at josephsmithpapers.org).
4. See Mosiah 3:19.

CHAPTER 1: ASK IN FAITH

1. Raffles, "Narrative of the Effects of the Eruption," 4–5, 19, 23–24.
2. Raffles, "Narrative of the Effects of the Eruption," 5, 7–8, 11.
3. Wood, *Tambora,* 97.
4. Wood, *Tambora,* 78–120; Statham, *Indian Recollections,* 214; Klingaman and Klingaman, *Year without Summer,* 116–18.
5. Wood, *Tambora,* 81–109; Klingaman and Klingaman, *Year without Summer,* 76–86, 115–20.
6. Klingaman and Klingaman, *Year without Summer,* 48–50, 194–203.
7. Joseph Smith History, 1838–56, volume A-1, 131; Lucy Mack Smith, History, 1844–45, book 2, [11]–book 3, [2]. **Topic: Joseph Smith's Leg Surgery**
8. Lucy Mack Smith, History, 1844–45, book 3, [3]; Stilwell, *Migration from Vermont,* 124–50.
9. Lucy Mack Smith, History, 1844–45, book 3, [4]; Bushman, *Rough Stone Rolling,* 18–19, 25–28. **Topic: Joseph Sr. and Lucy Mack Smith Family**
10. Lucy Mack Smith, History, 1844–45, book 3, [5], Joseph Smith History, 1838–56, volume A-1, 131–32.
11. Lucy Mack Smith, History, 1844–45, book 3, [2]; Joseph Smith History, 1838–56, volume A-1, 131.
12. Lucy Mack Smith, History, 1844–45, book 3, [5]–[6]; Lucy Mack Smith, History, 1845, 67; Joseph Smith History, 1838–56, volume A-1, 132. **Topic: Lucy Mack Smith**
13. Lucy Mack Smith, History, 1844–45, book 3, [6]–[7].
14. Lucy Mack Smith, History, 1844–45, book 3, [7]; Tucker, *Origin, Rise, and Progress of Mormonism,* 12. **Topic: Joseph Sr. and Lucy Mack Smith Family**
15. Cook, *Palmyra and Vicinity,* 247–61. **Topics: Palmyra and Manchester; Christian Churches in Joseph Smith's Day**
16. Joseph Smith History, circa Summer 1832, 1–2, in *JSP,* H1:11–12.
17. Joseph Smith—History 1:5–6; Joseph Smith History, 1838–56, volume A-1, [1]–2, in *JSP,* H1:208–10 (draft 2). **Topic: Religious Beliefs in Joseph Smith's Day**
18. Lucy Mack Smith, History, 1844–45, book 2, [1]–[6]; "Records of the Session of the Presbyterian Church in Palmyra," Mar. 10, 1830.

19. Asael Smith to "My Dear Selfs," Apr. 10, 1799, Asael Smith, Letter and Genealogy Record, 1799, circa 1817–46, Church History Library.
20. Lucy Mack Smith, History, 1844–45, miscellany, [5]; Anderson, *Joseph Smith's New England Heritage,* 161–62.
21. Joseph Smith—History 1:8–10; Joseph Smith History, 1838–56, volume A-1, 2, in *JSP,* H1:208–10 (draft 2). **Topic: Religious Beliefs in Joseph Smith's Day**
22. Lucy Mack Smith, History, 1844–45, book 3, [8]–[10]; Joseph Smith History, circa Summer 1832, 1, in *JSP,* H1:11. **Topic: Sacred Grove and Smith Family Farm**
23. **Topic: Awakenings and Revivals**
24. Acts 10:34–35; Joseph Smith History, circa Summer 1832, 2, in *JSP,* H1:12.
25. Neibaur, Journal, May 24, 1844, available at josephsmithpapers.org; Joseph Smith— History 1:10; Joseph Smith, "Church History," *Times and Seasons,* Mar. 1, 1842, 3:706, in *JSP,* H1:494.
26. Joseph Smith, Journal, Nov. 9–11, 1835, in *JSP,* J1:87; Joseph Smith—History 1:8–9; Joseph Smith History, 1838–56, volume A-1, 2, in *JSP,* H1:210 (draft 2).
27. "Wm. B. Smith's Last Statement," *Zion's Ensign,* Jan. 13, 1894, 6; James 1:5.
28. Joseph Smith—History 1:11–14; Joseph Smith History, 1838–56, volume A-1, 2–3, in *JSP,* H1:210–12 (draft 2); James 1:6.

CHAPTER 2: HEAR HIM

1. Joseph Smith—History 1:14; Joseph Smith History, 1838–56, volume A-1, 3, in *JSP,* H1:212 (draft 2); Interview, Joseph Smith by David Nye White, Aug. 21, 1843, in [David Nye White], "The Prairies, Nauvoo, Joe Smith, the Temple, the Mormons, &c.," *Pittsburgh Weekly Gazette,* Sept. 15, 1843, [3], available at josephsmithpapers.org.
2. Interview, Joseph Smith by David Nye White, Aug. 21, 1843, in [David Nye White], "The Prairies, Nauvoo, Joe Smith, the Temple, the Mormons, &c.," *Pittsburgh Weekly Gazette,* Sept. 15, 1843, [3], available at josephsmithpapers.org; Joseph Smith History, circa Summer 1832, 3, in *JSP,* H1:12.
3. Joseph Smith, Journal, Nov. 9–11, 1835, in *JSP,* J1:88.
4. Joseph Smith—History 1:15; Hyde, *Ein Ruf aus der Wüste,* 15–16; Joseph Smith History, 1838–56, volume A-1, 3, in *JSP,* H1:212 (draft 2).
5. Joseph Smith—History 1:16; Joseph Smith, Journal, Nov. 9–11, 1835, in *JSP,* J1:88; Joseph Smith History, 1838–56, volume A-1, 3, in *JSP,* H1:212 (draft 2).
6. Joseph Smith—History 1:16–17; Joseph Smith History, circa Summer 1832, 3, in *JSP,* H1:12–13; Joseph Smith History, 1838–56, volume A-1, 3, in *JSP,* H1:214 (draft 2); Joseph Smith, Journal, Nov. 9–11, 1835, in *JSP,* J1:88.
7. Joseph Smith History, circa Summer 1832, 3, in *JSP,* H1:13.
8. Interview, Joseph Smith by David Nye White, Aug. 21, 1843, in [David Nye White], "The Prairies, Nauvoo, Joe Smith, the Temple, the Mormons, &c.," *Pittsburgh Weekly Gazette,* Sept. 15, 1843, [3], available at josephsmithpapers.org.
9. Joseph Smith—History 1:5–26; Joseph Smith History, circa Summer 1832, 3, in *JSP,* H1:13; Levi Richards, Journal, June 11, 1843; Joseph Smith, "Church History," *Times and Seasons,* Mar. 1, 1842, 3:706, in *JSP,* H1:494.
10. Joseph Smith History, circa Summer 1832, 3, in *JSP,* H1:13.
11. Pratt, *Interesting Account,* 5, in *JSP,* H1:523.
12. Joseph Smith—History 1:20; Interview, Joseph Smith by David Nye White, Aug. 21, 1843, in [David Nye White], "The Prairies, Nauvoo, Joe Smith, the Temple, the Mormons, &c.," *Pittsburgh Weekly Gazette,* Sept. 15, 1843, [3], available at josephsmithpapers.org; Joseph Smith History, 1838–56, volume A-1, 3, in *JSP,* H1:214 (draft 2); Joseph Smith History, circa Summer 1832, 3, in *JSP,* H1:13.
13. Joseph Smith—History 1:20; Joseph Smith History, 1838–56, volume A-1, 3, in *JSP,* H1:214 (draft 2).

14. See Bushman, "Visionary World of Joseph Smith," 183–204.
15. Joseph Smith—History 1:21; Joseph Smith History, 1838–56, volume A-1, 3, in *JSP,* H1:216 (draft 2); Neibaur, Journal, May 24, 1844, available at josephsmithpapers.org. **Topic: Christian Churches in Joseph Smith's Day**
16. Joseph Smith—History 1:22, 27; Joseph Smith History, 1838–56, volume A-1, 4, in *JSP,* H1:216–18 (draft 2); Interview, Joseph Smith by David Nye White, Aug. 21, 1843, in [David Nye White], "The Prairies, Nauvoo, Joe Smith, the Temple, the Mormons, &c.," *Pittsburgh Weekly Gazette,* Sept. 15, 1843, [3], available at josephsmithpapers.org.
17. Joseph Smith—History 1:21–25; Joseph Smith History, 1838–56, volume A-1, 4, in *JSP,* H1:216–18 (draft 2).
18. Joseph Smith History, circa Summer 1832, 3, in *JSP,* H1:13; see also Historical Introduction to Joseph Smith History, circa Summer 1832, in *JSP,* H1:6.
19. Joseph wrote or supervised the writing of four accounts of this experience during his lifetime, the first being in Joseph Smith History, circa Summer 1832, 1–3, in *JSP,* H1:11–13. Five others who heard him speak of the experience wrote down their own accounts. The nine accounts can be found in "Primary Accounts of Joseph Smith's First Vision of Deity," Joseph Smith Papers website, josephsmithpapers.org. For an analysis of the similarities and differences between the accounts, see "First Vision Accounts," Gospel Topics, topics.lds.org. **Topic: Joseph Smith's First Vision Accounts**
20. Joseph Smith—History 1:26; Joseph Smith History, 1838–56, volume A-1, 4, in *JSP,* H1:218 (draft 2).

CHAPTER 3: PLATES OF GOLD

1. Joseph Smith History, 1838–56, volume A-1, 4–5, in *JSP,* H1:220 (draft 2); Joseph Smith History, circa Summer 1832, 1, in *JSP,* H1:11.
2. "Joseph Smith as Revelator and Translator," in *JSP,* MRB:xxi; Turley, Jensen, and Ashurst-McGee, "Joseph the Seer," 49–50; see also Mosiah 8:17; Alma 37:6–7, 41; and Doctrine and Covenants 10:1, 4 (Revelation, Spring 1829, at josephsmithpapers.org).
3. Bushman, *Rough Stone Rolling,* 48–49; Bushman, "Joseph Smith as Translator," 242. **Topic: Seer Stones**
4. Lucy Mack Smith, History, 1845, 95; see also Alma 37:23.
5. Joseph Smith History, circa Summer 1832, 4, in *JSP,* H1:13–14; Joseph Smith—History 1:28–29; Joseph Smith History, 1838–56, volume A-1, 5, in *JSP,* H1:218–20 (draft 2).
6. Lucy Mack Smith, History, 1844–45, book 3, [10].
7. Joseph Smith History, circa Summer 1832, 4, in *JSP,* H1:13–14; Joseph Smith—History 1:29–33; Joseph Smith History, 1838–56, volume A-1, 5, in *JSP,* H1:218–22 (draft 2); Pratt, *Interesting Account,* 6, in *JSP,* H1:524; Hyde, *Ein Ruf aus der Wüste,* 17–20. **Topic: Angel Moroni**
8. Joseph Smith, Journal, Nov. 9–11, 1835, in *JSP,* J1:88.
9. Joseph Smith—History 1:35; Joseph Smith History, 1838–56, volume A-1, 5, in *JSP,* H1:222 (draft 2); Joseph Smith History, circa Summer 1832, 4, in *JSP,* H1:14; Oliver Cowdery, "Letter IV," *LDS Messenger and Advocate,* Feb. 1835, 1:65–67; Turley, Jensen, and Ashurst McGee, "Joseph the Seer," 49–54; "Mormonism—No. II," *Tiffany's Monthly,* July 1859, 164. **Topic: Seer Stones**
10. Joseph Smith—History 1:36–41; Joseph Smith History, 1838–56, volume A-1, 5–6, in *JSP,* H1:222–26 (draft 2); Joseph Smith, Journal, Nov. 9–11, 1835, in *JSP,* J1:88–89.
11. Oliver Cowdery, "Letter IV," *LDS Messenger and Advocate,* Feb. 1835, 1:78–79; Lucy Mack Smith, History, 1844–45, book 3, [11].
12. Joseph Smith—History 1:42–43; Joseph Smith History, 1838–56, volume A-1, 6, in *JSP,* H1:226 (draft 2).
13. Lucy Mack Smith, History, 1844–45, book 3, [10]–[11]; Oliver Cowdery, "Letter IV," *LDS Messenger and Advocate,* Feb. 1835, 1:79–80; Oliver Cowdery, "Letter VII," *LDS*

Messenger and Advocate, July 1835, 1:156–57; Joseph Smith—History 1:44–46; Joseph Smith History, 1838–56, volume A-1, 6–7, in *JSP,* H1:230–32 (draft 2); Joseph Smith, Journal, Nov. 9–11, 1835, in *JSP,* J1:88–89.

14. Lucy Mack Smith, History, 1844–45, book 3, [11]; see also Smith, *William Smith on Mormonism,* 9.

15. Lucy Mack Smith, History, 1844–45, book 3, [11]; Smith, *Biographical Sketches,* 82; Joseph Smith—History 1:48–49; Joseph Smith History, 1838–56, volume A-1, 7, in *JSP,* H1:230–32 (draft 2); Joseph Smith, Journal, Nov. 9–11, 1835, in *JSP,* J1:89.

16. Joseph Smith, Journal, Nov. 9–11, 1835, in *JSP,* J1:89.

17. Oliver Cowdery, "Letter VIII," *LDS Messenger and Advocate,* Oct. 1835, 2:195–97. **Topic: Treasure Seeking**

18. Oliver Cowdery, "Letter VIII," *LDS Messenger and Advocate,* Oct. 1835, 2:195–97; Joseph Smith—History 1:51–52; Joseph Smith History, 1838–56, volume A-1, 6–7, in *JSP,* H1:230–32 (draft 2); see also Packer, "A Study of the Hill Cumorah," 7–10.

19. Joseph Smith—History 1:52; Joseph Smith History, 1838–56, volume A-1, 7, in *JSP,* H1:232 (draft 2). **Topic: Gold Plates**

20. Joseph Smith, "Church History," *Times and Seasons,* Mar. 1, 1842, 3:707, in *JSP,* H1:495.

21. Oliver Cowdery, "Letter VIII," *LDS Messenger and Advocate,* Oct. 1835, 2:197–98; see also Pratt, *Interesting Account,* 10, in *JSP,* H1:527–29.

22. Oliver Cowdery, "Letter VIII," *LDS Messenger and Advocate,* Oct. 1835, 2:198–99.

23. Knight, Reminiscences, 1; Joseph Smith, Journal, Nov. 9–11, 1835, in *JSP,* J1:89; Joseph Smith—History 1:53–54; Joseph Smith History, 1838–56, volume A-1, 7, in *JSP,* H1:232–34 (draft 2); see also Jessee, "Joseph Knight's Recollection of Early Mormon History," 31.

24. Joseph Smith, Journal, Aug. 23, 1842, in *JSP,* J1:116–17.

25. Lucy Mack Smith, History, 1844–45, book 3, [12]; book 4, [3]; Smith, *Biographical Sketches,* 83.

26. Lucy Mack Smith, History, 1844–45, book 4, [1]–[3]; Smith, *Biographical Sketches,* 86–87; see also Lucy Mack Smith, History, 1845, 89; and Bushman, *Refinement of America,* 425–27. **Topic: Joseph Sr. and Lucy Mack Smith Family**

27. Lucy Mack Smith, History, 1844–45, book 4, [3]–[5].

28. Lucy Mack Smith, History, 1844–45, book 4, [6]–[8]; "Wm. B. Smith's Last Statement," *Zion's Ensign,* Jan. 13, 1894, 6.

29. Lucy Mack Smith, History, 1844–45, book 4, [7]; Joseph Smith, Journal, Aug. 23, 1842, in *JSP,* J2:116–17.

30. Lucy Mack Smith, History, 1844–45, book 4, [2]–[3].

31. Lucy Mack Smith, History, 1844–45, book 4, [2]–[3]; Smith, *Biographical Sketches,* 85–86; Knight, Reminiscences, 1; Joseph Smith—History 1:54; Lucy Mack Smith, History, 1845, 88; see also Jessee, "Joseph Knight's Recollection of Early Mormon History," 31.

32. Smith, *Biographical Sketches,* 86.

CHAPTER 4: BE WATCHFUL

1. Agreement of Josiah Stowell and Others, Nov. 1, 1825, in *JSP,* D1:345–52.

2. Smith, *Biographical Sketches,* 91–92; Oliver Cowdery, "Letter VIII," *LDS Messenger and Advocate,* Oct. 1835, 2:200–202; Joseph Smith History, 1838–56, volume A-1, 7–8, in *JSP,* H1:234 (draft 2); Smith, *On Mormonism,* 10. **Topic: Treasure Seeking**

3. Agreement of Josiah Stowell and Others, Nov. 1, 1825, in *JSP,* D1:345–52.

4. Pratt, *Autobiography,* 47; Burnett, *Recollections and Opinions of an Old Pioneer,* 66–67; Woodruff, Journal, July 4, 1843, and Oct. 20, 1855; Emmeline B. Wells, "L.D.S. Women of the Past," *Woman's Exponent,* Feb. 1908, 36:49; Joseph Smith III, "Last Testimony of Sister Emma," *Saints' Herald,* Oct. 1, 1879, 289; see also Staker and

Ashton, "Growing Up in the Isaac and Elizabeth Hale Home"; and Ashurst-McGee, "Josiah Stowell Jr.–John S. Fullmer Correspondence," 108–17.

5. Baugh, "Joseph Smith's Athletic Nature," 137–50; Pratt, *Autobiography*, 47; Burnett, *Recollections and Opinions of an Old Pioneer*, 66–67; *Recollections of the Pioneers of Lee County*, 96; Youngreen, *Reflections of Emma*, 61, 67, 65, 69; Emmeline B. Wells, "L.D.S. Women of the Past," *Woman's Exponent*, Feb. 1908, 36:49.

6. Joseph Smith History, 1838–56, volume A-1, 8, in *JSP*, H1:234 (draft 2); Smith, *Biographical Sketches*, 92; Bushman, *Rough Stone Rolling*, 51–53; Staker, "Isaac and Elizabeth Hale in Their Endless Mountain Home," 104.

7. Joseph Smith History, 1838–56, volume A-1, 7–8, in *JSP*, H1:234–36 (draft 2); Knight, Reminiscences, 2; Joseph Smith III, "Last Testimony of Sister Emma," *Saints' Herald*, Oct. 1, 1879, 290.

8. William D. Purple, "Joseph Smith, the Originator of Mormonism," *Chenango Union*, May 2, 1877, [3]; see also An Act for Apprehending and Punishing Disorderly Persons (Feb. 9, 1788), *Laws of the State of New-York* (1813), 1:114. **Topic: Joseph Smith's 1826 Trial**

9. "Mormonism—No. II," *Tiffany's Monthly*, July 1859, 169.

10. Knight, Reminiscences, 2.

11. Lucy Mack Smith, History, 1844–45, 96; see also Knight, Reminiscences, 2.

12. See "The Original Prophet," *Fraser's Magazine*, Feb. 1873, 229–30.

13. Lucy Mack Smith, History, 1845, 97.

14. Knight, Reminiscences, 2; Joseph Smith III, "Last Testimony of Sister Emma," *Saints' Herald*, Oct. 1, 1879, 289.

15. Joseph Smith III, "Last Testimony of Sister Emma," *Saints' Herald*, Oct. 1, 1879, 289; Joseph Smith History, 1838–56, volume A-1, 8, in *JSP*, H1:236 (draft 2).

16. Joseph Smith III, "Last Testimony of Sister Emma," *Saints' Herald*, Oct. 1, 1879, 290; Joseph Lewis and Hiel Lewis, "Mormon History. A New Chapter, about to Be Published," *Amboy Journal*, Apr. 30, 1879, 1; see also Oliver Cowdery, "Letter VIII," in *LDS Messenger and Advocate*, Oct. 1835, 2:201.

17. Joseph Smith History, 1838–56, volume A-1, 8, in *JSP*, H1:236 (draft 2); Lucy Mack Smith, History, 1844–45, book 4, [11]–[12]; book 5, [1]–[3]. **Topic: Sacred Grove and Smith Family Farm**

18. "Mormonism—No. II," *Tiffany's Monthly*, July 1859, 167–68.

19. Lucy Mack Smith, History, 1844–45, book 5, [4]–[6].

20. Knight, Reminiscences, 2.

21. Lucy Mack Smith, History, 1844–45, book 5, [6].

22. Lucy Mack Smith, History, 1845, 105.

23. Lucy Mack Smith, History, 1844–45, book 6, [1].

24. "Mormonism—No. II," *Tiffany's Monthly*, June 1859, 165–66; Lucy Mack Smith, History, 1844–45, book 5, [6].

25. Lucy Mack Smith, History, 1844–45, book 5, [6]–[7]; Knight, Reminiscences, 2.

26. Lucy Mack Smith, History, 1844–45, book 5, [7]–[8].

27. Knight, Reminiscences, 2–3; Joseph Smith History, 1838–56, volume A-1, 5, in *JSP*, H1:222 (draft 2); see also Alma 37:23.

28. Lucy Mack Smith, History, 1844–45, book 5, [8]–[10]; "Mormonism— No. II," *Tiffany's Monthly*, Aug. 1859, 166; Smith, *Biographical Sketches*, 103; see also Genesis 25:29–34.

29. Lucy Mack Smith, History, 1844–45, book 5, [10] and adjacent paper fragment.

30. Lucy Mack Smith, History, 1844–45, book 5, [11]. **Topic: Gold Plates**

31. Lucy Mack Smith, History, 1844–45, book 5, [11].

32. "The Old Soldier's Testimony," *Saints' Herald*, Oct. 4, 1884, 643–44; Salisbury, "Things the Prophet's Sister Told Me," 1945, Church History Library; Ball, "The Prophet's Sister Testifies She Lifted the B. of M. Plates," 1954, Church History Library; Smith, *William Smith on Mormonism*, 11; Lucy Mack Smith, History, 1844–45, book 5, [11]; Joseph Smith III, "Last Testimony of Sister Emma," *Saints' Herald*, Oct. 1, 1879, 290.

33. Lucy Mack Smith, History, 1844–45, book 5, [11]–[12]. **Topic: Lucy Mack Smith**

CHAPTER 5: ALL IS LOST

1. Joseph Smith—History 1:59; Joseph Smith History, 1838–56, volume A-1, 8, in *JSP,* H1:236–38 (draft 2); Lucy Mack Smith, History, 1844–45, book 6, [1]–[2]; Knight, Reminiscences, 3.
2. Knight, Reminiscences, 3–4; Lucy Mack Smith, History, 1844–45, book 6, [1]–[3]; Joseph Smith History, circa Summer 1832, 1, in *JSP,* H1:11.
3. "Mormonism—No. II," *Tiffany's Monthly,* Aug. 1859, 167–68; Lucy Mack Smith, History, 1844–45, book 6, [3]–[4]; Joseph Smith History, 1838–56, volume A-1, 8, in *JSP,* H1:238 (draft 2). **Topic: Witnesses of the Book of Mormon**
4. "Mormonism—No. II," *Tiffany's Monthly,* Aug. 1859, 168–70.
5. Joseph Smith History, 1838–56, volume A-1, 8–9, in *JSP,* H1:238 (draft 2); Knight, Reminiscences, 3; "Mormonism—No. II," *Tiffany's Monthly,* Aug. 1859, 170.
6. Lucy Mack Smith, History, 1844–45, book 6, [6]; Lucy Mack Smith, History, 1845, 121.
7. "Mormonism—No. II," *Tiffany's Monthly,* Aug. 1859, 170.
8. "Mormonism—No. II," *Tiffany's Monthly,* Aug. 1859, 170; Joseph Smith History, 1838–56, volume A-1, 9, in *JSP,* H1:240 (draft 2).
9. Isaac Hale, Affidavit, Mar. 20, 1834, in "Mormonism," *Susquehanna Register, and Northern Pennsylvanian,* May 1, 1834, [1].
10. Joseph Smith History, 1838–56, volume A-1, 9, in *JSP,* H1:240 (draft 2); Knight, Reminiscences, 3.
11. Lucy Mack Smith, History, 1844–45, book 6, [3]; Joseph Smith History, 1838–56, volume A-1, 9, in *JSP,* H1:240 (draft 2); "Letter from Elder W. H. Kelley," *Saints' Herald,* Mar. 1, 1882, 68; see also Doctrine and Covenants 9:7–8 (Revelation, Apr. 1829–D, at josephsmithpapers.org).
12. Joseph Smith History, circa Summer 1832, 5, in *JSP,* H1:15; Knight, Reminiscences, 3. **Topic: Book of Mormon Translation**
13. Joseph Smith History, 1838–56, volume A-1, 9, in *JSP,* H1:238–40 (draft 2); Joseph Smith History, circa Summer 1832, 5, in *JSP,* H1:15.
14. MacKay, "Git Them Translated," 98–100.
15. Bennett, "Read This I Pray Thee," 192.
16. Joseph Smith History, 1838–56, volume A-1, 9, in *JSP,* H1:240 (draft 2); Bennett, Journal, Aug. 8, 1831, in Arrington, "James Gordon Bennett's 1831 Report on 'The Mormonites,'" 355.
17. [James Gordon Bennett], "Mormon Religion—Clerical Ambition—Western New York—the Mormonites Gone to Ohio," *Morning Courier and New-York Enquirer,* Sept. 1, 1831, [2].
18. Joseph Smith History, 1838–56, volume A-1, 9, in *JSP,* H1:240–42 (draft 2); Jennings, "Charles Anthon," 171–87; Bennett, "Read This I Pray Thee," 178–216.
19. Joseph Smith History, 1838–56, volume A-1, 9, in *JSP,* H1:244 (draft 2); Bennett, Journal, Aug. 8, 1831, in Arrington, "James Gordon Bennett's 1831 Report on 'The Mormonites,'" 355; Knight, Reminiscences, 4. **Topic: Martin Harris's Consultations with Scholars**
20. Joseph Smith History, circa Summer 1832, 5, in *JSP,* H1:15; Isaiah 29:11–12; 2 Nephi 27:15–19.
21. Lucy Mack Smith, History, 1844–45, book 6, [8]; Joseph Smith History, 1838–56, volume A-1, 9, in *JSP,* H1:244; Joseph Smith III, "Last Testimony of Sister Emma," *Saints' Herald,* Oct. 1, 1879, 289–90.
22. Joseph Smith History, 1838–56, volume A-1, 9, in *JSP,* H1:244 (draft 2); Isaac Hale, Affidavit, Mar. 20, 1834, in "Mormonism," *Susquehanna Register, and Northern Pennsylvanian,* May 1, 1834, [1]; Agreement with Isaac Hale, Apr. 6, 1829, in *JSP,* D1:28–34.
23. Briggs, "A Visit to Nauvoo in 1856," 454; see also Edmund C. Briggs to Joseph Smith, June 4, 1884, *Saints' Herald,* June 21, 1884, 396.

24. Joseph Smith III, "Last Testimony of Sister Emma," *Saints' Herald,* Oct. 1, 1879, 289–90; Briggs, "A Visit to Nauvoo in 1856," 454.
25. Joseph Smith History, 1838–56, volume A-1, 9, in *JSP,* H1:244 (draft 2); Isaac Hale, Affidavit, Mar. 20, 1834, in "Mormonism," *Susquehanna Register, and Northern Pennsylvanian,* May 1, 1834, [1].
26. Lucy Mack Smith, History, 1844–45, book 6, [8].
27. Lucy Mack Smith, History, 1844–45, book 6, [3]–[5], [8]–[9].
28. Lucy Mack Smith, History, 1844–45, book 6, [9]–[10]; Joseph Smith III, "Last Testimony of Sister Emma," *Saints' Herald,* Oct. 1, 1879, 289–90.
29. In a reminiscent account, Emma Smith said that she worked in the same room as Joseph and Oliver Cowdery while they completed the translation in 1829, and she was likely also present as Joseph and Martin translated in 1828. (Joseph Smith III, "Last Testimony of Sister Emma," *Saints' Herald,* Oct. 1, 1879, 290.)
30. William Pilkington, Affidavit, Cache County, UT, Apr. 3, 1934, in William Pilkington, Autobiography and Statements, Church History Library; "One of the Three Witnesses," *Deseret News,* Dec. 28, 1881, 10.
31. Briggs, "A Visit to Nauvoo in 1856," 454; Joseph Smith III, "Last Testimony of Sister Emma," *Saints' Herald,* Oct. 1, 1879, 289–90.
32. See Lucy Mack Smith, History, 1844–45, book 6, [10]; Joseph Smith History, 1838–56, volume A-1, 9, in *JSP,* H1:244; Joseph Smith History, circa Summer 1832, 5, in *JSP,* H1:15; Knight, Reminiscences, 5; and Historical Introduction to Preface to the Book of Mormon, circa Aug. 1829, in *JSP,* D1:92–93.
33. Joseph Smith History, 1838–56, volume A-1, 9, in *JSP,* H1:244 (draft 2); Lucy Mack Smith, History, 1844–45, book 6, [10].
34. Lucy Mack Smith, History, 1844–45, book 6, [10]–[11]; book 7, [1].
35. Joseph Smith History, circa Summer 1832, 5, in *JSP,* H1:15.
36. Joseph Smith History, 1838–56, volume A-1, 9–10, in *JSP,* H1:244–46 (draft 2); Lucy Mack Smith, History, 1844–45, book 7, [1]; Knight, Reminiscences, 5.
37. Joseph Smith History, 1838–56, volume A-1, 9–10, in *JSP,* H1:244–46 (draft 2).
38. Lucy Mack Smith, History, 1844–45, book 7, [1]–[2]. **Topic: Joseph and Emma Hale Smith Family**
39. Lucy Mack Smith, History, 1844–45, book 7, [1]–[2].
40. Lucy Mack Smith, History, 1844–45, book 7, [2]–[4].
41. Lucy Mack Smith, History, 1844–45, book 7, [5].
42. Lucy Mack Smith, History, 1844–45, book 7, [5]–[7]. **Topic: Lost Manuscript of the Book of Mormon**
43. Lucy Mack Smith, History, 1844–45, book 7, [7]. **Topic: Lucy Mack Smith**

CHAPTER 6: THE GIFT AND POWER OF GOD

1. Lucy Mack Smith, History, 1844–45, book 7, [9].
2. See Doctrine and Covenants 10:2 (Revelation, Spring 1829, at josephsmithpapers.org).
3. See Lucy Mack Smith, History, 1844–45, book 7, [5]–[7].
4. Lucy Mack Smith, History, 1844–45, book 7, [8]–[9].
5. Doctrine and Covenants 3:1 (Revelation, July 1828, at josephsmithpapers.org); Lucy Mack Smith, History, 1844–45, book 7, [8]–[9]; Joseph Smith History, 1838–56, volume A-1, 10, in *JSP,* H1:246 (draft 2).
6. Doctrine and Covenants 3 (Revelation, July 1828, at josephsmithpapers.org); Joseph Smith History, circa Summer 1832, [6], in *JSP,* H1:16; Lucy Mack Smith, History, 1844–45, book 7, [8]–[9].
7. Lucy Mack Smith, History, 1845, 138; Lucy Mack Smith, History, 1844–45, book 7, [8]–[11].

8. Preface to Book of Mormon, circa Aug. 1829, in *JSP,* D1:92–94; "Testamoney of Martin Harris," Sept. 4, 1870, [4], Edward Stevenson Collection, Church History Library; Lucy Mack Smith, History, 1844–45, book 8, [5]; Historical Introduction to Revelation, Mar. 1829 [D&C 5], in *JSP,* D1:14–16.

9. "Testamoney of Martin Harris," Sept. 4, 1870, [4], Edward Stevenson Collection, Church History Library; Lucy Mack Smith, History, 1844–45, book 6, [9]; book 8, [5].

10. Doctrine and Covenants 5 (Revelation, Mar. 1829, at josephsmithpapers.org).

11. Revelation, Mar. 1829 [D&C 5], in *JSP,* D1:17.

12. Isaac Hale, Affidavit, Mar. 20, 1834, in "Mormonism," *Susquehanna Register, and Northern Pennsylvanian,* May 1, 1834, [1]; "considered" in original changed to "consider."

13. Lucy Mack Smith, History, 1844–45, book 8, [6]–[7].

14. Lucy Mack Smith, History, 1844–45, book 7, [11].

15. Lucy Mack Smith, History, 1844–45, book 7, [12]; "Mormonism," *Kansas City Daily Journal,* June 5, 1881, 1; Morris, "Conversion of Oliver Cowdery," 5–8.

16. Lucy Mack Smith, History, 1844–45, book 7, [12]; Knight, Reminiscences, 5; Doctrine and Covenants 4 (Revelation, Feb. 1829, at josephsmithpapers.org); see also Darowski, "Joseph Smith's Support at Home," 10–14.

17. Lucy Mack Smith, History, 1844–45, book 7, [12].

18. Oliver Cowdery to William W. Phelps, Sept. 7, 1834, *LDS Messenger and Advocate,* Oct. 1834, 1:15.

19. Doctrine and Covenants 6 (Revelation, Apr. 1829–A, at josephsmithpapers.org); Lucy Mack Smith, History, 1844–45, book 7, [12]; book 8, [1].

20. Joseph Smith History, 1838–56, volume A-1, 15, in *JSP,* H1:284 (draft 2); Joseph Smith History, circa Summer 1832, [6], in *JSP,* H1:16; Lucy Mack Smith, History, 1844–45, book 8, [1]; see also Doctrine and Covenants 6:22–23 (Revelation, Apr. 1829–A, at josephsmithpapers.org).

21. Lucy Mack Smith, History, 1844–45, book 8, [3]–[4]; Joseph Smith History, circa Summer 1832, [6], in *JSP,* H1:16.

22. Lucy Mack Smith, History, 1844–45, book 8, [4]; Joseph Smith History, 1838–56, volume A-1, 13, in *JSP,* H1:276 (draft 2); Agreement with Isaac Hale, Apr. 6, 1829, in *JSP,* D1:28–34; Oliver Cowdery to William W. Phelps, Sept. 7, 1834, *LDS Messenger and Advocate,* Oct. 1834, 1:14.

23. Joseph Smith History, 1838–56, volume A-1, 18, in *JSP,* H1:296 (draft 2).

24. Joseph Smith History, 1838–56, volume A-1, 15, in *JSP,* H1:284 (draft 2); Lucy Mack Smith, History, 1844–45, book 8, [4]; Joseph Smith III, "Last Testimony of Sister Emma," *Saints' Herald,* Oct. 1, 1879, 290. **Topic: Daily Life of First-Generation Latter-day Saints**

25. "Book of Mormon Translation," Gospel Topics, topics.lds.org; Joseph Smith History, 1838–56, volume A-1, 15, in *JSP,* H1:284 (draft 2); Oliver Cowdery to William W. Phelps, Sept. 7, 1834, *LDS Messenger and Advocate,* Oct. 1834, 1:14; Joseph Smith III, "Last Testimony of Sister Emma," *Saints' Herald,* Oct. 1, 1879, 290; "Golden Bible," *Palmyra Freeman,* Aug. 11, 1829, [2]. **Topic: Book of Mormon Translation**

26. Doctrine and Covenants 10:45 (Revelation, Spring 1829, at josephsmithpapers.org); 1 Nephi 9:5; Words of Mormon 1; Doctrine and Covenants 3 (Revelation, July 1828, at josephsmithpapers.org).

27. Doctrine and Covenants 10:42–43 (Revelation, Spring 1829, at josephsmithpapers .org). **Topic: Lost Manuscript of the Book of Mormon**

28. Oliver Cowdery to William W. Phelps, Sept. 7, 1834, *LDS Messenger and Advocate,* Oct. 1834, 1:14; Mosiah 8:16–18; see also Omni 1:20; Mosiah 8:8–13; 28:11–15, 20; Alma 37:21, 23; and Ether 3:24–28.

29. Doctrine and Covenants 6:5, 11, 22–24 (Revelation, Apr. 1829–A, at josephsmithpapers.org).

30. Doctrine and Covenants 6:10–13 (Revelation, Apr. 1829–A, at josephsmithpapers.org); Doctrine and Covenants 8:4–8 (Revelation, Apr. 1829–B, at josephsmithpapers.org);

Historical Introduction to Revelation, Apr. 1829–B [D&C 8], in *JSP,* D1:44–45; Revelation Book 1, 13, in *JSP,* MRB:15.

31. Lucy Mack Smith, History, 1844–45, book 8, [1]; Paul and Parks, *History of Wells, Vermont,* 81; Historical Introduction to Revelation, 1829–B [D&C 8], in *JSP,* D1:44–45; see also Baugh, *Days Never to Be Forgotten;* Bushman, *Rough Stone Rolling,* 73; and Morris, "Oliver Cowdery's Vermont Years and the Origins of Mormonism," 106–29. **Topic: Divining Rods**

32. Doctrine and Covenants 6 (Revelation, Apr. 1829–A, at josephsmithpapers.org); Doctrine and Covenants 8 (Revelation, Apr. 1829–B, at josephsmithpapers.org); Joseph Smith History, 1838–56, volume A-1, 13–14, in *JSP,* H1:276–78 (draft 2); see also Book of Commandments 7:3; and Doctrine and Covenants 8:6–7.

33. Doctrine and Covenants 9 (Revelation, Apr. 1829–D, at josephsmithpapers.org); Oliver Cowdery to William W. Phelps, Sept. 7, 1834, *LDS Messenger and Advocate,* Oct. 1834, 1:14.

CHAPTER 7· FELLOW SERVANTS

1. Oliver Cowdery to William W. Phelps, Sept. 7, 1834, *LDS Messenger and Advocate,* Oct. 1834, 1:14; Staker, "Where Was the Aaronic Priesthood Restored?," 158, note 49.

2. 3 Nephi 8; Oliver Cowdery to William W. Phelps, Sept. 7, 1834, *LDS Messenger and Advocate,* Oct. 1834, 1:15–16; see also Kowallis, "In the Thirty and Fourth Year," 136–90.

3. 3 Nephi 9:13.

4. 3 Nephi 10:9; 11:1.

5. 3 Nephi 11:10; 15:21–24; see also John 10:16.

6. 3 Nephi 11:33.

7. 3 Nephi 11:23–33.

8. Oliver Cowdery to William W. Phelps, Sept. 7, 1834, *LDS Messenger and Advocate,* Oct. 1834, 1:15–16.

9. Doctrine and Covenants 13:1 (Joseph Smith History, 1838–56, volume A-1, 17–18, in *JSP,* H1:292–94 [draft 2]); Oliver Cowdery to William W. Phelps, Sept. 7, 1834, *LDS Messenger and Advocate,* Oct. 1834, 1:15; Staker, "Where Was the Aaronic Priesthood Restored?," 142–59. **Topic: Restoration of the Aaronic Priesthood**

10. Oliver Cowdery to William W. Phelps, Sept. 7, 1834, *LDS Messenger and Advocate,* Oct. 1834, 1:15.

11. Joseph Smith History, 1838–56, volume A-1, 17–18, in *JSP,* H1:292–94 (draft 2); "Articles of the Church of Christ," June 1829, in *JSP,* D1:371.

12. Joseph Smith History, 1838–56, volume A-1, 18, in *JSP,* H1:294–96 (draft 2).

13. "Mormonism," *Kansas City Daily Journal,* June 5, 1881, 1; James H. Hart, "About the Book of Mormon," *Deseret Evening News,* Mar. 25, 1884, [2]; Joseph F. Smith to John Taylor and Council of the Twelve, Sept. 17, 1878, draft, Joseph F. Smith, Papers, Church History Library; Joseph Smith History, 1838–56, volume A-1, 21, in *JSP,* H1:306 (draft 2).

14. Joseph Smith History, 1838–56, volume A-1, 18, in *JSP,* H1:296 (draft 2).

15. "Mormonism," *Kansas City Daily Journal,* June 5, 1881, 1; Dickinson, *New Light on Mormonism,* 250; "The Book of Mormon," *Chicago Tribune,* Dec. 17, 1885, 3; Joseph Smith History, 1838–56, volume A-1, 21, in *JSP,* H1:306 (draft 2).

16. Lucy Mack Smith, History, 1844–45, book 8, [8]; Orson Pratt and Joseph F. Smith, Interview with David Whitmer, Sept. 7–8, 1878, [10], in Joseph F. Smith to John Taylor and Council of the Twelve, Sept. 17, 1878, draft, Joseph F. Smith, Papers, Church History Library; Cook, *David Whitmer Interviews,* 26–27.

17. Orson Pratt and Joseph F. Smith, Interview with David Whitmer, Sept. 7–8, 1878, [10], in Joseph F. Smith to John Taylor and Council of the Twelve, Sept. 17, 1878, draft, Joseph F. Smith, Papers, Church History Library.
18. James H. Hart, "About the Book of Mormon," *Deseret Evening News,* Mar. 25, 1884, [2].
19. Skousen, "Another Account of Mary Whitmer's Viewing of the Golden Plates," 40; [Andrew Jenson], "Eight Witnesses," *Historical Record,* Oct. 1888, 621.
20. Orson Pratt and Joseph F. Smith, Interview with David Whitmer, Sept. 7–8, 1878, [10], in Joseph F. Smith to John Taylor and Council of the Twelve, Sept. 17, 1878, draft, Joseph F. Smith, Papers, Church History Library.
21. Skousen, "Another Account of Mary Whitmer's Viewing of the Golden Plates," 40; [Andrew Jenson], "Eight Witnesses," *Historical Record,* Oct. 1888, 621.
22. [Andrew Jenson], "Eight Witnesses," *Historical Record,* Oct. 1888, 621; Orson Pratt and Joseph F. Smith, Interview with David Whitmer, Sept. 7–8, 1878, [10], in Joseph F. Smith to John Taylor and Council of the Twelve, Sept. 17, 1878, draft, Joseph F. Smith, Papers, Church History Library; Stevenson, Journal, Dec. 23, 1877.
23. Whitmer, *Address to All Believers in Christ,* 30.
24. "Letter from Elder W. H. Kelley," *Saints' Herald,* Mar. 1, 1882, 68; see also Bushman, *Rough Stone Rolling,* 77.
25. Joseph Smith History, 1838–56, volume A-1, 34, in *JSP,* H1:352–54 (draft 2). **Topics: Book of Mormon Translation; Gold Plates**
26. 2 Nephi 3:7–19.
27. Joseph Smith History, circa Summer 1832, [5], in *JSP,* H1:15; 2 Nephi 26:16; 27:15–21.
28. Doctrine and Covenants 17 (Revelation, June 1829–E, at josephsmithpapers.org); Doctrine and Covenants 5:11–18 (Revelation, Mar. 1829, at josephsmithpapers.org); Joseph Smith History, 1838–56, volume A-1, 23, in *JSP,* H1:314–17 (draft 2).
29. Lucy Mack Smith, History, 1844–45, book 8, [11].
30. Joseph Smith History, 1838–56, volume A-1, 24–25, in *JSP,* H1:316–18 (draft 2).
31. "Letter from Elder W. H. Kelley," *Saints' Herald,* Mar. 1, 1882, 68; Joseph Smith History, 1838–56, volume A-1, 24–25, in *JSP,* H1:316–20 (draft 2); "Testimony of Three Witnesses," in Book of Mormon, 1830 edition, [589]. **Topic: Witnesses of the Book of Mormon**
32. Joseph Smith History, 1838–56, volume A-1, 25, in *JSP,* H1:320 (draft 2).
33. Lucy Mack Smith, History, 1844–45, book 8, [11]; book 9, [1].
34. Lucy Mack Smith, History, 1844–45, book 9, [1]; 2 Nephi 27:14.
35. "Testimony of Eight Witnesses," in Book of Mormon, 1830 edition, [590]. **Topic: Witnesses of the Book of Mormon**
36. Lucy Mack Smith, History, 1844–45, book 9, [2].

CHAPTER 8: THE RISE OF THE CHURCH OF CHRIST

1. Copyright for Book of Mormon, June 11, 1829, in *JSP,* D1:76–81.
2. "Prospect of Peace with Utah," *Albany Evening Journal,* May 19, 1858, [2]; "From the Troy Times," *Albany Evening Journal,* May 21, 1858, [2]; John H. Gilbert, Memorandum, Sept. 8, 1892, photocopy, Church History Library.
3. Doctrine and Covenants 19 (Revelation, circa Summer 1829, at josephsmithpapers .org); see also Historical Introduction to Revelation, circa Summer 1829 [D&C 19], in *JSP,* D1:85–89; and Knight, Reminiscences, 6–7.
4. McBride, "Contributions of Martin Harris," 1–9; Joseph Smith History, 1838–56, volume A-1, 34, in *JSP,* H1:352 (draft 2).
5. John H. Gilbert, Statement, Oct. 23, 1887, Church History Library; Indenture, Martin Harris to Egbert B. Grandin, Wayne County, NY, Aug. 25, 1829, Wayne County, NY, Mortgage Records, volume 3, 325–26, microfilm 479,556, U.S. and Canada Record Collection, Family History Library; Historical Introduction to Revelation, circa Summer 1829 [D&C 19], in *JSP,* D1:85–89.

6. Copyright for Book of Mormon, June 11, 1829, in *JSP*, D1:76–81; John H. Gilbert, Memorandum, Sept. 8, 1892, photocopy, Church History Library; Porter, "The Book of Mormon," 53–54.

7. John H. Gilbert, Memorandum, Sept. 8, 1892, photocopy, Church History Library; Lucy Mack Smith, History, 1844–45, book 9, [8]; Joseph Smith to Oliver Cowdery, Oct. 22, 1829, in *JSP*, D1:94–97.

8. John H. Gilbert, Memorandum, Sept. 8, 1892, photocopy, Church History Library; Lucy Mack Smith, History, 1844–45, book 9, [2]; "Printer's Manuscript of the Book of Mormon," in *JSP*, R3, Part 1:xxvi. **Topic: Printing and Publishing the Book of Mormon**

9. Oliver Cowdery to Joseph Smith, Nov. 6, 1829, in *JSP*, D1:100–101; Mosiah 3:18–19; 5:5–7; 4 Nephi 1:17; see also Oliver Cowdery to Joseph Smith, Dec. 28, 1829, in *JSP*, D1:101–4.

10. Thomas B. Marsh, "History of Thomas Baldwin Marsh," *LDS Millennial Star*, June 4, 1864, 26:359–60; June 11, 1864, 26:375–76.

11. Lucy Mack Smith, History, 1844–45, book 9, [9]. For examples of excerpts from the Book of Mormon published by Abner Cole, see "The Book of Mormon," *Reflector*, Sept. 16, 1829, 10; "Selected Items," *Reflector*, Sept. 23, 1829, 14; "The First Book of Nephi," *Reflector*, Jan. 2, 1830, 1; and "The First Book of Nephi," *Reflector*, Jan. 13, 1830, 1. **Topic: Critics of the Book of Mormon**

12. Lucy Mack Smith, History, 1844–45, book 9, [9]–[12]; Lucy Mack Smith, History, 1845, 166–68.

13. Chamberlin, Autobiography, 4–11.

14. Copyright for Book of Mormon, June 11, 1829, in *JSP*, D1:76–81; John H. Gilbert, Memorandum, Sept. 8, 1892, photocopy, Church History Library; "Book of Mormon," *Wayne Sentinel*, Mar. 26, 1830, [3]. Some books were also bound in sheepskin.

15. Title Page of Book of Mormon, circa early June 1829, in *JSP*, D1:63–65; see also Lucy Mack Smith to Solomon Mack, Jan. 6, 1831, Church History Library.

16. Testimony of Three Witnesses, Late June 1829, in *JSP*, D1:378–82; Testimony of Eight Witnesses, Late June 1829, in *JSP*, D1:385–87.

17. Tucker, *Origin, Rise, and Progress of Mormonism*, 60–61.

18. See Lucy Mack Smith to Solomon Mack, Jan. 6, 1831, Church History Library.

19. Joseph Smith History, circa Summer 1832, 1, in *JSP*, H1:10; Doctrine and Covenants 27:12–13 (Revelation, circa Aug. 1830, in Doctrine and Covenants 50:3, 1835 edition, at josephsmithpapers.org); Oliver Cowdery to Phineas Young, Mar. 23, 1846, Church History Library; "Joseph Smith Documents Dating through June 1831," in *JSP*, D1:xxxvii–xxxix; see also Cannon and others, "Priesthood Restoration Documents," 163–207. **Topic: Restoration of the Melchizedek Priesthood**

20. Joseph Smith History, 1838–56, volume A-1, 27, in *JSP*, H1:326–28 (draft 2).

21. Joseph Smith History, 1838–56, volume A-1, 37, in *JSP*, H1:364 (draft 2); Stevenson, Journal, Dec. 22, 1877; Jan. 2, 1887; An Act to Provide for the Incorporation of Religious Societies (Apr. 5, 1813), *Laws of the State of New-York* (1813), 2:212–19. **Topic: Founding Meeting of the Church of Christ**

22. Joseph Smith History, 1838–56, volume A-1, 37–38, in *JSP*, H1:364–71 (draft 2).

23. Joseph Smith History, 1838–56, volume A-1, 37, in *JSP*, H1:366; Doctrine and Covenants 21 (Revelation, Apr. 6, 1830, at josephsmithpapers.org); "History of Joseph Smith," *Times and Seasons*, Oct. 1, 1842, 3:928–29.

24. Lucy Mack Smith, History, 1844–45, book 9, [12]; Knight, Reminiscences, 8; see also Bushman, *Rough Stone Rolling*, 110.

25. Joseph Smith History, 1838–56, volume A-1, 38, in *JSP*, H1:372 (draft 2); Joseph Smith, "Latter Day Saints," in Rupp, *He Pasa Ekklesia*, 404–5, in *JSP*, H1:506.

26. Knight, Reminiscences, 7.

CHAPTER 9: COME LIFE OR COME DEATH

1. Joseph Smith History, 1838–56, volume A-1, 39, in *JSP,* H1:378 (draft 2).
2. See, for example, Mark 16:17–18. **Topic: Gifts of the Spirit**
3. Mosiah 3:19.
4. Joseph Smith History, 1838–56, volume A-1, 39, in *JSP,* H1:380 (draft 2); Knight, Reminiscences, 7; see also Historical Introduction to Revelation, Apr. 1830–E [D&C 23:6–7], in *JSP,* D1:136.
5. Joseph Smith History, circa June–Oct. 1839, [11]–[13] (draft 1); Joseph Smith History, 1838–56, volume A-1, 39–41 (draft 2); Joseph Smith History, circa 1841, 70–72 (draft 3), in *JSP,* H1:380–87. **Topic: Gifts of the Spirit**
6. Pratt, *Autobiography,* 30–37; Givens and Grow, *Parley P. Pratt,* 26–27.
7. Pratt, *Autobiography,* 37–38.
8. Pratt, *Autobiography,* 38–43.
9. Joseph Smith History, 1838–56, volume A-1, 42, in *JSP,* H1:390 (draft 2). **Topic: Emma Hale Smith**
10. Joseph Smith History, 1838–56, volume A-1, 42–43, in *JSP,* H1:390–94 (draft 2); Diedrich Willers to L. Mayer and D. Young, June 18, 1830, in Quinn, "First Months of Mormonism," 331. **Topic: Name of the Church**
11. Joseph Smith History, 1838–56, volume A-1, 43–44, 47, in *JSP,* H1:394–98, 412 (draft 2); Knight, Reminiscences, 8.
12. Joseph Smith History, 1838–56, volume A-1, 44–47, in *JSP,* H1:396–412 (draft 2); Knight, Reminiscences, 8; Bushman, *Rough Stone Rolling,* 116–18; see also Acts 4:1–3; 5:17–33; 6–7; 24–26.
13. Doctrine and Covenants 24:7, 9 (Revelation, July 1830–A, at josephsmithpapers.org).
14. Doctrine and Covenants 25:7, 9, 12 (Revelation, July 1830–C, at josephsmithpapers .org); see also Grow, "Thou Art an Elect Lady," 33–39. **Topic: Emma Hale Smith**
15. Joseph Smith History, 1838–56, volume A-1, 52–53, in *JSP,* H1:432 (draft 2). **Topic: Gifts of the Spirit**
16. Joseph Smith History, 1838–56, volume A-1, 53, in *JSP,* H1:436 (draft 2); Deed from Isaac and Elizabeth Hale, Aug. 25, 1830, in *JSP,* D1:167–71; Knight, Autobiography, 141.
17. Joseph Smith History, 1838–56, volume A-1, 53–54, in *JSP,* H1:436 (draft 2).
18. Knight, Autobiography, 146; Bushman, *Rough Stone Rolling,* 119–21.
19. Knight, Autobiography and Journal, 22; Knight, Autobiography, 145–47.
20. Knight, Autobiography, 145–47; Doctrine and Covenants 28 (Revelation, Sept. 1830–B, at josephsmithpapers.org); Covenant of Oliver Cowdery and Others, Oct. 17, 1830, in *JSP,* D1:204; see also Doctrine and Covenants 29 (Revelation, Sept. 1830–A, at josephsmithpapers.org); 3 Nephi 21:23–24; and Ether 13:3–10. The revelation said the place for the holy city would be "among the Lamanites" but was edited for publication to read "on the borders by the Lamanites." (Book of Commandments 30:9, in *JSP,* R2:80.) **Topics: American Indians; Zion/New Jerusalem; Gathering of Israel**
21. Joseph Smith History, 1838–56, volume A-1, 58, in *JSP,* H1:452 (draft 2); Minutes, Sept. 26, 1830, in *JSP,* D1:192.
22. Doctrine and Covenants 30:5–8 (Revelation, Sept. 1830–D, at josephsmithpapers.org); Doctrine and Covenants 32 (Revelation, Oct. 1830–A, at josephsmithpapers.org); Joseph Smith History, 1838–56, volume A-1, 60, in *JSP,* H1:458–60 (draft 2); Givens and Grow, *Parley P. Pratt,* 36.
23. Lucy Mack Smith, History, 1845, 189–90.
24. Pratt, *Autobiography,* 49. **Topics: Early Missionaries; Kirtland, Ohio**
25. Smith, "Copy of an Old Note Book," 31–35; Lucy Mack Smith, History, 1845, 186–87. **Topic: Early Missionaries**
26. Rigdon, "Life Story of Sidney Rigdon," 18; Keller, "I Never Knew a Time," 23; Joseph Smith History, 1838–56, volume A-1, 73.

27. "Sidney Rigdon and the Spaulding Romance," *Deseret Evening News,* Apr. 21, 1879, [2].
28. Joseph Smith History, 1838–56, volume A-1, 73; see also Maki, "Go to the Ohio," 70–73.
29. Rigdon, "Life Story of Sidney Rigdon," 19; Joseph Smith History, 1838–56, volume A-1, 73; "Mormonism," *Painesville Telegraph,* Feb. 15, 1831, [1].
30. Joseph Smith History, 1838–56, volume A-1, 72–73; 1 Thessalonians 5:21.
31. Rigdon, "Life Story of Sidney Rigdon," 17; Keller, "I Never Knew a Time," 24; "Records of Early Church Families," *Utah Genealogical and Historical Magazine,* Oct. 1936, 27:161–62.
32. Mather, "Early Days of Mormonism," 206–7; Joseph Smith History, 1838–56, volume A-1, 74; "Sidney Rigdon," *Millennial Harbinger,* Feb. 7, 1831, 100–101; see also Ezra Booth, "Mormonism—Nos. VIII–IX," *Ohio Star,* Dec. 8, 1831, 1.
33. Joseph Smith History, 1838–56, volume A-1, 75. **Topic: Kirtland, Ohio**

CHAPTER 10: GATHERED IN

1. Allen, Autobiographical Sketch, [1]–[2]; 1830 U.S. Census, Mentor, Geauga County, OH, 266; Smith and Allen, "Family History of Lucy Diantha (Morley) Allen"; see also Givens and Grow, *Parley P. Pratt,* 39. **Topic: Daily Life of First-Generation Latter-day Saints**
2. See Givens and Grow, *Parley P. Pratt,* 39–40; and Acts 2:44; 4:32. **Topic: Consecration and Stewardship**
3. Oliver Cowdery to Joseph Smith, Nov. 12, 1830, in *JSP,* D1:213.
4. Staker, *Hearken, O Ye People,* 5–9.
5. See Minute Book 2, Aug. 31, 1838; and Knutson, "Sheffield Daniels and Abigail Warren."
6. Oliver Cowdery to Joseph Smith, Nov. 12, 1830, in *JSP,* D1:211–14.
7. Joseph Smith History, 1838–56, volume A-1, 75–76; Pratt, *Autobiography,* 61; "Williams, Frederick Granger," Biographical Entry, Joseph Smith Papers website, josephsmithpapers.org.
8. Pratt, *Autobiography,* 54–55.
9. Partridge, Genealogical Record, 2, 5; Lucy Mack Smith, History, 1844–45, book 10, [11].
10. Lucy Mack Smith, History, 1844–45, book 10, [11].
11. Lucy Mack Smith, History, 1844–45, book 10, [11]–[12]; Lucy Mack Smith, History, 1845, 191. **Topic: Sacrament Meetings**
12. Doctrine and Covenants 36 (Revelation, Dec. 9, 1830, at josephsmithpapers.org).
13. *JSP,* D1:224, note 158; License for Edward Partridge, Dec. 15, 1830, Edward Partridge, Papers, Church History Library.
14. Doctrine and Covenants 35:20, 22 (Revelation, Dec. 7, 1830, at josephsmithpapers.org).
15. *JSP,* D1.151, note 207; see also Maki, "Joseph Smith's Bible Translation," 99–104. It may not have been until after receiving this revelation about Moses that Joseph Smith undertook his Bible translation; for more information, see Visions of Moses, June 1830, in *JSP,* D1:150–56. **Topic: Joseph Smith Translation of the Bible**
16. Moses 1 (Visions of Moses, June 1830, at josephsmithpapers.org).
17. Bible Used for Bible Revision, at josephsmithpapers.org; Old Testament Revision 1, at josephsmithpapers.org; Genesis 5:18–24.
18. 4 Nephi 1:1–18; Genesis 5:22–24; Moses 7:18–19, 62, 69 (Old Testament Revision 1, 16–19, at josephsmithpapers.org).
19. Moses 7:28, 62 (Old Testament Revision 1, 16–17, 19, at josephsmithpapers.org). **Topics: Zion/New Jerusalem; Consecration and Stewardship**
20. Doctrine and Covenants 37 (Revelation, Dec. 30, 1830, at josephsmithpapers.org).

21. Doctrine and Covenants 29:8 (Revelation, Sept. 1830–A, at josephsmithpapers.org). **Topic: Gathering of Israel**
22. Whitmer, History, 9, in *JSP*, H2:21; Joseph Smith History, 1838–56, volume A-1, 88.
23. Whitmer, History, 5–6, in *JSP*, H2:18.
24. Doctrine and Covenants 38:18–19, 32 (Revelation, Jan. 2, 1831, at josephsmithpapers .org). **Topic: Endowment of Power**
25. Whitmer, History, 9, in *JSP*, H2:21; Knight, Autobiography and Journal, 28. **Topic: Dissent in the Church**
26. Knight, Autobiography and Journal, 28.
27. [Elizabeth Ann Smith Whitney], "A Leaf from an Autobiography," *Woman's Exponent*, Sept. 1, 1878, 7:51; Lucy Mack Smith, History, 1844–45, book 10, [12]; Lucy Mack Smith, History, 1845, 190; Joseph Smith History, 1838–56, volume A-1, 92. **Topic: Joseph and Emma Hale Smith Family**
28. See Staker, *Hearken, O Ye People*, 74–81.
29. [Elizabeth Ann Smith Whitney], "A Leaf from an Autobiography," *Woman's Exponent*, Sept. 1, 1878, 7:51; Tullidge, *Women of Mormondom*, 41–42.
30. [Elizabeth Ann Smith Whitney], "A Leaf from an Autobiography," *Woman's Exponent*, Aug. 15, 1878, 7:41.
31. [Elizabeth Ann Smith Whitney], "A Leaf from an Autobiography," *Woman's Exponent*, Sept. 1, 1878, 7:51.
32. Staker, *Hearken, O Ye People*, 45. **Topic: Consecration and Stewardship**
33. Joseph Smith History, 1838–56, volume A-1, 112; Staker, *Hearken, O Ye People*, 139; Pratt, *Autobiography*, 65.
34. Whitmer, History, 26, in *JSP*, H2:38.
35. Hancock, Autobiography, 79; see also McBride, "Religious Enthusiasm among Early Ohio Converts," 105–11. **Topic: Gifts of the Spirit**
36. [Elizabeth Ann Smith Whitney], "A Leaf from an Autobiography," *Woman's Exponent*, Sept. 1, 1878, 7:51.
37. Orson F. Whitney, "Newel K. Whitney," *Contributor*, Jan. 1885, 125; [Elizabeth Ann Smith Whitney], "A Leaf from an Autobiography," *Woman's Exponent*, Sept. 1, 1878, 7:51.

CHAPTER 11: YE SHALL RECEIVE MY LAW

1. [Elizabeth Ann Smith Whitney], "A Leaf from an Autobiography," *Woman's Exponent*, Sept. 1, 1878, 7:51; Staker, *Hearken, O Ye People*, 226.
2. 1830 U.S. Census, Kirtland, Geauga County, OH, 268–73; Staker, *Hearken, O Ye People*, 402, 413; *JSP*, D1:530–31.
3. See 1 Corinthians 1:2.
4. Joseph Smith to Hyrum Smith, Mar. 3–4, 1831, in *JSP*, D1:272. **Topic: American Indians**
5. Jackson, "Chief Anderson and His Legacy."
6. Pratt, *Autobiography*, 56–60. **Topic: Lamanite Identity**
7. Joseph Smith to Hyrum Smith, Mar. 3–4, 1831, in *JSP*, D1:272. In this letter to Hyrum, Joseph copied the text of a January 29 letter he received from Oliver Cowdery.
8. "Mormonism," *Painesville Telegraph*, Feb. 15, 1831, [1]; Doctrine and Covenants 41:3 (Revelation, Feb. 4, 1831, at josephsmithpapers.org).
9. Doctrine and Covenants 41:9–11 (Revelation, Feb. 4, 1831, at josephsmithpapers.org). **Topic: Bishop**
10. Whitmer, History, 12, in *JSP*, H2:24; Historical Introduction to Revelation, Feb. 9, 1831 [D&C 42:1–72], in *JSP*, D1:247; see also Harper, "The Law," 93–98.
11. Doctrine and Covenants 42:1–72 (Revelation, Feb. 9, 1831, at josephsmithpapers.org).
12. Doctrine and Covenants 42:30–36 (Revelation, Feb. 9, 1831, at josephsmithpapers.org). **Topic: Consecration and Stewardship**
13. Doctrine and Covenants 42:61 (Revelation, Feb. 9, 1831, at josephsmithpapers.org).

14. Doctrine and Covenants 50:2–3, 21–25 (Revelation, May 9, 1831, at josephsmithpapers.org).
15. "History of Thos. Baldwin Marsh," *Deseret News,* Mar. 24, 1858, 18; Thomas Marsh and Elizabeth Godkin Marsh to Lewis Abbott and Ann Marsh Abbott, [circa Apr. 11, 1831], Abbott Family Collection, Church History Library. **Topic: Zion/New Jerusalem**
16. Faulring and others, *Joseph Smith's New Translation of the Bible,* 57. **Topic: Joseph Smith Translation of the Bible**
17. Genesis 17:5.
18. Old Testament Revision 1, 28 [Genesis 11:11–12:2], at josephsmithpapers.org.
19. Jacob 2:27–30.
20. "Report of Elders Orson Pratt and Joseph F. Smith," *LDS Millennial Star,* Dec. 16, 1878, 50:788; Doctrine and Covenants 132:1 (Revelation, July 12, 1843, at josephsmithpapers.org); "Plural Marriage in Kirtland and Nauvoo," Gospel Topics, topics.lds.org. **Topic: Joseph Smith and Plural Marriage**
21. Lucy Mack Smith, History, 1844–45, book 11, [2]; Knight, Autobiography and Journal, 28–29.
22. Lucy Mack Smith, History, 1844–45, book 11, [4]–[6]; Lucy Mack Smith, History, 1845, 196–97.
23. Lucy Mack Smith, History, 1844–45, book 11, [7]–[9].
24. Lucy Mack Smith, History, 1844–45, book 11, [11]–[12].
25. Lucy Mack Smith, History, 1845, 202–3.
26. Lucy Mack Smith, History, 1844–45, book 12, [2]. **Topic: Lucy Mack Smith**
27. Oliver Cowdery to "My Dearly Beloved Brethren and Sisters in the Lord," Apr. 8, 1831, in *JSP,* D1:292.
28. Pratt, *Autobiography,* 60; Rust, "Mission to the Lamanites," 45–49.
29. Oliver Cowdery to "Dearly Beloved Brethren," May 7, 1831, in *JSP,* D1:294–97; Richard W. Cummins to William Clark, Feb. 15, 1831, U.S. Office of Indian Affairs, Central Superintendency, Records, volume 6, 113–14; Pratt, *Autobiography,* 61.
30. Joseph Smith History, 1834–36, 9, in *JSP,* H1:28; Murdock, Autobiography, 197; Lucy Diantha Morley Allen, "Joseph Smith, the Prophet," *Young Woman's Journal,* Dec. 1906, 17:537. **Topic: Joseph and Emma Hale Smith Family**
31. Joseph Smith History, 1834–36, 9, in *JSP,* H1:28; Murdock, Autobiography, 9
32. Lucy Mack Smith, History, 1844–45, book 12, [6].

CHAPTER 12: AFTER MUCH TRIBULATION

1. Young, "What I Remember," 1–2.
2. Doctrine and Covenants 42:30–33 (Revelation, Feb. 9, 1831, at josephsmithpapers.org); Knight, Autobiography and Journal, 29–30; see also Darowski, "Journey of the Colesville Branch," 40–44.
3. Young, "What I Remember," 4; Partridge, Genealogical Record, 6, 64; Lyman, Journal, 8. **Topic: Daily Life of First-Generation Latter-day Saints**
4. Lyman, Journal, 8; Partridge, Genealogical Record, 6; Minutes, circa June 3–4, 1831, in *JSP,* D1:317–27; Doctrine and Covenants 44:1–2 (Revelation, Feb. 1831–B, at josephsmithpapers.org).
5. Doctrine and Covenants 52 (Revelation, June 6, 1831, at josephsmithpapers.org).
6. Doctrine and Covenants 52:42 (Revelation, June 6, 1831, at josephsmithpapers.org); Doctrine and Covenants 38:18 (Revelation, Jan. 2, 1831, at josephsmithpapers.org); Numbers 33:54; 34:2; Jeremiah 11:5.
7. Lyman, Journal, 8.
8. Partridge, Genealogical Record, 6.
9. Darowski, "Journey of the Colesville Branch," 41–42.

10. Knight, Reminiscences, 9; Knight, Autobiography, 288–89; see also Staker, *Hearken, O Ye People,* 138–39.
11. Whitmer, History, 26, 29, in *JSP,* H2:37, 41; Knight, Autobiography and Journal, 29–30; see also Doctrine and Covenants 49 (Revelation, May 7, 1831, at josephsmithpapers.org); and Historical Introduction to Revelation, May 7, 1831 [D&C 49], in *JSP,* D1:297–99.
12. Doctrine and Covenants 54:8 (Revelation, June 10, 1831, at josephsmithpapers.org).
13. Knight, Reminiscences, 9.
14. Knight, Autobiography and Journal, 33. **Topic: Zion/New Jerusalem**
15. Joseph Smith History, 1838–56, volume A-1, 126–27.
16. [William W. Phelps], "Extract of a Letter from the Late Editor," *Ontario Phoenix,* Sept. 7, 1831, [2]; Ezra Booth, "Mormonism—No. V," *Ohio Star,* Nov. 10, 1831, [3]. **Topic: Prophecies of Joseph Smith**
17. Ezra Booth, "Mormonism—No. VI," *Ohio Star,* Nov. 17, 1831, [3]; "History of Luke Johnson," *LDS Millennial Star,* Dec. 31, 1864, 834; see also Bushman, *Rough Stone Rolling,* 162, 168–69. **Topic: Independence, Missouri**
18. Joseph Smith History, 1838–56, volume A-1, 127–29; Anderson, "Jackson County in Early Mormon Descriptions," 275–76, 290–93; Ezra Booth, "Mormonism—No. V," *Ohio Star,* Nov. 10, 1831, [3]; Ezra Booth, "Mormonism—No. VI," *Ohio Star,* Nov. 17, 1831, [3]; [William W. Phelps], "Extract of a Letter from the Late Editor," *Ontario Phoenix,* Sept. 7, 1831, [2]; Edward Partridge to Lydia Clisbee Partridge, Aug. 5–7, 1831, Edward Partridge, Letters, Church History Library; Richard W. Cummins to William Clark, Feb. 15, 1831, U.S. Office of Indian Affairs, Central Superintendency, Records, volume 6, 113–14.
19. Joseph Smith History, 1838–56, volume A-1, 127.
20. Doctrine and Covenants 57:1–4 (Revelation, July 20, 1831, at josephsmithpapers.org); see also Woodworth, "The Center Place," 122–29. **Topics: Zion/New Jerusalem; Gathering of Israel**
21. Edward Partridge to Lydia Clisbee Partridge, Aug. 5–7, 1831, Edward Partridge, Letters, Church History Library; Joseph Smith History, 1838–56, volume A-1, 126–27; Doctrine and Covenants 57 (Revelation, July 20, 1831, at josephsmithpapers.org); Doctrine and Covenants 58:14–15 (Revelation, Aug. 1, 1831, at josephsmithpapers.org).
22. Ezra Booth, "Mormonism—No. VII," *Ohio Star,* Nov. 24, 1831, [1].
23. Doctrine and Covenants 58:3–4, 15–16 (Revelation, Aug. 1, 1831, at josephsmithpapers.org).
24. Edward Partridge to Lydia Clisbee Partridge, Aug. 5–7, 1831, Edward Partridge, Letters, Church History Library. **Topic: Bishop**
25. Knight, Reminiscences, 9; Whitmer, History, 31–32, in *JSP,* H2:43–45; Joseph Smith History, 1838–56, volume A-1, 137, 139.
26. Joseph Smith History, 1838–56, volume A-1, 139; Psalm 87:2–3.
27. Knight, Reminiscences, 9; Edward Partridge to Lydia Clisbee Partridge, Aug. 5–7, 1831, Edward Partridge, Letters, Church History Library.
28. Knight, Reminiscences, 9.
29. Doctrine and Covenants 59:1–2 (Revelation, Aug. 7, 1831, at josephsmithpapers.org).
30. Joseph Smith History, 1838–56, volume A-1, 142; Phelps, "A Short History of W. W. Phelps' Stay in Missouri," [2]; "Missouri River," Geographical Entry, Joseph Smith Papers website, josephsmithpapers.org.
31. Ezra Booth, "Mormonism—No. VII," *Ohio Star,* Nov. 24, 1831, [1]; Bushman, *Rough Stone Rolling,* 164; Historical Introduction to Revelation, Aug. 12, 1831 [D&C 61], in *JSP,* D2:37–39; Book of Commandments 62 [D&C 61], at josephsmithpapers.org; see also [William W. Phelps], "The Way of Journeying for the Saints of the Church of Christ," *The Evening and the Morning Star,* Dec. 1832, 53.
32. Ezra Booth, "Mormonism—No. VII," *Ohio Star,* Nov. 24, 1831, [1]; see also McBride, "Ezra Booth and Isaac Morley," 130–36.

33. Edward Partridge to Lydia Clisbee Partridge, Aug. 5–7, 1831, Edward Partridge, Letters, Church History Library; Doctrine and Covenants 57 (Revelation, July 20, 1831, at josephsmithpapers.org).
34. Edward Partridge to Lydia Clisbee Partridge, Aug. 5–7, 1831, Edward Partridge, Letters, Church History Library; Young, "What I Remember," 5.
35. Edward Partridge to Lydia Clisbee Partridge, Aug. 5–7, 1831, Edward Partridge, Letters, Church History Library. The original letter has "and shall for some time many privations here"; "have" added for clarity.
36. Edward Partridge to Lydia Clisbee Partridge, Aug. 5–7, 1831, Edward Partridge, Letters, Church History Library; Young, "What I Remember," 5. **Topic: Daily Life of First-Generation Latter-day Saints**
37. Young, "What I Remember," 5; Edward Partridge to Lydia Clisbee Partridge, Aug. 5–7, 1831, Edward Partridge, Letters, Church History Library.

CHAPTER 13: THE GIFT HAS RETURNED

1. Historical Introduction to Revelation, Aug. 12, 1831 [D&C 61], in *JSP*, D2:38–39.
2. Doctrine and Covenants 61:36–37 (Revelation, Aug. 12, 1831, at josephsmithpapers.org).
3. Joseph Smith History, 1838–56, volume A-1, 146; Historical Introduction to Revelation, Sept. 11, 1831 [D&C 64], in *JSP*, D2:61–63.
4. Ezra Booth, "For the Ohio Star," *Ohio Star*, Oct. 13, 1831, [3]; Staker, *Hearken, O Ye People*, 296–302; Minutes, Sept. 6, 1831, in *JSP*, D2:59–61. **Topic: Dissent in the Church**
5. Doctrine and Covenants 64:7–10, 21, 33–34 (Revelation, Sept. 11, 1831, at josephsmithpapers.org).
6. Elizabeth Godkin Marsh to Lewis Abbott and Ann Marsh Abbott, Sept. 1831, Abbott Family Collection, Church History Library; Isaiah 29:17; 35:1.
7. Elizabeth Godkin Marsh to Lewis Abbott and Ann Marsh Abbott, Sept. 1831, Abbott Family Collection, Church History Library. **Topic: Early Missionaries**
8. McLellin, Journal, Sept. 22, 1831; William McLellin to "Beloved Relatives," Aug. 4, 1832, photocopy, Church History Library; see also Shipps and Welch, *Journals of William E. McLellin*, 82–83.
9. McLellin, Journal, July 18, 1831.
10. McLellin, Journal, July 30–Aug. 19, 1831.
11. McLellin, Journal, Aug. 19–20, 1831.
12. McLellin, Journal, Aug. 20 and 24, 1831.
13. McLellin, Journal, Aug. 26–Oct. 4, 1831.
14. McLellin, Journal, Oct. 25–30, 1831; Shipps and Welch, *Journals of William E. McLellin*, 57, note 52; Doctrine and Covenants 66 (Revelation, Oct. 29, 1831, at josephsmithpapers.org); Godfrey, "William McLellin's Five Questions," 137–41.
15. Minutes, Nov. 1–2, 1831, in *JSP*, D2:94–98; Ezra Booth to Rev. Ira Eddy, Sept. 12, 1831, *Ohio Star*, Oct. 13, 1831, [3]; Ezra Booth, "Mormonism—No. II," *Ohio Star*, Oct. 20, 1831, [3]. **Topic: Dissent in the Church**
16. Whitmer, *Address to All Believers in Christ*, 54–55.
17. Minutes, Nov. 1–2, 1831, in *JSP*, D2:94–98; "Letter from Elder W H Kelley," *Saints' Herald*, Mar. 1, 1882, 67. **Topics: Book of Commandments; Revelations of Joseph Smith**
18. "Letter from Elder W H Kelley," *Saints' Herald*, Mar. 1, 1882, 67; Doctrine and Covenants 1 (Revelation, Nov. 1, 1831–B, at josephsmithpapers.org); Historical Introduction to Revelation, Nov. 1, 1831–B [D&C 1], in *JSP*, D2:103–4.
19. Doctrine and Covenants 1:38 (Revelation, Nov. 1, 1831–B, at josephsmithpapers.org).
20. Minutes, Nov. 1–2, 1831, in *JSP*, D2:97; Testimony, circa Nov. 2, 1831, in *JSP*, D2:110–14; Doctrine and Covenants 67 (Revelation, circa Nov. 2, 1831, at josephsmithpapers.org);

Historical Introduction to Revelation, circa Nov. 2, 1831 [D&C 67], in *JSP,* D2:108–9; Historical Introduction to Revelation, Nov. 1, 1831–B [D&C 1], in *JSP,* D2:103–4.

21. Doctrine and Covenants 1:24 (Revelation, Nov. 1, 1831–B, at josephsmithpapers.org).

22. Doctrine and Covenants 67:7–8 (Revelation, circa Nov. 2, 1831, at josephsmithpapers .org); Historical Introduction to Revelation, circa Nov. 2, 1831 [D&C 67], in *JSP,* D2:108–9.

23. Joseph Smith History, 1838–56, volume A-1, 162; "Manuscript Revelation Books," in *JSP,* MRB:xxx–xxxi.

24. Testimony, circa Nov. 2, 1831, in *JSP,* D2:110–14; Minutes, Nov. 1–2, 1831, in *JSP,* D2:94–98.

25. Minutes, Nov. 8, 1831, in *JSP,* D2:121–24.

26. See Brekus, *Strangers and Pilgrims,* 5, 213.

27. Towle, *Vicissitudes Illustrated,* 137. **Topic: Opposition to the Early Church**

28. Towle, *Vicissitudes Illustrated,* 138, 142.

29. Towle, *Vicissitudes Illustrated,* 141–45.

CHAPTER 14: VISIONS AND NIGHTMARES

1. Joseph Smith History, 1838–56, volume A-1, 204.

2. George A. Smith, "Sketch of Church History," *Deseret News,* supplement, Dec. 21, 1864, 90; Staker, *Hearken, O Ye People,* 282–85; see also Hinsdale, "Life and Character of Symonds Ryder," 250. **Topic: Healing**

3. Joseph Smith History, 1838–56, volume A-1, 183; Faulring and others, *Joseph Smith's New Translation of the Bible,* 58; see also John 5:29; and Staker, *Hearken, O Ye People,* 319–24. **Topic: Joseph Smith Translation of the Bible**

4. Historical Introduction to Vision, Feb. 16, 1832 [D&C 76], in *JSP,* D2:179–83; Dibble, "Recollections of the Prophet Joseph Smith," 303.

5. Doctrine and Covenants 76:11–24 (Vision, Feb. 16, 1832, at josephsmithpapers.org). **Topic: The Vision (D&C 76)**

6. 1 Corinthians 15:39–40; Doctrine and Covenants 76:50–112 (Vision, Feb. 16, 1832, at josephsmithpapers.org); Dibble, "Recollections of the Prophet Joseph Smith," 303–4; Historical Introduction to Vision, Feb. 16, 1832 [D&C 76], in *JSP,* D2:180–82.

7. Doctrine and Covenants 76:116 (Vision, Feb. 16, 1832, at josephsmithpapers.org).

8. Dibble, "Philo Dibble's Narrative," 81; Dibble, "Recollections of the Prophet Joseph Smith," 304.

9. "Phelps, William Wines," Biographical Entry, Joseph Smith Papers website, josephsmithpapers.org; Bowen, "Versatile W. W. Phelps."

10. William W. Phelps, *The Evening and the Morning Star Prospectus,* in *Evening and Morning Star,* June 1832 (published Jan. 1835), 1–2.

11. Murdock, Journal, 18; Brigham Young, in *Journal of Discourses,* May 18, 1873, 16:42; Brigham Young, Discourse, May 18, 1873, in Historian's Office, Reports of Speeches, 1845–85, Church History Library; Brigham Young, in *Journal of Discourses,* Aug. 29, 1852, 6:281; Wilford Woodruff, in *Journal of Discourses,* Apr. 9, 1857, 5:84; Joseph Young, "Discourse," *Deseret Weekly News,* Mar. 18, 1857, 11; "Items for the Public," *The Evening and the Morning Star,* July 1832, 25; see also McBride, "The Vision," 148–54.

12. Cahoon, Diary, Nov. 1831; Joseph Smith History, 1838–56, volume A-1, 205; see also Ezra Booth's letters printed weekly in the *Ohio Star* from Oct. 13 to Dec. 8, 1831. **Topic: Dissent in the Church**

13. Hayden, *Early History of the Disciples in the Western Reserve,* 220–21; Ryder, "A Short History of the Foundation of the Mormon Church," 3–4; Staker, *Hearken, O Ye People,* 344–49; Tullidge, *Women of Mormondom,* 404.

14. Joseph Smith History, 1838–56, volume A-1, 205–6; see also Staker, *Hearken, O Ye People,* 349–50.

15. Joseph Smith History, 1838–56, volume A-1, 206–7; "History of Luke Johnson," *LDS Millennial Star*, Dec. 31, 1884, 834–35; see also Staker, *Hearken, O Ye People*, 351–52. **Topic: Vigilantism**
16. Joseph Smith History, 1838–56, volume A-1, 207–8; "History of Luke Johnson," *LDS Millennial Star*, Dec. 31, 1884, 835.
17. Joseph Smith History, 1838–56, volume A-1, 208.
18. Joseph Smith History, 1838–56, volume A-1, 208–9; Joseph Smith III, "Last Testimony of Sister Emma," *Saints' Herald*, Oct. 1, 1879, 289. **Topic: Joseph and Emma Hale Smith Family**
19. Staker, *Hearken, O Ye People*, 354–55; Joseph Smith History, 1838–56, volume A-1, 209; Whitmer, History, 38–39, in *JSP*, H2:50–51; see also Minutes, Apr. 26–27, 1832, in *JSP*, D2:229–33; and Minutes, Apr. 30, 1832, in *JSP*, D2:237–40.
20. Doctrine and Covenants 72 (Revelation, Dec. 4, 1831–A, at josephsmithpapers.org); Doctrine and Covenants 78 (Revelation, Mar. 1, 1832, at josephsmithpapers.org). **Topic: Bishop**
21. Doctrine and Covenants 78:14 (Revelation, Mar. 1, 1832, at josephsmithpapers.org).
22. Doctrine and Covenants 82 (Revelation, Apr. 26, 1832, at josephsmithpapers.org); Historical Introduction to Revelation, Apr. 26, 1832 [D&C 82], in *JSP*, D2:233–35.
23. Doctrine and Covenants 82:15, 19 (Revelation, Apr. 26, 1832, at josephsmithpapers .org); see also Godfrey, "Newel K. Whitney and the United Firm," 142–47. **Topic: United Firm ("United Order")**
24. Joseph Smith History, 1838–56, volume A-1, 213; "Joseph Smith–Era Publications of Revelations," in *JSP*, R2:xxvi; Newel K. Whitney, Statement, circa 1842, Historian's Office, Joseph Smith History Documents, circa 1839–56, Church History Library.
25. Joseph Smith to William W. Phelps, July 31, 1832, in *JSP*, D2:257–71. **Topic: Dissent in the Church**
26. McLellin, Journal, Nov. 1831–Feb. 1832.
27. McLellin, Journal, Feb. 16, 1832.
28. McLellin, Journal, Feb. 25, 1832.
29. "History of Luke Johnson," *LDS Millennial Star*, Dec. 31, 1864, 26:835.
30. William McLellin to "Beloved Relatives," Aug. 4, 1832, photocopy, Church History Library; Joseph Smith to Emma Smith, June 6, 1832, in *JSP*, D2:251; Doctrine and Covenants 75:6–8 (Revelation, Jan. 25, 1832–A, at josephsmithpapers.org); see also Shipps and Welch, *Journals of William E. McLellin*, 79–85.
31. Joseph Smith to William W. Phelps, July 31, 1832, in *JSP*, D2:262; Corrill, *Brief History*, 18–19, in *JSP*, H2:146. **Topics: Bishop; Consecration and Stewardship**
32. William McLellin to "Beloved Relatives," Aug. 4, 1832, photocopy, Church History Library; see also Shipps and Welch, *Journals of William E. McLellin*, 83–84; and Isaiah 2:3.
33. "To His Excellency, Daniel Dunklin, Governor of the State of Missouri," *The Evening and the Morning Star*, Dec. 1833, [2].
34. "The Elders in the Land of Zion to the Church of Christ Scattered Abroad," *The Evening and the Morning Star*, July 1832, [5]; William McLellin to "Beloved Relatives," Aug. 4, 1832, photocopy, Church History Library; see also Shipps and Welch, *Journals of William E. McLellin*, 83.
35. Delilah Lykins to Isaac and Christina McCoy, Sept. 6, 1831, quoted in Jennings, "Isaac McCoy and the Mormons," 65–66.

CHAPTER 15: HOLY PLACES

1. Phebe Crosby Peck to Anna Jones Pratt, Aug. 10, 1832, Church History Library; see also Johnson, "Give Up All and Follow Your Lord," 93.
2. Phebe Crosby Peck to Anna Jones Pratt, Aug. 10, 1832, Church History Library; "A Vision," *The Evening and the Morning Star*, July 1832, [2]–[3]; Doctrine and Covenants 76

(Vision, Feb. 16, 1832, at josephsmithpapers.org); see also Johnson, "Give Up All and Follow Your Lord," 94–96.

3. Doctrine and Covenants 84:112–17 (Revelation, Sept. 22–23, 1832, at josephsmithpapers.org). **Topic: United Firm ("United Order")**

4. Doctrine and Covenants 84 (Revelation, Sept. 22–23, 1832, at josephsmithpapers.org); Joseph Smith History, 1838–56, volume A-1, 229.

5. Joseph Smith to Emma Smith, Oct. 13, 1832, in *JSP,* D2:304–14; see also Pasko, *Old New York,* 1–2.

6. Joseph Smith to Emma Smith, Oct. 13, 1832, in *JSP,* D2:304–14.

7. Brigham Young, Sermon, Nov. 20, 1864, George D. Watt Papers, Church History Library, as transcribed by LaJean Purcell Carruth; Joseph Young to Lewis Harvey, Nov. 16, 1880, Church History Library; Historian's Office, Brigham Young History Drafts, 1856–58, 3–4; "History of Brigham Young," *LDS Millennial Star,* July 11, 1863, 25:439.

8. **Topic: Joseph and Emma Hale Smith Family**

9. Historian's Office, Brigham Young History Drafts, 1856–58, 3–4; Joseph Young to Lewis Harvey, Nov. 16, 1880, Church History Library; see also 1 Corinthians 12–14; and Doctrine and Covenants 45 (Revelation, circa Mar. 7, 1831, at josephsmithpapers .org). **Topics: Gifts of the Spirit; Gift of Tongues**

10. News Item, *Painesville Telegraph,* Dec. 21, 1832, [3]; see also Woodworth, "Peace and War," 158–64.

11. Joseph Smith History, 1838–56, volume A-1, 244; Matthew 24; Joseph Smith—Matthew; Doctrine and Covenants 45 (Revelation, circa Mar. 7, 1831, at josephsmithpapers.org); see also "Revenge and Magnanimity," *Painesville Telegraph,* Dec. 21, 1832, [1]; and "The Plague in India," *Painesville Telegraph,* Dec. 21, 1832, [2].

12. Doctrine and Covenants 84:49, 117–18 (Revelation, Sept. 22–23, 1832, at josephsmithpapers.org).

13. Doctrine and Covenants 87 (Revelation, Dec. 25, 1832, at josephsmithpapers.org). **Topic: Prophecies of Joseph Smith**

14. Historical Introduction to Minutes, Dec. 27–28, 1832, in *JSP,* D2:331–33; Historical Introduction to Revelation, Dec. 27–28, 1832 [D&C 88:1–126], in *JSP,* D2:334–36; Joseph Smith to William W. Phelps, Jan. 11, 1833, in *JSP,* D2:364–67.

15. Minutes, Dec. 27–28, 1832, in *JSP,* D2:331–34.

16. Doctrine and Covenants 88:68, 118–19 (Revelation, Dec. 27–28, 1832, at josephsmithpapers.org). **Topics: School of the Prophets; Kirtland Temple**

17. Joseph Smith to William W. Phelps, Jan. 11, 1833, in *JSP,* D2:367.

18. See Hyde, *Orson Hyde,* 6, 9; "History of Orson Hyde," 1, in Historian's Office, Histories of the Twelve, 1856–58, 1861, Church History Library; Joseph Smith History, circa Summer 1832, 1, in *JSP,* H1:11; and Waite, "A School and an Endowment," 174–82.

19. Doctrine and Covenants 88:78–80 (Revelation, Dec. 27–28, 1832, at josephsmithpapers.org); Backman, *Heavens Resound,* 264–68.

20. Coltrin, Diary and Notebook, Jan. 24, 1833.

21. Minutes, Jan. 22–23, 1833, in *JSP,* D2:378–82.

22. Minutes, Jan. 22–23, 1833, in *JSP,* D2:378–82. **Topic: Washing of Feet**

23. School of the Prophets Salt Lake City Minutes, Oct. 3, 1883.

24. School of the Prophets Salt Lake City Minutes, Oct. 3, 1883; Brigham Young, Discourse, Feb. 8, 1868, in George D. Watt, Discourse Shorthand Notes, Feb. 8, 1868, Pitman Shorthand Transcriptions, Church History Library; see also Brigham Young, in *Journal of Discourses,* Feb. 8, 1868, 12:158. **Topic: Word of Wisdom (D&C 89)**

25. Woodworth, "Word of Wisdom," 183–91; Harper, *Word of Wisdom,* 45–49; Historical Introduction to Revelation, Feb. 27, 1833 [D&C 89], in *JSP,* D3:11–19.

26. Revelation, Feb. 27, 1833, at josephsmithpapers.org. The modern Doctrine and Covenants, based on another early copy of this revelation, has "A Word of Wisdom, for the benefit of the council of high priests, assembled in Kirtland, and the church,

and also the saints in Zion." (Doctrine and Covenants 89:1; see also Revelation Book 2, 49.)

27. Doctrine and Covenants 89 (Revelation, Feb. 27, 1833, at josephsmithpapers.org); Johnson, Notebook, [1]; "The Word of Wisdom," *Times and Seasons,* June 1, 1842, 3:800; Revelation Book 1, 168, in *JSP,* MRB:313. **Topic: Word of Wisdom (D&C 89)**

28. Doctrine and Covenants 89:1–4 (Revelation, Feb. 27, 1833, at josephsmithpapers .org); Minute Book 2, Jan. 26, 1838; Historical Introduction to Revelation, Feb. 27, 1833 [D&C 89], in *JSP,* D3:11–20.

29. School of the Prophets Salt Lake City Minutes, Oct. 3, 1883.

30. Minutes, Mar. 23, 1833–B, in *JSP,* D3:50–54; Joseph Smith History, 1838–56, volume A-1, 287.

31. Minutes, Apr. 2, 1833, in *JSP,* D3:55–56; Joseph Smith History, 1838–56, volume A-1, 283; Minutes, May 4, 1833, in *JSP,* D3:81–82.

32. Joseph Smith to "Brethren in Zion," Apr. 21, 1833, in *JSP,* D3:64–67; Historical Introduction to Revelation, Dec. 27–28, 1832 [D&C 88:1–126], in *JSP,* D2:334.

33. Doctrine and Covenants 95 (Revelation, June 1, 1833, at josephsmithpapers.org); Robison, *First Mormon Temple,* 8. **Topic: Kirtland Temple**

34. Lucy Mack Smith, History, 1844–45, book 14, [1]; Doctrine and Covenants 95:13 (Revelation, June 1, 1833, at josephsmithpapers.org); Minute Book 1, June 3, 1833.

35. "The Elders Stationed in Zion to the Churches Abroad," *The Evening and the Morning Star,* July 1833, [6].

36. Plat of the City of Zion, circa Early June–June 25, 1833, in *JSP,* D3:121–31; Hamilton, *Nineteenth-Century Mormon Architecture and City Planning,* 13–19.

37. Plat of the City of Zion, circa Early June–June 25, 1833, in *JSP,* D3:127–28. **Topic: Zion/New Jerusalem**

38. Joseph Smith to Church Leaders in Jackson County, MO, June 25, 1833, in *JSP,* D3:155–56.

CHAPTER 16: ONLY A PRELUDE

1. Young, "What I Remember," 6–7; "To His Excellency, Daniel Dunklin," *The Evening and the Morning Star,* Dec. 1833, [2]. **Topic: Jackson County Violence**

2. "The Elders Stationed in Zion to the Churches Abroad," *The Evening and the Morning Star,* July 1833, [6]–[7].

3. "Free People of Color," *The Evening and the Morning Star,* July 1833, [5]. **Topic: Slavery and Abolition**

4. "To His Excellency, Daniel Dunklin," *The Evening and the Morning Star,* Dec. 1833, [2]–[3].

5. Parley P. Pratt and others, "'The Mormons' So Called," *The Evening and the Morning Star,* Extra, Feb. 1834, [1]. **Topic: Opposition to the Early Church**

6. "To His Excellency, Daniel Dunklin," *The Evening and the Morning Star,* Dec. 1833, [2]–[3]; see also Breen, *The Land Shall Be Deluged in Blood;* and Oates, *Fires of Jubilee.* **Topic: Slavery and Abolition**

7. "To His Excellency, Daniel Dunklin," *The Evening and the Morning Star,* Dec. 1833, [2]–[3]; John Whitmer to Oliver Cowdery and Joseph Smith, July 29, 1833, in *JSP,* D3:191–94. **Topic: Vigilantism**

8. Reeve, *Religion of a Different Color,* 116–19; 2 Nephi 26:33; Staker, *Hearken, O Ye People,* 182–84.

9. *The Evening and the Morning Star,* Extra, July 16, 1833, [1]; Joseph Smith History, 1838–56, volume A-1, 326.

10. See "Race and the Priesthood," Gospel Topics, topics.lds.org.

11. "To His Excellency, Daniel Dunklin," *The Evening and the Morning Star,* Dec. 1833, [2]; see also Whitmer, History, 42, in *JSP,* H2:54–55.

12. See Joseph Smith to Church Leaders in Jackson County, MO, June 25, 1833, in *JSP,* D3:148.
13. "To His Excellency, Daniel Dunklin," *The Evening and the Morning Star,* Dec. 1833, [2]; Whitmer, History, 42, in *JSP,* H2:54–55.
14. [Edward Partridge], "A History, of the Persecution," *Times and Seasons,* Dec. 1839, 1:18, in *JSP,* H2:209. **Topic: Jackson County Violence**
15. "To His Excellency, Daniel Dunklin," *The Evening and the Morning Star,* Dec. 1833, [2]; Robert Weston, Testimony, Independence, MO, 581, Reorganized Church of Jesus Christ of Latter Day Saints v. Church of Christ of Independence, MO, and Others, typescript, Testimonies and Depositions, Church History Library.
16. "To His Excellency, Daniel Dunklin," *The Evening and the Morning Star,* Dec. 1833, [2]; Edward Partridge and others, Memorial to the Legislature of Missouri, Dec. 10, 1838; Edward Partridge, Affidavit, May 15, 1839, copy, Edward Partridge, Papers, Church History Library.
17. Minute Book 2, Dec. 10, 1838, 164; John Patten, Affidavit, Oct. 28, 1839, in Johnson, *Mormon Redress Petitions,* 517; "To His Excellency, Daniel Dunklin," *The Evening and the Morning Star,* Dec. 1833, [2]; [Edward Partridge], "A History, of the Persecution," *Times and Seasons,* Dec. 1839, 1:18, in *JSP,* H2:209.
18. [Edward Partridge], "A History, of the Persecution," *Times and Seasons,* Dec. 1839, 1:18, in *JSP,* H2:209; Young, "What I Remember," 8.
19. Young, "What I Remember," 9. **Topic: Book of Commandments**
20. "Mary Elizabeth Rollins Lightner," *Utah Genealogical and Historical Magazine,* 1926, 17:195–96.
21. Young, "What I Remember," 7–8.
22. Edward Partridge, Affidavit, May 15, 1839, copy, Edward Partridge, Papers, Church History Library. The original source has "If I must suffer for my religion it was no more than others had done before me."
23. Young, "What I Remember," 7; Joseph Smith History, 1838–56, volume A-1, 327; "To His Excellency, Daniel Dunklin," *The Evening and the Morning Star,* Dec. 1833, [2].
24. Joseph Smith History, 1838–56, volume A-1, 327–28; "To His Excellency, Daniel Dunklin," *The Evening and the Morning Star,* Dec. 1833, [2].
25. Edward Partridge, Affidavit, May 15, 1839, copy, Edward Partridge, Papers, Church History Library; "Tar and Feathers," *Deseret Weekly,* Dec. 23, 1893, 25–26; Young, "What I Remember," 7–8, 10; Joseph Smith History, 1838–56, volume A-1, 327–28. **Topic: Vigilantism**
26. Doctrine and Covenants 90:28–31 (Revelation Mar. 8, 1833, at josephsmithpapers.org); Vienna Jaques, Statement, Feb. 22, 1859, Church History Library.
27. Vienna Jaques, Statement, Feb. 22, 1859, Church History Library; Young, "What I Remember," 8.
28. "Mary Elizabeth Rollins Lightner," *Utah Genealogical and Historical Magazine,* 1926, 17:196; Young, "What I Remember," 9.

Chapter 17: Though the Mob Kill Us

1. "To His Excellency, Daniel Dunklin," *The Evening and the Morning Star,* Dec. 1833, [2]; Schaefer, *William E. McLellin's Lost Manuscript,* 167.
2. Schaefer, *William E. McLellin's Lost Manuscript,* 166–67.
3. Doctrine and Covenants 98:3 (Revelation, Aug. 6, 1833, at josephsmithpapers.org).
4. Oliver Cowdery to Church Leaders in Jackson County, MO, Aug. 10, 1833, in *JSP,* D3:238, 240.
5. John Whitmer to Joseph Smith, July 29, 1833, in *JSP,* D3:186–98; "To His Excellency, Daniel Dunklin," *The Evening and the Morning Star,* Dec. 1833, [2]–[3].

6. Oliver Cowdery to Church Leaders in Jackson County, MO, Aug. 10, 1833, in *JSP,* D3:238–43.
7. Historical Introduction to Letter to Church Leaders in Jackson County, MO, Aug. 18, 1833, in *JSP,* D3:260. "Doctor" was Hurlbut's first name, not a title. **Topic: Opposition to the Early Church**
8. Joseph Smith to Church Leaders in Jackson County, MO, Aug. 18, 1833, in *JSP,* D3:258–69; Revised Plat of the City of Zion, circa Early Aug. 1833, in *JSP,* D3:243–58. **Topic: Revelations of Joseph Smith**
9. [Edward Partridge], "A History, of the Persecution," *Times and Seasons,* Dec. 1839, 1:19, in *JSP,* H2:211; Historical Introduction to Letter, Oct. 30, 1833, in *JSP,* D3:331–35.
10. "To His Excellency, Daniel Dunklin," *The Evening and the Morning Star,* Dec. 1833, [2]–[3]; Joseph Smith to "Dear Brethren," Oct. 30, 1833, in *JSP,* D3:331–36; Edward Partridge to Joseph Smith, between Nov. 14 and 19, 1833, in *JSP,* D3:344–51.
11. Daniel Dunklin to Edward Partridge and others, Oct. 19, 1833, William W. Phelps, Collection of Missouri Documents, Church History Library; "To His Excellency, Daniel Dunklin," *The Evening and the Morning Star,* Dec. 1833, [3]; [Edward Partridge], "A History, of the Persecution," *Times and Seasons,* Dec. 1839, 1:19, in *JSP,* H2:212. **Topic: American Legal and Political Institutions**
12. William W. Phelps and others to William T. Wood and others, Oct. 30, 1833, copy, William W. Phelps, Collection of Missouri Documents, Church History Library.
13. [Edward Partridge], "A History, of the Persecution," *Times and Seasons,* Dec. 1839, 1:19, in *JSP,* H2:213.
14. Joseph Smith to "Dear Brethren," Oct. 30, 1833, in *JSP,* D3:336–41; "The Outrage in Jackson County, Missouri," *The Evening and the Morning Star,* Dec. 1833, [7].
15. Lydia B. [Hurlbut Whiting] English, Affidavit, in Johnson, *Mormon Redress Petitions,* 447–48. **Topic: Jackson County Violence**
16. [Edward Partridge], "A History, of the Persecution," *Times and Seasons,* Dec. 1839, 1:20, in *JSP,* H2:213–14.
17. Dibble, Reminiscences, [7]; Dibble, "Philo Dibble's Narrative," 82; [Edward Partridge], "A History, of the Persecution," *Times and Seasons,* Jan. 1840, 1:33, in *JSP,* H2:217. The Saint who died was Andrew Barber; the others killed were Thomas Linville and Hugh Breazeale. (*JSP,* H2:57, note 173.)
18. Dibble, "Philo Dibble's Narrative," 83; Philo Dibble, Affidavit, Adams Co., IL, May 13, 1839, Mormon Redress Petitions, 1839–45, Church History Library.
19. Dibble, "Philo Dibble's Narrative," 83–84; Dibble, Reminiscences, [8].
20. Dibble, Reminiscences, [8].
21. "From Missouri," *The Evening and the Morning Star,* Jan. 1834, [5]; [Edward Partridge], "A History, of the Persecution," *Times and Seasons,* Jan. 1840, 1:33, in *JSP,* H2:218.
22. "The Outrage in Jackson County, Missouri," *The Evening and the Morning Star,* Dec. 1833, [8]; [Edward Partridge], "A History, of the Persecution," *Times and Seasons,* Jan. 1840, 1:33, in *JSP,* H2:217–19.
23. "From Missouri," *The Evening and the Morning Star,* Jan. 1834, [5]; Pratt, *History of the Late Persecution,* 19.
24. [Edward Partridge], "A History, of the Persecution," *Times and Seasons,* Jan. 1840, 1:34–35, in *JSP,* H2:219–20; "From Missouri," *The Evening and the Morning Star,* Jan. 1834, [5].
25. [William W. Phelps] to "Dear Brethren," Nov. 6–7, 1833, in *JSP,* D3:341.
26. Pratt, *History of the Late Persecution,* 20–22; Young, "Incidents in the Life of a Mormon Girl," 75–76; Lyman, Journal, 9.
27. Dibble, "Philo Dibble's Narrative," 84–85; Dibble, Reminiscences, [8]. **Topic: Healing**
28. Edward Partridge to Joseph Smith, between Nov. 14 and 19, 1833, in *JSP,* D3:347; Emily Dow Partridge Young, "Autobiography," *Woman's Exponent,* Feb. 15, 1885, 13:138; Partridge, Autobiographical Writings, circa 1833–36, in Edward Partridge, Miscellaneous Papers, Church History Library; see also *JSP,* H1:192.
29. Joseph Smith, Journal, Nov. 13, 1833, in *JSP,* J1:16–17.

CHAPTER 18: THE CAMP OF ISRAEL

1. Joseph Smith, Journal, Nov. 14–19 and 25, 1833, in *JSP,* J1:18. **Topic: Revelations of Joseph Smith**
2. See Grua, "Joseph Smith and the 1834 D. P. Hurlbut Case," 35–37. **Topic: Opposition to the Early Church**
3. Joseph Smith, Journal, Nov. 25, 1833, in *JSP,* J1:20.
4. Joseph Smith to Edward Partridge and others, Dec. 10, 1833, in *JSP,* D3:375–81; see also Joseph Smith to Church Leaders in Jackson County, MO, Aug. 18, 1833, in *JSP,* D3:258–69; Joseph Smith to Emma Smith, June 6, 1832, in *JSP,* D2:246–57; Doctrine and Covenants 95 (Revelation, June 1, 1833, at josephsmithpapers.org); and Romans 8:38–39. The original has "When we learn your sufferings."
5. Doctrine and Covenants 101:1–5, 17–18 (Revelation, Dec. 16–17, 1833, at josephsmithpapers.org); see also Grua, "Waiting for the Word of the Lord," 196–201.
6. Doctrine and Covenants 101:43–62 (Revelation, Dec. 16–17, 1833, at josephsmithpapers.org).
7. Wight, Reminiscences, 5–6; Pratt, *Autobiography,* 114; Minutes, Feb. 24, 1834, in *JSP,* D3:453–57; "Elder John Brush," 23–24; William W. Phelps to "Dear Brethren," Dec. 15, 1833, in *JSP,* D3:383.
8. Minutes, Feb. 24, 1834, in *JSP,* D3:456–57. **Topic: Zion's Camp (Camp of Israel)**
9. Doctrine and Covenants 103:15, 27 (Revelation, Feb. 24, 1834, at josephsmithpapers.org); Woodruff, Journal, Apr. 1, 1834.
10. Woodruff, Journal, Apr. 1, 1834.
11. Woodruff, Journal, Apr. 11, 1834.
12. Woodruff, Journal, Apr. 26, 1834; Historian's Office, Brigham Young History Drafts, 1856–58, 3. **Topic: Daily Life of First-Generation Latter-day Saints**
13. Holbrook, Reminiscences, 34–35; Radke, "We Also Marched," 152–54, 160–61.
14. Woodruff, "History and Travels of Zion's Camp," 3–4; *JSP,* D4:138, note 182.
15. Holbrook, Reminiscences, 34; Woodruff, Journal, May 1, 1834; Joseph Smith History, 1838–56, volume A-1, 477–78.
16. William W. Phelps to Joseph Smith, Dec. 15, 1833, in *JSP,* D3:382–86; Robert W. Wells to Alexander Doniphan and David R. Atchison, Nov. 21, 1833, copy, William W. Phelps, Collection of Missouri Documents, Church History Library; Daniel Dunklin to David R. Atchison, Feb. 5, 1834, in "Mormon Difficulties," *Missouri Intelligencer and Boon's Lick Advertiser,* Mar. 8, 1834, [1]. **Topic: Zion's Camp (Camp of Israel)**
17. *It Becomes Our Duty to Address You on the Subject of Immediately Preparing* [Kirtland, OH: May 10, 1834], copy at Church History Library; Sidney Rigdon and Oliver Cowdery to "Dear Brethren," May 10, 1834, in Cowdery, Letterbook, 49–50; Sidney Gilbert and others to Daniel Dunklin, Apr. 24, 1834, copy, William W. Phelps, Collection of Missouri Documents, Church History Library.
18. Kimball, "Journal and Record," 8; see also Deuteronomy 1.
19. Joseph Smith to Emma Smith, June 4, 1834, in *JSP,* D4:52–59; Bradley, *Zion's Camp,* 27–28.
20. Joseph Smith to Emma Smith, June 4, 1834, in *JSP,* D4:54.
21. Joseph Smith to Emma Smith, June 4, 1834, in *JSP,* D4:52–59; "The Outrage in Jackson County, Missouri," *The Evening and the Morning Star,* June 1834, [8].
22. "Extracts from H. C. Kimball's Journal," *Times and Seasons,* Feb. 1, 1845, 6:788–89; George A. Smith, Autobiography, 29; Minutes, Aug. 28–29, 1834, in *JSP,* D4:125.
23. Minutes, Aug. 28–29, 1834, in *JSP,* D4:129–30.
24. Minutes, Aug. 28–29, 1834, in *JSP,* D4:129–30. **Topic: Dissent in the Church**
25. Kimball, "Journal and Record," 11; see also Crawley and Anderson, "Political and Social Realities of Zion's Camp," 413.
26. Kimball, "Journal and Record," 11; Joseph Smith History, 1838–56, volume A-1, 477–78.

27. Holbrook, Reminiscences, 36. The original source has this statement in the past tense: "if the sisters were willing to undergo a siege with the camp they could all go along with it."
28. Holbrook, Reminiscences, 36.
29. George A. Smith, Autobiography, 33; Pratt, *Autobiography*, 123–24; Daniel Dunklin to John Thornton, June 6, 1834, in "The Mormons," *Missouri Intelligencer and Boon's Lick Advertiser,* July 5, 1834, [2].
30. Rich, Diary, June 14, 1834.
31. George A. Smith, Autobiography, 36; "Extracts from H. C. Kimball's Journal," *Times and Seasons,* Feb. 1, 1845, 6:789. **Topic: Slavery and Abolition**
32. George A. Smith, Autobiography, 36–37; McBride, Reminiscences, 5; "Extracts from H. C. Kimball's Journal," *Times and Seasons,* Feb. 1, 1845, 6:789–90.
33. Hancock, Autobiography, 145; Holbrook, Reminiscences, 37.
34. George A. Smith, "My Journal," 216; George A. Smith, Autobiography, 37; McBride, Reminiscences, 5–6; "Extracts from H. C. Kimball's Journal," *Times and Seasons,* Feb. 1, 1845, 6:790.
35. "Extracts from H. C. Kimball's Journal," *Times and Seasons,* Feb. 1, 1845, 6:790; George A. Smith, Autobiography, 37; Woodruff, Journal, May 1834.
36. Joseph Smith History, 1838–56, volume A-2 (fair copy), 332.
37. Joseph Smith History, 1838–56, volume A-1, 496–97; "Extracts from H. C. Kimball's Journal," *Times and Seasons,* Feb. 1, 1845, 6:790.
38. Declaration, June 21, 1834, in *JSP,* D4:65–69; George A. Smith, Autobiography, 38; Holbrook, Reminiscences, 37–38; McBride, Reminiscences, 6; Joseph Smith History, 1838–56, volume A-1, 497–98; "Propositions, &c. of the 'Mormons,'" *The Evening and the Morning Star,* July 1834, [8].
39. George A. Smith, Autobiography, 39–40; McBride, Reminiscences, 6; Holbrook, Reminiscences, 38; Baldwin, Account of Zion's Camp, 13; Joseph Smith History, 1838–56, volume A-1, 497–98.
40. Doctrine and Covenants 105 (Revelation, June 22, 1834, at josephsmithpapers.org). **Topic: Endowment of Power**
41. See Historical Introduction to Revelation, June 22, 1834 [D&C 105], in *JSP,* D4:70–72.
42. Account with the Church of Christ, circa Aug. 11–29, 1834, in *JSP,* D4:135–55; Doctrine and Covenants 105 (Revelation, June 22, 1834, at josephsmithpapers.org).
43. Wilford Woodruff, in *Journal of Discourses,* Dec. 12, 1869, 13:158.
44. Wilford Woodruff, in *Journal of Discourses,* July 27, 1862, 10:14; Minute Book 2, Nov. 5, 1834.

Chapter 19: Stewards over This Ministry

1. Holbrook, "History of Joseph Holbrook," 17–18.
2. Woodruff, Journal, [June 1834].
3. Joseph Smith History, 1838–56, volume A-1, 505. **Topic: Healing**
4. Joseph Smith History, 1838–56, volume A-1, 506; addenda, 16, note 18.
5. "Afflicting," *The Evening and the Morning Star,* July 1834, [8]; Joseph Smith History, 1838–56, volume A-1, 509.
6. George A. Smith, in *Journal of Discourses,* Nov. 15, 1864, 11:8; Joseph Smith, Journal, Jan. 11, 1834, in *JSP,* J1:25; "A Mormon Battle," *Erie Gazette,* July 31, 1834, [3].
7. Note, Mar. 8, 1832, in *JSP,* D2:201–4; Minutes, Feb. 17, 1834, in *JSP,* D3:435–39. **Topics: First Presidency; Wards and Stakes**
8. Minutes, Feb. 17, 1834, in *JSP,* D3:435–39. **Topic: High Council**
9. Minutes and Discourse, circa July 7, 1834, in *JSP,* D4:90–96.
10. See Robison, *First Mormon Temple,* 45–58; Bushman, *Rough Stone Rolling,* 306–8; and Staker, *Hearken, O Ye People,* 401–34.

11. Kimball, "Journal and Record," 20.
12. Ames, Autobiography and Journal, [10]; see also Probert and Manscill, "Artemus Millet," 60–62.
13. Joseph Smith History, 1838–56, volume B-1, 553; Johnson, Reminiscences and Journal, 17–18; Staker, *Hearken, O Ye People,* 421–26, 436. **Topic: Kirtland Temple**
14. Kimball, "Journal and Record," 20.
15. Tippets, Autobiography, [9]–[10]; see also Doctrine and Covenants 101:67–73 (Revelation, Dec. 16–17, 1833, at josephsmithpapers.org).
16. Doctrine and Covenants 101:70–73 (Revelation, Dec. 16–17, 1833, at josephsmithpapers.org).
17. Tippets, Autobiography, [8]–[10]; Minutes, Nov. 28, 1834, in *JSP,* D4:182–88; Editorial Note and Joseph Smith, Journal, Nov. 29, 1834, in *JSP,* J1:46–47.
18. See Staker, *Hearken, O Ye People,* 412–28, 435–37.
19. See Doctrine and Covenants 90:28–29 (Revelation, Mar. 8, 1833, at josephsmithpapers .org); Tullidge, *Women of Mormondom,* 441; Staker, *Hearken, O Ye People,* 436, notes 8–9; Joseph Smith, Journal, Sept. 23, 1835, in *JSP,* J1:62; and Ames, Autobiography and Journal, [12].
20. Ames, Autobiography and Journal, [10]; Corrill, *Brief History,* 21, in *JSP,* H2:151; Joseph Young to Lewis Harvey, Nov. 16, 1880, Church History Library; Robison, *First Mormon Temple,* 50.
21. Tippets, Autobiography, [11]–[12]; Minute Book 1, Nov. 29–30, 1834; Editorial Note and Joseph Smith, Journal, Nov. 29, 1834, in *JSP,* J1:46–47.
22. Doctrine and Covenants 18 (Revelation, June 1829–B, at josephsmithpapers.org).
23. Doctrine and Covenants 102:30 (Revised Minutes, Feb. 18–19, 1834, at josephsmithpapers.org).
24. Young, *History of the Organization of the Seventies,* 1.
25. Minutes, Discourse, and Blessings, Feb. 14–15, 1835, in *JSP,* D4:219–28. **Topic: Quorum of the Twelve**
26. Patten, Journal, [1]–[2], [4]–[14].
27. See biographical entries for Luke Johnson, Lyman Eugene Johnson, Parley Parker Pratt, and Orson Pratt, Joseph Smith Papers website, josephsmithpapers.org.
28. See biographical entries for Orson Hyde, William Earl McLellin, John Farnham Boynton, and William B. Smith, Joseph Smith Papers website, josephsmithpapers.org.
29. Joseph Smith History, 1838–56, volume B-1, 574; Minutes and Blessings, Feb. 21, 1835, in *JSP,* D4:237–47.
30. Luke 10:1. **Topic: Quorum of the Seventy**
31. Minutes and Blessings, Feb. 28–Mar. 1, 1835, in *JSP,* D4:255–64; Joseph Smith History, 1838–56, volume B-1, 577–78; Minutes, Aug. 11, 1834, in *JSP,* D4:97–101; Minutes, Aug. 23, 1834, in *JSP,* D4:108–9; Minutes, Aug. 28–29, 1834, in *JSP,* D4:120–35; Sylvester Smith to Oliver Cowdery, Oct. 28, 1834, in *LDS Messenger and Advocate,* Oct. 1834, 1:10–11.
32. Young, *History of the Organization of the Seventies,* 14.

CHAPTER 20: DO NOT CAST ME OFF

1. William W. Phelps to Sally Waterman Phelps, June 2, 1835, in *JSP,* D4:335–36; William W. Phelps to Sally Waterman Phelps, in Historian's Office, Journal History of the Church, July 20, 1835; this entry was copied from the original letter in possession of a grandson of William W. Phelps. **Topic: Kirtland, Ohio**
2. Historical Introduction to Book of Abraham Manuscript, circa Early July–circa Nov. 1835–A [Abraham 1:4–2:6], in *JSP,* D5:71–77; "Egyptian Antiquities," *Times and Seasons,* May 2, 1842, 3:774.

3. Joseph Smith History, 1838–56, volume B-1, 595–96; "Egyptian Antiquities," *Times and Seasons,* May 2, 1842, 3:774; Oliver Cowdery to William Frye, Dec. 22, 1835, in Oliver Cowdery, Letterbook, 68–74; "Egyptian Mummies," *LDS Messenger and Advocate,* Dec. 1835, 2:234–35; Certificate from Michael Chandler, July 6, 1835, in *JSP,* D4:361–65.

4. "Egyptian Mummies," *LDS Messenger and Advocate,* Dec. 1835, 2:234–35; see also "Egyptian Papyri," at josephsmithpapers.org.

5. Historical Introduction to Certificate from Michael Chandler, July 6, 1835, in *JSP,* D4:362; Tullidge, "History of Provo City," 283; William W. Phelps to Sally Waterman Phelps, in Historian's Office, Journal History of the Church, July 20, 1835; Mormon 9:32.

6. Joseph Smith History, 1838–56, volume B-1, 596; Oliver Cowdery to William Frye, Dec. 22, 1835, in Oliver Cowdery, Letterbook, 68–74; Historical Introduction to Certificate from Michael Chandler, July 6, 1835, in *JSP,* D4:362; Tullidge, "History of Provo City," 283.

7. *JSP,* D4:363, note 9; Joseph Coe to Joseph Smith, Jan. 1, 1844, Joseph Smith Collection, Church History Library; Orson Pratt, in *Journal of Discourses,* Aug. 25, 1878, 20:65.

8. Joseph Coe to Joseph Smith, Jan. 1, 1844, Joseph Smith Collection, Church History Library; Peterson, *Story of the Book of Abraham,* 6–8.

9. William W. Phelps to Sally Waterman Phelps, in Historian's Office, Journal History of the Church, July 20, 1835. **Topic: Book of Abraham Translation**

10. Lyman and others, *No Place to Call Home,* 44.

11. William W. Phelps to Sally Waterman Phelps, in Historian's Office, Journal History of the Church, July 20, 1835; "The House of God," *LDS Messenger and Advocate,* July 1835, 1:147; see also Robison, *First Mormon Temple,* 153.

12. "Short Sketch of the Life of Levi Jackman," 17. **Topic: Sacrament Meetings**

13. Staker, *Hearken, O Ye People,* map 8, 413; Anderson, *Joseph Smith's Kirtland,* 155; Lysander Gee to Joseph Millet, July 18, 1885, copy, in Millet, Record Book, 34; Probert and Manscill, "Artemus Millet," 60.

14. Millet, "J. Millet on Cape Breton Island," 93–94; Probert and Manscill, "Artemus Millet," 64.

15. Minutes, Sept. 14, 1835, in *JSP,* D4:414–15; Doctrine and Covenants 25 (Revelation, July 1830–C, at josephsmithpapers.org); Minutes, Apr. 30, 1832, in *JSP,* D2:240; see also Hicks, *Mormonism and Music.* **Topic: Hymns**

16. *Collection of Sacred Hymns,* 120–21; Backman, *Heavens Resound,* 281–82; Robinson, "Items of Personal History," *Return,* Apr. 1889, 58; William W. Phelps to Sally Waterman Phelps, Sept. 16, 1835, Church History Library; Historical Introduction to Revelation, Aug. 2, 1833–B [D&C 94], in *JSP,* D3:203–4; William W. Phelps to Sally Waterman Phelps, May 26, 1835, William W. Phelps, Papers, Brigham Young University; Preface to Doctrine and Covenants, Feb. 17, 1835, in *JSP,* D4:234–37.

17. Minutes, Aug. 17, 1835, in *JSP,* D4:382–96. **Topics: Doctrine and Covenants; Lectures on Theology ("Lectures on Faith")**

18. Minutes, June 23, 1834, in *JSP,* D4:80–84; Joseph Smith, Journal, Oct. 29, 1835, in *JSP,* J1:76–77.

19. Joseph Smith, Journal, Oct. 29, 1835, in *JSP,* J1:77; Minutes, Oct. 29, 1835, in *JSP,* D5:26–29; see also Lucy Mack Smith, History, 1844–45, book 11, [4]–[5]. **Topic: Church Discipline**

20. Joseph Smith, Journal, Oct. 29 and 30, 1835, in *JSP,* J1:77–79.

21. Knight, Autobiography and Journal, [63]; Gates, *Lydia Knight's History,* 16–23; Hartley, "Newel and Lydia Bailey Knight's Kirtland Love Story," 10–14.

22. Knight, Autobiography and Journal, [56]. **Topic: Daily Life of First-Generation Latter-day Saints**

23. Gates, *Lydia Knight's History,* 26–27.

24. Knight, Autobiography and Journal, [60]–[63]; Gates, *Lydia Knight's History,* 10–12; Hartley, "Newel and Lydia Bailey Knight's Kirtland Love Story," 9–10.

25. Knight, Autobiography and Journal, [56]. The original source has "I told her I thought her situation, as well as mine was rather lonely."
26. Knight, Autobiography and Journal, [56]; Gates, *Lydia Knight's History,* 27.
27. Joseph Smith, Journal, Oct. 30, 1835, in *JSP,* J1:79.
28. Joseph Smith, Journal, Oct. 30–31, 1835, in *JSP,* J1:79–80.
29. Joseph Smith, Journal, Oct. 31, 1835, in *JSP,* J1:80.
30. Joseph Smith, Journal, Oct. 31 and Nov. 3, 1835, in *JSP,* J1:80, 83; Revelation, Nov. 3, 1835, in *JSP,* D5:32–36.
31. See Tyler, "Recollection of the Prophet Joseph Smith," 127–28. **Topic: Dissent in the Church**
32. Historical Introduction to Marriage License for John F. Boynton and Susan Lowell, Nov. 17, 1835, in *JSP,* D5:65–66; see also Bradshaw, "Joseph Smith's Performance of Marriages in Ohio," 23–69.
33. Knight, Autobiography and Journal, [56]–[59]; Gates, *Lydia Knight's History,* 28–31; Joseph Smith, Journal, Nov. 24, 1835, in *JSP,* J1:109–10; Hartley, "Newel and Lydia Bailey Knight's Kirtland Love Story," 6–22.
34. See Bushman, *Rough Stone Rolling,* 298–300; and Joseph Smith, Journal, Nov. 8 and Dec. 12, 1835; Jan. 16, 1836, in *JSP,* J1:86, 120, 158.
35. Joseph Smith, Journal, Nov. 18, Dec. 12 and 16, 1835, in *JSP,* J1:106, 120–21, 124.
36. Historical Introduction to Letter from William Smith, Dec. 18, 1835, in *JSP,* D5:112; Joseph Smith, Journal, Dec. 16, 1835, in *JSP,* J1:124; Joseph Smith History, 1834–36, 149–50, in *JSP,* H1:147–48; Joseph Smith to William Smith, circa Dec. 18, 1835, in *JSP,* D5:115–21.
37. William Smith to Joseph Smith, Dec. 18, 1835, in *JSP,* D5:109–15; Joseph Smith, Journal, Dec. 18, 1835, in *JSP,* J1:129–30.
38. William Smith to Joseph Smith, Dec. 18, 1835, in *JSP,* D5:114; Joseph Smith, Journal, Dec. 18, 1835, in *JSP,* J1:130.
39. Joseph Smith to William Smith, circa Dec. 18, 1835, in *JSP,* D5:115–21; Joseph Smith, Journal, Dec. 18, 1835, in *JSP,* J1:131–34.
40. Joseph Smith, Journal, Jan. 1, 1836, in *JSP,* J1:141.

CHAPTER 21: THE SPIRIT OF GOD

1. Robison, *First Mormon Temple,* 78–79; Staker, *Hearken, O Ye People,* 437. **Topic: Kirtland Temple**
2. Whitmer, History, 83, in *JSP,* H2:92; Joseph Smith, Journal, Nov. 12, 1835, in *JSP,* J1:97–98; Leviticus 8; Exodus 29:4–7.
3. Luke 24:49; Acts 1–2; see also Doctrine and Covenants 38 (Revelation, Jan. 2, 1831, at josephsmithpapers.org); and William W. Phelps to Sally Waterman Phelps, Apr. 1836, William W. Phelps, Papers, Brigham Young University. Spelling in Luke 24:49 standardized from "endued" to "endowed." **Topics: Endowment of Power; Gift of Tongues**
4. Joseph Smith, Journal, Jan. 21, 1836, in *JSP,* J1:166–71; Cowdery, Diary, Jan. 21, 1836; Partridge, Journal, Jan. 21, 1836.
5. Joseph Smith, Journal, Jan. 21, 1836, in *JSP,* J1:167–68; Doctrine and Covenants 137 (Visions, Jan. 21, 1836, at josephsmithpapers.org).
6. Joseph Smith, Journal, Jan. 21, 1836, in *JSP,* J1:168–71.
7. Joseph Smith, Journal, Mar. 27, 1836, in *JSP,* J1:200; Post, Journal, Mar. 27, 1836; William W. Phelps to Sally Waterman Phelps, Apr. 1–3, 1836, in Harper, "Pentecost and Endowment Indeed," 346.
8. Gates, *Lydia Knight's History,* 32.
9. Joseph Smith, Journal, Mar. 27, 1836, in *JSP,* J1:200–201; Gates, *Lydia Knight's History,* 32–33.

10. Joseph Smith, Journal, Mar. 27, 1836, in *JSP,* J1:200.
11. Minutes and Prayer of Dedication, Mar. 27, 1836, in *JSP,* D5:194–99; Joseph Smith, Journal, Mar. 27, 1836, in *JSP,* J1:203; Cowdery, Diary, Mar. 26, 1836. **Topic: Temple Dedications and Dedicatory Prayers**
12. Doctrine and Covenants 109 (Minutes and Prayer of Dedication, Mar. 27, 1836, at josephsmithpapers.org); Joseph Smith, Journal, Mar. 27, 1836, in *JSP,* J1:203–10.
13. Doctrine and Covenants 109:35–38 (Minutes and Prayer of Dedication, Mar. 27, 1836, at josephsmithpapers.org); Joseph Smith, Journal, Mar. 27, 1836, in *JSP,* J1:207.
14. Doctrine and Covenants 109:78 (Minutes and Prayer of Dedication, Mar. 27, 1836, at josephsmithpapers.org); Joseph Smith, Journal, Mar. 27, 1836, in *JSP,* J1:210.
15. *Collection of Sacred Hymns,* 120–21; Joseph Smith, Journal, Mar. 27, 1836, in *JSP,* J1:210. **Topic: Hymns**
16. Joseph Smith, Journal, Mar. 27, 1836, in *JSP,* J1:211; Minutes and Prayer of Dedication, Mar. 27, 1836, in *JSP,* D5:209; Gates, *Lydia Knight's History,* 33.
17. Benjamin Brown to Sarah M. Brown, Mar. 1836, Benjamin Brown Family Collection; *JSP,* J1:211, note 443; see also Harper, "Pentecost and Endowment Indeed," 336.
18. **Topic: Washing of Feet**
19. Joseph Smith, Journal, Mar. 27 and 30, 1836, in *JSP,* J1:211, 213–16; Post, Journal, Mar. 27–28 and 30, 1836; Cowdery, Diary, Mar. 27, 1836; William W. Phelps to Sally Waterman Phelps, Apr. 1836, William W. Phelps, Papers, Brigham Young University; Partridge, Journal, Mar. 27, 1836; Joseph Smith History, 1838–56, volume B-1, addenda, 3–4; see also Waite, "A School and an Endowment," 174–82. **Topics: Endowment of Power; Solemn Assemblies**
20. Joseph Smith, Journal, Apr. 3, 1836, in *JSP,* J1:219; see also *JSP,* J1:218.
21. Joseph Smith, Journal, Apr. 3, 1836, in *JSP,* J1:219; Doctrine and Covenants 110:1–3 (Visions, Apr. 3, 1836, at josephsmithpapers.org).
22. Joseph Smith, Journal, Apr. 3, 1836, in *JSP,* J1:219; Doctrine and Covenants 110:3, 6–7 (Visions, Apr. 3, 1836, at josephsmithpapers.org).
23. Doctrine and Covenants 110:8–10 (Visions, Apr. 3, 1836, at josephsmithpapers.org); Joseph Smith, Journal, Apr. 3, 1836, in *JSP,* J1:222.
24. Doctrine and Covenants 110:11–16 (Visions, Apr. 3, 1836, at josephsmithpapers.org); Malachi 4:6; Joseph Smith, Journal, Apr. 3, 1836, in *JSP,* J1:222; see also Robert B. Thompson, Sermon Notes, Oct. 5, 1840, Joseph Smith Collection, Church History Library; Coray, Notebook, Aug. 13, 1843; Joseph Smith, Journal, Aug. 27, 1843, in *JSP,* J3:86; and Woodruff, Journal, Mar. 10, 1844.
25. Joseph Smith, Journal, Apr. 3, 1836, in *JSP,* J1:222.
26. Woodruff, Journal, Jan. 21, 1844; see also Burgess, Journal, [303]–[6]; and Doctrine and Covenants 128:17–18 (Letter to "The Church of Jesus Christ of Latter Day Saints," Sept. 6, 1842, at josephsmithpapers.org). **Topic: Sealing**
27. Joseph Smith History, 1838–56, volume B-1, 728–29; Whitmer, History, 84, in *JSP,* H2:93.
28. Gates, *Lydia Knight's History,* 34–37; Knight, Autobiography and Journal, [67]–[68]. **Topic: Patriarchal Blessings**
29. Joseph Smith History, 1838–56, volume B-1, 733; see also *Collection of Sacred Hymns,* 120.

CHAPTER 22: TRY THE LORD

1. See, for example, Joseph Smith, Journal, Mar. 30, 1836, in *JSP,* J1:216.
2. Backman, *Heavens Resound,* 304–5; Tyler, "Incidents of Experience," 32.
3. Minutes, Mar. 30, 1836, in *JSP,* D5:219.
4. Doctrine and Covenants 105:28 (Revelation, June 22, 1834, at josephsmithpapers.org); Minutes, Apr. 2, 1836, in *JSP,* D5:223–24.
5. Minutes, Apr. 2, 1836, in *JSP,* D5:222–24.

6. "Anniversary of the Church of Latter Day Saints," *LDS Messenger and Advocate,* Apr. 1837, 2:488; Kimball, "Journal and Record," 33; Minute Book 1, June 16, 1836; see also Historical Introduction to Revelation, Aug. 6, 1836, in *JSP,* D5:272–74. **Topic: Canada**

7. Pratt, *Autobiography,* 141, 145; see also Givens and Grow, *Parley P. Pratt,* 82.

8. Pratt, *Autobiography,* 141–42.

9. See Givens and Grow, *Parley P. Pratt,* 71, 82, 91.

10. Pratt, *Autobiography,* 142, 145–46. The original source has "and see if anything was too hard for him."

11. Emily Dow Partridge Young, "Autobiography," *Woman's Exponent,* Feb. 15, 1885, 13:138.

12. Joseph Smith to Lyman Wight and Others, Aug. 16, 1834, in *JSP,* D4:102–8; Emily Dow Partridge Young, "Autobiography," *Woman's Exponent,* Mar. 1, 1885, 13:145; Partridge, History, Manuscript, circa 1839, [18].

13. Emily Dow Partridge Young, "Autobiography," *Woman's Exponent,* Feb. 15, 1885, 13:138. **Topic: Daily Life of First-Generation Latter-day Saints**

14. Partridge, Journal, June 29, 1836; Emily Dow Partridge Young, "Autobiography," *Woman's Exponent,* Feb. 15, 1885, 13:138; "Public Meeting," *LDS Messenger and Advocate,* Aug. 1836, 2:363–64; Partridge, History, Manuscript, circa 1839, [17]–[18].

15. Emily Dow Partridge Young, "Autobiography," *Woman's Exponent,* Feb. 15, 1885, 13:138.

16. Pratt, *Autobiography,* 146.

17. John Taylor, Sermon, Oct. 6, 1866, George D. Watt Papers, Church History Library, as transcribed by LaJean Purcell Carruth.

18. Pratt, *Autobiography,* 147.

19. John Taylor, Sermon, Oct. 6, 1866, George D. Watt Papers, Church History Library, as transcribed by LaJean Purcell Carruth.

20. Pratt, *Autobiography,* 164–65; "Diary of Joseph Fielding," book 1, 5. The original has "go over to meeting together."

21. "Diary of Joseph Fielding," book 1, 5; Pratt, *Autobiography,* 165–66.

22. Pratt, *Autobiography,* 166.

23. John Taylor, "History of John Taylor by Himself," 10–11, in Histories of the Twelve, Church History Library.

24. Jonathan Crosby, Autobiography, 14; Caroline Barnes Crosby, Reminiscences, [19].

25. Jonathan Crosby, Autobiography, 14–15; Caroline Barnes Crosby, Reminiscences, [15], [19]–[20].

26. Caroline Barnes Crosby, Reminiscences, [21]–[22].

27. Historical Introduction to Letter to William W. Phelps and Others, July 25, 1836, in *JSP,* D5:269; Partridge, Journal, June 29, 1836; "Public Meeting," *LDS Messenger and Advocate,* Aug. 1836, 2:359–61; Partridge, History, Manuscript, circa 1839, [17]–[18].

28. Sidney Rigdon and Others to William W. Phelps and Others, July 25, 1836, in *JSP,* D5:268–71.

29. Minutes, Apr. 2, 1836, in *JSP,* D5:222–24; Historical Introduction to Revelation, Apr. 23, 1834, in *JSP,* D4:19–22.

30. Minutes, June 16, 1836, in *JSP,* D5:247–53; Staker, "Raising Money in Righteousness," 144–53; Staker, *Hearken, O Ye People,* 445–46; Brigham Young, in *Journal of Discourses,* Oct. 9, 1852, 1:215; Oct. 8, 1855, 3:121.

31. Historical Introduction to Revelation, Aug. 6, 1836, in *JSP,* D5:271–75; see also Kuehn, "More Treasures Than One," 229–34.

32. Doctrine and Covenants 111:1, 5–6 (Revelation, Aug. 6, 1836, at josephsmithpapers.org). The word "on" was added; the original has "coming this journey."

CHAPTER 23: EVERY SNARE

1. Jonathan Crosby, Autobiography, 15; Caroline Barnes Crosby, Reminiscences, [53]–[54]; see also Lyman and others, *No Place to Call Home,* 46.

2. Historical Introduction to Constitution of the Kirtland Safety Society Bank, Nov. 2, 1836, in *JSP,* D5:300; "Part 5: 5 October 1836–10 April 1837," in *JSP,* D5:285–90; Staker, *Hearken, O Ye People,* 463. **Topic: Kirtland Safety Society**

3. Kirtland Safety Society Notes, Jan. 4–Mar. 9, 1837, in *JSP,* D5:331–40; Staker, *Hearken, O Ye People,* 463–64; Historical Introduction to Constitution of the Kirtland Safety Society Bank, Nov. 2, 1836, in *JSP,* D5:302.

4. Mortgage to Peter French, Oct. 5, 1836, in *JSP,* D5:293–99; Kirtland Safety Society, Stock Ledger, 1836–37; "Part 5: 5 October 1836–10 April 1837," in *JSP,* D5:285–86; Staker, *Hearken, O Ye People,* 464.

5. Historical Introduction to Constitution of the Kirtland Safety Society Bank, Nov. 2, 1836, in *JSP,* D5:303; *JSP,* D5:304, note 91; "Minutes of a Meeting," *LDS Messenger and Advocate,* Mar. 1837, 3:476–77; Staker, *Hearken, O Ye People,* 465.

6. Historical Introduction to Kirtland Safety Society Notes, Jan. 4–Mar. 9, 1837, in *JSP,* D5:331; Joseph Smith History, 1838–56, volume B-1, 750; Articles of Agreement for the Kirtland Safety Society Anti-Banking Company, Jan. 2, 1837, in *JSP,* D5:324, 329–31; see also Isaiah 60:9, 17; 62:1.

7. Woodruff, Journal, Jan. 6, 1837.

8. Jonathan Crosby, Autobiography, 14–15.

9. Caroline Barnes Crosby, Reminiscences, [39].

10. "Part 5: 5 October 1836–10 April 1837," in *JSP,* D5:286; Kirtland Safety Society Notes, Jan. 4–Mar. 9, 1837, in *JSP,* D5:331–35.

11. Woodruff, Journal, Jan. 6, 1837; Kirtland Safety Society Notes, Jan. 4–Mar. 9, 1837, in *JSP,* D5:331–40.

12. Editorial, *LDS Messenger and Advocate,* July 1837, 3:536; Willard Richards to Hepzibah Richards, Jan. 20, 1837, Levi Richards Family Correspondence, Church History Library; Historical Introduction to Mortgage to Peter French, Oct. 5, 1836, in *JSP,* D5:295; "Part 5: 5 October 1836–10 April 1837," in *JSP,* D5:286; Staker, *Hearken, O Ye People,* 481.

13. Ulrich, "Leaving Home," 451; see also Kirtland Safety Society, Stock Ledger, 1836–37.

14. Tullidge, *Women of Mormondom,* 412.

15. Woodruff, Journal, Apr. 1837. **Topic: Patriarchal Blessings**

16. Phebe Carter to Family, circa 1836, in Wilford Woodruff Collection, Church History Library.

17. Woodruff, Journal, Apr. 1837.

18. Woodruff, Journal, Apr. 10, 1837.

19. Staker, *Hearken, O Ye People,* 481–84.

20. Hall, *Thomas Newell,* 132–34; Adams, "Grandison Newell's Obsession," 160–63.

21. "The Court of Common Pleas," *Chardon Spectator and Geauga Gazette,* Oct. 30, 1835, 2; Eber D. Howe, Statement, Apr. 8, 1885; Maria S. Hurlbut, Statement, Apr. 15, 1885, in Collection of Manuscripts about Mormons, 1832–54, Chicago History Museum; Adams, "Grandison Newell's Obsession," 168–73.

22. Young, Account Book, Jan. 1837; "Our Village," *LDS Messenger and Advocate,* Jan. 1837, 3:444; Staker, *Hearken, O Ye People,* 482; see also Agreement with David Cartter, Jan. 14, 1837, in *JSP,* D5:341–43; and Agreement with Ovid Phinney and Stephen Phillips, Mar. 14, 1837, in *JSP,* D5:344–48. **Topic: Opposition to the Early Church**

23. An Act to Prohibit the Issuing and Circulating of Unauthorized Bank Paper [Jan. 27, 1816], *Statutes of the State of Ohio,* 136–39; "Part 5: 5 October 1836–10 April 1837," in *JSP,* D5:288–89.

24. Staker, *Hearken, O Ye People,* 468–77.

25. Staker, *Hearken, O Ye People,* 484; *JSP,* D5:287, note 19; 329, note 187.

26. Kirtland Safety Society, Stock Ledger, 219; Staker, *Hearken, O Ye People,* 391.

27. Woodruff, Journal, June 28, 1835; *JSP,* D4:72, note 334; "Parrish, Warren Farr," Biographical Entry, Joseph Smith Papers website, josephsmithpapers.org; see also Staker, *Hearken, O Ye People,* 465, 480.

28. Kimball, "History," 47–48; Staker, *Hearken, O Ye People,* 482–84; "A New Revelation— Mormon Money," *Cleveland Weekly Gazette,* Jan. 18, 1837, [3]; "Mormon Currency," *Cleveland Daily Gazette,* Jan. 20, 1837, 2; "Rags! Mere Rags!!," *Ohio Star,* Jan. 19, 1837; Jonathan Crosby, Autobiography, 16; Woodruff, Journal, Jan. 24 and Apr. 9, 1837; "Part 5: 5 October 1836–10 April 1837," in *JSP,* D5:287–90.

29. "Bank of Monroe," *Painesville Republican,* Feb. 9, 1837, [2]; "Monroe Bank," *Painesville Telegraph,* Feb. 24, 1837, [3]; "Kirtland,—Mormonism," *LDS Messenger and Advocate,* Apr. 1837, 3:490–91; "Part 5: 5 October 1836–10 April 1837," in *JSP,* D5:291; Staker, *Hearken, O Ye People,* 492–501.

30. Woodruff, Journal, Jan. 10 and 17, 1837; Feb. 19, 1837; Charges against Joseph Smith Preferred to Bishop's Council, May 29, 1837, in *JSP,* D5:393–97.

31. Woodruff, Journal, Feb. 19, 1837.

32. Woodruff, Journal, Apr. 6, 1837.

33. Joseph Smith, Discourse, Apr. 6, 1837, in *JSP,* D5:352–57.

34. Woodruff, Journal, Apr. 6, 1837.

35. "For the Republican," *Painesville Republican,* Feb. 16, 1837, [2]–[3]; Staker, *Hearken, O Ye People,* 498; "Joseph Smith Documents from October 1835 through January 1838," in *JSP,* D5:xxx.

36. Transcript of Proceedings, June 5, 1837, State of Ohio on Complaint of Newell v. Smith, Geauga County, Ohio, Court of Common Pleas Record Book T, 52–53, Geauga County Archives and Records Center, Chardon, Ohio; Woodruff, Journal, May 30, 1837; Hall, *Thomas Newell,* 135; Historical Introduction to Letter from Newel K. Whitney, Apr. 20, 1837, in *JSP,* D5:367–69.

37. Woodruff, Journal, Apr. 13, 1837; see also "The Humbug Ended," *Painesville Republican,* June 15, 1837, [2].

38. Historical Introduction to Letter from Emma Smith, Apr. 25, 1837, in *JSP,* D5:371.

39. Newel K. Whitney to Joseph Smith and Sidney Rigdon, Apr. 20, 1837, in *JSP,* D5:370.

40. Emma Smith to Joseph Smith, Apr. 25, 1837, in *JSP,* D5:372; Emma Smith to Joseph Smith, May 3, 1837, in *JSP,* D5:376. **Topic: Joseph and Emma Hale Smith Family**

41. Emma Smith to Joseph Smith, Apr. 25, 1837, in *JSP,* D5:372.

42. Emma Smith to Joseph Smith, May 3, 1837, in *JSP,* D5:375–76. **Topic: Emma Hale Smith**

43. Woodruff, Journal, Mar. 26, 1837; Pratt, *Autobiography,* 181–83; Givens and Grow, *Parley P. Pratt,* 92.

44. Pratt, *Autobiography,* 181–83, 188; Geauga County, Ohio, Probate Court, Marriage Records, 1806–1920, volume C, 220, May 14, 1837, microfilm 873,464, U.S. and Canada Record Collection, Family History Library; Givens and Grow, *Parley P. Pratt,* 93–95; Thomas B. Marsh and David W. Patten to Parley P. Pratt, May 10, 1837, in Joseph Smith Letterbook 2, 62–63.

45. Pratt, *Autobiography,* 183; Historical Introduction to Notes Receivable from Chester Store, May 22, 1837, in *JSP,* D5:383–84; Historical Introduction to Letter from Parley P. Pratt, May 23, 1837, in *JSP,* D5:386–87.

46. Historical Introduction to Letter from Parley P. Pratt, May 23, 1837, in *JSP,* D5:386–87.

47. See Givens and Grow, *Parley P. Pratt,* 97–98.

48. Parley P. Pratt to Joseph Smith, May 23, 1837, in *JSP,* D5:389–91. Parley's letter was first published the following year in an antagonistic newspaper. For further analysis, see Historical Introduction to Letter from Parley P. Pratt, May 23, 1837, in *JSP,* D5:386–89; and Pratt, *Autobiography,* 183–84.

49. Woodruff, Journal, May 28, 1831. **Topic: Dissent in the Church**

50. Woodruff, Journal, May 31 and July 16, 1837; Woodruff, *Leaves from My Journal,* 26; see also Ulrich, *House Full of Females,* 17–18. **Topic: Early Missionaries**

51. "Joseph Smith Documents from October 1835 through January 1838," in *JSP,* D5:xxxii.

52. Woodruff, Journal, May 28, 1837; West, *Few Interesting Facts,* 14.

53. Woodruff, Journal, May 28, 1837.

CHAPTER 24: TRUTH SHALL PREVAIL

1. Plewe, *Mapping Mormonism,* 48–49; "Joseph Smith Documents from October 1835 through January 1838," in *JSP,* D5:xxvi–xxvii; "Far West, Missouri," Geographical Entry, Joseph Smith Papers website, josephsmithpapers.org. **Topic: Zion/New Jerusalem**
2. Thomas B. Marsh and David W. Patten to Parley P. Pratt, May 10, 1837, in Joseph Smith Letterbook 2, 62–63.
3. Allen and others, *Men with a Mission,* 22. **Topic: Kirtland Safety Society**
4. Kimball, "History," 54; Whitney, *Life of Heber C. Kimball,* 116. **Topics: England; Early Missionaries**
5. Kimball, "History," 54.
6. Kimball, "History," 55.
7. Kimball, "History," 55.
8. Tullidge, *Women of Mormondom,* 113–15; Whitney, *Life of Heber C. Kimball,* 120–22.
9. Jonathan Crosby, Autobiography, 16; Joseph Smith and Others, Mortgage to Mead, Stafford & Co., July 11, 1837, in *JSP,* D5:404–10.
10. Jonathan Crosby, Autobiography, 16, Caroline Barnes Crosby, Reminiscences, [39]–[41].
11. Jonathan Crosby, Autobiography, 16–17. The original source has "provision" rather than "provisions"; it also has "make a present" rather than "make you a present."
12. Jonathan Crosby, Autobiography, 17; Caroline Barnes Crosby, Reminiscences, [41].
13. Mary Fielding to Mercy Fielding, circa June 1837, Mary Fielding Smith Collection, Church History Library; see also Whitney, *Life of Heber C. Kimball,* 112–14. **Topic: Dissent in the Church**
14. Mary Fielding to Mercy Fielding, circa June 1837, Mary Fielding Smith Collection, Church History Library.
15. John Taylor, "History of John Taylor by Himself," 15, in Historian's Office, Histories of the Twelve, Church History Library; see also Roberts, *Life of John Taylor,* 40; and Parley P. Pratt to Joseph Smith, May 23, 1837, in *JSP,* D5:386–91.
16. Joseph Smith History, 1838–56, volume B-1, 762; Mary Fielding to Mercy Fielding, circa June 1837, Mary Fielding Smith Collection, Church History Library.
17. Joseph Smith History, 1838–56, volume B-1, 763; Warren Parrish, Letter to the Editor, *Painesville Republican,* Feb. 15, 1838, [3].
18. Mary Fielding to Mercy Fielding, circa June 1837, Mary Fielding Smith Collection, Church History Library.
19. Fielding, Journal, 17; Kimball, "History," 60, 62; Watt, *Mormon Passage of George D. Watt,* 17; see also Ostler, "Photo Essay of Church History Sites in Liverpool and the Ribble Valley," 61–78. **Topic: England**
20. Whitney, *Life of Heber C. Kimball,* 133; Allen and others, *Men with a Mission,* 25–29.
21. Fielding, Journal, 17; "Mission to England," *LDS Millennial Star,* Apr. 1841, 12:290; Kimball, "History," 60; Whitney, *Life of Heber C. Kimball,* 134.
22. Joseph Fielding to Mary Fielding and Mercy Fielding Thompson, Oct. 2, 1837, Mary Fielding Smith Collection, Church History Library; "Mission to England," *LDS Millennial Star,* Apr. 1841, 12:290; Fielding, Journal, 17–18.
23. Givens and Grow, *Parley P. Pratt,* 101; Kirtland Safety Society, Stock Ledger, 47.
24. "History of Thomas Baldwin Marsh," 5, in Historian's Office, Histories of the Twelve, Church History Library.
25. Parley P. Pratt, "To the Public," *Elders' Journal,* Aug. 1838, 50–51.
26. Pratt, *Autobiography,* 183–84; John Taylor, "History of John Taylor by Himself," 15, in Historian's Office, Histories of the Twelve, Church History Library; see also Givens and Grow, *Parley P. Pratt,* 102.
27. "History of Thomas Baldwin Marsh," 5, in Historian's Office, Histories of the Twelve, Church History Library; Woodruff, Journal, June 25, 1857; see also Historical Introduction to Revelation, July 23, 1837 [D&C 112], in *JSP,* D5:410–12.
28. See Cook, "I Have Sinned against Heaven," 392–93; and Historical Introduction to Revelation, July 23, 1837 [D&C 112], in *JSP,* D5:410–11.

29. See Doctrine and Covenants 112:1–2 (Revelation, July 23, 1837, at josephsmithpapers.org).
30. Historical Introduction to Revelation, July 23, 1837 [D&C 112], in *JSP,* D5:410–14.
31. **Topics: First Presidency; Quorum of the Twelve**
32. Doctrine and Covenants 112 (Revelation, July 23, 1837, at josephsmithpapers.org); see also Darowski, "The Faith and Fall of Thomas Marsh," 54–60.

CHAPTER 25: MOVE ON TO THE WEST

1. Kimball, "History," 62–63; see also *Illustrated Itinerary of the County of Lancaster,* 159. **Topic: Healing**
2. Kimball, "History," 63–64.
3. Lucy Mack Smith, History, 1844–45, book 14, [8]; Snow, *Biography and Family Record of Lorenzo Snow,* 20–21; "Cowdery, Oliver," Biographical Entry, Joseph Smith Papers website, josephsmithpapers.org; see also Huntington, Diary and Reminiscences, 28–29. **Topic: Dissent in the Church**
4. Historical Introduction to Minutes, Sept. 3, 1837, in *JSP,* D5:420–22; Mary Fielding to Mercy Fielding Thompson, circa Aug. 30, 1837, Mary Fielding Smith Collection, Church History Library; Huntington, Diary and Reminiscences, 28–29; Esplin, "Emergence of Brigham Young," 295–96.
5. Minutes, Sept. 3, 1837, in *JSP,* D5:422–23. **Topic: Common Consent**
6. Mary Fielding to Mercy Fielding Thompson, Oct. 7, 1837, Mary Fielding Smith Collection, Church History Library; Minutes, Nov. 7, 1837, in *JSP,* D5:468–72; Minutes, Nov. 10, 1837, in *JSP,* D5:472–76; see also Minutes, Sept. 17, 1837-B, in *JSP,* D5:444–46. **Topic: Far West**
7. Historical Introduction to Revelation, Sept. 4, 1837, in *JSP,* D5:431–33; Thomas B. Marsh to Wilford Woodruff, *Elders' Journal,* July 1838, 36–38; Minute Book 2, Apr. 7, 1837.
8. Williams, "Frederick Granger Williams of the First Presidency of the Church," 256.
9. Oliver Cowdery to Lyman Cowdery, Jan. 13, 1834, in Cowdery, Letterbook, 19; Romig, *Eighth Witness,* 314–15.
10. Minutes, Sept. 17, 1837-A, in *JSP,* D5:442–43; Joseph Smith to John Corrill and the Church in Missouri, Sept. 4, 1837, in *JSP,* D5:426–31.
11. Hyrum Smith Family Bible. **Topic: Hyrum Smith**
12. Historical Introduction to Letter from Thomas B. Marsh, Feb. 15, 1838, in *JSP,* D6:12; Jenson, "Plural Marriage," *Historical Record,* May 1887, 6:232–33; "Report of Elders Orson Pratt and Joseph F. Smith," *LDS Millennial Star,* Dec. 16, 1878, 40:788. **Topic: Joseph Smith and Plural Marriage**
13. Lorenzo Snow, Affidavit, Aug. 28, 1869, Joseph F. Smith, Affidavits about Celestial Marriage, Church History Library; Tullidge, *Women of Mormondom,* 368.
14. Benjamin F. Johnson to George F. Gibbs, circa Apr.–circa Oct. 1903, Benjamin Franklin Johnson, Papers, Church History Library; Mosiah Hancock, Narrative, in Levi Hancock, Autobiography, circa 1896, 63; Historical Introduction to Minutes and Blessings, Feb. 28–Mar. 1, 1835, in *JSP,* D4:255; Minutes and Blessings, Feb. 28–Mar. 1, 1835, in *JSP,* D4:259; Young, *History of the Organization of the Seventies,* 4. **Topic: Fanny Alger**
15. Mosiah Hancock, Narrative, in Levi Hancock, Autobiography, circa 1896, 63; Historical Introduction to Letter from Thomas B. Marsh, Feb. 15, 1838, in *JSP,* D6:12; see also Andrew Jenson, Research Notes, Andrew Jenson Collection, Church History Library; Benjamin F. Johnson to George F. Gibbs, circa Apr.–circa Oct. 1903, Benjamin Franklin Johnson, Papers, Church History Library; Eliza Jane Churchill Webb to Mary Bond, Apr. 24, 1876; Eliza Jane Churchill Webb to Mary Bond, May 4, 1876, Biographical Folder Collection (labeled Myron H. Bond), Community of Christ Library-Archives; and Bradley, "Relationship of Joseph Smith and Fanny Alger," 14–58.
16. Mosiah Hancock, Narrative, in Levi Hancock, Autobiography, circa 1896, 63.

17. Mosiah Hancock, Narrative, in Levi Hancock, Autobiography, circa 1896, 63; Eliza Churchill Webb to Mary Bond, May, 4, 1876, Biographical Folder Collection (labeled Myron H. Bond), Community of Christ Library-Archives; Historical Introduction to Letter from Thomas B. Marsh, Feb. 15, 1838, in *JSP,* D6:13; Tullidge, *Women of Mormondom,* 368.
18. Benjamin F. Johnson to George F. Gibbs, circa Apr.–circa Oct. 1903, Benjamin Franklin Johnson, Papers, Church History Library.
19. Hales, *Joseph Smith's Polygamy,* 1:123.
20. Historical Introduction to Letter from Thomas B. Marsh, Feb. 15, 1838, in *JSP,* D6:13; see also Minutes, Apr. 12, 1838, in *JSP,* D6:91; and Oliver Cowdery to Warren Cowdery, Jan. 21, 1838, in Cowdery, Letterbook, 80–83.
21. Benjamin F. Johnson to George F. Gibbs, circa Apr.–circa Oct. 1903, Benjamin Franklin Johnson, Papers, Church History Library. This letter quotes what Fanny Alger said to others about her relationship with Joseph Smith.
22. Historical Introduction to Travel Account and Questions, Nov. 1837, in *JSP,* D5:478–80.
23. Woodruff, Journal, Aug. 18, 1837; Historical Introduction to Letter from Wilford Woodruff and Jonathan H. Hale, Sept. 18, 1837, in *JSP,* D5:447–48; Isaiah 11:11.
24. Woodruff, *Leaves from My Journal,* 34.
25. Woodruff, Journal, July 12 and Aug. 20, 1837; Woodruff, *Leaves from My Journal,* 30–31; Historical Introduction to Letter from Wilford Woodruff and Jonathan H. Hale, Sept. 18, 1837, in *JSP,* D5:447–48.
26. Woodruff, Journal, Aug. 8–18, 1837.
27. Woodruff, Journal, Aug. 20, 1837.
28. Woodruff, *Leaves from My Journal,* 33; Woodruff, Journal, Aug. 20–25, 1837.
29. Woodruff, Journal, Aug. 27, 1837; Hale, Journal, Aug. 27, 1837.
30. Woodruff, Journal, Aug. 27 and Sept. 3, 1837; Hale, Journal, Aug. 27 and Sept. 3, 1837.
31. Woodruff, *Leaves from My Journal,* 33–34; Woodruff, Journal, Sept. 3–4, 1837.
32. See Romig, *Eighth Witness,* 305–8.
33. Hyrum Smith Family Bible; Travel Account and Questions, Nov. 1837, in *JSP,* D5:480–81; Joseph Smith History, 1838–56, volume B-1, 775.
34. Minutes, Nov. 6, 1837, in *JSP,* D5:464–68; Minutes, Nov. 7, 1837, in *JSP,* D5:468–72.
35. Samuel Smith to Hyrum Smith, Oct. 13, 1837, Hyrum Smith, Papers, Church History Library; Obituary for Jerusha T. Smith, *Elders' Journal,* Oct. 1837, 16; Lucy Mack Smith, History, 1845, 34; Lucy Mack Smith, History, 1844–45, miscellany, [11].
36. Joseph Smith History, 1838–56, volume B-1, 775.
37. Oliver Cowdery to Warren Cowdery, Jan. 21, 1838, in Cowdery, Letterbook, 81.
38. Oliver Cowdery to Warren Cowdery, Jan. 21, 1838, in Cowdery, Letterbook, 81.
39. Joseph Smith History, 1838–56, volume B-1, 779; Samuel Smith to Hyrum Smith, Oct. 13, 1837, Hyrum Smith, Papers, Church History Library; Obituary for Jerusha T. Smith, *Elders' Journal,* Oct. 1837, 16; Lucy Mack Smith, History, 1845, 34; Lucy Mack Smith, History, 1844–45, miscellany, [11].
40. Smith, *Life of Joseph F. Smith,* 41–42, 120.
41. Mary Fielding to Mercy Fielding, circa June 1837; Mary Fielding to Mercy Fielding Thompson, July 8, 1837; Mary Fielding to Mercy Fielding Thompson and Robert Thompson, Oct. 7, 1837, Mary Fielding Smith Collection, Church History Library.
42. Hyrum Smith Family Bible; Geauga County, Ohio, Probate Court, Marriage Records, 1806–1920, volume C, 262, microfilm 873,461, U.S. and Canada Record Collection, Family History Library; Smith, *Life of Joseph F. Smith,* 120.
43. Vilate Murray Kimball to Heber C. Kimball, Jan. 19–24, 1838, Heber C. Kimball, Collection, Church History Library; Joseph Smith History, 1838–56, volume B-1, 779; Thomas B. Marsh to Wilford Woodruff, in *Elders' Journal,* July 1838, 36–37; John Smith and Clarissa Smith to George A. Smith, Jan. 1, 1838, George Albert Smith, Papers, Church History Library; Hepzibah Richards to Willard Richards, Jan. 18, 1838, Willard Richards, Journals and Papers, Church History Library.

44. Vilate Murray Kimball to Heber C. Kimball, Jan. 19–24, 1838, Heber C. Kimball, Collection, Church History Library; Historical Introduction to Revelation, Jan. 12, 1838–A, in *JSP,* D5:495–96.
45. Vilate Murray Kimball to Heber C. Kimball, Jan. 19–24, 1838, Heber C. Kimball, Collection, Church History Library. The original letter has "believe the Book of Mormon and covenants," referring to the Doctrine and Covenants.
46. Vilate Murray Kimball to Heber C. Kimball, Jan. 19–24, 1838; Marinda Johnson Hyde to Orson Hyde, Jan. 29, 1838, Heber C. Kimball, Collection, Church History Library; Joseph Smith History, 1838–56, volume B-1, 779; Thomas B. Marsh to Wilford Woodruff, in *Elders' Journal,* July 1838, 36–37; John Smith and Clarissa Smith to George A. Smith, Jan. 1, 1838, George Albert Smith, Papers, Church History Library; Hepzibah Richards to Willard Richards, Jan. 18, 1838, Willard Richards, Journals and Papers, Church History Library; Historical Introduction to Revelation, Jan. 12, 1838–A, in *JSP,* D5:495–96.
47. Warren Parrish to "The Editor of the *Painesville Republican," Painesville Republican,* Feb. 15, 1838, [3]; Warren Parrish to Asahel Woodruff, Sept. 9, 1838, Wilford Woodruff, Collection, Church History Library.
48. Vilate Murray Kimball to Heber C. Kimball, Jan. 19–24, 1838, Heber C. Kimball, Collection, Church History Library. The original letter has "there is some of them, that I love, and have a great feeling, and pity for them."
49. Vilate Murray Kimball to Heber C. Kimball, Jan. 19–24, 1838, Heber C. Kimball, Collection, Church History Library; see also Doctrine and Covenants 101:5 (Revelation, Dec. 16–17, 1833, at josephsmithpapers.org).
50. Joseph Smith History, 1838–56, volume B-1, 780; "History of Luke Johnson," *LDS Millennial Star,* Jan. 7, 1865, 27:5.
51. Revelation, Jan. 12, 1838–C, in *JSP,* D5:501–2.
52. Joseph Smith History, 1838–56, volume B-1, 780.
53. Joseph Smith History, 1838–56, volume B-1, 780; Historical Introduction to Revelation, Jan. 12, 1838–C, in *JSP,* D5:500–501.

CHAPTER 26: A HOLY AND CONSECRATED LAND

1. Oliver Cowdery to Joseph Smith, Jan. 21, 1838, in *JSP,* D5:502–5; Oliver Cowdery to Warren Cowdery and Lyman Cowdery, Feb. 4, 1838, in Cowdery, Letterbook, 83; Joseph Smith History, 1838–56, volume B-1, 780.
2. Oliver Cowdery to Joseph Smith, Jan. 21, 1838, in *JSP,* D5:502–5; Minute Book 2, Jan. 20, 1838.
3. Minute Book 2, Jan. 20 and 26, 1838; Oliver Cowdery to Warren Cowdery and Lyman Cowdery, Feb. 4, 1838, in Cowdery, Letterbook, 83–86; Phineas H. Young to Brigham Young and Willard Richards, Dec. 14, 1842, Brigham Young Office Files, Church History Library; see also Doctrine and Covenants 42:30–36 (Revelation, Feb. 9, 1831, at josephsmithpapers.org); Doctrine and Covenants 58:34–36 (Revelation, Aug. 1, 1831, at josephsmithpapers.org); and Doctrine and Covenants 105:28–29 (Revelation, June 22, 1834, at josephsmithpapers.org).
4. Minute Book 2, Jan. 26 and Feb. 5–9, 10, 1838; Oliver Cowdery to Warren Cowdery and Lyman Cowdery, Feb. 4, 1838; Oliver Cowdery to Warren Cowdery and Lyman Cowdery, Feb. 24, 1838, in Cowdery, Letterbook, 85, 87–90. **Topics: High Council; Church Discipline**
5. Oliver Cowdery to Warren Cowdery and Lyman Cowdery, Feb. 4, 1838, in Cowdery, Letterbook, 85–87.
6. Oliver Cowdery to Warren Cowdery and Lyman Cowdery, Feb. 24, 1838, in Cowdery, Letterbook, 88.

7. Oliver Cowdery to Warren Cowdery, Jan. 21, 1838; Oliver Cowdery to Warren Cowdery and Lyman Cowdery, Feb. 4, 1838; Oliver Cowdery to Warren Cowdery and Lyman Cowdery, Feb. 24, 1838, in Cowdery, Letterbook, 80–96; see also Bushman, "Oliver's Joseph," 1–13. **Topic: Oliver Cowdery**
8. Thompson, *Journal of Heber C. Kimball,* 65; Whitney, *Life of Heber C. Kimball,* 154.
9. See Pickup, *Pick and Flower of England,* 61–63.
10. Whitney, *Life of Heber C. Kimball,* 154–57.
11. Joseph Smith, Journal, Mar.–Sept. 1838, 16, in *JSP,* J1:237; Joseph Smith to the Presidency in Kirtland, Ohio, Mar. 29, 1838, in *JSP,* D6:57–59.
12. Joseph Smith to the Presidency in Kirtland, Ohio, Mar. 29, 1838, in *JSP,* D6:57–59.
13. Minutes, Apr. 12, 1838, in *JSP,* D6:83–94; Synopsis of Oliver Cowdery Trial, Apr. 12, 1838, in *JSP,* J1:251–55.
14. Minutes, Apr. 12, 1838, in *JSP,* D6:87–89; Synopsis of Oliver Cowdery Trial, Apr. 12, 1838, in *JSP,* J1:254.
15. Minutes, Apr. 12, 1838, in *JSP,* D6:91.
16. Minutes, Apr. 12, 1838, in *JSP,* D6:89–94; Synopsis of Oliver Cowdery Trial, Apr. 12, 1838, in *JSP,* J1:254–55. **Topics: Church Discipline; Oliver Cowdery**
17. Thompson, *Journal of Heber C. Kimball,* 76; Kimball, *On the Potter's Wheel,* 23.
18. Whitney, *Life of Heber C. Kimball,* 157; Richards, Journal, Mar. 22, 1838.
19. Allen and others, *Men with a Mission,* 17–19, 46–47. **Topics: Early Missionaries; England**
20. Allen and others, *Men with a Mission,* 9, 17, 19, 46–47; Whitney, *Life of Heber C. Kimball,* 174, 191.
21. Richards, Journal, Mar. 22, 1838; Thompson, *Journal of Heber C. Kimball,* 21; Kimball, "Journal and Record," 64; Allen and others, *Men with a Mission,* 61–62; Whitney, *Life of Heber C. Kimball,* 157.
22. Kimball, *Journal of Heber C. Kimball,* 32.
23. Fielding, Journal, 59–63; Allen and others, *Men with a Mission,* 52–53.
24. Doctrine and Covenants 115 (Revelation, Apr. 26, 1838, at josephsmithpapers.org). **Topics: Name of the Church; Far West**
25. Joseph Smith, Journal, May 18–June 1, 1838, in *JSP,* J1:270–71.
26. Walker, "Mormon Land Rights in Caldwell and Daviess Counties," 28–30.
27. LeSueur, "Missouri's Failed Compromise," 134–35.
28. Joseph Smith, Journal, May 18–June 1, 1838, in *JSP,* J1:270–71; "Part 1: 15 February–28 June 1838," in *JSP,* D6:163.
29. Joseph Smith, Journal, May 18–June 1, 1838, in *JSP,* J1:271; Doctrine and Covenants 107:53 (Revelation, circa Apr. 1835, at josephsmithpapers.org); Olmstead, "Far West and Adam-ondi-Ahman," 237–38; Doctrine and Covenants 27:11 (Revelation, circa Aug. 1835, at josephsmithpapers.org); Historical Introduction to Revelation, circa Aug. 1835, in *JSP,* D4:408–9.
30. Joseph Smith, Journal, May 18–June 1, 1838, in *JSP,* J1:271; Joseph Smith History, 1838–56, volume B-1, 798. **Topic: Adam-ondi-Ahman**
31. Minutes, June 28, 1838, in *JSP,* D6:162–67.

CHAPTER 27: WE PROCLAIM OURSELVES FREE

1. Woodruff, Journal, Apr. 26–June 12, 1838.
2. Woodruff, Journal, June 12 and July 1, 1838.
3. Woodruff, Journal, June 30, 1838.
4. Woodruff, Journal, July 1, 1838.
5. Woodruff, Journal, July 1, 1838.
6. Woodruff, Journal, July 3, 1838.
7. "History of John E. Page," *LDS Millennial Star,* Feb. 18, 1865, 27:103.

8. Kirtland Camp, Journal, Mar. 6, 10, and 13, 1838; Baugh, "Kirtland Camp, 1838," 58–61. **Topics: Gathering of Israel; Quorum of the Seventy**
9. "Celebration of the 4th of July," *Elders' Journal,* Aug. 1838, 60.
10. Synopsis of David Whitmer and Lyman Johnson Trials, Apr. 13, 1838, in *JSP,* J1:256–57.
11. Joseph Smith, Journal, May 11, 1838, in *JSP,* J1:268; "History of William E. Mc. Lellin," 2–3, in Historian's Office, Histories of the Twelve, Church History Library.
12. Corrill, *Brief History,* 30, in *JSP,* H2:165–66; Reed Peck to "Dear Friends," Sept. 18, 1839, 20–25, Henry E. Huntington Library, San Marino, CA; *JSP,* H2:97, note 295; see also Matthew 5:13. **Topic: Dissent in the Church**
13. Corrill, *Brief History,* 30, in *JSP,* H2:165–66; Reed Peck to "Dear Friends," Sept. 18, 1839, 22–23, Henry E. Huntington Library, San Marino, CA; *JSP,* H2:97, note 295.
14. *JSP,* D6:170, note 6; "Peace and Violence among 19th-Century Latter-day Saints," Gospel Topics, topics.lds.org. **Topic: Danites**
15. Corrill, *Brief History,* 30–31, in *JSP,* H2:166–67; Sampson Avard and Others to Oliver Cowdery and Others, circa June 17, 1838; Constitution of the Society of the Daughter of Zion, circa Early July 1838, Mormon War Papers, Missouri State Archives, Jefferson City; Joseph Smith, Journal, July 27, 1838; Editorial Note, in *JSP,* J1:274–75, 293; "Part 2: 8 July–29 October 1838," in *JSP,* D6:169–70.
16. "Celebration of the 4th of July," *Elders' Journal,* Aug. 1838, 60; Joseph Smith, Journal, July 4, 1838, in *JSP,* J1:275–76.
17. *Oration Delivered by Mr. S. Rigdon on the 4th of July, 1838,* 3–12. **Topic: Sidney Rigdon**
18. "Celebration of the 4th of July," *Elders' Journal,* Aug. 1838, 60; Pratt, *Autobiography,* 190; Ebenezer Robinson, "Items of Personal History of the Editor," *Return,* Oct. 1889, 149.
19. Eunice Ross Kinney to Wingfield Watson, Sept. 1891, 2–3, typescript, Wingfield Watson, Correspondence, Church History Library.
20. 1840 U.S. Census, Van Buren, Wayne Co., MI, 255[B]; 1850 U.S. Census, Burlington, Racine Co., WI, 152[B]; 1870 U.S. Census, Suamico, Brown Co., WI, 422[A]. Full biographical research for Eunice Ross Franklin (Kinney) and Charles O. Franklin in possession of editors. **Topic: Elijah Able**
21. Elder's Certificate for Elijah Able, Mar. 31, 1836, in Kirtland Elders' Certificates, 61; Nuttall, Diary, May 31, 1879, 29; Reeve, *Religion of a Different Color,* 196–97.
22. Eunice Ross Kinney to Wingfield Watson, Sept. 1891, 1–2, typescript, Wingfield Watson, Correspondence, Church History Library.
23. Eunice Ross Kinney to Wingfield Watson, Sept. 1891, 2–3, typescript, Wingfield Watson, Correspondence, Church History Library; 1 Peter 4:12.
24. Eunice Ross Kinney to Wingfield Watson, Sept. 1891, 3, typescript, Wingfield Watson, Correspondence, Church History Library.
25. See Kerber, "Abolitionists and Amalgamators," 28–30. **Topic: Slavery and Abolition**
26. Eunice Ross Kinney to Wingfield Watson, Sept. 1891, 3–4, typescript, Wingfield Watson, Correspondence, Church History Library.
27. Selections from *Elders' Journal,* Aug. 1838, in *JSP,* D6:216–17; Joseph Smith, Journal, Aug. 1–3, 1838, in *JSP,* J1:296; *Oration Delivered by Mr. S. Rigdon on the 4th of July, 1838* (Far West, MO: Journal Office, 1838).
28. Doctrine and Covenants 115:13 (Revelation, Apr. 26, 1838, at josephsmithpapers.org).
29. Historical Introduction to Revelation, July 8, 1838–C, in *JSP,* D6:184–87.
30. Minute Book 2, Dec. 6–7, 1837; Harper, "Tithing of My People."
31. Joseph Smith, Journal, July 6, 1838, in *JSP,* J1:278–80; Kimball, "History," 84.
32. See "Organizational Charts," in *JSP,* D6:672–74.
33. Doctrine and Covenants 117:5–6, 12–15 (Revelation, July 8, 1838–E, at josephsmithpapers.org). **Topic: Revelations of Joseph Smith**
34. Doctrine and Covenants 119 (Revelation, July 8, 1838–C, at josephsmithpapers.org); Joseph Smith, Journal, July 8, 1838, in *JSP,* J1:288. **Topics: Tithing; Consecration and Stewardship**

35. Doctrine and Covenants 118 (Revelation, July 8, 1838–A, at josephsmithpapers.org); see also Tait and Orton, "Take Special Care of Your Family," 242–49.
36. Doctrine and Covenants 118:6 (Revelation, July 8, 1838–A, at josephsmithpapers.org); Minutes, *Elders' Journal,* Aug. 1838, 61; Joseph Smith History, 1838–56, volume B-1, 803. **Topic: Quorum of the Twelve**
37. Woodruff, Journal, July 14, 1838.
38. Woodruff, Journal, July 16, 1838.
39. Woodruff, Journal, July 20, 1838.
40. Woodruff, Journal, July 30, 1838.
41. Woodruff, Journal, Aug. 9, 1838; Woodruff, *Leaves from My Journal,* 51.

CHAPTER 28: TRIED LONG ENOUGH

1. Butler, "Short History," 17–18; Hartley, *My Best for the Kingdom,* 39; Durham, "Election Day Battle at Gallatin," 39–40.
2. Butler, "Short History," 17; Hartley, *My Best for the Kingdom,* 48–50.
3. Butler, "Short History," 15–16; Hartley, *My Best for the Kingdom,* 39; Durham, "Election Day Battle at Gallatin," 39–40.
4. Butler, "Short Account of an Affray," [1]; Rigdon, *Appeal to the American People,* 17–18.
5. Britton, *Early Days on Grand River,* 6–7; Butler, "Short History," 18; Corrill, *Brief History,* 28, in *JSP,* H2:162–63.
6. Historian's Office, Journal History of the Church, Aug. 6, 1838; Butler, "Short History," 18; Butler, "Short Account of an Affray," [1].
7. John D. Lee and Levi Steward, Statement, circa 1845, in Joseph Smith History Documents, 1839–60, Church History Library; Butler, "Short Account of an Affray," [1]; see also Greene, *Facts Relative to the Expulsion,* 18.
8. Butler, "Short History," 18; Butler, "Short Account of an Affray," [1]; Hartley, *My Best for the Kingdom,* 11.
9. Butler, "Short History," 18; Butler, "Short Account of an Affray," [1].
10. Butler, "Short Account of an Affray," [1]–[4].
11. Butler, "Short History," 19.
12. Butler, "Short Account of an Affray," [4]; Butler, "Short History," 18. The original source has "They then said they must take me prisner" and "I told them I was a law abiding man, but I did not intend to be tried by a mob." **Topic: Mormon-Missouri War of 1838**
13. Butler, "Short History," 20.
14. Affidavit, Sept. 5, 1838, in *JSP,* D6:223–25; Joseph Smith, Journal, Aug. 7–9 and 10, 1838, in *JSP,* J1:298–301; see also *JSP,* J1:300, note 225. **Topic: Danites**
15. Joseph Smith, Journal, Aug. 11, 13, and 16–18, 1838, in *JSP,* J1:302–4; *JSP,* J1:303, note 234; 304, notes 237–38; see also "Public Meeting," *Missouri Republican,* Sept. 8, 1838, [1], "for the country" edition.
16. Historical Introduction to Discourse, Aug. 12, 1838, in *JSP,* D6:213; "The Mormons in Carroll County," *Missouri Republican,* Aug. 18, 1838, [2]; "Public Meeting," *Missouri Republican,* Sept. 3, 1838, [2]; Corrill, *Brief History,* 35, in *JSP,* H2:173–74; *JSP,* D6:534, note 326. **Topic: Vigilantism**
17. Recognizance, Sept. 7, 1838, in *JSP,* D6:226–28; "The Mormon Difficulties," *Niles' National Register,* Oct. 13, 1838, 103; Joseph Smith, Journal, Sept. 2, 4, and 7, 1838, in *JSP,* J1:312–13, 314, 316–17.
18. Joseph Smith to Stephen Post, Sept. 17, 1838, in *JSP,* D6:244.
19. Woodruff, Journal, Aug. 31, 1838.
20. Woodruff, Journal, Aug. 11, 1838.
21. "On Leaving Home," in Phebe Carter Woodruff, Autograph Book, Church History Library.

22. Woodruff, Journal, Sept. 11 and 25, 1838. The word "me" has been added for clarity.
23. Woodruff, Journal, Sept. 11 and 15; Sept. 25–Oct. 1, 1838.
24. Woodruff, Journal, Sept. 24–25, 1838.
25. Woodruff, Journal, Sept. 11, 22–25, 1838; Oct. 3–4, 1838; see also Ruth 1:15–16.
26. Joseph Smith History, 1838–56, volume B-1, 830; Rockwood, Journal, Oct. 1838–Jan. 1839, Oct. 29, 1838; "De Witt, Missouri," Geographical Entry, Joseph Smith Papers website, josephsmithpapers.org.
27. *History of Carroll County, Missouri*, 249–50; Murdock, Journal, 95; "Part 3: 4 November 1838–16 April 1839," in *JSP*, D6:365.
28. *History of Carroll County, Missouri*, 250–52; Joseph Dickson to Lilburn W. Boggs, Sept. 6, 1838; David Atchison to Lilburn W. Boggs, Sept. 17, 1838, Mormon War Papers, Missouri State Archives, Jefferson City; Joseph Smith History, 1838–56, volume B-1, 827–28; Citizens of De Witt, MO, to Lilburn W. Boggs, Sept. 22, 1838, copy, Mormon War Papers, Missouri State Archives.
29. "Biographies of the Seventies of the Second Quorum," 208–9, in Seventies Quorum Records, Church History Library; Horace G. Whitney, "Nauvoo Brass Band," *Contributor*, Mar. 1880, 134; Baugh, *Call to Arms*, 67.
30. "Biographies of the Seventies of the Second Quorum," 208–10, in Seventies Quorum Records, Church History Library; Joseph Smith History, 1838–56, volume B-1, 828, 831; Baugh, *Call to Arms*, 67; *History of Carroll County, Missouri*, 251–52; Murdock, Journal, 100–102.
31. Joseph Smith History, 1838–56, volume B-1, 833–35; *History of Carroll County, Missouri*, 253; Sidney Rigdon, Testimony, July 1, 1843, [3], Nauvoo, IL, Records, Church History Library.
32. Switzler, *Switzler's Illustrated History of Missouri*, [246].
33. Joseph Smith, Bill of Damages, June 4, 1839, in *JSP*, D6:496–97; Joseph Smith History, 1838–56, volume B-1, 834–35; see also Switzler, *Switzler's Illustrated History of Missouri*, [246]; *History of Carroll County, Missouri*, 255.
34. Joseph Smith History, 1838–56, volume B-1, 833–36; Joseph Smith, Bill of Damages, June 4, 1839, in *JSP*, D6:497–98.
35. "Biographies of the Seventies of the Second Quorum," 209, in Seventies Quorum Records, Church History Library.
36. Joseph Smith History, 1838–56, volume B-1, 836–37; Rockwood, Journal, Oct. 1838–Jan. 1839, Oct. 14, 15, and Nov. 11, 1838.
37. Reed Peck to "Dear Friends," Sept. 18, 1839, 78–80, Henry E. Huntington Library, San Marino, CA. **Topic: American Legal and Political Institutions**
38. Corrill, *Brief History*, 36, in *JSP*, H2:176. **Topic: Mormon-Missouri War of 1838**

Chapter 29: God and Liberty

1. Memorial to the U.S. Senate and House of Representatives, circa Oct. 30, 1839–Jan. 27, 1840, in *JSP*, 7:159–60.
2. Rigdon, *Appeal to the American People*, 41–42; *Document Containing the Correspondence*, 99, 124–26; Baugh, *Call to Arms*, 84–85.
3. Memorial to the U.S. Senate and House of Representatives, circa Oct. 30, 1839–Jan. 27, 1840, 22, in *JSP*, D7:162; Rigdon, *Appeal to the American People*, 43; Hyrum Smith, Testimony, July 1, 1843, Nauvoo, IL, Records, Church History Library; Rigdon, *Appeal to the American People*, 43; see also Baugh, *Call to Arms*, 85, 95, note 30.
4. Rigdon, *Appeal to the American People*, 43.
5. Rigdon, *Appeal to the American People*, 41–42; *Document Containing the Correspondence*, 99, 124–26; Baugh, *Call to Arms*, 84–86.
6. Historical Introduction to Agreement with Jacob Stollings, Apr. 12, 1839, in *JSP*, D6:417; Sampson Avard, Testimony, Nov. 12, 1838, 7, Mormon War Papers, Missouri

State Archives, Jefferson City; Corrill, *Brief History,* 37, in *JSP,* H2:177; Huntington, Diary and Reminiscences, 22–23.

7. Corrill, *Brief History,* 37, in *JSP,* H2:177; Reed Peck to "Dear Friends," Sept. 18, 1839, 85, Henry E. Huntington Library, San Marino, CA; Philip Covington, Statement, Sept. 2, 1838, Mormon War Papers, Missouri State Archives, Jefferson City; Huntington, Diary and Reminiscences, 22; J. H. McGee, Porter Yale, and Patrick Lynch, Testimonies, in *Document Containing the Correspondence,* 141–43, 145. **Topic: Mormon-Missouri War of 1838**

8. Baugh, *Call to Arms,* 87; see also Huntington, Diary and Reminiscences, 22.

9. George A. Smith, in *Journal of Discourses,* Apr. 6, 1856, 3:283–84.

10. "History of Brigham Young," *LDS Millennial Star,* June 25, 1864, 26:406.

11. See Thomas B. Marsh and Orson Hyde to Lewis Marsh and Ann Marsh Abbott, Oct. 25–30, 1838, in Joseph Smith Letterbook 2, 18–19; "Part 3: 4 November 1838–16 April 1839," in *JSP,* D6:268; Thomas B. Marsh, in *Journal of Discourses,* Sept. 6, 1857, 5:206–7.

12. Corrill, *Brief History,* 38, in *JSP,* H2:178; Baugh, *Call to Arms,* 99–102.

13. Thomas B. Marsh and Orson Hyde to Lewis Marsh and Ann Marsh Abbott, Oct. 25–30, 1838, in Joseph Smith Letterbook 2, 18–19.

14. See Thomas B. Marsh and Orson Hyde, Affidavit, Oct. 24, 1838, copy, Mormon War Papers, Missouri State Archives, Jefferson City; and Darowski, "The Faith and Fall of Thomas Marsh," 54–60. **Topic: Thomas B. Marsh**

15. Hales, *Windows,* 34–35.

16. Lilburn W. Boggs to John B. Clark, Oct. 27, 1838, copy, Mormon War Papers, Missouri State Archives, Jefferson City.

17. Hendricks, Reminiscences, 19.

18. Hendricks, Reminiscences, 19.

19. Hales, *Windows,* 35, 38; Pratt, *History of the Late Persecution,* 33; Thomas B. Marsh and Orson Hyde, Affidavits, Oct. 24, 1838, copy, Mormon War Papers, Missouri State Archives, Jefferson City; "History of Brigham Young," *LDS Millennial Star,* July 9, 1864, 26:440.

20. Pratt, *Autobiography,* 194–95; "History of Brigham Young," *LDS Millennial Star,* July 9, 1864, 26:440.

21. "History of Brigham Young," *LDS Millennial Star,* July 9, 1864, 26:440; Corrill, *Brief History,* 39, in *JSP,* H2:180; Holbrook, Reminiscences, 48.

22. Reed Peck to "Dear Friends," Sept. 18, 1839, 96–97, Henry E. Huntington Library, San Marino, CA; John Lockhart, Testimony, in *Senate Document 189,* 35–36.

23. Reed Peck to "Dear Friends," Sept. 18, 1839, 96–97, Henry E. Huntington Library, San Marino, CA; Baugh, *Call to Arms,* 47–48.

24. "The Mormons," *Missouri Argus,* Nov. 8, 1838, [2]; "History of Brigham Young," *LDS Millennial Star,* July 9, 1838, 26:441.

25. Holbrook, Reminiscences, 48; "History of Brigham Young," *LDS Millennial Star,* July 9, 1864, 26:441.

26. "History of Brigham Young," *LDS Millennial Star,* July 9, 1864, 26:440–41; Reed Peck to "Dear Friends," Sept. 18, 1839, 98, Henry E. Huntington Library, San Marino, CA; Corrill, *Brief History,* 39, in *JSP,* H2:180; Pratt, *History of the Late Persecution,* 35.

27. Pratt, *History of the Late Persecution,* 35–36; "History of Brigham Young," *LDS Millennial Star,* July 9, 1864, 26:441; see also *JSP,* H2:246, notes 163–64.

28. Hendricks, Reminiscences, 20.

29. "History of Brigham Young," *LDS Millennial Star,* July 9, 1884, 26:441; see also Samuel Bogart to David R. Atchison, Oct. 23, 1838, Mormon War Papers, Missouri State Archives, Jefferson City. **Topic: Mormon-Missouri War of 1838**

30. Samuel Bogart to David R. Atchison, Oct. 23, 1838, Mormon War Papers, Missouri State Archives, Jefferson City; Pratt, *History of the Late Persecution,* 37. **Topic: Vigilantism**

31. Sashel Woods and Joseph Dickson to "Sir," Oct. 24, 1838, Mormon War Papers, Missouri State Archives, Jefferson City.

32. Thomas B. Marsh, Affidavit, Oct. 24, 1838, Mormon War Papers, Missouri State Archives, Jefferson City.
33. Orson Hyde, Affidavit, Oct. 24, 1838, Mormon War Papers, Missouri State Archives, Jefferson City.
34. Lilburn W. Boggs to John B. Clark, Oct. 27, 1838, copy, Mormon War Papers, Missouri State Archives, Jefferson City. **Topic: Extermination Order**

CHAPTER 30: FIGHT LIKE ANGELS

1. See Baugh, "Joseph Young's Affidavit of the Massacre at Haun's Mill," 192; Greene, *Facts Relative to the Expulsion*, 22.
2. Tullidge, *Women of Mormondom*, 121; Smith, Notebook, 9–10; Baugh, "Rare Account of the Haun's Mill Massacre," 166; Baugh, *Call to Arms*, 118. The account in Tullidge, *Women of Mormondom*, quotes a first-person statement by Amanda Barnes Smith.
3. Smith, Notebook, 9–10; "Amanda Smith," *Woman's Exponent*, Apr. 1, 1881, 9:165; "History, of the Persecution," *Times and Seasons*, Aug. 1840, 1:145, in *JSP*, H2:260; Kirtland Camp, Journal, Oct. 24, 1838.
4. Smith, Notebook, 10; Tullidge, *Women of Mormondom*, 121; Amanda Smith, Affidavit, May 7, 1839, in Johnson, *Mormon Redress Petitions*, 538; Isaac Leany, Statement, Apr. 20, 1839, photocopy, United States Congress, Material Relating to Mormon Expulsion from Missouri, 1839–43, Church History Library; Baugh, "Rare Account of the Haun's Mill Massacre," 166. **Topic: Hawn's Mill Massacre**
5. Smith, Notebook, 9; "History, of the Persecution," *Times and Seasons*, Aug. 1840, 1:145, in *JSP*, H2:260; Baugh, *Call to Arms*, 116–17.
6. "History, of the Persecution," *Times and Seasons*, Aug. 1840, 1:145, in *JSP*, H2:261; Tullidge, *Women of Mormondom*, 121–22; Smith, Notebook, 10; "Amanda Smith," *Woman's Exponent*, Apr. 1 and 15, 1881, 9:165, 173; Amanda Smith, Affidavit, May 7, 1839, in Johnson, *Mormon Redress Petitions*, 538.
7. Lewis, Autobiography, 12; Smith, Notebook, 10–11; "History, of the Persecution," *Times and Seasons*, Aug. 1840, 1:146, in *JSP*, H2:261.
8. Smith, Notebook, 11; Tullidge, *Women of Mormondom*, 121–22, 126; "Amanda Smith," *Woman's Exponent*, Apr. 15 and May 1, 1881, 9:173, 181; Ellis Eamut, Statement, circa 1839, Joseph Smith History Documents, 1839–60, Church History Library; Baugh, *Call to Arms*, 120; Dunn, *Amanda's Journal*, 3.
9. Lewis, Autobiography, 12–14; Ellis Eamut, Statement, circa 1839, Joseph Smith History Documents, 1839–60, Church History Library; Baugh, "Rare Account of the Haun's Mill Massacre," 166; Smith, Notebook, 12.
10. "History, of the Persecution," *Times and Seasons*, Aug. 1840, 1:146, in *JSP*, H2:262; *History of Caldwell and Livingston Counties*, 147; Greene, *Facts Relative to the Expulsion*, 22; Baugh, *Call to Arms*, 120–23.
11. *Document Containing the Correspondence*, 82; Smith, Notebook, 13; Tullidge, *Women of Mormondom*, 123.
12. Smith, Notebook, 12; "History, of the Persecution," *Times and Seasons*, Aug. 1840, 1:147, in *JSP*, H2:263; Tullidge, *Women of Mormondom*, 127.
13. Tullidge, *Women of Mormondom*, 127.
14. Hyrum Smith, Testimony, July 1, 1843, 8, Nauvoo, IL, Records, Church History Library; Samuel D. Lucas to Lilburn W. Boggs, Nov. 2, 1838, Mormon War Papers, Missouri State Archives, Jefferson City. **Topic: Mormon-Missouri War of 1838**
15. Thorp, *Early Days in the West*, 88; Hyrum Smith, Testimony, July 1, 1843, 8–9, Nauvoo, IL, Records, Church History Library; Baugh, *Call to Arms*, 137–38; Corrill, *Brief History*, 40, in *JSP*, H2:183.
16. Durham, *Gospel Kingdom*, 354; Joseph Smith, Journal, Dec. 30, 1842, in *JSP*, J2:199–200.

17. "Mary Elizabeth Rollins Lightner," *Utah Genealogical and Historical Magazine*, July 1926, 199. The original source is a first-person account from Mary Lightner and has "our two families" rather than "your two families."

18. "Mary Elizabeth Rollins Lightner," *Utah Genealogical and Historical Magazine*, July 1926, 199. Original source has "I then said that he could go, and take the child with him, if he wanted to, but I would suffer with the rest."

19. Joseph Smith, Journal, Dec. 30, 1842, in *JSP,* J2:200.

20. Samuel D. Lucas to Lilburn W. Boggs, Nov. 2, 1838, Mormon War Papers, Missouri State Archives, Jefferson City.

21. "Lucas, Samuel D.," Biographical Entry, Joseph Smith Papers website, josephsmithpapers.org.

22. Ebenezer Robinson, "Items of Personal History of the Editor," *Return,* Jan. 1890, 2:206; Samuel D. Lucas to Lilburn W. Boggs, Nov. 2, 1838, Mormon War Papers, Missouri State Archives, Jefferson City.

23. James C. Owens, Testimony, Nov. 1838, [47], in State of Missouri, "Evidence"; Ebenezer Robinson, "Items of Personal History of the Editor," *Return,* Jan. 1890, 2:206; Burr Rigs, Testimony, in *Document Containing the Correspondence*, 135.

24. Corrill, *Brief History,* 40, in *JSP,* H2:183; George Hinkle, Testimony, in *Document Containing the Correspondence,* 127; Pratt, *History of the Late Persecution,* 39.

25. Baugh, "Rare Account of the Haun's Mill Massacre," 166–67; Baugh, *Call to Arms,* 123.

26. Baugh, "Rare Account of the Haun's Mill Massacre," 167; Tullidge, *Women of Mormondom,* 123.

27. Smith, Notebook, 13; Tullidge, *Women of Mormondom,* 123–24; Dunn, *Amanda's Journal,* 3–5.

28. Baugh, "Rare Account of the Haun's Mill Massacre," 167; Tullidge, *Women of Mormondom,* 123.

29. Tullidge, *Women of Mormondom,* 124; Baugh, "Rare Account of the Haun's Mill Massacre," 167; Dunn, *Amanda's Journal,* 4. **Topic: Healing**

30. Tullidge, *Women of Mormondom,* 124–25. **Topic: Amanda Barnes Smith**

31. Corrill, *Brief History,* 40–42, in *JSP,* H2:183–85; Baugh, *Call to Arms,* 139–40.

32. Foote, Autobiography and Journal, Oct. 30, 1838; Albert Perry Rockwood, Journal, Nov. 2, 1838; Hyrum Smith, Testimony, July 1, 1843, 11, Nauvoo, IL, Records, Church History Library.

33. Hyrum Smith, Testimony, July 1, 1843, 9–10, Nauvoo, IL, Records, Church History Library; Pratt, *Autobiography,* 219–24.

34. Corrill, *Brief History,* 41, in *JSP,* H2:183.

35. Corrill, *Brief History,* 41–42, in *JSP,* H2:183–86; Samuel D. Lucas to Lilburn W. Boggs, Nov. 2, 1838, Mormon War Papers, Missouri State Archives, Jefferson City; Baugh, *Call to Arms,* 140–41. **Topic: Extermination Order**

36. "Extract, from the Private Journal of Joseph Smith Jr.," *Times and Seasons*, Nov. 1, 1839, 1:5, in *JSP,* H1:477–79; Reed Peck to "Dear Friends," Sept. 18, 1839, Henry E. Huntington Library, San Marino, CA; Baugh, *Call to Arms,* 141.

37. Hyrum Smith, Testimony, July 1, 1843, 12–13, Nauvoo, IL, Records, Church History Library.

38. Hyrum Smith, Testimony, July 1, 1843, 12–13, Nauvoo, IL, Records, Church History Library; Pratt, *History of the Late Persecution,* 40; *JSP,* H2:251, note 181; Corrill, *Brief History,* 42, in *JSP,* H2:186; "Extract, from the Private Journal of Joseph Smith Jr.," *Times and Seasons,* Nov. 1, 1840, 1:5, in *JSP,* H1:477–79.

CHAPTER 31: HOW WILL THIS END?

1. Gates, *Lydia Knight's History,* 43–46.

2. Gates, *Lydia Knight's History,* 47.

3. Samuel D. Lucas to Lilburn W. Boggs, Nov. 2, 1838, Mormon War Papers, Missouri State Archives, Jefferson City; Ebenezer Robinson, "Items of Personal History of the Editor," *Return,* Feb. 1890, 210.

4. Gentry and Compton, *Fire and Sword,* 358–60.

5. Gates, *Lydia Knight's History,* 47.

6. Samuel D. Lucas to Lilburn W. Boggs, Nov. 2, 1838, Mormon War Papers, Missouri State Archives, Jefferson City.

7. Samuel D. Lucas to Lilburn W. Boggs, Nov. 2, 1838, Mormon War Papers, Missouri State Archives, Jefferson City; Hyrum Smith, Testimony, July 1, 1843, 11, Nauvoo, IL, Records, Church History Library; Brigham Young, Testimony, July 1, 1843, [2], Nauvoo, IL, Records, Church History Library; Kimball, "History," 94.

8. Gates, *Lydia Knight's History,* 48–49.

9. Ebenezer Page, "For Zion's Reveille," *Zion's Reveille,* Apr. 15, 1847, 55.

10. Kimball, "History," [88].

11. See Whitney, *Life of Heber C. Kimball,* 83.

12. Kimball, "History," [88].

13. Gates, *Lydia Knight's History,* 48; Hyrum Smith, Testimony, July 1, 1843, 13, Nauvoo, IL, Records, Church History Library.

14. Joseph Smith and Others to the Church and Edward Partridge, Mar. 20, 1839, 3, in *JSP,* D6:362; Hyrum Smith, Testimony, July 1, 1843, 13, 24; Brigham Young, Testimony, July 1, 1843, [2], Nauvoo, IL, Records, Church History Library; "Part 3: 4 November 1838–16 April 1839," in *JSP,* D6:271–72. **Topic: Mormon-Missouri War of 1838**

15. See "Mormonism," *United States' Telegraph,* Aug. 21, 1833, [2]; Hyrum Smith, Testimony, July 1, 1843, 13, Nauvoo, IL, Records, Church History Library; and Samuel D. Lucas to Lilburn W. Boggs, Nov. 2, 1838, Mormon War Papers, Missouri State Archives, Jefferson City.

16. Lyman Wight, Testimony, July 1, 1843, 20–21, 23, Nauvoo, IL, Records, Church History Library; Hyrum Smith, Testimony, July 1, 1843, 13, Nauvoo, IL, Records, Church History Library.

17. Lyman Wight, Testimony, July 1, 1843, 24, Nauvoo, IL, Records, Church History Library; "History of Lyman Wight," *LDS Millennial Star,* July 22, 1865, 29:457.

18. Lyman Wight, Journal, in *History of the Reorganized Church,* 2:260; "Part 3: 4 November 1838–16 April 1839," in *JSP,* D6:271; Hyrum Smith, Testimony, July 1, 1843, 13–14, Nauvoo, IL, Records, Church History Library; Eliza R. Snow to Isaac Streator, Feb. 22, 1839, photocopy, Church History Library; Alanson Ripley, Letter to the Editor, *Times and Seasons,* Jan. 1840, 1:37; see also Baugh, *Call to Arms,* 150–51.

19. Lyman Wight, Testimony, July 1, 1843, 24, Nauvoo, IL, Records, Church History Library.

20. *History of Caldwell and Livingston Counties,* 137; Lyman Wight, Testimony, July 1, 1843, 24, Nauvoo, IL, Records, Church History Library; "History, of the Persecution," *Times and Seasons,* July 1840, 1:130–31, in *JSP,* H2:258.

21. Hyrum Smith, Testimony, July 1, 1843, 14, Nauvoo, IL, Records, Church History Library; *History of Caldwell and Livingston Counties,* 137; Rigdon, *Appeal to the American People,* 51.

22. *History of Caldwell and Livingston Counties,* 137; see also Joseph Smith, Journal, Dec. 30, 1842, in *JSP,* J2:198; and Rigdon, "Lecture," 59–60.

23. Joseph Smith, Journal, Dec. 30, 1842, in *JSP,* J2:198.

24. Hyrum Smith, Testimony, July 1, 1843, 14–15, Nauvoo, IL, Records, Church History Library; Joseph Smith and Others to Edward Partridge and the Church, circa Mar. 22, 1839, in *JSP,* D6:395; Doctrine and Covenants 122:6; Joseph Smith, Bill of Damages, June 4, 1839, [6], in *JSP,* D6:502.

25. Joseph Smith, Journal, Dec. 30, 1842, in *JSP,* J2:198; Joseph Smith, Bill of Damages, June 4, 1839, [6], in *JSP,* D6:502; see also Lyman Wight, Testimony, July 1, 1843, 26, Nauvoo, IL, Records, Church History Library.

26. Hyrum Smith, Testimony, July 1, 1843, 15, Nauvoo, IL, Records, Church History Library; Lucy Mack Smith, History, 1844–45, book 16, [3].

27. Lucy Mack Smith, History, 1844–45, book 16, [3]–[4]; Lucy Mack Smith, History, 1845, 280–81. **Topic: Lucy Mack Smith**
28. Hyrum Smith, Testimony, July 1, 1843, 15–16, 18, Nauvoo, IL, Records, Church History Library; Parley P. Pratt to Willard Richards, Nov. 7, 1853, *Deseret News,* Nov. 12, 1853, [3].
29. Parley P. Pratt to Willard Richards, Nov. 7, 1853, *Deseret News,* Nov. 12, 1853, [3]; Pratt, *Autobiography,* 228–30.
30. Hyrum Smith, Testimony, July 1, 1843, 18, Nauvoo, IL, Records, Church History Library; see also "King, Austin Augustus," Biographical Entry, Joseph Smith Papers website, josephsmithpapers.org. **Topic: American Legal and Political Institutions**
31. Transcript of Proceedings, Richmond, MO, Nov. 1838, State of Missouri v. Joseph Smith and Others for Treason and Other Crimes, in State of Missouri, "Evidence"; "Part 3: 4 November 1838–16 April 1839," in *JSP,* D6:272–73; Madsen, "Joseph Smith and the Missouri Court of Inquiry," 93–136; *JSP,* H2:167, note 140.
32. *Document Containing the Correspondence,* 90; Gentry and Compton, *Fire and Sword,* 240, 408–9; Rigdon, *Appeal to the American People,* 66.
33. Sampson Avard, Testimony, Nov. 1838, [2]–[23], State of Missouri v. Joseph Smith and Others for Treason and Other Crimes, in State of Missouri, "Evidence"; *Document Containing the Correspondence,* 97, 99.
34. Pratt, *Autobiography,* 230; Parley P. Pratt, Testimony, July 1, 1843, 8, Nauvoo, IL, Records, Church History Library.
35. Hyrum Smith, Testimony, July 1, 1843, 18–19, Nauvoo, IL, Records, Church History Library; LeSueur, "High Treason and Murder," 7–13; Court Documents for State of Missouri v. Joseph Smith and Others for Treason and Other Crimes, in State of Missouri, "Evidence"; *Document Containing the Correspondence,* 97–151.
36. Pratt, *History of the Late Persecution,* 55; see also *Document Containing the Correspondence,* 150; and State of Missouri, "Evidence," [124]–[25].
37. Hyrum Smith, Testimony, July 1, 1843, 21, Nauvoo, IL, Records, Church History Library; Joseph Smith to Emma Smith, Dec. 1, 1838, in *JSP,* D6:293–94; Littlefield, *Reminiscences of Latter-day Saints,* 79–80; "Jail, Liberty, Missouri," Geographical Entry, Joseph Smith Papers website, josephsmithpapers.org.
38. Littlefield, *Reminiscences of Latter-day Saints,* 80. **Topic: Liberty Jail**

CHAPTER 32: THOUGH ALL HELL SHOULD ENDEAVOR

1. Joseph Smith History, 1838–56, volume C-1, 856–57; Greene, *Facts Relative to the Expulsion,* 13–14; "History, of the Persecution," *Times and Seasons,* Sept. 1840, 1:161–62, in *JSP,* H2:272–73.
2. John B. Clark to Lilburn W. Boggs, Nov. 10, 1838, Mormon War Papers, Missouri State Archives, Jefferson City; see also Esplin, "Emergence of Brigham Young," 348.
3. "Speech of General Clarke," Nov. 6, 1838, in Joseph Smith Letterbook 2, [i]–1; Greene, *Facts Relative to the Expulsion,* 26–27; see also John B. Clark, Report to Lilburn W. Boggs, Jefferson City, MO, Nov. 29, 1838, Mormon War Papers, Missouri State Archives, Jefferson City. The earliest copies of John B. Clark's discourse have "Never again organize yourselves with bishops, presidents, etc."
4. Smith, Notebook, 14–15; "Amanda Smith," *Woman's Exponent,* May 15, 1881, 9:189.
5. Tullidge, *Women of Mormondom,* 129; "Amanda Smith," *Woman's Exponent,* May 15, 1881, 9:189.
6. See Hartley, "Saints' Forced Exodus from Missouri," 347–90.
7. Woodruff, Journal, Oct. 1, 27, and 31, 1838; Historical Department, Journal History of the Church, Oct. 9, 1838.
8. Woodruff, Journal, Nov. 3, 7, 9, and 16, 1838.
9. Woodruff, Journal, Nov. 23–30, 1838; Historical Department, Journal History of the Church, Oct. 9, 1838.

10. Woodruff, Journal, Dec. 1–2, 1838; Historical Department, Journal History of the Church, Oct. 9, 1838.

11. Historical Department, Journal History of the Church, Oct. 9, 1838. **Topic: Healing**

12. "Clay County, Missouri," *Historical Record,* Dec. 1888, 7:670; "Liberty Jail," history .lds.org; Joseph Smith to Isaac Galland, Mar. 22, 1839, in *JSP,* D6:380; Joseph Smith to Emma Smith, Apr. 4, 1839, in *JSP,* D6:403; Hyrum Smith, Testimony, July 1, 1843, 21–22; Lyman Wight, Testimony, July 1, 1843, 30–31, Nauvoo, IL, Records, Church History Library; Bray, "Within the Walls of Liberty Jail," 258–59. **Topic: Liberty Jail**

13. *History of the Reorganized Church,* 2:309.

14. Joseph Smith to the Church in Caldwell County, MO, Dec. 16, 1838, in *JSP,* D6:294–310.

15. Hyrum Smith Family Bible; *History of the Reorganized Church,* 2:315; Thompson, Autobiographical Sketch, 3–4.

16. *History of the Reorganized Church,* 2:315; Thompson, Autobiographical Sketch, 2, 4.

17. "Recollections of the Prophet Joseph Smith," *Juvenile Instructor,* July 1, 1892, 27:398.

18. Thompson, Autobiographical Sketch, 4; "Recollections of the Prophet Joseph Smith," *Juvenile Instructor,* July 1, 1892, 27:398.

19. Joseph Smith and Others to Heber C. Kimball and Brigham Young, Jan. 16, 1839, in *JSP,* D6:310–16. **Topic: Quorum of the Twelve**

20. Minute Book 2, Dec. 13, 1838.

21. Albert P. Rockwood to "Dear Beloved Father," Jan. 1839, in Jessee and Whittaker, "Albert Perry Rockwood Journal," 34; Joseph Smith and Others to Heber C. Kimball and Brigham Young, Jan. 16, 1839, in *JSP,* D6:310–16.

22. Far West Committee, Minutes, Jan. 29 and Feb. 2, 1839; Joseph Smith History, 1838–56, volume C-1, 881–83.

23. Huntington, Diary and Reminiscences, 45; Joseph Smith History, 1838–56, volume C-1, 884; Hartley, "Saints' Forced Exodus from Missouri," 347–90.

24. In a March 22, 1839, letter to Isaac Galland, Joseph Smith refers to "five children." The fifth child was apparently Johanna Carter, an orphan who would have been about fifteen in 1839. There is some evidence that Johanna was staying with the Smiths in Far West and that she was still with Emma Smith in Quincy; Joseph again mentioned Johanna among his children in an April 4, 1839, letter to Emma. (Joseph Smith to Isaac Galland, Mar. 22, 1839, in *JSP,* D6:382; Joseph Smith to Emma Smith, Apr. 4, 1839, in *JSP,* D6:404; see also *JSP,* D6:382, note 674; 404, note 817.)

25. Joseph Smith History, 1838–56, volume C-1, 884; Mary Audentia Smith Anderson, "Memoirs of President Joseph Smith," *Saints' Herald,* Nov. 6, 1934, 1416; Cooper, "Spiritual Reminiscences.—No. 2," 18. **Topic: Emma Hale Smith**

26. Joseph Smith History, 1838–56, volume C-1, 885; Mary Audentia Smith Anderson, "Memoirs of President Joseph Smith," *Saints' Herald,* Nov. 6, 1934, 1416; see also Cooper, "Spiritual Reminiscences.—No. 2," 18.

27. Leonard, *Nauvoo,* 33; Hartley, "Winter Exodus from Missouri," 18; Bennett, "Study of the Mormons in Quincy," 103–18.

28. Emma Smith to Joseph Smith, Mar. 7, 1839, in *JSP,* D6:339–40.

29. Tullidge, *Women of Mormondom,* 128–29.

30. *Collection of Sacred Hymns,* 112; see also "How Firm a Foundation," *Hymns,* no. 85. Amanda Barnes Smith's account in Tullidge's *Women of Mormondom* has a few wording changes to the hymn text: "That soul who on Jesus hath leaned for repose, I cannot, I will not desert to its foes."

31. Tullidge, *Women of Mormondom,* 129–30.

32. Smith, Notebook, 25; Tullidge, *Women of Mormondom,* 128, 131–32; "Amanda Smith," *Woman's Exponent,* May 15, 1881, 9:189; Baugh, "Rare Account of the Haun's Mill Massacre," 168; Baugh, "I'll Never Forsake," 338. **Topic: Amanda Barnes Smith**

33. Hendricks, Reminiscences, 20–22.

34. Woodruff, Journal, Mar. 13–16, 1839; see also Woodruff, Journal, Sept. 12 and 25, 1838; Oct. 1, 1838. **Topic: Quincy, Illinois, Settlement**

35. Hartley, "Saints' Forced Exodus from Missouri," 347–90; Edward Partridge to Joseph Smith and Others, Mar. 5, 1839, in *JSP,* D6:326–31.
36. Edward Partridge to Joseph Smith and Others, Mar. 5, 1839, in *JSP,* D6:329; Woodruff, Journal, Mar. 16, 1839.
37. Woodruff, Journal, Mar. 17–18, 1839; Joseph Smith History, 1838–56, volume C-1, 898–99.
38. Woodruff, Journal, Mar. 18, 1839.
39. Joseph Smith History, 1838–56, volume C-1, 884, 888, 891–92, 894. **Topic: Gathering of Israel**

CHAPTER 33: O GOD, WHERE ART THOU?

1. See Jessee, "Walls, Grates and Screeking Iron Doors," 26; and Baugh, "Joseph Smith in Northern Missouri," 329.
2. Hyrum Smith, Diary, Oct. 29, 1838–Feb. 5, 1839; Report, *Saints' Herald,* Aug. 2, 1884, 490; "Part 3: 4 November 1838–16 April 1839," in *JSP,* D6:276; Joseph Smith to Isaac Galland, Mar. 22, 1839, in *JSP,* D6:379; Sidney Rigdon, Testimony, July 1, 1843, [22]–[23], Nauvoo, IL, Records, Church History Library.
3. Hyrum Smith, Diary, Mar. 18 and 31, 1839; Apr. 3, 1839; Hyrum Smith, Testimony, July 1, 1843, 22, Nauvoo, IL, Records, Church History Library; Joseph Smith to Isaac Galland, Mar. 22, 1839, in *JSP,* D6:380; see also Jessee, "Walls, Grates and Screeking Iron Doors," 28.
4. Hyrum Smith to Mary Fielding Smith, Mar. 16, 1839, Mary Fielding Smith Collection, Church History Library; Jessee, "Walls, Grates and Screeking Iron Doors," 30–31.
5. See Joseph Smith and Others to the Church and Edward Partridge, Mar. 20, 1839, in *JSP,* D6:361–62.
6. Joseph Smith and Others to the Church and Edward Partridge, Mar. 20, 1839, in *JSP,* D6:362; Doctrine and Covenants 121:1–2; see also Psalms 44:23–24; 77:6–9.
7. Woodruff, Journal, Apr. 17, 1839; Doctrine and Covenants 118:5 (Revelation, July 8, 1838–A, at josephsmithpapers.org); Historian's Office, Brigham Young History Drafts, 21.
8. See Historical Introduction to Letter to Heber C. Kimball and Brigham Young, Jan. 16, 1839, in *JSP,* D6:311–12.
9. Historian's Office, Brigham Young History Drafts, 21. The original source is in the past tense: "The Lord God had spoken . . . it was our duty to obey, and leave the event in his hands."
10. Edward Partridge to Joseph Smith and Others, Mar. 5, 1839, in *JSP,* D6:326–31; Don Carlos Smith and William Smith to Joseph Smith, Mar. 6, 1839, in *JSP,* D6:331–34; Emma Smith to Joseph Smith, Mar. 7, 1839, in *JSP,* D6:338–40; Historical Introduction to Letter from Edward Partridge, Mar. 5, 1839, in *JSP,* D6:328.
11. Joseph Smith and Others to the Church and Edward Partridge, Mar. 20, 1839, in *JSP,* D6:356–72, Jessee and Welch, "Joseph Smith's Letter from Liberty Jail," 125–45; Bray, "Within the Walls of Liberty Jail," 256–63.
12. Joseph Smith and Others to the Church and Edward Partridge, Mar. 20, 1839, in *JSP,* D6:363; Doctrine and Covenants 121:5.
13. Joseph Smith and Others to Edward Partridge and the Church, circa Mar. 22, 1839, in *JSP,* D6:393–94; Doctrine and Covenants 121:34–39.
14. Joseph Smith and Others to Edward Partridge and the Church, circa Mar. 22, 1839, in *JSP,* D6:394; Doctrine and Covenants 121:41–46.
15. Joseph Smith and Others to the Church and Edward Partridge, Mar. 20, 1839, in *JSP,* D6:362; Doctrine and Covenants 121:1–3.
16. Joseph Smith and Others to the Church and Edward Partridge, Mar. 20, 1839, in *JSP,* D6:366; Doctrine and Covenants 121:7–8.

17. Joseph Smith and Others to Edward Partridge and the Church, circa Mar. 22, 1839, in *JSP,* D6:395; Doctrine and Covenants 122:7–9; see also Alma 7:12. **Topic: Liberty Jail**
18. Far West Committee, Minutes, Mar. 17–18, 1839; Kimball, "History," 99; Theodore Turley, Memoranda, circa Feb. 1845, Joseph Smith History Documents, 1839–60, Church History Library.
19. Kimball, "History," 99; Theodore Turley, Memoranda, circa Feb. 1845, Joseph Smith History Documents, 1839–60, Church History Library.
20. Kimball, "History," 99–100.
21. Joseph Smith and Others to the Church and Edward Partridge, Mar. 20, 1839, in *JSP,* D6:371.
22. Joseph Smith and Others to Edward Partridge and the Church, circa Mar. 22, 1839, in *JSP,* D6:398; Doctrine and Covenants 123:1–6, 13, 16–17.
23. Joseph Smith to Emma Smith, Apr. 4, 1839, in *JSP,* D6:404–5.
24. Hyrum Smith, Diary, Apr. 7–8, 1839; Hyrum Smith, Testimony, July 1, 1843, 23–25, Nauvoo, IL, Records, Church History Library.
25. Bill of Damages, June 4, 1839, in *JSP,* D6:504; Joseph Smith History, 1838–56, volume C-1, 921; Hyrum Smith, Testimony, July 1, 1843, 25–26, Nauvoo, IL, Records, Church History Library.
26. Hyrum Smith, Diary, Apr. 14, 1839.
27. Burnett, *Old California Pioneer,* 40–41; see also Baugh, "Gallatin Hearing and the Escape of Joseph Smith," 62–63.
28. Bushman, *Rough Stone Rolling,* 382; Leonard, *Nauvoo,* 38–39.
29. Hyrum Smith, Testimony, July 1, 1843, 26, Nauvoo, IL, Records, Church History Library; Hyrum Smith, Diary, Apr. [16], 1839; Joseph Smith History, 1838–56, volume C-1, 921–22; see also Historical Introduction to Promissory Note to John Brassfield, Apr. 16, 1839, in *JSP,* D6:422–26.
30. Historian's Office, Brigham Young History Drafts, 21–22; Woodruff, Journal, Apr. 18, 1839.
31. John Taylor to "Dear Sir," in *LDS Millennial Star,* May 1841, 2:13; Woodruff, Journal, Apr. 26, 1839; Kimball, "History," 102.
32. Woodruff, Journal, Apr. 26, 1839; Historian's Office, General Church Minutes, Apr. 26, 1839; *Collection of Sacred Hymns,* 29–30; see also "Adam-ondi-Ahman," *Hymns,* no. 49. **Topic: Zion/New Jerusalem**
33. Woodruff, Journal, Apr. 27, 1839.
34. Dimick B. Huntington, Statement, circa 1854–56, Joseph Smith History Documents, 1839–60, Church History Library; Joseph Smith, Journal, Apr. 22–23, 1839, in *JSP,* J1:336.
35. Dimick B. Huntington, Statement, circa 1854–56, Joseph Smith History Documents, 1839–60, Church History Library.
36. Joseph Smith History, 1838–56, volume C-1, 922.
37. Dimick B. Huntington, Statement, circa 1854–56, Joseph Smith History Documents, 1839–60, Church History Library; Joseph Smith, Journal, Apr. 22–23, 1839, in *JSP,* J1:336; Joseph Smith History, 1838–56, volume C-1, 924.

CHAPTER 34: BUILD UP A CITY

1. Joseph Smith History, 1838–56, volume C-1, 930; *JSP,* J1:336, note 14; Joseph Smith to Isaac Galland, Mar. 22, 1839, in *JSP,* D6:388.
2. Far West Committee, Minutes, Feb. 1839; Leonard, *Nauvoo,* 55.
3. David W. Rogers, Statement, Feb. 1, 1839, Church History Library; Joseph Smith, Journal, Apr. 13, 1843, in *JSP,* J2:354; see also Plewe, *Mapping Mormonism,* 53–54. **Topic: Nauvoo (Commerce), Illinois**
4. Woodruff, Journal, May 20, 1839; Woodruff, *Leaves from My Journal,* 61.

5. See Rollins and others, "Transforming Swampland into Nauvoo," 125–57; Flanders, *Nauvoo,* 38–44, 116.

6. Woodruff, Journal, June 27, 1839; Bushman, *Rough Stone Rolling,* 386–89; Esplin, "Emergence of Brigham Young," 398–402.

7. Richards, "Pocket Companion," 17.

8. Woodruff, Journal, July 2, 1839.

9. Joseph Smith, Journal, June 27, 1839, in *JSP,* J1:343; Woodruff, Journal, June 25–27, 1839.

10. Woodruff, Journal, July 12, 1839; Givens and Grow, *Parley P. Pratt,* 158–65.

11. Woodruff, Journal, July 12 and 19, 1839; Historian's Office, Brigham Young History Drafts, 25; Historian's Office, "History of Brigham Young," 35; Woodruff, *Leaves from My Journal,* 62.

12. Woodruff, *Leaves from My Journal,* 62–63; Joseph Smith, Journal, July 22–23, 1839, in *JSP,* J1:349; Historian's Office, Brigham Young History Drafts, 25; Woodruff, Journal, July 22, 1839; Pratt, *Autobiography,* 324.

13. Woodruff, Journal, July 22, 1839; Pratt, *Autobiography,* 324–25.

14. Kimball, "History," 110; Woodruff, *Leaves from My Journal,* 63; Historian's Office, Brigham Young History Drafts, 25–26; Pratt, *Autobiography,* 325.

15. Woodruff, Autobiographical Sketch, 3. **Topic: Healing**

16. Tullidge, *Women of Mormondom,* 213–14.

17. Gates, *History of the Young Ladies' Mutual Improvement Association,* 16; see also "Mother in Heaven," Gospel Topics, topics.lds.org. **Topic: Mother in Heaven**

18. Woodruff, Journal, Aug. 8, 1839; see also Woodruff, Journal, May 30, 1840; and Alexander, *Heaven and Earth,* 85.

19. Pratt, *Autobiography,* 325; George A. Smith to Bathsheba Wilson Bigler, Jan. 14, 1841, George A. Smith, Collection, Church History Library; "History of George Albert Smith," 15, in Historian's Office, Histories of the Twelve, Church History Library; Allen and others, *Men with a Mission,* 8, 277, 288–89.

20. Historian's Office, Brigham Young History Drafts, 26; "Biography of Mary Ann Angell Young," *Juvenile Instructor,* Jan. 15, 1891, 26:56–57; Kimball, "History," 111.

21. Historian's Office, Brigham Young History Drafts, 26–27; Historian's Office, "History of Brigham Young," 35; Kimball, "History," 111.

22. Brigham Young, in *Journal of Discourses,* July 17, 1870, 13.211; Kimball, "History," 111.

23. Johnson, *Mormon Redress Petitions,* xix, xxiii–xxv; McBride, "When Joseph Smith Met Martin Van Buren," 150; Joseph Smith, Discourse, Apr. 7, 1840, in *JSP,* D7:258–60. **Topic: American Legal and Political Institutions**

24. Sidney Rigdon to Martin Van Buren, Nov. 9, 1839; Memorial to the United States Senate and House of Representatives, circa Oct. 30, 1839–Jan. 27, 1840; Joseph Smith, Discourse, Apr. 7, 1840, in *JSP,* D7:57–59, 138–74, 258–60.

25. Reynolds, *My Own Times,* 574–75; Joseph Smith and Elias Higbee to Hyrum Smith and Nauvoo high council, Dec. 5, 1839, in *JSP,* D7:69; Monkman, *White House,* 93–94; Seale, *President's House,* 212–15.

26. Joseph Smith History, 1838–56, volume C-1, 972; Joseph Smith to Emma Smith, Nov. 9, 1839; Sidney Rigdon to Martin Van Buren, Nov. 9, 1839, in *JSP,* D7:55–59; Reynolds, *My Own Times,* 575; see also Sidney Rigdon to Joseph Smith and others, Apr. 10, 1839, in *JSP,* D6:408–9; and Bushman, *Rough Stone Rolling,* 391–93.

27. Freidel, *Presidents of the United States of America,* 22–23; Joseph Smith and Elias Higbee to Hyrum Smith and Nauvoo high council, Dec. 5, 1839, in *JSP,* D7:69–70; Reynolds, *My Own Times,* 575.

28. Joseph Smith, Discourse, Mar. 1, 1840, in *JSP,* D7:202; compare *History of the Church,* 4:80.

29. McBride, "When Joseph Smith Met Martin Van Buren," 150–58; Joseph Smith and Elias Higbee to Hyrum Smith and Nauvoo high council, Dec. 5, 1839; Joseph Smith, Discourse, Apr. 7, 1840, in *JSP,* D7:69–70, 260.

30. Joseph Smith, Discourse, Apr. 7, 1840, in *JSP,* D7:260; compare *History of the Church,* 4:80; Joseph Smith and Elias Higbee to Hyrum Smith and Nauvoo high council, Dec. 5, 1839, in *JSP,* D7:69.

31. Joseph Smith and Elias Higbee to Hyrum Smith and Nauvoo high council, Dec. 5, 1839; Joseph Smith and Elias Higbee to Seymour Brunson and Nauvoo high council, Dec. 7, 1839, in *JSP,* D7:70, 78–81; *Journal of the Senate of the United States of America,* 138; Bushman, *Rough Stone Rolling,* 397.

32. See Minutes and Discourse, Jan. 13, 1840, in *JSP,* D7:111–15; and Joseph Smith to Robert D. Foster, Dec. 30, 1839, in *JSP,* D7:89–93.

33. Woodruff, Journal, Jan. 11–13, 1840; Woodruff, *Leaves from My Journal,* 75; Bitton, *George Q. Cannon,* 33–38; John Taylor to Leonora Taylor, Jan. 30, 1840, John Taylor, Collection, Church History Library.

34. Woodruff, Journal, Jan. 13–18, 1840.

35. Woodruff, Journal, Mar. 2–4, 1840; Woodruff, *Leaves from My Journal,* 77–78.

36. Woodruff, Journal, Mar. 4, 1840; Woodruff, *Leaves from My Journal,* 78–81.

37. Woodruff, Journal, Mar. 5–7, 1840; Woodruff, *Leaves from My Journal,* 79–81; Allen and others, *Men with a Mission,* 126.

38. Wilford Woodruff to Willard Richards, Mar. 31, 1840, Willard Richards, Journals and Papers, Church History Library; see also Allen and others, *Men with a Mission,* 126–28. **Topics: England; Early Missionaries**

39. Matthew L. Davis to Mrs. Matthew [Mary] L. Davis, Feb. 6, 1840, Church History Library; Bushman, *Rough Stone Rolling,* 394–95.

40. Joseph Smith to Emma Smith, Jan. 20–25, 1840, in *JSP,* D7:136.

41. Joseph Smith to Emma Smith, Oct. 13, 1832, in *JSP,* D2:313.

42. Hales, *Joseph Smith's Polygamy,* 1:201–2.

43. Pratt, *Autobiography,* 329–30; see also Givens and Grow, *Parley P. Pratt,* 173–74.

44. Joseph Smith and Elias Higbee to Hyrum Smith and Nauvoo high council, Dec. 5, 1839, in *JSP,* D7:72.

45. John C. Calhoun to Joseph Smith, Dec. 2, 1843, Joseph Smith Collection, Church History Library; Joseph Smith History, 1838–56, volume C-1, 1016.

46. Historian's Office, Joseph Smith History Draft Notes, Mar. 4, 1840; Report of the Senate Committee on the Judiciary, Mar. 4, 1840, in *JSP,* D7:539–43; McBride, "When Joseph Smith Met Martin Van Buren," 154–58; Bushman, *Rough Stone Rolling,* 396–98.

47. Elias Higbee to Joseph Smith, Mar. 24, 1840, in *JSP,* D7:232–34.

CHAPTER 35: A BEAUTIFUL PLACE

1. "Autobiography of Emily D. P. Young," *Woman's Exponent,* July 15, 1885, 14:26; Lyman, Journal, 12; Obituary for Harriet Partridge, *Times and Seasons,* June 1, 1840, 1:128.

2. Obituary for Edward Partridge, *Times and Seasons,* June 1, 1840, 1:127–28; Lyman, Journal, 12.

3. "Autobiography of Emily D. P. Young," *Woman's Exponent,* Aug. 1, 1885, 14:37.

4. Obituary for Edward Partridge, *Times and Seasons,* June 1, 1840, 1:127–28. **Topic: Church Periodicals**

5. "Autobiography of Emily D. P. Young," *Woman's Exponent,* July 15, 1885, 14:26; Lyman, Journal, 13.

6. "Nauvoo" and "Immigration," *Times and Seasons,* June 1840, 1:122–24; Joseph Smith History, 1838–56, volume C-1, 1060; Bushman, *Rough Stone Rolling,* 405; Leonard, *Nauvoo,* 60–61.

7. "Proclamation, to the Saints Scattered Abroad," *Times and Seasons,* Jan. 15, 1841, 2:273–74; see also Leonard, *Nauvoo,* 59. **Topic: Nauvoo (Commerce), Illinois**

8. See Leonard, *Nauvoo,* 91.

9. William W. Phelps to Joseph Smith, June 29, 1840, in *JSP,* D7:303–5.

10. Joseph Smith to William W. Phelps, July 22, 1840, in *JSP,* D7:345–48.
11. Woodruff, Journal, July 28, 1844; see also Joseph Smith to Presendia Huntington Buell, Mar. 15, 1839, in *JSP,* D6:354–56; and Esplin, "Joseph Smith's Mission and Timetable," 280–319.
12. **Topic: Bishop**
13. John C. Bennett to Joseph Smith, July 25, 1840, in *JSP,* D7:348–50; Bushman, *Rough Stone Rolling,* 411; "Bennett, John Cook," Biographical Entry, Joseph Smith Papers website, josephsmithpapers.org.
14. John C. Bennett to Joseph Smith and Sidney Rigdon, July 27, 1840, in *JSP,* D7:350–53; see also John C. Bennett to Joseph Smith, July 30, 1840, in *JSP,* D7:368–70.
15. John C. Bennett to Joseph Smith, July 30, 1840, in *JSP,* D7:370. The earliest copy of this letter has "My anxiety to be with is daily increasing."
16. Joseph Smith to John C. Bennett, Aug. 8, 1840, in *JSP,* D7:370–74.
17. Joseph Smith, Discourse, circa July 19, 1840, in *JSP,* D7:340–45. **Topics: Gathering of Israel; Zion/New Jerusalem; Nauvoo Temple**
18. Lucy Mack Smith, History, 1844–45, book 17, [7]; book 18, [1]–[10]; Funeral Address, *Times and Seasons,* Sept. 1840, 1:170–73; Vilate Murray Kimball to Heber C. Kimball, Sept. 6, 1840, Heber C. Kimball, Church History Library; Obituary for Seymour Brunson, *Times and Seasons,* Sept. 1840, 1:176.
19. Jane Neyman, Statement, Nov. 29, 1854, Historian's Office, Joseph Smith History Documents, Church History Library; Historical Department, Journal History of the Church, Aug. 15, 1840; Brunson, "Short Sketch of Seymour Brunson, Sr.," 3–4; Doctrine and Covenants 137 (Visions, Jan. 21, 1836, at josephsmithpapers.org); see also Tobler, "Saviors on Mount Zion," 186, note 12.
20. 1 Corinthians 15:29.
21. Simon Baker, "15 Aug. 1840 Minutes of Recollection of Joseph Smith's Sermon," Joseph Smith Collection, Church History Library.
22. Jane Neyman, Statement, Nov. 29, 1854, Historian's Office, Joseph Smith History Documents, Church History Library. **Topic: Baptism for the Dead**
23. Joseph Smith to John C. Bennett, Aug. 8, 1840, in *JSP,* D7:372–73; "Mormonism—Gen. Bennett, &c.," *Times and Seasons,* Oct. 15, 1842, 3:955; "Bennett, John Cook," Biographical Entry, Joseph Smith Papers website, josephsmithpapers.org; News Item, *Times and Seasons,* Dec. 1, 1840, 2:234.
24. Lucy Mack Smith, History, 1844–45, book 17, [7]; book 18, [3]–[4].
25. Lucy Mack Smith, History, 1844–45, book 18, [3]–[9]; Lucy Mack Smith, History, 1845, 296, 301; Smith, *Biographical Sketches,* 267. **Topic: Joseph Smith Sr.**
26. Vilate Kimball to Heber C. Kimball, Oct. 11, 1840, Vilate M. Kimball, Letters, Church History Library.
27. Conference Minutes, *Times and Seasons,* Oct. 1840, 1:185–87; Vilate Kimball to Heber C. Kimball, Oct. 11, 1840, Vilate M. Kimball, Letters, Church History Library; Nauvoo Temple, Baptisms for the Dead, book A, 149, microfilm 183,376, U.S. and Canada Record Collection, Family History Library; Black and Black, *Annotated Record of Baptisms for the Dead,* 6:3361; see also Nauvoo Temple, Baptisms for the Dead, 1840–45, Church History Library.
28. Vilate Kimball to Heber C. Kimball, Oct. 11, 1840, Vilate M. Kimball, Letters, Church History Library.
29. Isaac Hale, Affidavit, Mar. 20, 1834, in "Mormonism," *Susquehanna Register, and Northern Pennsylvanian,* May 1, 1834, [1].
30. Nauvoo Temple, Baptisms for the Dead, book A, 45.
31. Act to Incorporate the City of Nauvoo, Dec. 16, 1840, in *JSP,* D7:472–88; Conference Minutes, *Times and Seasons,* Oct. 1840, 1:186.
32. News Item, *Times and Seasons,* Jan. 15, 1841, 2:287. **Topic: Early Missionaries**
33. "Report from the Presidency," *Times and Seasons,* Oct. 1840, 1:188.

34. Act to Incorporate the City of Nauvoo, Dec. 16, 1840, in *JSP,* D7:472–88; Joseph Smith and others, Proclamation, Jan. 15, 1841, in *JSP,* D7:503–4; see also Bushman, *Rough Stone Rolling,* 410–12.
35. Doctrine and Covenants 124:19, 91–96, 127 (Revelation, Jan. 19, 1841, at josephsmithpapers.org). **Topic: Hyrum Smith**
36. Doctrine and Covenants 124:16–17 (Revelation, Jan. 19, 1841, at josephsmithpapers.org).
37. Doctrine and Covenants 124:22–24, 49–54, 60–61 (Revelation, Jan. 19, 1841, at josephsmithpapers.org).
38. Doctrine and Covenants 124:40 (Revelation, Jan. 19, 1841, at josephsmithpapers.org); see also Smith, "Organizing the Church in Nauvoo," 264–71. **Topic: Nauvoo Temple**
39. Doctrine and Covenants 124:29–38 (Revelation, Jan. 19, 1841, at josephsmithpapers.org). **Topic: Baptism for the Dead**
40. Doctrine and Covenants 124:41–42 (Revelation, Jan. 19, 1841, at josephsmithpapers.org); see also Smith, "Organizing the Church in Nauvoo," 264–71.
41. Doctrine and Covenants 124:55 (Revelation, Jan. 19, 1841, at josephsmithpapers.org).
42. "Municipal Election," *Times and Seasons,* Feb. 1, 1841, 2:309; "Inaugural Address," *Times and Seasons,* Feb. 15, 1841, 2:316–18; "Trial of Elder Rigdon," *Times and Seasons,* Sept. 15, 1844, 5:655; An Act to Incorporate the City of Nauvoo [Dec. 16, 1840], *Laws of the State of Illinois,* p. 55, section 16; "Bennett, John Cook," Biographical Entry, Joseph Smith Papers website, josephsmithpapers.org.
43. "Memoirs of President Joseph Smith," *Saints' Herald,* Jan. 8, 1935, 49.

CHAPTER 36: INCLINE THEM TO GATHER

1. Maughan, Autobiography, [29]–[34].
2. Maughan, Autobiography, [29]–[34]; Allen and others, *Men with a Mission,* 302, note 37; Winters, Reminiscences, 10; see also Minutes, Apr. 6, 1841, in *LDS Millennial Star,* Apr. 1841, 1:302.
3. Allen and others, *Men with a Mission,* 225–26.
4. Allen and Thorp, "Mission of the Twelve to England," 503, 510–14; Givens and Grow, *Parley P. Pratt,* 182–83.
5. See, for example, Richard Livesey, *Exposure of Mormonism* (Preston: J. Livesey, 1838); see also "Mission to England," *LDS Millennial Star,* Apr. 1841, 1:295; Givens and Grow, *Parley P. Pratt,* 183, 186; and Foster, *Penny Tracts and Polemics.*
6. "From England," *Times and Seasons,* June 1840, 1:119–22. **Topic: Church Periodicals**
7. Maughan, Autobiography, [30]–[31], [35]–[38]; see also "Proclamation to the Saints Scattered Abroad," *LDS Millennial Star,* Mar. 1841, 1:270–71; and "Epistle of the Twelve," *LDS Millennial Star,* Apr. 1841, 1:310–11.
8. "Celebration of the Anniversary" and "Communication," *Times and Seasons,* Apr. 15, 1841, 2:375–77, 380–83; Report, *Warsaw Signal,* June 9, 1841, [2].
9. *Biographical Review of Hancock County, Illinois,* 109; see also Hamilton, "Thomas Sharp's Turning Point," 19.
10. See Report, *Western World,* Jan. 20, 1841, [2].
11. "Celebration of the Anniversary" and "Communication," *Times and Seasons,* Apr. 15, 1841, 2:375–77, 380–83; "The Mormons," *Western World,* Apr. 7, 1841, [3]; Report, *Warsaw Signal,* June 9, 1841, [2]; "Life of Norton Jacob," 6; see also Leonard, *Nauvoo,* 233–34.
12. "Celebration of the Anniversary" and "Communication," *Times and Seasons,* Apr. 15, 1841, 2:375–77, 380–83. **Topic: Nauvoo Temple**
13. Report, *Warsaw Signal,* June 9, 1841, [2]; Joseph Smith, Journal, Jan. 29, 1843, in *JSP,* J2:253.
14. "The Mormons," *Western World,* Apr. 7, 1841, [3]; Joseph Smith, Letter to the Editors, *Times and Seasons,* May 15, 1841, 2:414.

15. See Whitney, *Why We Practice Plural Marriage,* 23–24; Esplin, "Joseph Smith's Mission and Timetable," 298–99, 303–4; and "Plural Marriage in Kirtland and Nauvoo," Gospel Topics, topics.lds.org.
16. Pratt, *Autobiography,* 329; Doctrine and Covenants 132:19 (Revelation, July 12, 1843, at josephsmithpapers.org). **Topic: Sealing**
17. Jacob 2:27, 30.
18. Doctrine and Covenants 132:29–37, 63 (Revelation, July 12, 1843, at josephsmithpapers .org); Genesis 16:3–12; 17. **Topic: Joseph Smith and Plural Marriage**
19. Nauvoo City Council Minute Book, Mar. 1, 1841, 13. The ordinance specifically mentioned "Mahommedans," a common nineteenth-century term for Muslims.
20. See, for example, Doctrine and Covenants 98:3–6 (Revelation, Aug. 6, 1833, at josephsmithpapers.org); and Doctrine and Covenants 134 (Declaration on Government and Law, circa Aug. 1835, at josephsmithpapers.org).
21. "Plural Marriage in Kirtland and Nauvoo," Gospel Topics, topics.lds.org.
22. Temple Lot Transcript, part 3, 395, questions 40–41; Joseph Bates Noble, Affidavit, June 6, 1869, in Affidavits about Celestial Marriage, 1:38; "Plural Marriage," *Historical Record,* May 1887, 221.
23. Temple Lot Transcript, part 3, 395, questions 40–41.
24. Joseph Bates Noble, Affidavit, June 6, 1869, in Affidavits about Celestial Marriage, 1:38.
25. Joseph Bates Noble, Affidavit, June 6, 1869, in Affidavits about Celestial Marriage, 1:38; Temple Lot Transcript, part 3, 395–96, questions 43–49; Franklin D. Richards, Journal, Jan. 22, 1869; Charles Lowell Walker, Diary, June 17, 1883, in Larson and Larson, *Diary of Charles Lowell Walker,* 2:610; see also Woodruff, Journal, Jan. 22, 1869.
26. See "The Mormon Plot and League," *Sangamo Journal,* July 8, 1842, [2]; and "Trouble among Judge Ford's Constituents," *Alton Telegraph and Democratic Review,* July 2, 1842, [2].
27. "Appointment," *Warsaw Signal,* May 19, 1841, [2].
28. "The Mormons," *Warsaw Signal,* May 19, 1841, [2].
29. "Highly Important," *Warsaw Signal,* June 2, 1841, [2]; see also "The Warsaw Signal," *Times and Seasons,* June 1, 1841, 2:431–33.
30. "Highly Important," *Warsaw Signal,* June 2, 1841, [2]; "The Mormons," *Warsaw Signal,* May 19, 1841, [2].
31. "Read and Ponder," *Warsaw Signal,* June 9, 1841, [2].
32. "The Warsaw Signal," *Times and Seasons,* June 1, 1841, 2:431–33.
33. Britton, *Bath and Bristol,* 6. **Topics: England; Gathering of Israel**
34. Maughan, Autobiography, [38]–[44], [48]–[49]; "Bristol to Quebec, 10 May 1841–12 July 1841," Mormon Migration website, mormonmigration.lib.byu.edu; "Phelps, William Wines," Biographical Entry, Joseph Smith Papers website, josephsmithpapers.org. **Topic: Kirtland, Ohio**
35. Maughan, Autobiography, [38]–[44], [48]–[49]
36. *Tullidge's Histories,* volume 2, supplement, 34–35.
37. Maughan, Autobiography, [52]–[53]; see also Ward, "John Needham's Nauvoo Letter: 1843," 41; and Pratt, *Autobiography,* 47.
38. Hyde, *Voice from Jerusalem,* 7, 16; see also Bartlett, *Walks about the City and Environs of Jerusalem,* 14.
39. Hyde, *Voice from Jerusalem,* 7–19, 27–28.
40. Hyde, *Voice from Jerusalem,* 28–29; see also Joseph Smith—Matthew 1:3; Luke 19:44; 21:6; Mark 13:2; and Matthew 24:2.
41. Hyde, *Voice from Jerusalem,* 28–32; 3 Nephi 20:29–37.
42. Hyde, *Voice from Jerusalem,* 30, 32–33. **Topic: Dedication of the Holy Land**

CHAPTER 37: WE WILL PROVE THEM

1. Joseph Smith to Edward Hunter, Jan. 5, 1842, Joseph Smith Collection, Church History Library; Joseph Smith, Journal, Jan. 5, 1842, in *JSP,* J2:21.
2. See Doctrine and Covenants 109:69 (Prayer of Dedication, Mar. 27, 1836, at josephsmithpapers.org); and Doctrine and Covenants 124:9 (Revelation, Jan. 19, 1841, at josephsmithpapers.org).
3. See Woodruff, Journal, Feb. 19, 1842; and "A Translation," *Times and Seasons,* Mar. 1, 1842, 3:704–6. **Topic: Book of Abraham Translation**
4. Abraham 3:25–26; "The Book of Abraham," *Times and Seasons,* Mar. 15, 1842, 3:720.
5. Joseph Smith, Journal, Jan. 6, 1842, in *JSP,* J2:26; see also Revelation 5:10; Doctrine and Covenants 124:39–41 (Revelation, Jan. 19, 1841, at josephsmithpapers.org); *JSP,* J2:54, note 198; and Bushman, *Rough Stone Rolling,* 448–49. **Topic: Temple Endowment**
6. Heber C. Kimball, Discourse, Sept. 2, 1866, George D. Watt Papers, Church History Library, as transcribed by LaJean Purcell Carruth.
7. Brigham Young, in *Journal of Discourses,* July 14, 1855, 3:266; John Taylor, "Sermon in Honor of the Martyrdom," June 27, 1854, George D. Watt Papers, Church History Library, as transcribed by LaJean Purcell Carruth; "Scenes and Incidents in Nauvoo," *Woman's Exponent,* Oct. 15, 1881, 10:74; Whitney, *Life of Heber C. Kimball,* 336.
8. See Crocheron, *Representative Women of Deseret,* 26; "Plural Marriage in Kirtland and Nauvoo," Gospel Topics, topics.lds.org. **Topic: Joseph Smith and Plural Marriage**
9. Though it is possible Joseph Smith fathered children within plural marriage, genetic testing of potential descendants has so far been negative. (See "Plural Marriage in Kirtland and Nauvoo," Gospel Topics, topics.lds.org.)
10. "Plural Marriage in Kirtland and Nauvoo," Gospel Topics, topics.lds.org.
11. Mary Elizabeth Rollins Lightner, Remarks, Apr. 14, 1905, 3–5, Church History Library; Mary Elizabeth Rollins Lightner, Affidavit, Mar. 23, 1877, Collected Material Concerning Joseph Smith and Plural Marriage, Church History Library; Mary Elizabeth Rollins Lightner to Wilford Woodruff, Salt Lake City, Oct. 7, 1887; "Mary Elizabeth Rollins Lightner," *Utah Genealogical and Historical Magazine,* July 1926, 26:197, 203.
12. Mary Elizabeth Rollins Lightner, Remarks, Apr. 14, 1905, 3–5, Church History Library.
13. Mary Elizabeth Rollins Lightner, "Mary Elizabeth Rollins," copy, Susa Young Gates Papers, Utah State Historical Society, Salt Lake City.
14. See Mary Elizabeth Rollins Lightner, Remarks, Apr. 14, 1905, 2, Church History Library.
15. Mary Elizabeth Rollins Lightner, Remarks, Apr. 14, 1905, 7, Church History Library.
16. Mary Elizabeth Rollins Lightner, "Mary Elizabeth Rollins," copy, Susa Young Gates Papers, Utah State Historical Society, Salt Lake City; Mary Elizabeth Rollins Lightner, Remarks, Apr. 14, 1905, 4, Church History Library; Mary Elizabeth Rollins Lightner to Emmeline B. Wells, summer 1905, Mary Elizabeth Rollins Lightner, Collection, Church History Library.
17. Mary Elizabeth Rollins Lightner, Remarks, Apr. 14, 1905, 4–7, Church History Library.
18. Mary Elizabeth Rollins Lightner, Remarks, Apr. 14, 1905, 4–7, Church History Library; Mary Elizabeth Rollins Lightner, "Mary Elizabeth Rollins," copy, Susa Young Gates Papers, Utah State Historical Society, Salt Lake City.
19. Mary Elizabeth Rollins Lightner, Affidavit, Mar. 23, 1877, Church History Library; Mary Elizabeth Rollins Lightner, "Mary Elizabeth Rollins," copy, Susa Young Gates Papers, Utah State Historical Society, Salt Lake City; see also Mary Elizabeth Rollins Lightner to John Henry Smith, Jan. 25, 1892, George A. Smith Family Papers, Marriott Library, University of Utah, Salt Lake City, quoted in Hales, *Joseph Smith's Polygamy,* 1:436, note 90; and Mary Elizabeth Rollins Lightner, Statement, Feb. 8, 1902, Mary Elizabeth Rollins Lightner, Collection, Church History Library.
20. Abraham 3:1, 23–24; 4:1–28; see also "A Translation," *Times and Seasons,* Mar. 1, 1842, 3:703–18; and "The Book of Abraham," *Times and Seasons,* Mar. 15, 1842, 3:719–34. **Topic: Book of Abraham Translation**
21. Gregg, *History of Hancock County, Illinois,* 296–98.

22. Leonard, *Nauvoo*, 249. **Topic: Wards and Stakes**
23. Clayton, History of the Nauvoo Temple, 3–4, 6, 13–14, 20–21; Sarah M. Kimball, Reminiscence, Mar. 17, 1882, in Derr and others, *First Fifty Years of Relief Society*, 495; Joseph Smith History, volume C-1, addenda, 44; Maughan, Autobiography, [54]; see also McGavin, *Nauvoo Temple*, 50–51. **Topics: Nauvoo Temple; Baptism for the Dead**
24. Crocheron, *Representative Women of Deseret*, 26–27.
25. Sarah M. Granger Kimball, "Auto-biography," *Woman's Exponent*, Sept. 1, 1883, 12:51; compare Sarah M. Kimball, Reminiscence, Mar. 17, 1882, in Derr and others, *First Fifty Years of Relief Society*, 495; see also 6–7.
26. Sarah M. Kimball, Reminiscence, Mar. 17, 1882, in Derr and others, *First Fifty Years of Relief Society*, 495.
27. Nauvoo Relief Society Minute Book, Mar. 17, 1842, in Derr and others, *First Fifty Years of Relief Society*, 28–30.
28. See Derr and others, *Women of Covenant*, 29–30. For biographical information on these women and other members of the Female Relief Society of Nauvoo, see churchhistorianspress.org.
29. Joseph Smith, Journal, Mar. 16, 1842, in *JSP*, J2:45; Woodruff, Journal, Mar. 15, 1843; Nauvoo Masonic Lodge Minutes, Mar. 15–16, 1842.
30. Nauvoo Relief Society Minute Book, Mar. 17, 1842, in Derr and others, *First Fifty Years of Relief Society*, 28–31; see also "Joseph Smith's Teachings about Priesthood, Temple, Women," Gospel Topics, topics.lds.org.
31. Joseph Smith, Journal, Mar. 17, 1842, in *JSP*, J2:45; Nauvoo Relief Society Minute Book, Mar. 17, 1842, in Derr and others, *First Fifty Years of Relief Society*, 32–34; Doctrine and Covenants 25:3 (Revelation, July 1830–C, at josephsmithpapers.org); "Joseph Smith's Teachings about Priesthood, Temple, Women," Gospel Topics, topics.lds.org.
32. Nauvoo Relief Society Minute Book, Mar. 17, 1842, in Derr and others, *First Fifty Years of Relief Society*, 34–36; *Daughters in My Kingdom*, 11–14; Derr and others, *Women of Covenant*, 26–31; see also 1 Corinthians 13:3. **Topics: Female Relief Society of Nauvoo; Emma Hale Smith**
33. Nauvoo Relief Society Minute Book, Mar. 31, 1842, in Derr and others, *First Fifty Years of Relief Society*, 42. The original source has "Said he was going to make of this Society a kingdom of priests an in Enoch's day— as in Pauls day." **Topic: Temple Endowment**
34. Nauvoo Relief Society Minute Book, Mar. 31, 1842; Copied Documents, Mar. 31, 1842, in Derr and others, *First Fifty Years of Relief Society*, 42, 97–99; Joseph Smith, Journal, Mar. 31, 1842, in *JSP*, J2:48.
35. Woodruff, Journal, Apr. 10, 1842.
36. Nauvoo Relief Society Minute Book, Apr. 28, 1842, in Derr and others, *First Fifty Years of Relief Society*, 59.
37. Lucius N. Scovil, Letter to the Editor, Jan. 2, 1884, *Deseret Evening News*, Feb. 11, 1884, [2]; Launius and McKiernan, *Joseph Smith, Jr.'s Red Brick Store*, 28; see also McBride, *House for the Most High*, 100, note 10.
38. Joseph Smith, Journal, May 4, 1842, in *JSP*, J2:53–54; Joseph Smith History, 1838–56, volume C-1, 1328.
39. See Genesis 3:21; Exodus 40:12–13; and Historian's Office, Joseph Smith History, draft notes, May 4, 1842. **Topic: Temple Endowment**
40. Abraham 3–5; Facsimile no. 2, fig. 3.
41. See Joseph Smith, Journal, May 1, 1842, in *JSP*, J2:53; Historian's Office, Joseph Smith History draft notes, May 4, 1842; Joseph Smith History, 1838–56, volume C-1, 1328; see also Brigham Young, in *Journal of Discourses*, Apr. 6, 1853, 2:31.
42. Heber C. Kimball to Parley P. Pratt, June 17, 1842, Parley P. Pratt Correspondence, Church History Library; Historian's Office, Joseph Smith History, draft notes, May 4, 1842; Joseph Smith History, 1838–56, volume C-1, 1328. **Topic: Anointed Quorum ("Holy Order")**
43. Nuttall, Diary, Feb. 7, 1877.

44. Godfrey, "Joseph Smith and the Masons," 83; Harper, "Freemasonry and the Latter-day Saint Temple Endowment Ceremony," 143–57; Joseph Smith, Journal, Mar. 15, 1842, in *JSP,* J2:45; Heber C. Kimball to Parley P. Pratt, June 17, 1842, Parley P. Pratt Correspondence, Church History Library. **Topic: Masonry**
45. Heber C. Kimball to Parley P. Pratt, June 17, 1842, Parley P. Pratt Correspondence, Church History Library.

CHAPTER 38: A TRAITOR OR A TRUE MAN

1. Boggs, "Short Biographical Sketch of Lilburn W. Boggs," 107–8; "A Foul Deed," *Daily Missouri Republican,* May 12, 1842, [2]; "Governor Boggs," *Jeffersonian Republican,* May 14, 1842.
2. Boggs, "Short Biographical Sketch of Lilburn W. Boggs," 107–8; Joseph Smith, Letter to the Editor, *Quincy Herald,* June 2, 1842, [2]; Launius, "Boggs, Lilburn W.," in Christensen and others, *Dictionary of Missouri Biography,* 92; Hill, "Honey War," 81–88; Gordon, "Public Career of Lilburn W. Boggs," 110–12, 138; Walker, "Lilburn W. Boggs and the Case of Jacksonian Democracy," 81–82; Baugh, "Missouri Governor Lilburn W. Boggs and the Mormons," 116.
3. "A Foul Deed," *Daily Missouri Republican,* May 12, 1842; "Governor Boggs," *Jeffersonian Republican,* May 14, 1842, [2]; Boggs, "Short Biographical Sketch of Lilburn W. Boggs," 107–8; see also Thurston, "The Boggs Shooting," 7–11.
4. "Affidavit of Hyrum Smith," *Times and Seasons,* Aug. 1, 1842, 3:870–71; see also *JSP,* J2:xxviii, note 64; and Hales, *Joseph Smith's Polygamy,* 1:560–62.
5. "Affidavit of Hyrum Smith," *Times and Seasons,* Aug. 1, 1842, 3:870–71; Nauvoo Stake High Council Minutes, May 25, 1842; George Miller, "To the Church of Jesus Christ," *Times and Seasons,* July 1, 1842, 3:839–42; Smith, *Saintly Scoundrel,* 78–79.
6. George Miller, "To the Church of Jesus Christ," *Times and Seasons,* July 1, 1842, 3:840; "Affidavit of Hyrum Smith," *Times and Seasons,* Aug. 1, 1842, 3:870; Smith, *Saintly Scoundrel,* 79–80; see also "Letter from L. D. Wasson," *Times and Seasons,* Aug. 15, 1842, 3:892.
7. "Affidavit of Hyrum Smith," *Times and Seasons,* Aug. 1, 1842, 3:870, 872; Notice, May 11, 1842, Joseph Smith Collection, Church History Library; "Notice," *Times and Seasons,* June 15, 1842, 3:830; see also *JSP,* J2:55, note 207.
8. "Affidavit of Hyrum Smith," *Times and Seasons,* Aug. 1, 1842, 3:870–71. In Hyrum Smith's account, Joseph also asked John Bennett, "Have I ever taught you that fornication and adultery was right, or polygamy or any such practices?" to which Bennett answered, "You never did." Chapter 40 explains that Saints viewed their divinely sanctioned plural marriages as distinct from polygamy.
9. "New Election of Mayor, and Vice Mayor, of the City of Nauvoo," *Wasp,* May 21, 1842, [3]; *JSP,* J2:58, note 222.
10. Joseph Smith, Journal, May 19, 1842, in *JSP,* J2:58–60; "New Election of Mayor, and Vice Mayor, of the City of Nauvoo," *Wasp,* May 21, 1843, [3]; see also "Affidavit of Hyrum Smith," *Times and Seasons,* Aug. 1, 1842, 3:872.
11. "Assassination of Ex-Governor Boggs of Missouri," *Quincy Whig,* May 21, 1842, [3]; see also "A Foul Deed," *Daily Missouri Republican,* May 12, 1842, [2]; and "Governor Boggs," *Jeffersonian Republican,* May 14, 1842. **Topic: Missouri Extradition Attempts**
12. Joseph Smith, Letter to the Editor, *Quincy Whig,* June 4, 1842, [2]; see also Joseph Smith, Journal, May 22, 1842, in *JSP,* J2:62; and Joseph Smith, Letter to the Editor, May 22, 1842, *Quincy Herald,* June 2, 1842, [2].
13. Joseph Smith, Journal, May 21, 1842, in *JSP,* J2:62; Nauvoo Stake High Council Minutes, May 20–28, 1842.

14. Catherine Warren, Testimony, May 25, 1842, Testimonies in Nauvoo High Council Cases, Church History Library; Nauvoo Stake High Council Minutes, May 20–28, 1842; see also "Chauncy L. Higbee," *Nauvoo Neighbor,* May 29, 1844, [3]. **Topic: Church Discipline**

15. Historian's Office, Joseph Smith History, draft notes, May 25, 1842; see also Joseph Smith, Journal, May 26, 1842, in *JSP,* J2:63; and "Affidavit of Wm. Law," *Times and Seasons,* Aug. 1, 1842, 3:873.

16. Historian's Office, Joseph Smith History, draft notes, May 26, 1842; "Affidavit of Hyrum Smith," *Times and Seasons,* Aug. 1, 1842, 3:872; Joseph Smith, Journal, May 11 and 26, 1842, in *JSP,* J2:55, 63; see also 55, note 207.

17. Nauvoo Relief Society Minute Book, May 26, 1842, in Derr and others, *First Fifty Years of Relief Society,* 69–71.

18. See Smith, *Saintly Scoundrel,* 91.

19. Nauvoo Relief Society Minute Book, Apr. 28 and May 27, 1842, in Derr and others, *First Fifty Years of Relief Society,* 52–54, 72–77. **Topic: Female Relief Society of Nauvoo**

20. Nauvoo Relief Society Minute Book, May 27, 1842, in Derr and others, *First Fifty Years of Relief Society,* 75–76; see also 75, note 188.

21. Alexander, *Things in Heaven and Earth,* 103–4.

22. Woodruff, Journal, May 29, 1842.

23. See Nauvoo Relief Society Minute Book, May 19–June 9, 1842, in Derr and others, *First Fifty Years of Relief Society,* 65–79.

24. "Affidavit of Hyrum Smith," *Times and Seasons,* Aug. 1, 1842, 3:872; "Notice," *Times and Seasons,* June 15, 1842, 3:830; Joseph Smith, Journal, May 26, 1842, in *JSP,* J2:63; see also 63, note 249; and "Affidavit of Wm. Law," *Times and Seasons,* Aug. 1, 1842, 3:872–73.

25. Discourse, June 18, 1842, as reported by Wilford Woodruff, at josephsmithpapers.org.

26. "Affidavit of Hyrum Smith," *Times and Seasons,* Aug. 1, 1842, 3:872; Nauvoo Relief Society Minute Book, June 23, 1842, in Derr and others, *First Fifty Years of Relief Society,* 84–85; see also 84, note 206.

27. Joseph Smith, Letter to the Church, June 23, 1842, *Times and Seasons,* July 1, 1842, 3:839–42.

28. "Astounding Mormon Disclosures! Letter from Gen. Bennett," *Sangamo Journal,* July 8, 1842, [2]; "Further Mormon Developments!! 2d Letter from Gen. Bennett" and "Gen. Bennett's Third Letter," *Sangamo Journal,* July 15, 1842, [2]; "Gen. Bennett's 4th Letter," *Sangamo Journal,* July 22, 1842, [2]; Smith, *Saintly Scoundrel,* 98.

29. Lilburn W. Boggs Affidavit, July 20, 1842, in *JSP,* J2:379–80; see also Introduction to Appendix 1, in *JSP,* J2:377.

30. Thomas Reynolds, Requisition, July 22, 1842, in *JSP,* J2:380–81.

31. Joseph Smith, Journal, May 6, 1842, in *JSP,* J2:54; Nauvoo Female Relief Society, Petition to Thomas Carlin, circa July 22, 1842, in Derr and others, *First Fifty Years of Relief Society,* 136–41; Nauvoo City Council Minute Book, July 22, 1842, 95–97; Nauvoo City Council Draft Minutes, July 22, 1842, 36; Joseph Smith History, 1838–56, volume C-1, 1359.

32. Eliza R. Snow, Journal, July 29, 1842; Introduction to Nauvoo Female Relief Society, Petition to Thomas Carlin, circa July 22, 1842, in Derr and others, *First Fifty Years of Relief Society,* 137; Thomas Carlin, Proclamation, Sept. 20, 1842, in *JSP,* J2:381–82.

33. Orrin Porter Rockwell, by S. Armstrong, to Joseph Smith, Dec. 1, 1842, Joseph Smith Collection, Church History Library; Writ of Habeas Corpus for Joseph Smith, Aug. 8, 1842, copy, Nauvoo, IL, Records, Church History Library; Joseph Smith, Journal, Aug. 8–10, 1842, in *JSP,* J2:81–83; see also 81, note 319; and "Persecution," *Times and Seasons,* Aug. 15, 1842, 3:886–89.

CHAPTER 39: THE SEVENTH TROUBLE

1. Joseph Smith, Journal, Aug. 8–11, 1842, in *JSP,* J2:83.
2. Joseph Smith, Journal, Aug. 8–11 and 16, 1842, in *JSP,* J2:81–84, 93–94; Orrin Porter Rockwell, by S. Armstrong, to Joseph Smith, Dec. 1, 1842, Joseph Smith Collection, Church History Library.
3. Joseph Smith, Journal, Aug. 11, 1842, in *JSP,* J2:83–84; Joseph Smith History, 1838–56, volume D-1, 1364; see also Thomas Carlin, Writ, Aug. 2, 1842, Ex Parte Joseph Smith for Accessory to Boggs Assault, copy, Nauvoo, IL, Records, Church History Library.
4. Joseph Smith, Journal, Aug. 11 and 16, 1842, in *JSP,* J2:83–85, 93–95; on the "seventh trouble," see Job 5:19. **Topic: Emma Hale Smith**
5. Joseph Smith, Journal, Aug. 13–14 and Sept. 9, 1842, in *JSP,* J2:85–89, 143. **Topic: Missouri Extradition Attempts**
6. Joseph Smith, Journal, Aug. 15, 1842, in *JSP,* J2:90–92; Rowley, "Mormon Experience in the Wisconsin Pineries," 121.
7. Joseph Smith to Emma Smith, Aug. 16, 1842, in *JSP,* J2:107–10; see also Joseph Smith, Journal, Aug. 16, 1842, in *JSP,* J2:93.
8. Emma Smith to Joseph Smith, Aug. 16, 1842, in *JSP,* J2:110–11.
9. Emma Smith to Thomas Carlin, Aug. 16, 1842, in *JSP,* J2:111–14.
10. Thomas Carlin to Emma Smith, Aug. 24, 1842, in *JSP,* J2:126–28.
11. Emma Smith to Thomas Carlin, Aug. 27, 1842, in *JSP,* J2:128–30.
12. Joseph Smith, Journal, Aug. 29, 1842, in *JSP,* J2:122; see also Eliza R. Snow, Journal, Aug. 14–Sept. 4, 1842.
13. Maughan, Autobiography, [51], [54].
14. See Leonard, *Nauvoo,* 154–61.
15. Maughan, Autobiography, [55]; Joseph Smith, Journal, Jan. 12–16, 1842, in *JSP,* J2:24.
16. Maughan, Autobiography, [54].
17. See Givens, *In Old Nauvoo,* 154–55, 158, 187–88, 221–22. **Topic: Daily Life of First-Generation Latter-day Saints**
18. Joseph Smith, Journal, Aug. 23–29, 1842, in *JSP,* J2:119–24.
19. Joseph Smith, Journal, Aug. 31, 1842, in *JSP,* J2:124; Nauvoo Relief Society Minute Book, Aug. 31, 1842, in Derr and others, *First Fifty Years of Relief Society,* 93.
20. Joseph Smith, Journal, Sept. 3, 1842, in *JSP,* J2:124–26.
21. Joseph Smith to "all the Saints in Nauvoo," Sept. 1, 1842, in *JSP,* J2:131–33; Doctrine and Covenants 127; "Tidings," *Times and Seasons,* Sept. 15, 1842, 3:919–20. **Topic: Baptism for the Dead**
22. Joseph Smith to "the Church of Jesus Christ of Latter-day Saints," Sept. [7], 1842, in *JSP,* J2:149–50; Doctrine and Covenants 128:18–24; "Letter from Joseph Smith," *Times and Seasons,* Oct. 1, 1842, 3:934–36; see also McBride, "Letters on Baptism for the Dead," 272–76; and *JSP,* J2:143, note 491.
23. Thomas Carlin to Emma Smith, Sept. 7, 1842, in *JSP,* J2:151–53.
24. Bennett, *History of the Saints;* "On Marriage," *Times and Seasons,* Oct. 1, 1842, 3:939–40; Smith, *Saintly Scoundrel,* 114–22; see also "The Discussion by General Bennett about Joe Smith and the Mormons," *New York Herald,* Aug. 31, 1842, [2].
25. See Joseph Smith to James Arlington Bennet, Sept. 8, 1842, in *JSP,* J2:137–43; and Joseph Smith, Journal, Oct. 5, 1842, in *JSP,* J2:161.
26. Thomas Ford to Joseph Smith, Dec. 17, 1842, in *JSP,* J2:179–81.
27. Joseph Smith, Journal, Dec. 26, 1842, in *JSP,* J2:193–94; see also Editorial Note, *JSP,* J2:194.
28. "From the Editor," *Alton Telegraph and Democratic Review,* Jan. 7, 1843, [2]; "Important from Illinois—Arrest of Joe Smith," *New York Herald,* Jan. 18, 1843, [2].
29. Arnold, *Reminiscences of the Illinois Bar,* 3; "Important from Illinois—Arrest of Joe Smith," *New York Herald,* Jan. 18, 1843, [2]; Joseph Smith, Journal, Jan. 4, 1843, in *JSP,* J2:216.

30. Arnold, *Reminiscences of the Illinois Bar,* 3; Joseph Smith, Journal, Jan. 4, 1843, in *JSP,* J2:216–27; Court Ruling, Jan. 5, 1843, in *JSP,* J2:401. **Topic: Missouri Extradition Attempts**
31. Joseph Smith, Journal, Jan. 4, 1843, in *JSP,* J2:222–24.
32. Joseph Smith, Journal, Jan. 5, 1843, in *JSP,* J2:227–34; Court Ruling, Jan. 5, 1843, in *JSP,* J2:391–402. **Topic: American Legal and Political Institutions**

CHAPTER 40: UNITED IN AN EVERLASTING COVENANT

1. Joseph Smith, Journal, Jan. 10 and 18, 1843, in *JSP,* J2:243, 245–46.
2. Joseph Smith, Journal, Apr. 16, 1843, in *JSP,* J2:360.
3. Woodruff, Journal, Jan. 22, 1843; Doctrine and Covenants 130:20–21 (Instruction, Apr. 2, 1843, as reported by Willard Richards and William Clayton, at josephsmithpapers.org).
4. See Haven, "A Girl's Letters from Nauvoo," 616–38; and Joseph Smith, Journal, Jan. 11, 1843, in *JSP,* J2:243.
5. Woodruff, Journal, Mar. 1, 1843; Nauvoo Relief Society Minute Book, Sept. 28, 1842–June 16, 1843, in Derr and others, *First Fifty Years of Relief Society,* 96–100; Emily Dow Partridge Young, "Autobiography," *Woman's Exponent,* Aug. 1, 1885, 14:37–38; Young, "Incidents in the Life of a Mormon Girl," 51; Lyman, Journal, 13; see also Jeffress, "Mapping Historic Nauvoo," 274–75; and Trustees Land Book A, White Purchase, block 146, lot 2.
6. "Young, Emily Dow Partridge," Biographical Entry, First Fifty Years of Relief Society website, churchhistorianspress.org; Nauvoo Relief Society Minute Book, Apr. 28, 1842, in Derr and others, *First Fifty Years of Relief Society,* 53; "Huntington, William, Sr.," Biographical Entry, Joseph Smith Papers website, josephsmithpapers.org; "Married," *Times and Seasons,* Oct. 1840, 1:191; "Plural Marriage in Kirtland and Nauvoo," Gospel Topics, topics.lds.org; Temple Lot Transcript, part 3, 373, 385, questions 532–34, 770; "Nauvoo Journals, December 1841–April 1843," in *JSP,* J2:xxix–xxx.
7. Young, Diary and Reminiscences, 1–2, Young, "Incidents in the Life of a Mormon Girl," 54.
8. Young, Diary and Reminiscences, 1–2, Young, "Incidents in the Life of a Mormon Girl," 54.
9. Young, Diary and Reminiscences, 1–2; Young, "Incidents in the Life of a Mormon Girl," 54.
10. Lyman, Journal, 13; Eliza Partridge Kimball, Affidavit, July 1, 1869, in Affidavits about Celestial Marriage, 2:32. **Topics: Sealing; Joseph Smith and Plural Marriage**
11. See Brigham Young, Discourse, Oct. 1866, George D. Watt, Discourse Shorthand Notes, Oct. 8, 1866, George D. Watt, Papers, as transcribed by LaJean Purcell Carruth, copy at Church History Library.
12. Brigham Young, Discourse, Oct. 1866, George D. Watt, Discourse Shorthand Notes, Oct. 8, 1866, George D. Watt, Papers, as transcribed by LaJean Purcell Carruth, copy at Church History Library.
13. "Biography of Mary Ann Angell Young," *Juvenile Instructor,* Jan. 15, 1891, 26:57–58; Arrington, *Brigham Young,* 102; Lucy Ann D. Young, Affidavit, July 10, 1869, in Affidavits about Celestial Marriage, 1:48.
14. Brigham Young, Discourse, Oct. 1866, George D. Watt, Discourse Shorthand Notes, Oct. 8, 1866, George D. Watt, Papers, as transcribed by LaJean Purcell Carruth, copy at Church History Library; see also Richards, Scriptural Items, 1843; and Woodruff, Journal, Jan. 22, 1843.
15. Brigham Young, Discourse, Oct. 1866, George D. Watt, Discourse Shorthand Notes, Oct. 8, 1866, George D. Watt, Papers, as transcribed by LaJean Purcell Carruth, copy at Church History Library.

16. "Clayton, William," Biographical Entry, Joseph Smith Papers website, josephsmithpapers.org. **Topic: Wards and Stakes**
17. Joseph Smith, Journal, Apr. 1, 1843, in *JSP,* J2:321.
18. Joseph Smith, Journal, Apr. 1–2, 1843, in *JSP,* J2:321–23.
19. Joseph Smith, Journal, Apr. 2, 1843, in *JSP,* J2:323–25; Doctrine and Covenants 130:1, 3.
20. Joseph Smith, Journal, Apr. 2, 1843, in *JSP,* J2:326; Doctrine and Covenants 130:22; Joseph Smith History, 1838–56, volume D-1, 1511. The word "and" was added to the original.
21. Joseph Smith, Journal, Apr. 2, 1843, in *JSP,* J2:325; Doctrine and Covenants 130:18–19.
22. Clayton, Journal, Apr. 2 and May 16, 1843; Instruction, May 16, 1843, as reported by William Clayton, at josephsmithpapers.org; Doctrine and Covenants 131:1–4; see also McBride, "Our Hearts Rejoiced to Hear Him Speak," 277–80. **Topic: Sealing**
23. Maughan, Autobiography, [52]–[54].
24. Joseph Smith, Journal, Apr. 6, 1843; Haven, "A Girl's Letters from Nauvoo," 624.
25. See Doctrine and Covenants 76:70–81 (Vision, Feb. 16, 1832, at josephsmithpapers.org); Mace, Autobiography, 120; Revelation 12:1. **Topic: Nauvoo Temple**
26. McBride, *House for the Most High,* 21–27, 91–95.
27. Maughan, Autobiography, [56].
28. "Mary Elizabeth Rollins Lightner," *Utah Genealogical and Historical Magazine,* July 1926, 17:202.
29. Mary Audentia Smith Anderson, "The Memoirs of Joseph Smith III," *Saints' Herald,* Feb. 19, 1935, 240; Mar. 17, 1936, 338.
30. See Temple Lot Transcript, part 3, 350–52, questions 22–24; see also George A. Smith to Joseph Smith III, Oct. 9, 1869, copy, George A. Smith, Papers, Church History Library; "More Testimony," *Ogden Herald,* May 21, 1886, 1; "Celestial Marriage," *Woman's Exponent,* June 1, 1886, 15:1–2.
31. See Eliza R. Snow to Joseph F. Smith, no date, Joseph F. Smith, Papers, Church History Library.
32. Amasa Lyman, in *Journal of Discourses,* Apr. 5, 1866, 11:198–208; "Plural Marriage in Kirtland and Nauvoo," Gospel Topics, topics.lds.org.
33. "Plural Marriage in Kirtland and Nauvoo," Gospel Topics, topics.lds.org. **Topics: Emma Hale Smith; Joseph Smith and Plural Marriage**
34. Young, Diary and Reminiscences, 2.
35. Temple Lot Transcript, part 3, 351, questions 31–32; Emily Dow Partridge Young, Statement, *Historical Record,* May 1887, 240; Young, "Incidents in the Life of a Mormon Girl," 51; Lyman, Journal, 13.
36. Young, "Incidents in the Life of a Mormon Girl," 54; Emily Dow Partridge Smith Young, "Testimony That Cannot Be Refuted," *Woman's Exponent,* Apr. 1, 1884, 12:165; Temple Lot Transcript, part 3, 351, 353–62, 371–72, questions 31–32, 47–272, 488–93.
37. Young, "Incidents in the Life of a Mormon Girl," 54; Emily Dow Partridge Smith Young, "Testimony That Cannot Be Refuted," *Woman's Exponent,* Apr. 1, 1884, 12:165; Temple Lot Transcript, part 3, 353–62, 371–72, questions 47–272, 488–93. **Topic: Joseph Smith and Plural Marriage**
38. Hyrum Smith, Discourse, in Levi Richards, Journal, May 14, 1843; Jacob 2:23–30.
39. Hyrum Smith, Discourse, in Levi Richards, Journal, May 14, 1843; Temple Lot Transcript, part 3, 373, 385, questions 532–34, 770.
40. Watson, *Brigham Young Addresses,* volume 5, Oct. 8, 1866; compare Brigham Young, Discourse, Oct. 8, 1866, George D. Watt, Discourse Shorthand Notes, Oct. 8, 1866, George D. Watt, Papers, as transcribed by LaJean Purcell Carruth, copy at Church History Library; see also Clayton, Journal, May 26, 1843. **Topic: Hyrum Smith**
41. Joseph Smith, Journal, May 28, 1843, in *JSP,* J3:25; see also Joseph Smith to Emma Smith, Nov. 12, 1838, in *JSP,* D6:290–93; and Emma Smith Blessing, 1844, Church History Library.
42. Joseph Smith, Journal, May 29, 1843, in *JSP,* J3:25–26; see also 25, note 89.
43. Joseph Smith History, 1838–56, volume E-1, 1987.

44. Joseph Smith, Journal, May 29, 1843, in *JSP,* J3:25–26; Historian's Office, Brigham Young History Drafts, 69; "Reminiscence of Mercy Rachel Fielding Thompson," quoted in Madsen, *In Their Own Words,* 195; see also Woodworth, "Mercy Thompson and the Revelation on Marriage," 281–93.
45. Joseph Smith, Journal, May 29, 1843, in *JSP,* J3:25–26; "Reminiscence of Mercy Rachel Fielding Thompson," quoted in Madsen, *In Their Own Words,* 195; see also Woodworth, "Mercy Thompson and the Revelation on Marriage," 281–93.
46. Joseph Smith, Journal, May 29, 1843, in *JSP,* J3:25–26. **Topic: Sealing**

CHAPTER 41: GOD MUST BE THE JUDGE

1. Pratt, Journal and Autobiography, 107–8.
2. Cannon, "Tahiti and the Society Island Mission," 334; Pratt, Journal and Autobiography, 107–8.
3. Pratt, Journal and Autobiography, 107–8; Joseph Smith History, 1838–56, volume D-1, 1568.
4. Quorum of the Twelve Apostles, Minutes, May 23, 1843.
5. Joseph Smith, Journal, June 13, 1843, in *JSP,* J3:36; "Missouri *vs* Joseph Smith," *Times and Seasons,* July 1, 1843, 4:242; Nauvoo Relief Society Minute Book, June 16, 1843, in Derr and others, *First Fifty Years of Relief Society,* 100.
6. Joseph Smith, Journal, June 11, 1843, in *JSP,* J3:31–35; Woodruff, Journal, June 11, 1843; Nauvoo Relief Society Minute Book, June 16, 1843, in Derr and others, *First Fifty Years of Relief Society,* 100.
7. Nauvoo Relief Society Minute Book, June 16, 1843, in Derr and others, *First Fifty Years of Relief Society,* 100–102. Sister Chase could have been either Phebe Ogden Ross Chase or Tirzah Wells Chase; see biographical entries for both women at churchhistorianspress.org.
8. Joseph Smith, Journal, June 16 and 18, 1843, in *JSP,* J3:37, 38; Clayton, Journal, June 18, 1843; Warrant for Joseph Smith, June 17, 1843, copy, Joseph Smith Collection, Church History Library; Joseph Smith History, 1838–56, volume D-1, 1581.
9. "Missouri *vs* Joseph Smith," *Nauvoo Neighbor,* July 5, 1843, [2]; Joseph Smith History, 1838–56, volume D-1, 1582. **Topic: Missouri Extradition Attempts**
10. Clayton, Journal, June 23, 1843; Joseph Smith History, 1838–56, volume D-1, 1583–88; *JSP,* J3:39, note 153; "Missouri *vs* Joseph Smith," *Times and Seasons,* July 1, 1843, 4:243.
11. Burbank, Autobiography, 43–44; Peter Conover, Statement, Sept. 26, 1854, Historian's Office, Joseph Smith History Documents, Church History Library; Joseph Smith, Journal, July 1–4, 1843, in *JSP,* J3:48–52; "Missouri *vs* Joseph Smith," *Times and Seasons,* July 1, 1843, 4:243; Joseph Smith History, 1838–56, volume D-1, 1591.
12. Clayton, Journal, June 30, 1843; Joseph Smith History, 1838–56, volume D-1, 1593; Joseph Smith, Journal, June 30, 1843, in *JSP,* J3:42; Peter Conover, Statement, Sept. 26, 1854, Historian's Office, Joseph Smith History Documents, Church History Library.
13. Joseph Smith, Journal, July 1, 1843, in *JSP,* J3:48; Nauvoo Municipal Court Docket Book, 55–87.
14. James, Autobiography, [1]; Wolfinger, *Test of Faith,* 1–3; Platt, "Early Branches of the Church of Jesus Christ of Latter-day Saints," 41. **Topic: Slavery and Abolition**
15. James, Autobiography, [1]. **Topic: Gift of Tongues**
16. James, Autobiography, [1]; Nauvoo Stake High Council Minutes, Dec. 9, 1843. **Topic: Jane Elizabeth Manning James**
17. Young, "Incidents in the Life of a Mormon Girl," 54; Lovina Smith Walker, Certificate, June 16, 1869, in Affidavits about Celestial Marriage, 1:30.
18. Clayton, Journal, July 12, 1843; William Clayton, Affidavit, Feb. 16, 1874, in Affidavits about Celestial Marriage, Church History Library; "Another Testimony—Statement of William Clayton," *Deseret Evening News,* May 20, 1886, [2].

19. Doctrine and Covenants 132:7–19 (Revelation, July 12, 1843, at josephsmithpapers.org).
20. Doctrine and Covenants 132:20 (Revelation, July 12, 1843, at josephsmithpapers.org).
21. Doctrine and Covenants 132:1–20, 29–37 (Revelation, July 12, 1843, at josephsmithpapers.org).
22. Jacob 2:27–30; see also Doctrine and Covenants 132:63 (Revelation, July 12, 1843, at josephsmithpapers.org).
23. Doctrine and Covenants 132:52–56 (Revelation, July 12, 1843, at josephsmithpapers.org).
24. Clayton, Journal, July 12, 1843; William Clayton, Statement, Feb. 16, 1874, in Affidavits about Celestial Marriage, Church History Library; William Clayton to Madison M. Scott, Nov. 11, 1871, copy, Church History Library.
25. William Clayton, Affidavit, Feb. 16, 1874, in Affidavits about Celestial Marriage, Church History Library; "Another Testimony—Statement of William Clayton," *Deseret Evening News,* May 20, 1886, [2]; Clayton, Journal, July 12, 1843. **Topics: Emma Hale Smith; Joseph Smith and Plural Marriage**
26. Joseph Smith, Journal, July 13, 1843, in *JSP,* J3:57–59; Clayton, Journal, July 13, 1843; see also *JSP,* J3:57, note 262.
27. Joseph Smith, Journal, July 13, 1843, in *JSP,* J3:57–59; Clayton, Journal, July 12–15, 1843; William Clayton, Affidavit, Feb. 16, 1874, in Affidavits about Celestial Marriage, Church History Library; "Another Testimony—Statement of William Clayton," *Deseret Evening News,* May 20, 1886, [2]; Trustees Land Book B, White Purchase, 241–44, 246, 249, 251, 259–61, 265; Galland Purchase, 267–71, 273; see also *JSP,* J3:57, note 262.
28. See "Nauvoo Journals, May 1843–June 1844," in *JSP,* J3:xix–xx; see also 57–59, notes 259 and 262.
29. Joseph Smith, Journal, Aug. 31, Sept. 15, and Oct. 3, 1843, in *JSP,* J3:91, 99, 105; "Nauvoo Mansion," Geographical Entry, Joseph Smith Papers website, josephsmithpapers.org; Smith, *Biographical Sketches,* 274; see also *JSP,* J3:91, note 421.
30. **Topic: Slavery and Abolition**
31. James, Autobiography, [1]–[4]; "Joseph Smith, the Prophet," *Young Woman's Journal,* Dec. 1905, 551–52. **Topic: Jane Elizabeth Manning James**
32. See Clayton, Journal, June 23, 1843; July 12, 1843; Aug. 3, 16, and 23, 1843.
33. Doctrine and Covenants 25:13–15 (Revelation, July 1830–C, at josephsmithpapers.org).
34. Emily Dow Partridge Smith Young, "Testimony That Cannot Be Refuted," *Woman's Exponent,* Apr. 1, 1884, 12:165.
35. Emily Dow Partridge Young, "Autobiography," *Woman's Exponent,* Aug. 1, 1885, 14:38; Young, "Incidents in the Life of a Mormon Girl," 186; Young, Diary and Reminiscences, 2.
36. Young, Diary and Reminiscences, 2–3; Emily Dow Partridge Young, "Autobiography," *Woman's Exponent,* Aug. 1, 1885, 14:38; see also Lyman, Journal, 13.
37. Young, Diary and Reminiscences, 5.
38. Emily Dow Partridge Smith Young, "Testimony That Cannot Be Refuted," *Woman's Exponent,* Apr. 1, 1884, 12:165. **Topic: Emma Hale Smith**
39. Young, "Incidents in the Life of a Mormon Girl," 177; see also Young, Diary and Reminiscences, 5.

CHAPTER 42: ROUND UP YOUR SHOULDERS

1. Woodruff, Journal, Nov. 4, 1843; see also Woodruff, Journal, Jan. 16, 17, 18, and 19, 1844.
2. Wilford Woodruff to Phebe Carter Woodruff, Oct. 1843, Emma S. Woodruff, Collection, Church History Library; see also Woodruff, Journal, Oct. 8, 1843.
3. Woodruff, Journal, Nov. 11, 1843.
4. Joseph Smith, Journal, Sept. 28, 1843, in *JSP,* J3:104–5; Clayton, Journal, Oct. 19, 1843; see also "Nauvoo Journals, May 1843–June 1844," in *JSP,* J3:xx–xxi; Nauvoo

Relief Society Minute Book, Mar. 30, Apr. 28, and Aug. 31, 1842, in Derr and others, *First Fifty Years of Relief Society,* 43, 59, 94; and Doctrine and Covenants 132:7–20 (Revelation, July 12, 1843, at josephsmithpapers.org).

5. Joseph Smith, Journal, Sept. 28 and Oct. 1, 1843, in *JSP,* J3:104, 105; "Part 1: 1830, 1842–1854," in Derr and others, *First Fifty Years of Relief Society,* 10. **Topic: Emma Hale Smith**

6. Joseph Smith, Journal, Oct. 8 and Nov. 1, 1843, in *JSP,* J3:109, 123; Young, Journal, Nov. 1, 1843, 21; Helen Mar Whitney, "Scenes in Nauvoo," *Woman's Exponent,* July 1, 1883, 12:[18]; Bathsheba W. Smith, Affidavit, Nov. 19, 1903, Church History Library; Whitney, *Plural Marriage,* 14.

7. Joseph Smith, Journal, Dec. 2, 1843, in *JSP,* J3:138; Woodruff, Journal, Dec. 2 and 23, 1843.

8. "Nauvoo Journals, May 1843–June 1844," in *JSP,* J3:xx–xxi; Joseph Smith, Journal, Sept. 28 1843; Oct. 1, 8, 12, and 29, 1843; Nov. 1, 1843; and Dec. 2, 9, 17, and 23, 1843; in *JSP,* J3:104–5, 108–9, 112, 122, 123, 138, 142–43, 146, 150; Clayton, Journal, Dec. 2, 1843; Ehat, "Joseph Smith's Introduction of Temple Ordinances," 98–100, 102–3; "Quorum, The," Glossary entry, Joseph Smith Papers website, josephsmithpapers.org. **Topic: Anointed Quorum ("Holy Order")**

9. Neibaur, Journal, May 24, 1844; Council of Fifty, "Record," [290], in *JSP,* CFM:192; see also 192, note 596; and Cook, *William Law,* 25–27, note 84.

10. "Dr. Wyl and Dr. Wm. Law," *Salt Lake Daily Tribune,* July 31, 1887, [6]; Neibaur, Journal, May 24, 1844; see also Cook, *William Law,* 24–25.

11. McMurrin, "An Interesting Testimony," 507–9.

12. Neibaur, Journal, May 24, 1844; Council of Fifty, "Record," [290], in *JSP,* CFM:192; see also 192, note 596; and Cook, *William Law,* 25–27, note 84.

13. Clayton, Journal, June 12, 1844; see also Cook, *William Law,* 25.

14. Joseph Smith, Journal, Dec. 30, 1843, in *JSP,* J3:154; see also 154, note 692.

15. "Dr. Wyl and Dr. Wm. Law," *Salt Lake Daily Tribune,* July 31, 1887, [6].

16. Law, Record of Doings, Jan. 8, 1844, in Cook, *William Law,* 46–47; Joseph Smith, Journal, Jan. 8, 1844, in *JSP,* J3:159; see also 159, note 707. No manuscript version of Law's "Record of Doings" has been located. For more analysis, see "Essay on Sources," in *JSP,* J3:491–92.

17. Woodruff, Journal, Jan. 21, 1844.

18. "Great Meeting of Anti Mormons!," *Warsaw Message,* Sept. 13, 1843, [1]–[2]; Joseph Smith History, 1838–56, volume E-1, 1687; Ford, *History of Illinois,* 319. **Topic: American Legal and Political Institutions**

19. Joseph Smith, Journal, Nov. 4 and Dec. 27, 1843; May 5, 1844, in *JSP,* J3:124, 152, 243; 152, note 683; 166, note 738; 243, note 1102; Henry Clay to Joseph Smith, Nov. 15, 1843; Lewis Cass to Joseph Smith, Dec. 9, 1843; John C. Calhoun to Joseph Smith, Dec. 2, 1843, Joseph Smith Collection, Church History Library.

20. Joseph Smith, Journal, Jan. 29, 1844, in *JSP,* J3:169–71; "Who Shall Be Our Next President?," *Times and Seasons,* Feb. 15, 1844, 5:439–41; Robertson, "Campaign and the Kingdom," 164–65. **Topic: Joseph Smith's 1844 Campaign for United States President**

21. Addison Pratt, Journal, Jan. 13, 1844; Ellsworth, *Journals of Addison Pratt,* 114–15. **Topic: Patriarchal Blessings**

22. Addison Pratt, Journal, Oct. 6, 1843; Dec. 3 and 7, 1843; Jan. 12 and 19, 1844; Perrin, "Seasons of Faith," 202–3.

23. Addison Pratt, Journal, Jan. 26, 1844.

24. Addison Pratt, Journal, Jan. 19, 1844.

25. Thompson, Autobiographical Sketch, 7–9; see also Doctrine and Covenants 85:1–3 (Joseph Smith to William W. Phelps, Nov. 27, 1832, at josephsmithpapers.org). After Mercy Fielding Thompson's sealing to her deceased husband, Robert, in May 1843, he appeared to Joseph Smith in vision and asked to have Mercy marry Hyrum Smith

for time. Joseph sealed Hyrum and Mercy on August 11, 1843. (Woodworth, "Mercy Thompson and the Revelation on Plural Marriage," 281–93.)

26. "To the Sisters of the Church of Jesus Christ in England," *LDS Millennial Star,* June 1844, 5:15; see also Introduction to Boston Female Penny and Sewing Society, Minutes, Jan. 28, 1845, in Derr and others, *First Fifty Years of Relief Society,* 163.

27. Joseph Smith, Journal, Jan. 29, 1844; Feb. 8, 19, and 25, 1844; Mar. 7, 1844, in *JSP,* J3:171, 175, 179, 183, 194.

28. Joseph Smith, *General Smith's Views of the Powers and Policy of the Government of the United States* (Nauvoo, IL: John Taylor, 1844); see also *JSP,* J3:168, note 748; 173, note 775. **Topic: Joseph Smith's 1844 Campaign for United States President**

29. Joseph Smith, Journal, Feb. 20, 1844, in *JSP,* J3:180; "The Council of Fifty in Nauvoo, Illinois," in *JSP,* CFM:xxvi–xxxix; "Early Discussions of Relocating," Joseph Smith Papers website, josephsmithpapers.org.

30. "The Council of Fifty in Nauvoo, Illinois," in *JSP,* CFM:xxiii; Council of Fifty, "Record," Mar. 10–11, 1844, in *JSP,* CFM:17–45. **Topic: Council of Fifty**

31. Council of Fifty, "Record," Mar. 11, 1844, in *JSP,* CFM:39–45; "The Council of Fifty in Nauvoo, Illinois," in *JSP,* CFM:xxxvii.

32. Orson Hyde, Statement about Quorum of the Twelve, circa late March 1845, Brigham Young Office Files, Church History Library; Baugh and Holzapfel, "I Roll the Burthen and Responsibility," 15, 18; Brigham Young, Sermon, Oct. 6, 1866, George D. Watt, Discourse Shorthand Notes, Oct. 6, 1866, George D. Watt, Papers, as transcribed by LaJean Purcell Carruth, copy at Church History Library; Parley P. Pratt to the Church of Jesus Christ of Latter-day Saints, Jan. 1, 1845, in *Prophet,* Jan. 4, 1845, 33.

33. Orson Hyde, Statement about Quorum of the Twelve, circa late March 1845, Brigham Young Office Files, Church History Library; Baugh and Holzapfel, "I Roll the Burthen and Responsibility," 18; Holzapfel and Harper, "This Is My Testimony," 112–16. **Topic: Succession of Church Leadership**

34. Brigham Young, Sermon, Oct. 6, 1866, George D. Watt, Discourse Shorthand Notes, Oct. 6, 1866, George D. Watt, Papers, as transcribed by LaJean Purcell Carruth, copy at Church History Library; Parley P. Pratt to the Church of Jesus Christ of Latter-day Saints, Jan. 1, 1845, in *Prophet,* Jan. 4, 1845, 33. **Topic: Quorum of the Twelve**

35. Orson Hyde, Statement about Quorum of the Twelve, circa late March 1845, Brigham Young Office Files, Church History Library; Woodruff, Journal, Aug. 25, 1844; Wilford Woodruff, Testimony, Mar. 19, 1897, Church History Library; Historian's Office, General Church Minutes, McEwan copy, Sept. 8, 1844; Clayton copy, Sept. 8, 1844; Nauvoo Stake High Council Minutes, Nov. 30, 1844; "Trial of Elder Rigdon," *Times and Seasons,* Sept. 15, 1844, 5:650–51; Parley P. Pratt, "Proclamation," *LDS Millennial Star,* Mar. 1845, 5:151; Wilford Woodruff, "To the Officers and Members of the Church of Jesus Christ of Latter-day Saints in the British Islands," *LDS Millennial Star,* Feb. 1845, 5:136; Council of Fifty, "Record," Mar. 18 and 25, 1844, in *JSP,* CFM:337–38, 379; George A. Smith, Sermon, Dec. 25, 1874, 2–4, Saint George Utah Stake, General Minutes, Church History Library; Johnson, "A Life Review," 96; Benjamin F. Johnson to George F. Gibbs, Apr.–Oct. 1903, 1911, Benjamin Franklin Johnson, Papers, Church History Library; see also Historian's Office, General Church Minutes, Sept. 30, 1855.

CHAPTER 43: A PUBLIC NUISANCE

1. Law, Record of Doings, Mar. 29 and Apr. 15, 1844, in Cook, *William Law,* 47–49.

2. Woodruff, Journal, Mar. 24, 1844; Affidavits of A. B. Williams and M. G. Eaton, *Nauvoo Neighbor,* Apr. 17, 1844, [2].

3. Woodruff, Journal, Mar. 24, 1844.

4. Orson Hyde, Statement about Quorum of the Twelve, circa Late Mar. 1845, Brigham Young Office Files, Church History Library; Bushman, *Rough Stone Rolling,* 532–34.

5. Cummings, "Conspiracy of Nauvoo," *Contributor,* Apr. 1884, 252.

6. "Conference Minutes," *Times and Seasons,* Aug. 15, 1844, 5:612–13; Historian's Office, General Church Minutes, Clayton copy, Apr. 7, 1844, 11; Bullock copy, Apr. 7, 1844, 14; Joseph Smith, Journal, Apr. 7, 1844, in *JSP,* J3:217.
7. "Conference Minutes," *Times and Seasons,* Aug. 15, 1844, 5:613–14; Historian's Office, General Church Minutes, Clayton copy, Apr. 7, 1844, [12]–14; Bullock copy, Apr. 7, 1844, 15–17. The original quotation is slightly different, reading "although the earthly tabernacle shall be dissolved, that they shall rise in immortal glory."
8. Historian's Office, General Church Minutes, Bullock copy, Apr. 7, 1844, 17; Woodruff, Journal, Apr. 7, 1844; "Conference Minutes," *Times and Seasons,* Aug. 15, 1844, 5:617.
9. "Conference Minutes," *Times and Seasons,* Aug. 15, 1844, 5:616–17; Historian's Office, General Church Minutes, Bullock copy, Apr. 7, 1844, 19–22; see also Joseph Smith, Journal, May 21 and June 11, 1843, in *JSP,* J3:20, 31; Joseph Smith History, 1838–56, volume D-1, 1556.
10. Joseph Smith, Journal, Apr. 7, 1844, in *JSP,* J3:217–22; Historian's Office, General Church Minutes, Bullock copy, Apr. 7, 1844, 22; "Conference Minutes," *Times and Seasons,* Aug. 15, 1844, 5:617; see also "Accounts of the 'King Follett Sermon,'" Joseph Smith Papers website, josephsmithpapers.org. **Topic: King Follett Discourse**
11. Ellen Briggs Douglas to Family Members, Apr. 14, 1844, in Derr and others, *First Fifty Years of Relief Society,* 157–62; George Douglas and Ellen Briggs Douglas to "Father and Mother," June 2, 1842, Ellen B. Parker, Letters, Church History Library. One line is slightly different in the original source: "fetched me such a present as I never received before from no place in the world." **Topic: Female Relief Society of Nauvoo**
12. Cummings, "Conspiracy of Nauvoo," *Contributor,* Apr. 1884, 252–53.
13. "Resolutions," *Nauvoo Expositor,* June 7, 1844, [2]. **Topic: Dissent in the Church**
14. "The New Church," *Warsaw Signal,* May 15, 1844, [2]; Joseph Smith, Journal, Feb. 21, 1843, in *JSP,* J2:271–73; see also 239, note 1074.
15. Nauvoo City Council Draft Minutes, June 8, 1844, 13–15; Nauvoo Stake High Council Minutes, May 20 and 24, 1842; *JSP,* J3:245, note 1108; 246, note 1116; see also Joseph Smith History, 1838–56, volume E-1, 1949.
16. Cummings, "Conspiracy of Nauvoo," *Contributor,* Apr. 1884, 253–57.
17. Cummings, "Conspiracy of Nauvoo," *Contributor,* Apr. 1884, 257–59.
18. Council of Fifty, "Record," Apr. 11, 1844, in *JSP,* CFM:95–96; see also Revelation 1:6.
19. Council of Fifty, "Record," Apr. 11, 1844, in *JSP,* CFM:97–101. **Topic: Council of Fifty**
20. Law, Record of Doings, Apr. 19–22, 1844, in Cook, *William Law,* 50–52; Joseph Smith, Journal, Apr. 18, 1844, in *JSP,* J3:231–32; see also 232, note 1037.
21. Joseph Smith, Journal, Apr. 28, 1844, in *JSP,* J3:238.
22. Law, Record of Doings, June 1, 1844, in Cook, *William Law,* 54; Joseph Smith, Journal, Apr. 28, 1844, in *JSP,* J3:239; see also 239, note 1074; and "The New Church," *Warsaw Signal,* May 15, 1844, [2].
23. "Why Oppose the Mormons?," *Warsaw Signal,* Apr. 25, 1844, [2]; see also *JSP,* J3:238, note 1068.
24. *Prospectus of the Nauvoo Expositor* [Nauvoo, IL: May 10, 1844], copy at Church History Library.
25. Joseph Smith, Journal, May 6, 1844, in *JSP,* J3:245; Subpoena for Wilson and William Law, May 27, 1844, State of Illinois v. Joseph Smith for Adultery [Hancock County Circuit Court 1844], Illinois State Historical Library, Circuit Court Case Files, 1830–1900, microfilm, Church History Library; see also *JSP,* J3:245, note 1108; 261, note 1189. **Topic: Nauvoo Expositor**
26. Joseph Smith, Discourse, May 12, 1844, Joseph Smith Collection, Church History Library; Joseph Smith, Journal, May 12, 1844, in *JSP,* J3:248–49.
27. Joseph Smith, Journal, May 17, 1844, in *JSP,* J3:253; see also 253, note 1147.
28. Clayton, Journal, May 21, 1844; Joseph Smith, Journal, May 21, 25, and 27, 1844, in *JSP,* J3:256, 260–61, 263.
29. Joseph Smith, Journal, May 27, 1844, in *JSP,* J3:263–65.
30. Thomas Sharp, Editorial, *Warsaw Signal,* May 29, 1844, [2].

31. Pratt, Journal and Autobiography, 108–13.
32. "Preamble" and "Resolutions," *Nauvoo Expositor,* June 7, 1844, [1]–[2].
33. Francis M. Higbee to "Citizens of Hancock County," June 5, 1844, in *Nauvoo Expositor,* June 7, 1844, [3].
34. Joseph Smith, Journal, June 8, 1844, in *JSP,* J3:274–76; Nauvoo City Council Draft Minutes, June 8, 1844, 18.
35. Nauvoo City Council Draft Minutes, June 8, 1844, 19.
36. Nauvoo City Council Draft Minutes, June 10, 1844, 19–31; Joseph Smith, Journal, June 10, 1844, in *JSP,* J3:276–77.
37. Nauvoo City Council Draft Minutes, June 10, 1844, 27; see also Oaks, "Suppression of the *Nauvoo Expositor,*" 862–903; William Blackstone, *Commentaries on the Laws of England* (New York: W. E. Dean, 1840).
38. Nauvoo City Council Draft Minutes, June 10, 1844, 30–31; Nauvoo City Council Minute Book, June 10, 1844, 210–11; Joseph Smith, Journal, June 10, 1844, in *JSP,* J3:276. One member of the city council, Benjamin Warrington, spoke against the resolution; he argued that the council should first try fining the publisher of the *Expositor.* (*JSP,* J3:276–77, note 1258.)
39. Joseph Smith, Journal, June 10, 1844, in *JSP,* J3:276–77; Joseph Smith, Order to Nauvoo City Marshal, June 10, 1844, Joseph Smith Collection, Church History Library; "Unparalleled Outrage at Nauvoo," *Warsaw Signal,* June 12, 1844, [2]. **Topic: Nauvoo Expositor**
40. "Unparalleled Outrage at Nauvoo," *Warsaw Signal,* June 12, 1844, [2].

Chapter 44: A Lamb to the Slaughter

1. "Preamble and Resolutions," *Warsaw Signal,* Extra, June 14, 1844; Sarah D. Gregg to Thomas Gregg, June 14, 1844, copy, Illinois State Historical Society Papers, Church History Library; James Robbins to Leanna Robbins, June 16, 1844, James Robbins Letters, Church History Library; Joseph Smith, Proclamation to John P. Greene, June 17, 1844; Joseph Smith to Jonathan Dunham, June 17, 1844, Joseph Smith Collection, Church History Library.
2. Joseph Smith, Journal, June 13, 1844, in *JSP,* J3:280–81; see also 281, note 1284.
3. Maughan, Autobiography, [57]–[58]; "History of Joseph Smith," *LDS Millennial Star,* Nov. 9, 1861, 23:720; see also *JSP,* J3:8, note 14; 16, note 39.
4. Maughan, Autobiography, [57]–[58]; *Peter Maughan Family History,* 17–18.
5. Clayton, Journal, June 11, 1844; *JSP,* J3:279, note 1272; see also Joseph Smith, Journal, June 11, 1844, in *JSP,* J3:277–79.
6. Joseph Smith, Journal, June 11–12, 1844, in *JSP,* J3:279; Warrant for Joseph Smith and Others, June 11, 1844, State of Illinois v. Joseph Smith and Others for Riot, copy, Joseph Smith Collection, Church History Library.
7. Joseph Smith, Journal, June 12–13, 1844, in *JSP,* J3:279–82; Warrant for Joseph Smith and Others, June 11, 1844, State of Illinois v. Joseph Smith and Others for Riot, copy, Joseph Smith Collection, Church History Library; Nauvoo Municipal Court Docket Book, 108–12.
8. Joseph Smith, Journal, June 14, 1844, in *JSP,* J3:282; Clayton, Daily Account of Joseph Smith's Activities, June 14, 1844, in *JSP,* J3:333–34; Joseph Smith to Thomas Ford, June 14, 1844, Joseph Smith Collection, Church History Library; Sidney Rigdon to Thomas Ford, June 14, 1844, Sidney Rigdon Collection, Church History Library; see also Joseph Smith History, 1838–56, volume F-1, 97–98.
9. Joseph Smith, Journal, June 16–18, 1844, in *JSP,* J3:286–92; Joseph Smith, Proclamation, June 17, 1844, Joseph Smith Collection, Church History Library; *JSP,* J3:294–95, note 1357; Hyrum Smith and Joseph Smith to Brigham Young, June 17, 1844, Joseph Smith Collection, Church History Library.

10. Joseph Smith, Journal, June 18, 1844, in *JSP,* J3:290–91; Joseph Smith History, 1838–56, volume F-1, 118–19.
11. Oaks, "Suppression of the *Nauvoo Expositor,*" 891–903.
12. Thomas Ford to Joseph Smith, June 22, 1844, Joseph Smith Collection, Church History Library. **Topic: American Legal and Political Institutions**
13. Joseph Smith to Thomas Ford, June 22, 1844, Joseph Smith Collection, Church History Library; Editorial Note, in *JSP,* J3:301–2.
14. Joseph Smith History, 1838–56, volume F-1, 147; Richards, Journal, June 23, 1844, in *JSP,* J3:305.
15. Joseph Smith to Emma Smith, June 23, 1844, copy, Joseph Smith Collection, Church History Library.
16. Joseph Smith History, 1838–56, volume F-1, 148; Richards, Journal, June 23, 1844, in *JSP,* J3:305.
17. Briggs, "A Visit to Nauvoo in 1856," 453–54; Joseph Smith History, 1838–56, volume F-1, 148.
18. Briggs, "A Visit to Nauvoo in 1856," 453–54.
19. Joseph Smith History, 1838–56, volume F-1, 149; "Pleasant Chat," *True Latter Day Saints' Herald,* Oct. 1, 1868, 105; Christensen, "Edwin Rushton," 3. **Topic: Joseph and Emma Hale Smith Family**
20. Christensen, "Edwin Rushton," 3; John Bernhisel to George A. Smith, Sept. 11, 1854, in Historian's Office, Joseph Smith History Documents, Church History Library; Doctrine and Covenants 135:4 (Account of the Martyrdom, circa July 1844, at josephsmithpapers.org); Joseph Smith History, 1838–56, volume F-1, 149–51; Richards, Journal, June 24, 1844, in *JSP,* J3:305; Clayton, Journal, June 24, 1844.
21. Joseph Smith History, 1838–56, volume F-1, 151; Richards, Journal, June 24, 1844, in *JSP,* J3:305.
22. Richards, Journal, June 24, 1844, in *JSP,* J3:306; Joseph Smith History, 1838–56, volume F-1, 151–52; see also "Awful Assassination of Joseph and Hyrum Smith," *Times and Seasons,* July 1, 1844, 5:560; "Statement of Facts," *Times and Seasons,* July 1, 1844, 5:563; and *JSP,* J3:306, note 6.
23. Leonora C. Taylor, Statement, circa 1856, Church History Library; Clayton, Journal, June 24, 1844.
24. Emma Smith Blessing, 1844, typescript, Church History Library. The original blessing Emma wrote is lost. Historian Juanita Brooks reported that she studied the original in about 1946, compared the handwriting to Emma's, and sent transcripts of the blessing to George Albert Smith and Joseph K. Nicholes. (See Juanita Brooks to Joseph K. Nicholes, Apr. 29, 1946, Joseph K. Nicholes Collection, Church History Library; Juanita Brooks to George Albert Smith, Apr. 29, 1946, Joseph Fielding Smith, Papers, Church History Library; and Emma Smith to Joseph Heywood, Oct. 18, 1844, Church History Library.) **Topic: Emma Hale Smith**
25. Joseph Smith History, 1838–56, volume F-1, 154; Richards, Journal, June 24, 1844, in *JSP,* J3:306.
26. Joseph Smith History, 1838–56, volume F-1, 155–56; Richards, Journal, June 25, 1844, in *JSP,* J3:307–8.
27. Richards, Journal, June 25, 1844, in *JSP,* J3:307, 311–14; Joseph Smith History, 1838–56, volume F-1, 158–61; "Statement of Facts," *Times and Seasons,* July 1, 1844, 5:561–62; Dan Jones, "Martyrdom of Joseph Smith and His Brother Hyrum!," in Dennis, "Martyrdom of Joseph Smith and His Brother Hyrum," 87–88; Joseph Smith to Emma Smith, June 25, 1844, copy, Joseph Smith Collection, Church History Library.
28. Dennis, "Dan Jones, Welshman," 50–52.
29. Dan Jones, "Martyrdom of Joseph Smith and His Brother Hyrum!"; Dan Jones to Thomas Bullock, Jan. 20, 1855, in Dennis, "Martyrdom of Joseph and Hyrum Smith," 89, 101.
30. Dan Jones, "Martyrdom of Joseph Smith and His Brother Hyrum!"; Dan Jones to Thomas Bullock, Jan. 20, 1855, in Dennis, "Martyrdom of Joseph and Hyrum Smith," 89, 101. **Topic: Prophecies of Joseph Smith**

31. Joseph Smith to Emma Smith, June 27, 1844, copy, Joseph Smith Collection, Church History Library; Richards, Journal, June 27, 1844, in *JSP,* J3:323; Dan Jones, "Martyrdom of Joseph Smith and His Brother Hyrum!," in Dennis, "Martyrdom of Joseph Smith and His Brother Hyrum," 90; Joseph Smith History, 1838–56, volume F-1, 174–76.

32. Clayton, Journal, June 26, 1844; Joseph Smith to Emma Smith, June 27, 1844, copy, Joseph Smith Collection, Church History Library; Richards, Journal, June 27, 1844, in *JSP,* J3:323; see also Richards, Journal, June 26, 1844, in *JSP,* J3:314–23.

33. Joseph Smith to Emma Smith, June 27, 1844, copy, Joseph Smith Collection, Church History Library.

34. Ford, *History of Illinois,* 346; Joseph Smith History, 1838–56, volume F-1, 186.

35. Joseph Smith History, 1838–56, volume F-1, 186; Mace, Autobiography, 107; Clayton, Journal, June 27, 1844.

36. Clayton, Journal, June 27, 1844; Mace, Autobiography, 107–8; Ford, *History of Illinois,* 346–47; Joseph Smith History, 1838–56, volume F-1, 192.

37. Richards, Journal, June 27, 1844, in *JSP,* J3:327; Joseph Smith History, 1838–56, volume F-1, 182; "Statement of Facts," *Times and Seasons,* July 1, 1844, 5:563.

38. Richards, Journal, June 27, 1844, in *JSP,* J3:327; John Fullmer to George A. Smith, Nov. 27, 1854; Cyrus Wheelock to George A. Smith, Dec. 29, 1854, Historian's Office, Joseph Smith History Documents, Church History Library; *JSP,* J3:327, note 128; "History of Joseph Smith," *LDS Millennial Star,* June 14, 1862, 24:375; Stephen Markham to Wilford Woodruff, June 20, 1856, Historian's Office, Joseph Smith History Documents, Church History Library.

39. Richards, Journal, June 27, 1844, in *JSP,* J3:326; Carruth and Staker, "John Taylor's June 27, 1854, Account of the Martyrdom," 59; Joseph Smith History, 1838–56, volume F-1, 180–81; *A Collection of Sacred Hymns* [1840], 254–57; see also "A Poor Wayfaring Man of Grief," *Hymns,* no. 29. **Topic: Hymns**

40. Richards, Journal, June 27, 1844, in *JSP,* J3:326–27; Joseph Smith History, 1838–56, volume F-1, 181–82.

41. Richards, Journal, June 27, 1844, in *JSP,* J3:327; Joseph Smith History, 1838–56, volume F-1, 182; Ford, *History of Illinois,* 353.

42. Richards, Journal, June 27, 1844, in *JSP,* J3:327; Joseph Smith History, 1838–56, volume F-1, 182.

43. Richards, Journal, June 27, 1844, in *JSP,* J3:327; Joseph Smith History, 1838–56, volume F-1, 182–83.

44. Richards, Journal, June 27, 1844, in *JSP,* J3:329; Willard Richards, "Two Minutes in Jail," *Nauvoo Neighbor,* July 24, 1844, [3]; John Taylor, "The Martyrdom of Joseph Smith," in Burton, *City of the Saints,* 537; see also "Two Minutes in Jail," *Times and Seasons,* Aug. 1, 1844, 5:598–99; and Joseph Smith History, 1838–56, volume F-1, 182–83.

45. Joseph Smith History, 1838–56, volume F-1, 183; Willard Richards, "Two Minutes in Jail," *Nauvoo Neighbor,* July 24, 1844, [3]; see also "Two Minutes in Jail," *Times and Seasons,* Aug. 1, 1844, 5:598–99. **Topic: Deaths of Joseph And Hyrum Smith**

CHAPTER 45: AN ALMIGHTY FOUNDATION

1. Mary Audentia Smith Anderson, "The Memoirs of President Joseph Smith," *Saints' Herald,* Jan. 29, 1935, 143.

2. Call, Autobiography and Journal, 12.

3. Mary Audentia Smith Anderson, "The Memoirs of President Joseph Smith," *Saints' Herald,* Jan. 29, 1835, 143; "The Prophet's Death!," *Deseret Evening News,* Nov. 27, 1875, [2]–[3].

4. "The Prophet's Death!," *Deseret Evening News,* Nov. 27, 1875, [2]–[3].

5. Joseph Smith History, 1838–56, volume F-1, 188; "The Prophet's Death!," *Deseret Evening News,* Nov. 27, 1875, [3].

6. Lucy Mack Smith, History, 1845, 312.

7. Joseph Smith History, 1838–56, volume F-1, 183; Willard Richards, "Two Minutes in Jail," *Nauvoo Neighbor,* July 24, 1844, [3]. **Topic: Prophecies of Joseph Smith**

8. *Portrait and Biographical Record of Hancock, McDonough and Henderson Counties, Illinois,* 135–36; see also Carruth and Staker, "John Taylor's June 27, 1854, Account of the Martyrdom," 31.

9. Willard Richards and John Taylor to Thomas Ford and Others, June 27, 1844, Willard Richards, Journals and Papers, Church History Library; Joseph Smith History, 1838–56, volume F-1, 185; see also Roberts, *Life of John Taylor,* 144–45.

10. Joseph Smith History, 1838–56, volume F-1, 188; Vilate Murray Kimball to Heber C. Kimball, June 30, 1844, Church History Library; "The Prophet's Death!," *Deseret Evening News,* Nov. 27, 1875, [3].

11. Joseph Smith History, 1838–56, volume F-1, 188; Clayton, Journal, June 28, 1844; Zina D. H. Young, Diary, June 28, 1844.

12. Mace, Autobiography, 110; "Who Are the Rebels?," *LDS Millennial Star,* Mar. 20, 1858, 20:179.

13. Lucy Mack Smith, History, 1845, 312–13; "The Prophet's Death!," *Deseret Evening News,* Nov. 27, 1875, [3]; Joseph Smith History, 1838–56, volume F-1, 188–89; Mary Audentia Smith Anderson, "The Memoirs of President Joseph Smith," *Saints' Herald,* Jan. 29, 1935, 143.

14. Lucy Mack Smith, History, 1845, 312–13.

15. "The Prophet's Death!," *Deseret Evening News,* Nov. 27, 1875, [3]; Joseph Smith History, 1838–56, volume F-1, 189.

16. Phelps, Funeral Sermon of Joseph and Hyrum Smith, 1855, Church History Library.

17. Mary Ann Angell Young to Brigham Young, June 30, 1844, Brigham Young Office Files, Church History Library; see also Vilate Murray Kimball to Heber C. Kimball, June 30, 1844, Church History Library. Original source has "Our dear brother Joseph Smith and Hyrum has fell victims to a ferocious mob."

18. Vilate Murray Kimball to Heber C. Kimball, June 30, 1844, Church History Library.

19. Phebe Carter Woodruff to "Dear Parents," July 30, 1844, Church History Library; see also Mahas, "Remembering the Martyrdom," 299–306.

20. Historian's Office, Brigham Young History Drafts, 98–100; "History of Brigham Young," *Deseret News,* Mar. 24, 1858, 1; Historian's Office, Manuscript History of Brigham Young, book G, 103.

21. "History of Brigham Young," *Deseret News,* Mar. 24, 1858, 1; Historian's Office, Brigham Young History Drafts, 99; Woodruff, Journal, July 18, 1844.

22. Woodruff, Journal, July 18, 1844.

23. Clayton, Journal, July 2–4, 7, and 12, 1844; Oaks and Bentley, "Joseph Smith and Legal Process," 735–82; for an example of a deed prepared to separate Joseph's personal property from church property, see Bond from Joseph Smith, Sidney Rigdon, and Hyrum Smith, Jan. 4, 1842, at josephsmithpapers.org. **Topic: Emma Hale Smith**

24. Clayton, Journal, July 12, 1844; Obituary for Samuel H. Smith, *Times and Seasons,* Aug. 1, 1844, 5:606–7; Lucy Mack Smith, History, 1845, 313–14.

25. Clayton, Journal, July 4–8, 1844.

26. Clayton, Journal, July 12, 1844; *JSP,* J3:163, note 726.

27. Pratt, *Autobiography,* 371–73; Clayton, Journal, July 14, 1844.

28. Pratt, *Autobiography,* 372; Joseph Smith History, 1838–56, volume F-1, 293; Doctrine and Covenants 100:9 (Revelation, Oct. 12, 1833, at josephsmithpapers.org); Council of Fifty, "Record," May 6, 1844, in *JSP,* CFM:157–59.

29. "Nauvoo Journals, May 1843–June 1844," in *JSP,* J3:xxiii; *JSP,* J3:79–80, notes 364–66; "Continuation of Elder Rigdon's Trial," *Times and Seasons,* Oct. 1, 1844, 5:660–66; Wilford Woodruff to the "Church of Jesus Christ of Latter-day Saints," Oct. 11, 1844,

Times and Seasons, Nov. 1, 1844, 5:698–700; "Special Meeting," *Times and Seasons,* Sept. 1, 1844, 5:637–38.

30. Joseph Smith History, 1838–56, volume F-1, 293; addenda, 10; *Speech of Elder Orson Hyde,* 13. **Topic: Sidney Rigdon**
31. Willard Richards, Journal, Aug. 4, 1844; Joseph Smith History, 1838–56, volume F-1, 293.
32. Woodruff, Journal, July 24 and Aug. 5–6, 1844.
33. Woodruff, Journal, Aug. 7, 1844.
34. Joseph Smith History, 1838–56, volume F-1, 294.
35. Joseph Smith History, 1838–56, volume F-1, 295–96; Doctrine and Covenants 100:9–11 (Revelation, Oct. 12, 1833, at josephsmithpapers.org); see also Doctrine and Covenants 76 (Vision, Feb. 16, 1832, at josephsmithpapers.org).
36. Woodruff, Journal, Aug. 7, 1844.
37. Joseph Smith History, 1838–56, volume F-1, 296.
38. Historian's Office, General Church Minutes, Dec. 5, 1847; see also Walker, "Six Days in August," 181; Joseph Smith History, 1838–56, volume F-1, 296.
39. Sidney Rigdon, Discourse, Aug. 8, 1844, Historian's Office, General Church Minutes, Church History Library; Jensen and Carruth, "Sidney Rigdon's Plea to the Saints," 133–37; Joseph Smith History, 1838–56, volume F-1, 296. The original has "There is a spirit who shall be greatest in our midst."
40. Brigham Young, Discourse, Aug. 8, 1844, Historian's Office, General Church Minutes, Church History Library; Jensen and Carruth, "Sidney Rigdon's Plea to the Saints," 138–39; Joseph Smith History, 1838–56, volume F-1, 297–98; "Special Meeting," *Times and Seasons,* Sept. 1, 1844, 5:637–38; see also Brigham Young, Journal, Aug. 8, 1844.
41. Hoyt, Reminiscences and Diary, volume 1, 7, 9–10, 16–17, 19–21; Jorgensen, "Mantle of the Prophet Joseph," 139–42; Whitney, *History of Utah,* 4:303.
42. Joseph Smith History, 1838–56, volume F-1, 296; "Special Meeting," *Times and Seasons,* Sept. 1, 1844, 5:637; Brigham Young, Journal, Aug. 8, 1844.
43. Joseph Smith History, 1838–56, volume F-1, 298; Woodruff, Journal, Aug. 8, 1844; Afternoon Meeting, Aug. 8, 1844, Historian's Office, General Church Minutes, as transcribed by Sylvia Ghosh, copy at Church History Library.
44. Hoyt, Reminiscences and Diary, volume 1, 20–21; see also Jorgensen, "Mantle of the Prophet Joseph," 130, 142.
45. Joseph Smith History, 1838–56, volume F-1, 298–99. **Topic: Succession of Church Leadership**
46. Joseph Smith History, 1838–56, volume F-1, 302; Hoyt, Reminiscences and Diary, volume 1, 20–21; Woodruff, Journal, Aug. 8, 1844; Afternoon Meeting, Aug. 8, 1844, Historian's Office, General Church Minutes, as transcribed by Sylvia Ghosh, copy at Church History Library. **Topic: Common Consent**
47. Joseph Smith History, 1838–56, volume F-1, 303.
48. Hoyt, Reminiscences and Diary, volume 1, 20–21; see also Jorgensen, "Mantle of the Prophet Joseph," 125–204.
49. Hoyt, Reminiscences and Diary, volume 1, 21.
50. Woodruff, Journal, Aug. 9, 1844; Brigham Young, Journal, Aug. 9, 1844.
51. Woodruff, Journal, Aug. 12, 1844.
52. Woodruff, Journal, Aug. 18, 1844; "Letter from Joseph Smith to James J. Strang," *Voree Herald,* Jan. 18, 1846, [1]; "Strang, James Jesse," Biographical Entry, Joseph Smith Papers website, josephsmithpapers.org. **Topic: Latter Day Saint Movements**
53. Woodruff, Journal, Aug. 18, 1844.
54. Woodruff, Journal, Aug. 27, 1844.
55. Woodruff, Journal, Aug. 28, 1844; see also "Jones, Dan," Biographical Entry, Joseph Smith Papers website, josephsmithpapers.org.

CHAPTER 46: ENDOWED WITH POWER

1. "An Epistle of the Twelve," *Times and Seasons,* Oct. 1, 1844, 5:668. **Topic: Nauvoo Temple**
2. Peter Maughan to Willard Richards, Sept. 21, 1844, Willard Richards, Journals and Papers, Church History Library; Maughan, Autobiography, [59]–[60].
3. Clayton, Journal, Dec. 7, 1845; Historian's Office, History of the Church, 1838–circa 1882, volume 13, Sept. 24 and 29, 1844; Brigham Young, Journal, Aug. 25, 1844; see also Taylor, Journal, Dec. 25, 1844.
4. Gregory, "Sidney Rigdon," 51; Brigham Young, Journal, Sept. 8–9, 1844; Orson Hyde to "Dear Brethren," Sept. 12, 1844, Brigham Young Office Files, Church History Library; William Clayton to Wilford Woodruff, Oct. 7, 1844, Wilford Woodruff, Journals and Papers, Church History Library; William Player, Statement, Dec. 12, 1868, Church History Library; Letter to the Editor, *Nauvoo Neighbor,* May 21, 1845, [3].
5. Clayton, Journal, Aug. 15, 1844; Historian's Office, History of the Church, 1838–circa 1882, History of Brigham Young, volume 13, Aug. 19, 1844; Lucy Meserve Smith, Statement, undated, Church History Library.
6. Leonard, *Nauvoo,* 503; "Part 2: February–May 1845," in *JSP,* CFM:209. The exact number of women to whom Joseph Smith was sealed in his lifetime is unknown because the evidence is fragmentary. Careful estimates put the number between thirty and forty; see "Plural Marriage in Kirtland and Nauvoo," Gospel Topics, topics.lds.org.
7. "The Mormon Troubles" and "The Carthage Assassins," *Nauvoo Neighbor,* June 4, 1845, 1, [2], Brigham Young to Parley P. Pratt, May 26, 1845, Church History Library; *Journal of the Senate . . . of Illinois,* Dec. 19, 1844, 80–81; Oaks and Hill, *Carthage Conspiracy,* 79, 184–86; Leonard, *Nauvoo,* 464–74.
8. Young, Journal, Jan. 24, 1845.
9. "The Council of Fifty in Nauvoo, Illinois," in *JSP,* CFM:xl–xliii; Council of Fifty, "Record," Mar. 1, 1845, in *JSP,* CFM:251–52, 255, 256–57; see also "Dana (Denna), Lewis," Biographical Entry, Joseph Smith Papers website, josephsmithpapers.org. **Topic: American Indians**
10. Council of Fifty, "Record," Mar. 1, 1845, in *JSP,* CFM:257–58.
11. Council of Fifty, "Record," Mar. 1, 1845, in *JSP,* CFM:262.
12. Council of Fifty, "Record," Mar. 1, 4, 18, and 22, 1845; Apr. 11, 1845, in *JSP,* CFM:257, 273–76, 290–91, 328, 350, 394–96, 399.
13. Council of Fifty, "Record," Apr. 22, 1845, in *JSP,* CFM:436; "Tindall, Solomon," Biographical Entry, Joseph Smith Papers website, josephsmithpapers.org; *JSP,* CFM:436, note 757.
14. Phineas Young, Journal, Apr. 23–May 12, 1845.
15. Pratt, Journal, June 1, July 22, and Sept. 5, 1844; Jan. 5, Mar. 23, and Apr. 6, 1845; "Extract of a Letter," *LDS Millennial Star,* Aug. 1, 1845, 6:59; see also Garr, "Latter-day Saints in Tubuai," 4–9.
16. Pratt, Journal, Apr. 6, 1845.
17. Pratt, Journal, July 1, 1845.
18. Pratt, Journal, July 9, 1845; Ellsworth, *Journals of Addison Pratt,* 238–39; "From the Islands of the Sea," *Times and Seasons,* Dec. 15, 1844, 5:739–40.
19. Pratt, Journal, July 1, 1845.
20. Pratt, Journal, July 9–13, 1845. **Topic: French Polynesia**
21. Pratt, Journal and Autobiography, 124; Ellsworth, *History of Louisa Barnes Pratt,* 75; "Mobbing Again in Hancock!," *Nauvoo Neighbor,* Sept. 10, 1845, [2]; see also Historian's Office, History of the Church, 1838–circa 1882, History of Brigham Young, volume 14, Sept. 16, 1845.
22. Pratt, Journal and Autobiography, 124; Ellsworth, *History of Louisa Barnes Pratt,* 75–76; "Mobbing Again in Hancock!," *Nauvoo Neighbor,* Sept. 10, 1845, [2]; "Historic Sites and Markers: Morley's Settlement," 153–55.

23. Brigham Young, Journal, Sept. 16, 1845; Historian's Office, History of the Church, volume 14, Sept. 11, 1845.
24. Pratt, Journal and Autobiography, 125; see also Ellsworth, *History of Louisa Barnes Pratt,* 76.
25. Foote, Autobiography and Journal, Oct. 6, 1845; McBride, *House for the Most High,* 231–33.
26. "Conference Minutes," *Times and Seasons,* Nov. 1, 1845, 6:1008.
27. Oaks and Hill, *Carthage Conspiracy,* 184–86.
28. Council of Fifty, "Record," Sept. 9, 1845, in *JSP,* CFM:467–75. **Topic: Council of Fifty**
29. "Conference Minutes," *Times and Seasons,* Nov. 1, 1845, 6:1010–11; see also "First Meeting in the Temple," *Times and Seasons,* Nov. 1, 1845, 6:1017. **Topic: Departure from Nauvoo**
30. Tullidge, *Women of Mormondom,* 321; Norton, Reminiscence and Journal, Nov. 3, 17, and 26, 1845; Kimball, Diary, Nov. 24, 26, and 29, 1845; Leonard, *Nauvoo,* 252–55; McBride, *House for the Most High,* 253–61. **Topic: Temple Endowment**
31. **Topic: Baptism for the Dead**
32. Brigham Young, "Speech," *Times and Seasons,* July 1, 1845, 6:954–55.
33. Kimball, Diary, Nov. 29 and Dec. 9, 1845; Brigham Young, Journal, Dec. 10, 1845; McBride, *House for the Most High,* 264–65.
34. Historian's Office, History of the Church, volume 14, Dec. 27, 1845; Lee, Journal, Dec. 10, 1845; see also McBride, *House for the Most High,* 286.
35. "Pen Sketch of an Illustrious Woman," *Woman's Exponent,* Oct. 15, 1880, 9:74; Kimball, Diary, Dec. 10 and 20, 1845; Thompson, Autobiographical Sketch, 10. **Topic: Anointed Quorum ("Holy Order")**
36. Cowan, *Temple Building: Ancient and Modern,* 29. **Topic: Sealing**
37. Young, Journal, Jan. 12 and 31, 1846; Doctrine and Covenants 128:18 (Letter to "The Church of Jesus Christ of Latter Day Saints," Sept. 6, 1842, at josephsmithpapers.org).
38. Reports of the U.S. District Attorneys, 1845–50, Report of Suits Pending, Circuit Court of the District of Illinois, Dec. 1845 term, Dec. 17–18, 1845, microfilm, Records of the Solicitor of the Treasury, copy at Church History Library; Brigham Young, in *Journal of Discourses,* July 23, 1871, 14:218–19; Stout, Reminiscences and Journals, Dec. 23–24, 1845.
39. Ford, *History of Illinois,* 404, 410–13; Historian's Office, History of the Church, volume 15, Jan. 27, 1846.
40. Council of Fifty, "Record," Jan. 11, 1846, in *JSP,* CFM:510–21; George A. Smith, in *Journal of Discourses,* June 20, 1869, 13:85.
41. Council of Fifty, "Record," Jan. 13, 1846, in *JSP,* CFM:521–22; Lee, Journal, Jan. 13, 1846; see also Isaiah 11:12.
42. Historian's Office, History of the Church, volume 15, Jan. 31–Feb. 2, 1846.
43. Young, Journal, Feb. 3, 1846; Historian's Office, History of the Church, volume 15, Feb. 3–7, 1846.
44. Lee, Journal, Feb. 4, 1846; Historian's Office, History of the Church, volume 15, Feb. 8, 1845. **Topics: Nauvoo Temple; Departure from Nauvoo**
45. See McBride, *House for the Most High,* 320–22.
46. Pratt, Journal and Autobiography, 126.
47. Young, Diary and Reminiscences, 3.
48. Young, Diary and Reminiscences, 3; "Last Testimony of Sister Emma," *Saints' Herald,* Oct. 1, 1879, 289–90. **Topic: Emma Hale Smith**
49. Young, Diary and Reminiscences, 3–4; Lyman, Journal, 14.
50. Rich, Autobiography and Journal, 72.

NOTE ON SOURCES

This volume is a work of narrative nonfiction based on more than five hundred historical sources. Utmost care has been taken to ensure its accuracy. The early Latter-day Saints wrote many letters, journals, newspaper articles, and autobiographies. As a result, much of Church history between 1815 and 1846 is remarkably well documented. Readers should not assume, however, that the narrative presented here is perfect or complete. The records of the past, and our ability to interpret them in the present, are limited.

All sources of historical knowledge contain gaps, ambiguities, and biases. They often convey only their creator's point of view. Consequently, witnesses of the same events experience, remember, and record them differently, and their diverse perspectives enable varied ways of interpreting history. The challenge of the historian is to assemble known points of view and piece together an accurate understanding of the past through careful analysis and interpretation.

Saints is a true account of the history of The Church of Jesus Christ of Latter-day Saints, based on what we know and understand at the present time from existing historical records. It is not the only possible telling of the Church's sacred history, but the scholars who researched, wrote, and edited this volume know the historical sources well, used them thoughtfully, and documented them in the endnotes and list of sources cited. Readers are invited to evaluate the sources themselves, many of which have been digitized and linked to the endnotes. It is probable that the discovery of more sources, or new readings of existing sources, will in time yield other meanings, interpretations, and possible points of view.

The narrative in *Saints* draws on primary and secondary sources. Primary sources contain information about events from those who witnessed them firsthand. Some primary sources, like letters and journals, were written at the time of the events they describe. These contemporaneous sources reflect what people thought, felt, and did in the moment, revealing how the past was interpreted when it was the present. Other primary sources, like autobiographies, were written after the fact. These reminiscent sources reveal what the past came to mean to the writer over time, often making them better than contemporary sources at recognizing the significance of past events. Since they rely on memory, however, reminiscent sources can include inaccuracies and be influenced by the author's later understandings and beliefs.

Secondary historical sources contain information from people who did not witness the events described firsthand. Such sources include later family histories and academic works. This volume is indebted to many such sources, which proved valuable for the broader contextual and interpretive work they provided.

Every source in *Saints* was evaluated for credibility, and each sentence was repeatedly checked for consistency with the sources. Lines of dialogue and other quotations come directly from historical sources, word for word. Spelling, capitalization, and punctuation in direct quotations have been silently modernized for clarity. In rare instances, more significant modifications, like shifting from the past tense to present tense or standardizing grammar, have been made to quotations to improve readability. In these cases, endnotes describe the changes made.

Choices about which sources to use and how to use them were made by a team of historians, writers, and editors who based decisions on both historical integrity and literary quality.

Lucy Mack Smith's memoir, for instance, is a vital source for the early chapters of this volume. Lucy composed it between 1844 and 1845 at age sixty-nine, with the help of Martha Jane Knowlton Coray and Martha's husband, Howard. As a reminiscent source, Lucy's history is not free of errors, but it has been found to be generally reliable. It is used judiciously in this volume and cited mostly for events Lucy witnessed. For more about this history, see "Lucy Mack Smith" at saints.lds.org.

Some antagonistic sources were used to write this volume and are cited in the notes. These sources were primarily used to characterize early opposition to the Church. Though largely hostile to Joseph Smith and the Church, these documents sometimes contain details that were not recorded elsewhere. Some of these details were used when other records confirmed their general accuracy. Facts from these antagonistic records were used without adopting their hostile interpretations.

As a narrative history written for a general audience, this volume presents a foundational history of the Church in a coherent, accessible format. While drawing on the techniques of popular storytelling, it does not go beyond information found in historical sources. When the text includes even minor details, such as facial expressions or weather conditions, it is because these details are found in or reasonably deduced from the historical record.

To maintain the readability of the narrative, the volume rarely addresses challenges in or to the historical record in the text itself. Rather, it relegates such source-based discussions to topical essays on saints.lds.org. Readers are encouraged to consult these essays as they study Church history.

SOURCES CITED

This list serves as a comprehensive guide to all sources cited in the first volume of *Saints: The Story of the Church of Jesus Christ in the Latter Days*. In entries for manuscript sources, dates identify when the manuscript was created, which is not necessarily the time period the manuscript covers. Volumes of *The Joseph Smith Papers* are listed under "JSP." Many sources are available digitally, and links are found in the electronic version of the book, available at saints.lds.org and in Gospel Library.

The following abbreviations are used in this list of sources cited:

BYU: L. Tom Perry Special Collections, Harold B. Lee Library, Brigham Young University, Provo, Utah

CHL: Church History Library, The Church of Jesus Christ of Latter-day Saints, Salt Lake City

FHL: Family History Library, The Church of Jesus Christ of Latter-day Saints, Salt Lake City

Abbott Family Collection, 1831–2000. CHL.

Adams, Dale W. "Grandison Newell's Obsession." *Journal of Mormon History* 30, no. 1 (2004): 159–88.

Albany Evening Journal. Albany, NY. 1830–63.

Alexander, Thomas G. *Things in Heaven and Earth: The Life and Times of Wilford Woodruff, a Mormon Prophet*. Salt Lake City: Signature Books, 1991.

Allen, James B., Ronald K. Esplin, and David J. Whittaker. *Men with a Mission, 1837–1841: The Quorum of the Twelve Apostles in the British Isles*. Salt Lake City: Deseret Book, 1992.

Allen, James B., and Malcom R. Thorp. "The Mission of the Twelve to England, 1840–41: Mormon Apostles and the Working Class." *BYU Studies* 14, no. 4 (Summer 1975): 499–526.

Allen, Lucy M. Autobiographical Sketch, no date. CHL.

Alton Telegraph and Democratic Review. Alton, IL. 1836–55.

Amboy Journal. Amboy, IL. 1870–1913.

Ames, Ira. Autobiography and Journal, 1858. CHL.

Anderson, Karl Ricks. *Joseph Smith's Kirtland: Eyewitness Accounts*. Salt Lake City: Deseret Book, 1989.

Anderson, Richard Lloyd. "Jackson County in Early Mormon Descriptions." *Missouri Historical Review* 65, no. 3 (Apr. 1971): 270–93.

———. *Joseph Smith's New England Heritage: Influences of Grandfathers Solomon Mack and Asael Smith*. Rev. ed. Salt Lake City: Deseret Book; Provo, UT: Brigham Young University Press, 2003.

Arnold, Isaac N. *Reminiscences of the Illinois Bar Forty Years Ago: Lincoln and Douglas as Orators and Lawyers*. Chicago: Fergus Printing, 1881.

Arrington, Leonard J. "James Gordon Bennett's 1831 Report on 'The Mormonites.'" *BYU Studies* 10 (Spring 1970): 353–64.

Ashurst-McGee, Mark. "The Josiah Stowell Jr.–John S. Fullmer Correspondence." *BYU Studies* 38, no. 3 (1999). 108–17.

Backman, Milton V., Jr. *The Heavens Resound: A History of the Latter-day Saints in Ohio, 1830–1838*. Salt Lake City: Deseret Book, 1983.

Baldwin, Nathan Bennett. Account of Zion's Camp, 1882. Typescript. CHL.

Ball, Isaac Birkenhead. "The Prophet's Sister Testifies She Lifted the B. of M. Plates," Aug. 31, 1954. CHL.

Bartlett, W. H. *Walks about the City and Environs of Jerusalem*. London: Hall, Virtue, 1840.

Baugh, Alexander L. *A Call to Arms: The 1838 Mormon Defense of Northern Missouri*. Dissertations in Latter-day Saint History. Provo, UT: Joseph Fielding Smith Institute for Latter-day Saint History; BYU Studies, 2000.

————, ed. *Days Never to Be Forgotten: Oliver Cowdery.* Provo, UT: Religious Studies Center, Brigham Young University, 2009.

————. "'I'll Never Forsake': Amanda Barnes Smith (1809–1886)." In *Women of Faith in the Latter Days.* Vol. 1, *1775–1820,* edited by Richard E. Turley Jr. and Brittany A. Chapman, 450–60. Salt Lake City: Deseret Book, 2011.

————. "Joseph Smith in Northern Missouri." In *Joseph Smith, the Prophet and Seer,* edited by Richard Neitzel Holzapfel and Kent P. Jackson, 291–346. Provo, UT: Religious Studies Center, Brigham Young University; Salt Lake City: Deseret Book, 2010.

————. "Joseph Smith's Athletic Nature." In *Joseph Smith: The Prophet, The Man,* edited by Susan Easton Black and Charles D. Tate Jr., 137–50. Provo, UT: Religious Studies Center, Brigham Young University, 1993.

————. "Joseph Young's Affidavit of the Massacre at Haun's Mill." *BYU Studies* 38, no. 1 (1999): 188–202.

————. "Kirtland Camp, 1838: Bringing the Poor to Missouri." *Journal of Book of Mormon Studies* 22, no. 1 (2013): 58–61.

————. "Missouri Governor Lilburn W. Boggs and the Mormons." *John Whitmer Historical Association Journal* 18 (1998): 111–32.

————. "A Rare Account of the Haun's Mill Massacre: The Reminiscence of Willard Gilbert Smith." *Mormon Historical Studies* 8, nos. 1 and 2 (2007): 165–71.

————. "'We Took Our Change of Venue to the State of Illinois': The Gallatin Hearing and the Escape of Joseph Smith and the Mormon Prisoners from Missouri, April 1839." *Mormon Historical Studies* 2, no. 1 (2001): 59–82.

Baugh, Alexander L., and Richard Neitzel Holzapfel. "'I Roll the Burthen and Responsibility of Leading This Church off from My Shoulders on to Yours': The 1844/1845 Declaration of the Quorum of the Twelve regarding Apostolic Succession." *BYU Studies* 49, no. 3 (2010): 5–19.

Benjamin Brown Family Collection, 1835–1983. CHL.

Bennett, Richard E. "'Quincy—the Home of Our Adoption': A Study of the Mormons in Quincy, Illinois, 1838–40." *Mormon Historical Studies* 2, no. 1 (2001): 103–18.

————. "'Read This I Pray Thee': Martin Harris and the Three Wise Men of the East." *Journal of Mormon History* 36 (Winter 2010): 178–216.

Bible. See *Holy Bible.*

Biographical Review of Hancock County, Illinois, Containing Biographical and Genealogical Sketches of Many of the Prominent Citizens of To-Day and Also of the Past. Chicago: Hobart, 1907.

"Biography of Mary Ann Angell Young." *Juvenile Instructor* 26, no. 2 (Jan. 15, 1891): 56–58.

Bitton, Davis. *George Q. Cannon: A Biography.* Salt Lake City: Deseret Book, 1999.

Black, Susan Easton, and Harvey Bischoff Black. *Annotated Record of Baptisms for the Dead, 1840–1845, Nauvoo, Hancock County, Illinois.* 7 vols. Provo, UT: Center for Family History and Genealogy, Brigham Young University, 2002.

Blackstone, William. *Commentaries on the Laws of England: In Four Books; with an Analysis of the Work. By Sir William Blackstone, Knt. One of the Justices of the Court of Common Pleas. In Two Volumes, from the Eighteenth London Edition. . . . 2 vols.* New York: W. E. Dean, 1840.

Boggs, William M. "A Short Biographical Sketch of Lilburn W. Boggs, by His Son." *Missouri Historical Review* 4, no. 2 (Jan. 1910): 106–10.

A Book of Commandments, for the Government of the Church of Christ, Organized according to Law, on the 6th of April, 1830. Zion [Independence], MO: W. W. Phelps, 1833.

The Book of Mormon: An Account Written by the Hand of Mormon, upon Plates Taken from the Plates of Nephi. Palmyra, NY: E. B. Grandin, 1830.

The Book of Mormon: Another Testament of Jesus Christ. Salt Lake City: The Church of Jesus Christ of Latter-day Saints, 2013.

Bowen, Walter D. "The Versatile W. W. Phelps—Mormon Writer, Educator and Pioneer." Master's thesis, Brigham Young University, 1958.

Bradley, Don. "Mormon Polygamy before Nauvoo? The Relationship of Joseph Smith and Fanny Alger." In *Persistence of Polygamy: Joseph Smith and the Origins of Mormon Polygamy,* edited by Newell G. Bringhurst and Craig L. Foster, 14–58. Independence, MO: John Whitmer Books, 2010.

Bradley, James L. *Zion's Camp 1834: Prelude to the Civil War.* Logan, UT: By the author, 1990.

Bradshaw, M. Scott. "Joseph Smith's Performance of Marriages in Ohio." *BYU Studies* 39, no. 4 (2000): 23–69.

Bray, Justin R. "Within the Walls of Liberty Jail: D&C 121, 122, 123." In *Revelations in Context: The Stories behind the Sections of the Doctrine and Covenants,* edited by Matthew McBride and James Goldberg, 256–63. Salt Lake City: The Church of Jesus Christ of Latter-day Saints, 2016.

Breen, Patrick H. *The Land Shall Be Deluged in Blood: A New History of the Nat Turner Revolt.* New York: Oxford University Press, 2016.

Brekus, Catherine A. *Strangers and Pilgrims: Female Preaching in America, 1740–1845.* Chapel Hill: University of North Carolina Press, 1998.

Briggs, Edmund C. "A Visit to Nauvoo in 1856." *Journal of History* 9, no. 4 (Oct. 1916): 446–62.

Brigham Young Office Files, 1832–78. CHL.

Britton, John. *Bath and Bristol, with the Counties of Somerset and Gloucester, Displayed in a Series of Views; including the Modern Improvements, Picturesque Scenery, Antiques, &c.* London: Jones and Company, 1829.

Britton, Rollin J. *Early Days on Grand River and the Mormon War.* Columbia: State Historical Society of Missouri, 1920.

Brunson, Lewis. "Short Sketch of Seymour Brunson, Sr." *Nauvoo Journal* 4 (1992): 3–4.

Burbank, Daniel M. Autobiography, 1863. CHL.

Burgess, James. Journal, 1841–48. CHL.

Burnett, Peter H. *An Old California Pioneer.* Oakland, CA: Biobooks, 1946.

———. *Recollections and Opinions of an Old Pioneer.* New York: D. Appleton, 1880.

Burton, Richard F. *The City of the Saints, and Across the Rocky Mountains to California.* New York: Harper and Brothers, 1862.

Bushman, Richard Lyman. "Joseph Smith as Translator." In *Believing History: Latter-day Saint Essays,* edited by Reid L. Neilson and Jed Woodworth, 233–47. New York: Columbia University Press, 2004.

———. *Joseph Smith: Rough Stone Rolling.* With the assistance of Jed Woodworth. New York: Knopf, 2005.

———. "Oliver's Joseph." In *Days Never to Be Forgotten: Oliver Cowdery,* edited by Alexander L. Baugh, 1–13. Provo, UT: Religious Studies Center, Brigham Young University, 2009.

———. *The Refinement of America: Persons, Houses, Cities.* New York: Knopf, 1992.

———. "The Visionary World of Joseph Smith." *BYU Studies* 37, no. 1 (1997–98): 183–204.

Butler, John L. "A Short Account of an Affray That Took Place between the Latter Day Saints and a Portion of the People of Davis County Mo," 1859. CHL.

———. "A Short History," Autobiography, circa 1859. CHL.

Cahoon, Reynolds. Diaries, 1831–32. CHL.

Call, Anson. Autobiography and Journal, circa 1856–89. CHL.

Cannon, Brian Q., and BYU Studies Staff. "Priesthood Restoration Documents." *BYU Studies* 35, no. 4 (1995–96): 163–207.

Cannon, Eugene M. "Tahiti and the Society Island Mission." *Juvenile Instructor* 32, no. 11 (June 1, 1897): 334–36.

Carruth, LaJean Purcell, and Mark Lyman Staker. "John Taylor's June 27, 1854, Account of the Martyrdom," *BYU Studies* 50, no. 3 (2011): 25–62.

Chamberlin, Solomon. Autobiography, circa 1858. CHL.

Chardon Spectator and Geauga Gazette. Chardon, OH. 1833–35.

Chenango Union. Norwich, NY. 1847–1975.

Chicago Tribune. Chicago. 1847–.

Christensen, Edith Rushton. "Edwin Rushton: Bridge Builder and Faithful Pioneer." Salt Lake City: N.p., 1941.

The Church Historian's Press. Church History Department, The Church of Jesus Christ of Latter-day Saints. http://churchhistorianspress.org.

Church History Department Pitman Shorthand Transcriptions, 2013–17. CHL.

Clayton, William. History of the Nauvoo Temple, circa 1845. CHL.

———. Journals, 1842–45. CHL.

———. Letter to Madison M. Scott, Nov. 11, 1871. Copy. CHL.

Cleveland Daily Gazette. Cleveland. 1836–37.

Cleveland Weekly Gazette. Cleveland. 1837.

Collected Material concerning Joseph Smith and Plural Marriage, circa 1870–1912. CHL.

Collection of Manuscripts about Mormons, 1832–1954. Chicago History Museum.

A Collection of Sacred Hymns, for the Church of the Latter Day Saints. Edited by Emma Smith. Kirtland, OH: F. G. Williams, 1835.

A Collection of Sacred Hymns, for the Church of Jesus Christ of Latter-day Saints, in Europe. Selected by Brigham Young, Parley P. Pratt, and John Taylor. Manchester, England: W. R. Thomas, 1840.

Coltrin, Zebedee. Diaries and Notebook, 1832–34. CHL.

Cook, Lyndon W., ed. *David Whitmer Interviews: A Restoration Witness.* Orem, UT: Grandin Book, 1991.

———. " 'I Have Sinned against Heaven, and Am Unworthy of Your Confidence, but I Cannot Live without a Reconciliation': Thomas B. Marsh Returns to the Church." *BYU Studies* 20, no. 4 (Summer 1980): 389–400.

———. *William Law: Biographical Essay, Nauvoo Diary, Correspondence, Interview.* Orem, UT: Grandin Book, 1994.

Cook, Thomas L. *Palmyra and Vicinity.* Palmyra, NY: Palmyra Courier-Journal, 1930.

Cooper, F. M. "Spiritual Reminiscences.—No. 2." *Autumn Leaves* 4, no. 1 (Jan. 1891): 17–20.

Coray, Martha Jane Knowlton. Notebook, circa 1850. CHL.

Corrill, John. *A Brief History of the Church of Christ of Latter Day Saints, (Commonly Called Mormons;) Including an Account of Their Doctrine and Discipline; with the Reasons of the Author for Leaving the Church.* St. Louis: By the author, 1839.

Cowan, Richard O. *Temple Building: Ancient and Modern.* Provo, UT: Brigham Young University Press, 1971.

Cowdery, Oliver. Diary, Jan.–Mar. 1836. CHL. Also available as Leonard J. Arrington, "Oliver Cowdery's Kirtland, Ohio, 'Sketch Book,' " *BYU Studies* 12, no. 4 (Summer 1972): 410–26.

———. Letterbook, 1833–38. Henry E. Huntington Library, San Marino, CA.

———. Letter to Phineas Young, Mar. 23, 1846. CHL.

Crawley, Peter, and Richard L. Anderson. "The Political and Social Realities of Zion's Camp." *BYU Studies* 14 (Summer 1974): 406–20.

Crocheron, Augusta Joyce. *Representative Women of Deseret, a Book of Biographical Sketches, to Accompany the Picture Bearing the Same Title.* Salt Lake City: J. C. Graham, 1884.

Crosby, Caroline Barnes. Reminiscences, no date. In Jonathan and Caroline B. Crosby Papers, circa 1871–75. Copy at CHL.

Crosby, Jonathan. Autobiography, 1850–52. In Jonathan and Caroline B. Crosby Papers, circa 1871–75. Copy at CHL.

Cummings, Horace. "Conspiracy of Nauvoo." *Contributor,* Apr. 1884, 251–60.

Daily Missouri Republican. St. Louis. 1822–1919.

Daniels, William M. *Correct Account of the Murder of Generals Joseph and Hyrum Smith, at Carthage. On the 27th Day of June, 1844.* Nauvoo, IL: John Taylor, 1845.

Darowski, Joseph F. "The Journey of the Colesville Branch: D&C 26, 51, 54, 56, 59." In *Revelations in Context: The Stories behind the Sections of the Doctrine and Covenants,* edited by Matthew McBride and James Goldberg, 40–44. Salt Lake City: The Church of Jesus Christ of Latter-day Saints, 2016.

Darowski, Kay. "Joseph Smith's Support at Home: D&C 4, 11, 23." In *Revelations in Context: The Stories behind the Sections of the Doctrine and Covenants,* edited by Matthew

McBride and James Goldberg, 10–14. Salt Lake City: The Church of Jesus Christ of Latter-day Saints, 2016.

Daughters in My Kingdom: The History and Work of Relief Society. Salt Lake City: The Church of Jesus Christ of Latter-day Saints, 2011.

Davis, Matthew L. Letter to Mrs. Matthew [Mary] L. Davis, Feb. 6, 1840. CHL.

Dennis, Ronald D. "Dan Jones, Welshman." *Ensign,* Apr. 1987, 50–56.

———. "The Martyrdom of Joseph Smith and His Brother Hyrum." *BYU Studies* 24, no. 1 (Winter 1984): 78–109.

Derr, Jill Mulvay, Janath Russell Cannon, and Maureen Ursenbach Beecher. *Women of Covenant: The Story of Relief Society.* Salt Lake City: Deseret Book; Provo, UT: Brigham Young University Press, 1992.

Derr, Jill Mulvay, Carol Cornwall Madsen, Kate Holbrook, and Matthew J. Grow, eds. *The First Fifty Years of Relief Society: Key Documents in Latter-day Saint Women's History.* Salt Lake City: Church Historian's Press, 2016.

Deseret News. Salt Lake City. 1850–.

"Diary of Joseph Fielding." 1963. Typescript. CHL.

Dibble, Philo. "Philo Dibble's Narrative." In *Early Scenes in Church History,* Faith-Promoting Series 8, 74–96. Salt Lake City: Juvenile Instructor Office, 1882.

———. "Recollections of the Prophet Joseph Smith." *Juvenile Instructor* 27, no. 10 (May 15, 1892): 302–4.

———. Reminiscences, no date. Typescript. CHL.

Dickinson, Ellen E. *New Light on Mormonism.* New York: Funk and Wagnalls, 1885.

Dictionary of Missouri Biography. Edited by Lawrence O. Christensen, William E. Foley, Gary R. Kremer, and Kenneth H. Winn. Columbia: University of Missouri Press, 1999.

The Doctrine and Covenants of The Church of Jesus Christ of Latter-day Saints: Containing Revelations Given to Joseph Smith, the Prophet, with Some Additions by His Successors in the Presidency of the Church. Salt Lake City: The Church of Jesus Christ of Latter-day Saints, 2013.

Document Containing the Correspondence, Orders, &c., in Relation to the Disturbances with the Mormons; and the Evidence Given before the Hon. Austin A. King, Judge of the Fifth Judicial Circuit of the State of Missouri, at the Court-House in Richmond, in a Criminal Court of Inquiry, Begun November 12, 1838, on the Trial of Joseph Smith, Jr., and Others, for High Treason and Other Crimes against the State. Fayette, MO: Boon's Lick Democrat, 1841.

Dunn, Lura S., comp. *Amanda's Journal.* Provo, UT: Lura S. Dunn, [1977?].

Durham, G. Homer, ed. *The Gospel Kingdom: Selections from the Writings and Discourses of John Taylor.* Salt Lake City: Bookcraft, 1943.

Durham, Reed C., Jr. "The Election Day Battle at Gallatin." *BYU Studies* 13, no. 1 (1973): 36–61.

Ehat, Andrew F. "Joseph Smith's Introduction of Temple Ordinances and the 1833 Mormon Succession Question." Master's thesis, Brigham Young University, 1981.

Ellsworth, S. George, ed. *The History of Louisa Barnes Pratt, Being the Autobiography of a Mormon Missionary Widow and Pioneer. . . .* Life Writings of Frontier Women 3. Logan: Utah State University Press, 1998.

———, ed. *The Journals of Addison Pratt, Being a Narrative of Yankee Whaling in the Eighteen Twenties, a Mormon Mission to the Society Islands. . .* Salt Lake City: University of Utah Press, 1990.

"Elder John Brush." *Autumn Leaves* 4, no. 1 (Jan. 1891): 21–24.

Elders' Journal of the Church of Latter Day Saints. Kirtland, OH, Oct.–Nov. 1837; Far West, MO, July–Aug. 1838.

Emma Smith Blessing, 1844. CHL.

Erie Gazette. Erie, PA. 1820–59.

Esplin, Ronald K. "The Emergence of Brigham Young and the Twelve to Mormon Leadership, 1830–1841." PhD diss., Brigham Young University, 1981. Also available as *The Emergence of Brigham Young and the Twelve to Mormon Leadership, 1830–1841,* Dissertations in

Latter-day Saint History (Provo, UT: Joseph Fielding Smith Institute for Latter-day Saint History; BYU Studies, 2006).

————. "Joseph Smith's Mission and Timetable: 'God Will Protect Me until My Work Is Done.'" In *The Prophet Joseph: Essays on the Life and Mission of Joseph Smith*, edited by Larry C. Porter and Susan Easton Black, 280–319. Salt Lake City: Deseret Book, 1988.

Evening and Morning Star. Edited reprint of *The Evening and the Morning Star*. Kirtland, OH. Jan. 1835–Oct. 1836.

The Evening and the Morning Star. Independence, MO, July 1832–July 1833; Kirtland, OH, Dec. 1833–Sept. 1834.

Far West Committee. Minutes, Jan.–Apr. 1839. CHL.

Faulring, Scott H., Kent P. Jackson, and Robert J. Matthews, eds. *Joseph Smith's New Translation of the Bible: Original Manuscripts*. Provo, UT: Religious Studies Center, Brigham Young University, 2004.

Fielding, Joseph. Journals, 1837–59. CHL.

Flanders, Robert Bruce. *Nauvoo: Kingdom on the Mississippi*. Urbana: University of Illinois Press, 1956.

Foote, Warren. Autobiography and Journal, 1837–79. Warren Foote Papers, 1837–1941. CHL.

Ford, Thomas. *A History of Illinois, from Its Commencement as a State in 1818 to 1847. Containing a Full Account of the Black Hawk War, the Rise, Progress, and Fall of Mormonism, the Alton and Lovejoy Riots, and Other Important and Interesting Events.* Chicago: S. C. Griggs; New York: Ivison and Phinney, 1854.

Foster, Craig L. *Penny Tracts and Polemics: A Critical Analysis of Anti-Mormon Pamphleteering in Great Britain (1837–1860)*. Salt Lake City: Greg Kofford Books, 2002.

Freidel, Frank, with Hugh S. Sidney. *The Presidents of the United States of America*. 15th ed. Washington, DC: White House Historical Association, 1999.

Gates, Susa Young. *History of the Young Ladies' Mutual Improvement Association of the Church of Jesus Christ of Latter-day Saints, from November 1869 to June 1910*. Salt Lake City: Deseret News, 1911.

————. [Homespun, pseud.]. *Lydia Knight's History*. Noble Women's Lives Series 1. Salt Lake City: Juvenile Instructor Office, 1883.

————. Papers, 1852–1932. Utah State Historical Society, Salt Lake City.

Geauga County Archives and Records Center, Chardon, OH.

Gentry, Leland Homer, and Todd M. Compton. *Fire and Sword: A History of the Latter-day Saints in Northern Missouri, 1836–39*. Salt Lake City: Greg Kofford Books, 2010.

Gilbert, John H. Memorandum, Sept. 8, 1892. Photocopy. CHL.

————. Statement, Oct. 23, 1887. CHL.

Givens, George W. *In Old Nauvoo: Everyday Life in the City of Joseph*. Salt Lake City: Deseret Book, 1990.

Givens, Terryl L., and Matthew J. Grow. *Parley P. Pratt: The Apostle Paul of Mormonism*. New York: Oxford University Press, 2011.

Godfrey, Kenneth W. "Joseph Smith and the Masons." *Journal of the Illinois State Historical Society* 64, no. 1 (Spring 1971): 79–90.

Godfrey, Matthew C. "Newel K. Whitney and the United Firm: D&C 70, 78, 82, 92, 96, 104." In *Revelations in Context: The Stories behind the Sections of the Doctrine and Covenants,* edited by Matthew McBride and James Goldberg, 142–47. Salt Lake City: The Church of Jesus Christ of Latter-day Saints, 2016.

————. "William McLellin's Five Questions: D&C 1, 65, 66, 67, 68, 133." In *Revelations in Context: The Stories behind the Sections of the Doctrine and Covenants,* edited by Matthew McBride and James Goldberg, 137–41. Salt Lake City: The Church of Jesus Christ of Latter-day Saints, 2016.

Gordon, Joseph. "The Public Career of Lilburn W. Boggs." Master's thesis, University of Missouri, 1949.

"Gospel Topics." The Church of Jesus Christ of Latter-day Saints. http://lds.org/topics.

Greene, John P. *Facts Relative to the Expulsion of the Mormons or Latter Day Saints, from the State of Missouri, under the "Exterminating Order."* Cincinnati: R. P. Brooks, 1839.

Sources Cited

Gregg, Sarah D. Letter to Thomas Gregg, June 14, 1844. Copy. Illinois State Historical Society Papers, 1840–45. CHL.

Gregg, Thomas. *History of Hancock County, Illinois, together with an Outline History of the State, and a Digest of State Laws.* Chicago: Charles C. Chapman, 1880.

Gregory, Thomas J. "Sidney Rigdon: Post Nauvoo." *BYU Studies* 21, no. 1 (Winter 1981): 51–67.

Grua, David W. "Joseph Smith and the 1834 D. P. Hurlbut Case." *BYU Studies* 44, no. 1 (2005): 33–54.

———. "Waiting for the Word of the Lord: D&C 97, 98, 101." In *Revelations in Context: The Stories behind the Sections of the Doctrine and Covenants,* edited by Matthew McBride and James Goldberg, 196–201. Salt Lake City: The Church of Jesus Christ of Latter-day Saints, 2016.

Grow, Matthew J. "'Thou Art an Elect Lady': D&C 24, 25, 26, 27." In *Revelations in Context: The Stories behind the Sections of the Doctrine and Covenants,* edited by Matthew McBride and James Goldberg, 33–39. Salt Lake City: The Church of Jesus Christ of Latter-day Saints, 2016.

Hales, Brian C. *Joseph Smith's Polygamy.* 3 vols. Salt Lake City: Greg Kofford Books, 2013.

Hales, Kenneth Glyn, ed. *Windows: A Mormon Family.* Tucson, AZ: Skyline Printing, 1985.

Hall, Mary A. Newell. *Thomas Newell, Who Settled in Farmington, Conn., A.D. 1632. And His Descendants.* Southington, CT: Cochrane Brothers, 1878.

Hamilton, C. Mark. *Nineteenth-Century Mormon Architecture and City Planning.* New York: Oxford University Press, 1995.

Hamilton, Marshall. "Thomas Sharp's Turning Point: Birth of an Anti-Mormon." *Sunstone* 13, no. 5 (Oct. 1989): 16–22.

Hancock, Levi. Autobiography, circa 1854. CHL.

Harper, Steven C. "Freemasonry and the Latter-day Saint Temple Endowment Ceremony." In *A Reason for Faith,* edited by Laura Harris Hales, 143–57. Provo, UT: Religious Studies Center, Brigham Young University; Salt Lake City: Deseret Book, 2016.

———. "The Law: D&C 42." In *Revelations in Context: The Stories behind the Sections of the Doctrine and Covenants,* edited by Matthew McBride and James Goldberg, 93–98. Salt Lake City: The Church of Jesus Christ of Latter-day Saints, 2016.

———. "'A Pentecost and Endowment Indeed': Six Eyewitness Accounts of the Kirtland Temple Experience." In *Opening the Heavens: Accounts of Divine Manifestations, 1820–1844,* edited by John W. Welch, 327–71. Salt Lake City: Deseret Book; Provo, UT: Brigham Young University Press, 2005.

———. *Setting the Record Straight: The Word of Wisdom.* Orem, UT: Millennial Press, 2007.

———. "'The Tithing of My People': D&C 119, 120." In *Revelations in Context: The Stories behind the Sections of the Doctrine and Covenants,* edited by Matthew McBride and James Goldberg, 250–55. Salt Lake City: The Church of Jesus Christ of Latter-day Saints, 2016.

Hartley, William G. "'Almost Too Intolerable a Burthen': The Winter Exodus from Missouri, 1838–39." *Journal of Mormon History* 18, no. 2 (1992): 6–40.

———. *My Best for the Kingdom: History and Autobiography of John Lowe Butler, a Mormon Frontiersman.* Salt Lake City: Aspen Books, 1993.

———. "Newel and Lydia Bailey Knight's Kirtland Love Story and Historic Wedding." *BYU Studies* 39, no. 4 (2000): 7–22.

———. "The Saints' Forced Exodus from Missouri." In *Joseph Smith, the Prophet and Seer,* edited by Richard Neitzel Holzapfel and Kent P. Jackson, 347–90. Provo, UT: Religious Studies Center, Brigham Young University; Salt Lake City: Deseret Book, 2010.

Haven, Charlotte. "A Girl's Letters from Nauvoo." *Overland Monthly* 16, no. 96 (Dec. 1890): 616–38.

Hayden, Amos Sutton. *Early History of the Disciples in the Western Reserve, Ohio; with Biographical Sketches of the Principal Agents in Their Religious Movement.* Cincinnati: Chase and Hall, 1875.

Hendricks, Drusilla D. Reminiscences, circa 1877. CHL.

Hicks, Michael. *Mormonism and Music: A History.* Urbana: University of Illinois Press, 1989.

Hill, Craig. "The Honey War." *Pioneer America* 14, no. 2 (July 1982): 81–88.

Hinsdale, B. A. "Life and Character of Symonds Ryder." In Amos S. Hayden, *Early History of the Disciples in the Western Reserve, Ohio; with Biographical Sketches of the Principal Agents in Their Religious Movement*, 245–57. Cincinnati: Chase and Hall, 1875.

Historian's Office. Brigham Young History Drafts, 1856–58. CHL.

———. General Church Minutes, 1839–77. CHL.

———. Histories of the Twelve, 1856–58, 1861. CHL.

———. "History of Brigham Young." In Manuscript History of Brigham Young, circa 1856–60, vol. 1, 1–104. CHL.

———. History of the Church, 1838–circa 1882. 69 vols. CHL.

———. Joseph Smith History Documents, 1839–60. CHL.

———. Joseph Smith History Draft Notes, circa 1840–80. CHL.

———. Manuscript History of Brigham Young, 1856–62. CHL.

———. Reports of Speeches, 1845–85. CHL.

Historical Department. Journal History of the Church, 1896–2008. CHL.

The Historical Record, a Monthly Periodical, Devoted Exclusively to Historical, Biographical, Chronological and Statistical Matters. Salt Lake City. 1882–90.

"Historic Sites and Markers: Morley's Settlement." *Nauvoo Journal* 11, no. 1 (Spring 1999): 153–55.

History of Caldwell and Livingston Counties, Missouri, Written and Compiled from the Most Authentic Official and Private Sources. . . . St. Louis: National Historical Co., 1886.

History of Carroll County, Missouri, Carefully Written and Compiled from the Most Authentic Official and Private Sources. . . . St. Louis: Missouri Historical Company, 1881.

History of the Church / Smith, Joseph and others. *History of the Church of Jesus Christ of Latter-day Saints.* Edited by B. H. Roberts. Salt Lake City: Deseret News, 1902–12 (vols. 1–6), 1932 (vol. 7).

The History of the Reorganized Church of Jesus Christ of Latter Day Saints. 8 vols. Independence, MO: Herald Publishing House, 1896–1976.

Holbrook, Joseph. "History of Joseph Holbrook." In Joseph Holbrook, Autobiography and Journal, circa 1860–71. Typescript. CHL.

———. Reminiscences, not before 1871. In Joseph Holbrook, Autobiography and Journal, circa 1860–71. Private possession. Copy at CHL.

The Holy Bible, Containing the Old and New Testaments Translated Out of the Original Tongues: And with the Former Translations Diligently Compared and Revised, by His Majesty's Special Command. Authorized King James Version with Explanatory Notes and Cross References to the Standard Works of The Church of Jesus Christ of Latter-day Saints. Salt Lake City: The Church of Jesus Christ of Latter-day Saints, 2013.

Holzapfel, Richard Neitzel, and Steven C. Harper. "'This Is My Testimony, Spoken by Myself into a Talking Machine': Wilford Woodruff's 1897 Statement in Stereo." *BYU Studies* 45, no. 2 (2006): 112–16.

Hoyt, Emily S. Reminiscences and Diary, 1851–93. 7 vols. CHL.

Huntington, Oliver B. Diary and Reminiscences, 1843–1900. Typescript. CHL.

Hyde, Myrtle Stevens. *Orson Hyde: The Olive Branch of Israel.* Salt Lake City: Agreka Books, 2000.

Hyde, Orson. *Ein Ruf aus der Wüste, eine Stimme aus dem Schoose der Erde: Kurzer Ueberblick des Ursprungs und der Lehre der Kirche "Jesus Christ of Latter Day Saints" in Amerika, gekannt von Manchen unter der Benennung: "Die Mormonen."* Frankfurt: Im Selbstverlage des Verfassers, 1842. Excerpts also available in German and in English translation on the Joseph Smith Papers website, josephsmithpapers.org.

———. *A Voice from Jerusalem, or a Sketch of the Travels and Ministry of Elder Orson Hyde, Missionary of the Church of Jesus Christ of Latter Day Saints, to Germany, Constantinople, and Jerusalem.* . . . Liverpool: P. P. Pratt, 1842.

Hyrum Smith Family Bible, 1834. In Hyrum Smith, Papers, circa 1832–44. BYU.

Illinois State Historical Library. Circuit Court Case Files, 1830–1900. Microfilm. CHL.

An Illustrated Itinerary of the County of Lancaster. London: How and Parsons, 1842.

It Becomes Our Duty to Address You on the Subject of Immediately Preparing. [Kirtland, OH: May 10, 1834]. Copy at CHL.

Jackman, Levi. "A Short Sketch of the Life of Levi Jackman." Typescript. CHL.

Jackson, Stephen T. "Chief Anderson and His Legacy." Madison County Historical Society. Accessed Mar. 21, 2018. http://andersonmchs.com.

James, Jane Manning. Autobiography, circa 1902. CHL.

Jaques, Vienna. Statement, Feb. 22, 1859. CHL.

Jeffress, Melinda Evans. "Mapping Historic Nauvoo." *BYU Studies* 32, nos. 1 and 2 (1992): 269–75.

Jennings, Erin B. "Charles Anthon: The Man behind the Letters." *John Whitmer Historical Association Journal* 32, no. 2 (Fall/Winter 2012): 171–87.

Jennings, Warren A. "Isaac McCoy and the Mormons," *Missouri Historical Review* 61, no. 1 (Oct. 1966): 62–82.

Jensen, Robin S., and LaJean P. Carruth. "Sidney Rigdon's Plea to the Saints: Transcription of Thomas Bullock's Shorthand Notes from the August 8, 1844, Morning Meeting." *BYU Studies Quarterly* 53, no. 2 (2014): 121–39.

Jenson, Andrew. Collection, circa 1841–1942. CHL.

Jessee, Dean. "Joseph Knight's Recollection of Early Mormon History." *BYU Studies* 17, no. 1 (Autumn 1976): 29–39.

———. "'Walls, Grates and Screeking Iron Doors': The Prison Experience of Mormon Leaders in Missouri, 1838–1839." In *New Views of Mormon History: Essays in Honor of Leonard J. Arrington,* edited by Davis Bitton and Maureen Ursenbach Beecher, 19–42. Salt Lake City: University of Utah Press, 1987.

Jessee, Dean C., and John W. Welch. "Revelations in Context: Joseph Smith's Letter from Liberty Jail, March 20, 1839." *BYU Studies* 39, no. 3 (2000): 125–45.

Jessee, Dean C., and David J. Whittaker. "The Last Months of Mormonism in Missouri: The Albert Perry Rockwood Journal." *BYU Studies* 28, no. 1 (1988): 5–41.

Johnson, Benjamin Franklin. "A Life Review," circa 1885–94, 1923. Benjamin Franklin Johnson, Papers, 1852–1923. CHL.

———. Papers, 1852–1911. CHL.

Johnson, Clark V., ed. *Mormon Redress Petitions: Documents of the 1833–1838 Missouri Conflict.* Religious Studies Center Monograph Series 16. Provo, UT: Religious Studies Center, Brigham Young University, 1992.

Johnson, Janiece. "'Give Up All and Follow Your Lord': Testimony and Exhortation in Early Mormon Women's Letters, 1831–1839." *BYU Studies* 41, no. 1 (2002): 77–107.

Johnson, Joel H. Notebook, not before 1879. Joel Hills Johnson, Papers, circa 1877–79. CHL.

———. Reminiscences and Journals, 1835–82. Joel Hills Johnson, Papers, circa 1835–82. CHL.

Jorgensen, Lynne Watkins. "The Mantle of the Prophet Joseph Passes to Brother Brigham: A Collective Spiritual Witness." *BYU Studies Quarterly* 36, no. 4 (1996): 125–204.

Joseph Smith Letterbook 2 / Smith, Joseph. "Copies of Letters, &c. &c.," 1839–43. Joseph Smith Collection. CHL.

The Joseph Smith Papers. Church History Department, The Church of Jesus Christ of Latter-day Saints. http://josephsmithpapers.org.

Journal of Discourses. 26 vols. Liverpool: F. D. Richards, 1855–86.

Journal of the Senate of the Fourteenth General Assembly of the State of Illinois, at Their Regular Session, Begun and Held at Springfield, December 2, 1844. Springfield, IL: Walters and Weber, 1844.

Journal of the Senate of the United States of America, Being the First Session of the Twenty-Sixth Congress, Begun and Held at the City of Washington, December 2, 1839. Washington, DC: Blair and Rives, 1839.

JSP, CFM / Grow, Matthew J., Ronald K. Esplin, Mark Ashurst-McGee, Gerrit J. Dirkmaat, and Jeffrey D. Mahas, eds. *Council of Fifty, Minutes, March 1844–January 1846.* Administrative Records series of *The Joseph Smith Papers,* edited by Ronald K. Esplin, Matthew J. Grow, and Matthew C. Godfrey. Salt Lake City: Church Historian's Press, 2016.

JSP, D1 / MacKay, Michael Hubbard, Gerrit J. Dirkmaat, Grant Underwood, Robert J. Woodford, and William G. Hartley, eds. *Documents, Volume 1: July 1828–June 1831.* Vol. 1 of the Documents series of *The Joseph Smith Papers,* edited by Dean C. Jessee, Ronald K. Esplin, Richard Lyman Bushman, and Matthew J. Grow. Salt Lake City: Church Historian's Press, 2013.

JSP, D2 / Godfrey, Matthew C., Mark Ashurst-McGee, Grant Underwood, Robert J. Woodford, and William G. Hartley, eds. *Documents, Volume 2: July 1831–January 1833.* Vol. 2 of the Documents series of *The Joseph Smith Papers,* edited by Dean C. Jessee, Ronald K. Esplin, Richard Lyman Bushman, and Matthew J. Grow. Salt Lake City: Church Historian's Press, 2013.

JSP, D3 / Dirkmaat, Gerrit J., Brent M. Rogers, Grant Underwood, Robert J. Woodford, and William G. Hartley, eds. *Documents, Volume 3: February 1833–March 1834.* Vol. 3 of the Documents series of *The Joseph Smith Papers,* edited by Ronald K. Esplin and Matthew J. Grow. Salt Lake City: Church Historian's Press, 2014.

JSP, D4 / Godfrey, Matthew C., Brenden W. Rensink, Alex D. Smith, Max H Parkin, and Alexander L. Baugh, eds. *Documents, Volume 4: April 1834–September 1835.* Vol. 4 of the Documents series of *The Joseph Smith Papers,* edited by Ronald K. Esplin, Matthew J. Grow, and Matthew C. Godfrey. Salt Lake City: Church Historian's Press, 2016.

JSP, D5 / Rogers, Brent M., Elizabeth A. Kuehn, Christian K. Heimburger, Max H Parkin, Alexander L. Baugh, and Steven C. Harper, eds. *Documents, Volume 5: October 1835–January 1838.* Vol. 5 of the Documents series of *The Joseph Smith Papers,* edited by Ronald K. Esplin, Matthew J. Grow, and Matthew C. Godfrey. Salt Lake City: Church Historian's Press, 2017.

JSP, D6 / Ashurst-McGee, Mark, David W. Grua, Elizabeth A. Kuehn, Brenden W. Rensink, and Alexander L. Baugh, eds. *Documents, Volume 6: February 1838–August 1839.* Vol. 6 of the Documents series of *The Joseph Smith Papers,* edited by Ronald K. Esplin, Matthew J. Grow, and Matthew C. Godfrey. Salt Lake City: Church Historian's Press, 2017.

JSP, D7 / Godfrey, Matthew C., Spencer W. McBride, Alex D. Smith, and Christopher James Blythe, eds. *Documents, Volume 7: September 1839–January 1841.* Vol. 7 of the Documents series of *The Joseph Smith Papers,* edited by Ronald K. Esplin, Matthew J. Grow, and Matthew C. Godfrey. Salt Lake City: Church Historian's Press, 2018.

JSP, H1 / Davidson, Karen Lynn, David J. Whittaker, Richard L. Jensen, and Mark Ashurst-McGee, eds. *Histories, Volume 1: Joseph Smith Histories, 1832–1844.* Vol. 1 of the Histories series of *The Joseph Smith Papers,* edited by Dean C. Jessee, Ronald K. Esplin, and Richard Lyman Bushman. Salt Lake City: Church Historian's Press, 2012.

JSP, H2 / Davidson, Karen Lynn, Richard L. Jensen, and David J. Whittaker, eds. *Histories, Volume 2: Assigned Historical Writings, 1831–1847.* Vol. 2 of the Histories series of *The Joseph Smith Papers,* edited by Dean C. Jessee, Ronald K. Esplin, and Richard Lyman Bushman. Salt Lake City: Church Historian's Press, 2012.

JSP, J1 / Jessee, Dean C., Mark Ashurst-McGee, and Richard L. Jensen, eds. *Journals, Volume 1: 1832–1839.* Vol. 1 of the Journals series of *The Joseph Smith Papers,* edited by Dean C. Jessee, Ronald K. Esplin, and Richard Lyman Bushman. Salt Lake City: Church Historian's Press, 2008.

JSP, J2 / Hedges, Andrew H., Alex D. Smith, and Richard Lloyd Anderson, eds. *Journals, Volume 2: December 1841–April 1843.* Vol. 2 of the Journals series of *The Joseph Smith Papers,* edited by Dean C. Jessee, Ronald K. Esplin, and Richard Lyman Bushman. Salt Lake City: Church Historian's Press, 2011.

JSP, J3 / Hedges, Andrew H., Alex D. Smith, and Brent M. Rogers, eds. *Journals, Volume 3: May 1843–June 1844.* Vol. 3 of the Journals series of *The Joseph Smith Papers,* edited by Ronald K. Esplin and Matthew J. Grow. Salt Lake City: Church Historian's Press, 2015.

JSP, MRB / Jensen, Robin Scott, Robert J. Woodford, and Steven C. Harper, eds. *Manuscript Revelation Books.* Facsimile edition. First volume of the Revelations and Translations series of *The Joseph Smith Papers,* edited by Dean C. Jessee, Ronald K. Esplin, and Richard Lyman Bushman. Salt Lake City: Church Historian's Press, 2009.

JSP, R2 / Jensen, Robin Scott, Richard E. Turley Jr., and Riley M. Lorimer, eds. *Revelations and Translations, Volume 2: Published Revelations.* Vol. 2 of the Revelations and Translations series of *The Joseph Smith Papers,* edited by Dean C. Jessee, Ronald K. Esplin, and Richard Lyman Bushman. Salt Lake City: Church Historian's Press, 2011.

JSP, R3, Part 1 / Skousen, Royal, and Robin Scott Jensen, eds. *Revelations and Translations, Volume 3, Part 1: Printer's Manuscript of the Book of Mormon, 1 Nephi 1–Alma 35.* Facsimile edition. Part 1 of vol. 3 of the Revelations and Translations series of *The Joseph Smith Papers,* edited by Ronald K. Esplin and Matthew J. Grow. Salt Lake City: Church Historian's Press, 2015.

Kansas City Daily Journal. Kansas City, MO. 1878–96.

Keller, Karl. "'I Never Knew a Time When I Did Not Know Joseph Smith': A Son's Record of the Life and Testimony of Sidney Rigdon." *Dialogue: A Journal of Mormon Thought* 1, no. 4 (1966): 15–42.

Kerber, Linda K. "Abolitionists and Amalgamators: The New York City Race Riots of 1834." *New York History* 48, no. 1 (Jan. 1967): 28–39.

Kimball, Heber C. Collection, 1837–98. CHL.

———. Diary, 1845. BYU.

———. "History of Heber Chase Kimball by His Own Dictation," circa 1842–56. Heber C. Kimball, Papers, 1837–66. CHL.

———. "The Journal and Record of Heber Chase Kimball an Apostle of Jesus Christ of Latter Day Saints," circa 1842–58. Heber C. Kimball, Papers, 1837–66. CHL.

Kimball, Stanley B., ed. *On the Potter's Wheel: The Diaries of Heber C. Kimball.* Salt Lake City: Signature Books, 1987.

Kimball, Vilate Murray. Letters, 1840. CHL.

———. Letter to Heber C. Kimball, June 30, 1844. CHL.

Kirtland Camp. Journal, Mar.–Oct. 1838. CHL.

Kirtland Elders' Certificates / Kirtland Elders Quorum. "Record of Certificates of Membership and Ordinations of the First Members and Elders of the Church of Jesus Christ of Latter Day Saints Dating from March 21st 1836 to June 18th 1838 Kirtland Geauga Co. Ohio," 1836–38. CHL.

Kirtland Safety Society. Stock Ledger, 1836–37. Collection of Manuscripts about Mormons, 1832–1954. Chicago History Museum.

Klingaman, William K., and Nicholas P. Klingaman. *The Year without Summer: 1816 and the Volcano That Darkened the World and Changed History.* New York: St. Martin's Griffin, 2014.

Knight, Joseph, Sr. Reminiscences, no date. CHL.

Knight, Newel. Autobiography, circa 1871. CHL.

———. Autobiography and Journal, circa 1846. CHL.

Knutson, Phyllis. "Sheffield Daniels and Abigail Warren." FamilySearch. Compiled by The Church of Jesus Christ of Latter-day Saints. Accessed Mar. 21, 2018. https://familysearch.org.

Kowallis, Bart J. "In the Thirty and Fourth Year: A Geologist's View of the Great Destruction in 3 Nephi." *BYU Studies* 37, no. 3 (1997–98). 136–90.

Kuehn, Elizabeth. "More Treasures Than One: D&C 111." In *Revelations in Context: The Stories behind the Sections of the Doctrine and Covenants,* edited by Matthew McBride and James Goldberg, 229–34. Salt Lake City: The Church of Jesus Christ of Latter-day Saints, 2016.

Larson, A. Karl, and Katharine Miles Larson, eds. *Diary of Charles Lowell Walker.* 2 vols. Logan: Utah State University Press, 1980.

Latter Day Saints' Messenger and Advocate. Kirtland, OH. 1834–37.

Latter-day Saints' Millennial Star. Liverpool. 1840–1970.

Launius, Roger D., and F. Mark McKiernan. *Joseph Smith, Jr.'s Red Brick Store.* Macomb: Western Illinois University, 1985.

Laws of the State of Illinois, Passed by the Eleventh General Assembly, at Their Special Session, Began and Held at Springfield, on the Ninth of December, One Thousand Eight Hundred and Thirty-Nine. Springfield, IL: William Walters, 1840.

Laws of the State of New-York, Revised and Passed at the Thirty-Sixth Session of the Legislature, with Marginal Notes and References. . . . 2 vols. Albany, NY: H. C. Southwick, 1813.

Lee, John D. Journal, Feb.–Aug. 1846. John D. Lee, Journals, 1844–53. CHL.

Leonard, Glen M. *Nauvoo: A Place of Peace, a People of Promise.* Salt Lake City: Deseret Book; Provo, UT: Brigham Young University Press, 2002.

LeSueur, Stephen C. "'High Treason and Murder': The Examination of Mormon Prisoners at Richmond, Missouri, in November 1838." *BYU Studies* 26, no. 2 (1986): 3–30.

———. "Missouri's Failed Compromise: The Creation of Caldwell County for the Mormons." *Journal of Mormon History* 31, no. 3 (Fall 2005): 113–44.

Levi Richards Family Correspondence, 1827–48. CHL.

Lewis, David. Autobiography, 1854. CHL.

"Liberty Jail." Historic Sites, Church History Department, The Church of Jesus Christ of Latter-day Saints. Accessed Mar. 21, 2018. http://history.lds.org.

"The Life of Norton Jacob." No date. Typescript. CHL.

Lightner, Mary Elizabeth Rollins. Collection, 1865–1914. BYU.

———. Remarks, Apr. 14, 1905. Typescript. CHL.

Littlefield, Lyman Omer. *Reminiscences of Latter-day Saints. Giving an Account of Much Individual Suffering Endured for Religious Conscience.* Logan, UT: Utah Journal, 1888.

Livesey, Richard. *An Exposure of Mormonism, Being a Statement of Facts Relating to the Self-Styled "Latter Day Saints," and the Origin of the Book of Mormon.* Preston, England: J. Livesey, 1838.

Lyman, Edward Leo, Susan Ward Payne, and S. George Ellsworth, eds. *No Place to Call Home: The 1807–1857 Life Writings of Caroline Barnes Crosby, Chronicler of Outlying Mormon Communities.* Life Writings of Frontier Women, edited by Maureen Ursenbach Beecher. Logan: Utah State University Press, 2005.

Lyman, Eliza Partridge. Journal, 1846–85, 1927. CHL.

Mace, Wandle. Autobiography, circa 1890. CHL.

MacKay, Michael Hubbard. "'Git Them Translated': Translating the Characters on the Gold Plates." In *Approaching Antiquity: Joseph Smith and the Ancient World,* edited by Lincoln H. Blumell, Matthew J. Grey, and Andrew H. Hedges, 83–116. Provo, UT: Religious Studies Center, Brigham Young University, 2015.

Madsen, Carol Cornwall. *In Their Own Words: Women and the Story of Nauvoo.* Salt Lake City: Deseret Book, 1994.

Madsen, Gordon A. "Joseph Smith and the Missouri Court of Inquiry: Austin A. King's Quest for Hostages." *BYU Studies* 43, no. 4 (2004): 92–136.

Mahas, Jeffrey. "Remembering the Martyrdom: D&C 135." In *Revelations in Context: The Stories behind the Sections of the Doctrine and Covenants,* edited by Matthew McBride and James Goldberg, 299–306. Salt Lake City: The Church of Jesus Christ of Latter-day Saints, 2016.

Maki, Elizabeth. "'Go to the Ohio': D&C 35, 36, 37, 38." In *Revelations in Context: The Stories behind the Sections of the Doctrine and Covenants,* edited by Matthew McBride and James Goldberg, 70–73. Salt Lake City: The Church of Jesus Christ of Latter-day Saints, 2016.

———. "Joseph Smith's Bible Translation: D&C 45, 76, 77, 86, 91." In *Revelations in Context: The Stories behind the Sections of the Doctrine and Covenants,* edited by Matthew McBride and James Goldberg, 99–103. Salt Lake City: The Church of Jesus Christ of Latter-day Saints, 2016.

"Mary Elizabeth Rollins Lightner." *Utah Genealogical and Historical Magazine* 17 (1926): 193–205, 250–60.

Mary Elizabeth Rollins Lightner Family Collection. 1833–1973. CHL.

Mather, Frederic G. "The Early Days of Mormonism." *Lippincott's Magazine of Popular Literature and Science* 26 (Aug. 1880): 198–211.

Maughan, Mary Ann Weston. Autobiography. Vol. 1, 1894. CHL.

McBride, Matthew. "Contributions of Martin Harris: D&C 3, 5, 10, 17, 19." In *Revelations in Context: The Stories behind the Sections of the Doctrine and Covenants,* edited by

Matthew McBride and James Goldberg, 1–9. Salt Lake City: The Church of Jesus Christ of Latter-day Saints, 2016.

———. "Ezra Booth and Isaac Morley: D&C 57, 58, 60, 61, 62, 63, 64, 71, 73." In *Revelations in Context: The Stories behind the Sections of the Doctrine and Covenants,* edited by Matthew McBride and James Goldberg, 130–36. Salt Lake City: The Church of Jesus Christ of Latter-day Saints, 2016.

———. *A House for the Most High: The Story of the Original Nauvoo Temple.* Salt Lake City: Greg Kofford Books, 2007.

———. "Letters on Baptism for the Dead: D&C 127, 128." In *Revelations in Context: The Stories behind the Sections of the Doctrine and Covenants,* edited by Matthew McBride and James Goldberg, 272–76. Salt Lake City: The Church of Jesus Christ of Latter-day Saints, 2016.

———. " 'Our Hearts Rejoiced to Hear Him Speak': D&C 129, 130, 131." In *Revelations in Context: The Stories behind the Sections of the Doctrine and Covenants,* edited by Matthew McBride and James Goldberg, 277–80. Salt Lake City: The Church of Jesus Christ of Latter-day Saints, 2016.

———. "Religious Enthusiasm among Early Ohio Converts: D&C 46, 50." In *Revelations in Context: The Stories behind the Sections of the Doctrine and Covenants,* edited by Matthew McBride and James Goldberg, 105–11. Salt Lake City: The Church of Jesus Christ of Latter-day Saints, 2016.

———. " 'The Vision': D&C 76." In *Revelations in Context: The Stories behind the Sections of the Doctrine and Covenants,* edited by Matthew McBride and James Goldberg, 148–54. Salt Lake City: The Church of Jesus Christ of Latter-day Saints, 2016.

McBride, Reuben, Sr. Reminiscences, no date. CHL.

McBride, Spencer W. "When Joseph Smith Met Martin Van Buren: Mormonism and the Politics of Religious Liberty in Nineteenth Century America." *Church History: Studies in Christianity and Culture* 85, no. 1 (Mar. 2016): 150–58.

McGavin, Elmer C. *The Nauvoo Temple.* Salt Lake City: Deseret Book, 1962.

McLellin, William E. Journal, Nov. 16, 1831–Feb. 25, 1832. William E. McLellin, Papers, 1831–36, 1877–78. CHL. Also available in Jan Shipps and John W. Welch, eds., *The Journals of William E. McLellin, 1831–1836* (Provo, UT: BYU Studies; Urbana: University of Illinois Press, 1994).

———. Letter, Independence, MO, to "Beloved Relatives," Carthago, TN, Aug. 4, 1832. Photocopy. CHL.

McMurrin, Joseph W. "An Interesting Testimony." *Improvement Era* 6, no. 7 (May 1903): 507–10.

Millennial Harbinger. Bethany, VA. 1830–70.

Millet, Joseph. "J. Millet on Cape Breton Island," 1927. CHL.

———. Record Book, circa 1850–1947. CHL.

Minute Book 1 / "Conference A," 1832–37. CHL.

Minute Book 2 / "The Conference Minutes and Record Book of Christ's Church of Latter Day Saints," 1838, 1842, 1844. CHL.

Missouri, State of. "Evidence." Hearing Record, Richmond, MO, Nov. 12–29, 1838, State of Missouri v. Joseph Smith and Others for Treason and Other Crimes. Eugene Morrow Violette Collection, 1806–1921, Western Historical Manuscript Collection. University of Missouri and State Historical Society of Missouri, Ellis Library, University of Missouri, Columbia.

Missouri Argus. St. Louis. 1835–41.

Missouri Intelligencer and Boon's Lick Advertiser. Franklin, MO, 1819–27; Fayette, MO, 1827–30; Columbia, MO, 1830–35.

Missouri Republican. St. Louis. 1822–1919.

Monkman, Susan C. *The White House: Its Historic Furnishings and First Families.* 2nd ed. Washington, DC: White House Historical Association, 2014.

Mormon Migration. Brigham Young University. Accessed Mar. 21, 2018. https://mormonmigration.lib.byu.edu.

Mormon Redress Petitions, 1839–45. CHL.

Mormon War Papers, 1838–41. Missouri State Archives, Jefferson City.

Morning Courier and New-York Enquirer. New York City. 1829–61.

Morris, Larry E. "The Conversion of Oliver Cowdery." *Journal of Book of Mormon Studies* 16, no. 1 (2007): 4–17.

———. "Oliver Cowdery's Vermont Years and the Origins of Mormonism." *BYU Studies* 39, no. 1 (2000): 106–29.

Murdock, John. Autobiography, circa 1859–67. CHL.

———. Journal, circa 1830–59. CHL.

Nauvoo, IL. Records, 1841–45. CHL.

Nauvoo City Council Draft Minutes, 1841–44. Nauvoo, IL, Records, 1841–45. CHL.

Nauvoo City Council Minute Book / Nauvoo City Council. "A Record of the Proceedings of the City Council of the City of Nauvoo Handcock County, State of Illinois, Commencing A.D. 1841," circa 1841–45. CHL.

Nauvoo Expositor. Nauvoo, IL. 1844.

Nauvoo Masonic Lodge Minute Book / "Record of Na[u]voo Lodge under Dispensation," 1842–46. CHL.

Nauvoo Municipal Court Docket Book / Nauvoo, IL, Municipal Court. "Docket of the Municipal Court of the City of Nauvoo," circa 1843–45. In Historian's Office, Historical Record Book, 1843–74, 51–150 and 1–19 (second numbering). CHL.

Nauvoo Neighbor. Nauvoo, IL. 1843–45.

Nauvoo Stake High Council Minutes, 1839–45. CHL.

Nauvoo Temple. Baptisms for the Dead, 1840–45. CHL.

Neibaur, Alexander. Journal, 1841–62. CHL.

Newell, Linda King, and Valeen Tippetts Avery. *Mormon Enigma: Emma Hale Smith.* 2nd ed. Urbana: University of Illinois Press, 1994.

New York Herald. New York City. 1835–1924.

Nicholes, Joseph K. Collection, circa 1930–50. CHL.

Niles' National Register. Washington, DC. 1837–49.

Norton, Jacob. Reminiscence and Journal, 1844–52. CHL.

Nuttall, L. John. Diary, 1876–84. Typescript. In L. John Nuttall, Papers, 1854–1903. CHL.

Oaks, Dallin H. "The Suppression of the *Nauvoo Expositor.*" *Utah Law Review* 9 (Winter 1965): 862–903.

Oaks, Dallin H., and Joseph I. Bentley. "Joseph Smith and Legal Process: In the Wake of the Steamboat *Nauvoo.*" *Brigham Young University Law Review,* no. 3 (1976): 735–82.

Oaks, Dallin H., and Marvin S. Hill. *Carthage Conspiracy: The Trial of the Accused Assassins of Joseph Smith.* Urbana: University of Illinois Press, 1975.

Oates, Stephen B. *The Fires of Jubilee: Nat Turner's Fierce Rebellion.* New York: Harper and Row, 1975.

Ogden Herald. Ogden, UT. 1881–87.

Ohio Star. Ravenna, OH. 1830–54.

Olmstead, Jacob W. "Far West and Adam-ondi-Ahman: D&C 115, 116, 117." In *Revelations in Context: The Stories behind the Sections of the Doctrine and Covenants,* edited by Matthew McBride and James Goldberg, 235–41. Salt Lake City: The Church of Jesus Christ of Latter-day Saints, 2016.

Ontario Phoenix. Canandaigua, NY. 1828–32.

Oration Delivered by Mr. S. Rigdon, on the 4th of July, 1838. Far West, MO: Journal Office, 1838. Also available in Peter Crawley, "Two Rare Missouri Documents," *BYU Studies* 14 (Summer 1974): 502–27.

"The Original Prophet. By a Visitor to Salt Lake City." *Fraser's Magazine* 7, no. 28 (Feb. 1873): 225–35.

Ostler, Craig James. "Photo Essay of Church History Sites in Liverpool and the Ribble Valley." In *Regional Studies in Latter-day Saint Church History: The British Isles,* edited by Cynthia Doxey, Robert C. Freeman, Richard Neitzel Holzapfel, and Dennis A. Wright, 61–78. Provo, UT: Religious Studies Center, Brigham Young University, 2007.

Sources Cited

Packer, Cameron J. "A Study of the Hill Cumorah: A Significant Latter-day Saint Landmark in Western New York." Master's thesis, Brigham Young University, 2002.

Painesville Republican. Painesville, OH. 1836–41.

Painesville Telegraph. Painesville, OH. 1831–38.

Palmyra Freeman. Palmyra, NY. 1828–29.

Parker, Ellen B. Letters, 1842–51. In Martha G. Boyle, Family Papers, 1842–1972. CHL.

Partridge, Edward. History, Manuscript, circa 1839. CHL.

———. Journal, Jan. 1835–July 1836. CHL.

———. Letters, 1831–35. CHL.

———. Miscellaneous Papers, circa 1839–May 1840. CHL.

———. Papers, 1818–39. CHL.

Partridge, Edward, Jr. Genealogical Record, 1878. CHL.

Pasko, W. W. *Old New York: A Journal Relating to the History and Antiquities of New York City.* New York: By the author, Feb. 1890.

Patten, David Wyman. Journal, 1832–34. CHL.

Paul, Hiland, and Robert Parks. *History of Wells, Vermont, for This First Century after Its Settlement.* Rutland, VT: Tuttle, 1869.

The Pearl of Great Price: A Selection from the Revelations, Translations, and Narrations of Joseph Smith, First Prophet, Seer, and Revelator to The Church of Jesus Christ of Latter-day Saints. Salt Lake City: The Church of Jesus Christ of Latter-day Saints, 2013.

Peck, Phebe Crosby. Letter to Anna Jones Pratt, Aug. 10, 1832. CHL.

Peck, Reed. Letter, Quincy, IL, to "Dear Friends," Sept. 18, 1839. Henry E. Huntington Library, San Marino, CA.

Perrin, Kathleen C. "Seasons of Faith: An Overview of the History of the Church in French Polynesia." In *Pioneers in the Pacific,* edited by Grant Underwood, 201–18. Provo, UT: Religious Studies Center, Brigham Young University, 2005.

Peter Maughan Family History. Logan, UT: Peter Maughan Family Organization, 1971.

Peterson, H. Donl. *The Story of the Book of Abraham: Mummies, Manuscripts, and Mormonism.* Springville, UT: Cedar Fort International, 2008.

Phelps, William W. Collection of Missouri Documents, 1833–37. CHL.

———. Funeral Sermon of Joseph and Hyrum Smith, 1855. CHL.

——— Letter to Sally Waterman Phelps, May 26, 1835. William W. Phelps, Papers, 1835–65. BYU.

———. Letter to Sally Waterman Phelps. In Historian's Office, Journal History of the Church, July 20, 1835. CHL.

———. Letter to Sally Waterman Phelps, Sept. 16, 1835. CHL.

———. Letter to Sally Waterman Phelps, Apr. 1836. William W. Phelps, Papers, 1835–65. BYU.

———. "A Short History of W. W. Phelps' Stay in Missouri," 1864. CHL.

Pickup, David M. W. *The Pick and Flower of England: The Illustrated Story of the Mormons in Victorian England.* Lancashire, England: Living Legend, 2001.

Pilkington, William. Autobiography and Statements, 1934–39. CHL.

Pitman Shorthand Transcriptions, 1998–2013. CHL.

Pittsburgh Weekly Gazette. Pittsburgh. 1841–59.

Platt, Lyman D. "Early Branches of the Church of Jesus Christ of Latter-day Saints 1830–1850." *Nauvoo Journal* 3 (1991): 3–50.

Player, William. Statement, Dec. 12, 1868. CHL.

Plewe, Brandon S., ed. *Mapping Mormonism: An Atlas of Latter-day Saint History.* Provo, UT: Brigham Young University Press, 2012.

Porter, Larry C. "The Book of Mormon: Historical Setting for Its Translation and Publication." In *Joseph Smith: The Prophet, the Man,* edited by Susan Easton Black and Charles D. Tate Jr., 49–64. Provo, UT: Religious Studies Center, Brigham Young University, 1993.

Portrait and Biographical Record of Hancock, McDonough and Henderson Counties, Illinois; Containing Biographical Sketches of Prominent and Representative Citizens of the

County; together with Biographies and Portraits of All the Presidents of the United States. Chicago: Lake City, 1894.

Post, Stephen. Journal, 1835–39. Stephen Post, Papers, 1835–1921. CHL.

Pratt, Addison. Journal, Sept. 1843–Oct. 1844. Addison Pratt, Autobiography and Journals, 1843–52. CHL.

Pratt, Louisa Barnes. Journal and Autobiography, 1850–80. CHL.

Pratt, Orson. *A[n] Interesting Account of Several Remarkable Visions, and of the Late Discovery of Ancient American Records.* Edinburgh: Ballantyne and Hughes, 1840.

Pratt, Parley P. *The Autobiography of Parley Parker Pratt, One of the Twelve Apostles of the Church of Jesus Christ of Latter-day Saints, Embracing His Life, Ministry and Travels, with Extracts, in Prose and Verse, from His Miscellaneous Writings.* Edited by Parley P. Pratt Jr. New York: Russell Brothers, 1874.

———. Correspondence, 1842–55. CHL.

———. *History of the Late Persecution Inflicted by the State of Missouri upon the Mormons, in Which Ten Thousand American Citizens Were Robbed, Plundered, and Driven from the State, and Many Others Imprisoned, Martyred, &c. for Their Religion, and All This by Military Force, by Order of the Executive. By P. P. Pratt, Minister of the Gospel. Written during Eight Months Imprisonment in That State.* Detroit: Dawson and Bates, 1839.

Probert, Josh E., and Craig K. Manscill. "Artemus Millet: Builder of the Kingdom," *Mormon Historical Studies* 5, no. 1 (Spring 2004): 53–86.

The Prophet. New York City, NY. May 1844–Dec. 1845.

Prospectus of the Nauvoo Expositor. Nauvoo, IL. 10 May 1844. Copy at CHL.

Quincy Herald. Quincy, IL. 1841–before 1851.

Quincy Whig. Quincy, IL. 1838–57.

Quinn, D. Michael, ed. "The First Months of Mormonism: A Contemporary View by Rev. Diedrich Willers." *New York History* 54 (July 1973): 317–33.

Quorum of the Twelve Apostles. Minutes, 1840–44. CHL.

Radke, Andrea G. "We Also Marched: The Women and Children of Zion's Camp, 1834." *BYU Studies* 39, no. 1 (2000): 147–65.

Raffles, Thomas Stamford. "Narrative of the Effects of the Eruption from the Tomboro Mountain in the Island of Sumbawa on the 11th and 12th of April 1815,—Communicated by the President." In A. H. Hubbard, *Verhandelingen van het Bataviaasch Genootschap, der Kunsten en Wetenschappen,* 1–25 (eleventh numbering). Batavia, Dutch East Indies: By the author, 1816.

Recollections of the Pioneers of Lee County. Dixon, IL: Inez A. Kennedy, 1893.

"Recollections of the Prophet Joseph Smith." *Juvenile Instructor* 27, no. 13 (July 1, 1892): 398–400.

"Records of the Session of the Presbyterian Church in Palmyra," 1828–48. Microfilm 900, no. 59. BYU.

Records of the Solicitor of the Treasury / National Archives Reference Service Report, Sept. 23, 1964. "Record Group 206, Records of the Solicitor of the Treasury, and Record Group 46, Records of the United States Senate: Records relating to the Mormons in Illinois, 1839–1848 (Records Dated 1840–1852), including Memorials of Mormons to Congress, 1840–1844, Some of Which Relate to Outrages Committed against the Mormons in Missouri, 1831–1839." Microfilm. Washington, DC: National Archives and Records Service, General Services Administration, 1964. Copy at CHL.

Reeve, W. Paul. *Religion of a Different Color: Race and the Mormon Struggle for Whiteness.* New York: Oxford University Press, 2015.

Reflector. Palmyra, NY. 1829–31.

Reorganized Church of Jesus Christ of Latter Day Saints v. Church of Christ of Independence, Missouri, and Others (Circuit Court of the Western District of Missouri 1894). Testimonies and Depositions, 1892. Typescript. CHL.

Return. Davis City, IA, 1889–91; Richmond, MO, 1892–93; Davis City, 1895–96; Denver, 1898; Independence, MO, 1899–1900.

Reynolds, John. *My Own Times: Embracing Also, the History of My Life.* N.p., 1855.

Rich, Charles Coulson. Diary, May–July 1834. Typescript. CHL. Original in Western Americana Collection, Beinecke Rare Book and Manuscript Library, Yale University, New Haven, CT.

Rich, Sarah P. Autobiography and Journal, 1885–90. CHL.

Richards, Franklin D. Journals, 1844–99. Vol. 16, Jan. 1, 1868–Jan. 29, 1869. Richards Family Collection, 1837–1961. CHL.

———. Scriptural Items, circa 1841–44. CHL.

Richards, Levi. Journals, 1840–53. Levi Richards, Papers, 1837–67. CHL.

Richards, Willard. Journals and Papers, 1821–54. CHL.

———. "Willard Richards Pocket Companion Written in England," circa 1838. Willard Richards, Papers, 1821–54. CHL.

Rigdon, John Wickliff. "Lecture on the Early History of the Mormon Church," 1906. CHL.

———. "Life Story of Sidney Rigdon," no date. CHL.

[Rigdon, Sidney]. *An Appeal to the American People: Being an Account of the Persecutions of the Church of Latter Day Saints; and of the Barbarities Inflicted on Them by the Inhabitants of the State of Missouri.* Cincinnati: Glezen and Shepard, 1840.

Robbins, James. Letters, 1836 and 1844. CHL.

Roberts, B. H. *The Life of John Taylor, Third President of the Church of Jesus Christ of Latter-day Saints.* Salt Lake City: George Q. Cannon and Sons, 1892.

Robertson, Margaret C. "The Campaign and the Kingdom: The Activities of the Electioneers in Joseph Smith's Presidential Campaign." *BYU Studies* 39, no. 3 (2000): 147–80.

Robison, Elwin C. *The First Mormon Temple: Design, Construction, and Historic Context of the Kirtland Temple.* Provo, UT: Brigham Young University Press, 1997.

Rockwood, Albert Perry. Journal Entries, Oct. 1838–Jan. 1839. Photocopy. CHL.

Rogers, David W. Statement, Feb. 1, 1839. CHL.

Rollins, Kyle M., Richard D. Smith, M. Brett Borup, and E. James Nelson. "Transforming Swampland into Nauvoo, the City Beautiful." *BYU Studies* 45, no. 3 (2006): 125–57.

Romig, Ronald E. *Eighth Witness: The Biography of John Whitmer.* Independence, MO: John Whitmer Books, 2014.

Rowley, Dennis. "The Mormon Experience in the Wisconsin Pineries, 1841–1845." *BYU Studies* 32, nos. 1 and 2 (1992): 119–48.

Rupp, Israel Daniel, ed. *He Pasa Ekklesia* [The whole church]. *An Original History of the Religious Denominations at Present Existing in the United States, Containing Authentic Accounts of Their Rise, Progress, Statistics and Doctrines. Written Expressly for the Work by Eminent Theological Professors, Ministers, and Lay-Members, of the Respective Denominations.* Philadelphia: James Y. Humphreys; Harrisburg, PA: Clyde and Williams, 1844.

Rust, Richard Dilworth. "A Mission to the Lamanites: D&C 28, 30, 32." In *Revelations in Context: The Stories behind the Sections of the Doctrine and Covenants,* edited by Matthew McBride and James Goldberg, 45–49. Salt Lake City: The Church of Jesus Christ of Latter-day Saints, 2016.

Ryder, Hartwell. "A Short History of the Foundation of the Mormon Church." 1902. Typescript. Hiram College Collection, 1909–73. CHL.

Saint George Utah Stake. General Minutes, 1864–1977. CHL.

Saints' Herald. Independence, MO. 1860–.

Salisbury, Herbert Spencer. "Things the Prophet's Sister Told Me," 1945. CHL.

Salt Lake Daily Tribune. Salt Lake City. 1871–.

Sangamo Journal. Springfield, IL. 1831–47.

Schaefer, Mitchell K., ed. *William E. McLellin's Lost Manuscript.* Salt Lake City: Eborn Books, 2012.

School of the Prophets Salt Lake City Minutes, Apr.–Dec. 1883. CHL.

Seale, William. *The President's House: A History.* Vol. 1. Baltimore: Johns Hopkins University Press, 2008.

Senate Document 189. Testimony Given before the Judge of the Fifth Judicial Circuit of the State of Missouri, on the Trial of Joseph Smith, Jr., and Others, for High Treason,

and Other Crimes against That State. Photomechanical reprint. Salt Lake City: Modern
Microfilm, 1965. Copy at CHL.

Seventies Quorum Records, 1844–1975. CHL.

Shipps, Jan, and John W. Welch, eds. *The Journals of William E. McLellin, 1831–1836.* Provo,
UT: BYU Studies; Urbana: University of Illinois Press, 1994.

Skousen, Royal. "Another Account of Mary Whitmer's Viewing of the Golden Plates."
Interpreter: A Journal of Mormon Scripture 10 (2014): 35–44.

Smith, Alex D. "Organizing the Church in Nauvoo: D&C 124, 125." In *Revelations in Context:
The Stories behind the Sections of the Doctrine and Covenants,* edited by Matthew
McBride and James Goldberg, 264–71. Salt Lake City: The Church of Jesus Christ of
Latter-day Saints, 2016.

Smith, Amanda Barnes. Notebook, 1854–66. CHL.

Smith, Andrew F. *The Saintly Scoundrel: The Life and Times of Dr. John Cook Bennett.* Urbana
and Chicago: University of Illinois Press, 1997.

Smith, Asael. Letter and Genealogy Record, 1799, circa 1817–46. CHL.

Smith, Emma. Letter to Joseph Heywood. Oct. 18, 1844. CHL.

Smith, George Albert. Autobiography, circa 1860–82. In George Albert Smith, Papers,
1834–82. CHL.

———. "My Journal." *Instructor,* May 1946, 212–18.

———. Papers, 1834–82. CHL.

Smith, Hyrum. Diary, Mar.–Apr. 1839, Oct. 1840. CHL.

———. Papers, 1834–43. CHL.

Smith, Joseph. Collection, 1827–46. CHL.

———. *General Smith's Views of the Powers and Policy of the Government of the United
States.* Nauvoo, IL: John Taylor, 1844.

———. History, circa Summer 1832 / Smith, Joseph. "A History of the Life of Joseph Smith Jr.,"
circa Summer 1832. In Joseph Smith, "Letterbook A," 1832–35, 1–[6] (earliest numbering).
Joseph Smith Collection. CHL.

———. History, [circa June–Oct. 1839]. Draft. CHL.

———. History, circa 1841. Draft. CHL.

Smith, Joseph, and others. History, 1834–36. In Joseph Smith and others, History, 1838–56,
vol. A-1, back of book (earliest numbering), 9–20, 46–187. CHL.

Smith, Joseph, and others. History, 1838–56. Vols. A-1–F-1 (original), A-2–E-2 (fair copy). In
Historian's Office, History of the Church, 1839–circa 1882. CHL. The history for the period after August 5, 1838, was composed after the death of Joseph Smith. Also available
on the Joseph Smith Papers website, josephsmithpapers.org.

Smith, Joseph F. Papers, 1854–1918. CHL.

Smith, Joseph Fielding, comp. *Life of Joseph F. Smith, Sixth President of the Church of Jesus
Christ of Latter-day Saints.* Salt Lake City: Deseret News, 1938.

———. Papers, 1893–1973. CHL.

Smith, Leslie, and B. Larry Allen. "Family History of Lucy Diantha (Morley) Allen."
FamilySearch. Compiled by The Church of Jesus Christ of Latter-day Saints. Accessed
Mar. 21, 2018. https://familysearch.org.

Smith, Lucy Mack. *Biographical Sketches of Joseph Smith the Prophet, and His Progenitors for
Many Generations.* Liverpool: S. W. Richards, 1853.

———. "Copy of an Old Note Book." Typescript, 1945. BYU.

———. History, 1844–45. 18 books. CHL. Also available on the Joseph Smith Papers website,
josephsmithpapers.org.

———. History, 1845. CHL. Also available on the Joseph Smith Papers website,
josephsmithpapers.org.

———. Letter to Solomon Mack, Jan. 6, 1831. CHL.

Smith, Lucy Meserve. Statement, undated. CHL.

Smith, Mary Fielding. Collection, circa 1832–48. CHL.

Smith, William. *William Smith on Mormonism.* . . . Lamoni, IA: Herald Steam Book and Job
Office, 1883.

Sources Cited

Snow, Eliza R. *Biography and Family Record of Lorenzo Snow, One of the Twelve Apostles of the Church of Jesus Christ of Latter-day Saints.* Salt Lake City: Deseret News, 1884.

———. Journal, 1842–44. CHL.

———. Letter to Isaac Streator, Feb. 22, 1839. Photocopy. CHL.

Speech of Elder Orson Hyde, Delivered before the High Priests' Quorum, in Nauvoo, April 27th 1845, upon the Course and Conduct of Sidney Rigdon, and upon the Merits of His Claims to the Presidency of the Church of Jesus Christ of Latter-day Saints. Liverpool: James and Woodburn, 1845.

Staker, Mark Lyman. *Hearken, O Ye People: The Historical Setting of Joseph Smith's Ohio Revelations.* Salt Lake City: Greg Kofford Books, 2009.

———. "Isaac and Elizabeth Hale in Their Endless Mountain Home." *Mormon Historical Studies* 15, no. 2 (Fall 2014): 1–105.

———. "Raising Money in Righteousness: Oliver Cowdery as Banker." In *Days Never to Be Forgotten: Oliver Cowdery,* edited by Alexander L. Baugh, 143–253. Provo, UT: Religious Studies Center, Brigham Young University, 2009.

———. "Where Was the Aaronic Priesthood Restored?: Identifying the Location of John the Baptist's Appearance, May 15, 1829." *Mormon Historical Studies* 12, no. 2 (Fall 2011): 142–59.

Staker, Mark Lyman, and Curtis Ashton. "Emma's Susquehanna: Growing Up in the Isaac and Elizabeth Hale Home." Priesthood Restoration Site, Church History Department, The Church of Jesus Christ of Latter-day Saints. Published Aug. 25, 2015. http://history.lds.org.

Statham, J. *Indian Recollections.* London: Samuel Bagster, 1832.

State of Missouri. See Missouri, State of.

Statutes of the State of Ohio, of a General Nature, in Force, December 7, 1840; Also, the Statutes of a General Nature, Passed by the General Assembly at Their Thirty-Ninth Session, Commencing December 7, 1840. Columbus, OH: Samuel Medary, 1841.

Stevenson, Edward. Collection, 1849–1922. CHL.

———. Journal, 1852–92. CHL.

Stilwell, Lewis D. *Migration from Vermont.* Montpelier: Vermont Historical Society, 1948.

Stout, Hosea. Reminiscences and Journals, 1845–69. CHL.

Susquehanna Register, and Northern Pennsylvanian. Montrose, PA. 1831–36.

Switzler, William F. *Switzler's Illustrated History of Missouri, from 1541 to 1877.* St. Louis: C. R. Barns, 1879.

Taylor, John. Collection, 1829–94. CHL.

———. Journal, Dec. 1844–Sept. 1845. CHL.

Taylor, Leonora Cannon. Statement, circa 1856. CHL.

Temple Lot Transcript / United States Circuit Court (8th Circuit). Reorganized Church of Jesus Christ of Latter Day Saints v. Church of Christ of Independence, Missouri, and Others, Testimonies and Depositions, 1892. Typescript. CHL.

Thompson, Mercy Rachel Fielding. Autobiographical Sketch, 1880. CHL.

Thompson, Robert B. *Journal of Heber C. Kimball, an Elder of the Church of Jesus Christ of Latter Day Saints. Giving an Account of His Mission to Great Britain. . . .* Nauvoo, IL: Robinson and Smith, 1840.

Thorp, Joseph. *Early Days in the West, Along the Missouri One Hundred Years Ago.* Liberty, MO: Irving Gilmer, 1924.

Thurston, Morris A. "The Boggs Shooting and Failed Extradition: Joseph Smith's Most Famous Case." *BYU Studies Quarterly* 48, no. 1 (2009): 4–56.

Tiffany's Monthly. New York City. 1856–59.

Times and Seasons. Commerce/Nauvoo, IL. Nov. 1839–Feb. 1846.

Tippets, John H. Autobiography, circa 1882. CHL.

Tobler, Ryan G. "'Saviors on Mount Zion': Mormon Sacramentalism, Mortality, and the Baptism for the Dead." *Journal of Mormon History* 39, no. 4 (2013): 182–238.

Towle, Nancy. *Vicissitudes Illustrated, in the Experience of Nancy Towle, in Europe and America.* Charleston, SC: James L. Burgess, 1832.

True Latter Day Saints' Herald. See *Saints' Herald.*

Trustees Land Books / Trustee-in-Trust, Church of Jesus Christ of Latter-day Saints. Land Books, 1839–45. 2 vols. CHL.

Tucker, Pomeroy. *Origin, Rise, and Progress of Mormonism: Biography of Its Founders and History of Its Church.* New York: D. Appleton, 1867.

Tullidge, Edward W. "History of Provo City." *Tullidge's Quarterly Magazine* 3, no. 3 (July 1884): 233–85.

———. *Tullidge's Histories.* Vol. 2. *Containing the History of all the Northern, Eastern and Western Counties of Utah; also the Counties of Southern Idaho.* Salt Lake City: Juvenile Instructor Office, 1889.

———. *The Women of Mormondom.* New York: Tullidge and Crandall, 1877.

Turley, Richard E., Jr., Robin S. Jensen, and Mark Ashurst-McGee. "Joseph the Seer." *Ensign,* Oct. 2015, 48–55.

Tyler, Daniel. "Incidents of Experience." In *Scraps of Biography,* Faith-Promoting Series 10, 20–46. Salt Lake City: Juvenile Instructor Office, 1883.

———. "Recollections of the Prophet Joseph Smith." *Juvenile Instructor* 27, no. 4 (Feb. 15, 1892): 127–28.

Ulrich, Laurel Thatcher. *A House Full of Females: Plural Marriage and Women's Rights in Early Mormonism, 1835–1870.* New York: Knopf, 2017.

———. "'Leaving Home': Phebe Whittemore Carter Woodruff (1807–1885)." In *Women of Faith in the Latter Days.* Vol. 1, *1775–1820,* ed. Richard E. Turley Jr. and Brittany A. Chapman, 450–60. Salt Lake City: Deseret Book, 2011.

United States' Telegraph. Washington, DC. 1826–37.

U.S. and Canada Record Collection. FHL.

U.S. Bureau of the Census. Population Schedules. Microfilm. FHL.

U.S. Congress. Material Relating to Mormon Expulsion from Missouri, 1839–43. CHL.

U.S. Office of Indian Affairs, Central Superintendency. Records, 1807–55. Kansas State Historical Society, Topeka. Also available at kansasmemory.org.

Utah Genealogical and Historical Magazine. Salt Lake City. 1910–40.

Voree Herald. Voree, Wisconsin Territory. Jan.–Oct. 1846.

Waite, Nathan. "A School and an Endowment: D&C 88, 90, 95, 109, 110." In *Revelations in Context: The Stories behind the Sections of the Doctrine and Covenants,* edited by Matthew McBride and James Goldberg, 174–82. Salt Lake City: The Church of Jesus Christ of Latter-day Saints, 2016.

Walker, Jeffrey N. "Mormon Land Rights in Caldwell and Daviess Counties and the Mormon Conflict of 1838: New Findings and New Understandings." *BYU Studies* 47, no. 1 (2008): 4–55.

Walker, Robert John. "Lilburn W. Boggs and the Case for Jacksonian Democracy." Master's thesis, Brigham Young University, 2011.

Walker, Ronald W. "Six Days in August: Brigham Young and the Succession Crisis of 1844." In *A Firm Foundation: Church Organization and Administration,* edited by David J. Whittaker and Arnold K. Garr, 161–96. Provo, UT: Religious Studies Center, Brigham Young University, 2011.

Ward, Maurine Carr. "John Needham's Nauvoo Letter: 1843." *Nauvoo Journal* 8, no. 1 (Spring 1996): 38–42.

Warsaw Message. Warsaw, IL. 1843–44.

Warsaw Signal. Warsaw, IL. 1841–43.

The Wasp. Nauvoo, IL. Apr. 1842–Apr. 1843.

Watson, Eldon J. *Brigham Young Addresses.* 6 vols. N.p., 1979–84.

Watson, Wingfield. Correspondence, 1891, 1908. CHL.

Watt, George D. Papers, circa 1846–65. CHL. Transcriptions by LaJean Purcell Carruth found in Church History Department Pitman Shorthand Transcriptions, 2013–17. CHL.

Watt, Ronald G. *The Mormon Passage of George D. Watt: First British Convert, Scribe for Zion.* Logan: Utah State University Press, 2009.

Wayne Sentinel. Palmyra, NY. 1823–52, 1860–61.

Sources Cited

Webb, Eliza Churchill. Letter to Mary Bond, May 4, 1876. Biographical Folder Collection (labeled Myron H. Bond). Community of Christ Library-Archives, Independence, MO.

———. Letter to Mary Bond, Apr. 24, 1876. Biographical Folder Collection (labeled Myron H. Bond). Community of Christ Library-Archives, Independence, MO.

West, William S. *A Few Interesting Facts, Respecting the Rise Progress and Pretensions of the Mormons.* N.p., 1837.

Western World. Warsaw, IL. 1840–41.

Whitmer, David. *An Address to All Believers in Christ.* Richmond, MO: By the author, 1887.

Whitmer, History / Whitmer, John. "The Book of John Whitmer Kept by Commandment," circa 1835–46. Community of Christ Library-Archives, Independence, MO.

Whitney, Helen Mar. *Plural Marriage, as Taught by the Prophet Joseph. A Reply to Joseph Smith, Editor of the Lamoni (Iowa) "Herald."* Salt Lake City: Juvenile Instructor Office, 1882.

———. *Why We Practice Plural Marriage.* Salt Lake City: Juvenile Instructor Office, 1884.

Whitney, Horace G. "Nauvoo Brass Band." *Contributor,* Mar. 1880, 134.

Whitney, Orson F. *History of Utah.* 4 vols. Salt Lake City: George Q. Cannon and Sons, 1904.

———. *Life of Heber C. Kimball, an Apostle; the Father and Founder of the British Mission.* Salt Lake City: Kimball Family, 1888.

———. "Newel K. Whitney." *Contributor,* Jan. 1885, 123–32.

Wight, Orange L. Reminiscences, 1903. CHL.

Williams, Frederick G. "Frederick Granger Williams of the First Presidency of the Church." *BYU Studies* 12, no. 3 (Spring 1972): 243–61.

Winters, Mary Ann Stearns. Reminiscences, no date. Typescript. Church History Library.

Wolfinger, Henry J. *A Test of Faith: Jane Elizabeth James and the Origins of the Utah Black Community.* Washington, DC: National Archives and Records Service, 1975. Copy at CHL.

Woman's Exponent. Salt Lake City. 1872–1914.

Wood, Gillen D'Arcy. *Tambora: The Eruption That Changed the World.* Princeton, NJ: Princeton University Press, 2014.

Woodruff, Emma S. Collection, 1832–1919. CHL.

Woodruff, Phebe Carter. Autobiographical Sketch, 1880. In University of California (Berkeley) Bancroft Library and Hubert H. Bancroft, Utah and the Mormons Collection, before 1889. Microfilm. CHL.

———. Autograph Book, 1838–44, 1899. CHL.

———. Letter to "Dear Parents," July 30, 1844. CHL.

Woodruff, Wilford. Collection, 1831–1905. CHL.

———. "The History and Travels of Zion's Camp, Led by the Prophet Joseph Smith from Kirtland Ohio to Clay County Missoura in the Spring of 1838," 1882. CHL.

———. Journals, 1833–98, in Wilford Woodruff, Journals and Papers, 1828–98. CHL.

———. Journals and Papers, 1828–98. CHL.

———. *Leaves from My Journal.* Faith-Promoting Series 3. Salt Lake City: Juvenile Instructor Office, 1881.

———. Testimony, Mar. 19, 1897. CHL.

Woodworth, Jed. "The Center Place: D&C 52, 57, 58." In *Revelations in Context: The Stories behind the Sections of the Doctrine and Covenants,* edited by Matthew McBride and James Goldberg, 122–29. Salt Lake City: The Church of Jesus Christ of Latter-day Saints, 2016.

———. "Mercy Thompson and the Revelation on Marriage: D&C 132." In *Revelations in Context: The Stories behind the Sections of the Doctrine and Covenants,* edited by Matthew McBride and James Goldberg, 281–93. Salt Lake City: The Church of Jesus Christ of Latter-day Saints, 2016.

———. "Peace and War: D&C 87." In *Revelations in Context: The Stories behind the Sections of the Doctrine and Covenants,* edited by Matthew McBride and James Goldberg, 158–64. Salt Lake City: The Church of Jesus Christ of Latter-day Saints, 2016.

———. "The Word of Wisdom: D&C 89." In *Revelations in Context: The Stories behind the Sections of the Doctrine and Covenants,* edited by Matthew McBride and James Goldberg, 183–91. Salt Lake City: The Church of Jesus Christ of Latter-day Saints, 2016.

Young, Brigham. Account Book, 1836–46. CHL.

———. Journals, 1832–77. Brigham Young Office Files, 1832–78. CHL.

———. Letter to Parley P. Pratt, May 26, 1845. CHL.

Young, Emily Dow Partridge. Diary and Reminiscences, Feb. 1874–Nov. 1883. CHL.

———. "Incidents in the Life of a Mormon Girl," circa 1884. CHL.

———. "What I Remember," 1884. Typescript. CHL.

Young, Joseph, Sr. *History of the Organization of the Seventies. Names of the First and Second Quorums. Items in Relation to the First Presidency of the Seventies. Also, a Brief Glance at Enoch and His City. Embellished with a Likeness of Joseph Smith, the Prophet, and a View of the Kirtland Temple.* Salt Lake City: Deseret News, 1878.

———. Letter to Lewis Harvey, Nov. 16, 1880. CHL.

Young, Phineas H. Journal, Apr.–May 1845. CHL.

Young, Zina Diantha Huntington. Diaries, 1844–45, 1886, 1889. CHL.

Youngreen, Buddy. *Reflections of Emma: Joseph Smith's Wife.* Orem, UT: Grandin Book, 1982.

Young Woman's Journal. Salt Lake City. 1889–1929.

Zion's Ensign. Independence, MO, 1891–97.

Zion's Reveille. Voree, Wisconsin Territory. 1846–47.

ACKNOWLEDGMENTS

Hundreds of people contributed to this new history of the Church, and we are grateful to each one of them. We are indebted to the generations of historians employed by the Church who have meticulously collected and preserved the records on which this book is based. All staff members, missionaries, and volunteers in the Church History Department contributed directly or indirectly. Special thanks to James Goldberg, David Golding, Elizabeth Mott, Jennifer Reeder, and Ryan Saltzgiver for creating the supplemental materials online. The digitization of sources on the Church History Catalog was led by Audrey Spainhower Dunshee and Jay Burton.

The historical analysis in the book depends particularly on *The Joseph Smith Papers*. We acknowledge the reviews of historians with that project, including Matthew Godfrey, Mark Ashurst-McGee, Elizabeth Kuehn, David Grua, Spencer McBride, and Alex Smith. Jenny Lund and Mark Staker of the Historic Sites Division also provided careful reviews and corrections. R. Eric Smith, editorial manager of the Publications Division, made sizable contributions, as did Alison Palmer and Stephanie Steed. The members of the Church Historian's Press Editorial Board provided ongoing support.

In shaping the literary structure of the book, we consulted with Ardis Parshall, Chris Crowe, Angela Hallstrom, the late Jonathan Langford, the late Eric C. Olson, Brandon Sanderson, Laurel Barlow, Kathleen and Dean Hughes, H. B. Moore, Kimberley Heuston Sorenson, and Gale Sears. Historians Alex Baugh and Melissa Wei-Tsing Inouye also provided important assistance, as did Frank Rolapp. Greg Newbold created the engaging artwork and maps.

John Heath, Debra Abercrombie, and Miryelle Resek contributed to the outreach effort. Kiersten Olson, Jo Lyn Curtis, Andrea Maxfield, and Debi Robins provided administrative assistance. Lizzie Saltsman provided project management.

Members of other Church departments likewise contributed, including a cross-departmental team made up of Irinna Danielson, Alan Paulsen, Karlie Guymon, Robert Ewer, Jen Ward, Drew Conrad, David Dickson, and Paul Murphy. Other contributors include Eliza Nevin, Patric Gerber, Nick Olvera, Paul VanDerHoeven, Randall Pixton, Brooke Frandsen, David Mann, Alan Blake, Jeff Hutchings, Gary Walton, Matt Evans, Scott Welty, and Jeff Hatch. Kelly Haws, Mark Eastmond, Casey Olson, and Tom Valletta spent many hours reviewing the manuscript. Translators carefully prepared the entire text in thirteen languages as well as the first eight chapters in dozens of additional languages.

Hundreds of volunteer readers from all around the world reviewed the narrative and provided feedback that improved the book and helped ensure that it would speak to the minds and hearts of Saints everywhere.

INDEX

Aaron, 63, 233
Aaronic Priesthood, 67, 97, 197, 235
Able, Elijah, 315–19
Abraham, 121, 233–34, 433, 503. *See also* book of
    Abraham
abuse, physical, 223–24
Adam, 234, 310, 411
Adam-ondi-Ahman, Missouri, 310, 324,
    335–38
Adams, James, 453
adoption sealing, 580. *See also* sealing
African Americans. *See* black people
alcohol, 85, 167–68, 224, 238, 324–25, 393
Alger, Fanny, 291–92, 295, 305
Allen, Charles, 179–80
America, 22, 93, 98, 108. *See also* United States of
    America
American Indians, 98, 105, 115–17, 123–24, 571–72,
    577
angel
    angels at First Vision, 16
    John the Baptist, 66–67
    Joseph Smith gives plates to, 75
    Joseph Smith told to practice plural marriage
        by, 290–91
    Joseph Smith tutored by, 86
    in Kirtland, 234–35, 237, 239, 247
    Mary Lightner sees, 445–46
    Peter, James, and John, 84
    Phebe Woodruff sees, 373–74
    Three Witnesses see, 73–75
    See also Moroni
Angell, Mary Ann. *See* Young, Mary Ann Angell
Anthon, Charles, 46–48, 72
Atonement of Jesus Christ, 79, 90, 440
Avard, Sampson, 327, 368–69

Bailey, Calvin, 224–25
Bailey, Lydia. *See* Knight, Lydia Bailey
Baldwin, Caleb, 369–70, 384
Ball, Joseph, 322
baptism, 66–67, 86, 94, 104–5, 234, 286–87, 410,
    481, 573
baptism for the dead, 421, 424, 447, 464, 476–77,
    578
Beaman, Louisa, 435, 444, 496
Beaman, Mary. *See* Noble, Mary Beaman
Bear Creek, Illinois, 575
Benbow, Jane, 410, 464
Benbow, John, 410, 464
Benbow, William, 410
Benjamin, King, 90

Bennett, John
    anti-Mormon activities of, 466, 474, 478, 484
    joining church, 419–20
    leadership positions of, 422, 425, 427, 431, 435
    misconduct and excommunication of, 457–62,
        465–66
    revelation instructs, 426
Bible
    Book of Mormon and, 72, 255, 485
    church teachings follow, 252–55
    Joseph Smith reads, 12
    more scripture than, 83, 100–101
    seeking for truth found in, 79, 303
Bible, Joseph Smith's inspired translation, 107–8,
    121, 146–47, 502
Big Blue River, 182, 190
Bigler, Bathsheba. *See* Smith, Bathsheba Bigler
bishop, 118, 126, 130, 154, 233, 289, 319–20, 419, 447
bishop's council, 305–6, 313
bishop's storehouse, 294
Black, Adam, 327
black people, 172–75, 316, 318, 500. *See also*
    slavery
blessing
    of children, 277, 308, 542
    Emma Smith writes, 543–44
    of healing, 402–3, 505
    James Hendricks receives, 380
    Joseph Smith receives, 233
    Joseph Smith Sr. gives on deathbed, 422–23
    Parley Pratt receives, 249–50, 283
    patriarchal, 242–43, 263, 514
    Phebe Woodruff receives, 373–74, 568
Boggs, Lilburn, 331, 345–46, 350, 456–57, 460,
    466–67, 479
book of Abraham, 220, 446, 453
Book of Commandments, 140–42, 148, 177–81, 222
Book of Mormon
    Abner Cole mocks, 80–81
    and Bible, 72, 255, 485
    British edition, 429
    dissenters' belief in, 297, 302, 526
    Emma Smith's belief in, 585
    Joseph Smith testifies of, 412, 546
    Martin Harris loses manuscript, 51–53
    missionaries teach to American Indians, 116
    plural marriage in, 121, 433, 491
    publication of, 76–80, 83
    testifies of Christ, 72, 83
    testimony of doubted, 182–83
    testimony of received, 92–93, 99–101, 139–40,
        253–54, 271
    See also gold plates

Preston, England, 281–82
priest, 528
priesthood
    and administering ordinances, 160
    endowment as ordinance of, 454
    held by Joseph Smith, 528, 564
    keys of, 240–41, 559
    and marriage, 228, 413, 502
    new and everlasting covenant as order of, 487
    power of, 389
    Relief Society organized after pattern of, 448, 451
    restoration of, 86
    See also Aaronic Priesthood; Melchizedek
        Priesthood
printing office
    Independence, 148, 154, 177–78
    Kirtland, 221, 233, 236
    Nauvoo, 538
property. *See* land and property
prophecy
    about church in Missouri, 128–29, 140–41
    about gathering, 109, 292, 518–19
    about sealed book, 72
    at baptism of Joseph Smith and Oliver
        Cowdery, 67
    of Brigham Young, 578
    of Daniel in Bible, 369
    of ensign to the nations, 572, 582
    at time of Joseph Smith's death, 543, 554, 568
    at time of Kirtland endowment, 234–35, 238–39
prophet
    in Book of Mormon, 61–62, 66
    Brigham Young on importance of, 484–86
    Elijah as, 240
    Hyrum Smith as, 426
    Joseph Smith as, 55, 142, 157, 280, 528
    Saints question Joseph Smith's role as, 266,
        297–98, 530

Quincy, Illinois, 377, 381–82, 467
Quorum of the Seventy, 217–18, 238–39, 249, 313,
    570
Quorum of the Twelve Apostles
    campaigns for Joseph Smith as U.S.
        president, 514
    dissent and reconciliation in, 275, 283–85
    endowed with power in Kirtland
        temple, 238–39
    Joseph Smith instructs, 217–18, 401, 491
    journey to Far West temple site, 321, 386–87,
        393–95
    keys bestowed on, 519–20, 559, 563, 565
    and leadership succession, 560–62, 566–67
    and location for church settlements, 518

missionary work by, 249
mission to England, 274–75, 395, 404–5
organization of, 214–17
restoring members to, 230, 401
vacancies filled in, 320–21
washing of feet in Kirtland, 238

Ramus, Illinois, 486–87
record keeping, 85, 487
redemption of the dead, 422, 476
redress for Missouri losses, 391–92, 406–8, 414,
    513–14, 555
Relief Society. *See* Female Relief Society of Nauvoo
religious freedom, 433, 529
Repa, 573
repentance, 20, 55, 65, 78, 168, 230, 277, 283, 298, 462
Restoration, 18, 72, 83, 115, 241, 433, 463, 477
resurrection, 147–48, 403, 487
revelations to Joseph Smith
    for church, 97–98
    corrections to, 143
    divine source of, 528
    harmonious with Bible, 255
    publishing, 140–41, 148–49, 222
    recording, 56, 516
    threatening to Missourians, 174
    through Urim and Thummim, 55
    truth of despite imperfections, 142–43
    as words of Jesus Christ, 58
revivals in Palmyra area, 4, 9, 11–12, 55
Reynolds, John, 407–8
Reynolds, Thomas, 466–67
Ribble, River, 281, 287, 306
Rich, Charles, 342, 344
Richards, Ellin, 302
Richards, Jennetta Richards, 286–88, 302–3, 307,
    409, 492–93, 510
Richards, John, 302–3
Richards, Willard
    accompanies bodies of Joseph and Hyrum
        Smith, 554–55
    calling to Quorum of the Twelve, 321, 387
    in Carthage jail, 549–50
    endowed in Nauvoo, 453–54
    and leadership succession, 560–62
    marriage to Jennetta Richards, 307, 409, 492–93
    mission in England, 277, 306, 308, 410–11
    scribe to Joseph Smith, 448, 479, 547
Richmond, Missouri, 367–69
Rigdon, Nancy, 449
Rigdon, Phebe, 101
Rigdon, Sidney
    and Book of Commandments preface, 141
    conversion of, 99–101

Lake Superior

WISCONSIN
TERRITORY

Mississippi River

Lake Michigan

IOWA
TERRITORY

MICHIG

ILLINOIS

NAUVOO

INDIANA

• FAR WEST
INDEPENDENCE

Missouri River

ST LOUIS

MISSOURI

KENTUC

ARK.

Mississippi River

TENNESSEE

UNITED STATE
OF AMERICA

MISS.   ALA.